BENNETT

BENNETT

THE REBEL WHO CHALLENGED
AND CHANGED A NATION

JOHN BOYKO

KEY PORTER BOOKS

Library and Archives Canada Cataloguing in Publication

Boyko, John, 1957-
  Bennett : the rebel who challenged a nation / John Boyko.

ISBN 978-1-55470-248-0

1. Bennett, R. B. (Richard Bedford), 1870-1947. 2. Canada--Politics and government--1930-1935. 3. Prime ministers--Canada--Biography. 4. Legislators--Alberta--Biography. I. Title.

FC576.B45B69 2010   971.062'3092   C2009-905834-0

ONTARIO ARTS COUNCIL
CONSEIL DES ARTS DE L'ONTARIO

The publisher gratefully acknowledges the support of the Canada Council for the Arts and the Ontario Arts Council for its publishing program. We acknowledge the support of the Government of Ontario through the Ontario Media Development Corporation's Ontario Book Initiative.

We acknowledge the financial support of the Government of Canada through the Book Publishing Industry Development Program (BPIDP) for our publishing activities.

Key Porter Books Limited
Six Adelaide Street East, Tenth Floor
Toronto, Ontario
Canada M5C 1H6

www.keyporter.com

Text design: Martin Gould
Electronic formatting: Marijke Friesen

Printed and bound in Canada

10 11 12 13 14 5 4 3 2 1

Mixed Sources
Cert no. SW-COC-001271
© 1996 FSC
FSC

This book is dedicated to Shirley, Sue, Jennifer and Kenzie
—the women who make me whole.

CONTENTS

ACKNOWLEDGEMENTS

I AM INDEBTED to a number of people who devoted their energies and talents to the creation of this book. My kind and hard working literary agent is Daphne Hart of the Helen Heller Agency. Daphne first saw merit in the idea of exploring Bennett's life and career and took it to Jordan Fenn and the good people at Key Porter Books. Editor-in-Chief Linda Pruessen patiently and skillfully shepherded the manuscript through several drafts and oversaw the book's development. John English not only wrote a fine foreword but also read an early draft and made a number of excellent suggestions. Liba Berry and Marie-Lynn Hammond did impressive work in eagle-eyed copyediting and proofreading, Martin Gould created a tremendous design, and Jennifer Fox developed a fine marketing plan. I am grateful to the folks who assisted me with research and the collection of photographs at Trent University's Thomas J. Bata Library in Peterborough, the Glenbow Museum in Calgary, and Ottawa's Library and Archives Canada. I thank my students, whose humour keeps me humble and whose questions keep me curious. And as with all else I do, the book would not have been possible without the support of my dear wife Sue, to whom I owe everything.

FOREWORD

BY JOHN ENGLISH

THERE HAS BEEN NO FULL BIOGRAPHY of R. B. Bennett, a major Canadian political figure and Canada's prime minister during the first years of the Depression. This absence is explained partly by Bennett's decision to destroy many of his public papers and partly, I would suggest, by Bennett's apparently contradictory views. Although Richard Wilbur long ago argued that Bennett's New Deal was more than a deathbed conversion at a time when his political death seemed inevitable, there has been no full study of Bennett's remarkable business and political career. The distinguished historian Peter Waite has written an excellent short study of Bennett, but Ernest Watkin's dated biography has remained the major source for Bennett's full career. Lord Beaverbrook's personal memoir of his friendship with Bennett is fascinating but, like its author, often unreliable.

John Boyko's biography of Bennett is, therefore, a most welcome addition to prime ministerial biographies. Using Bennett's papers, contemporary documents, and secondary works, Boyko has written a lively and highly readable account of a largely unknown prime minister. Boyko's major contribution is his analysis of Bennett's conservatism or, more accurately, Bennett's peculiar, Canadian definition of conservatism. At its core was the British connection, and Bennett's perception of the British imperial idea. Bennett, like many British conservative imperialists, believed that the empire possessed a moral force, a responsibility to improve not only the "lesser breeds" beyond the law but also the worker, the farmer, and the hardy yeoman who were the empire's strengths. They fought its wars and, in peacetime, bore its message of duty and commitment.

And yet, the British imperialist Bennett was North American, and his British-Canadian perspective was complicated by his immersion in the laissez-faire world of North American capitalism. That world opposed the tradition of working class conservatism espoused by Benjamin Disraeli in Britain and John A. Macdonald in Canada. While highly successful in business, Bennett's strong religious beliefs, his youthful penury, his experience of the frontier with its sense of common purpose, and, not least, his highly romantic view of the British monarchy combined to create a political outlook that was distinct and fascinating. In tracing Bennett's intellectual and emotional development, Boyko has convincingly demonstrated that Bennett's New Deal was not a whimsical or desperate response to the Depression but rather a reflection of a profound and enduring commitment to an enhanced role for the state in the emerging industrial economy.

Like the British Empire, Bennett's conservatism has passed as if in a dream. Boyko's book illuminates corners of Canada's and the Conservative Party's past that have been shaded for too long. If we are to understand Canada's past, we must probe the darkened parts more deeply. John Boyko has ably guided us toward a better understanding of a past and a person we barely know today. R. B. Bennett was not a great prime minister, but he was a remarkable Canadian. Because of John Boyko, we now know him much better.

BENNETT

IT WAS A SAD SIGHT, REALLY. To walk the streets of London in the shadow of the Second World War was to be moved by the broken buildings, mounds of rubble, and too many widows attempting but not quite mustering the stiff upper lip of the newsreel propaganda. But the particularly piteous sight that afternoon was not the ruins of a city ravaged by madness; it was a man. He would have stood out. He was a big man, just over six feet tall and well over 200 pounds. A bowler hat topped a large head on which once-proud features were lined now with age and worry, and high cheekbones sagged to jowls. The bright, brown eyes had faded to grey. But the clothes told the tale of a still fiercely independent and well-to-do gentleman. The pinstriped suit with high-waisted pants, swallowtail jacket falling to tails, stiff collar, and bold tie spoke of another era. Londoners would no doubt have noticed him. But they would likely have passed him by with nary a glance, not sure if he was from the House of Lords—which he was.

A Canadian, on the other hand, would have recognized him in an instant. For here on a London afternoon, leaving one theatre and on his way to another, was a man who less than a dozen years before had been the prime minister of Canada. Richard Bedford Bennett, now Viscount Bennett of Mickleham, Calgary, and Hopewell, and permanent resident of the posh Juniper Hill estate, had led his country through the most treacherously dangerous period of its short, eighty-year history. He had been welcomed by presidents and kings and toasted by his countrymen. He had been lauded for his stunning intelligence, polymath prowess, and boundless generosity. But now here he was—a gloomy anachronism.

Like any man's, Bennett's life had many chapters. He was a teacher, a principal, and a lawyer. He was a naturally gifted businessman who enjoyed success in land speculation and clever investments while playing a leading role in merging small businesses into large corporations. He was the president of several companies and on the boards of even more. His business acumen, connections, and sheer good luck rendered him a multi-millionaire who hobnobbed with Canada's economic elite. But from his early days in New Brunswick to his adulthood in Alberta, he had yearned to serve. He was a town alderman, territorial representative, provincial party leader, and member of Parliament, and he held several federal cabinet posts. He did all of that and more before he became leader of the Conservative Party in 1927 and prime minister three years later.

To understand Bennett's five years as prime minister one must understand the Depression, for it shaped every decision he made throughout his term in office and, in turn, shaped his legacy. The Depression was an era of dizzying paradox. Men left home to save their families. Farmers who had helped feed the world went hungry, and police committed criminal acts while criminals became folk heroes. It was a time when, for millions of people, every morning presented a new struggle to survive while every evening offered Hollywood glamour and Busby Berkeley musicals. Suddenly, the rules seemed to have changed and all that had been certain was up for grabs. The Depression was a time when quintuplets born to a dirt-poor Ontario mother were a miracle ruined by a greedy provincial government that transformed them into a freak show. And just when many came to be inspired by the decency of a man of the earth named Grey Owl, he was revealed as a fraud. One could rely on nothing.

In the last year of the Dirty Thirties, Toto invited Dorothy to look behind the curtain and see the truth. Her glance revealed that everything she and her three companions had believed to be real was a sham and all their heroic efforts a waste. *The Wizard of Oz* was well received because everyone understood it. The Depression invited Canadians to peek behind the curtain and see that the country's social, political, and economic superstructure was nothing more than the puffing, flaming face of a false wizard. The Depression had been caused by overproduction, insane speculation, unsustainable debt, and insatiable avarice, and then brought to its knees by collapsing commodity prices and financial paralysis.

Canadians ached for a return to stability, prosperity, and predictability. They did not want handouts; they wanted fairness. They did not want bromides; they wanted the truth. They wanted the dignity of work and the pride of independence. They did not demand a perfect government but expected empathy and a state that would allow them to do their best with at least an even chance at success. People were eager to work and willing to sacrifice, but they needed to be helped out of the morass into which the false wizard had led and then abandoned them. They needed someone to show them the way home. In the summer of 1930, with everything sliding into chaos, but the worst of times not yet visited upon the land, Canadians turned to R. B. Bennett as that leader.

Bennett's fiery speeches, bold ideas, and audacious confidence had inspired Canadians and won their support. But winning office mainly on the promise to fix an economy in turmoil does not guarantee long-term public support. Bennett was soon blamed for causing the Depression that he had inherited. He was condemned for failing to quickly turn things around. What had been seen as intelligence morphed into apparent arrogance. His personal wealth came to be seen as a reflection of his ignorance of the tribulations of the common man. Farmers removed engines from old cars they could no longer afford, hitched them to horses, and called them Bennett buggies. Homeless people pulled newspapers over themselves to ward off the night's chills and called them Bennett blankets. A bitter, ersatz brew of wheat or barley was dubbed Bennett coffee. Shantytowns housing the transient unemployed were called Bennett boroughs.

Despite the storms of criticism and a near absence of credit, Prime Minster Bennett did a great deal of good. With the American market shrinking due to its own problems and its self-defeating protectionist legislation, Bennett initiated international conferences and other actions that increased trade. Later, with a vigorous new president hinting at a promise of new openness, he did what he could to move Canadian products over the southern border. He created the Canadian Broadcasting Corporation (CBC) and the Bank of Canada, both of which immediately played indispensable social and economic roles. He advanced negotiations that led to Canada's growing independence from Britain and hastened the building of the St. Lawrence Seaway. He saved the national railway system. He helped the unemployed with emergency relief and then a massive infrastructure program. He helped urban workers, who were assisted through the institution of a higher minimum wage and regulated hours of work. He made farm credit easier to attain and created systems that stabilized the price and sale of wheat and grain. He presented legislation to vastly improve old-age pensions and unemployment insurance. In the last year of his mandate, he outlined a daring new plan that was prescient in how it promised to restructure the relationship between the government, the people, and the economy with social and economic assistance and regulatory programs that Canadians would later claim as their birthright. The plan's boldness was such that it initiated constitutional reform that led to the independence of Canada's Supreme Court and the ability of the federal government to do much that Canadians came to expect of it.

But there was more. A leader's effectiveness is measured not only by what he does but also by what he avoids. The global Depression had led the people of some countries to turn in desperation to fascism, communism, socialism, or strong men claiming to be one thing or another but similar only in their race to ruination. Canada had its share of those willing to promote, others eager to exploit, and still others ready to try just about any political option imaginable. Canada avoided extremism as enormous demands were met by a strong, determined, and resilient people. It all could have gone another way.

Regardless of everything that had been avoided and accomplished, and of the recovery that was finally being felt in most parts of the land, just five years after Canadians had greeted Bennett as a hero, they could not wait to vote against him. He was attacked from the political left and right. Critics said he was a dictator and ran a one-man government. An old friend and trusted cabinet colleague had abandoned him, formed his own populist party, and spoke of Bennett's betraying core principles. He was dubbed "Iron Heel" by those who said he either ordered or allowed the RCMP to trample the rights of workers and then the workers themselves. They said he instigated riots and cavalierly jailed or deported those with whom he disagreed. He was pilloried for succumbing to a red scare. He was criticized for ignoring the United States when trying to foster greater trade with Britain and other Commonwealth countries, but then attacked for attempting to create new American markets for Canadian goods. Many in the business community condemned him for creating more regulation to control greed and malfeasance in Canada's banks and financial institutions. In the last months of his administration, he was ridiculed as a cynical opportunist for five radio addresses in which he used incendiary rhetoric in an attempt to explain problems and present solutions. Those who called the program of reform and restructuring Bennett's New Deal did so as a form of derision.

In the fall of 1935, the good people of Calgary West returned Bennett to Ottawa, but as the leader of His Majesty's Loyal Opposition. His majority government had been defeated. His caucus had been demolished. Most of his cabinet had been turfed. The voters returned to the prime minister's office the same man whom Bennett had replaced five years before, a man no one really understood or liked, the wily William Lyon Mackenzie King. All Mackenzie King had needed to do to win was not be Bennett.

Just three years after Canadians had rejected him, Bennett turned his back on Canadians. He purchased a large estate in Great Britain, next door to Lord Beaverbrook, another expatriate Canadian and lifelong friend. He did good and valuable work during the war. He accepted his peerage. As a member of the House of Lords, he made valuable contributions to the war effort, played a hand in the creation of Britain's postwar social welfare state, and due to his work in the aviation industry was offered the chairmanship of BOAC. Through it all, he made tremendously generous donations to individuals, to a great number of schools, and to a host of charitable causes. Other than brief visits, he never returned home. He was not missed. He is the only Canadian prime minister whose grave lies outside the country.

He was admired but condemned, and honoured but forgotten. Few really knew him. Bennett was a complex man whose character was defined by his contradictions. To difficult issues he brought his keen intellect and lawyer's ability to rationally deconstruct complexity and quickly discern pith and substance. His prodigious memory astounded all and served to assist him in the determination of an issue's core problem and options for solutions. He was sometimes sabotaged by his intelligence, for it was coupled with an impatience with others who seemed unable to keep up. During meetings, he would often have already determined the root of a problem, weighed options, and decided upon the best course while others were still wrestling to understand the issue. He acted as though he was the smartest person in the room because he usually was. Dr. R.J. Manion, who served in the cabinets of Borden, Meighen, and Bennett, and who knew Mackenzie King and Laurier, observed that of all the prime ministers with whom he was acquainted, Bennett was by far the brightest.[1]

Throughout his life he never mastered the art of patience: of waiting while others caught up. Sometimes that impatience surfaced in an explosive temper that served to make enemies of those who would have been allies, and associates of those who could have been friends. He could be friendly, funny, charitable, and grandiloquently charming. Unfortunately, those stung by rebukes or rebuffed by intransigence were less warmed by his smile than chilled by his glare.

He always worked harder than those around him and so found it difficult to compliment others whom he saw as simply doing their share or their duty. He sought no thanks or praise and was thus stingy about doling it out. He could blast out orders but also consult, listen, admit error, and change his mind. He could rankle by speaking for ministers in the House or ordering their staffers to report first to him. But he also allowed ministers great latitude in running their departments and often suggested that important bills be introduced by others if such a move increased the potential for success.

Bennett was rapaciously ambitious. It was this ambition that rendered him a school principal when he was just slightly older than his students and then led him to seek adventure and fortune in what was at the time Canada's Wild West. His talent, determination—and timing—made him rich. But he saw wealth and power as a means rather than an end, and public service as a duty. His ambition was fuelled not by greed but rather by both a sincere desire to serve and a philanthropic impulse to help. Together, those motives led him to policies and charitable giving that supported hard-working people who deserved a hand up and a fair deal.

Like all effective leaders, his decisions were informed by an adherence to a core set of principles. His mother would have been proud of his Christian heart that saw money as a tool to help others. His political heroes, such as Benjamin Disraeli, would have applauded his Tory mind. Throughout his long public life, Bennett saw government as a vehicle to responsibly intervene in the marketplace in an effort to counterweight corporate power and thereby advance the common good.

Bennett's intelligence and the clarity and consistency of his personal values and ideological principles allowed him to do as all great leaders must, and see beyond the issues of the day. Even as a young man he seemed to understand that while others scramble with tactics, a successful person and effective leader must develop and remain focused on long-range strategies by seeing farther and more clearly. This essential element of his character was revealed through nearly all that he said and did. For example, Bennett was one of six leaders who addressed an international audience through an American radio hookup on Remembrance Day 1934. Unlike the others, he did not celebrate the years of peace since the First World War but, rather, issued a prescient warning. Five years before the Second World War—and decades before the terrible events of 9/11 saw Canada allow its citizens to be kidnapped and tortured while freedom-loving Americans casually tossed aside their civil rights for the Patriot Act's false security and the initiation of a perpetual war against a tactic—Bennett said,

> Loss of self-confidence; national regimentation on a scale hitherto unknown; the surrender of liberty for the most ephemeral and makeshift protection—all this is evidence that a great portion of the human family prefers the mere illusion of security to facing the real causes of the world's present state of fear. But the eternal truth remains that there can be no real security until the spectre of fear is banished from the minds of the great masses of men and women whose social, political, and economic problems are incapable of solution in the international atmosphere of suspicion, doubt and misunderstanding.[2]

That these words inspire reflection so many decades later suggests that Bennett possessed another essential attribute of leadership: the ability to communicate. His facility with words was legendary. He recognized his talents in this area when in elementary school but then worked hard to hone his abilities. His courtroom experience helped and his steady climb from municipal, to territorial, to provincial, then finally to federal politics meant that by the time he was prime minister his outlier's mastery of the power of the spoken word was something to behold. He seldom read a speech but rather relied on a single sheet of paper on which were scratched the few points that he wished to make. From those few words he could fashion full and perfect paragraphs. He used his prodigious memory to employ accurate statistics and perfectly rendered quotes. Historian Bruce Hutchison observed that Bennett ". . . could utter 220 words a minute, as registered by a stopwatch, never missing a syllable or misplacing a predicate. Without a note to guide him, his language glowed like a purling brook."[3]

His intelligence, work ethic, ambition, values, vision, and oratorical skills were important, but all of it together would have been an empty bag without courage. Bennett demonstrated courage in all aspects of his life. In 1914, for instance, he was a rookie member of Parliament who could have cleverly guarded his chances for advancement by staying quiet about an initiative that he believed was wrong. But rather than take the safer and perhaps smarter route, he stood in the House and spoke against his own government. He was publicly rebuked by the prime minister and the cabinet minister in charge, who was his rival for advancement. He knew that his principled action could end his career in federal politics before it had really begun, but he did it anyway.

Bennett's life is full of similar moments—moments in which he was willing to forgo his career trajectory or the chance for profit before abandoning his principles or surrendering to expediency. To delegates at the 1927 Conservative Party convention that had just elected him their leader, he said, "To hold convictions and principles is more important than power. . . . Power is the last consideration that should influence us except to the extent that power may enable us to realize the instrument we have in our hands and see that our policies grow into fruition, and it matters not whether we achieve power or not in that sense."[4]

All of this means that he was an effective leader; it does not mean that he was always a nice guy. In many ways and moments he was not even close. Nor was he immune to silly mistakes or grand misjudgments. He sometimes joked when he should have been serious, lost his temper when he should have remained calm, wavered when he should have been decisive, and was stubborn when he needed only to be strong. He was, in short, as human as the rest of us. But his human foibles do not negate his admirable qualities, the importance of his contributions, or the value of the lessons he offers us still.

In 1935, with the election lost and Bennett in humiliated defeat, Sir Robert Borden, past prime minister and former boss, summarized his thoughts on the man. Borden wrote,

> His splendid ability, his keen grasp of general conditions, both national and international, his complete devotion to public duty and to the welfare of our country, the admirable resourcefulness and fine courage with which he has faced the overwhelming difficulties of the past five years, entitle him to the respect, admiration and gratitude of all right thinking Canadians.[5]

Borden's words were kind but they do not accurately reflect Bennett's legacy, and that's a shame. Historian Jeffrey Simpson was once in a British pub and an elderly patron asked, "What on earth did you Canadians do to R. B. Bennett? You seem to have forced him out, almost as if you wanted to drive him into exile. Why? He was the nicest man imaginable."[6] Why indeed.

The premise of this book is that the consensus about Bennett is fundamentally flawed. That consensus leans upon a false stereotype, a misreading of the depth and consistency of his political principles, and a refusal to acknowledge that he should be celebrated as an outstanding Canadian for his lifetime of daring and enduring accomplishments. That his life and legacy have been afforded short shrift is evidenced by the fact that this book is Bennett's first comprehensive biography.

The first attempt to examine Bennett was a short 1935 book by his office assistant, Andrew MacLean. In 1959 came a thin volume by his friend Lord Beaverbrook. Both were full of compliments and anecdotes but little analysis. A slim 1963 book by Ernest Watkins skimmed over Bennett's life and career as a pebble on a pond. In 1992, James Gray and Peter Waite both contributed valuable and insightful works, but neither were complete examinations of the man's life. The next year, Larry Glassford turned his master's thesis into a scholarly piece examining the Conservative Party's policies under Bennett's leadership. Glassford characterized Bennett's term as having three phases: implementation of campaign promises, defence of the social order, and an attempt at long-term reform. The book was a serious attempt to wring from an analysis of Bennett the emotion that has too often warped interpretation, but it was still not an examination of the man's entire life.

Most historians have dealt with Bennett only tangentially, and few have been kind. Some are blunt in their assessment, such as Blair Neatby who, in 1972, wrote, "As a politician he was a failure."[7] Some appear almost gleeful in their attacks. Michael Bliss, for instance, wrote in 2004 that Bennett was ". . . a plutocrat of plutocrats [possessing] either a messiah complex or horrible judgement, perhaps both."[8] Not yet done, Bliss went on to call him ". . . bombastic, pompous, a near tragic figure . . . Bennett was rich, fat, self-satisfied, and, in some of his policies apparently uncaring."[9] Perhaps Gordon Donaldson hit the mark when he concluded that the problem with Canadians then, and many historians later, was that Bennett's wealth, personality, and even his style of dress made him too tempting a target. Donaldson observed in 1994, "Bennett was the perfect cartoon capitalist—a top-hatted, carnationed exploiter of the masses—a Marxist's dream villain."[10] This is not to suggest that Bennett's policies and actions are not fair game. Jim Struthers, for instance, labelled Bennett's actions regarding unemployment and relief deeply flawed due mostly to policy inconsistencies.[11] His analysis, and those like it, is valuable because, like Glassford, he avoided character assassination and the disparagement of motives.

Most Canadians are introduced to Bennett in school. Many secondary school textbooks present negative interpretations based on misleading ideas or utterly demonstrable falsehoods. Secondary school students given the textbook *Canada: A North American Nation*, for instance, read that Mackenzie King and Bennett both adopted laissez-faire attitudes toward the Depression and that Bennett was unaware of the consequences of his actions—neither is true. These students probably passed tests by aping the text's assertion that Bennett was indifferent to the needs of Canadians and did nothing for much of his time in office until his last year—also not true.[12] Students instead reading *The North*

Americans could not be blamed for believing that Bennett was essentially asleep for the first four years of his administration. It reports, "Finally in January of 1935, the prime minister decided to act."[13] According to the text, Mackenzie King was responsible for increasing the power of the central government and for creating the Bank of Canada and the CBC—more falsehoods. While students may learn little of the man and some of what they do learn may be wrong, all seem to emerge from secondary school history courses knowing exactly what a Bennett buggy was.

Bennett came back into focus in the fall of 2008. The skyrocketing price of oil and the actions of a greedy few led to a worldwide financial, then economic, collapse. Canadians were awed by the degree to which all that was once certain suddenly vanished. Venerable corporations that produced goods and provided jobs that had helped define the country for generations threatened to disappear. The economic and political assumptions that had long guided decisions made in Parliament, boardrooms, and around kitchen tables were gone. Beginning in 2009, Canadians set out to play a new game with rules that had yet to be written. Canadians came to know a little about how 1930 felt.

Pundits and politicians stumbled over themselves in comparing current challenges to the Great Depression. Some journalists fell back to the old misinformed stereotypes, but others demonstrated a clearer understanding of what Bennett and his administration had truly been about. In October 2008, for example, Thomas Walkom wrote in the *Toronto Star*, "In popular mythology, Bennett is remembered as an apostle of laissez-faire, a well-heeled lawyer who could only shrug as the poor starved. In fact, he was one of the most interventionist prime ministers the country has seen. Somewhat of a Red Tory (he approved of old-age pensions), Bennett was compelled by events to become more radical over time and, in the end, to redefine government's economic role."[14]

There is more to Bennett than the Bennett buggy. He was more than the stereotype and more than a straw man available for those of the far right or left, both at the time and later, to tear asunder in lazily making a point. Throughout his political career he stood as a rebel with views that were often divorced from the priorities, policies, and commonly held beliefs of the day. His success in business was similarly owed mostly to his being able to see opportunities others were too blind to see or too timid to exploit. Bennett's bold vision regarding the manner in which the country could evolve, and his fierce passion that inspired him to urge others to share that vision, led to a remarkable life and career in which he challenged and changed Canada.

Bennett is among Canada's most intriguing citizens and influential prime ministers, with a great deal of value to teach us all. Exploring his life affords a better understanding of the country that Canadians enjoy today and of challenges to be conquered tomorrow. R. B. Bennett is a case study in political leadership during a time of national and global crisis. He is whispering to us through time. We owe it to ourselves to listen.

CHAPTER ONE

THE EARLY YEARS

1870–1910

C APTAIN DAVID STILES must have been a hell of a man. A bit of a rogue and raconteur, he spun grand tales of his life as a sea captain whose adventures took him around the world. And if this were not enough, he regaled those who would listen with fascinating stories of his family having fought the French at the battle of Louisburg and again on the Plains of Abraham. The captain often surrendered to the siren song of the sea. But when the winds managed to blow him home it was to Albert County on the picturesque Bay of Fundy. It must have been something to have heard the yarns. Among those who did was the captain's grandson Richard.

Richard Bedford Bennett was born on July 3, 1870, to Captain Stiles's daughter, the sprightly Henrietta. Henrietta welcomed her new son in the bedroom of her parents' modest wooden frame house at Hopewell Hill, just a short walk up from her and her husband's home in Hopewell Cape. The town is minutes from what is now New Brunswick's much photographed and scampered-upon Hopewell Rocks. At the time of Richard's birth, Hopewell Cape was a town of about five hundred souls. It boasted shops, a stone courthouse, a small school, and tidy, comfortable, brightly coloured frame houses. The endless rhythm of 45-foot tides saw the 3-mile-wide Petitcodiac River regularly surrender to reveal glistening adobe-red mud flats.

The town was also home to a large, stone Methodist church that played an important role in the lives of Henrietta Bennett and her growing family. She gave up her teaching career with Richard's arrival and two years later gave birth to Henry, who died only four years later. Evelyn was born in 1874, then Ronald in 1876, George in 1881, and finally Mildred in 1889. All of Henrietta's children attended church once and sometimes twice each Sunday. Under her strict guidance they were taught to adhere to its stern Wesleyan beliefs. Gambling, drinking, and smoking were to be avoided in lives guided by the often-discussed virtues of honesty, hard work, tolerance, and generosity. Like all Henrietta's children, Richard soaked in everything that came from the pulpit and which was reinforced by his mother. Avoiding temptation and maintaining strict self-discipline in all matters in one's life became a source of pride from his days as a tall, freckled child onward. Henrietta would have been pleased with the degree to which her oldest son internalized those teachings.

As Richard grew up, the small town remained home to hard-working folks who fished, farmed, or worked in the local shipbuilding industry. Unfortunately for Henrietta, the work ethic exhibited by nearly all around her was largely lost on her husband. Henry Bennett married Henrietta on January 22, 1869. Like the Stiles family, the Bennetts were proud of their British heritage. The first Bennett to find his way to the New World was Samuel, who arrived in Massachusetts in 1635. The late 1750s saw the embers of discontent fanned to flames by pamphleteers, rebels, and opportunists. Samuel's son Zadoc was loyal to the king and wise enough to read the writing on the wall, and so he came north from Lyme, Connecticut, to Nova Scotia in 1759. King George II showed his gratitude to the Connecticut Loyalists by issuing 500-acre land grants to the head of each family.

By the time the American Revolution ended in 1783, 50,000 to 60,000 loyalists had fled north, and about 30,000 had found their way to the Maritimes. The hardscrabble farmers of the Annapolis Valley and the independently minded fishermen and entrepreneurs of the growing towns of Halifax and Lunenburg warily welcomed the newcomers. They saw their colony's population suddenly double. Towns became infused with upper- and middle-class families used to hard work but accustomed as well to the deference owed to those whose efforts had won them a particular rank in society. Established Methodist communities soon found themselves in the minority as predominately Anglican Loyalists assumed prominent civil society positions. The construction of grand churches announced the newcomers' wealth and permanence.

Soon after the Loyalists' thunderous arrival in the early 1780s, an application was made to split Nova Scotia into two colonies in order that the 12,000 Loyalists who had settled among the 2,500 British settlers and 1,500 Acadians in territory west of the peninsula could have their own government. Still reeling from the world war that had resulted in the loss of lives, treasure, status, and the American colonies, the British government quickly approved the division. The idea was to keep the Canadian colonies small, divided, and weak. The king certainly did not want another troublesome powerhouse such as Virginia. And so New Brunswick was created in 1784.

It was in this climate of opportunity, challenge, and change that the industrious Zadoc Bennett bought and sold land until his death in 1810 at age 77. His estate saw his twelve children share an impressive inheritance. His son Benjamin shared his father's skill at real estate investment and at his death at age one hundred he left tracts of land to each of his children. Shipbuilding was an integral part of the nineteenth-century Maritime economy. Benjamin's second child, Nathan, worked his inherited land wealth into a new shipbuilding venture at Hopewell Cape. His enterprising spirit turned the Bennett shipyards into a stunning success. The first ship produced was *Albert*, a 56-foot schooner, and the second a 127-footer called the *Alice Bentley*. By the 1850s, the company had become quite prosperous and then famous for having sold a Bennett clipper ship, named the *Emma*, to the White Star Line, later notorious for its unsinkable *Titanic*. Bennett ships were sailing the world's oceans and the *Emma* was delivering the mail between Britain and Australia. It was knowledge of his family's shipbuilding heritage that made Prime Minister Bennett's chest swell with pride when in October 1930, the good people of Lunenburg cheered as the champagne bottle crashed and a fishing schooner christened the *R. B. Bennett* slid into the bay's choppy waters for her maiden voyage.

Henry Bennett was born in 1842. He inherited the family business when its best days were already behind it. Henry earned a reputation as an honest man and for years he served with distinction as the county's justice of the peace and Hopewell Cape's port warden. But he could not save the company from its slow downward spiral—owed partly to the replacement of wood and sails by steel and steam, but also to the fact that he loved a good laugh and a strong drink more than a full day's work. More affable than ambitious and more forgiving than firm, Henry was eventually to find part-time work as a blacksmith and that, plus the sale of vegetables from his small farm became the family's main source of income.

Henry's eldest son, Richard, consequently, was raised in a household with tales of wealth and adventure but little money and fewer prospects. He grew up learning that good times can be won but never taken for granted, that hard work is rewarded and sloth punished, that drink is a thief, and piety its own reward. He later told a friend, "I'll always remember the pit from which I was [dug] and the long uphill road I had to travel. I'll never forget one step."[1]

Young Richard, or Dick as he was called by all, was a shy, quiet, and introspective child who did not like or often participate in the games of childhood, preferring instead the solitude of the garden or a book and the company of his protective mother. He could always be relied upon to do his chores, which consisted mostly of the daily milking and leading the small herd from one field to another for pasture. The Methodist church was a source of both spiritual sustenance and community fellowship where he enjoyed and participated joyfully in socials, festivals, and teas.

Richard worked well at school and Henrietta drilled him again at home each evening. He did alright but did not excel. Nonetheless, at twelve years of age his scholastic achievements were adequate to earn him a spot at Fredericton's Provincial Normal School for teacher training. He coasted through courses, relying mostly on a prodigious memory that revealed itself early in his life and would serve him well through to its end. In the days of rote learning he found that while others struggled he was easily able to commit to memory long poems and large passages of prose. Also noteworthy, and something which would forever both serve and hinder him, was a natural verbal acuity and willingness to exploit that ability for gain. Schoolmates wrote a small poem about him that captured his proficiency and personality and perhaps an early shimmering of arrogance:

First there came Bennett, conceited and young,
Who never knew quite when to hold his quick tongue.[2]

By the age of fifteen Bennett had graduated with a second-class cer-
tificate. He accepted a position teaching elementary school at Irishtown,
near Moncton. He worked hard, lived frugally, and saved his money.

The summer after his first year of teaching provided Bennett with his
first taste of politics. In the 1887 federal election he volunteered with the
Liberal-Conservative Party that was trying to send Richard Weldon to
Ottawa.[3] Bennett began by stuffing envelopes but Weldon quickly recognized that his young volunteer was capable of much more and soon
Bennett was delivering speeches for the candidate. The verbal gifts Bennett
had shown in school were transferred easily to the stump and he found
that despite being only seventeen he could hold his own not only in delivering a political message but also in handling the rough and tumble of the
inevitable hecklers.[4] Weldon won his seat and Bennett won a mentor.

Meanwhile, Bennett had been completing courses that in 1888
earned him a first-class teaching certification, allowing him to apply for
administrative positions and affording him a much-needed raise. The
certification and his talents led to an appointment as school principal in
Douglastown, on the Miramichi River's north bank. Only eighteen, he
was responsible for four teachers, in four different schools, ministering
to 159 children.

Personality traits that would inform his maturing character were
seen in his prudent and skilful handling of such an enormous responsibility. His officiousness and unwillingness to suffer fools were clear in
the stern manner in which he ran his charge. Discipline was strict, and
staff and students were expected to work diligently. He demanded respect and expected obedience and zeal, but employed persuasion rather
than corporal punishment for miscreants. At the time, his must have
been the only principal's office in the land without a well-worn leather
strap. An Inspector of Schools report stated that Bennett was doing
splendid work and that his ideas regarding the revision of courses for
improving instruction in secondary schools were well received.[5]

He was doing fine but he was impatient. Bennett was seldom satisfied with things as they were and constantly sought not comfort but
challenge and improvement. This habit, as well as a bold, perhaps
haughty, self-confidence, coupled with a youthful inability to differentiate honesty from insult, was revealed in a letter the nineteen-year-old
Bennett wrote to school board trustees:

During a stay of nearly two years in this place, I have come to the conclusion that the material is not lacking here to produce pupils of more than ordinary ability but while I feel that such is the case I cannot but remark that unless the parents are aroused and awakened from the apathy with which they now view all matters connected with the school work, the fine abilities of their children will never be shown.

I would remark that the school officers are sadly deficient in their duties. During my stay here I have not been favoured by a visit from one of the trustees.[6]

Meanwhile, Bennett's staid, fastidious lifestyle allowed him to save more than half his annual five-hundred-dollar principal's salary. For recreation, and for the stipend allowance attached, he joined the local militia. However, the non-athletic young man proved himself a rather inept soldier. He was eventually assigned to the paymaster's office. He sometimes inadvertently found himself in places where drinking and dancing took place but was quite proud of his yielding to neither temptation.[7]

Bennett was often seen in the company of young women and enjoyed a number of relationships of various lengths and emotional depths. He showed particular romantic interest in Frances Snowball, the daughter of a New Brunswick senator, and then later in a nurse in Calgary known only as Miss Knight. Evelyn Windsor, the daughter of a Montreal rector, once turned his thoughts to romance, and later he even asked Edith Cochrane's father, a minister in Borden's government, for his daughter's hand. But for reasons unknown it was denied.

The woman that most people believed would someday become Bennett's wife was the witty and vivacious Jennie Shirreff, whom he met when he was a twenty-three-year-old lawyer in Chatham, New Brunswick. The warm relationship peaked at friendship, however, when Jennie left the province for Quebec to marry prominent industrialist Ezra Eddy; everybody called him E. B. After the death of her husband, in February 1906, the friendship was renewed as Bennett helped the widow with inheritance, business, and legal issues, and was rewarded with company stock, a directorship, and warm personal letters. When Bennett was in Ottawa, the two often found time to dine and to enjoy each other's company. Jennie died in 1921. Bennett died a bachelor.

A rumour that was later to grow more salacious with each telling was that Bennett remained unmarried due to a health problem. It was whispered that he had phimosis, which is a tight foreskin resulting in intensely painful erections.[8] Another is that he suffered from Peyronie's disease, which involves a thickening of the penile shaft resulting in painful and misshapen erections.[9] Despite the popularity and persistence of the rumours, and another that he had had his problem dealt with through surgery in London, there is no evidence that Bennett ever mentioned either disease or that any of the women with whom he was romantically inclined discussed it with anyone.

From his first days as a teacher to his term as principal, Bennett maintained his austere lifestyle in one modest boarding house or another. Landlords noticed that his worldly possessions were crammed into one small black trunk and that its contents were nearly all books. Reading, that most detached and solitary of pursuits, was his only form of recreation and even then he read to be informed rather than entertained. He saw novels as a waste of time, preferring political biography and history. His Bible was always at his bedside and he read from it every night. Not yet having grown out of the young man's urge to show off, he was a little too eager to demonstrate his ability to accurately quote chapter and verse. He would never be attracted to a hobby or sport, either as spectator or participant. He avoided exercise, believing that a short walk on Sunday afternoon was sufficient. He preferred to walk with only his thoughts for company.

Perhaps his monastic lifestyle and yearning for privacy were expressions of his shyness. However, Bennett could also roar with an infectious laugh, enjoy funny stories, and even participate in practical jokes. As prime minister he once called Alice Millar, his personal secretary, and disguising his voice, tried every tactic he could imagine to secure an interview with himself. On another occasion he worked a stenographer late into the evening then called her at home to ask her to return early the next morning for more work. When she agreed he laughed and told her that he was only joking and had just wanted to thank her for her dedication.

Bennett had but one lifelong friend. In 1879, Max Aitken was born in Maple, Ontario, but the next year his minister-father moved his young family to the Presbyterian manse in Newcastle, New Brunswick. Max would later become a lawyer, businessman, and owner of several newspapers and other businesses in Canada and England. He would serve in Britain's House of Commons and in the cabinet of Prime Minister David Lloyd George. In 1916, he became Lord Beaverbrook and took his place in the House of Lords and in Churchill's cabinet, where he continued to wield considerable influence in business, politics, and the arts until the end of his long and meritorious life in 1964.

In the spring of 1889, the two met on a wharf, awaiting the 6-mile steamship journey down the Miramichi River from Douglastown to Aitken's Newcastle home. The precocious ten-year-old Aitken was taken by the nineteen-year-old Bennett, standing there in his banker's suit and banker's hat, and he boldly introduced himself. Bennett was amused then fascinated by the boy, who looked no more than seven or eight, and so engaged him where other, older boys might have simply walked away. One acted older than he was and the other was trying to look older than he was and both were quickly as enthralled with each other as they were with themselves. They chatted amiably during the trip and agreed to meet again. The two became close friends and confidants. Bennett was a regular dinner guest at the Aitken home, which was always filled with lively, informed conversation and the energy and laughter of nine children.

In 1959, Lord Beaverbrook wrote a slim volume that chronicled his business dealings with Bennett, from which both benefited, and their political principles, which were nearly always identical. The book told of a deep and enduring friendship in such simpering, sycophantic terms that it would most probably have mightily embarrassed Bennett. The hero-worshipping idolization of his older friend was such that as a young man Aitken adopted Bennett's speaking patterns, many of his favourite phrases, and even altered his handwriting to ape that of his friend/mentor/idol. He wrote, for instance, of a visit Bennett paid to him in Halifax over the Christmas holidays of 1904, at which Bennett stayed at his flat: "I saw him off by train at ten the next night, heartened by his visit and saddened by his departure. How I liked and admired him."[10]

The picture Aitken paints of his close friend reveals the degree to which Bennett consciously and successfully reinvented himself. Aitken noted that Bennett had a mercurial temper but that when the storm passed he would remonstrate that his mother had warned him that he would not amount to much if he could not learn to control his emotions. He wrote that the young Bennett worked to be polite but that sometimes it reached the point where he flattered those around him so much that he appeared insincere. He took pride in his memory but sometimes could not avoid showing off, often quoting from Scripture, poetry, or the words of men he admired. Aitken rather interestingly recalled that one time he looked up a Disraeli quote that Bennett had ostentatiously pronounced and found that his friend had botched a line or two. He revealed perhaps more than he intended in defending Bennett's sometimes casual relationship with accuracy, observing, "Bennett never deceived others. He sometimes deceived himself."[11]

The dapper appearance that had first caught young Aitken's attention was a part of Bennett's conscious reinvention of himself and something in which he took great pride. He was tall and thin, with bright auburn hair, which he often had cut twice a week. In public he was always in a three-piece suit and wore a bowler hat when first it appeared presumptuous on such a young man and then long after the style had fallen from fashion. In his early twenties he began to eat three sumptuous and fat-laden meals a day in a determined effort to gain weight. He explained to Aitken that he believed he could present a more impressive appearance if he were larger. He was successful in attaining the girth for which he yearned and later, when gravity and a slowing metabolism found him, he significantly reduced his daily caloric intake. Neither his love of fine food nor his waistline followed the trend. Perhaps it was the pound or so of chocolate that he enjoyed each evening that was his undoing.

Bennett enjoyed his time as a school principal in Douglastown. While jealously protecting his privacy and still enjoying solitary pursuits he was nonetheless part of the social scene, and occasionally took pleasure in wagon rides with young women. He also involved himself in church and community affairs. The temperance movement was sweeping the Maritimes and was something for which he had a natural affinity. He joined the local Sons of Temperance Lodge and spoke at a number of meetings, extolling the virtues of an alcohol-free life for individuals and the benefits of an alcohol-free society. Pledges were signed and many proudly wore a blue ribbon indicating their dedication to abstinence. He also continued to work with the local Conservative riding association making speeches on behalf of Weldon and the party.

THE LAW AND POLITICS

Bennett was a good educator and careful administrator but he grew somewhat bored with the prospect of repeating the same routines year after year. Even as a boy he had told a teacher that he wanted someday to become a lawyer. Among the many people he had met in Douglastown was Lemuel John Tweedie, who had established a thriving law practice in nearby Chatham. Bennett impressed Tweedie to the point that he offered the ambitious young man a chance to clerk in his office. Every weekend Bennett would take the ferry to Chatham, stay with the Tweedie family, and article in the office until returning to his school duties each Monday morning. Despite this harried schedule, Bennett still found time each week to teach Sunday school, get elected as a church trustee, and serve as the Sunday School Committee secretary. His reading turned exclusively to the law. This punishing pace showed the determination, drive, and indefatigable capacity for work that all of Canada would later come to know.

In 1890, Bennett left the teaching profession and entered Dalhousie University in Halifax to study law. Old friend and Albert County member of Parliament Dr. Richard Weldon had founded and was the dean of the Dalhousie Law School. It was through his good graces that Bennett was appointed law school librarian—an early lesson in the value of favours earned and loyalty respected. The library post enabled the twenty-year-old voracious reader to be surrounded by his beloved books while also earning some much-needed money.

Like many others who find secondary school tedious, Bennett excelled in university. Not surprisingly, he played no sports and joined no clubs. He read, he studied, and he worked. He spent summers articling with Tweedie and saving money. Upon graduation in 1893, Bennett moved to Chatham and became the junior partner in the law firm Tweedie and Bennett. He took his old room in Tweedie's large home. Tweedie left many of the day-to-day activities of the practice to young Bennett as he was increasingly active in the Conservative Party. His political work would later lead to his becoming the premier of New Brunswick and still later its lieutenant-governor, rendering him yet another well-placed friend for the ambitious Bennett.

Tweedie was helpful in introducing his determined young protegé to people who would help him to realize his political ambitions. Helpful as well was Aitken who, inspired by Bennett, had registered as a law student in the provincial capital, passed oral exams, and was articling at Tweedie and Bennett. Aitken was also showing an uncanny ability to make money. While fulfilling his duties at the law office he was also an insurance salesman and wrote articles for newspapers across the province, with some placed as far afield as the *Montreal Star*. If Tweedie was Bennett's new mentor, then Aitken remained his cheerleader.

When in 1896 Chatham received its charter as a town, Bennett convinced himself that he could be successful in a run for the position of alderman. Tweedie offered his advice but Aitken gave his heart to the campaign. Aitken, only seventeen years old but already an old hand at ingratiating himself with those who could prove to be advantageous, had become friends with J. L. Stewart, who owned the *Chatham World* newspaper. He persuaded Stewart to run a series of articles lauding Bennett's virtues and qualifications. Leaflets were printed and Aitken and Bennett took turns on the candidate's bicycle until every door in town had been knocked upon and a leaflet shoved into every hand.

There were also public meetings. The boy who had shown his ability with words in school was now a young man finding new ways to stir a crowd. He had for years been attending political meetings and noting oratorical tricks that worked well and he now adapted them for his presentations. Aitken heard all of Bennett's speeches and later wrote, "... he would speak for an hour or more with fire and fury. My efforts to record these speeches in shorthand failed entirely. So thrilled was I by his oratory and so excited by his domination over his audience that my notes were forgotten."[12]

The election saw Bennett win by only one vote; but he had won. Rather than a glorious blastoff into public life, however, Bennett's time as alderman was as unspectacular as his margin of victory. Municipal politics is unique in that people are governed by their neighbours. Municipal leaders make decisions and then see the results of those decisions quickly, such as a sidewalk being laid or a road paved. So too, municipal politicians are few in number and often long serving in a transparent arena where personalities, family ties, tradition, and unwritten rules can win the day. Bennett was new and seemed unwilling to acknowledge the delicate web of feelings and understandings. He quickly gained a reputation for stepping on toes and hurting himself by commenting on every issue whether big or small. He became unpopular with fellow aldermen and a feud developed, as none would support actions that Bennett wanted and he would support none of his fellow aldermen's ideas. Only three months into his two-year term he resigned his seat. No tears were shed.

His short and unsuccessful foray into politics portended issues of personality that would be seen throughout both his public and private careers. He was either a man who did his homework, determined the best road forward, and did what he could to bring to fruition the best available option, or he was bullheadedly arrogant; maybe he was both. Regardless, his brief appearance on the public stage was the first step on a long and circuitous path that would take him to the prime minister's office. Even while poring over staff reports regarding problems and opportunities affecting only the people of Chatham, New Brunswick, it seems clear that young Bennett had his eye on that prize.

There is a fascinating sculpture in downtown Saskatoon, marking the occasion in 1910 when a ten-year-old newspaper boy named John Diefenbaker met Prime Minister Wilfrid Laurier. According to the speech Laurier delivered later that evening, the young Diefenbaker had told him categorically that someday he too would be prime minister. Although there was no such meeting in Bennett's life, his goal and determination to attain it were as unambiguous as those of his prairie compatriot. One of the teachers that he supervised as principal later told the story that she and the eighteen-year-old Bennett had shared a wagon ride with a Mr. Brown and that she listened quietly as the two engaged in a heated discussion about religion. Later on the journey, Bennett entertained them with a recitation of Marc Antony's funeral piece from *Julius Caesar*. Impressed with his debating skill and memory, she told Bennett that he should consider a career in public life. He responded: "Some day I'm going to be Prime Minister of Canada."[13]

That his boyhood expression of political ambition was not just a brash teenager's attempt to impress a girl is seen in the fact that he repeated his audacious goal to others. While at Dalhousie, for example, Bennett and a classmate named W. H. Trueman, who would later become a member of the Manitoba Court of Appeals, took a horse-and-buggy ride to a public meeting to hear Sir John A. Macdonald. On the way home Bennett told his companion that one day he too would be prime minister.[14] That Bennett had told his friend Aitken about his political ambitions is made evident by the fact that voters in the Chatham municipal election were told by Aitken that they should support the young lawyer, for one day he would be prime minister.

When does healthy ambition became rapaciousness? When does a dream become a plan? Does any person become the leader of his country without the burning determination to do so lodged at the centre of his being? When does the story of Diefenbaker's encounter with Laurier or Bennett's much less public declarations to Brown, Trueman, or Aitken move from cute to interesting to egotistical? In 1930, Trueman visited Prime Minister Bennett in his Winnipeg hotel room and asked with a smile if he remembered the night he swore he would become prime minister. Bennett appeared hurt at Trueman's jocular tone and replied flatly, "I said I would, didn't I?"[15]

CALGARY

As the cool autumn evenings of 1896 were turning New Brunswick hardwoods to impressionist art, a visitor arrived at Chatham from faraway Calgary. For some time Calgary had been little more than a mounted police outpost with an attitude. It was named by Colonel James McLeod as a nod to his Scottish highland home and existed only because Kicking Horse Pass, with its gradient more forgiving than its alternative, had won the day among Canadian Pacific Railway (CPR) engineers and, consequently, the line had swung north. The tiny Hudson's Bay Company fort perched precariously at the confluence of the Elbow and Bow rivers got lucky. The rails had arrived in 1883 and with them the town burst with energy and potential. By 1896 it was an ambitious young man's dream with a growing population of about 4,000 and surrounded by prosperous farms and ranches run by hard-working adventurers who had come from eastern Canada and western Europe seeking land, freedom, and opportunity. The town was soon shipping wheat and beef to the East, and more of what Interior Minister Clifford Sifton had dubbed "stalwart peasants in sheep skin coats" were arriving every day. Since the great fire of 1886, more and more buildings were being constructed of sandstone and brick, so the city was slowly developing a statelier look and feel. But much of Calgary still had the appearance of every cowboy town we have come to know in every western movie we have ever seen: horses, mostly dirt streets and wooden sidewalks, and wooden two-storey buildings.

The visitor to Chatham that day was frontier lawyer James Lougheed. He had been born in Brampton, Ontario, but followed the steel rail west, literally encamping in Medicine Hat and running his first law office from beneath a canvas ceiling. Two events encouraged him to move his practice to Calgary in 1883 and contributed to his quick success. First, he encountered a rattlesnake in his tent, and he hated snakes. Second, he married well. Isabella (Belle) Hardisty was from a powerful Métis family; her father had been the Hudson Bay Company's Chief Factor. One of her uncles was Donald Smith, who later became Lord Strathcona. Smith was a man of wealth and influence who sat on a number of boards, held a significant number of shares in Canada's most important companies, and enjoyed political and business ties to the country's power elites. In Smith's impressive portfolio were shares of the Canadian Pacific Railway and many of the companies upon which it depended. It was Lougheed's connection to Smith that enabled him to secure an appointment with the CPR's President William Van Horne. Lougheed left the meeting as the railway's lawyer. From that retainer he established his Calgary practice and watched it, along with his profits from land speculation, grow at the same breakneck pace as his newly adopted city.

Another of Isabella's uncles was Richard Hardisty, one of the Northwest Territories' wealthiest men and its senator. When the senator died in 1889, Sir John appointed Lougheed to succeed him. His responsibilities in Ottawa grew just as his firm was becoming a substantial power in Calgary, with more clients and lucrative opportunities in land speculation. He needed help. Lougheed had contacted his old friend, Dalhousie's Dean Weldon, to see if there were any young lawyers that he could recommend as a partner to take some of the pressure from his shoulders. Weldon knew just the young man. Lougheed took the train from Ottawa to Chatham and met with Bennett.

After less than an hour of conversation, Lougheed was sufficiently impressed that he offered Bennett a partnership. But the young man demurred, and from a position of no strength whatsoever he summoned the temerity to negotiate. Lougheed was impressed again. As a result of the deal to which they eventually agreed, Lougheed Bennett would see the junior partner earn 20 per cent of the firm's income for the first $3,750 and 30 per cent on each additional dollar. The deal was sweetened by 5 per cent in the second year. There were many other law firms in Calgary at the time, so competition for cases and clients would be fierce, but Bennett was assured that since Lougheed had already bagged the biggest elephant in town with his CPR deal, more corporate clients could be won. Further, Lougheed promised that Bennett would have great sway in the affairs of the firm, as his political responsibilities in Calgary and Ottawa would often have him absent from the office. It was an offer much too good for the motivated young man to refuse.

Bennett quickly wrapped up his business dealings in Chatham and spent Christmas back with his family in Hopewell Cape. The first days of 1897 found him aboard a CPR train for the long journey to the Northwest Territories and to a city and country he had never seen. He was twenty-six years old.

It was late January. Bennett's train was scheduled to arrive at 3 a.m., but a storm delayed it until eight o'clock. It was dark. It was 40 below zero. One freezing hand held tight to a coat that was too light and the other to a grip that was too heavy. He lurched his way to the platform and asked for a cab but a porter laughed and told him that there were no such conveniences in Calgary. He left to slowly shuffle his way along Stephens Avenue through the cold and snow and past empty lots piled with freezing horse manure, horses tethered in the numerous livery stables, and finally a motley collection of stone, brick, and ramshackle wooden buildings that were struggling to form themselves into a downtown.

The Alberta Hotel's small lobby must have seemed like an oasis of warmth and welcome. As he was at the desk checking into the third-floor rooms that Lougheed had arranged, Bennett met more Calgarians. According to an often-regaled story, a roughly dressed man approached and offered to warm the young stranger with a drink but was told that he did not drink. Another offered him a cigar but was informed he did not smoke. A third reportedly snorted, "Boy oh boy, there's a guy who's got no future in this man's town."[16]

That evening, Lougheed took Bennett to the Calgary Opera House where Madam Albani performed. It was so cold even inside that a patron helped the shivering singer by placing his coat over her shoulders so that she could continue. The next morning Bennett set out and on the street asked the location of the nearest church. As he made his way through the bitter cold he heard one woman say to another, "Poor boy, he won't keep that up."[17] He had to fight an urge to scamper back to New Brunswick.

In no time, however, Bennett had established a routine that he would maintain for years. He would be up and to work early and arrive back at his rented rooms late. When not lunching at his office desk he took all three meals at the hotel dining room. He continued his habit of gorging himself and was becoming increasingly successful in his quest to gain weight. Two years later, in 1899, he moved to a Fourth Street rooming house kept by a pair of widows. But he continued, as a young man observing an older man's habits, to take his meals at his favourite corner table at the Alberta Hotel.

The Methodist church again became the centre of his social life. It offered fellowship and through contacts in the congregation he quickly built a social network in the bustling city. He became active in the church's support for Prohibition. He also renewed his membership with the Masonic lodge, which was something he had begun through following his father's footsteps back in Hopewell Cape. Through the church, the lodge, the firm, and Lougheed's active introductions, he quickly established a range of friends and acquaintances and was a regular in Calgary's small but growing social scene. But he showed little interest in women and spent most evenings alone with his work or books.

In Lougheed Bennett's Clarence Block second-floor offices, just down the street from his hotel, Bennett continued to make an impression on his partner and others with his work ethic, ability to synthesize large volumes of facts, and his remarkable memory. As cases came his way and were dispatched quickly and successfully, Bennett's workload increased, but it was never onerous. He impressed judges and other lawyers with his abilities and also with what was seen as a burning desire to win. He employed the arsenal of his memory and ability to think quickly on his feet and to speak in eloquent full paragraphs to his advantage, but these were often still undisciplined weapons used sometimes merely to harangue witnesses, juries, and opponents. One lawyer was so incensed by Bennett's badgering that he leapt over a table and physically attacked him. Bennett was humiliated when he was knocked to the ground by the much smaller man, but while he lost the fight he won the case.

His cockiness was on public display one evening at a political meeting at which the keynote speaker was Edmonton Liberal Member of Parliament Frank Oliver. Bennett heckled and interrupted Oliver to the point where members of the audience began to taunt Bennett. People suggested that if he truly believed that he could do better than Oliver, then he should stand and speak. Bennett did just that and, with detailed and witty extemporaneous remarks, quickly bested the carefully prepared Oliver. He was rude, but he was smart, and he was becoming well respected by some and well known by many.

As his notoriety increased, Bennett was mocked by a local entertainer at a fundraising dinner. Some men might have been amused and perhaps flattered, but Bennett endured the show in silent rage. In the professions of law and politics it is often said that one benefits from developing the skin of a rhinoceros. But Bennett never did. He was and would always be sensitive to even a perceived slight. Despite the importance he placed and the pride that he took in controlling his human urges, Bennett never really learned to turn the other cheek. A beast of a temper always seemed to lurk within him. Aitken observed that even as a young man, "He would burst out in angry indignation against slights and injustice, fancied or real, using tough and tiresome language."[18] And he did so that night, controlling himself during the performances but later in his hotel exploding in a thunderous rage.

Also haunting the shadows of his character, and a cousin to his arrogance, was a stubborn refusal to admit error. In 1935, Bennett's secretary, Andrew MacLean, wrote a charming little book that was obviously meant to extol his boss's virtues for a public that would soon be going to the polls. Even so, MacLean could not help but make a point often made by others regarding that quirk. MacLean observed, "Like many others of unusual powers, he is intellectually vain. He would rather do almost anything than admit he was wrong. He will twist and wriggle endlessly in order to becloud the fact that he has made a mistake."[19]

RETURN TO POLITICS

Only a year after bidding his friend goodbye, in the spring of 1898 Max Aitken found his prospects too limited in Chatham, and law school too tedious in Saint John. He purchased a train ticket and followed Bennett to Calgary. The two friends met each other with a joyful reunion. Aitken set to work helping in the law office, writing articles for newspapers, speculating in real estate and small businesses, and again demonstrating the greatest key to his success: his ability to curry favour with others. He was pleased with how quickly Bennett had become a part of Calgary's business, social, and political life. He attended speeches that Bennett was making both in the city and surrounding communities in support of a Wesleyan Methodist lifestyle based on self-denial and, most specifically, an abstinence from tobacco and alcohol. He noted how his friend's already terrific speaking ability had improved.

Bennett's ambition was having a tough time locating opportunity, but the two would soon meet. At that moment, the politics and governance structure of the territory was in flux. The Northwest Territories had been Rupert's Land, then the property of the Canadian government, then from 1875 a legal territory of the Dominion. It was ruled by a legislative assembly, which met in Regina. The government worked under the not inconsiderable influence of the lieutenant-governor with a council that he appointed. It operated much like a municipal council in terms of the limited powers it possessed and in that it was ostensibly without political parties while roiling with partisanship that gurgled just beneath the surface. The territory's political structure was as unsustainable as Calgary's potential was unstoppable.

A territorial election was scheduled for November 1898. Bennett consulted Aitken who, not surprisingly, encouraged his candidacy for one of Calgary's seats and pledged assistance in running the campaign. Lougheed also enthusiastically supported his partner. He promised to use his substantial influence in the local Conservative Party to do all he could to help. At that time the Conservatives had yet to recover from Sir John A. Macdonald's 1891 death and the sad parade of intelligent, well-meaning but ineffective leaders that followed—Abbott, Thompson, Bowell, and Tupper. The party was especially weak on the western frontier with Lougheed nearly single-handedly holding it together from his seat in the Senate and through the force of his personality. Bennett's party membership and election to office could only help Lougheed's organizational efforts. But his support was also based on a sincere appreciation for Bennett and his potential. In 1910, Lougheed wrote of Bennett's political skills and made a prescient prediction:

Bennett can solve any problem he puts his mind to. No man is quicker to strip a problem of unnecessary verbiage and translate it into a simple and understandable language. Some day Bennett will be called upon to solve the greatest problems in Canada. Some day Canada will turn to him to get the country out of its difficulties.[20]

Bennett paid the hundred-dollar candidacy fee in August for the November election and worked hard throughout the long campaign. He promised to bring greater prosperity to his city and to turn the territory into a province with Calgary, rather than Regina, as its capital. These were bold promises boldly pronounced, but few heard them: his first public meeting drew only seven people. His next, although widely advertised, drew the same seven people. It was not a propitious start. Newspapers were at best lukewarm to Bennett's candidacy. Some stories noted that he had lived in the city for less than two years while others wondered if he was simply being foisted upon the people as a mouthpiece for the CPR. Still others warned about the possibility of too much political power resting in the law offices of Lougheed Bennett.[21]

His opponents were all much older, better known, and more experienced men: W. W. Stuart, James Muir, and James Riley. Few believed Bennett stood much of a chance. But his campaign caught fire during a debate in the town of Olds. Bennett lashed out at what he called the tired old men who had been ruling the territory and were running against him. He turned the criticism of his youth and inexperience to his advantage by proposing that new ideas and new people were needed to move the territory forward. Muir was in the audience and rose to defend not only himself but the others of his generation who had been and were continuing to provide service to the public. Bennett would have none of it and carried on his boisterous assault. The spontaneous debate became so raucous that RCMP officers intervened and warned Bennett that they would need to take drastic action if tempers did not cool. Bennett threw gas on the fire by accusing the police of overstepping their bounds and all but daring them to arrest him. Muir shouted that he was willing to end the debate by taking Bennett outside and giving him the beating he deserved. The audience loved it. The papers reported it. Bennett had succeeded in not only injecting excitement into what had been a moribund campaign, but more important, he had established its narrative. Like the 1968 Canadian federal election that pitted Pierre Trudeau against Robert Stanfield, and the 2008 American presidential election that saw Barack Obama opposing John McCain, Bennett's 1898 territorial campaign began as a contest about ideas and issues but ended up being about people's desire for political and generational change and the power of personality.

The fourth of November dawned frighteningly cold in Calgary. The snow was already piling up. It was Election Day and the results were far from certain. Bennett sat nervously but with quiet confidence in the Alberta Hotel's telegraph office, encamped with Aitken and others from his law office, including George Tempest, George Cloakey, and his secretary, Miss Cameron, all of whom had helped in the campaign. Early results came slowly to the intrepid group and they appeared positive. The city seemed to be going to Bennett. It soon became clear that even rural areas were supporting the young newcomer.

The final tally saw Bennett win 291 votes to Stuart's 205, Muir's 169, and Riley's disappointing 47. After only twenty-four months in Calgary, Bennett was a well-known, successful, and respected partner in the city's largest firm and its member in the Territorial Assembly.

Bennett sprang to his new duties in Regina with great relish. For two years he worked hard and learned that in politics, as in most professions, the way to get things done is to understand that progress is never a straight road. Those who move forward are those who understand that friends and allies must be nurtured, enemies recognized, and that while black-and-white rules are important, political success grows only in a great garden of grey. That Bennett understood all of this was seen even before the legislature's first meeting in early April 1899. He had organized an evening for five fellow MLAS who were scheduled to spend the night in Calgary while en route to Regina. He picked up the tab for a lavish dinner at the Alberta Hotel and then the six retired to Lougheed's home where everyone except Bennett enjoyed scotch and cigars.

Once in the legislature, however, Bennett reverted to the unfortunate habits he had demonstrated as a Chatham alderman. He ignored the procedures and understandings of the past and immediately demonstrated what some could consider political intelligence, but what others might deem ruthlessness. He did so with a direct attack on Frederick Haultain, who for years had been the de facto premier of the territories.

Haultain was born in London to a military family that in 1860 moved to Peterborough, Ontario, when he was three. After earning his law degree, he moved to Fort Macleod to practise. He served in a number of important positions in the territorial government before being appointed president of the Executive Council, or premier, in 1897. Haultain was a slight man with dark, slicked-back hair and a thin moustache. He had won the respect of all with his tireless dedication to the territory that he hoped would someday form a large province that he wanted to call Buffalo. He had no idea that the young rookie from Calgary somehow saw himself as the new sheriff in town.

Haultain had made it his practice to begin each new legislative session by allowing every member to speak and then rising in response to all that had been said, thereby presenting his own remarks as the Speech from the Throne. But this time was different. After each member but Bennett had spoken, Haultain looked to Bennett's chair and found it was empty. He had no option but to rise and speak. No sooner had he done so than Bennett strolled into the chamber, drew all eyes to himself as he took his place, and then made voluminous notes throughout the speech. When Haultain was finished, Bennett rose to lambaste all that had been said. He saved his most vitriolic language for a personal attack on Haultain and then on his government for lacking vision and refusing to push harder for provincial status.

Bennett's long and damning speech was widely reported and lavishly praised, even by the Liberal *Calgary Herald* that noted, "After Mr. Haultain had concluded his speech, Mr. Bennett replied in what is conceded to have been one of the most eloquent speeches ever heard in this house."[22] The *Regina Leader* argued that Bennett was ". . . the most fluent speaker whose voice ever sounded within the walls of the Territorial chamber."[23] The next day the *Calgary Herald* again wrote of Bennett, opining that he was quickly making a name for himself in Regina but warning that the brash young MLA was being carried away by the "the exuberance of his verbosity."[24] Bennett's quick wit and silver tongue, although untamed and undisciplined, were rendering him widely known.

But he had not yet learned to pick his battles. Bennett was heard on every issue. Although he could speak extemporaneously, weaving articulate and powerful phrases, he seemed to revel in the satisfaction of defeating an opponent in debate and being the first member on his feet rather than in seeking compromise or allies to move an issue forward. He still seemed to misunderstand the connection between oratory and persuasion or tactics and strategy.[25]

Bennett's time in the territorial legislature was important for the degree to which he established himself as a friend of the farmer and working class who would champion their interests over those of the powerful corporate elite. Bennett's support for those without power remained constant throughout his political career. In his maiden speech, he argued that the main benefit of provincial status would be the ability to raise capital for a competing rail line that would end the CPR's monopoly and thereby reduce freight rates. In the months that followed, he supported many bills that sought to limit the power of the CPR and to improve the lot of workers, including those who worked for the railway and its subsidiaries.

His acting on the behalf of the people rather than the CPR was interesting given that at that time Bennett had moved his law office a block and a half down the road from Lougheed Bennett to the CPR land offices. There, he was overseeing the sectioning off and sale of thousands of acres of CPR land for the benefit of both the company and himself. He made a commission of 25 cents for every acre he sold. He also made a practice of purchasing and flipping many sections on his own. Further, he had renegotiated his retainer so that the company was paying him a substantial personal fee of $7,500 a year. At the same time, Lougheed Bennett had secured many other corporate clients. including the Bank of Montreal, the Royal Bank, the Bank of Nova Scotia, Merchants Bank, the Bank of Commerce, Crown Trust, Union Trust, Massey Harris, R. G. Dun, and insurance companies Crown Life and Great West Life. As a private citizen Bennett pocketed money directly and indirectly from the CPR and these major financial corporations. As a public servant he spoke aggressively against corporate power and for the rights of working people.

Bennett did not see a contradiction between his corporate ties and his defence of labour. He explained his belief in a capitalist system that is fair to both the needs of corporations and the working class in his support of the July 1902 carpenters' union strike. He spoke at a mass meeting of Calgary's carpenters and fellow tradesmen. He argued with great rhetorical flourishes that he supported capitalism and the right of business people to make a fair profit, but also that all workers deserved the right to organize themselves into unions, set reasonable prices for their labour, and earn a decent living through which they could raise their families. As in all industrialized democracies, Bennett argued, Canadian business and labour needed each other and so the interests of both had to be protected. To the cheering union men he said, "So long as I live I will give my best efforts to any labour organization which endeavours to uphold right causes, make better the homes of the people and helps to build a strong and reliant race."[26]

Over a year and a half, beginning shortly after his arrival at the Northwest Territories Legislative Assembly in April 1899, Bennett also demonstrated his concern for the conditions under which working-class people toiled with his efforts as an impassioned legislator. He played a significant role with six pieces of legislation. First he moved an amendment that sought to restrict miners to eight hours underground during any twenty-four-hour period and to strengthen other provisions to further protect their interests and safety. The amendment was initially defeated but later adopted as part of other legislation. Second, he introduced a private member's bill that offered compensation for workers injured on the job. It went nowhere, but later he heartily supported a government initiative based on his idea. Third, he proposed a measure that would protect working men and women from having their property confiscated if they were having trouble paying small debts. The bill was debated in the Assembly but died. Fourth, Bennett proposed a law that would have improved workplace safety by making employers liable for unsafe practices, machinery, or buildings. This bill also died a quick death. Fifth, he worked to stop a bill that sought to remove the ability of landowners to sue if the government offered unfair value for land it expropriated. The legislation passed without Bennett's amendment. Finally, he opposed a bill that sought to give the territory the power to administer newly created villages without first considering the desire of residents for self-government. He argued that too much power was being placed in the hands of government-appointed commissioners and won a partial victory when an amendment reduced their power. The failure of the bills to make substantive changes in the lives of working people is secondary to their importance in illustrating the core political beliefs to which Bennett would remain true.

After two years in the legislature, and with his name known through-out the territory, Bennett wondered about taking the next step with his political career. He consulted with friends and colleagues and then flung his hat into the ring, seeking the nomination as one of four Conservative candidates in the upcoming 1900 federal election.

The campaign was a daunting one, for Bennett had to fight on two fronts. The Conservative Party was in the midst of tearing itself up over a number of issues. Hard feelings hovered regarding whether party power would rest with those in Edmonton or Calgary. Power had been slowly shifting to Edmonton, which threatened to leave Bennett's candidacy an orphan within his own party as money and attention drifted north. This trend meant that while Bennett was the most well-known Conservative in the race, his nomination fight was ugly. Although he eventually won, there were plenty of wounds that needed to be salved before going outside the party to win votes.

While this internal struggle was playing itself out, Bennett faced a powerful opponent in the well-respected and well-connected Edmonton Liberal Frank Oliver. Oliver was an Ontario-born newspaperman who had learned his craft at the *Globe* under George Brown. With this experience, and his ownership of the *Edmonton Bulletin*, Oliver knew well how to use the press to his advantage. He was also an experienced legislator, having served in the Legislative Assembly for nearly fifteen years. Oliver also had the advantage of a well-organized and financed Liberal Party.

Bennett had his work cut out for him. He opened his six-week campaign with a two-hour speech to a packed Calgary Opera House. He then worked tirelessly, delivering speeches to large crowds in big towns while also taking time to chat with farmers over rail fences. He demonstrated once again his uncanny ability to remember names, his bottomless reservoir of energy, and his insatiable desire to win. He spoke of the need for the territory to become a province, but beyond that there were few big issues in the campaign. It was nearly all about personality and character, youth versus experience, and promise versus achievement. Consistent with such a campaign, Liberal newspapers wrote not of policy differences but personal habits. Bennett was criticized for claiming to be a religious man but allowing his campaign staff to work Sundays. Articles wondered about his support of temperance while some of his workers plied potential supporters with alcohol. Bennett fought back and decried not only the individual charges but also the distractions that the charges represented, but the attacks continued. The Liberal *Calgary Herald* supported Oliver, as one might expect, but then the *Alberta Tribune* changed ownership and quickly switched sides to also support him. Bennett was not only without a real party but also without a paper.

Election Day was November 7. There was no polling, of course, but everyone seemed to know what the results would be. None was surprised when the votes were tallied. Oliver won 5,203 votes to Bennett's 4,029. The brash young lawyer had been handed a devastating loss. His defeat was part of a sweep in which all four territorial seats went to the Liberals.

Bennett had little time to mourn his fate, however, for the by-election that had been made necessary by his resigning to run as a federal candidate was nigh. At first it was not clear that he would contend for his old territorial seat, and so four other Conservative candidates had begun to organize. But once he announced his candidacy, the others immediately withdrew.

What seemed for a moment might be easy quickly turned terribly difficult. The by-election proved to be as bitterly fought as the federal contest had been. Bennett again spoke at meeting after meeting and reminded Calgarians of his record. He spoke of his standing up for the "little guy" and against powerful interests. Premier Haultain played a major role in the campaign, often coming to the riding and speaking against Bennett and for his opponent, the well-known and well-liked C. A. Stuart.

A number of public debates were set up and Bennett approached each as performance theatre. He outdid himself one evening in which he was to debate both Stuart and Haultain. With the hall filled and Stuart, Haultain, and the moderator waiting onstage, Bennett was nowhere to be seen. While the candidates fumed and the crowd murmured, Bennett was outside. He paced the sidewalk, patiently waiting for the perfect moment to make his entrance. And he made them wait longer. Finally, Bennett crashed open the back doors, swept into the hall, and with every gaze upon him he methodically took his time to shake hands and kibitz with supporters as he inched toward the stage.

When the debate finally began, Stuart and Haultain found that every time they spoke, Bennett would laugh, roll his eyes, or interrupt. The tricks lacked class but they were effective; he won the crowd. All of his opponents' well-honed arguments could not trump Bennett's bombast and shameless theatrics.

On March 22, 1901, the people of Calgary returned Bennett to Regina. He had increased his margin of victory by winning 562 of the 849 votes cast. Bennett and his exuberant supporters celebrated with a small but boisterous party at the Alberta Hotel, which included the fire brigade band. He would serve the riding for the next four years.

GROWING NOTORIETY

The most important issue facing the territorial government at the turn of the century remained its application to become a province. Without provincial status, control of millions of acres of crown land and of all natural resources rested with the federal government. Further, the territorial government could not make the infrastructure improvements that it needed, as it could neither charter companies nor borrow money. Haultain had led the government for six years and claimed to see winning provincehood as his first priority. Bennett and nearly all members agreed with that goal, disagreeing only on the pace of that progress and the tactics used to advance it.

Bennett also disagreed with Haultain and the majority of members who argued that partisan interests were a distraction and so parties should have no place in the territorial government. In staking such a position, Haultain and his supporters were advocating a system that had been in place from the beginning of the democratic governance of the territories in 1887 and, it is worth noting, is the system now employed, with a twist, by the territorial government of Nunavut. But to Bennett, the thought of politics without parties was unthinkable. He had weaned himself on the heroic fights of British statesmen such as Benjamin Disraeli, Rudyard Kipling, Cecil Rhodes, and Joseph Chamberlain— Conservatives all. Further, Lougheed had schooled him on the power of patronage while bemoaning the adept manner with which Laurier played the game. Bennett wanted parties in the Regina assembly, but his fight would prove an uphill battle.

The session was important for the degree to which Bennett demonstrated a considerable measure of political maturation. Realizing that his rickety stature as a young member with a minority opinion regarding the two signal issues of the day was a flimsy political base indeed, he for once held his tongue and worked smarter. He remembered the clever moves he had made in Calgary before he had first arrived at the territorial capital, and began to focus his attention on creating a network of allies that would support the idea of a territorial Conservative Party convention. He was finally realizing that the most important decisions made at meetings are often made before the meeting begins, and that a legislature is nothing more than a long and large meeting. He was beginning to think strategically to win larger goals rather than tactically to win points that, in the end, no one ever tallied.

Bennett's work was interrupted by a snap election. Haultain decided upon May 21, 1902, as voting day because he wanted it over in time to attend the coronation of King Edward VII. The campaign would be Bennett's third in less than two years. He was tiring but he nonetheless revved up the machine one more time. Showing his growing ability to see the political horizon, he publicly stated his support for Premier Haultain and pledged to campaign at his side. Haultain turned Bennett's brash and transparent offer down but, conspicuously, for once he did not campaign against him. The results were a foregone conclusion. Liberal Thomas Riley put up a nominal effort as Bennett's opponent, but Calgary's newspapers wrote that the seat might just as well be given to Bennett by acclamation and spoke glowingly of Bennett's record. It was the first time he enjoyed newspaper support.

Bennett spoke at only two public meetings. In both cases he ignored his opponent and devoted his time to explaining the various advantages that would accrue to the people of Calgary if the territory were to become a province. He argued that provincial status would end the practice of ceding territorial lands to the federal government. He spoke of the day when a new province would be able to control public lands and through that raise funds for public works while also exerting influence over the laying of new rail lines. The two meetings were important not only in clarifying his policy positions but also for the opportunity he took to publicly attack Arthur and Clifford Sifton. The speeches marked the public beginning of a long and bitter battle between him and the powerful Liberal brothers.

The severe and rather humourless Sifton brothers were born in Ontario but moved west in their early twenties to practise law. Arthur was the older of the two and first to enter territorial politics, where he rose quickly to serve in a number of important cabinet-level positions. Clifford also entered public service and would find his place in Laurier's government where, as interior minister, he was primarily responsible for the policies that filled the West with immigrants in the decades shouldering the turn of the twentieth century. Both were also successful businessmen and owned newspapers that were callously and shamelessly pro-Liberal. Bennett and Arthur first met as opposing counsels in a minor February 1897 trial involving an illegal billiard table. Both fought harder to win than the case deserved and left with a personal dislike for one another. Their mutual enmity spilled into politics as the Liberal brothers and Conservative Bennett seemed to disagree on just about every issue, and every spat turned personal. The *Albertan*, a Sifton newspaper, was the only paper that railed against both of Bennett's 1902 campaign speeches. A long fuse was lit in the Bennett-Sifton feud and the sparks would flicker and flare for years.

On Election Day, hundreds of Calgarians trudged through muddy streets, and farmers whipped horses to haul wagons through boglike roads as four days of steady rain turned green to brown and blue to grey. But the foregone conclusion had been foregone indeed. Bennett won 436 votes to Riley's 172, his most decisive victory to date. He returned to the legislature determined to introduce party politics into public debate and to turn the Northwest Territories into a province.

In September 1902, Bennett met the newly chosen federal Conservative Party leader, Robert Borden. Borden was a tall, handsome man with a shock of unruly greying hair that he parted in the middle. He had dark eyes and a tremendous smile topped by a thick and bushy moustache. He was a fellow Maritimer, having been born in Grand Pré. Like Bennett, he had worked as a teacher, later took up the law, and had established a thriving practice. He was first elected to office as an MP for Halifax in 1896, avoiding the Laurier sweep, and became the leader of his party only five years later. Borden would offer Bennett not only his first responsibilities and praise as a federal member of Parliament, but also frustrations that threatened to end Bennett's political career. The two quite different men would become amicable but never close.

Borden had come west as part of a grand tour meant to introduce himself to western voters and kick to life the dead horse that was the Conservative Party on the prairies. Bennett spent three days with the new leader, visiting Edmonton and surrounding ridings and introducing him to local business people and party loyalists. Borden was quite impressed with Bennett, noting later that he was "overflowing with energy and enthusiasm" and full of "valuable and useful suggestions," and predicted a great future for the talented thirty-two-year-old.[27]

In January 1903, as part of a more concerted effort to rejuvenate the party in the West, Borden announced that a series of policy conventions would take place in a number of towns, with a culminating convention in Moose Jaw in March. Bennett worked hard, along with his political and business friends, to organize the Calgary convention. In a series of letters, he promised that Lougheed would take care of transportation costs for men of loyalty and virtue who wished to attend. A week later he published and distributed a circular and another flurry of personal letters. Many concluded with the blunt exhortation "We must make this Convention a success" [underline Bennett's].[28] When the inevitable squabbling began regarding precise policy positions, Bennett sent forth another circular and a third raft of letters that asked all involved to put aside petty disagreements and simply attend with open minds. He pleaded with all to concern themselves only with the ultimate good of the party and territory. He urged his correspondents to do what could be done to arrange for a full delegation from each district to be present at the convention.[29]

As a grassroots organizer, Bennett grew frustrated with those who would offer their time and talents only with the expectation of rewards. Dedication to party and through it to one's country must, he believed, be deeper than greed. He expressed his beliefs in this matter in a letter to a wavering party supporter in which he complained, "The country is full of those who are prepared to do work when the party is in power and be on deck when there is a big time [power and its many perks] expected but what is wanted now is men who are prepared to work and fight in the face of strong opposition with very slim chances of reward. . . ."[30] The letter, and the effort of which it was a part, is further evidence of the degree to which Bennett's beliefs in selfless and patriotic effort were well established long before he tasted substantial political success.

Bennett also wrote a number of letters directly to Borden. In some he tried to defuse misunderstandings possibly caused by others who had written to the leader proposing policy positions or wondering about the wisdom of the Moose Jaw convention. In others he explained in careful detail the work that was being done to gather delegates to ensure the convention's success. He detailed his beliefs regarding the territory and its special needs. In each letter Bennett thanked Borden for his support of the territory and for agreeing to the small conventions leading to the culminating convention. In each letter he adopted a sycophantic tone in praising Borden's leadership.

Bennett was in British Columbia on business when Borden arrived in Calgary, and it fell to Lougheed to play host. Upon his return, Bennett impressed Borden and his staff with his graciousness, attention to detail, the number of people he knew, and the enthusiasm of his introduction at each of Borden's speaking engagements.[31] In both his introductions and private conversations, Bennett presented the federal leader with his version of why and how the territory should become a province while simultaneously impressing a future boss with his political skills.

The conventions began in late January 1905 at Yorktown. A draft party platform was forged that ratified what had already been understood to be Conservative Party stands. For example, it stated the party's call for continued support for British foreign policy and for an extension of Macdonald's old National Policy which would result in higher protective tariffs. With respect to the West, it supported the creation of a western port, the abolition of land grants to railway companies, and the granting of provincial status to the territory. It also stated that candidates should campaign in the next territorial election as a party and that those elected under the party banner should sit as Conservatives. It was everything Bennett had wanted. He played a significant role in the convention and was its keynote speaker. He spoke powerfully in support of a number of concerns and ideas but saved the majority of his time for the issue of provincehood.

A week later, Calgary hosted a second policy convention, and Bennett repeated his keynote remarks. Beyond the well-received speech, Bennett worked the backrooms in bringing supporters to his causes. He also influenced those responsible for choosing delegates who would represent the territories in discussions with Ottawa. He ensured that he and the other three Calgary delegates to the final party convention were cut from the same political cloth.

Finally, the culminating convention began in Moose Jaw on March 26. Bennett was everywhere. He was a presence on the stage and in the backrooms, as a Calgary delegate, member of the Resolutions Committee, on the Alberta Executive Committee, and on the Southern Alberta Organizing Committee. His influence was seen clearly when Haultain arranged for a motion to be brought forward stating that nothing passed by convention delegates could later be brought forward as legislation. It was a cute trick meant to emasculate the entire affair, but Bennett would have none of it. He worked the rooms until he was able to relax after watching the motion defeated on the floor. He noted that if Haultain had been either more popular or more clever the result would have been different.[32]

The 140 delegates passed thirteen resolutions. Included among them were that the territories should be granted provincehood and that the next territorial election should be contested along partisan lines. Bennett was getting good; he was becoming powerful. Part of that power and his adroit use of it was seen in the fact that he had not delivered a speech from the podium or uttered a word from the floor. Bennett's silence underscored the degree to which he was coming to understand the fundamentals of political power and effective leadership.

EMERGING ON THE NATIONAL STAGE

Following the convention, Bennett arranged for letters of thanks to be sent to every delegate. He sat for interviews with reporters and wrote a long letter to Borden offering his appraisal of all that had happened. Borden asked Bennett's opinion on the possible division of constituencies if the Northwest Territories should become a province and Bennett provided a detailed analysis with pre-emptive gerrymandering that promised an increased possibility of a Conservative victory in each of the ridings he proposed.[33]

The November 1904 federal election returned Laurier and the Liberals to office with another majority. Among the prime minister's campaign promises had been a vow to create a new western province.

Two months before the election, on September 30, Laurier had written to Premier Haultain informing him that he wished to begin negotiations regarding provincehood. Haultain had avoided a debate in the legislature by holding the letter for more than two weeks and announcing it four days after the legislature had been prorogued.

Bennett was saddened that he had been robbed of the opportunity to debate in the legislature and to weigh in on the negotiations that he had played a role in initiating. He was later angered that even before talks had begun, Laurier had been persuaded that the territories were too vast to be made into one province and so divided it into two: Alberta and Saskatchewan. Bennett was also disappointed that the federal government was to maintain control of Crown lands and natural resources. But he and many others saved singular outrage for Clause 16 of the Autonomy Act.

Clause 16 was based on the precedent established at the 1864 Confederation debates and then later applied to Manitoba. That is, religious minorities must be granted the right to create their own separate religious-based schools. The clause had led to heated debate in the House of Commons and a rift in the Liberal caucus. Clifford Sifton had resigned his post. Laurier remained adamant, knowing that the clause was as much about maintaining the deal between French and English that was at the heart of the Confederation agreement itself than about the Catholics who actually lived in what would become the two new provinces. In this courageous stance, Laurier demonstrated that he could see beyond partisanship and expediency to the broader principles at stake.

Clause 16 brought Bennett to one of the fundamental issues of his country's very being. It lay at the junction of religion, ethnicity, and prejudice, where tolerance and bigotry battle for ascendancy and where identity and, ultimately, national survival is at stake. With Laurier modelling the thoughts and actions of a principled leader, but with his constituency split, Bennett had a decision to make. He said nothing. The controversy raged, but with Laurier's firmness and Haultain's refusal to inflame the issue, it slowly receded. In saying nothing, Bennett had avoided involving himself in an issue that could have scarred him.

But public silence did not mean he was doing nothing. Behind the scenes he was again acting the political organizer and pushing those in the ridings to gather volunteers and consider candidates for the first provincial election. He maintained his contact with Borden and broadened his network of political contacts.

In November, Bennett took ill with flulike symptoms that a doctor, mistakenly, as it turned out, diagnosed as appendicitis. Concerns were sufficiently serious as to necessitate a hospital stay. He was then some weeks recovering at home. The illness was never diagnosed. Even from his sickbed he kept up with correspondence dealing with political, business, and legal matters.

While Bennett was still recovering, a convention was held in Calgary, and Bennett's name was placed in nomination as a candidate for the upcoming provincial election. Bennett had not sought the nomination and stated that the demands of his business were such that he had to decline the honour. He nonetheless promised to continue to devote what time he could to work for the party's success.

That Bennett's refusal to accept the nomination could not be interpreted as a turning of his back on politics was seen in the fact that he took time out while visiting his mother for Christmas to sit with a reporter from the *Saint John Star*. He used a statement he prepared for the paper to break his silence on the matter that was gripping much of the country. He bemoaned the fact that important legislation was being slowed or ignored due to the controversy surrounding the Catholic- and French-school question. He then criticized the federal government for taking up the language-in-schools issue at all when education was clearly a provincial responsibility.

Taking advantage of his being east, federal party strategists invited Bennett to participate in two Ontario by-elections. In both campaigns, with the anti-Catholic Orange Lodge still a powerful presence, the controversy surrounding separate schools was playing a considerable part. Laurier had reworded the more controversial provisions of the legislation to render them more vague without actually changing their intent. The feint was successful in that opposition waned and the Liberal rift was repaired. Sifton rejoined the caucus, although not the cabinet.

However, Laurier's tinkering allowed Bennett to take to the stump in Ontario and claim with some validity that the Conservatives had stood up to the Liberals in this important manner and forced Laurier to finally acknowledge the importance of provincial rights. Bennett argued that his party had also forced Laurier to recognize the legitimacy of the

Protestant majority in determining the type of society in which they wished to live while still allowing for minority rights. In Bennett's mind, the issue had become simply a legal question regarding the constitutional division of powers and would only be put to rest when religion was removed from the equation.[34] This perceived inability of some people to divorce passion from reason would irritate Bennett throughout his life.

Bennett's Ontario speeches were insignificant in themselves. In fact, the ridings in which he spoke all voted Liberal. But they were important in signalling that the federal Conservative Party brass recognized the potential of the young westerner and, further, that his name was becoming known in yet another province. Borden continued to write and seek his opinion on western matters and Bennett was forthright in dictating long and detailed letters regarding policies he might pursue or even topics that he might address in the House.[35]

On March 10, 1905, Bennett's father died. He was only sixty-three. It was a short illness and he suffered little. There is little evidence of the two having being especially close, but Bennett returned to New Brunswick where for nearly a month he acted the family patriarch in dealing with the funeral and the legalities of the will. Except for his sister Mildred, with whom Bennett shared a special love, the family tragedy did nothing to change the cordial but never warm relationships with his other siblings. The death did, however, fortify the already strong bond with his mother. Bennett allowed himself very little time to grieve. By month's end he was back in Calgary and working the fourteen-hour days and living the monastic life that had become, for him, normal.

ALBERTA

Alberta became a province in July 1905. Bennett again witnessed the power that power allowed when Laurier appointed Liberal George H. V. Bulyea as the province's first lieutenant-governor and he, in turn, asked Liberal stalwart Alexander Rutherford to form a government. Constituency lines were drawn to the advantage of Liberal candidates and an election was set for November 9.

Meanwhile, with the help of Lougheed's influence, the firm's money, and a decided lack of passion among Alberta Conservatives, a convention in Red Deer had chosen Bennett as the new province's first Conservative Party leader. He really had no competition as neither Haultain nor anyone else of consequence wanted the job. It was a significant honour but a pyrrhic victory, for the party existed more in name than reality. There was little time, less money, and trifling interest in doing much about the problems the party faced before the impending election. With the creation of two provinces out of the old territory, Conservatives had lost the most important issue around which they had rallied. Haultain, who had become a Conservative, although either party would have welcomed him, was not helping matters by wavering not only on whether he would again run for office, but also in what riding, and even in which province. Meanwhile, both infant provinces were suddenly awash in new Liberal money and new Liberal projects that were being showered upon them through partisan largess. Further, the whole country was enjoying yet another year of what many newspapers had taken to calling the Laurier prosperity. Bennett's uphill road was more like a vertical cliff.

As the fall campaign began, however, Bennett remained confident in his party's prospects. He also felt good about his chances to retain his seat. He was pleased with his reception wherever he went and bolstered by the number of known Liberals who not only listened during his speeches but actually shook his hand afterwards with expressions of support.[36]

While Bennett had to travel the province speaking at small gatherings and nomination meetings in attempts to lend his name and talents to lesser and often unknown candidates, his Liberal opponent, lawyer William Cushing, was at home in Calgary working. He tirelessly canvassed the streets and knocked on doors in the best retail politics tradition. Every day, Cushing reminded Calgarians that while he and Laurier stood for the building of a second transcontinental line, Bennett's connections with the CPR prevented him from ever supporting such a policy. Cushing ignored the fact that Bennett had supported the Conservative Party platform plank that advocated ending the CPR's monopoly and its tax-free status. Cushing was sure, however, to remind listeners of his opponent's large retainer and of the fact that just two months before, Bennett had been in British Columbia as the CPR's lawyer, negotiating the purchase of one and a half million acres of land on Vancouver Island for the extension of a railway line from Nanaimo. Cushing also spoke of

Bennett's investments in and legal involvement with a number of other powerful Calgary corporations. He ignored Bennett's promise to resign all his corporate directorships if he became premier. Despite Bennett's history of supporting unions and legislation that sought to help working people while standing against unbridled corporate power, the label of big-business lackey that had been foisted on Bennett before and that Cushing was ruthlessly exploiting seemed to resonate with reporters and voters. Then, as now, perception mattered more than fact, and negative campaigning seemed to work.

Bennett continued to work hard throughout the campaign, delivering speech after speech, but he found himself speaking to dwindling crowds. Things became even worse when a Labour candidate entered the race. Now his support was buffeted not only by Cushing's attacks but by the splitting of the labour vote. The religious-schools question grew in importance as the effectiveness of Bennett's constitutional argument faded. He was appealing to logic as the crowds increasingly reacted with emotion. The wheels were falling off the campaign.

There was no party organization from which to draw support or advice, and Bennett had either inadequate time or inclination to delegate authority or seek proper help. He was acting as party leader, local and provincial campaign director, candidate, and through his chequebook, fundraiser. Further, he was also maintaining obligations at his law practice. It was a punishing pace for anyone, even someone of Bennett's prodigious energy.

It was a Liberal landslide. The Conservatives returned members in only Rosebud and High River. Bennett lost his own seat. Despite all that was stacked against him and all the advantages of the Liberal candidate, the Calgary numbers were surprisingly close. Cushing won 906 votes to Bennett's 890. The Labour candidate, A. D. Macdonald, won 354. There were 300 spoiled ballots. If the Labour candidate had not entered the race, Bennett would most certainly have carried the day. Because the results were so close and due to the unprecedented number of spoiled ballots, a recount was automatically undertaken. The effort only changed the margin of Cushing's victory, which rose from 16 to 37.

Borden wrote to console Bennett and received a response that was typical of the man. He expressed no regret for having entered the battle and having fought the good fight but grumbled that the Liberals played dirty, spent outrageous amounts of money, and that the people of Alberta had made a choice that they would soon regret.[37] The contradictory emotions of humble resignation and bitter anger were rolled into a ball and hurled with the urgency of his disappointment at the painful defeat. A similar self-destructive ball would be thrown at every loss with which he was presented.

But there was one more letter. Bennett informed Borden that he was quitting politics—and he did. He returned to his law office and complex business involvements with what appeared to be a shooting star of a political career destined to be a mere footnote for his resumé. He was to spend the next four years in the political wilderness.

Losing a contest is seldom a tragedy for a man of confidence, principle, and faith. Such men recognize the difference between battles and wars. And in that recognition a loss can become a teacher, offering the redemptive development of one's character and a healthy reconsideration of the tactics needed to pursue a goal still firmly envisioned. In Bennett's case, this development was coupled with his prideful refusal to accept defeat. Together, the two greased the wheels of his return.

But his return would have to wait. The voracious reader continued to use mail order to purchase an impressive number of books from England and Toronto. He even began to occasionally read novels. He sometimes teared up reading the novels of Robert Louis Stevenson.[38] Bennett also maintained his practice of quiet generosity. He heard, for instance, about a high school football team doing well and so sent them an unsolicited $10.[39] He mailed another $10 to a church in need of repair in the tiny town of Bowden.[40] He sent $10 to a church in Olds, which earlier in the year he had helped to incorporate as a town.[41]

All the while, despite a small fire in the law office that destroyed many important documents, he continued to build his firm and professional reputation. His intelligence, vision, luck, connections, alliance with Max Aitken, and his fourteen-hour days had combined with Calgary's boom years to make Lougheed Bennett the most prosperous law firm in the city. In July 1904, he boasted in a letter to Aitken that of the twenty-four cases on the June docket, his firm had twenty and had lost but one.[42] The CPR remained the firm's premier client and Bennett's personal retainer had climbed to what at that time was a staggering $10,000 a year. This connection led to the winning of other clients of note, which, beyond the banks and insurance companies already mentioned, included the Canadian Pacific's Western Division and the British Columbia Land and Irrigation departments. Bennett and Lougheed had also renegotiated the terms of their partnership so that the senior partner, who was spending precious little time on the firm's affairs, received an annual payment of $3000 a year while the rest of the proceeds went to Bennett. As the firm continued to expand, Bennett hired H. A. Allison in 1902, W. T. Taylor in 1905, and W. H. McLaws in 1907.

Aitken and Bennett were shrewd businessmen and financial entrepreneurs. They were ideal partners. Aitken was terrific at making friends and finding investors. Bennett was adept at seeing opportunities and recognizing potential in new or small companies. Both were able to see where amalgamations would create economic synergy. This marriage of skills led to a successful pattern. Bennett and Aitken would negotiate the deals, and then Aitken would sell stocks and bonds to eastern and British business people, with Bennett personally overseeing the growth of the ideas and new companies. They would then share the profits. There were always profits.

There were many deals, but three of special significance involved Canada Cement, Calgary Power, and Alberta Pacific Grain Company. All were wildly successful as Bennett and Aitken were outliers in the perfect place at the perfect time and at the perfect age to cash in on the explosion of economic activity that had gripped the prairies in the first decades of the twentieth century. Bennett served as legal counsel for Calgary Cement and for a time the company president. Besides his salary and fees, he earned an annual dividend of $33,000. For ten years Bennett was president of the Calgary Power Company, which began as a small electrical-generating plant on the Bow River, supplying power to a Calgary Cement plant. Under Bennett's leadership, it grew so that it was providing electricity to most of the city. The success of the Alberta Pacific Grain Company cashed in on the enormous increase in wheat and grain production that the influx of immigrants had brought to the prairies beginning in 1897. Its success can be measured by the fact that when the company was sold to Britain's Spillers Milling and Associated Industries in 1924, Bennett earned a capital gain of $1.35 million.[43]

In these and other business arrangements with which the two were involved, Bennett's hands remained clean and his reputation unsullied, while the Canadian and later the British business community's opinion of Aitken grew increasingly suspect. The merger that created Canada Cement, for instance, was a complex and nasty affair that began with Sir Sanford Fleming, the CPR, and the Bank of Montreal seeking to take advantage of Aitken, but ended with him cleverly besting them all and winning an overwhelming stake in the lucrative Canadian industry. The stock and bond issue that created the new company was the largest Canada had seen to that point.[44] He was terrific at ingratiating himself with older and more powerful men, but equally adept at making enemies. Aitken would suffer the indignity of being seen by many in the business and political elite as a clever usurper, casual with the truth, seldom to be trusted, and always out for the next big deal. H.G. Wells once quipped, "When Max dies, he will be kicked out of paradise for trying to set up a merger between heaven and hell."[45] Through it all, Bennett remained a father figure for Aitken and the greatest influence in his life.[46] But, much to Bennett's consternation, although Aitken benefitted from their many deals, he never included his friend as a full partner.

An initiative that did not work out was Bennett's attempt to do as many of his political rivals had done, most notably Clifford Sifton, and purchase a newspaper. With Lougheed, Bennett bought 46 per cent of Calgary's *Albertan*. On seeing what the two Conservatives were up to, however, Liberal W. M. Davidson, who was the editor of the paper, put together a group that held on to the remaining shares. Bennett later had to suffer the indignity of a newspaper in which he was heavily invested trashing him in its editorials and affording lavish coverage of his Liberal opponents. Bennett told a friend, "No dividend for me ever came out of 'The Albertan' except curses."[47] Bennett was later able to divest himself of the *Albertan* shares and purchase a controlling interest in the *Regina Star*. Although this created a Conservative mouthpiece in Saskatchewan, it was another poor investment. Bennett tried for years to dump the stock and finally sold it in 1939 at a loss that he estimated at approximately $100,000.[48]

Despite occasional disappointments, his law practice, land deals, and business activities meant that by 1911 Bennett was rich. He was collecting about $50,000 a year in dividends while earning legal fees, retainers, and income from his directorships. At forty-one, he no longer needed to worry about making a living and so was able to concern himself with matters beyond his personal well-being. And the only matters that interested him were political. Bennett made no secret of the fact that he wished to someday return to politics. While tending to business activities, he also took actions that demonstrated his desire to take more control of the manner in which the press portrayed him. This effort was seen in his seeking out a relationship with an important Calgary opinion maker, Bob Edwards.

Edwards was a short, hard-drinking, plain-spoken newspaperman who had brought from his native Scotland both a rolling brogue on his tongue and a thick chip on his shoulder. His *Eye Opener* was modelled on the scurrilous yellow journals that were popular in Britain at the time and still command a wide readership through selling titillating tales of the rich and famous.

Like many of his readers, Edwards was repulsed by the power of the CPR that allowed it to set freight rates and own or control so much land. Edwards attacked the corporation whenever and however he could, including through sketches and horrid details of every train accident he could find, especially those that took place at dangerous CPR crossings that bisected downtown Calgary. When a week went by without an accident, he would make that the blaring headline. Edwards often personally attacked Bennett as the company's most well-known spokesperson. One front page had a picture of a train mishap in downtown Calgary and beside it a photograph of Bennett. The caption under the accident photo was "A Train Wreck" and under the picture of Bennett was "Another Train Wreck."

Always sensitive to the slightest slight, Bennett was enraged to find his name being not only slandered in columns but also in the derogatory cartoons that sometimes made their way to the front page. Bennett forbade the paper from being sold on CPR property and Edwards found himself to be the only newspaperman in Alberta without a free CPR rail pass. Following these actions, Edwards focused even more vitriolic attacks on Bennett as the face of the otherwise faceless CPR. Bennett had not yet learned the lesson of the truism that one should never pick a fight with someone who buys ink by the barrel.

After his slim defeat in 1905, however, Bennett pondered the degree to which the *Eye Opener* had soured public opinion on his candidacy. He decided to do something about it in a way that his younger self would not have contemplated. He asked good friend and prominent Conservative Paddy Nolan to go to the Sunday-morning Salvation Army service that Edwards was known to attend and invite the newspaperman to lunch at the Alberta Hotel. Edwards arrived to find not only Nolan and Bennett but several of Bennett's business and political friends already dug in and waiting. Handshakes and jovial introductions brought Edwards into the circle. He demonstrated his quick wit in responding to Bennett's invitation to say grace by clearing his throat and whispering, "Mr. Chairman, I'd prefer that the good Lord didn't know I was here."[49] Great laughter greeted Edwards's quip. The mood remained light as the luncheon proceeded with Bennett and his cronies relating a number of self-deprecating anecdotes. Bennett told a story of Paddy Nolan refusing to take a case in which a farmer wanted to sue the CPR after a train had run down several of his horses. Nolan explained that if the man's horses could not outrun a CPR train then he was better to be rid of them.

Although Bennett touched not a drop, the gin, scotch, and wine flowed with the stories and by the end of the long and sumptuous meal a corner had been turned. After that day, the *Eye Opener* printed not a single damning story about Bennett. In fact, when Bennett returned to the political arena, Bob Edwards was one of his staunchest supporters. He even worked on his campaigns. Much later, Bennett was the executor of Edwards's will.

Bennett's growing political maturity bred a wisdom that spawned caution. And it was this caution that led him to refuse offers to become a candidate in the 1908 federal election. The time was not right. Business demands were too heavy, he explained, plus the chances for victory were slim. He also resisted pressure to resume his position as Alberta's Conservative Party leader.

Finally, in February 1909, with his business affairs in order and after having satisfied himself that he had a reasonable chance for victory, he accepted the nomination of his party as a candidate in the upcoming provincial election. At that time, two members represented each riding and so Dr. T.H. Blow became his Conservative running mate. Bennett campaigned vigorously but seemed resigned to a poor showing for his party overall. His speeches often asked voters to return more Conservatives to Edmonton in order to form a more potent opposition

to what he conceded would be yet another Rutherford Liberal administration. He criticized the Liberals for favouring Edmonton over Calgary
and, again ignoring his work for the CPR, for doing little to combat outrageous railway rate hikes.

When the votes were counted in March 1909, the Liberals had
won 32 seats in the province, with one independent, and only two
Conservatives. Bennett was one of the two. His somewhat surprising
support cut across class lines and across the urban-rural cleavage. He
won 2,579 votes, only 153 behind first-place finisher and incumbent
Liberal W. H. Cushing. Bennett became the junior member for
Calgary and in February 1910 took his seat in the provincial legislature.
His political career was back on track.

BACK IN THE ARENA

Bennett had no sooner made his way up to Edmonton when a great
scandal erupted that provided an opportunity for him to demonstrate
his emergent political skills. The Alberta and Great Waterways Railway
had been created by the Rutherford government in the previous session.
It was meant to fill gaps in service left by the CPR, Grand Trunk, and
Canadian Northern, none of which saw the value in extending lines into
the province's sparsely populated southern plains. While Rutherford's
idea was fine, problems arose when it came to light that the syndicate
created to carry out the financing and construction of the lines was tied
to a Liberal member from Peace River, that businessmen from Kansas
stood to make outrageous profits, and further, that the province had
waived the usual provision that a company must meet proscribed financial limits in terms of credit and cash on hand in order to offer shares.
Ironically, a Liberal member began it all with seemingly innocuous
questions that surprisingly led to the embarrassed premier literally fleeing the House.

All legislative activity screeched to a halt as the Opposition tore into
the government. Bennett bided his time. Then word went out that the
great orator was planning to speak. The galleries filled and an overflow
crowd gathered outside the legislature building. As he walked to his
seat, he was welcomed by a standing ovation from the boisterous galleries that ignored the speaker's pleas for order.

When he was recognized and rose to begin, the House dramatically fell silent. Bennett then demonstrated the beauty and power that oratory can wield when style meets substance. He began quietly, slowly, reviewing the facts of the case that were then known. He meticulously built detail upon detail, arguing that the scandal was merely one example of the shady manner in which the Rutherford government conducted all of the people's business. Then, demonstrating the well-honed prosecutorial style he had developed, and the articulate phrasing with which he had seemingly been born, he tore into the government with example after example of corruption and graft. He savaged cabinet members involved in the scheme not only for their insalubrious, if not illegal, deal making, but also for the unfulfilled contracts that had rendered obscenely high and yet fully paid fees. He laid out evidence proving that the deal had left the province holding all of the risk while able to reap few of the potential rewards.

Bennett then returned to the theme of broader corruption. He went up and down the government benches relating sordid tales about one red-faced member after another. He scolded Liberal MLA Jack Hopkins, for instance, for having demanded from the Calgary business community a $12,000 donation to the Liberal Party as the price for his government paying the cost of staffing a telephone switchboard system which was then being contemplated for the city.

Bennett was interrupted many times for applause. There were many shouts and taunts from the government benches but he pressed relentlessly on until finally, five hours after he had begun, he took his seat to the sound of thunderous and sustained applause from his benches and the public galleries. A government had been shamed. A star had been born.

The *Calgary Herald* reported the next day, "When Bennett finished his wonderful speech, he had torn the contract and agreement to shreds."[50] The *Edmonton Journal* wrote, "Never before had the members of the legislature and those who crowded into every nook of the building witnessed such a display of forensic eloquence as was given in the afternoon and evening session . . . in the splendour of the diction and the physical endurance of the orator it established a high water mark for Parliamentary debate in Alberta . . . He held his listeners spellbound from start to finish."[51]

Although the government was rocked, it reacted with the old trick of appointing a commission to steal the heat and light from the legislature and front pages. The commission was charged with investigating the legality of the contracts and the probity of the ministers involved in their negotiation. The premier and cabinet ministers were able to avoid sticky questions by asking for patience as the commission did its work. Four months of government bobbing and weaving ended when Lieutenant-Governor Bulyea appeared unexpectedly in the House one afternoon and announced that he had accepted Rutherford's resignation. Several cabinet ministers had quit as well. Arthur Sifton was asked to form a government and the House was immediately prorogued. Newspapers printed condemnations of the actions and Conservatives screamed. But as the media and parties learned in late 2008 and again in 2010 when another leader on the run used prorogation to buy time and escape political peril, there was nothing that could be done.

The three-person commission took its time and eventually reported that while many members of the government had been incompetent, none had been criminal. As apparently ironclad as Bennett's case had seemed, and as brilliant as his speech had been, when the House finally reconvened in late November he was unable to move sufficient votes to carry the Opposition's motion that would have effectively ended the government. And so it limped on.

The episode was crucial to Bennett's career for the role it played in introducing so many more Canadians to him and his talents while acting as yet another learning opportunity for the young politician. Bennett was improving and was impressive, but his handling of the scandal demonstrated that he was still suffering from a malady that is common among those with a keen wit, an extraordinary memory, and dexterity with language. That is, they are sometimes perceived by others to be more concerned with displaying their skills than committed to the content of their argument. The *Herald* made that very point after the government had saved itself by salvaging enough support to survive crucial confidence votes. In its summary of another torrid week in the House, it reported,

> Bennett had a handicap, which is granted to few men in debate. His
> ability is recognized to such an extent that even when he lays a problem
> bare, talking in language that any man can understand, the rank and file
> of the remaining Government supporters, though they can see the

picture of what he painted as clearly as if it stood before them, refused to be influenced by him because they feared his cleverness was simply twisting things to appear his way.[52]

It is a burden to be respected for one's intelligence and eloquence while not being trusted due to those very same qualities. But another of Bennett's qualities was soon to be demonstrated: his steely determination to see justice done, as he perceived it, and his stubborn refusal to accept defeat until all options had been fully played out.

While the assembly was prorogued, Premier Arthur Sifton had made a fateful decision. He noticed that the $7.4 million that had been raised for the then defunct Alberta and Great Waterways Railway project was still resting as cash in three Edmonton banks while also sitting as debt on the province's books. He decided that the money could be used for whatever purpose his cabinet deemed appropriate. Consequently, at the first session of the new assembly he proposed a bill to allow the expenditure of the money, and his Liberal majority saw it quickly passed. The next day, representatives from the government appeared at three banks to collect the booty. All three had already consulted lawyers and determined that the government was acting illegally, and so they refused to release the funds. Having anticipated the banks' refusal to fork over the cash, the government had already filed a statement of claim with the Alberta Supreme Court naming the Royal Bank of Canada, the largest of the three, as the defendant. It was the first time a province had sued a bank.

Bennett took the lead in the Conservative Party's response to this newest twist in the now months-old scandal. He also offered himself and was quickly accepted by the Royal Bank to appear as its lead counsel. His detailed and impassioned case before Mr. Justice Stuart was based upon two arguments. First, he maintained that the original payment from investors on the bonds in question technically still resided with the investor's bank, the Bank of Montreal in Quebec, and so the Royal Bank was quite within its rights to refuse to forward money that it did not have to the government. Second, and more politically and legally damning, was that Sifton's government was acting beyond its constitutional powers in passing a bill that demanded that the bank transfer funds to the province's general revenue fund. The law constituted a rewriting of banking rules and procedures, and banking was a federal responsibility.

The trial that ensued allowed Bennett to shine yet again, but this time he managed to do so by sticking to facts and avoiding rhetorical flourishes. He picked the government's arguments apart. The scandal became even tawdrier as it was revealed that the railway company had done many things that Rutherford and Sifton had claimed it had not done, most significantly, submitting plans directly to the government regarding lines to be constructed and kickbacks to be paid. The embarrassed Rutherford squirmed when it was shown that his government had indeed received the documents but that they had been mislaid, only to be found months later crammed under the Speaker's chair. But revelations such as this and many others were political, not legal, and the legality of the case was Judge Stuart's only concern. He decided that both of Bennett's arguments were without merit and so he found for the government. His judgment even provided for interest on the funds that had been tied up since the case had begun.

Bennett was appalled, but he would not surrender, and so continued the fight for years. He prepared an appeal that took some time to be heard until finally, in April 1912, three judges unanimously dismissed Bennett's arguments. At that point the Royal Bank could have cut its losses and saved more legal bills, but Bennett encouraged one last move—an application to what at that time was Canada's court of last resort, Westminster's Judicial Committee of the Privy Council.

In the late winter of 1912 Bennett was in England arguing the case once again, but this time before Privy Council justices who were far removed both in terms of distance, time, and experience from the messy partisanship of Alberta politics. Bennett was victorious. In the case of *Rex v. Royal Bank*, Lord Chancellor Huldane handed down a unanimous verdict that vindicated Bennett. Huldane's January 1913 ruling stated that the money that had been invested was for one specific purpose, that the funds legally lay with the bank in Montreal, and that when the venture for which the funds had been raised and invested had ended, the government had lost all claim to those funds. The decision stated that the Alberta government's bill was unconstitutional as it attempted to rewrite federal Bank Act rules to allow the moving of funds from one bank to another and then to its own accounts. Its actions, in short, constituted an attempt to illegally and unconstitutionally steal money, just as Bennett had contended from the start.

Bennett's victory had taken steadfast patience, legal skill, and years, but it was absolute. The corruption in the government had been revealed and the company had been exposed for the fraud it had always been. The Alberta and Great Waterways Railway Company later defaulted on $7.4 million of its bonds, leaving taxpayers to pick up the sordid pieces.

Bennett's notoriety had increased again and this time through a national and then international victory. He took pride in the triumph and great satisfaction from a note he received from Lord Macnaghten, who was among the most learned and respected members of the Privy Council. Macnaghten wrote, "May I take the liberty of congratulating you on your appearance before this P.C. this afternoon. I thought you argued your point extremely well—and I may add we all thought so."[53] From his speech in the House to his arguments two years later in London, Bennett had been like a pit bull with a bone in its mighty jaws. That tenacity would prove to be both a strength and weakness as his career proceeded.

TO OTTAWA

As the railway scandal and its court challenges were playing themselves out, Calgary boomed. Still based on the wealth of the farming community that surrounded it and the financial, manufacturing, and railway interests that supported it, the city boasted a population of around 47,000. More of its streets were paved and more of the old wooden structures were gone, replaced by many of the multi-storey brick and sandstone buildings that remain today. Even its social scene was improving, with more plays, operas, and vaudeville shows making their way to small venues and to the new 1,500-seat Sherman Grand Theatre. But it was still a western town. Its heart was in the rodeos and related outdoor shows that would later become the famous Stampede.

The vibrancy of the young city stirred plans and dreams within those who were fuelling its spectacular development, and among them was Bennett. The Great Waterways Railway scandal had brought his name to the headlines and his court challenges were keeping it there. As the 1911 federal election drew near, he was a viable federal candidate. Bennett was ready to seek the challenge of federal politics. He had grown tired of serving as the head of an Alberta Conservative Party that had no real prospects of ever forming a government.[54]

Beyond personal ambition, the issue that spurred his desire to run in the federal election—and one that would remain a motivating factor in his political career—was his concern about the continental pull of the United States. He saw it as a negative force that was drawing Canada away from its historical and familial ties to Britain and the economic and military security of the Empire. Bennett made the necessary moves to have himself nominated as the federal Conservative candidate for his Calgary West riding.

The 1911 campaign became a referendum on Prime Minister Laurier's support for the free trade agreement that he had negotiated with the United States. In April, a special session of the American Congress had been convened to ratify the reciprocity agreement, and President William Howard Taft had signed it. The deal had aroused fears in many Canadians who wondered if Canada could withstand the onslaught of unfettered American imports. Union Jacks were unfurled as arguments were heard about the reciprocity agreement tying the country too closely to its southern neighbour while turning its back on mother Britain. This was a time, it must be recalled, when British Canadians grew from childhood hearing stories at home and at school about British heroes, studied British history, read British literature, and pledged loyalty to the British royal family. Bennett was among those who came to maturity at a time when the British Empire was number one in the world, with no apparent or significant competition. The tales of Rudyard Kipling and the notions of the "white man's burden" did not induce the uncomfortable squirming they do today, but rather a swelling in the breast of those proud to count themselves among a people so powerful and noble.

It was from this emotional core at the centre of Canada's dominant political and social culture that was heard the contention that the free trade agreement was nothing but a giant step toward annexation and a repudiation of all things British and thus all things good. President Taft had hurt Laurier's and free trade's cause by remarking that reciprocity would ". . . make Canada only an adjunct of the United States."[55] In case any had missed the president's remarks, Conservative papers delighted in printing the comments of House of Representatives Speaker Champ Clarke who said, "We are preparing to annex Canada."[56]

The Liberal Party disintegrated as Clifford Sifton led eighteen MPs to sign a manifesto condemning the free trade agreement. Further, Laurier's Naval Service Act angered some supporters. In pledging that Britain could employ Canada's tiny navy in times of trouble it promised too much, while not providing the cash to build dreadnoughts, as Westminster had requested, led others to argue that it did too little. In Quebec, the Liberal's electoral stronghold, Henri Bourassa and his nationalists were successfully encouraging Quebecers to dismiss Laurier and the Liberals as acting against the interests of the province.

Bennett did not need instruction from his party to oppose reciprocity and closer ties to the United States. His campaign allowed him to bring to the fore his lifelong support for an increased Canadian role in the British Empire and his visceral beliefs about the importance of Canada's links to the mother country. Bennett believed as a young man, and maintained throughout his life, that Canada's future in foreign affairs, including international trade, should be forged as a strong and independent Dominion within a strong and united Empire. In this belief he found inspiration and leadership from British statesmen such as influential Tory Joseph Chamberlain. In 1903, Chamberlain had summarized his party's notions on the subject as "Commercial Union on the basis of preferences between Britain and the Dominions and Colonies."[57] Upon reading of the Tory's renewed emphasis on developing imperial ties, Bennett wrote a personal letter of support to Chamberlain. Aitken later observed, "Bennett believed fervently that Canada's future lay with the Founderland across the ocean. He, too, looked East and turned his eyes away from the dazzling prospects held out by the nation to the South—the United States."[58]

Bennett was not anti-American but rather pro-Canadian. He saw the maintenance of British ties as the only way Canada could survive, given the enormity of American economic and social might. His desire to forge greater links to Britain reflected neither an overweening, blind love for the Empire nor visceral hatred of the United States, but rather his Canadian nationalism and patriotic pride.

In private letters written throughout his life, Bennett explained his unflinching belief in protecting and enhancing Canada's future through the development of imperial commercial ties. On November 13, 1910, for instance, he argued,

If the Empire is to endure, the self-governing nations which compose it must in some way be federated. I believe that Canada awaits the coming of a man with a vision, a statesman with a revelation, one who sees our destiny and who will arouse the latent patriotism and pride of our race and by appealing to all that is best within us lead us to an Imperial Federation where among the nations that comprise the Union Canada must take a foremost place and in time direct the larger destinies of our world-wide Empire.[59]

In the spring of 1911, with Laurier's reciprocity negotiations under way but the election yet to be called, Aitken had written a series of letters to Bennett encouraging him to initiate negotiations with Borden regarding the creation of an Imperial Preference Party. He argued that the party would do some good in promoting the idea among Canadians but that even if it was not altogether successful, ". . . we can subsequently retire from the Canadian Parliament and be welcomed in England. . . . This is a great chance to carry on the fight and force England's hand."[60] Bennett rejected this idea but the exchanges left little doubt as to his fealty to the notion of an imperial commercial union. It was as a proponent of that idea, and fervent opponent of Laurier's continentalist vision, that he entered the 1911 contest and through it became a voice on the federal stage. It was also one of the many instances in which the notion of moving to England played in his mind.

Despite significant reservations about and opposition to Laurier's reciprocity agreement in most parts of the country, Bennett's stand against it was a politically courageous one for an Alberta politician. The West was at the time, and for decades would remain, very much an agrarian society. And farmers were generally pleased with Laurier's reciprocity deal. It would see their wheat open to the great American market a hundred miles south rather than having to suffer what many believed were criminally unfair freight rates that ate their profits when they shipped their crops over a thousand miles east. In Alberta's farming communities, this economic consideration was at war with the spiritual ties to Britain. The spiritual tug remained strong across the vast prairie that, despite the waves of European settlers Clifford Sifton had directed west, was still predominately British and Protestant. Discussions that took place in newspapers, barbershops, and over farm fences weighed the power of money against this sentimental yearning. Liberal politicians were advocating head over heart while Bennett tried to link the two. His goal was to challenge voters to see the congruity between maintaining emotional ties to Britain while addressing Canada's trade concerns through the adoption of imperial trade preferences that would open more markets to Canadian commodities. It would be a trick, for in the West his was a brave but lonely voice.

Laurier was sixty-nine years old but still energetic and charismatic and many were moved by his invitation to, according to his campaign slogan, follow his white plume. But Henri Bourassa's actions in Quebec, the fears about reciprocity nearly everywhere, and the novelty of Robert Borden's relatively new presence on the national stage were more than the old leader and tired Liberals, who after all had been in power for fifteen years, could handle. One could sense a shift in the public mood.

That shift could be felt in Calgary. Bennett had worked hard to win the support of the city's press and had been successful in doing so. He was amused by a backhanded compliment afforded him by the *Eye Opener*, which continued to enjoy influence that belied the size of its readership or the quality of its writing. On August 12, the paper's subscribers read,

> The storms of political conflict have gentled him and he is not the uproarious, dictatorial, flamboyant individual of the old days. It may be putting it crudely, but nevertheless truthfully, to say that Bennett is psychologically ready for the job. . . . Were we to be asked what is Bennett's chief qualification to represent a western constituency in the Dominion parliament, we should say that it was his clear discernment of popular rights and his gift of fighting eloquence. This is a powerful combination.[61]

Bennett's campaign also benefited from the ridiculously one-sided reporting of the anti free trade *Calgary Herald*. Bennett's speeches were reprinted on the front page while his opponents were ignored. His events were advertised beforehand then lavishly praised afterwards. Meanwhile, the paper would run only paid Liberal ads; other than that, it was as if the Liberal Party did not exist. Only the *Albertan* maintained its staunch anti-Bennett stance.

Bennett ran against Liberal candidate I. S. G. Van Wart, a successful Calgary businessman and president of the chamber of commerce. He was able to compete with Bennett in winning business supporters while also rallying pro-reciprocity farmers to his candidacy. However, Van Wart was unimpressive as a speaker and clumsy in his personal politicking. Bennett campaigned assiduously. He often spoke at two or more events a day. His mainstreeting techniques were well honed and his uncanny ability to remember names helped him to connect with voters. His speeches were often interrupted by hecklers but his fiery passion, faultless memory, and ruthless wit often rendered the interjections the highlights of his events. Those who doubted Bennett's version of the facts were bombarded with statistics. Questions regarding his patriotic devotion were turned aside with detailed explanations of his being a fourth generation and proud Canadian. Taunts about his wealth and corporate connections invited long reviews of the legislation he had championed and actions he had taken in support of working people. A nickname he had acquired in the 1898 territorial election, and that had surfaced from time to time over the years, returned—Bonfire Bennett. And many a heckler was burned.

So much interest was aroused by the campaign that on voting day a thousand people blocked traffic as they huddled before a large up-to-the-minute-results board erected by the *Calgary Herald*. By six o'clock the individual poll tallies were not all in but the verdict was clear. Bennett had crushed his Liberal rival. In the end he won with a plurality of 2,500 votes.

Bennett was cheered as he made his way down Centre Street to the *Herald* office. Another cheer rose as a second-floor window opened and Bennett leaned out to deliver an unscripted victory speech. He ended with an invitation to the crowd to join him on a ten-block walk to a celebratory party at the Sherman Rink. Bennett rode most of the way on the shoulders of joyous supporters who stepped along to the refrains of a band that played jaunty tunes through the night.

While Bennett celebrated in Calgary, Conservatives across the country were also able to smile. One hundred and thirty-three ridings had elected Conservative members and there were only eighty-eight Liberals. Canadians did not trust the free trade deal and seemed to be as tired of Laurier as he had looked throughout the campaign. For other voters, the Liberals had simply been in power for too long and it was time for a change. Benefiting from the Canadian habit of kicking a government out as much as voting a new one in, the Conservative Party recovered from the slide it had been on since the death of the iconic Sir John A. Macdonald in 1891.

Bennett had reason to be proud of his Calgary West win, for the Alberta Conservative Party was indeed a shabby beast on which to latch one's political wagon. Many of the province's constituencies did not even have viable riding associations. Bennett had personally financed his entire campaign. He was the only successful Conservative candidate in the province.

While wise enough never to express the opinion in public, Bennett and his supporters were confident that his political, business, and legal experience, personal ties to Borden, and, perhaps more important, the political need to assuage Alberta would result in a cabinet appointment. But Borden had other plans. Senator James Lougheed was appointed minister without portfolio. He had been the Conservative leader of the Senate and the appointment rendered him the first Alberta Conservative to serve as a member of a federal cabinet. He retained his leadership role in the Senate and his cabinet post until the Conservatives were voted from office in 1921.

So while Bennett was happy to be travelling to Ottawa to take the next step in his political career, he went hurt and resentful. He needed to swallow that negative emotion so as to remain respectful to his leader while also appearing pleased for his friend and business partner. He also needed to maintain a wariness of other young men whose ambitions burned as fervently as his own. In Ottawa, the Opposition is the known enemy and thus one against which an easy defence can be made. The more dangerous foes are those in one's own caucus whose aspirations render them at once both voting sheep and Machiavellian jackals. A smile is often more dangerous than a sneer.

CHAPTER TWO

PUBLIC FIGURE, PRIVATE MAN
1911–1925

O TTAWA IN 1911 exuded the feel of the rough lumber town that it still very much was. Before and around Parliament Hill were more wooden structures than brick or stone, linked by a good many dirt roads that were choked with dust in the summer and sodden mud every spring. Two blocks from the Hill was the wicked ByWard Market where for sale or rent was every temptation the lonely or lecherous could conjure. Log booms plied the river below the towering cliffs. The smell of pulp mills fouled the air and filled the nostrils of rookie members of Parliament who arrived in the Capitol with their new suits and callow dreams. Most found that in Ottawa, politics was a business like any other and that, like in any other, only the smart and strong survived. But sometimes even brains and brawn were not enough.

When Bennett arrived that fall to take his place as the Conservative member of Parliament from Calgary West, the country had celebrated but forty-four Dominion days. Laurier was the opposition leader and Macdonald had been dead only twenty years. Bennett took his seat in the old House of Commons, which had only a few sessions left before a careless smoker would accidentally burn all but the library to the ground.

Like all rookie MPs, Bennett initially had trouble with the pace and procedures of the Hill. But he quickly adjusted. A popular political axiom claims that in your first year as a new member of Parliament you marvel how you got there; in the second you begin to get some work done; and in the third you look around and wonder how all the others ever got there. Bennett seemed to skip the first steps, for he immediately showed not only the confidence of a veteran but also the emotional intelligence to remain quiet while adjusting to his new environment. He had learned to watch others and pick his battles.

An MP's maiden address to the House is always nerve-racking and carefully scrutinized. It is an indicator as to whether a new member will be simply a puff of smoke to be ignored for the wisp of time he will take to fade or perhaps a force with which to be reckoned. Bennett's maiden speech was rendered even more stressful for him as he had been afforded the honour of speaking to the government's Speech from the Throne. Bennett wrote to Max Aitken expressing pride in having been chosen and admitted to being quite nervous.[1] He spent a great deal of time writing his remarks and practising his delivery.

Bennett stood before the House on November 20, 1911, and spoke with the booming voice upon which he had partly built his reputation. The ideas that he expressed were fascinating for they situated him as a red Tory; that is, on the left of the Conservative Party, a supporter of Borden's Halifax platform and far from the mainstream thought that dominated the Canadian civil society of the day. His rebellious ideas and core, guiding principles were important, for not only were they true to the conventions upon which Bennett was constructing his nascent public career but they also foreshadowed those upon which he would rely in steering the country when, nineteen years later, he placed his hands on the ship of state's tiller. Bennett's was a lonely voice among Conservatives in challenging many party members, and through them all Canadians, to consider government power as a force for good and a judicious use of that power as an essential element in the forging of a progressive society.

The speech also demonstrated that Bennett understood the challenges and pitfalls not only of the moment but of issues that are with us still. For instance, accurately predicting the dilemma faced by twenty-first-century western leaders contemplating increased trade with China, he observed, "In my judgement, in this complex civilization of ours, the greatest struggle of the future will be between human rights and property interests; and it is the duty and the function of government to provide that there shall be no undue regard for the latter that limits or lessens the other."[2]

Given that the election that had brought him to Ottawa had focused on the issue of a new trade arrangement with the United States, it was perhaps to be expected that Bennett would devote a good deal of time to trade and tariffs. Again, the point he made was prescient, for it addressed issues with which he would deal as prime minister and with which the country still wrestles. Bennett said, ". . . what is the great weapon with which nations must fight the battles of commerce? . . . and these battles will be just as fierce [as wars] and even though there is no bloodshed, just as deadly in some respects, as the battles of the past. The only weapon we have is the weapon of the tariff."[3] He implored the House to turn from the folly of reduced or eliminated tariffs with the United States and see a bright and prosperous future in preferential trade arrangements with Britain and the Dominions of the Empire. He advocated the creation of a government tariff commission to oversee and regulate trade in a rational way, or, as he called it, scientifically.

Finally, with a nod to problems that awaited the country in 1929 and again in 2009, he returned to his belief in positive government intervention in the marketplace. He argued that Canada needed to modernize its financial and securities regulations. Perhaps, he said, fluctuations in the market could be reduced, investors could be protected from fraudulent practices, and companies could be protected from themselves through the establishment of an investment protection agency.[4] By the end of his speech, anyone who believed that the rich corporate lawyer would be a staunch advocate of laissez-faire and a mouthpiece for big business should have been disabused.

He took his seat to applause from the Conservative benches but there was no follow-up. His words were quickly lost in the sparring between Borden and Laurier. He received scant mention in newspapers the next day. It was a stark welcome to the life of a backbencher, where the work is often tedious and the spotlight's glare is nearly always absent or, at best, fleeting.

Used to a workaholic pace, Bennett dove into his duties as an MP. Letters were answered quickly and with attention to the details of each correspondent's inquiry. He read reports and dutifully did his time in the House. He found his ability to speak without notes and to pivot like a skilled linebacker in debate an advantage that few other rookies seemed to enjoy. However, he sometimes still fell into the old habit of losing himself in wordy diatribes that were impressive as oratorical displays but failed to persuade. He sometimes talked himself out on a limb.

One afternoon in the House, for instance, after lambasting the Liberals with torrents of words, he paused and uttered, "And now I will tell you the truth."[5] The response from across the aisle was as raucous and merciless as one might expect.

He knew he needed to improve and worked hard to do so. A friend from Calgary named George Robinson helped by coaching Bennett. He taught him to reduce his volume and speed and the number of points made in a single speech. He even used a stopwatch to try to lasso his verbose friend. Robinson, a real estate and insurance broker, was one of few friends who went to great lengths to shake Bennett from his shell of self-control. For instance, he hated bowler hats but always wore one to Bennett's office just to tease his friend about the overly formal way in which R.B. dressed. Bennett was always amused but maintained parsimonious priggishness.

Bennett involved himself in a number of political and policy issues. His support for activist, interventionist economic policies was seen in his enthusiastic endorsement of the government's attempts to reform the two-decades-old Bank Act. The reforms were designed to, among other things but of special interest to Bennett, allow farmers easier access to credit. He spoke of the need for the amendments and criticized the Liberal-dominated Senate for blocking them. He went as far as arguing that its tactics proved that the upper house needed to be significantly reformed or perhaps even abolished.

His speeches advocating Bank Act changes again demonstrated his belief that the immoderate power of business interests should stop at the foot of Parliament Hill. The country's elected representatives should base their decisions not only on what was best for big business but also for the country as a whole. Decrying what he saw as the corporate, financial, and business elite having too much power in the halls of Parliament was a theme to which he returned many times. Two years later, in 1913, for instance, he said in the House, "The vital question is whether or not a few capitalists shall control the action of this Parliament. . . . the Bank Act of 1913 is the Bank Act of twenty years ago without any change, without any single step forward or one motion towards progress and reform . . . and I say [this] is not in accordance with the spirit of our institutions."[6]

Later in the same speech Bennett detailed his support for the progressive and populist idea that not only should the government have more regulatory power over banks and banking, but also that monetary policy should be the purview of the government and not that of Canada's chartered banks. Years later, this belief would lead to his creation of the Bank of Canada. Consider these words, spoken twenty years before he designed that now-respected and indispensable institution and nearly one hundred years before banks and financial investment houses would be primarily responsible for the devastating economic crash of 2008:

> Shall or shall not Parliament impose a restriction on the rate of interest the banks may charge? . . . I think there should be a restriction. . . . Parliament has a right to hold a bank to the strictest account, and in the exercise of those powers this Parliament must stipulate that they shall be exercised for the public interest and not for the benefit purely of private individuals.[7]

PRINCIPLES AND COURAGE

Bennett knew that if he were to ever fulfill his dream to become prime minister, his first step must be to get himself appointed to cabinet. Upon arriving in Ottawa he surveyed the competition and saw as his main rival a man four years younger than himself but already with three years' experience as the member of Parliament for Portage la Prairie, Manitoba. Arthur Meighen was a tall, fit, handsome man with thin lips and cold eyes. He had been born in Ontario but like Bennett had been drawn to the West. Also like Bennett, Meighen was a lawyer, had been successful in business, possessed a keen mind, and was an exceptionally talented speaker. Meighen's memory was such that as a parlour trick he would accurately recite long poems and Shakespearean sonnets. Those who tested him found hardly ever a word misspoken. In 1913, Meighen was appointed Solicitor General.

Bennett already felt that he was being left behind. Rather than surrendering, however, he took a step that both led to his being noticed and risked his needing to leave the race altogether. It began with a speech that articulated his core political beliefs and demonstrated his political courage.

The occasion was precipitated by the transcontinental Canadian Northern Railway (CNR) project that had been initiated by the Laurier government. The skilled financier William Mackenzie and adroit lobbyist

Donald Mann had been joined by the legally masterful, and magnificently named, Zebulon Lash. They had put together the money and politicians that would see a new line built from ocean to ocean. But after nearly seven years, the complex international and government-backed conglomerate had constructed less than one hundred miles of track in rural Manitoba running from nowhere to nowhere. In 1911, the CNR had asked the government for $30,000 in loan guarantees. The next year it asked for another $15 million and a year after that for yet another $44 million. Despite a near absence of assets, the watering of shares to laughable levels, and a colossal inability to match achievement to promise, first the Laurier and then the Borden government continued to grant land, subsidies, and loan guarantees to the Northern Railway.

In the spring of 1914, company officials were back in the prime minister's office with caps in hand. Borden had little faith in Mackenzie and Mann, but had become convinced that to allow the CNR to fail would negatively affect the economy and hurt the federal and many provincial governments that would be left to pay the interest on guaranteed bonds. Consequently, a complex arrangement was designed to consolidate the company's lines into one and streamline its financial and corporate structure, thereby rendering it more stable. It proposed the creation of more stringent regulations and the federal government's ownership of 40 per cent of company stock.

When the complicated deal was explained to the Conservative caucus, it was accepted with few questions, but then Bennett stood and expressed outrage that Mackenzie and Mann were being handed a lifeline. Borden later met privately with Bennett and found him quite agitated. He believed that Bennett was upset about the deal mostly because his expertise had not been called up to create it, and that he was jealous of the role Meighen was playing in the issue.[8] Borden confided in his diary that, with respect to the railways issue, he believed Bennett's mind was becoming affected.[9]

On May 13, Prime Minister Borden moved the long and complicated railway motion in the House. Meighen made a detailed speech seconding and supporting it. Perfunctory comments followed, and it appeared that the bill was headed for easy passage. The next day, however, William Nickle, Conservative member for Kingston, stood and made a short speech opposing the extension of yet more loan guarantees for the CNR and noted that Bennett would soon rise to express his objection. Everyone knew of Bennett's speaking ability, ties to big business and the CPR, and news had leaked about his firm opposition to the bill. Everyone was waiting for the main show. The galleries filled over the lunch break. Many were left waiting in line. He did not disappoint.

Bennett stood to speak in the early afternoon and was still on his feet when the House rose for dinner at six. He carried on at eight and did not wrap up until he had spent nearly four and a half hours dissecting the intricacies of the Northern Railway operations. Bennett's experience with the CPR, and with the corporate mergers undertaken by him and Aitken, allowed him to understand and deconstruct the complex web that Mackenzie and Mann had woven. His courtroom experience and dexterity with words allowed him to lay it out in a way that all could understand. He explained how the conglomerate had been set up so that its properties and other assets were hidden in a tangle of separate corporate names, with each protecting their true owners, while each issued ridiculously overvalued stock based on little or nothing at all. He explained that each of the separate corporate entities held debt in such a way that each asset was used as collateral for a number of different loans. The CNR was exposed as not really a railway company but a financing scam.

With the tawdry corporate structure and manoeuvrings laid bare, Bennett then moved on to condemn members of the House, including those of his own party, and even his own leader, for failing to peek behind the elaborate but obvious facade. He criticized those in the House who were at that moment planning to cast a vote to perpetuate the swindle and spoke of the place at which private misdeed meets public irresponsibility. He accused both parties of supporting the CNR for no other reason than to receive campaign donations. He thundered that the history of the debauched relationship between the syndicate and two governments was

> . . . nothing but a long trail of parliamentary corruption, of lobbying, of degradation of parliamentary institutions, of the lowering of the morale of public life and the degrading of those standards by which public life should be truly measured. . . . Just a few days before a General Election, one party proposes and the other acquiesces. They are bound to ask a few

questions in order that the contributions to party funds may be large enough. Let us look the business square in the face . . . we must decide whether we will continue to add to the predatory wealth of promoters or whether we shall strike a blow for the people of the country.[10]

Then, shutting down accusations of hypocrisy before they could be launched, he said,

Last year and the year before we were induced to grant extensive aid . . . to this Canadian Northern system. I voted for it on a statement of facts that, I am bound to say, I did believe. . . . I failed in my duty as a member of this House last year . . . but I am not going to fail again.[11]

As Bennett's speech continued and the case against the Canadian Northern and the men and governments that had supported it became increasingly damning, there were more and more interruptions. Interestingly, the Liberals seemed to recognize Napoleon's dictum about not attacking while an enemy is in the midst of destroying himself. They stayed relatively quiet, enjoying the angry shouts from the government benches. Finally, even Meighen could stay silent no longer. As Solicitor General and as the seconder of the motion that had set Bennett off in the first place, it was obvious to him and to all listening that much of the mud being flung at Mackenzie and Mann was splattering on him.

At first, Bennett ignored the jibes coming from his colleagues. But finally, with the sun long since set and his patience long worn thin, he controlled his mercurial temper but cut into his younger rival. He glared at Meighen and said, "I am glad to see that the Solicitor-General has become the advocate of these two men. Before I finish he will regret that he has become their apologist."[12] Minutes later Bennett was sarcastically dismissive of Meighen in a response to another of his taunts: "I will not be diverted from my argument by the impertinent interruptions of this young man."[13] Bennett then called Meighen "the gramophone of Mackenzie and Mann," thus handing the Liberals and the press a sound-bite they would ruthlessly exploit.[14]

He came to the summation of his remarks with a recommendation that the bill be defeated, not another cent be forwarded to or guaranteed for the syndicate, and that a Royal Commission be established to investigate the entire matter. He concluded with a final plea to parliamentarians to act for the good of the country and not merely as pawns in the hands of a group of shady financiers in particular and big business in general.

When finally it was over, Bennett took his seat to silence. When the motion was eventually called, the Canadian Northern Railway Aid Bill passed, with only he and Nickle voting nay. Mackenzie and Mann got their loans and the Northern Railway continued to raise and spend money without laying much track or significantly advancing the progress of the Canadian West.

The speech was noticed and commented upon favourably in newspapers across the country. In his diary, Mackenzie King wrote, "It was fearless, full of information and convincing, a terrific indictment of the Co., [Northern Railway] a powerful plea to the Gov't.—a statesman's speech."[15]

Less than a year later, as Bennett had predicted, Mackenzie and Mann reappeared at the prime minister's door and again Borden approved the spending of even more taxpayer cash. Mackenzie and Mann made out like the bandits they were. Within two years, however, the demands of the war plus the stress on the Canadian railway infrastructure were such that the government could no longer avoid taking action. The Royal Commission that Bennett had advocated was finally appointed to investigate the corporate inefficiencies and corruption that had wasted so much time, robbed Canada of so much potential, and squandered so much public money. The tangled financial web that Mackenzie and Mann had constructed, and that Bennett had exposed, was a significant part of the investigation. The 1917 *Report of the Royal Commission to Inquire into Railways and Transportation in Canada, King's Parties* vindicated all that Bennett had said about both the syndicate and its ties to two governments and both political parties. It demonstrated that the CN Railway was, in fact, bankrupt. It was first placed in receivership and then nationalized. The Canadian National Railway thus became a Crown corporation.

Bennett's role in the creation of the new CN again helped to propel his career through the demonstration of his intelligence, disdain for the power of money in Parliament and politics, and his belief in the necessity of the state to stand against business interests when those interests stood in contrast to those of the country. The episode was yet another indication of the innate political courage that allowed Bennett to put his career on the line in a determination to do what was right rather than what was simply safe or expedient. As he stated in his speech on that long day in May, "Let us begin right . . . and not be deterred from our duty because the action which that duty lays upon us seems temporarily unpopular."[16]

Another issue that demonstrated Bennett's political principles and courage while also advancing his career involved the plight of western farmers. His interest in the agricultural industry was somewhat natural as an Alberta MP It was important in his political and personal education as well, for a good deal of the suffering that the 1930s depression would bring to all Canadians would be visited most destructively upon farmers. In his 1911 maiden speech to the House, he had spoken of the many challenges facing those who worked the land, and called for the government to construct and regulate grain elevators that would assist in the storage and marketing of wheat.

The summer of 1913 brought a drought to much of the prairies. Bennett had spoken in caucus and written letters to the prime minister arguing the need for the federal government to assist those who, due to no fault of their own, were suffering hardship. Bennett requested that the government provide low-interest loans and, in the spring, arrange to send western farmers a supply of cheap and plentiful seed grain to allow crops to be planted.

In February 1914, Bennett said in the House, "It is even true that the children of the farmers in some instances have been suffering from the pangs of hunger, almost starvation, and under these circumstances the Government relief is absolutely needed. . . . Even if the Government should expend several millions more than was anticipated at first, it seems to me that this duty devolves upon them fairly."[17]

Bennett's advocacy of using the power of the government as a tool to improve the lot of Canadians was consistent with the Social Gospel sentiment that was at that time sweeping parts of Canada and was especially powerful in the West. The Social Gospel came from reformers who sought to bring a Christian sensibility to the myriad ills that for decades the industrial revolution had been visiting upon the urban poor. Its goals and means naturally applied to rural folks as well. Leaders such as Ontario's John J. Kelso and Manitoba's J. S. Woodsworth promoted the notion that the work of Jesus should be done to help individuals through addressing broad social problems. You help individuals, it was argued, by improving society as a whole. Bennett never openly espoused the Social Gospel or imposed his Christian beliefs on others. But a good deal of what Bennett did through the policies he supported echoed both the ideas of that movement and the personal religious values that he had learned at his mother's side in the polished oak pews of the small Hopewell Cape church.

As the drought ended and conditions slowly improved, the need for immediate aid for farmers waned. The issue was also overwhelmed as the drumbeats of war filled the summer of 1914. But as attention shifted, Bennett's dedication to the needs of farmers, and their respect for him, was not forgotten.

Remembered as well, during interminable sessions and long nights far from home, was the excitement of the business world that Bennett had left for the tedium of life as a backbencher. It was not like today when members of Parliament use free or radically reduced airfare to fly home nearly every weekend. Bennett was stuck in Ottawa throughout the length of the parliamentary session. That the city offered few distractions or entertainments mattered little to a young man of Bennett's fastidious habits and prim attitudes, but he missed the challenge of difficult work and suffered the malady of many rookie back-benchers who find themselves at the periphery of power. He wrote to Aitken, "I am sick of it here. There is little or nothing to do and what there is to do is that of a party hack or departmental clerk or messenger. I will probably leave here. There must be more doing that counts than is at present apparent."[18]

Aitken offered a respite from Bennett's funk. In 1903, Aitken's business interests and contacts had taken him to London where he wiggled his way into the newspaper business and then into London's political and economic circles of influence. In December 1910, he had used business favours and what was becoming his fortune to win election as the member of Parliament for Ashton-under-Lyne. In August 1912, after numerous invitations, Bennett finally visited Aitken at his handsome estate near the quiet village of Mickleham in Surrey and found that his friend had arranged for a grand public meeting. Bennett took to the stage and electrified his audience with calls for a stronger union between Britain and her dominions. Bennett argued that closer ties were becoming increasingly necessary not only for the economic benefits that would accrue to all, but also in light of what all observers recognized as the dark clouds of war on the horizon.

As was nearly always the case, Bennett's sister Mildred was his supportive travelling companion on his trip to Britain. Mildred was nineteen years younger than her brother, witty, quick with a smile, and as fun-loving as he was staid. They were as close as siblings could be and all saw how much they loved each other and each other's company. She offered spirited conversation and encouraged adventurous outings, such as a trip to Stonehenge, where Bennett might have otherwise remained ensconced with a book. They later shopped in London's most fashionable districts, with Mildred directing his purchases of clothing and him searching out rare books. He later relaxed with Aitken, and then was able to relax again on the long transatlantic journey home. It was an idyllic summer blessed with beautiful weather. But trouble was coming.

No one could have predicted the length or savagery of the First World War, or the collapse of empires that would be its blood-soaked legacy. But few could deny that the nationalistic militarism that was accelerating the arms race between the great European powers was creating pressure that would be relieved one way or the other, and in no way that would be good. It was precisely because of this pressure, Bennett argued, that imperial ties with the dominions needed to be enhanced.

WAR YEARS

In the summer of 1914 the short-sighted insatiable greed of some and the angry pride of others led Europe to sleepwalk into a family squabble that turned into a stupid war, fought in a stupid way, for stupid reasons. When Britain declared war on Germany in August 1914, Canada was automatically in a state of war too. It began as a great adventure. Canadian recruiting centres could not keep up with the thousands who were signing on, most believing it all would be over by Christmas. By the end of 1915, more than 100,000 Canadians were in uniform and in Europe. This number is astounding when one considers that there were only 8 million people in all of Canada and only 1.5 million men of military age. Borden and his minister of militia, the fascinating and perhaps unstable Sir Sam Hughes, were insistent that Canadians fight not as British soldiers but as Canadians. And fight they did. They fought the German army. They fought leaders who couldn't lead and rifles that wouldn't shoot. They fought disease, rats, lice, dysentery, and they fought the mud. It was hours of boredom punctuated by moments of terror linked by days of inhuman misery. Their bravery earned them tremendous respect from allies and foes alike. After the long and dreadful battle of the Somme, British Prime Minister Lloyd George remarked, "The Canadians played a part of such distinction that thence forward they were marked out as storm troopers and for the remainder of the war they were brought along to head the assault in one great battle after another. Whenever the Germans found the Canadian Corps coming into the line they prepared for the worst."[19]

In July 1914, before war had even been declared, Bennett had attempted to enlist, but at age forty-four and with only his time in the Chatham militia as experience, he was turned down. He quickly found that his money allowed him to contribute in a more substantive way than carrying a rifle. He wrote to Sam Hughes and received permission to pledge $100,000 from his personal savings to raise a regiment in Calgary. He wrote to Governor General the Duke of Connaught and received permission to name the regiment in honour of his daughter, the Princess Patricia. Alas, Bennett's grand plan did not work out: Montreal millionaire Andrew Gault had already been granted permission to raise a regiment. Since the government did not need two, Bennett surrendered the name and the honour. Nonetheless, due partly to his efforts, in August, four hundred young Calgarians boarded a train bound for training in Valcartier, Quebec, where they joined the Princess Patricia Light Infantry Division. On that troop train was a young man who had been among the first to enlist: Bennett's youngest brother, George.

Bennett also sought to contribute to the war effort by accepting an invitation to become a part of the Alberta Red Cross and was soon appointed president. He participated fully in its fundraising efforts and related activities. Over the years he would attend a number of Red Cross conferences across Canada, and in 1919 he would represent Canadians at an international conference in Geneva. He also accepted an invitation to become a member of the board of the Southern Alberta Patriotic

Fund, which raised money to support the families of fighting men. This organization took him not only across the province but across the country, where he spoke at fundraising rallies and strong-armed those who he knew could afford to contribute.

But those activities lay in his future. With the war just under way, Bennett delivered a number of stirring speeches intended to boost morale, inspire giving, and urge recruitment. One such speech was planned for early September 1914 at Calgary's Victoria Arena, but when organizers found they were swamped by people wanting to attend, they split the event in two, with a second rally taking place at the Sherman Rink. More than five thousand people showed up at the two venues. Speakers were shuttled between the two locations, with Bennett as the keynote at both. He closed the events with inspired speeches that left the crowds roaring approval.

Tragedy struck when on the first of October 1914 Bennett's mother died. Henrietta Bennett was seventy years old. She died in the same Hopewell Cape house in which she had raised her family and in which her husband had passed away ten years before. Her forty-one-year-old daughter Evelyn, a schoolteacher, was sharing the house with her at the time of her death, as was twenty-five-year-old Mildred, who had just returned from graduating with a bachelor of arts degree at Mount Allison University.

Bennett returned to Hopewell Cape and again led his family through a difficult period. He handled Henrietta's modest will and arranged it so that Evelyn could remain in the house. He also took the lead in organizing his mother's small funeral. As was always the case, Bennett kept his emotions to himself, as his mother had taught him to do. Few saw any outward signs of grieving as he adjusted to the fact that the woman who had meant so much to him was gone.

The special bond between him and Mildred that had always been evident had grown deeper since their father's death. Bennett had paid for her education and the two were regular and warm correspondents. In 1929, she would move to Calgary and to a room in his elegant suite at the Palliser Hotel. Mildred was often on his elbow at business and political events and his companion on nearly all of his transatlantic trips.

She and her husband, Bill Herridge, would play major roles in Bennett's life.

In the spring of 1915, Evelyn married a Methodist minister from Fredericton named Dr. Horace Coates. Soon afterwards, he accepted a parish in Vancouver. Bennett paid for the couple's moving expenses and bought them a small bungalow. His visits to New Brunswick became somewhat sporadic after his mother's death, and Christmas found him at Evelyn's home. Evelyn had one child and named him Richard Bedford Coates. Years later, Bennett paid his nephew's tuition and expenses at Dalhousie. When young Richard's dream of becoming a doctor did not pan out, his uncle wrote letters that allowed him entrance to Montreal's business community.

Bennett's brother Ronald entered the military early in his life and proudly served Canada in a distinguished career. He retired a captain. He enjoyed a long and happy marriage and proudly saw two sons follow his footsteps into military service. Tragically, both boys were killed at Normandy in the Second World War. Ronald, or R. V. as he came to be known, was a respected member of the Sackville, New Brunswick, community. His brother Richard made news in the small town when as prime minister he once visited Ronald's unpretentious York Street home. Ronald made frequent and generous donations to a number of charities and served on several community boards. He was especially interested in promoting excellence in education and spent time and donated money to improve the University of New Brunswick and Mount Allison. In 1931, he stood proudly at the opening of the UNB's Bonar Law–Bennett Library Building named after his brother and Andrew Bonar Law, a fellow New Brunswicker and the only non-British-born person to serve as British prime minister. Although the library was later moved to other facilities the building still houses the provincial archives. In 1979, Ronald's Sackville home was bequeathed to Mount Allison University and became the Centre for Canadian Studies. In 1998, the university's new Centre for Learning Technologies was named in his brother's and his son's honour. His was a life well lived.

Brother George was a special case. He had gone to war in 1914 with Calgary's Patricia Pats and had made it to France. Before seeing action, however, he fell ill with enteritis. Bennett pulled strings to expedite his return home, where he spent months in and out of hospitals. It was while recovering that George developed a relationship with the bottle. He eventually found work in Fort McMurray, married a young woman he met there, and together they welcomed a daughter. Bennett purchased a house for the young couple and helped them with their bills. Things were looking up. But George's drinking turned to alcoholism. He eventually left his family, and his wife left the child. Bennett opened his mail one morning to find a letter from Ronald informing him that their young niece, Joan Bennett, was at Toronto's St. Joseph's College Academy with no means of support. Bennett arranged to pay for all the expenses regarding her upbringing and education. The bills were always paid, but the growing girl and Bennett never met nor exchanged as much as a card.

Meanwhile, George's life continued to spiral down, with Bennett receiving news from time to time that he was in jail after a bender in Calgary or Edmonton. He always paid the legal and travel costs needed to get his brother back to Fort McMurray. Bennett set up a $20,000 endowment from which George could draw interest and also had $125 deposited to his brother's bank account on the first of every month. He also paid all maintenance expenses for George's small house. Despite many angry letters in which the elder Bennett threatened to cut his brother adrift, the largess continued despite George's unrepentant profligate ways. More than once Alice Millar saved George from the law when informed that he had again tried to pass a bad cheque. Without informing Bennett, she arranged for money to be transferred to the bank in question and the trouble, for a time, to fade. The two brothers went years without speaking. George died in Fort McMurray in 1938. His brother Richard did not attend the funeral. He did not even send flowers.

Bennett's relationship to his family, and especially to his brother George and niece, reveals a good deal about the man. His ability to compartmentalize his mind enabled Bennett to simultaneously juggle myriad personal, business, and political challenges and, with respect to his family, to meet responsibilities without the emotion that familial ties might, in most others, arouse. This facility to divorce himself from emotional commitment impressed many and infuriated more.

He was self-aware. When the lure of war took a number of important young men from his Calgary law firm, Bennett wrote to Aitken,

"The loss of these men leaves me absolutely heartbroken in so far as it is possible for a man of my type and temperament (sic) to be heartbroken about anything."[20] It was this chilly intellectual capacity that Pierre Trudeau would later call reason over passion and it left people unable to truly understand him, just as colleagues, friends, and family could never truly comprehend Bennett. Trudeau's wife, Margaret, once described her husband in terms that perfectly describe Bennett and perhaps explain Bennett's aloof support for his rogue brother and hapless niece. Margaret Trudeau said, "Behind the silky, charming manner and the absolute confidence that had given him such a reputation for arrogance, was a curiously solitary figure."[21] Late in life Trudeau gave himself fulsomely to his three children. Bennett, on the other hand, was an absolute solitary man who was an engaged citizen and supportive family member but offered himself wholly to no one.

As the fall of 1914 turned to winter and the spring found fresh flowers brightening Canadian gardens, the new warmth brought only stinking mud to the young men in France. The mobile ground war had been short lived and the wretched stalemate of the trenches settled over the front. The Western Front's trench system had become so elaborate that it was said one could walk from the North Sea to Switzerland without going above ground. But with the trenches came more death.

Bennett read of the thousands of young men dying and was sickened by the waste. He mourned for the men, but also for the country as a generation was needlessly slaughtered. He wrote to Aitken,

> And when I think of the multiplication of the loss to the State of the men that are dying, of the blood that is being spilled, of the economic waste that is going on; when I see the best men of the Empire being drained from it; when I see the population of the province in which I live being lessened day after day by the men who are so willingly, so gladly, so nobly, so patriotically giving their services for the cause of freedom, I ask myself; where will it end?[22]

In 1915, Prime Minister Borden had put together a team of business leaders and his most respected political colleagues to travel to Europe.

They would meet with the British prime minister to discuss strategy, with his generals to discuss tactics, and with the brave men who had to face the horror of carrying out orders whether inspired or, as was more often the case, asinine. Already the courageous soldiers were being called lions led by donkeys.

Bennett was chosen to be part of the Canadian contingent. By this time, Aitken had been afforded that most British of honours and become Lord Beaverbrook. Besides his peerage, Beaverbrook had also talked his way into an appointment by Borden as a special envoy for the Canadian government in London, was given the honorary rank of lieutenant colonel, and led the newly created Canadian War Records Office that kept Canadian contributions to the war before the eyes of the British public and decision makers. It was Beaverbrook, therefore, who welcomed the Canadians to the Empire's capital and led the group to, and sometimes through, its rounds of discussions. Bennett participated in a number of the high-level, bilateral military and political meetings. Beaverbrook also ensured that Bennett spent time with Britain's political elite, including Bonar Law, Lloyd George, and Rudyard Kipling, whom Bennett embarrassed at a dinner with an all-too-effusive toast. Kipling had been named godfather to Beaverbrook's son Peter, and Bennett had made far too much of the honour. Bennett also travelled to France, where he toured rear trenches that were close enough to hear, smell, and sense the horrors of the Western Front.

When Borden and the others returned home, Bennett arranged to stay two weeks longer. He treasured his time in London with Mildred, who loved few things more than shopping in that most cosmopolitan of cities. On the sprees that would be a part of every trip to Britain, beyond a couple of rare books, Bennett bought little or nothing but approved of the purchases Mildred made for him or on his behalf. Bennett also again took the time to repair to Beaverbrook's estate where the two old friends enjoyed pleasant afternoons of long walks and evenings of quiet conversation.

While neither spoke or wrote about the substance of their conversations, it is a good bet that business was discussed. By 1915, Bennett had become firmly established as one of Canada's most successful businessmen. His interests were varied and complex. He had a knack for land speculation. Shortly after arriving in Calgary in 1897 he had purchased the mortgage on 94 acres on the city's southwest boundary that the Agricultural Association had owned but allowed to fall into arrears. In 1901, when its financial stability returned, it offered to buy it back, but Bennett held out for $7,000—much more than market value and far beyond what he had paid. There was a great deal of negotiation, but in the end Bennett got his price. It is this transaction that gave Bennett the financial foothold he needed to build his wealth.[23]

After his initial success, real estate remained a source of interest and profit. Bennett bought and flipped farms and houses that had fallen into default and purchased land on Calgary's outskirts that was flipped as the city continued to expand at breakneck speed in the first decades of the new century. Bennett was not above using his insider knowledge with the CPR to purchase land that was to be developed. His buying land in the small town of Wetaskiwin in 1904, for instance, may have seemed odd to observers, but not later when the CPR chose the town as a terminus for a new line and land prices soared.

In 1911, he had resigned his position as vice-president of CPR's Irrigation Colonization Company and with the acceptance of a $5,000 cheque in lieu of a pension, surrendered his $10,000 annual retainer. He was, however, still president and principal shareholder of the Calgary Power Company. The company had grown so that it not only supplied all Calgary's electricity but had also created subsidiaries that generated power for Medicine Hat and Edmonton. In 1917, the board of Calgary Power rewarded Bennett's efforts by presenting him with $50,000 in stock. He was still president and principal shareholder of the Canada Cement Company. He still owned shares in the E. B. Eddy Company and was the solicitor for both Jennie Eddy and E. B.'s grandson Ezra.

Bennett was still pocketing 40 per cent of the net proceeds from Lougheed Bennett, which was continuing to make more money from insurance, mortgages, and real estate than from law. Bennett always thought in the long term. For instance, when handling the legal affairs of business clients, he sought stock in lieu of fees. Bennett continued to find and invent lucrative business ventures. The amalgamation of six companies that in 1912 had become the Alberta Pacific Grain Company was continuing to grow in wealth and influence. It owned and operated seventy-seven grain elevators in or around Fort Macleod, Vancouver, Red Deer, and Calgary. A single transaction in 1917 netted Bennett $90,000. The Alberta Pacific Grain Company would become the most profitable business in which he was involved.

One spring afternoon in 1912, a rancher in Alberta's Turner Valley, just south of Calgary, had stood pointing at a hole in one of his fields. He showed an amazed Bennett a small crack that was spewing forth a steady stream of hot gas. He demonstrated its heat by frying an egg on the emission. Bennett quickly formed a partnership with local businessman Archibald Dingman and together they created the Calgary Petroleum Products Company. A financing arrangement was put together and drilling soon began.

On the fourteenth of May 1914, the same day Bennett was on his feet in the House of Commons delivering his blistering attack on the Canadian Northern Railway boondoggle, the Dingman well hit. And it hit big. The oil flowed and the money flowed with it. At that time, the Imperial Oil Company was reaping astronomical profits from a series of wells in Montana, and it was not long before company officials learned of Bennett's success. Its representatives found their way to the offices of Lougheed Bennett where after intense negotiations they created a subsidiary called the Royalite Oil Company. Bennett was its president and majority shareholder. He was also given a seat on the board of Imperial Oil. The legal transactions were handled through Lougheed Bennett and the sale of shares through Montreal's Alliance Trust Company, which had been put together by Beaverbrook and where Bennett was board director and president. Money from fees, commissions, and gas and oil profits from three companies criss-crossed before ending up in Bennett's bulging pockets.

Despite his growing fortune and notoriety earned both through business and politics, Bennett maintained a frugal lifestyle. He purchased one car and on his first day careened it into a tree. He sold the wreck and never drove again. He spent lavishly only on travel, books, and clothing. When in Ottawa he lived in a suite at the Château Club and in Calgary he maintained even more spartan quarters at the same rooming house at 222 Fourth Street at which he had lived for years. In 1922, he would move to a suite of rooms at the Ranchman's Club and then the next year to a somewhat larger suite on the seventh floor of the

Palliser Hotel. He still worked long hours and enjoyed nothing more than an evening with a good book. He amassed an impressive seven hundred–volume library that he arranged to keep at his Fourth Street rooming house until 1929 when he finally had the collection moved to the Palliser.

Bennett was also growing physically larger due to his lack of exercise and his seemingly insatiable appetite for three sumptuous meals that he continued to enjoy every day. The broadening of his girth was also helped along by the pound of Moires Candy Company chocolate creams that he continued to polish off each night.

As Bennett's fortune and waistline grew, so too did his generosity. Many churches, libraries, and schools opened envelopes to find small and sometimes large unsolicited donations to capital projects or worthwhile programs. When Calgary was working to create a Sick Children's hospital, for example, Bennett purchased a large house in which it could be located. When it outgrew that space, he purchased a mansion on Eighteenth Avenue and donated it to the hospital. Every Christmas he gave boxes of chocolates to every member of the Palliser Hotel staff as well as to the staffs of hospitals and children's homes. He gave about 10 per cent of his annual income to charity, an amount his tithing mother would have recognized as honourable.

Bennett believed that affording a young person a good education was the greatest gift one could bestow. He donated money to a number of schools and universities, with Dalhousie University in Halifax his personal favourite. His donations landed him a position on the Dalhousie board. He persuaded Jennie Eddy to donate $1 million to Dalhousie and saw that the money was used partly to purchase a large house near the campus to become the university's first student residence for women. His goal was to encourage more young women to seek a university education. He provided the money needed for medals and certificates for deserving secondary school students in Calgary, and when possible, attended commencement ceremonies to bestow the awards himself. He wrote large cheques to many who could not have otherwise afforded university. For some deserving students he provided help with tuition and even clothing allowances. Every year he helped others by composing effusive letters of reference. Sometimes the grateful young recipients were those he knew, such as his four nephews or the children of friends and colleagues. Often he helped young people whom he would learn about one way or another but whom he would never meet. Bennett explained once to a skeptical reporter who cynically wondered about his benevolence, "I still think that hard work is the solvent for most of our troubles. But all the hard work in the world won't give that vitally important first chance. . . . Getting your feet off the ground and onto the first rung of the ladder."[24]

He seldom simply gave money to those wanting to start a business or farm, but he signed many loan guarantees to help hard-working people to get a footing on that first rung. There are many examples of his taking such action, but one is particularly interesting. Reverend William Irving was a socialist who played an important role in the Winnipeg General Strike of 1919 and then was elected to the House of Commons as a member of the Labour Party representing the people of Calgary East. When he lost his seat, he decided to turn to farming and approached Bennett for help. Bennett signed a loan guarantee for $8,000. During the Depression, like thousands of others, Irving's farm failed to provide an income and so Bennett gave permission to the bank to allow Irving to overdraw on the fund. Meanwhile, Irving had returned to politics, this time as a member of the United Farmers of Alberta Party, and sat across the aisle from Bennett and the Conservatives who at that time formed the government. Despite their political differences, neither man publicly spoke of their financial arrangement. By 1935, Irving had lost his farm and defaulted on the loan, leaving Bennett on the hook for $8,579. He paid the bank without private complaint or public comment.

While Bennett's various business and personal responsibilities took up much of his time, he remained a hard-working member of Parliament—and the primary focus of Parliament remained the war. Borden had said in his 1916 New Year's message to the country that Canada would raise another 600,000 soldiers. It was soon apparent to all, however, that recruitment was slowing to the point that the prime minister's goal would be tremendously difficult to meet, while dwindling numbers would soon affect the fighting capability of soldiers already overseas. Further, a growing shortage of labour was affecting war-material production. In October, Borden created the National Service Board to address both problems. Its mandate was to urge more men into uniform while simultaneously keeping essential skilled workers at home and perhaps even moving them to where their skills could best serve the war effort.

The board was created by an order-in-council on October 3, with Sir Thomas Tait in charge. He was to receive no remuneration. Tait wanted G. M. Murray, the secretary of the Canadian Manufacturers' Association, to be appointed secretary to the new board, but because Murray had publicly savaged the government in its handling of the recruitment issue, Borden felt that he could not appoint him to the post. When Tait was told of the decision, he quit in a huff. Tait's departure, which Borden later admitted was actually a good thing, allowed him to appoint Bennett as the board's director general.

Borden had written to Laurier explaining that the board would split the country into twelve National Service districts and that while he would appoint directors for seven of the districts, the Liberal leader was invited to appoint the remaining five. Laurier suspected a political trap, however, and refused to participate.[25] Two political foxes were demonstrating their cleverness through calculated caution regarding every aspect of the board's work. Both knew that most Canadians, and especially Quebecers and farmers, were vigorously opposed to any action that threatened to take their sons from the fields or to fight in what most Quebecers had begun to call Britain's war. Borden had written to a trusted friend that "Registration means, in end, conscription and that might mean civil war in Quebec."[26] Bennett, on the other hand, motivated by his visceral ties to empire, rapacious ambition, and either his political courage or egotist's refusal to see risk, charged into the challenge.

Bennett split Canadians into four categories: nineteen- to twenty-five-year-olds able to enlist, workers, farmers, and bureaucrats. He deemed all necessary to win the war and pondered how to put people into the positions and areas of the country where they could do the most good. In one of the first meetings of the new board, Bennett brought up the notion of conscription. When he took the idea to Borden, however, he found that the prime minister would not consider it. While Borden had mused publicly and in a July cabinet meeting about the option, and he still did not want conscription at the moment, he did concede that if the war lasted longer than expected it might become necessary. To prepare for that possibility, Bennett argued, the government should implement a policy demanding the completion of a compulsory military registration card for all military-age Canadians. Again, recognizing the political costs of the suggestion, Borden said no and even refused Bennett's request to take it to cabinet.

But politics is chess, not checkers, and Bennett was becoming a shrewd player. A few weeks later he returned to the prime minister's office and was successful in having Borden and then the cabinet approve a registration drive that would focus more on the need to harness labour than on preparing to conscript soldiers. Ten days before Christmas, 150,000 prominent Canadians received a letter from Bennett. Many others saw newspaper ads and found 8 x 10 inch posters in post offices and other public buildings throughout the country entitled "National Service." The letters, ads, and posters all stated that under the authority of the War Measures Act, the government would be undertaking an inventory of every male between the ages of sixteen and sixty-five. Canadians could expect National Service cards to arrive by mail and they were to complete them and return them to the post office within ten days. At the bottom of the poster was printed "R. B. Bennett, Director General," and in bold underlined print—"**God Save the King**."[27]

The small brown cardboard cards that Canadians soon began pulling from their mailboxes posed twenty-four questions. They asked everything from name, health details, and occupation, to the nationality of not only the man filling it out but also his parents. Two interesting questions were, "Would you be willing to change your present work for other necessary work at the same pay during the war?" and "Are you willing, if your railway fare is paid, to leave where you now live and go to some other place in Canada to do such work?"[28] Eighty per cent of the cards were filled out and returned.

With cards filling mail bags from and to Ottawa, Borden and Bennett set out on a cross-country tour to try to stir up interest in service and sacrifice. Their biggest challenge was in Quebec where opposition to the war was greatest, and they bravely began their tour there. They met with provincial and municipal leaders as well as with Cardinal Begin and Bishop Williams, who both promised support. At a well-attended meeting at Quebec City's Garrison Club, Bennett delivered a rousing speech, albeit in English, followed by a somewhat more pedestrian address from the prime minister. It was then off to the West where they addressed meetings in Winnipeg, Brandon, Regina, Edmonton, Calgary, Kamloops, and Vancouver. The three-week tour ended rather anticlimactically with a poorly organized and sparsely attended meeting in Toronto. At every stop, provincial politicians of both parties pledged their support for the cause. Bennett could look at his directorship of the National Service initiative with pride; a great deal had been accomplished in just a few short weeks.

After he took a well-deserved but short Christmas break Bennett was back in Ottawa keeping the indefatigable Alice Millar and himself busy with a mountain of business, political, and personal correspondence. The number of letters he composed on any particular day, coupled with the range of topics addressed, suggest a dexterous mind and ability to accomplish a great deal in limited time.

Boxing Day 1916 found Bennett in the prime minister's office. He urged Borden to consider a Maritime tour and again raised the question of conscription. Borden agreed to the first but continued to resist all arguments regarding mandatory military service. Bennett expressed concern with what he told Borden were disappointing results with national registration. He was especially peeved with the lack of what he considered an adequate response from Quebec. Bennett demonstrated a rookie's reaction to his annoyance when he suggested to Borden that they needed to threaten to punish Quebec in order to inspire Quebecers. He suggested that if the number of recruits from the province did not meet the quota he had set then it should be deprived of one of its cabinet ministers. Borden wisely told him that such a move would be neither wise nor generous.[29]

The Western Front had become a catastrophic quagmire. Young men had their valour wasted in launching countless suicidal frontal assaults against gas, shells landing accurately from miles behind the line, and the deadly incessant spray of machine-gun fire. They fought for generals who employed twentieth-century technology but first-century tactics. And yet, as in all wars, the generals screamed for more troops. A new government took office in London and among its first actions was to call for more men from the dominions.

Canada did its best to answer the call, but despite Bennett's best efforts and a steadily increasing number of valiant recruits, it was becoming evident to all in the early spring of 1917 that Canada could not meet the demands of the British government or Borden's pledge, let alone those of Canadian military leaders, with an all-volunteer army. It had become painfully apparent to Borden that the only way to meet the country's military commitment would be through the imposition of conscription.[30] He still understood the political risk and the price that would be paid in national unity, but Borden swallowed hard and announced to the House that if Canada was to meet its commitment to play a significant role in the winning of the war then it must impose conscription. Borden introduced the Military Services Act on May 18. The prime minister, Meighen, and others then took part in the spirited debate, but it was Bennett whom Borden later described as being most effective in defending the government's policy.[31] In a powerful speech, Bennett made legal points that essentially differentiated between rights and responsibilities and between citizenship and enfranchisement. He never once gloated that it was he who had seen the need for conscription two years before. As the public debate caught fire, both Laurier and Montreal's Monseigneur Bruchési sent private notes to Borden warning him that there could be a violent reaction if the conscription bill was passed. It was too late to turn back.

Shortly after what for many had been a surprise announcement came yet another. Borden floated the notion that in order to bring about conscription and present a united domestic front to meet all of the war's other needs, the Liberals and Liberal-Conservatives should form a coalition government. A number of rogue Liberals, led by Arthur and Clifford Sifton, met in Winnipeg to discuss the idea and found it curiously appealing. Later in the month, the Governor General sat with Borden and the venerable and still widely respected Sir Wilfrid Laurier. The old man listened carefully while the prime minister made his pitch. Borden even offered to postpone conscription and delay the next election if Laurier would join him. But Sir Wilfrid would not bite. He left Government House and walked into the hot Ottawa sunshine with his head bowed.

Since he could not win Laurier, Borden went around him and recruited a number of Liberal MPs to join what he had begun to call a Union government. In June and July, many fell in line after Clifford Sifton and *Winnipeg Free Press* editor John Dafoe joined the growing chorus of support for the unprecedented new coalition. With their support the deal was all but done. There was consternation among many people, especially Conservatives, who believed they had elected a Conservative government and were suddenly getting a coalition. With adjustments that saw ten Liberals join the cabinet, the Union government was in place. The establishment of the Union government covered Borden's political flanks and allowed him to move boldly. Parliament passed the Military Voters Act, allowing soldiers and their wives to vote, while disenfranchising those deemed enemy aliens. It passed the War Time Elections Act, which extended the government's life beyond the constitutionally mandated five years. With this done, Borden was able to postpone the election until the new government was firmly in place. He finally dropped the writ, with Canadians to go to the polls on December 17, 1917.

While pleased with Borden's decision regarding conscription, Bennett was upset by the idea of bringing Liberals to the cabinet table. He believed that the Liberal Party was rife with men bereft of scruples. He thought that the presence of Liberals in the government would lead to inter-cabinet partisan bickering. He warned about manoeuvring that would derail Canada's attempts to meet its war obligations with honour and later hamper the task of rebuilding a postwar economy. Bennett saw Borden's actions as desperate measures that would ultimately destroy the Conservative Party that he had worked diligently and for years to build and one that he sincerely believed represented Canada's best hope for the future. Bennett believed that conscription and income tax were both needed but that a Union government was not necessary to bring about either.[32]

Part of the reason for his growing anger with Borden was also the degree to which Clifford Sifton and J. W. Dafoe were playing an increasingly significant role in Borden's political stage management, while Arthur Sifton became a Union cabinet minster from Alberta. A character flaw that Bennett carried with him to his grave was his difficulty in forgiving and his inability to forget. Bennett was absolutely Olympian in his ability to carry a grudge and the one he toted with regard to the Sifton family was gargantuan. He simply could not abide being in the same government with one of the detested brothers.

Bennett wrote to Aitken commenting on the unusual political situation in Canada and the state of the West, and reserved special venom for Clifford Sifton. He observed, "The degradation of the public life in

Western Canada is directly attributable to the influence of one man, and that man is Sifton."[33] He went on to accuse him of theft and corruption in his public dealings—something for which he was indeed being investigated at the time, but was later exonerated. In a concluding jab, Bennett wrote, "He is now a Knight Commander of St. Michael and St. George and, if money compensates for lack of honour, I suppose he is one of the most powerful and least influential citizens of this new democracy."[34]

Despite his growing political acumen Bennett's passion and rebellious nature, often disguised as arrogance, kept him from keeping opinions to himself, even when he probably should have done so. He expressed his worries about the Union coalition government to Borden in letters that began with polite expressions of concern. When they went unanswered he turned to accusations of political piracy. Bennett wrote in one letter that was both impolitic and too rude by half, "... it was a grave responsibility for any man who had been placed in the position of prime minister by the united efforts of the members of a great party to destroy that party."[35]

The Military Service Bill was approved by the House on 24 July 1917. When it was afforded royal assent on 28 August, the rage that had been simmering beneath the surface in Quebec exploded in two days of riots, the worst of which were in Montreal's Victoria Square and in Phillips Square. Windows were smashed, cars were overturned and streetcars destroyed as 150 police struggled to quell the violence. The army was eventually called in and by the time order was restored, hundreds had been injured and four people were dead.

Perhaps if Borden had acceded to Bennett's argument and considered conscription sooner, the Canadian people might have been consulted and allowed time to digest the necessity for the action. Violence and the widening of the French-English cleavage might have been avoided or at least mitigated. Bennett never publicly raised the idea.

A TIME TO LEAVE

In January 1917, with Borden moving toward a serious consideration of conscription, and the work of the National Service Board all but complete, Bennett had resigned his directorship. It was his first step out of the political door. For months, he had been confiding to friends that he was growing increasingly disenchanted with life as an MP and was considering leaving public life.

Borden had often been frustrated by Bennett and had once confided to his diary that "Bennett has much ability and great facility of speech but…lacks common sense."[36] However, Borden had accepted his resignation from the National Service Board with a handwritten letter that was effusive in praise for the work Bennett had done. The prime minister wrote, in part,

> You are already aware of my most grateful appreciation of your splendid labours in the cause of National Service. . . . The tremendous energy that you have executed, the wonderful organization that you have built up, the marvellous effort which you have thus been enabled to fuel, faith in the fine forethought and broad vision which you have displayed throughout, your untiring industry and your unfailing devotion to the cause, all these entitle you to the thanks of the Canadian people.[37]

Bennett was forty-seven years old; an age when a man is too young to retire but nearly too old to start all over again. In a letter to Beaverbrook, Bennett confessed concern and confusion regarding his options and admitted to casting about for guidance regarding the next stage in his life. The only thing about which he was certain was his desire to serve in the Senate. He wrote,

> My present intention is to retire from the House of Commons at the next election and to be appointed to the Senate. I desire, after the war, to visit the Dominions Overseas and other sections of the British Empire. I do not desire to be entirely dissociated with the public life of my own country. I am very anxious to arrive at sound and sane conclusions about many matters affecting our National and Imperial well-being, and perhaps the Canadian Senate may afford me a medium through which to express independent opinions that would be denied me as a Party man in the House of Commons.[38]

Beaverbrook understood and supported Bennett's desire to retire his seat in the House but urged him to resist the Senate, seeing no value in a seat in the red chamber. He suggested that his friend consider instead perhaps the lieutenant-governorship of Alberta or New Brunswick, a position which would allow him to move later to Britain.

As it turned out, none of the options would be in Bennett's immediate future, for it was at that point that he instigated an unfortunate and totally avoidable tiff with Borden. Although the two men later differed in their memory of what exactly was said and promised, both agreed that following an exchange of letters, Bennett had sat with Borden and discussed his future. Bennett recalled asking about an appointment to the Senate. Bennett said that there were two vacancies at that time and that Lougheed was Alberta's lone senator so he was in a perfect position to fill one of the spots. Bennett was convinced, although Borden was less so, that the prime minister then promised that the appointment was his and would be made before the upcoming election. Bennett left the prime minister's office and informed the Calgary West riding association president that he would not be placing his name in nomination for the 1917 election. When asked by caucus colleagues about his decision, he explained that he was quitting because Borden wanted him in the Senate.

But then, with Borden's promise in his pocket and having announced his plans to colleagues and friends and through them the press, he could not keep his mouth shut. The Conservative Party's last caucus meeting before the election should have been a time for reflection, offering thanks to members, and mixing careful plans with a pep talk. And it began that way. But then Bennett stood up. He cleared his throat and began a long and detailed criticism of Borden and the decision to create a coalition government. He argued that Borden had effectively destroyed the old party and for no good reason. Borden grew increasingly peeved with Bennett's remarks and finally retorted with a rare show of public temper. While Borden was still raging, a caucus colleague whispered to Bennett that he knew of one man who would not be appointed to the Senate and that Bennett was that man.

That very afternoon, coincidentally, Laurier stated in the House that despite the fact that there were Liberals in the new Union government, two Senate seats were vacant and that it was only fair that both should come from Conservative Party ranks. Laurier's generous offer and Bennett's resumé meant that Borden's ability to appoint Bennett would probably have been without opposition or controversy. But it would not happen. The next day Borden announced the Senate appointments of Edward Michener, a Conservative who had served two quite undistinguished terms in the Alberta legislature, and Liberal Party hack Bill Harmer, who had been a backroom adviser to Arthur Sifton. Not getting the appointment would have been bad enough, but to lose it to Michener and especially to Harmer was almost more than Bennett could take.

One can understand Borden's reasoning: why would he have wanted an angry senator whose negative opinions of both him and his Union government were well known? And one can also understand Bennett feeling anger, confusion, betrayal, and humiliation. But just as emotion has no place in business, it is an orphan in politics. Bennett had his things packed and took the train to Calgary. As he watched Ontario's rugged shield give way to endless prairie, it was quite far from certain that he would ever see Ottawa again.

In April 1918, Bennett sat down and, over the course of a week, hand wrote an eleven-page letter to Borden that outlined his view of what had happened. The remarkable letter began with a detailed account of his public service. He claimed, in a sentence that foretold his future, that after losing an election in 1905, "I resolved to devote myself to the practice of my profession, accumulate a reasonable competence and occupy the leisure of my later life in travel and study, possibly settling and to some extent taking an interest in politics in Great Britain."[39] Bennett went on to remind Borden of his having encouraged him to return to politics and that he had left a lucrative practice, financed his own election, and become the only Alberta Conservative elected to office. Regardless, he continued, at no time did he seek a position in the government. He reminded Borden of his reluctantly accepting the appointment as director general of the National Service Board and explained that he had been encouraged by others to resign when Borden refused to consider his advice regarding compulsory service, but that his loyalty and duty kept him at his post. Only when conscription seemed to be inevitable, Bennett explained, and he and his colleagues recognized that they had no further role to play, did he resign. Bennett then came to the nub of the letter and recounted his calling on the prime minister and asking to be appointed to the Senate. Bennett wrote, "Not only did you readily promise to comply with my request but you expressed the opinion that I had claims to consideration which could not be disregarded or overlooked."[40] It was with this promise in hand, Bennett continued, that he had not placed his name in nomination for re-election. Bennett concluded, "As this letter marks the formal termination of such friendship as has heretofore existed between us—a friendship seemingly on your part more apparent than real . . ."[41] The letter was at once a rebuke and a sulk. It was an act of political suicide.

Borden did not reply. In his memoirs he mentioned neither the Senate incident nor the harsh letter. But he did take one action. The British government had created a new award called the Order of British Empire (OBE) for those in the dominions who were doing exemplary work in the war effort. Bennett was among those whom Borden had put on the list to receive the award. With Bennett's love of empire the award would have been an exceptional honour. Shortly after Bennett mailed his long missive to the prime minister, however, his name was dropped from the list of OBE recipients.

Bennett turned his attention back to business and the law. But public issues would not leave him alone. In early May he was dealing with paperwork at his desk, when a local farmer was shown into his office. The gentleman asked if there was anything that could be done about the fact that his son, Norman Lewis, had been conscripted. Bennett was moved by the story of the hardships that the loss of the son would bring to the man's family and he went to work. Farmers across the country had been trying to win exemptions by arguing that taking their sons from them would hurt the war effort by hindering food production. On May 14, five thousand farmers had protested on Parliament Hill. It was an argument to which Bennett was sympathetic, but Borden was not. The prime minister made it clear in response to the farmers' protests that he had to choose between food production and troop replacement and that he had decided on the troops.

Bennett, on the other hand, looked beyond Borden's false choice and considered the case strictly on its legal merits. Perhaps, too, he was motivated by his bitterness toward Borden. He presented the Lewis case to Alberta's Supreme Court. He noted that the Military Services Act as originally passed had exempted farmers from conscription but that an order-in-council passed in April had ended that exemption. Bennett argued that the order-in-council was *ultra vires*, or beyond the cabinet's legal authority, since the House had been in session at the time. Further, he contended that taking Lewis into what was, in effect, custody violated the young man's right of *habeas corpus*. On June 18, 1918, the court found for Bennett.

The federal government reacted quickly and announced that it would appeal to Canada's Supreme Court while continuing to conscript young farmers. Meanwhile, a new order-in-council was passed stating that the Alberta court's decision was to be ignored. Lieutenant Colonel Philip Moore, who was in charge of conscription in Calgary, was thus left in the untenable position of obeying the federal government by ignoring the Alberta courts. He also needed to act in the face of growing and increasingly angry crowds who formed every day outside recruiting offices and at Calgary armouries. Just when tension was reaching a snapping point, a writ for Moore's arrest was issued and Calgary's sheriff arrived at Moore's office at the Victoria Park barracks to serve it. Armed soldiers would not let him in. Guns were cocked and the crowd hushed. The wise sheriff turned and left.

Meanwhile, in province after province, lawyers had hopped on the Bennett bandwagon and brought the constitutional and *habeas corpus* arguments to their courts. More and more young farmers were refusing to become soldiers. Finally, on July 20, the Supreme Court ruled in an Ontario case that the Alberta court had been wrong; Borden's order-in-council ending the exemption for farmers was constitutional. Young men, including Norman Lewis, could be legally conscripted.

Bennett had been energized by the legal fight but for months his mood remained dark. In December 1918, he composed a letter to Beaverbrook that revealed the seething anger that was still souring his heart, and asked what his old friend thought of his moving to England to run for office in the upcoming election there. The letter was black and sad and desperate.[42] If running for office was not a possibility, he wrote, then perhaps he could just deliver a few speeches in support of the prime minister. The Borden and Beaverbrook letters together reveal a middle-aged man who had seen his dreams shattered but was still too close to the shards to be able to reflect on the role that he had himself played in the demolition. The Beaverbrook letter also shows that an escape to England seemed to rise in Bennett's mind whenever his fortunes fell.

His childhood dream seemed to have been dashed. As Christmas drew near, the first Christmas of peace in so long, Bennett and Mildred made the slow train ride from Calgary to their sister's home in Vancouver. No one, least of all he himself, would have predicted that within ten years he would be back in Ottawa as the leader of the Conservative Party, and that three years later he would be prime minister.

PRIVATE MAN

It was a rather embittered and despondent Bennett who welcomed the new year, alone in the hotel suite Bennett called home. It was January 1919. Although he had impressed many and done some important work, Ottawa had not been what he had expected. To make matters worse, while in Vancouver for the holidays he had contracted a case of erysipelas, an infection caused by streptococcal bacteria. The condition tortured him with red, itchy blotches on his skin, a fever, and headaches, all of which made sleep impossible; it would incapacitate him for several days then go away only to return a week later. This was the second bout of ill health he had suffered, for in June 1917 he had checked himself into Montreal's Royal Victoria Hospital where he had undergone abdominal surgery. He was back to work in a matter of weeks but then back in hospital in early August with complications. The Montreal surgery and the bout of erysipelas were the first indications that his strong constitution was no longer able to sustain the long hours, massive stress, lack of exercise, and questionable diet. But like others of his day, Bennett did nothing to change the lifestyle that was beginning to affect his health. When the ravages of his latest illness finally left him, he felt utterly fatigued. He laboured under a general feeling of malaise that haunted him for nearly a year. Being forced to address his age and mortality was the last thing he needed as he faced an uncertain future.

While fitfully recovering his health, Bennett caught up with a mountain of correspondence and discovered that all had not been as he had presumed at the firm during his absence. As his strength slowly returned, he dug deeper into the affairs of Lougheed Bennett and grew increasingly irritated as he did. The war had robbed the firm of several important men, including George Robinson who was a trusted friend, gifted attorney, and Bennett's political organizer. Further, in 1909, long-time partner Senator James Lougheed had formed a separate brokerage firm called Lougheed and Taylor to handle mortgages, loans, and insurance while also providing employment for his son. Bennett had felt robbed, as it was business that could have gone through Lougheed Bennett, but he had said little, secure in the belief that there were plenty of clients to go around. While in Ottawa, Bennett had surrendered Lougheed Bennett's day-to-day control to four young lawyers named W. H. McLaws, L. M. Roberts, H. A. Allison, and W. T. Taylor. Taylor was doing double duty with Lougheed's new firm. While preparing for the National Service tour, Bennett had received a rather startling letter from Lougheed asking that the old partnership be dissolved. Bennett was shaken. He suggested, and the two agreed, to postpone decisions regarding the firm's future until he could return to Calgary.

Now Bennett found that for months, Lougheed and the others had been acting as if the firm were either already dissolved or indeed had no future. A great deal of new business was being diverted to the new firm while many poorly thought-out decisions were being made at the old one. For instance, Lougheed Bennett had made a number of loans that Bennett later deemed to have been far too risky, and had put the firm in a precarious position. One particular loan, for instance, had been to a client who had skipped the country and left the firm responsible for full repayment of a considerable sum. At a stormy meeting, he announced to Allison and Taylor that he was displeased, that their powers were being curtailed, and that he would be taking a much more active role in all decisions. By mid-March he was back at the office every day and back in control. While his various business interests took up much of his time and remained profitable, the firm's future was uncertain.

On August 9, 1921, Jennie Eddy (née Shirreff) passed away. She had suffered with peritonitis and after enduring extreme pain for some time she died peacefully in her sleep. She was only fifty-seven. She and Bennett had met in New Brunswick, but Jennie had left to marry Ezra Butler Eddy. He was a fascinating man who had begun his business career in Vermont, then later found success with a modest match-making venture in the back offices of lumber magnate J. R. Booth. While he served in the Quebec legislature and also as an alderman and mayor of Hull, his genius was business. He slowly built a multi-million-dollar company, housed on over 20 acres of sprawling factories and power-generating plants on the banks of the Ottawa River, right across from Parliament Hill. The company manufactured matches for the world but also a host of wood products. It turned pulp to newsprint that supplied newspapers across North America. In February 1906, Eddy had died. His will had placed control of the company and its considerable wealth into a ten-year trust with five-eighths held for his wife and the rest for his grandson Ezra and four company officials. The company men plotted while Ezra immediately embarked upon what seemed to be a race to see how quickly he could burn through his inheritance.

Jennie was much wiser than them all. She was an intelligent woman who had learned the business well before her husband's death. She turned to Bennett for legal advice and he was instrumental in negotiating a deal with the Quebec government regarding the payment of an exorbitant $700,000 in inheritance taxes. Their business dealings led to a renewal of their close friendship and Jennie arranged for Bennett to be given Eddy stock and a place on the board. Their obvious affection for each other was clear to all, but their busy lives invited space and time to trump their hearts. This did not stop the spread of a rumour that Mildred was actually the daughter of Bennett and Jennie. It was as cruel as it was false.[43]

Bennett was not the only prominent political figure to be smitten by Mrs. Eddy's charm and grace. In a whimsical diary note dated August 28, 1907, an obviously gobsmacked Mackenzie King related a tumble of misunderstandings between him and Laurier's wife that occurred in his adolescent-like attempt to secure an invitation to a theatre production in order to spend some time with the recently widowed Jennie Eddy. The note also somewhat sadly betrays his steely determination to control his desire for anything beyond companionship. King wrote, "Mrs. Shirreff is what Sir Wilfrid says is a fine girl, the makings of a fine woman, kind, generous I should think, gentle disposition and all that. Unless she can surpass in my judgement any woman I have yet seen as the one with whose nature my nature could best blend, I will not allow wealth, position, or aught else to tempt me."[44] But despite the fact that Jennie rubbed elbows with Canada's elite, including captains of industry and prime ministers, only Bennett remained her true friend and trusted confidant.

In 1917, Jennie had sensed that something fishy was going on and called on Bennett for help. He soon discovered that the four trustees were untrustworthy. They had voted to increase their dividends beyond what the will had stipulated. Bennett acted on Jennie's behalf and the four repaid the company what they had stolen. The repayment was made just in time for the tenth anniversary of the trust's creation, which allowed Jennie to inherit controlling interest in the company. Jennie was a rich and powerful woman and Bennett was her rich and powerful ally.

At the time of Jennie's death, the E. B. Eddy Company was among the most successful in the country. Bennett naturally handled her will and discovered that she had split her shares of the company and related wealth among her brother, sister, a few other relatives, a number of charities, and to endowments at McGill and Dalhousie universities. She left Bennett 500 of her 1,507 shares. He became the most influential member of the Eddy board and quickly used that power to have the president fired. He then hand picked G. H. Millen as the new company president. Millen did not make a major decision without consulting Bennett.

The Eddy inheritance was a boost to Bennett's power and bank account, but Jennie's death left him truly alone. Shortly after her passing he burned all of their letters. Upon his mother's death he had also burned all of the correspondence between them that he had kept and carefully filed. Pop psychologists might enjoy pondering the fact that, as with the letters to and from Jennie Eddy, he did not just throw them away but rather made a point of carefully consigning them to the flames. Both acts of wilful destruction would have taken time and effort and would have been emotionally wrenching. In addition, they robbed historians of the chance to pry into Bennett's personal thoughts and learn a little more about the man. Maybe that is exactly what he had in mind.

Only a month after Jennie's death in 1921, before the will had been settled and while tending to his overlapping and all-consuming business interests, Bennett received a series of enticing cables from Ottawa. After his departure from the federal scene, the Union government had seen its way through the end of the war. Borden had done well in Versailles in securing a place for Canada at the grown-ups' table. Canada took part in negotiations, signed the treaty, and took a seat in the League of Nations. Due to the country's dedication to the war effort and the valour of its women that worked at home and as nurses at the front and its fighting men on the fields of battle, especially in the spectacular victory at Vimy Ridge, Canada was recognized by all. Perhaps most important, their country was recognized by Canadians themselves as a mature and independent state. In a country where census forms still had no box to check one's self off as Canadian, people began to proudly declare themselves just that. Macdonald might have created the state, but Vimy created the nation.

After his return from the international stage, Borden had announced that it was time for him to step down. He visited the Governor General on July 10, 1920, and his successor, Manitoba's Arthur Meighen, was asked to become prime minister. Meighen was an intense man who was as dedicated to his family as his career, but who allowed no one to peek behind the austere image that he offered to the world. A brilliant administrator and adept speaker and debater, his nature was such that few warmed to him. A naturally shy man, he hated the interaction with strangers on the campaign trail and was not good at it. Reporters openly spoke of Meighen's struggling to stay interested in the hand shaking and baby kissing that is a part of running for office, the rarity of a smile, and the death stare that sometimes welcomed crowds.

The forty-six-year-old Meighen carried a number of liabilities with him up the marble stairs to the prime minister's corner office. First was that while Conservatives in the Union government supported his leadership, the Liberals in the cabinet did not. They had argued for Sir Thomas White, who would have won favour with both parties. Second, and more important, was that Meighen had been a loyal cabinet man. As solicitor general and later justice minister, he had been the government's face for hugely unpopular acts. The tainted and expensive acquisitions of the Grand Trunk and Northern Railways had pleased few observers. The Military Services Act brought conscription to Canada and riots to the streets of Montreal. The War Time Elections Act had allowed soldiers and their wives to vote, which most saw as good. But it also had soldiers cast ballots only for a party and allowed the government to allocate them to whatever riding needed Conservative-Union votes, which most saw as underhanded.

Meighen possessed an intellectual arrogance that allowed him to sincerely believe that it was the role of the political elite to lead. The people's task was simply to choose their representatives, then be quiet and subserviently complacent until asked to do so again four or five years later. He never deigned to explain himself or ask for support from the people or the House. Mackenzie King was cynically delighted in

Borden's choice. He confided to his diary, "I could not help exclaiming Good for him when I read of Meighen having won out, and achieved his ambition, immediately I added walking up and down with feelings of satisfaction it is too good to be true."[45]

With the end of the war that had justified the Union government's creation, and with the ascension of Meighen to leadership, the government began to slowly unravel. The coalition had weakened the Liberal and Conservative parties and new parties such as the Progressives had risen to steal support from both. The postwar recession led many workers and recent immigrants to see value in the socialist ideas of Labour parties, while many farmers turned to parties geared specifically to their interests. Conscription had widened the French-English cleavage to a state not seen since Macdonald had allowed French-Catholic hero Louis Riel to hang in 1885. No one knew what would emerge from an age of uncertainty where the old political alliances were being made obsolete and all that had been certain was up for grabs.

Through it all, Meighen appeared unwilling or unable to do what was needed to inspire loyalty. Within months there were resignations by Liberal after Liberal and only one Liberal replaced those jumping ship. Mackenzie King was gaining strength as he moved adroitly to bring disaffected Liberals to his side. He had enjoyed a successful swing through the Maritimes in January, then Ontario and Quebec in the summer and autumn. He had also been skilfully rebuilding the political fences that had once been erected between Liberals and Progressives in the West and, in so doing, outflanking the Conservatives. All four western provinces had Liberal governments and Mackenzie King's most enthusiastic audiences were in Alberta, in Bennett's backyard.

It was from within this perilous political environment that Meighen had swallowed hard and in May 1921 sent a cable to Bennett. He asked his old rival to join the cabinet as minister of railways and canals. The two had never been close. The CNR affair had stung Meighen as Bennett had intended it to. But the new prime minister was in a difficult spot and needed friends. Bennett pondered the offer. He was still peeved with having had a promised Senate seat snatched from him, plus his business responsibilities were enormous. Only weeks before he had turned down an offer to be chief justice for the province of Alberta. But this was another matter. Meighen's offer was a chance to re-enter federal politics and rekindle his childhood dream. Bennett weighed the offer against his business responsibilities. He said no.

Within days, a second cable arrived that promised him the Interior Ministry. That portfolio was even more tempting. Bennett was considering the new offer when a third cable arrived. Meighen stated that if the Interior Ministry did not thrill him then perhaps he would be interested in becoming the minister of justice. Meighen was on his knees. Bennett paced his office for an hour weighing options. At midnight he cabled Meighen and accepted the position. In a follow-up letter that was mailed the next day, Bennett spoke of the many challenges that stood before the Canadian people and of his eagerness to confront them. He wrote, "I should not like to think that I had shrunk from discharging my duties merely because the problems that confront us are difficult, the conditions of life onerous, or the outlook of the future dark and gloomy. . . . I have therefore concluded . . . to place my services loyally and unreservedly, under your Premiership, at the disposal of the country."[46]

Bennett was thrilled. He saw the position as one that would make every lawyer in the country salivate with envy. It offered him the opportunity to make, as well as practise, the law.[47] He wrote to Beaverbrook, explaining his decision to join the Meighen administration as motivated by a desire to put his talents on the side of "law, order, and constituted authority."[48] He also confided that he was entering the race with no expectation that the government would survive the next election, believing that the Conservatives would find no support in Quebec or the Maritimes. So it was with an idealist's desire to serve and a realist's misgivings about the length of that service, packed along with his ever-present books and always stylish clothes that Bennett was soon on the train to Ottawa. It appeared that the young country offered even middle-aged men a second act.

While the post was a good one, Bennett soon learned that he had joined a cabinet that resembled a pick-up team. It comprised twelve recent appointees, most of whom were of rather limited capabilities, with not a single French-speaking member. He was among those whose duties were made more difficult to completely fulfill as he held no Commons seat and thus could not participate in committee work, vote, or appear at question period. Still, for six months Bennett put in his typically long days serving as Canada's minister of justice and then, due to a resignation, he also took on the position of attorney general. But it was a government held together with binder twine and old glue. It could not hold.

The election was finally called for December 6, 1921. It was the first to be fought by the new Liberal leader. William Lyon Mackenzie King would play a central role in the rest of Bennett's political career. Mackenzie King is Canada's longest-serving prime minister and among its most fascinating. Even as a young man, Mackenzie King appeared old. Short, mashed-potato soft, with thin, comb-over hair and grey eyes, he was a staunch and determined bachelor.

Mackenzie King was the proud descendant of Upper Canadian rebel William Lyon Mackenzie. Born in Kitchener (then called Berlin), Ontario, Mackenzie King was educated at the universities of Toronto, then Chicago, then earned his master's and Ph.D. in political economy at Harvard. He specialized in labour law and worked as the Deputy Minister of Labour and then for the Rockefeller Foundation. Mackenzie King first won federal office as the MP for Waterloo North in 1908 and quickly caught the eye of Wilfrid Laurier as an intelligent and hard-working administrator with palpable ambition. In 1919, as an MP for Prince, in Prince Edward Island, Mackenzie King became Laurier's successor as Liberal leader.

The 1921 campaign saw a number of issues discussed in the West, including immigration, freight rates, and grain marketing. Foremost in most westerners' minds, though, seemed to be Meighen's tireless support of high tariffs and Mackenzie King's hammering of the Conservatives' blemished record. There was a palpable and growing desire for change. One must respect Meighen for his refusal to parse words or try to re-write his record. He went to Quebec and stated that he had supported conscription and would do it again. He went to Manitoba and declared that he supported high protective tariffs that might hurt farmers. As a man who admired the beauty and power of oratory, he was infuriated with Mackenzie King's slippery language and teased him at one point, saying that King had spoken against tariffs but for tariff revenue. Not the first or last to be exasperated by Mackenzie King's crafty ability to speak without saying a thing, Meighen sputtered, "Those words are just the circular pomposity of a man who won't say what he means. He might as well say he favours a perambulating tariff, or an atmospheric tariff, or a dynamic tariff."[49] Observers were treated to the sad view of a train wreck in slow motion. Meighen and the Conservatives were headed for a crash.

Meanwhile, Bennett was having just about as much fun as his leader, who was out munching bad chicken dinners in small sweaty church basements, shaking hands with people he did not really want to meet, and scowling at crowds he would rather not address from one end of the cold snow-covered and subzero-degree country to the other. Bennett enjoyed the cut and thrust more than Meighen ever would, but he had been away from politics and Calgary too long. He was rusty. He had sat out the 1917 election and all but ignored the constituency. Its Conservative riding association had been allowed to disintegrate. In the bustling city there were many new people; so many of the old ones upon whom he could rely before were gone.

Bennett had written to Beaverbrook in November stating that he knew the campaign would be a tough one and even predicted his defeat.[50] Regardless, he campaigned vigorously. But his efforts found little traction. Bennett was in the heart of Liberal Alberta and in a city where, like elsewhere, a growing number of immigrant and urban workers saw credibility in the words and ideas of labour and socialist candidates. At the same time, the United Farmers of Alberta and the Progressive Party were poaching what had been reliable Conservative rural votes.

Bennett ignored the lack of an Alberta Conservative party organization, personally financed his campaign, and ran the show himself. His efforts were not helped by the fact that for much of the campaign he was dealing with cabinet responsibilities in Ottawa and delivering speeches for other promising Conservative candidates in Alberta and Saskatchewan. Further, he was at the same time representing the city of Calgary in hearings dealing with a public utilities board. As if all of that were not enough, the people of Calgary were, like other Canadians, being jolted by the postwar labour upheavals, recession, and the terror of the Spanish flu pandemic. Returning soldiers spread the virus quickly and without antibiotics there was little doctors could do to stop it. The 1918–20 pandemic killed between 50 to 100 million people world-wide and took 30,000 to 50,000 Canadians—nearly as many as the war. In Calgary, whole families succumbed to the disease.

At the Beaver Indian Reserve, northeast of Calgary, 85 per cent of the population perished.

Meanwhile, wheat prices, still the foundation of Alberta's economy, had fallen from $2.80 a bushel in 1919 to only $1.21 a bushel at the time of the election. Even the weather had turned. In 1915, every acre under cultivation had produced thirty bushels of wheat; in 1921, those same acres were producing only ten bushels. All these factors meant that the voters' mood did not bode well for incumbent candidates. The Labour Party's Joseph Shaw, a lawyer, built slowly and used a populist appeal to win the working class and farm vote. Liberal candidate Edward Ryan, another lawyer, sank along with Bennett.

The election results were closer than anyone expected. When the votes were finally counted on December 14, it appeared that Bennett had won 7,372 to Shaw's 7,366. Shaw naturally appealed to the district court of the province for a recount. Judge W. R. Winter discovered that there was a good deal of uncertainty in the voting as twenty-three ballots had been marked in ink and nine in coloured pencil rather than black pencil as prescribed by law. Further, it was found that twenty-nine ballots had been marked with a single stroke rather than an X, and that a Mrs. Laird had somehow voted for Shaw twice. Her votes were thrown out, as were those marked in ink, but the others were allowed. On December 23, Judge Winter announced that Shaw had won by 16 votes. If all the others had been counted or if all the other irregular votes had been thrown out, Bennett would have won. Most estimates had him winning the election by ten. The decision regarding the votes marked in pen had done it. Newspapers called it the fountain pen election.

Bennett was bitter and, as was often his wont, he blamed others. He claimed that the countryside had been against him and the city part of the riding had been strongly in his camp, yet his small group of campaign volunteers had not organized properly to pull the urban vote. He estimated that about six thousand urban voters had not gone to the polls when only a handful would have made the difference.[51]

As Shaw had before, Bennett refused to accept the decision and demanded that the Supreme Court of Alberta count the ballots yet again. Judge W. W. Stuart sided with Winter and announced that indeed Shaw had won by 16 votes. Bennett was still not satisfied. He took it to the Supreme Court of Canada, which, in June 1922, sided with Winter's first decision. Shaw was sworn in as the MP for Calgary West. While maintaining a brave public face, Bennett was bitter in the protracted defeat.

Bennett's Calgary West riding mattered to him and Shaw, of course, but the final result would have no effect on the overall outcome of the national election. Meighen's Conservative government had been soundly trounced. The Liberals were back in power, one seat short of a majority, with the Progressives winning 69 seats and the Conservatives reduced to 50. Bennett's brief foray back into federal politics had seen him hold two cabinet posts but his time had been so brief that he'd played only a managerial role. There had been no opportunity for leadership or accomplishment. The people of Calgary West had decided that he should be a private man rather than a public figure, and so he gathered his talents and ambitions and turned them again to the world of business and finance.

BITTER DIVISION

Bennett allowed himself little time to ruminate over the last recount's final decision. He poured himself into matters at the firm and with the many other companies and investments with which he was involved. Just a few months later, in the late spring of 1923, Bennett found himself on a ship to England where he was to act as lead counsel in an appeal to the Privy Council. The case involved the damages awarded to the widow of a Calgary doctor named W. J. Chambers who had been killed in a train accident while in western Ontario. In the midst of arguing the case, Bennett's focus was tested when he received an abrupt but disturbing telegram from James Lougheed. The telegram prompted proceedings that are debated to this day among Alberta law students.

He and Lougheed had discussed their partnership and the future of the firm on at least two occasions before Bennett's latest departure for England. They had agreed that the firm was changing and growing to meet the evolving needs of Calgary's development. They had finally conceded that the 1897 partnership agreement that had been reviewed and extended each year since needed to be substantially restructured, and that they would begin discussions upon Bennett's return. It was with this plan in mind that Bennett read the telegram and felt the sting of betrayal. The July 21 Great North Western telegram read, "Acting on Ottawa conversation Sinclair will purchase your interest as mentioned and organize new firm. Unless immediate steps taken dissolution probable. Cable reply."[52]

Lougheed and his cohorts had been busy. They visited each of the firm's clients attempting to persuade them to leave Bennett and move to the new, and what they promised would be, improved firm. Room would be created in the new entity for William McLaws who had articled with Bennett but had been let go in 1918. There would also be a place for Lougheed's son Edgar.

Bennett was hurt and angry. He carefully planned his response. He made no communication with Lougheed but sent a number of carefully worded telegrams to trustworthy allies. On August 24, Bennett returned to Calgary but ignored his office, instead setting up headquarters in his rooms at the Palliser. Alice Millar and other friends and colleagues spent hours with Bennett, relaying their versions of what had happened, trading gossip, and helping to plan his counterattack. All of Calgary knew what was happening and awaited the battle of the titans.

Lougheed had placed Lougheed Bennett in receivership. Horace Howard of the Calgary Trusts and Guaranty Company had been appointed by the court to oversee it all. Bennett carefully planned his move then pounced. He called Lougheed's bluff. Bennett summoned Howard to his room and demanded, in his capacity as one of the firm's partners, that the court's decision be carried out immediately and completely. That day, the Clarence Block offices were stripped to the bare walls. Everything was boxed up then carted away to be stored, locked, and guarded in the attic of the nearby Southam Building. When Howard returned to the Palliser to report on the action, Bennett was unsatisfied. He castigated the poor man and demanded that he return and remove the brass plaque inscribed with the words "Lougheed and Bennett" from the door. Bennett's actions deprived Lougheed and his new partners of their offices, furniture, equipment, and even more important, their files. There was to be no turning back.

Lougheed set up a new legal firm called Lougheed McLaws Sinclair and Redman, with the clients he and his partners had stolen. He began to build anew. Bennett did the same and with loyal employees Alexander Hannah and Percy Sanford founded Bennett Hannah and Sanford with new offices on the sixth floor of the Lancaster Building, only a block from his old offices. It is interesting that all of the secretaries, support staff, and associate attorneys E. J. Chambers, O. E. Might, and H. G. Nolan were given the choice and every one of them went with Bennett. He also discovered that the majority of major clients, excluding the Bank of Montreal, had decided to remain with him.

The legal wrangling that was necessary to dissolve the partnership continued for some time. The next step in the saga involved Bennett's response to the Statement of Claim that Lougheed had filed on August 1. The document outlined the history of the firm in a way that Bennett found offensive. For instance, its second paragraph stated that William McLaws became a partner in the firm that was subsequently called Lougheed, Bennett, McLaws and Company but that he retired in 1918, which returned the firm to its original partnership of Lougheed and Bennett. It portrayed McLaws as the aggrieved party. Bennett found the paragraph instructive, and assumed, although it was never proven, that it was McLaws who had been manipulating events from behind the scenes and had turned Lougheed against him.

Bennett's response was a twenty-two-page document filed on December 2, 1922. It was at once both a carefully argued legal brief and the cry of a hurt and bitter associate who had assumed friendship. While the document's fifth paragraph admitted that the firm changed names and brought McLaws to prominence for a time, its third paragraph attacked Lougheed's honesty in charging, "This Defendant denies that the Defendant, McLaws, at any time became a member of the said partnership of Lougheed and Bennett."[53]

Two other paragraphs were even more scathing in reproving Lougheed's character and reputation as a lawyer, public servant, and as a man. Bennett claimed that his former partner had used underhanded tricks to rob him of his firm and that such action was beneath the behaviour of a gentleman.

Bennett must have known that the accusations and personal barbs would hurt and he must also have known that they would not be allowed to stand. Indeed, Lougheed filed a Notice of Motion with the court asking that the personally insulting paragraphs be struck as they were, ". . . scandalous, embarrassing and tending to prejudice or delay the fair trial of this action, and as contravening the provisions of the Rule of Practice in regard to pleadings generally . . . ."[54] The judge agreed and paragraphs 45 and 46 were removed.

The case dragged on for year after painful year. In November 1925, with the case still pending, Senator James Lougheed died. It was Lougheed's son Clarence who finally approached Bennett and the final arrangements were made to put it all to a close. As in most cases motivated more by emotion than logic, neither side really won; they just stopped fighting. Lougheed and Bennett had seen each other only once between the London telegram and the senator's death. They sat and sipped tea in Bennett's Palliser suite and, according to Alice Millar, who was listening in the next room, they quietly and politely disagreed with each other's recollection of events. They left each other's company for the last time with a solemn handshake. It is said that upon his Ottawa deathbed, Lougheed was brought news that Bennett, who by that time had re-entered politics, had won an election and would again represent Calgary West. Lougheed smiled and said, "Isn't that just fine."[55]

In the midst of the wrangle with Lougheed, Bennett had stirred intrigue in the city when he took ownership of a fabulous three-storey sandstone house. The Prospect Avenue house boasted a commanding view of Calgary from atop Mount Royal. Rumours quickly spread that Bennett had purchased it in advance of a pending marriage. There were, in fact, a number of women to whom Bennett was romantically linked in those years. The name bandied about at that moment was Edith Cochrane, the daughter of Ontario Conservative Party leader Frank Cochrane. Indeed, the two enjoyed a number of evenings together in Ottawa and Toronto, but nothing came of the relationship. The tongues stopped wagging when Bennett rented the house and remained in his rooms at the Palliser. A less romantic story finally came to light. The house had come to Bennett from L. M. Roberts in lieu of payment for debts owed as part of the dissolving of Bennett Lougheed.

Meanwhile, Bennett Hannah and Sanford thrived quickly and well. Everyone in Calgary called it simply the Bennett firm. It remains a powerful institution today and is called Bennett Jones. Interesting and perhaps ironic is that among the many lawyers who have been associated with the firm was the Honourable Peter Lougheed, from 1971 to 1985 Alberta's mercurial and respected premier, and James Lougheed's grandson.

The fight with Lougheed had been tough financially and emotionally. As much or perhaps more than the defeats he had suffered at the hands of the voters, the frustrations he experienced with Sifton and Meighen, and the snub he had been handed by Borden, the struggle with James Lougheed had torn at something deep within him. In 1925, Bennett was fifty-five years old, rich beyond his dreams, and respected in his community. But the Lougheed challenge had re-awakened within him the desire to fight for what was in his mind right and fair.

In June 1925, with the Lougheed struggle entering its final stages, Bennett received a cable from Meighen. As he had before, he asked Bennett to leave private life and run for office. Without mentioning a particular post, he promised a seat at his cabinet table.[56] It was a bold offer from a not very popular or powerful leader of a small and ineffectual Opposition who had done little to ingratiate himself with Canadians to a retired Conservative living in a Liberal province in a Labour riding. Bennett thought for two days then cabled back that his responsibilities with his new legal firm, his other businesses and directorships, and his growing responsibilities with the Eddy Company were such that he could not contemplate leaving private life and would not be a candidate. He was gracious and wished Meighen well and promised to help in any way that he could.[57] One wonders if Bennett allowed himself the anticipatory tingle of pondering whether his answer was final or if his days as a public figure were truly over.

CHAPTER THREE

ON TO LEADERSHIP

1925–1927

THE 1920S ARE OFTEN SEEN through the prism of the prosperity that by mid-decade most regions of the country enjoyed. They are recalled as an exciting time of new technological wizardry, of bush planes and automobiles that opened wilderness to tourists, and of rollicking popular culture through which Canadians were outraged by flappers, amused by Charlie Chaplin, and later enthralled by talkies. Canadians cheered at their radios as the Ottawa Senators won yet another Stanley Cup. They cheered again as province after province revoked prohibition laws, allowing them to hoist their first legal pint in years. Of course, the American Constitution still dictated thirst, so many adventurous maritime fishermen ran rum down the coast, earning more in a night with their booty of booze than in a year with their nets. Samuel Bronfman continued to bootleg his way to wealth and the Seagram's empire. Al Capone was apparently in tunnels beneath Moose Jaw, although when asked about Canada he claimed to not even know what street it was on.

But not far beneath the veneer of exciting times, the country was splintering. The First World War had been devastating. Just over 60,000 of Canada's young men lay slaughtered on the fields of France and Belgium. Their bravery on every field of battle, coupled finally with the genius of their own generals at Vimy Ridge, had earned respect among both allies and enemies and caused Canadian chests to swell in a way they had never done before—with patriotism that was not British but Canadian. Even beyond the loss of so many from that generation who were killed or suffered physical or emotional wounds from which they would never recover, the country had been torn by the decision to enact conscription. Thousands mourned the loss of loved ones taken by the flu. The country had surrendered to the devil's call of racism and nativism and imprisoned thousands of loyal Ukrainian, Italian, and German Canadians who were suddenly deemed enemy aliens. Further, like every other country involved in the war, a decision had been made to turn away from long-established economic practices and gold-standard rules in order to allow inflation and debt to pay for it all. Everyone would worry about costs later. But then later arrived.

So the postwar years began as if the country were waking up with a hangover from a party it had not really enjoyed. Income tax had been implemented as a temporary measure to deal with the shortage of revenue, but the initiative did not take effect until 1920. Even then the amount was so low as to be a nuisance rather than a source of substantial government income. Like every other country that had involved itself in the war, Canada slid into a postwar recession as it adjusted to changes and challenges none had ever known.

The economic hard times and readjustments were felt to different degrees and in different ways in various regions of the country, but none was untouched. The angst that challenge and change were visiting upon people was at the heart of the violent 1919 Winnipeg General Strike and the dramatic rise in the size and power of labour unions everywhere from British Columbia's lumber camps to Ontario's manufacturing Golden Horseshoe to Cape Breton's coal mines. With the emergent influence of organized labour came new political parties that sought to speak for the growing working class. The Communist Party of Canada was born in a Guelph, Ontario, barn in 1921, but soon its power would be seen in the sway it held in a number of industrial unions. Its leader, the charismatic and irascible Tim Buck, would become a household name. And from the hardscrabble streets of Winnipeg's north end came Methodist minister J. S. Woodsworth and labour organizer A. A. Heaps, who as Labour Party candidates running under the banner "Human Needs Before Property Rights," were elected to federal office that same year.

The West was especially hard hit. While he continued to increase his wealth, Bennett noted the difficult time fellow westerners were experiencing. In a 1922 Christmas letter to Beaverbrook's secretary he called the situation on the prairies ". . . the worst it has ever been in the history of this country."[1] Bennett reported that the population of Calgary and Alberta was actually shrinking, that the province was $40 million in debt, and that the city of Calgary's debt had topped $25 million. There were crop failures causing troubled times to the point of starvation in some rural areas. He wrote of reports that cattle were being shot because they could not be fed. The postwar recession was the prime motivating factor in the creation of cooperative movements such as the Alberta Wheat Pool. In 1923, under the leadership of the charismatic Henry Wise Wood, it sold one-dollar shares to farmers who were pleased to be taking control of their livelihood after years of what they saw as eastern and corporate greed.

Proving that the war's Union government had truly broken the traditional parties' hold on Canadians, the United Farmers of Ontario formed the country's largest provincial government under the leadership of Ernest (E. C.) Drury in 1919. Then in 1922, proving that that success was not a regional fluke, John Bracken led the United Farmers of Manitoba to victory and formed another province's government. Meanwhile, upset by what he believed was the Borden government's unwillingness to adequately address agrarian issues, Minister of Agriculture Thomas Crerar split from both the Union government and the Liberals. He returned to Winnipeg, and in 1920 became the first leader of the Progressive Party. In the 1921 federal election, the new party sent sixtynine MPS to Ottawa not only from the west but also from Ontario, New Brunswick, and Nova Scotia.

The 1920s were roaring alright. They roared with widows, orphans, and the shattered minds and bodies of veterans. They roared with economic instability, violent strikes, and the redrawing of the political map in ways that left nothing that could be safely predicted. At least Chaplin was funny.

1925 ELECTION

It was in this mixed-up and topsy-turvy milieu in which everyone seemed to be changing his or her mind about something that Richard Bennett changed his. With no apparent consultation with anyone, and certainly no explanation, Bennett reconsidered Meighen's repeated and insistent invitations to run. He decided to end his declared retirement from public life and offer himself in the 1925 federal election.

Prime Minister Mackenzie King began the campaign with a confident slogan that spoke to people's growing unease and desire for stability: "Unity—Moderation—Progress." Like so many of his speeches the slogan hinted at a promise of something while actually saying nothing. While the smaller parties did what they could to attract attention to their particular areas of concern, Mackenzie King and Meighen seemed content to ignore the cleavages of class, gender, and race and argue the old issues of taxation, tariffs, railways, and immigration.[2] In so doing, they sought votes by asking people to join them on a journey with their eyes not on the horizon before them but on the dust behind.

As the campaign began, the theme that emerged in the West and was soon felt throughout the country was anti-Americanism. In 1922, the American Congress had passed, and President Harding had signed, the Fordney-McCumber Act. The new legislation had raised tariffs on a host of goods from around the world including products that Canadian companies had been selling over the southern border. Most important among them were the essential staples upon which the Canadian economy relied—wheat, lumber, and fish. National political leaders stumbled over one another in criticizing the protectionist action and in making pledges to address it with retaliatory actions of their own. World tariffs and non-tariff barriers began to rise.

The Fordney-McCumber Act was among the first major steps world governments took to win votes at home by enacting protectionist policies that pretended to guard domestic jobs but in the end resulted in destroying those jobs by slowing international trade and commerce. In January 2009, economic and political leaders met at the annual World Economic Forum held at Davos, Switzerland, and were united in urging one another to avoid the temptation to repeat the protectionist errors their predecessors had made. They knew then what world leaders had no way of knowing in the 1920s: that by the decade's end, protectionist trade policies and practices played a major role in turning what could have been a minor challenge into a devastating global disaster.

Bennett had won his Calgary West nomination by acclamation. Meanwhile, Joseph Shaw, the Labour candidate who had defeated Bennett in the controversial 1921 contest, had proven unspectacular as a member of Parliament and constituency man. Further, the Progressive Party was in trouble. Its leader had resigned and a number of Alberta and Saskatchewan members had become Liberals as Mackenzie King deftly stole Progressive policies and thus the party's raison d'être. Further, like a dog that had finally caught the car it had been chasing, the United Farmers of Alberta was imploding due to internal party squabbling.

Bennett was quick and effective in exploiting the political problems of those around him. He focused primarily on his Liberal opponent. Confident in the support of the business community and Calgary's urban working class, with which he had spent the last year re-establishing himself, he spent a good deal of time in the rural townships west of the city. He stirred the anti-American pot, although he was always careful to speak of the American government or American polices and not Americans themselves. He was the only candidate to speak against the growing resentment that many Albertans were expressing about eastern Canadians. Then as now, there was a perception among many westerners that Ottawa unfairly catered to Ontario's needs due to its being the country's financial capital and its containing more House of Commons seats than any other province. Just as he would not play to religious or racial cleavages, Bennett did not and never played to regional divisions to win votes.

Two days before Halloween the votes were cast. Bennett earned 10,256 votes to Shaw's second-place 6,040. He had easily won the city and his work in the rural areas had paid off handsomely with 55 per cent of the farm vote. He had spent his own money on posters and newspaper ads. He had knocked on doors. He had organized volunteers to pull the vote. He had promised little and sold his experience as his greatest asset. He had simply outworked the other candidates and earned his victory.

Canadians awoke on October 30 to find surprising results in a national campaign that had seemed to promise no surprises at all. Meighen's Conservatives had rebounded from only 50 seats in the last Parliament to win 116. The Liberals won 101 and the fading Progressives 25. Woodsworth and Heaps returned as members of the Labour Party and the venerable Henri Bourassa was back in the House as one of four independents. The election was doubly disappointing for Mackenzie King in that not only had his government been defeated but he had also lost his own riding. The Conservatives had won, and for the second time since Confederation, Canadians had created a minority government.

Then the fun began. The Conservatives had elected more members and so Canadians assumed that they had elected Meighen as their prime minister. But in the Canadian democratic system voters do not choose a government, they assemble a parliament. It is the members of that parliament who decide which party or coalition of parties commands the confidence of the House and thus which can form the government.

It is this tradition that Prime Minister Stephen Harper either failed to grasp or boldly lied about in December 2008 when a Liberal–NDP coalition threatened to pass a motion of non-confidence that could have removed his minority government and replaced it with one that had the votes in the House. Harper huffed and puffed and claimed in a bizarre television address to the nation on December 3 that the Opposition's actions were akin to a coup that violated the democratic wishes of the voters. Harper said, in part, ". . . Canada's Government has always been chosen by the people. . . . Unfortunately, even before the Government has brought forward its budget, and only seven weeks after a general election, the opposition wants to overturn the results of that election."[3] He was as desperate as he was wrong.

In 1926, Mackenzie King and Meighen offered the civics lesson that Harper and many Canadians could have used eighty-two years later. Canadians had built a parliament that gave Prime Minister Mackenzie King's Liberals fifteen fewer MPs than Meighen's Conservatives. But as was his right he refused to step down. He told Governor General Baron Lord Byng of Vimy that he could, even with his diminished numbers in the House, and even with leading from the curtains behind the benches, form a government and that that government could enjoy the confidence of the House.

Byng was no fool. He was a well-read, intelligent man with an Eton education. He was a blue-blooded English aristocrat and an experienced military man, the heel at Gallipoli but the hero of Ypres and Vimy, who was used to straight talk and holding men at their word. It was Byng's wife, by the way, who upon seeing her first hockey game, recoiled at the brutality and offered a trophy in her name to the most gentlemanly player. Byng shook Mackenzie King's hand when his prime minister offered to meet Parliament and prove that he could govern. He assumed Mackenzie King meant that he would resign and Meighen would become prime minister, based on the election just held, if the confidence of the House was lost. Mackenzie King, on the other hand, assumed that Byng understood he had really meant that if he lost the confidence of

the House he could, as prime minister, ask for dissolution and be granted another election. This sincere misunderstanding or ruthless ploy, depending on whether one believes Mackenzie King or Byng, led to the
constitutional crisis that was to ensue.

Like most Canadians, Bennett had assumed that Meighen would be
forming a government and that he himself would soon be at the cabinet
table, but Byng's decision foiled those dreams and plans. Bennett had
not re-entered the political arena to languish in Opposition. Compared
to the challenge of his many business interests, a stint in Opposition
held little appeal. Those interests had, in fact, been growing steadily
more complex and lucrative. In Bennett's day, politicians were not expected to surrender their financial holdings through sales, resignations,
or blind trusts. If there was trust at all, it was that they would make decisions based upon the desires of their constituents, the good of the country, and the dictates of their conscience, rather than considerations of
personal benefit. It was naive perhaps, but until politicians were paid a
decent salary for their efforts, and that was decades away, Bennett, like
his contemporaries, would continue to sit on boards, collect dividends,
and make investments as a private citizen. And with respect to business,
Bennett was better at it than most.

In 1924, Bennett's position as a major shareholder and influential
board member at E. B. Eddy allowed him to oversee a major corporate
expansion. The complex initiative led to $3 million in capital improve-
ments to the Hull facilities and a 50 per cent increase in the workforce
so that the company came to employ over 1,400 people. In May 1926,
Jennie Eddy's brother, J. T. (Harry) Shirreff, unexpectedly died. He and
Bennett had made a deal whereby the first to die would bequeath his
Eddy shares to the other, and so with J. T.'s death Bennett won ownership
of another 1,007 shares, which were then valued at $1,500 each. The inher-
itance meant that Bennett came to own 1,508 of Eddy's 3,000 shares at a
value of $2.2 million.

An annoyance at the time came in the actions of Jennie's sister Edith
Richardson, who convinced herself that Bennett had done something
illegal and swindled her family out of capital stock. She threatened a law-
suit. But soon she showed her true colours in demanding through her
lawyer that she would go away for a lump sum payment from Bennett of
$250,000. Jennie had already set her up with a $375,000 trust fund that

was paying her $19,000 a year, but it was apparently not enough. Bennett hired a lawyer who quickly dealt with the matter and with not a penny paid. The avaricious Mrs. Richardson disappeared from the scene.

By this time, Bennett's success in running businesses, land speculation, and financial entrepreneurialism, coupled with his nationally known and respected name, earned through principled political activity, had resulted in his being invited to join a number of boards, including Canadian General Electric and Metropolitan Life. Beaverbrook had introduced Bennett to the Royal Bank's president, Sir Herbert Holt, who already knew Bennett through his work on the *Rex v. Royal Bank* case. Bennett was invited to join the board of the Royal Bank of Canada. Meanwhile, he still owned a substantial number of shares in a number of successful businesses, was seeing great success in his stock market investments, and was reaping growing profits from his law firm. In 1924, he had sold the Alberta Pacific Grain Company to a British firm, affording him a capital gain of $1.35 million.[4] Meanwhile, he remained president of Calgary Power, which was still supplying electricity to Alberta's major cities. He was also president of Canadian Cement, which had grown even more successful after winning the contract to help rebuild Halifax after the tragic December 1917 explosion in which two ships had collided in the harbour. The ensuing blast flattened the city and took the lives of 1,900 people, while leaving 4,000 injured and 6,000 homeless. Bennett had been doing quite well for years, but by the mid-1920s he had moved from rich to wealthy.

With business interests and political affairs duelling for his attention, Bennett boarded the train in Calgary and was off to Ottawa and his old suites at the Château Club. He quickly settled into his new east wing office, met his staff, and established routines. Every night he left Parliament Hill after dark and walked to his rooms, where he pored over briefing books until midnight. He continued to eat too much, work too much, and read too much, while exercising too little. He still loved his chocolate.

While as an Opposition backbencher Bennett had little power to influence legislation, it is interesting to examine the questions that he raised and the proposals he made to the shaky Mackenzie King minority government. They indicate that his fundamental beliefs about government's positive role in society were becoming more finely honed and persuasively articulated. His very first question was perhaps most prescient of all. He queried the interior minister about unemployment insurance, wondering about the amounts that the provinces and the federal government had pledged for relief. He feigned surprise and disappointment in the minister's declaration that unemployment relief was a provincial matter and that the federal government had no role to play.[5] Bennett ridiculed the minister, insisting that a commitment to a federal relief plan was essential for the well-being of Canadians. Later, in a linked matter, he brought attention to the problems of farmers. He asked about the amount of help being offered to those in need not only in the West but across the country. Again he attacked the government for what he said was an inadequate response to growing problems on the prairies.

On another day he noted that it was under the Borden government that the Canadian National Railway Corporation was created but that no allowance had been made for a meeting of the shareholders as is the standard practice for all corporations. He suggested that a representative from each of the nine provinces should be assembled as a board of directors. He suggested that the board could act independently of Parliament in protecting the investment that Canadians had made as the corporation's owners. The idea was not Bennett's—it had its origins in Borden's 1907 Halifax Platform—but it was the first time it had been brought to the House. In airing the idea, Bennett was once again stating his support for more transparency in the affairs of an activist state.

Bennett also asked about the idea of old age pensions. In a speech regarding the issue, he demonstrated that he was among those who, even in the 1920s, were coming to accept the fundamental assumptions that would decades later form the basis of Canada's present Canada Pension Plan (and similar plan in Quebec) and the notion of tax incentives for retirement savings.[6]

In bringing the idea to light he also showed his wisdom in warning about two problems that are present with all of today's social programs. First, he advocated the ideas without abandoning his core belief in the need for people to be self-reliant. Pensions, he said, should deal with the tragedy of people working their entire lives only to find themselves struggling in retirement against the wolf of poverty. But they should never be interpreted as replacing personal sacrifice, investments, and savings, lest the government create a culture of dependency. He said,

I want to see in this country a system for providing for . . . [an] old age pension. But in this new country, with its resources untouched and undeveloped, where we are endeavouring to develop a hardy spirit of enterprise on the part of our citizens, where we want them to look upon the government as an instrument for their well-being and not something on which they are to depend for sustenance.[7]

Bennett's second warning, couched within his advocacy of helping Canadians to face retirement with financial security and dignity, is one that all past and present provincial premiers would applaud. For example, since the 1980s, provincial governments have had to shoulder a greater and greater percentage of health care costs. The federal government, which had at the outset of the program in the 1960s promised to provide 50 per cent of needed funds, sought to balance its books partly by reducing that percentage on the backs of provincial taxpayers. As if seeing this trick coming, Bennett warned the Liberal finance minister, and those in his caucus who shared his enthusiasm for unemployment and retirement support ideas, that once the federal government enacted the national scheme, it would be on the hook for it and must never shirk its fiduciary responsibility. He said, "Once you enact a law and place it on the statute book, and once you incur financial responsibility, you cannot lightly shake it off, as you would an overcoat."[8] Premiers from Mike Harris on the right to Bob Rae on the left and all in between would agree.

KING, BYNG, AND THE END OF MEIGHEN

While Bennett and his colleagues worked to bring ideas to the House through proposals, questions, and committee work, Prime Minister Mackenzie King watched nervously from behind the government benches. He knew there was a trap waiting for him and his government in the simmering scandal regarding the customs ministry. He waited for the trap to be sprung.

It was really Henry Ford's fault. The Customs scandal had its genesis in the growing number of automobiles in Canada and the United States, resulting in more goods crossing the border on roads rather than solely through ports or rail stations. As is always the case when technological advances move faster than legislation and bureaucratic processes, it was a free-for-all. As the amount of smuggled goods increased and as illegal booze became a bigger and bigger part of that aggregate amount, some customs officials scrambled to react while others cashed in.

Before the 1925 election, some Opposition members had raised questions about the Mackenzie King government's involvement in the manufacture, transport, and illicit sale of liquor involving Canada, the West Indies, Saint-Pierre and Miquelon, and the United States. The minister in charge, the hapless Jacques Bureau, was, according to popular opinion, either corrupt or incompetent. Mackenzie King had tried to stop the questions by promoting him to the Senate and replacing him with Quebec's George Boivin, but his expectation that a new minister would change the subject was soon dashed. The questions and accusations continued.

Meighen saw an opportunity to sting the government and appointed Vancouver's Harry Stevens to lead the Conservative Party's investigation into the Customs Department scandal. Stevens was a tall, fit, handsome man with thinning and greying hair and round frameless glasses. Having sharpened his skills in the tough and taxing world of Vancouver municipal politics, he had been elected to federal office in 1911 and had quickly earned respect on both sides of the aisle as a hard-working parliamentarian. During Stevens's first session in Ottawa, Bennett was happy to share with him both an office and a Commons desk. It was as a respected colleague, and with a nod to his experience as an investigative attorney, that Stevens chose Bennett to work with him on his customs committee. At that point, neither man could have guessed what their relationship would later turn into and the nationally significant consequences of that turning. But that's for later.

Stevens and Bennett unearthed so much damning evidence so quickly that they surprised even themselves. On February 2, Stevens rose in the House, with Mackenzie King squirming impotently from behind the curtains, and in a five-hour tirade laid out in excruciating detail fact after sordid fact. The blatantly corrupt activities and the depth of the sleaze was such that had not been seen since the Pacific Scandal that had brought down the venerable Sir John A. The Liberal government did the only thing it could and called for the formation of a Select Committee of the House to conduct a full investigation. Stevens and Bennett were among the four Conservative members of the committee, serving with four Liberals and Progressive Donald Kennedy as the chair.

From February until June 1926 the committee heard from 225 witnesses. The evidence demonstrated that, as Bennett and Stevens had suspected, there had indeed been a complex system of bribes paid to Liberal hacks and to the Liberal Party itself in return for department officials turning a blind eye to the illegal international liquor trade. At one point Customs Minister Jacques Bureau had even used his influence to try to pressure a judge to go easy on one of the convicted rumrunners, who had close ties to the Liberal Party.

Throughout the 115 days of proceedings, Bennett acquitted himself quite well. His ability to synthesize a mass of facts and boil them to their essence allowed him to unravel devastating lines of questioning that led witnesses far down incriminating roads before realizing they had even begun a journey. Admissions and confessions were inadvertently made as a result of Bennett's tactical cleverness and acuity with a phrase.

Bennett was again gaining national attention and once again his ability to speak intelligently, fluidly, and without notes was being observed. The *Montreal Evening Standard*, for instance, wrote of admiration for his oratorical skill but, as a Liberal paper, could not help taking a swipe. The article described him as ". . . the most gifted of Canadian orators, but his speeches seldom have any strain of humour in them. . . . They are purely and simply rhetorical, and are delivered with great rapidity of utterance."[9]

To review Hansard, the official record of all that is said in the House of Commons, is to be amazed with Bennett's ability. It is common to find three single-spaced double-columned pages filled with his blistering oratory. Bennett spoke off the top of his head better than most professional writers can compose with time on their hands. His speaking notes often consisted of four or five scribbled points that he planned to cover. Such a skill is needed and widely admired in any democracy and, as Barack Obama proved in the 2008 presidential campaign and then later in shepherding difficult legislation through Congress, one that can help a great deal in the pursuit of political goals.

In March, Mackenzie King had won a by-election in Prince Albert, Saskatchewan, defeating a young lawyer named John Diefenbaker, and was back in the House. Canadians, of course, carried on with their lives and as is the case today mostly ignored the backroom machinations on Parliament Hill. But in Ottawa and among the chattering class there was Christmas Eve-like quivering anticipation regarding the customs committee's findings. On June 18, 1926, it reported to the House. It found that the former Customs Bureau minister had spectacularly failed in his duties and that there was a great deal that other members of cabinet, including the prime minister, should have known and should have stopped. The minister primarily responsible was gone but the committee report suggested that legal action against him should be contemplated.

But this was Ottawa, where everything is always political, and so the Opposition was less interested in seeing a minister's backside in court than in seeing their own on the government benches. On the twenty-second, the political fight began as Stevens moved beyond what the report had suggested and led the Conservative push to have it amended so as to censure the prime minister for both what he had done and what he had failed to do. Stevens demanded that the government resign. For two days, one procedural amendment after another was presented and defeated. Party whips worked overtime as alliances between the parties were forged then broken.

Knowing that he did not have the votes to keep the fight going for long but ever the brilliant tactician, Mackenzie King went to the Governor General, resigned, and asked for the dissolution of Parliament before the Stevens amendment was called. Byng refused. Mackenzie King could not believe his ears. No Governor General had ever refused the request of a prime minister to dissolve Parliament and set an election date. Byng was an intelligent and proud man who had been following the circus in the House closely. He knew both his constitutional powers and the agreement he believed he had made with Mackenzie King just months before. He dismissed Mackenzie King and summoned Meighen, who, after all, had more members in the House than the Liberals. He asked Meighen to form a government.

Meighen had options before him, but the one he chose and how he chose to operationalize it ended his career as prime minister and Conservative party leader while yawning open the door of opportunity for Bennett. After the 1925 election Bennett had quickly become one of Meighen's closest and most trusted advisers and the deputy leader of the Opposition. But Meighen was unable to discuss this critical decision with Bennett, for at that moment Bennett was home in Calgary, having accepted an invitation from Alberta Conservative leader and old friend A. A. McGillivary to help in the provincial election. The Alberta Conservatives did not have a snowball's chance of forming the government, but, like everyone else, Meighen had not seen the political tsunami coming and had given Bennett permission to go.

Bennett was immediately contacted and began to make arrangements to return to Ottawa, but the whole thing was over so fast that he ended up missing the entire affair. Meighen later told a friend that this happenstance was important, for he believed that if Bennett had been present in the House with his tough talk, shrewd mind, and fighting spirit, things might have worked out differently.[10] If Meighen's assessment was correct, then Bennett's absence changed Canadian history.

Meighen decided to form a government and was dutifully sworn in as prime minister. He could have then adjourned the House and gone to the country as prime minister, probably acquitting himself quite well against the corruption-tainted Liberals. Instead, he decided to renew the session in order to pass the Stevens amendment, thereby smearing the tar of censure on Mackenzie King and his government. That was his fatal error.

At that time, any sitting member who was appointed to cabinet had to resign his seat and run in a by-election, presumably so that his constituents could decide if they wanted to share his time between them and the country. Knowing that if he allowed the resignation of so many Conservative members his government would not have the votes to survive until lunch the first day, Meighen told Byng that he would resign his seat. But he asked the Governor General to appoint five of his caucus as acting ministers to handle the administrative duties of the entire cabinet. His understanding was that as acting ministers they would not need to resign their seats.

As he could no longer be in the House, Meighen needed a strong House leader. Bennett was best suited for the job but could not get back to Ottawa in time. Stevens declined the honour. Meighen was left with his third choice and appointed the long-serving Sir Henry Drayton. After a weekend of behind-the-scenes political intrigue, the likes of which the country, or for that matter, no Commonwealth dominion had ever known, a new government was ready to govern. By Monday evening Canada had a new prime minister, again watching from behind the House of Commons curtains, and a new, although small and

quite inexperienced, cabinet. In his absence, Bennett had been appointed acting minister of justice.

Mackenzie King was too smart and ruthless for all that chicanery.
The House met on Tuesday and took up the debate about the Customs
scandal as if nothing had happened. The same votes went up and down
as before the major parties had switched sides of the House. Mackenzie
King then feinted by moving that the House consider tariff policy. The
motion went nowhere but it did as he had hoped, and split the
Progressives. Even better than he had hoped, the gambit played a role in
leading to the resignation of their leader, ex-Liberal Robert Forke. The
strategy was brilliant. But the real show had yet to begin.

On Wednesday evening, now June 30, Mackenzie King rose and began to ask a series of seemingly innocuous questions. In a quiet voice, he
asked whether Drayton had taken the oath of office. Meighen stood behind the curtain at the back of the government benches and saw what
was about to happen but was unable to stop it. Drayton said no. Mackenzie
King then repeated his question to each of the acting ministers—Harry
Stevens, Hugh Guthrie, Sir George Perley, and Robert Manion—and
each dutifully admitted to not having taken an oath. As members came
running into the House from offices and smoke- and gin-filled lounges,
every Conservative member protested loudly, but the jig was up. As
Mackenzie King droned on in a detailed review of the remarkable events
that had brought them to that point, Meighen watched his infant government die. It was painted as illegitimate and unconstitutional. The Customs
scandal that had begun it all no longer mattered.

At two o'clock in the morning a vote was finally called to decide the
future of the Meighen government. The Conservative Party whip had
met with his Liberal counterpart and told him that Bennett was still in
Calgary and would miss the vote. Following a parliamentary tradition
called twinning, the Progressive whip agreed that he would choose a
member to miss the vote as well. When the vote was called, it was obvious that the double cross was in, for there sat the Progressive Party's
Reverend Thomas Bird. Bird had been twinned with Bennett and should
have absented himself, but there he was. Conservative members howled
protests, to no avail. The Conservatives lost the confidence motion by
Bird's single vote: 96 to 95. Meighen was left with no option but to ask the
Governor General for dissolution. This time Byng acceded. The election

would be held on September 14. It was the first time that a Canadian government had fallen on a confidence motion. Meighen's government had lasted just three days.

Still in Calgary, Bennett received a wire telling him to stay there as another campaign was on. Mackenzie King was brilliant in the battle that followed. With 14 per cent of the electorate having voted in the last election for splinter party candidates or independents, he knew that moving those voters to the Liberals was the key to electoral success. He had already stolen or adopted all the Progressive Party policy ideas that he could possibly cram under the Liberal tent. The Progressives seemed to sense that their time was up and did all they could to help their new Liberal allies. In many strong Conservative ridings, for instance, they did not run a candidate so as to avoid vote splitting. In Manitoba, not a single riding saw a Liberal compete with a Progressive and in many Ontario and Maritime ridings candidates ran as Liberal Progressives.

Meighen presented no new policy ideas, having opted to run instead on the issue of Liberal corruption. Mackenzie King decided that the constitutional question was key. He argued that Canada needed to be independent of the Governor General—a British-appointed peer of the realm who had ignored the will of the people in saying no to a prime minister—and also that the scandal had proven Meighen to be a power-hungry scoundrel who could not be trusted. Only near the campaign's end did Meighen seem to realize that his message was failing to resonate and begin talking about the constitutional issues that had put him before the people in the first place. Not since Confederation, and not again until the 1970s, would the Constitution be the primary issue in a national campaign.

When the counting was over it was clear that Mackenzie King had sensed the mood of the country faster and better. He had outcampaigned Meighen as decidedly on the hustings as he had outfoxed him in the House. Despite having won 83,051 fewer votes, the Liberals won 118 seats. Meighen's Conservatives limped over the finish line with only 91. The party had been completely shut out of Saskatchewan and Manitoba and Meighen had even lost his own Portage la Prairie riding. It was the second election in a row in which a sitting prime minister was left without a seat. Mackenzie King had again defeated the thirty-year-old Diefenbaker to win in Prince Albert.

In Alberta, the United Farmers of Alberta had rallied and won 11 seats while the Conservatives took only one riding—Bennett's Calgary West. Bennett had again run an enthusiastic campaign and had again financed it with his own money. He won both the city and the townships and decisively defeated Liberal Harry Lunney by 2,449 votes. The plurality was less than the year before but a win is a win and he was soon on an eastbound train heading back to his Château Club suite and a desk on the Opposition side of the House.

Bennett had gone to the people believing that the Customs scandal and King's constitutional game playing would anger voters and lead to a Conservative victory, but he had misread the mood of the country.[11] Bennett confided to friends that he blamed himself for much of the constitutional and electoral morass into which Meighen had allowed himself to slide. He later explained that if he had been in Ottawa, he would have advised Meighen to refuse Byng's offer to form a government.[12] This was despite the fact that Meighen later said that he based his decision to accept the Governor General's offer on his belief that had he declined, Canada would have been without a government. Further, if he had said no to Byng, the Governor General would have been left with the alternatives of either humiliatingly begging Mackenzie King to reconsider or perhaps offering Woodsworth or the Progressives a chance to tape together a coalition. In Meighen's mind, either option would have irreparably harmed Byng, which mattered a little; the office of the Governor General, which mattered more; and the entire concept of a constitutional monarchy, which mattered most of all. Bennett might have avoided the trap into which Sir Henry Drayton inadvertently waltzed. But given Meighen's desire to protect the monarch's voice and dignity in Canada, no matter how indirect, it is by no means certain that Bennett could have changed his leader's mind and kept him from accepting the offer to form a government.

Grant Dexter of the *Winnipeg Free Press* later asked Bennett what he would have done differently had he been in Ottawa at the time. Bennett explained that as a competent House of Commons man he would have allowed Mackenzie King to pose his queries but would have refused to answer them. Instead, Bennett claimed, he would have turned the debate back to the Customs scandal or perhaps to the tariff questions that were at that time splitting the Progressives and scattering the independents. Dexter wrote, "I am a good Liberal, but I am very much inclined to think he was right. He was exactly the kind of debater that could have done this."[13]

Until the victory in 1926, Mackenzie King's hold on the Liberal leadership was tenuous at best. At the beginning of the campaign there had been open talk among the Liberal rank and file about his paling in comparison to Laurier and about a mistake having been made in placing him in a position of leadership. Charles Dunning, the nattily dressed, ruggedly handsome, moustached former farmer, was being touted by many as a suitable successor. Those planning the palace coup had even set up Ernest Lapointe to act as Dunning's Quebec lieutenant, reminiscent of the old Macdonald-Cartier ministry.[14] But their plans evaporated when the conspirators found that Mackenzie King's parliamentary manoeuvrings had worked and he had become a much improved campaigner. When Mackenzie King was introducing his cabinet to the new Governor General he did so secure in the knowledge that his leadership of the party was unchallenged.

Whether Mackenzie King had reacted to unpredicted events cleverly or had set the elaborate scheme up from the beginning mattered little to Meighen after the election. Meighen was devastated by how everything that he had worked so long and so hard for had unravelled so quickly and in so unexpected a fashion. His leadership and party were in tatters. There was really only one decision left for him to make. He was only fifty-two years old and in bracingly good health. He could have found a new seat and carried on. But sometimes the writing on the wall is too vivid for anyone to ignore. There were no public calls for his resignation, but also, even more important in such a circumstance, there were few for him to stay. At a lunch meeting at the Ottawa Club he announced that he would immediately step down as leader. A career noted more for its potential than its accomplishment appeared to be over.

LEADERSHIP

The Conservative Party's disgraced leader was leaving. It had been rejected at the polls. It had new rebellious parties and movements competing for voter support and it faced a re-invigorated Liberal Party and leader who had earned loyalty and legitimacy. The party had little money and few immediate prospects. It needed to rebuild itself quickly or risk sinking beneath the political waves as the Progressive Party was in the midst of doing and other parties in the past had done. There is, after all, nothing in Canada's political culture that guarantees that a party will last forever. Ask the Union Nationale, the CCF, the Social Credit, or the Reform Party. Something dramatic needed to be done to save the party of Macdonald.

In the meantime, the party also needed to deal with the spring session of Parliament. Mackenzie King presented his new government's budget to the House in early February 1927. The humbled Meighen said little in response, leaving Bennett to lead the Conservatives through the ensuing debate. Bennett avoided attacking what had been proposed and instead chose to ignore the Liberal plan and advance one of his own. After consulting with caucus colleagues, he delivered a speech in which he presented a number of what at the time were novel ideas. Most interesting among them was his argument that Canadian businesses would be better able to compete internationally, sell less expensive products domestically, and thereby create more employment, if certain taxes were removed from businesses and instead paid by consumers on things they purchased—a national sales tax.[15] He had presaged the Good and Services Tax (GST)—which Canadians hate but which helps businesses and thus the economy—by over sixty years. While his tax ideas and other notions went nowhere, they received significant national attention.

Bennett also garnered a good deal of ink for his attack on a Liberal private member's bill supporting the extension of a charter to a conglomerate intent on pushing forward with the creation of the Georgian Bay Canal Project. The idea was to build a series of canals linking Lake Huron to Montreal. Different combinations of business people had been trying to put together public and private financing to start construction since 1894. Bennett criticized extending the charter, as the canal scheme would bring enormous costs with little benefit. He was also aghast that Clifford and Arthur Sifton were part of the new Montreal, Ottawa, and Georgian Bay Canal Company that was seeking government largess. The plan was eventually killed and for the role he played in its death, Bennett was again seen as a powerful and articulate spokesperson for his party.

The short spring session ended in late April, allowing Bennett to travel to England. Once again he enjoyed the company of his sister Mildred on the long cruise over and back. He was able to spend time with Beaverbrook at his friend's luxurious estate and through his good graces to meet with many of Britain's political and business leaders. It was a rare year that Bennett did not make England part of his travel plans. Alice Millar, Bennett's secretary and personal assistant, either accompanied him on his many trips or stayed home tending his offices. Either way he was, through her, in constant contact with his businesses. The mammoth flow of correspondence makes clear that even when on vacation, Bennett's mind was never far from work.

The long parliamentary recess allowed Conservative Party leaders to plan. Throughout the summer, uncoordinated discussions were held among party brass and large donors and at the grassroots. Many ideas were floated. Finally, at a party caucus held in Ottawa on October 11, 1927, it was decided that the widely respected Guelph MP Hugh Guthrie would act as interim leader. Guthrie was a man of fierce intelligence with rugged, leading-man good looks. He had begun his career as a Liberal but came to the Union government and then became a Conservative. He was among those who supported a brave and risky decision: new party policies and a new party leader would be chosen at a national convention.

Conventions were a relatively novel phenomenon in Canada. After a few provincial conventions, the Liberals held the first federal convention in 1893 and then another to choose Mackenzie King in 1919. Ontario Conservatives had just staged a convention to choose Howard Ferguson as their new leader. But for the federal Conservative Party a convention would be new.

There were dangers. As the backroom doors were flung open, those who led and those who bankrolled the party would surrender much of their control in choosing both the platform and leader. But there were advantages too. A convention could stir interest at the riding level across the country and, in grabbing national headlines, stimulate political discussions that could invigorate interest in the Liberal-Conservative brand, while affording the legitimacy of democratic selection to a new leader. It was deemed worth the risk.

Major General A. D. McRae was chosen to work closely with Guthrie and oversee the meeting's organization. He had distinguished himself as the quartermaster general for the Canadian expeditionary force in Europe during the First World War and been loaned to the British to work as the assistant minister of information, where he learned to generate, disseminate, and appreciate propaganda. Once home, he entered public life, won a Vancouver seat, and quickly earned respect on both sides of the aisle as a wise member, a sympathetic but firm House whip, and a good constituency man. He was a man who could get things done.

A number of Conservative clubs wrote to Guthrie and McRae explaining why their city was best suited to host the convention. Finally, it was decided that it would be held in the centre of the country—in Winnipeg. A number of organizing committees were struck, delegates were chosen, people appointed, and procedures established. It was decided that delegates would need to pay the approximately $200 it took to attend the conference on their own, without party funding, effectively limiting the delegates according to class. It was also decided that delegate numbers would be allocated according to population, which spoke to the importance of region.

In a nod to gender, it was determined that at least 25 per cent of the delegates had to be women. The goal was not reached, but not for a lack of trying. Guthrie's first job was to form a thirty-six-person organizing committee based on representation by population. He determined that with the advances that women had been making in Canada—as seen most directly in the winning of the right to vote in federal elections that was legislated in 1919—this committee must include women from every province. Some provinces were quick to appoint women to the list. Ontario, for instance, without prodding, had included Mrs. Fallis of Peterborough and Mrs. Edwards of London. Other provinces were less receptive to the idea of women at the convention at all, let alone on such an important committee, which forced Guthrie to write repeatedly to some, insisting on female representation. New Brunswick was especially intransigent until finally delegation chair George Jones surrendered and included Mrs. Price on the province's list. Mildred Bennett became involved in the convention. With Bennett's approval she met with McRae and was put to work encouraging women to participate fully in the planning of the convention and then later in the convention itself. In the end, nine of the thirty-six members of the organizing committee were women—a good start. The committee established as one of its goals the seeking of powerful, independently minded women to attend the convention.

On the morning of Monday, October 10, 1927, Winnipeg's Amphitheatre Rink prepared itself to host and witness three days of political theatre. The rink was a large, boxy, three-storey building that was decorated with Arabian-style red-and-white bunting, which was popular at the time. As delegates entered, they were given identification cards to carry and badges to wear. Each bore a picture of Sir John A. Macdonald.

The stage was far from the made-for-television set pieces that a modern eye would recognize. It was a simple affair, crowded with dark wooden tables and chairs that would have been at home in an old public library. But the platform party was chosen to impress. There were two former prime ministers; three Conservative provincial premiers representing Ontario, Nova Scotia, and New Brunswick, nine provincial party leaders; and six former lieutenant-governors, as well as former cabinet ministers, including Bennett. In all, thirty-one people were seated on the stage. Most of the time, however, the platform chairs rested empty.

Hugh Guthrie brought down the gavel to begin the proceedings at eleven o'clock. Despite months of careful preparations meant to appease all and offend few, the very first words from his mouth welcomed the delegates to the Liberal Party convention. Red faced and engulfed by shouts and laughter, he quickly recovered, began again, and welcomed the 1,700 delegates to the Liberal-Conservative convention. The Lord's Prayer was recited in English, then again in French, followed by the singing of "God Save the King" and then "O Canada"—but only in English.

The honour of the convention's first major speech went to Sir Robert Borden. Always a charming man with a self-deprecating sense of humour, Borden was warmly received. His full shock of thick grey hair was carefully combed and his long grey moustaches tried but failed to hide a beaming smile. It was a speech short on nostalgia and long on advice for the future. Borden emphasized that the creation of a party platform was important but that the selection of a party leader was more important by far. With more than a hint to the memories of those who had left him after the conscription and Union government decisions, as well as to those who left Meighen for decisions of less significance, Borden said, "Select your leader, and after you have selected him, stand by him. Being human, he may not always be right. Perhaps it would be well for you sometimes to remember that you are also human, and that occasionally when you think he is wrong he may be right."[16]

After lunch and some housekeeping issues, Arthur Meighen was given a chance to make a departing speech. Oddly, and sadly, instead of choosing to fade from view and leave gracefully, he used his allotted time to defend an old stance. In 1925, in Hamilton, Ontario, Meighen had made an ill-advised speech in which he had proposed that the only way a government should be able take the country to war in the future should be to dissolve Parliament and hold an election on the issue. The notion was a bald gesture toward Quebec voters, many of whom had defied the urgings of Laurier and the church and had opposed Canada's following Britain to war in 1914. Meighen's idea was boneheaded not only because it would lose more support across the country than it would win in Quebec, but also because it was improbable, impractical, and constitutionally unwarranted. The speech had been roundly criticized at the time by Liberals, Conservatives, and the media, and should have been forgotten. But there he was in Winnipeg, before Conservative delegates and the country, reiterating and defending all he had said. As the stunned audience listened, Meighen went on to dismiss Mackenzie King's actions at, and the issues emanating from, the 1923 Imperial Conference. This attack was blunder number two, for those actions had been widely celebrated in Canada as another step toward political maturity as all Britain's dominions had been promised constitutional independence.

As delegates, many of whom had hoped that Meighen might save the day and succeed himself as leader, sat in stunned silence, the proud but foolish man appeared to commit political suicide. Several times the hall erupted in applause, but as he went on and on the audience fell silent. Things grew worse as some began to heckle. Meighen went on. He responded with an angry monotone and the cold "death stare" for which he had become known. Then things got even worse.[17]

Behind him, in the front row of the platform party, sat Ontario premier Howard Ferguson. Ferguson was a short, soft, chubby man with cropped hair, who peered at the world through small eyes and large, round wire-framed glasses. He was seen by many to be an excellent choice as leader and one who might just win a majority of delegates if he played his cards intelligently. Ferguson had sat with Meighen before he had delivered his Hamilton remarks in 1925 and had tried to talk him out of it. He saw the idea as wrong-headed, constitutionally unnecessary, with the potential to split the country and negatively affect Canada's ability to carry out foreign policy efficiently in times of crisis. Further, he had argued that Meighen's idea would hurt the party, especially in Quebec where it would be dismissed as a cynical ploy, and among imperialists in the rest of the country as akin to treason. Ferguson had said after the 1925 election that the Hamilton speech had cost the party at least twenty seats and thus the government. And now, to his shock and horror, Meighen was delivering and defending the speech again!

Several times Ferguson left his chair and joined the hecklers in shouting at Meighen. When Meighen finally concluded, Ferguson abruptly commandeered the microphone and delivered a rough, impulsive attack on the former leader and the ideas he had presented. Ferguson told the delegates how two years before he had privately begged Meighen not to deliver the Hamilton speech. Now he literally shouted his objections. As he fumed on, he was interrupted by hisses, boos, catcalls, and shouts to sit down and shut up. Twice was heard three cheers for Meighen. Undaunted, Ferguson continued. When he finally took his seat it was clear that his chances at taking up the mantle of leadership had vanished. Further, where and when the cheers had come in reaction to Borden, Meighen, and Ferguson had made it clear that the party was regionally divided. Today we can see the incident as a demonstration of a time when politics was more spontaneous rather than stage-managed for television. But to Conservatives at the time it was a terrible start to what all had hoped would be a show of promise and unity.

When Ferguson retook his seat, the man he sat beside was R. B. Bennett. He had been visibly upset by Meighen's speech and had applauded Ferguson. Bennett had been told beforehand that Meighen was to speak and he had opposed it. When he heard the topic of the speech, he'd opposed it even more fervently and sent a message to Meighen asking him to reconsider. Meighen's ignoring his advice ended a feeble relationship that had started as rivals in ambition and had turned to allies in expediency. There was nothing left that either could do for or to the other. When the convention was over, Meighen sat in his

Toronto office and penned a warm letter of congratulations to Bennett. It went unanswered.[18]

Meighen's unfortunate speech and Ferguson's tempestuous reaction had effectively removed them as viable leadership candidates. On the top of the list of others left to be considered was Harry Stevens. He was forty-eight years old, talented, articulate, had served in two cabinet posts, and led the customs committee that had brought the scandal to Canadians' attention and precipitated the King-Byng two-step. However, he had told any who would listen that he was not interested, and his sincerity was demonstrated by his not organizing support before or at the convention. Not widely known at the time was that his personal finances had suffered through the bankruptcy of the Manufacturer's Finance Company in which he had been heavily invested. He believed that he might soon have to leave politics to make some money.[19]

When the first-ballot voting began, there were six men from whom the delegates had to choose. Later, Bennett stated rather disingenuously in a note to Beaverbrook that he had not really sought the nomination, but that it had been thrust upon him by friends within the party.[20] Bennett's white lie was consistent with the traditions of the day. Neither he nor any of the six leadership candidates could be seen to be degrading themselves or the office by shamelessly campaigning for it. All six, however, were active behind the scenes. Ferguson worked tirelessly on Bennett's behalf as did McRae. Both spoke from the podium and twisted arms on the floor and in hotel rooms. Perhaps even more important, Stevens spoke to delegate after delegate promoting Bennett as the party's best choice. When it was all over Bennett said to Stevens, "Harry, I owe this entirely to you. You are the one that put me here."[21]

Seven men were nominated but declined to accept: Stevens, Perley, Currie, Rhodes, Baxter, Meighen, and Ferguson. Six allowed their names to stand, but among Bennett's five opponents two were of little consequence. Sir Henry Drayton had served in the cabinet under Borden and Meighen but was blamed by many for not stopping Mackenzie King's questioning that led to the fall of the Conservative government while he was House leader. He further doomed his candidacy by arriving in Winnipeg having done little in preparation for the convention and then doing very little to gather support while there. Manitoba's Robert Rogers was another of Borden's cabinet ministers. His credibility was tainted by the fact that he had resigned from cabinet in 1917, then, after sitting out the next election, was defeated in both 1921 and 1926. He came to Winnipeg without a seat or financial backing.

While Bennett could safely ignore Drayton and Rogers, he could not dismiss the appeal or potential of Dr. Robert J. Manion, Charles Cahan, or Hugh Guthrie. R.J. Manion wore a look of constant good cheer and appeared younger than his years with baby fat still filling his cheeks and a teenager's unruly dark curls. Manion was a doctor and decorated First World War veteran with a command of French. As the Liberal MP from Fort William, he had served in the Union government as the minister of soldiers' civil re-establishment, and then, having switched to the Conservative Party, was Meighen's Postmaster General. Manion was a charismatic man and an effective debater and stump speaker. But he was the youngest of the candidates, and his youth was emphasized by his often appearing somewhat tempestuous and injudicious in some of his pronouncements. He was also without personal wealth or substantial financial backers. Further, Manion was late in organizing in preparation for and then later at the convention. He saw his expected Quebec base taken by Cahan, and the support he had assumed was his from Ontario stolen by Bennett.

After leading the Nova Scotia Conservative Party while editor of the *Halifax Herald*, Charles Cahan had joined a prestigious law firm in Montreal. He thrived as a corporate lawyer and made many strong business connections in the city. He had worked hard as the chair of Quebec's convention committee in gathering delegates from every constituency in the province and, in so doing, winning votes for his candidacy. He was smart and well respected. He was the oldest of the candidates and yet he was relatively new, having only entered Parliament in 1925. He was popular with those pleased that he could bring dollars to the party, but others worried that before winning his seat he had lost three elections in a row. His past should have allowed him to draw support from two provinces, but as the convention began there seemed to be no tide toward him from either. Solidly built with a square jaw and dark eyes, he looked like the no-nonsense man that he was. Cahan did not help his cause with a weak speech delivered in a faltering and often cracking voice.

Hugh Guthrie had served the Borden government as Solicitor General and later was minister of militia and defence with both Borden and Meighen. He had become nationally known when appointed interim party leader after Meighen's resignation. He had impressed many with his gentle nature but firm stand on a number of issues. He had first been elected in the Ontario riding of South Wellington in 1900 and no opponent had come close to him in any subsequent contest. He was unable, however, to recover from his opening gaffe in welcoming delegates to the *Liberal* convention. Many would have forgiven him if not for the fact that for the first seventeen years of his political career he had been a Liberal. He also hurt his cause by arguing too many times that the country could be won without Quebec, which reminded people of Meighen's inability to make inroads in that populous province that seated so many MPS in the House.

In Manion, Cahan, Guthrie, and Bennett, the delegates had four viable candidates. Despite the strengths and weaknesses each presented, at an open convention anything can happen and so all had a chance to win. All were careful in whom they chose both to nominate them and to second that nomination. Bennett chose New Brunswick member of Parliament Leonard Tilley. Tilley was an old friend with whom Bennett had attended elementary school and university. Tilley's presence allowed Bennett to emphasize his Maritime roots but, more than that, it afforded a vicarious connection to Macdonald, as Tilley's grandfather had been at the table in Charlottetown back in 1864, when between the grand balls and consumption of gallons of liquor he and the other fathers of Confederation forged the deal that led to the creation of Canada. Tilley was an inspired orator whose message to those who yearned to see the party back in power was blunt. He said, "I nominate a gentleman whom, I believe, will be a winner."[22]

Bennett chose Alberta MLA Alexander McGillivary as his seconder. Tilley and McGillivary symbolized Bennett's ties to both the Maritimes and western Canada. In their speeches both emphasized Bennett's political experience and support for farmers and working people. Appealing to the Conservative base, they also spoke highly of his legal background and success in business.

Bennett accepted the nomination with a strong and stirring speech. He reviewed the history of the Conservative Party and noted that the genius of Confederation was in the uniting of regions and peoples. He presented himself as a Macdonald-style uniter, noting of the Fathers of

Confederation that "They realised that Federation, the Constitution, is a great federal pact—a great treaty between men and women of diverse races, religions and creeds, coming together under a federal union, respecting one another's races, religions and customs—conserving by adequate and complete legislation the supremacy of the rights of minorities and majorities."[23]

Of all who spoke that day, Bennett was, unsurprisingly, the most effective in both style and substance. With the speeches done, the slow process of voting began. The votes cast in the first and second ballots showed that Bennett had been the man to beat from the outset, and further, that he was the second choice of those gathered in the over-heated hall. Needing 777 votes for a majority and a win, the first ballot gave him 594, which was 249 more than second-place Guthrie and more than enough to destroy the hopes of all the others. Between the first and second ballots McRae, Stevens, and Ferguson visited every provincial delegation and worked to sell their man. Unlike in later conventions, the last-place finisher, Drayton, was allowed to stay in the contest, so the race was on to have all those who saw Bennett as their second choice to abandon their candidate and come to his camp. Ferguson was able to swing many of the Ontario votes. Rogers, Drayton, and McRae were inadvertently effective in drawing Quebec votes from Cahan.

On the second ballot every other candidate lost support, allowing Bennett to sneak over the top with 780 votes. Bennett was fifty-seven years of age, the second-youngest of the leadership candidates; his victory represented a significant step up the ladder to the prime minister's office that, decades before, he had identified as his ultimate goal.

	First Ballot	Second Ballot
Bennett	594	780
Guthrie	345	320
Cahan	310	266
Manion	170	148
Rogers	114	37
Drayton	31	3
	1,564	1,554[24]

The chair had not finished reading the full results when the stage filled with people all trying to shake Bennett's hand. Uproarious applause met each candidate who worked, one by one, to get to the microphone to withdraw in the old tradition of making the vote unanimous. Even greater applause washed over Bennett as he slowly weaved his way through the people and heavy tables and chairs to the front of the crowded platform to accept his prize. He shook every hand until he finally stood in the cramped space between the tables and the crowded floor. He beamed out at the cheering crowd from behind a large pie-plate-sized microphone that was hooked up to transmit his words to a national radio audience. There was no lectern.

With the stage finally brought back to order and the delegates hushed, Bennett began by reading quietly from papers he held in his hands. He humbly accepted the decision of the delegates. Like all great orators he began slowly, haltingly, earning the crowd's attention through volume, pace, and pauses. He even offered a lame joke, stating, "One night, not long ago, I had a dream (and I don't believe particularly in dreams because they usually represent just bad digestion) . . ."[25] But then he warmed to his main message. Even reading it today invites one to hear the tempo quickening, the pitch rising, and the volume increasing. He called for work and sacrifice. He told the delegates and radio audience that democracy would not succeed and their party would not succeed if people of goodwill did not work, and organize, and put forth sincere effort. He argued that a political party is merely an instrument designed to accomplish a purpose. He said that that purpose must be ". . . the health, the happiness, the prosperity of the Canadian people. Measures of social justice, measures of fiscal reform, measures that will make for the interest and happiness of all the people that call themselves Canadians. . . ."[26]

At the end of his speech, he returned to the importance of sacrifice, noting that he was personally putting aside much that would materially benefit him in order to serve the party and the country. He then roared to his conclusion with powerful and sweeping images and phrases, exclaiming,

> Promise here and now, as you walk out of yonder door, that you will be
> missionaries for the great cause, missionaries for the great party to which

we belong, missionaries from the greatest political convention ever held in the Dominion of Canada—and if you are missionaries your efforts will be crowned with success, and you will have a government, at Ottawa, reflecting your principles, your convictions, hopes and aspirations.[27]

Bennett was moved by the outpouring of support, and from some, genuine affection. He later wrote to Beaverbrook, "What ever may be the result of my efforts, I will always have at least the memories of hundreds of wonderful messages of good will from men and women of every shade of political opinion and from all parts of Canada and beyond."[28]

McRae had assured good press coverage through the radio broadcast and by having the party pick up the transportation and accommodation costs for one reporter from every newspaper in the country. Coverage of Bennett's victory was generally positive. The staunchly Conservative *Globe* was, perhaps not unexpectedly, especially effusive in its praise: "Mr. Bennett has an abundance of energy. . . . His legal acumen and his business ability are of a high order. He has had long experience in legislative halls."[29] *Saturday Night* magazine, most often in the Liberals' corner, recognized the ideological underpinnings of Bennett's actions and applauded him for his political courage. An article said, "In his political philosophy Bennett is a Tory of the Left. . . . His whole record shows that he reverences tradition, but that he is not afraid to break new ground when met with new conditions."[30]

The *Vancouver Sun*, however, touched on a note of caution that was seen in many other papers. Its article the next day wondered,

> Has this rich autocratic bachelor the qualities that would ever permit him
> to assume leadership of the Canadian people? There are snobbish
> elements that would welcome his elevation to such a post. There are
> financial interests that might find profit in raising him to political power.
> But the mass of Canadians, in east or west, will never find in this cold,
> aloof intellectual the sympathies and sincerity essential in the Prime
> Minister of Canada.[31]

After the last hand was shaken and the last thank-you note signed, Bennett needed to get to work to unite the party, raise some money, and organize both for the House and for the next election. The job would not be an easy one; like after every convention, there was healing to be done and bruised egos to soothe. But the party had a rich history and there was an invigorated base from which to build. The question was, What was he building and what was he leading?

THE PARTY

Sociologists and political scientists have for years argued about the purpose and, in fact, the very definition of a political party. In his seminal 1915 book entitled *Political Parties: A Sociological Study of the Oligarchical Tendencies of Modern Democracy*, sociologist Robert Michels argues that political parties exist to organize people and groups so as to attain political power and that an oligarchy ultimately controls what the party does and the ideas for which it stands. The notion that a party exists simply to attain power differentiates parties from movements. By way of illustration, sociologist Leo Zakuta wrote about the western-based Cooperative Commonwealth Federation which was formed in 1932 as a combination of Fabian socialists, trade unionists, farmers, and eastern intellectuals. He contended that it started as a movement that entailed an ideologically based fight to move Canada toward the acceptance of certain ideas. It slowly transformed itself, he argued, into a party interested only in winning office. He wrote that the changes ". . . turned rebels into reformers and prophets into politicians."[32] Zakuta's thoughtful argument added nuance to Michels's by positing the following question: Can a political party that exists primarily to attain office remain principled?

The question lends credence to and borrows from the conventional consensus among political scientists and sociologists that political parties grow from and are linked to particular cleavages within a society. Canadian cleavages involve region, ethnicity, language, class, race, and gender. The existence of these cleavages leads to brokerage politics as parties create policies designed to either exploit or heal a particular division. Even the most principled parties thereby become quite pragmatic and studiously avoid taking doctrinaire stances that might restrict their flexibility or place them too far over any divide.[33]

Further, political parties, like all organizations, acquire institutional memories. Decisions are influenced by a desire to prolong or recapture what they perceive to be glory days by seeking leaders that remind them of leaders long gone. In the case of the Conservatives, with every change of leader, this tendency led to the seeking of someone akin to the autocratic, decisive charmer Sir John A. Macdonald.[34] And once in place, a party leader must deliver electoral success or be thrown to one side.

Finally, political parties reflect the dominant ideological beliefs of the society from which they spring and which they try to lead. Sir John A. created the Liberal-Conservative Party as an unlikely coalition of moderate Upper Canadian Tories and moderate Quebec Liberals along with others from Montreal's English business elite. As it evolved, the party seemed to represent ideas more in keeping with those expressed by urban rather than rural people and more with the business than working class. When in office, it tended to support policies that drew more support from English than French and seemed to champion loyalty to Britain and the imperial connection more than surrendering to the social and economic pull of the United States.[35]

More important, with the creation of the Liberal-Conservative coalition, Macdonald tapped into what socialist Gad Horowitz called the Tory tradition. Horowitz argued that it arrived in Canada with the United Empire Loyalists, who rejected the Jeffersonian liberalism that stressed the power of the individual and suspicion of the state. In fleeing the American Revolution, or in being tarred and feathered and then kicked out, the new un-American Canadians chose a unique brand of British Toryism that placed value in social hierarchy, deference to authority, and a desire for law and order.[36] It is this Tory tradition that led to the broad public support for the state's crackdown in Saskatchewan in 1885, in Winnipeg in 1919, in Regina in 1935, in Montreal in 1970, and in Oka in 1990.

Further, it is this Tory tradition at the heart of Canadian political culture that led to an acceptance of—in fact, a patriotic pride in—governments actively supporting businesses and people who need help, whether it be Macdonald's CPR or Pearson's health care initiatives. It is this Tory tinge that has resulted in Canada's Conservative Party—even when tempted to the right by the Reform Party challenges of the 1990s—still being to the left of most American Democrats. And it keeps Canada a part of the British Commonwealth with the Governor General ensconced in Rideau Hall and the monarch on its coins.

The Canadian constitution and Sir John's successive Liberal-

Conservative administrations put flesh on that skeleton and thus were embodiments of that Tory tradition. They made permanent Canada's allegiance to the Crown through establishing the queen as Canada's head of state. They made definite its protection of privilege through the creation of an appointed Senate. They made evident its belief in an activist government through the purchase of the Hudson's Bay land, which at the time was greater than the size of what was then Canada; the enormity of the government's investment in the creation of the CPR; and in the National Policy that injected the government into the economy to assist in the development of Canadian business, finance, and trade opportunities. They made certain the dominant power of the central government by affording it the right of disallowance, enabling it to overturn provincial legislation that was deemed *ultra vires*.

But Macdonald's treatment of Louis Riel, Charles Tupper's handling of the Manitoba Schools Question, Laurier's ascension to the Liberal Party leadership, and Borden's imposition of conscription and the Union government had combined to rob the Conservative Party of much of its rural and French Quebec bases. With those voting blocs and Macdonald gone, the party's troubles were inevitable. It experienced dissension in a self-defeating struggle to redefine itself. Borden's Halifax Platform harked back to the ideals of Conservatives past. In office he remained solidly pro-British, but rendered the relationship with the mother country more nuanced when he moved away from the traditional Tory ties to Britain by ending peerages and demanding greater Canadian autonomy from Britain at both Versailles and the League of Nations.

Meighen did nothing to re-establish the party's Quebec or rural base or stem its ideological drift. With Meighen, the forces moving it to the right appeared to gain ascendency. The party seemed to lose site of the Tory element that for years had anchored it to the collectivist values that informed much of Canada's civil society. Whether realizing it or not, Canadian voters sent the party from power to think for a little while, and that's okay. In a vibrant and healthy democracy, every party needs a good spanking from time to time.

The party's proud history and recent hardships rendered Bennett's election in Winnipeg tremendously significant. It was the election of not just another Liberal-Conservative leader but a new *Tory* leader—a leader in the Macdonald tradition. Bennett's personal views, as seen in many of his speeches and in the public policy stands he had taken throughout his career, were Tory at their core. The platform that he had helped to create, drawing from the Halifax Platform ideals, and then reshape as prime minister was a reflection of that Toryism—a Red Toryism—a belief in the positive power of government intervention to help people in need, balanced by a fiscal conservatism that respected the vitality of a free market and individual responsibility.

Neither Bennett nor the platform that the convention created was of the left-populist wing of the party that saw corporate power as evil and sought to use the state's power to assist the little guy through improving his material reality while protecting him from the wrath of big business. That became the constituency of Stevens. Nor were Bennett and the Winnipeg platform of the right laissez-faire wing of the party—a group that saw Canada through the eyes of enlightenment philosopher and political economist Adam Smith and believed that the state acted best when it acted least and that the populace would be helped most when the state allowed them and corporations to pursue their own self-interests. That became the constituency of Charles Cahan.

Bennett's middle ground—his Tory grounding—was reflected not only in all that he had already said and done in his political career but also in his Winnipeg convention speeches and again in an article he penned in 1933 in which he observed,

> . . . the state regulation of individual activities has been and will continue to be a part of the program of any Conservative Government. It was so with respect to the restriction on hours of labour and against the laissez faire opinions of their opponents. The Conservative party has always taken the view that the order of regulation of individual activity may be of interest to the government as a whole.[37]

One sees the Tory tradition in all that Bennett did and in the people and policies he opposed. This is not to suggest that he was an ideologue who blindly sought to fit every round peg of a problem into one square ideological hole. He was too smart and too responsible for that. But neither would he abandon his Tory principles or allow events or elections to tempt him to lurch from one point to another on the political spectrum. He was too ethical for that.

Bennett's Tory ideas led him to do as Borden had suggested and reshape some of the planks that comprised the party platform while ignoring others. Twenty-two resolutions were presented, debated, and ultimately adopted. A 150-member resolutions committee was formed and split into various subcommittees. Each resolution was evaluated, rewritten, or amalgamated into others. While this sounds impressive on its face, the process was actually quite chaotic. At one point, for instance, A. D. McRae was seen sitting in his messy, crowded, and smoke-filled hotel room, reading resolution after resolution that had been submitted by riding associations and simply throwing the ones he did not like into the wastebasket.[38] Committees worked past midnight and into the twilight hours fuelled by too much coffee, bad food, and alcohol.

When most resolutions came to the convention floor they were read to a half-empty hall with few delegates actually listening. Most were then passed with little explanation or discussion. Many resolutions had been vetted through so many people that they seemed to have been drained of their lifeblood. One such anemic resolution was entitled Party Policy. It claimed to express exactly what the party stood for but said,

> The Liberal Conservative Party whose founders have brought about
> Confederation and cemented its Provinces into an harmonious political
> whole, based upon common interest, common ideas, and mutual respect
> and affection of all its elements, stands everlastingly pledged to a policy
> which will at all times bring prosperity, contentment, and peace to all its
> citizens irrespective of boundaries and of origins.[39]

Despite the slapdash process and the political pabulum that passed for policy, the committees and delegates actually created a platform that was startlingly prophetic. Many of the ideas presented addressed issues that were to be at the heart of Canada's national conversation for decades to come. Prime Minister Trudeau, for instance, would have smiled and Alberta premier Peter Lougheed would have grimaced to notice a resolution supporting the need for a "national fuel policy." Sir John would have approved but Mulroney squirmed at the support given to national tariffs as a way to protect manufacturing. St. Laurent would have liked and

Lévesque puffed himself into a tizzy when delegates voted to create a system of canals on the St. Lawrence to be owned and operated solely by the federal government. Socialists from the CCF's Woodsworth to the NDP's Layton would have applauded the platform's support for more worker rights, an eight-hour workday, the end to child labour, and equal pay for work of equal value for women. So too would they have cheered the party's tepid but nonetheless clearly stated support for federally controlled pensions and what was called "social legislation" to alleviate the worst problems associated with illness, unemployment, and alcohol abuse.

The two resolutions that caused the most furious debates on the floor also presaged arguments that would rattle Canadians in the future. Those of the old Reform Party would have loved in one way, and those of the Parti Québécois welcomed in another, the arguments revolving around the idea that all Canadians should declare their loyalty to the Union Jack and the English language. The resolution was eventually allowed to die.

A resolution that was unfortunately not dropped involved immigration and race. Somewhat ironically, in that the Conservative Party delegates were in a province that had been built upon the backs of immigrants, the resolution came to the floor warning of the dangers of letting too many people and too many of the "wrong" people into Canada. The resolution had eight parts. The second stated that Canada's immigration policy must have the attraction of an increased percentage of British immigrants as its goal. The eighth part had only two words: "Oriental exclusion."[40]

There was furious debate. Sir George Foster was the first on his feet, moving that the eighth part should be sent back for further consideration. Tilley came to the microphone to explain that the committee had devoted three hours to arguing over those two words and that sending it back would change nothing. He also said that the only delegation that asked for its inclusion and would veto its being dropped or softened was British Columbia. There ensued a long and heated debate in which a number of blatantly racist and anti-Oriental opinions smudged the air.

Among the most vehement in his support of part eight was Harry Stevens. He argued that to remove it would jeopardize every Conservative seat in British Columbia. Stevens knew that from the first arrival of Asian immigrants, attracted by the Fraser Valley gold rush, anti-Asian racism had been central to British Columbia's political culture. The province had seen municipalities pass racist bylaws and the provincial government enact racist legislation and then pressure the federal government, sometimes successfully, to enact racist immigration policies and procedures. Vancouver and Victoria had suffered race riots. Stevens himself, despite the fact that few whispered about it in Winnipeg that fall, had been one of the founders and leaders of the blatantly racist Oriental Exclusion League. His speeches had been among those that had sparked a 1907 rampage by a white mob that had torn through Vancouver's Chinese district. The party seemed intent on ignoring all of this, just as there was no mention made of the fact that Prime Minister Borden had once approved as the party slogan in B.C. "White Power."[41]

The vote was taken and Oriental exclusion was adopted as party policy. The blatantly racist clause was the elephant in the living room that betrayed the party's otherwise progressive and inclusive social policy platform. Those who voted for it were those who would support Mackenzie King's locking up innocent Japanese Canadians only a few years hence. But Pierre Trudeau and all those who would later support a multicultural and non-racist Canada would have shuddered when the plank was nailed down. Bennett chose to pick his fights carefully and so ignored it.

Meanwhile, in a Canada that still spoke of French and English as two races, there was an attempt to reach out to Quebec. It was determined that all proceedings would be recorded in both languages, that the Lord's Prayer that opened the convention would be recited in both French and English, and that the co-chairs would be Anglophone Nova Scotia premier Edgar Rhodes and francophone senator Charles Beaubien.

In the end, the twisting of arms and raising of hands created a policy document that reflected the sometimes contradictory beliefs of the delegates, the big-tent party in which they found a political home, and the ideas that they hoped would be supported by an adequate number of Canadians to turn their resolutions to votes. For a news release that many newspapers reprinted verbatim, the platform was condensed and summarized into eight pledges:

1. We pledge ourselves to a policy of protection for Canadians in the development of our national resources, our agriculture and industrial life, and our consumers from exploitation.

2. We pledge ourselves to foster and develop agriculture and the livestock and dairy industries now so sadly neglected.

3. We pledge ourselves to the stabilization of economic conditions and to the continuity of trade and freedom from the manipulation of home and foreign tariffs.

4. We pledge ourselves to the development of inter-provincial trade, and of a Canadian fuel policy and the development of a foreign market.

5. We pledge ourselves to the improvement of the whole scheme of Canadian transportation and to the establishment of a national highway system.

6. We pledge ourselves to foster and support a plan for greater Empire trade based on mutual advantage.

7. We pledge ourselves to a national Old Age Pensions scheme.

8. We pledge ourselves to such compensation adjustment as will ensure the benefit of the above policies to every Canadian of every part.[42]

Bennett approved the wording of the eight points. They reflected not only the most significant platform planks that had been approved by the delegates but also his personal and political beliefs and priorities. Demonstrating that he disapproved of the racist elements of the party platform, he ensured that the anti-Oriental immigration clauses were not stated in the summary. It is interesting to read the eight. Many are anachronisms stuck in the issues of their times, but many more are marvellously visionary and would find themselves reflected in policies enacted by both Liberal and Conservative governments of the future.

However, Bennett had for years and in many circumstances proven himself to be a principled but also pragmatic politician. There were realists present who reminded delegates even before they had left the hall that while the platform was important, the ideas of the leader were more significant still. The platform would be there to inform him of the party's beliefs but not to restrict his ability to intelligently react to changing times and circumstances. The point was brought home by the widely respected old chieftain Robert Borden, who rose early in their deliberations to patiently urge, "You must not forestall too much, a leader who will be responsible to you, to parliament, and to the country, for the policy which is put before the people."[43] That Bennett agreed with Borden's assessment was seen in an *Ottawa Journal* interview published only three months later in January 1928. The still-new party leader made the point that while the Winnipeg resolutions were important, the details of the party policies would be shaped through consultations between the leader and caucus members.[44] With Borden's blessing, Bennett would pull the party toward his Red Tory vision.

As the Amphitheatre Rink's floors were being swept and train cars filled with tired delegates chugged east and west from Winnipeg, Bennett was left with the fierce burden of the prize he had so long cherished and just won. As he sat resting back home at his Palliser Hotel suites, answering each letter of congratulations with similar messages and phrases, he faced a challenge like none he had known before. He was used to being the boss, to holding all power and thus being obeyed. But political power is dependent more upon consent than coercion. Political power is not demanded from above but temporarily offered from below. Its fleeting nature makes it less a bookstore than a library.

Like all party leaders, he had supporters who would turn on him with the first decision that threatened a favourite hobby horse or mistake that allowed an opening through which they could advance their own careers. He had reporters, especially those in the Liberal newspapers, anxiously waiting to pounce. It is a naive politician, and one in for a short and trying career, who treats reporters as anything other than jackals there to seek then feed on political weakness. He had the cunning Mackenzie King, whose diary entries reveal that his respect for the new leader was growing, but who also knew that his success depended partly on Bennett's failure and would do what he could to bring it to fruition. President Harry Truman once said that if you want a friend in politics you should buy a dog.

And so there he was as fall turned to winter in 1927. Bennett's job was to find his way through the dangerous maze of those who temporarily wished him well and those who would always wish him ill. If he could do that, he might just persuade Canadians to concern themselves with the things about which he had always cared so much.

CHAPTER FOUR

OPPOSITION TO PRIME MINISTER

1927–1930

WINNING THE STANLEY CUP must be a marvellous feeling. We have all seen the goofy grins on the young players as they hoist the thirty-four-and-a-half-pound trophy over their heads to circle the ice in triumph and later, in various states of sweaty undress, deliriously gurgle beer from the chalice like dishevelled Arthurian knights who have found the Grail. But the next morning, sore from the bruises of battles fought and slightly hungover from booze, pride, and adulation, they rise knowing that they have but a scant while to rest before being tested again and needing to prove that the victory won was truly deserved.

That fourth period, as it were, of reflection and rejuvenation is not afforded the winners of political contests. The celebrations among supporters may be as raucous, and with television, phone cameras, and YouTube having all but erased privacy, they may now be as public. But unlike in hockey, the political champion must swallow the temptation to rejoice too much. Joy and gratitude can be expressed, but dignity must be maintained. And what is more, the morning after the race is won, political victors cannot rest. Rather, they must immediately begin to work even harder than during the contest that brought them to the summit of their ambition. A political victory is not an end but a beginning; it is less a triumph than an invitation.

Bennett's victory in Winnipeg rendered him leader of the federal Liberal-Conservative Party and also of His Majesty's Loyal Opposition. As such, he was a juggler with four balls to keep aloft. First, five men had run against him and at least two others could have launched legitimate campaigns. Those seven each believed that they would have been a better choice, and that opinion was shared by hundreds and perhaps thousands of their political and financial friends, allies, and supporters. Bennett had to convince the seven—and the thousands—that he was worthy of their support and loyalty.

Second, Bennett had a ninety-one-member caucus. There were twelve from Nova Scotia, one from PEI, seven from New Brunswick, only four from Quebec and, forming the core of Conservative power, fifty-three from Ontario. Twelve members called British Columbia home and there was one from the territories. The party's wasteland was the prairies. Bennett was the only member from Alberta and there was not a single Conservative MP from Manitoba or Saskatchewan. He had to convince all ninety-one current Conservative MPS and those considering a candidacy in the next election that the delegates at Winnipeg had made the right decision.

Third, Bennett knew, as all leaders of parties that are out of office know, that the next federal campaign had already begun. Campaigns, after all, never really end. To wage its next phase meant that he needed to organize the party federally, in each province, and in each riding, so that the electorate would know and support him and the party's ideas as he would shape them. He needed to persuade people to join him because without grassroots volunteers a political leader is not really a leader at all.

Fourth, Bennett needed to carry out his responsibilities as Opposition leader, holding the government's feet to the fire in the House and in committees. He needed to ensure that proposed legislation was improved where it could be, supported when it should be, and opposed when it needed to be. In so doing, he would have to differentiate strategy from tactics while on the one hand balancing political with legislative actions and on the other determining what was best for the country, himself, and the party. And he had to make it all look easy.

All of this rested upon one goal more than any other. Bennett needed to convince his caucus, his former rivals and their supporters, the media, and ultimately the Canadian public that he was qualified and ready to be prime minister and that the people he had around him were a government in waiting.

But the first thing Bennett had to do was get himself to Ottawa. He spent a week cleaning up files in Calgary, passing on active cases, and doing what he could to wrap up cold ones. He left his suites in Calgary's Palliser Hotel and upon his arrival at the Ottawa train station simply walked across Wellington Street to his new home on the Château Laurier's second floor.

Within days, a rumour circulated that he was going to purchase a house and in no time he was receiving letters from real estate agents and others who were only too willing to find an appropriate place. There was even pressure exerted on him to live in Hull so as to promote his electoral chances in Quebec.[1] Bennett responded politely to each inquiry and offer with the assurance that he would not be purchasing or leasing a home in Ottawa, but the rumours and consequently the solicitations continued for weeks.

PARTY ORGANIZATION

The Conservative Party organization that Bennett inherited was broken and broke. Bennett knew that while there were political junkies out there who would have followed the Winnipeg convention on the radio and in the papers, the vast majority of Canadians would have paid it no mind. He had rebuilding to do that would begin with introducing himself and his progressive message to Canadians. He pulled $500,000 from his personal bank account to offset part of the costs of the convention and to finance a cross-country tour.

Bennett began a back-breaking speaking junket in the Maritimes that would take him eventually to the Pacific. In Ontario alone he made countless stops and delivered twenty-four major addresses. At each city, town, and village he was well received by audiences and the local press. He spoke with Canadians at outdoor picnics and in church basements. He sat in the parlours of the elite and in farm kitchens. He received advice from party leaders, members of Parliament, potential candidates, significant donors, and Canadians from all walks of life. People came to know him, but just as importantly he came to know the country in a deeper and more profound way than he had before. He was off to a good start, but it would not be enough.

In each of the previous four elections, the party had tried to bring a representative to Ottawa from each provincial organization as part of an ad hoc national committee to coordinate efforts. It was a good idea that had never really worked. The Winnipeg delegates had supported a new idea of establishing for the next election a permanent central party organization. It had been decided that to create the necessary structure, a Dominion Council would be established. The process would begin with party representatives from across the country meeting in Ottawa in April 1928 to map out how the new party organization should look and what needed to be done to create and run a modern, national party. These decisions and plans, coupled with Bennett's energetic tour, were evidence of a party no longer nostalgically yearning for a lost past or speaking only to its shrinking traditional base. Rather, it was vigorously seeking to re-invent itself to serve a new Canada in a new way with a new leader.

At the convention, Bennett had supported the idea of a permanent federal party organization and the notion of the council, but he became quite worried as the Ottawa meeting approached. He was afraid that the council would simply make public the various rifts within the party and publicize the sad state of its organization and finances. Further, he feared that it might lead to the establishment of a structure that would have the power it needed but then grow to assume a larger role.[2] In expressing this worry he was sharing a concern that Borden had expressed in Winnipeg. That is, he needed to finely balance the creation of an influential national council to build a party almost from scratch while at the same time ensuring that the council would not emasculate him and future leaders. To allay this fear Bennett saw to it that he would chair the executive council and appoint its members and national party director. The national party director would coordinate provincial associations and report directly to the leader. There was little objection.

Bennett's first and only choice for national party director was Vancouver MP General A. D. McRae, the richly experienced and adroit lead organizer of the Winnipeg convention. Unfortunately, McRae had slipped on some ice and fractured his skull, which meant he was unable to begin his duties until he had recovered. Valuable weeks were lost. But when he took the reins, he did so with energy and aplomb. McRae hired Redmond Code as the council's general secretary, and former *Winnipeg Telegram* journalist Robert Lipset to oversee public relations. He hired secretarial and support staff. He rented space on Ottawa's Wellington

Street, close to Parliament Hill. He also saw that office space was rented and staff hired in nine cities, which established a presence in each
province.

McRae and Code then became itinerant teachers. They spent much
of the next year on the road. At each stop they met with provincial staff
and the volunteers who ran riding associations. At meetings that were
large in some places and convened around kitchen tables elsewhere,
they spoke of the need and ways to coordinate messages, gather volunteers, and create and spread positive news. In each riding, they visited
and evaluated potential candidates. They supported some, dissuaded
others, and were quite blunt with both Bennett back in Ottawa and with
volunteers in some ridings when they believed a particular person
should be supported and when another should be dropped and a replacement sought. They declared some ridings lost causes and suggested
that no time or money be wasted upon them.[3]

Bennett's biggest challenge was Quebec. Its population afforded it
sixty-five ridings, second only to Ontario. However, in the four elections fought from 1917 to 1926, the party had been unable to win more
than four. Quebec mattered. The Quebec Organization Committee's
work was closely monitored by both Bennett and McRae. While McRae
led the efforts in the affairs of all other provinces, he called on Bennett
to intercede directly in Quebec. Bennett's work there would not be easy.
At the Winnipeg convention, interim party leader Hugh Guthrie had
advised the delegates, including the Quebec delegation that was seated
immediately before the stage, that the party should forget about trying
to woo Quebec voters and concentrate instead on the rest of the country
and especially the West. This was not a new position for him. Just ten
months before, he had stood before the Conservative Business Men's
Club in Toronto and said much the same thing.[4] The fact that the party
had chosen to hold its convention in Winnipeg was seen as confirma-
tion by some Quebecers, including Montreal's Charles Cahan, that
the party elite was following Guthrie's advice and abandoning the
province.[5]

Bennett disagreed with Guthrie. He believed that the party could
and must win the support of Quebecers and that Quebec had to play
a role in Canada's future if that future was to be one in which the country was united and strong. In his acceptance speech, Bennett bluntly

announced his rejection of the Guthrie strategy and reached out not only to Quebec but to new Canadians as well.

Bennett claimed to friends that he did not understand the province but he nonetheless set out to win Quebec.[6] He knew that he faced five major challenges. First, he was the leader of a party that had been rejected by Quebecers after the enormously unpopular decisions of Macdonald, Tupper, and Borden. Second, he knew that in Winnipeg the vast majority of the Quebec delegation had voted for native son Cahan on both the first and second ballots and that out of the four hundred Quebec delegates he had won only 77 votes. Third, as part of the Borden government he had promoted the notion of conscription and then his work with the National Service Board had seen the registration of thousands of Quebec's young men. Fourth, he had made it clear in speech after speech that he was a firm believer in the emotional, military, and economic ties between Canada and the British Empire and that his hopes for the future saw those ancestral ties growing stronger. Finally, the ragtag Conservative Party in Quebec was split into rival factions based on personalities and tensions between leaders in Quebec City and Montreal, and between urban and rural riding associations.

After a great deal of consultation, Bennett decided upon a plan. Its implementation began with his appointing Montreal business executive and former MP Joseph Rainville to lead a provincial committee to oversee provincewide organizing. Rainville proved himself quite effective in establishing and running the federal office in Montreal. He was skilful too in hiring Thomas Mahar to run the party's Quebec City office then carefully managing and coordinating his efforts. Mahar often bristled at the restrictions put on his activities from Montreal and Ottawa but never for long and never publicly. Mahar and Rainville worked well in papering over the many hard feelings that had previously hampered the party's efforts to organize in the province.

With these appointments made and beginning to pay dividends, Bennett began to impose his leadership upon the province in quite a wise fashion. He could have led from the front, as an orchestra leader instructing each player. However, he chose to lead from behind, as a cowboy, slowly and patiently nudging the herd toward a destination of his choosing. With McRae and Rainville in place, Bennett moved behind the scenes. He allowed events to play themselves out, knowing that both sides in any familial split often want reconciliation and that clumsy, active intervention only slows and complicates that process.[7]

He spoke in Quebec only three times between the end of the convention and the beginning of the next parliamentary session on January 26, 1928. On each occasion he charmed his audiences with warm speeches about national reconciliation and unified purposes. He studiously avoided mentioning partisan politics or the party's rift in the province. In all three cases he peppered his speeches with French that he could manage if he read it carefully. He was introducing himself and letting the elite and the grassroots come to him.

Then Bennett spoke in the House in favour of the federal government's funding of improvements to the Quebec City harbour, the importance of bilingualism in immigration matters, and the necessity of saving the country from being swamped by American business interests and cheap agricultural products. These stances were not just political expediency, they were consistent with beliefs he had held for years and ideas and priorities upon which he would later base policies when in power. However, he ensured that his articulation of those beliefs was widely reported in Quebec. They were quite well received and added substance to his charm.

Among the first stops on Bennett's national speaking tour were Quebec's Eastern Townships. McRae and Rainville worked together and well to advance the tour, and Bennett found hundreds at some events and thousands at others. The first took place at La Prairie's Kempton Park Racetrack. Four thousand supporters applauded as he entered from the back and slowly made his way through the crowd. He smiled, shook hands, and slapped backs while offering greetings and small talk. Signs proclaiming "Vive Bennett" and "Bennett is the Farmer's Friend" fluttered among Canadian Red Ensign and Quebec fleur-de-lis flags and the red, white, and blue bunting. He delivered a rousing speech extolling Quebec pride, national unity, and patriotism, tinged with that old Canadian standby, anti-Americanism.

Bennett skilfully moved from parish to parish in a way that demonstrated that he understood the province better than past Conservative leaders and much better than he had tried to have others believe that he understood it. At each stop he spoke with local organizers and potential candidates and attempted to inspire them with his knowledge of their particular challenges. He left them convinced that their work was essential for the party's success and that through their efforts the party would win.

All of these activities, when coupled with McRae's propaganda campaign, were effective at moving the party organization out from the cities and into the large rural ridings. In so doing, the efforts were helping to heal the rift in the party. Bennett was simply going around those who had caused and were perpetuating it. He made his final attempt to address the schisms by announcing in speeches throughout the tour that he would not employ the traditional tactic of designating a Quebec lieutenant. There would be no Cartier to his Macdonald. He believed the practice to be divisive.[8] By removing the prize for which many Quebec politicians were salivating, he stole one of the reasons for the factionalism. Bennett then appointed members to a new Quebec Organization Committee whose mandate was to oversee preparations for the upcoming election. He carefully selected representatives from both factions and then wrote letters and met personally with each of them, essentially ordering them to play nice. But they were not quite ready to share their toys.

The first conference of the Quebec Organization Committee was held in Montreal in May 1929 and nearly fell apart in rancorous infighting. It took Bennett's personal intervention to fix it. He said nothing until the shouting and insults subsided. Then he spoke to the delegates in hushed tones and quietly called for repose and dignity. He reminded them of why they were there and of their shared beliefs and goals. Things calmed and productive work was eventually done. The lines between the factions were still evident but they were beginning to blur.

Bennett made an unfortunate and avoidable misstep when in July 1929 he ignored Rainville's advice and involved himself in the selection of a new provincial party leader. Bennett believed that University of Montreal professor Edouard Montpetit was best suited for the job and made his views known. He was quickly embarrassed when Montpetit announced that he did not want the job but, more devastatingly, that he was a Liberal. Bennett's error angered Camillien Houde, the charismatic and bombastic mayor of Montreal, who had been coveting and eventually won the position. Houde could have been an ally but instead was embittered. He declared privately to supporters that he would ensure that neither he nor provincial Conservatives in Quebec would lift a finger to help elect Bennett or his federal candidates. Fortunately, the good work that Bennett, McRae, Rainville, Mahar, and others had done, and the alliances that had been forged, more than made up for Houde's destructive intentions.

Bennett's patience, charm, tact, and political adroitness had laid the foundation for rebuilding the party in Quebec. The manner and success with which he had intervened had made the organization tighter and the party stronger, and increased its chances of success in the upcoming election. In all that he had cleverly done and not done he had created for himself a bastion of strength and authority and unquestionably established himself as leader.

While all of that determined effort in Quebec had been going on, of course, Bennett had also been dealing with the rest of the country. Quebec had 65 seats in the House, but Ontario had 82. The other seven provinces had only 98 among them. That arithmetic meant that Ontario was of special importance. Fortunately for Bennett, Conservative Howard Ferguson was the very popular premier of the province and he had built and carefully nurtured a robust political organization. It was split into regions then into carefully supervised riding associations. William Clysdale had demonstrated exceptional talent as a full-time party organizer working with two influential cabinet ministers to ensure that volunteers were plentiful, engaged, and happy, and that money was sufficient and being spent when and where it would do the most good. Just as Ontario premier Bill Davis would four decades later lend his "Big Blue Machine" to the federal Conservative Party, Ferguson promised to offer up his mailing and volunteer lists to his old friend Bennett.

Bennett supported McRae's decision to have Clysdale work in the federal wing of the party as well. In choosing potential federal candidates, for instance, McRae worked through Clysdale and he, in turn, consulted Ferguson about every decision. This arrangement meant that Bennett merely signed the papers of the candidates whom Ferguson had approved.[9] Ferguson's loyalty, efforts, and organization left Bennett with scant preparatory work to do in Canada's most populous province. Ferguson's popularity and the power of his machine was shown in October 1929 when 57 per cent of Ontarians returned him to the premier's office.

The 1926 federal election had sent twelve Conservative MPs to Ottawa from British Columbia's fourteen ridings, so it was another province of special interest. As a Vancouver MP, McRae knew the province well. He was disheartened, though, by the fact that B.C.'s Conservative government under Premier Simon Fraser Tolmie, which had been elected in a landslide in July 1928, was drawing criticism for incompetence. British Columbia had already become notorious for electing colourful premiers. The reputation was established with its first, an enigmatic Nova Scotian named Bill Smith who, after working as a photographer in the California gold rush, moved to Vancouver, opened a virulently racist newspaper, and changed his name to Amor De Cosmos—lover of the universe. At least Tolmie kept his own name. But in mishandling one issue after another he was becoming something of a joke and threatening to take the party down with his sinking ship.

Despite Tolmie's bumbling, however, the province's federal party organization was sound. It benefited from the popularity of Harry Stevens and McRae himself. While Bennett had learned from the Ontario experience that the federal party could profit from forging closer ties with a Conservative premier, he demonstrated his flexibility as a tactician in expressing his understanding that in B.C. the party would benefit from distancing itself from Tolmie. Ever blunt in his communications, Bennett wrote to Tolmie, stating, "Today, if the Liberal Party were in power in the Province the fortunes of our Party federally would be brighter than they are now."[10]

The situation in New Brunswick was similar in that having a Conservative government in office did not help Bennett's efforts. Premier John Baxter was cool to the opening of a federal office in Fredericton and offered little assistance when asked to coordinate his provincial organization with the barely existent federal one. After unsuccessful meetings with the premier and with party leaders in a number of ridings, McRae wrote to Bennett stating that he would need to rely upon his personal connections to pull volunteers and money from the hinterlands when election time came.

In Nova Scotia, on the other hand, Conservative premier Edgar Rhodes believed in the efficacy of a good political organization. Following the near defeat of his government in October 1928, he had led a drive to bring structure to the provincial party. When McRae arrived in Halifax he found much of his work already done. He opened and staffed a federal office but worked with Rhodes to coordinate the two organizations so that they supported each other, much as in Ontario.

In June 1929, the Saskatchewan Conservatives had usurped the Liberals and struck a strategic alliance with the Progressives in a number of ridings. The combination of their shared efforts—and desire among the people for change after years of a tired and corrupt provincial Liberal administration—had placed a Conservative government in Regina. McRae's challenge in Saskatchewan was to build on the advantage of Conservatives controlling patronage in the province while extracting the party from its ties to the Progressives, who had made it clear that they would not support Conservatives in a federal election.

At the same time, Bennett had to rely upon many Saskatchewan volunteers who had helped the party win based partly on its support of anti-Catholic sentiments while simultaneously selling them on the notion that such ideas would doom the party in vast, vote-rich regions of the country. The problem was made trickier by the fact that the provincial Conservatives had been so venomous in their anti-Catholic pronouncements that even the Ku Klux Klan had publicly supported Conservative candidates. Bennett had spoken passionately against the Klan and the vile bigotry for which it stood. He did all that he could to ensure that it played no role in the party. Despite his efforts, there were persistent rumours about the KKK's strength in the party's Saskatchewan wing.

With that flurry of activity demanding attention, McRae also had to create organizations in provinces without a Conservative government. His visits to PEI convinced him that Charlottetown's federal office could essentially organize the whole island without attempting to create structures in each of the four tiny ridings. Money flowed to the office from Ottawa and some staff were shared with Halifax. In many parts of Alberta and Manitoba, Bennett and McRae found it virtually impossible to create riding associations, while in others the quality of the people who were willing to stand as candidates was somewhat abysmal. Despite the opening of offices in Charlottetown, Calgary, and Winnipeg, and progress in a number of ridings, Bennett held little hope for an electoral turnaround in PEI, Alberta, and Manitoba.[11]

Meanwhile, the Ottawa office had become a hectic hub of activity.

From only four employees when it began, it had grown so that by February 1930 it employed twenty-seven full-time people. The activity was good but it cost money, while each provincial office needed money too. Rainville had predicted that it would take $65,000 a year for his Quebec offices and expenses.[12] As the party's operations grew, McRae, J. D. Chaplin, Sir George Perley, and Bennett himself each dug into their own pockets to defray costs. Bennett donated $2,500 a month to keep the central office and its operations running.[13] Despite Perley's fundraising efforts, the costly organization was constantly short of resources. Beyond his monthly stipend, Bennett often had to make large cash advances to keep it all afloat. In May 1930, for instance, he wrote a personal cheque to the party for $50,000.[14]

SHAPING THE MESSAGE

While McRae and often Bennett were on the road creating offices, spreading and trying to raise money and interest, Robert Lipset was in the Ottawa office doing work that revealed him to be a political genius. He met often with Bennett and the two grew so close that Lipset became one of the very few who called him Dick. As the director of the newly established Research and Publicity Bureau, Lipset understood that the key to political organization is information. The party needed to control information both coming in and going out. He set to work to create systems whereby the party would have access to accurate information from each of the ridings as well as detailed research on issues of the day. He also created a way to bypass newspapers and radio and disseminate information directly to party supporters.

To begin, Lipset had Redmond Code conduct interviews with each member of the Conservative caucus and stress to each the importance of his project. He asked them to provide detailed information about their ridings that was to include the newspapers and radio stations, with the political bent of each, plus a summary of the riding's history, economic and social conditions, and finally a list of voters that included names, addresses, party affiliation or voting habits, and influential organizations to which each belonged. When some MPs were slow in getting him the information, follow-up letters were written and phone calls made. Bennett personally nudged those who still did not respond. Soon, reams of paper were being analyzed in Code's office. He and Lipset came to understand each riding as they had never been understood before. They established a mailing list of over 160,000 names.[15]

But Lipset and Code were not done. Code had read about a machine called an addressograph. It had been invented in Sioux City, Iowa, in 1896. It allowed addresses to be printed on envelopes, letters, pamphlets, or printed matter of any kind. American businesses had been using them for years and in the 1928 presidential election that had just placed Herbert Hoover in the White House, the Republican Party became the first to use the machine in politics. Lipset purchased an addressograph.

They soon found that in the little office on Wellington Street they could transfer the names and addresses from the lists the MPS had helped to develop to multi-graph plates. They could then print 250,000 personally addressed pamphlets every three days. In the 1930 election, the machine allowed them to hear about a mass mailing the Liberals were preparing, write a response, print it, and have it in the hands of Conservative supporters before the Liberal mailing even arrived.

Lipset then turned his attention to content. He had research material arriving on a regular basis. It was combined with the information gleaned from Conservative MPS and senators who informed him exactly what parts of what ridings would be most receptive to hearing about particular issues. He hired a team of writers and established the National News Service. Every week saw articles written and then mailed to specific groups in a particular riding or even to particular individuals. Articles were printed in a number of languages in an appeal to immigrant communities.

The National News Service also sent full articles to ninety-nine newspapers every week. Simultaneously, it blanketed the country with letters to the editor and other short political pieces sent to 165 newspapers a week. Lipset also targeted specific articles to particular papers. By 1930, there were 645 newspapers receiving free articles from the service, which translated to a national readership of approximately 750,000.[16] Newspaper editors, especially small-town editors, were happy to receive the space-filling articles. Even free editorial cartoons were provided. Many editors wrote the National News Service asking for more copy. Lipset bragged to Bennett that he was especially proud of the articles that were written in a way that was pro-Conservative but appeared non-partisan so that no editor seemed to catch on to the fact that they were from the party. Lipset told Bennett of the mountain of thank-you notes he had on file from grateful editors.[17] The operation was of paramount importance given that in that era of blatantly partisan papers, only eleven could be counted as Conservative.[18]

In addition to the newspaper work, the National News Service also produced a small magazine called *The Canadian*. Published nine times before and during the 1930 election, it was sent to candidates and important Conservative supporters and used to explain party policies and offer tips for responding to criticism.

A bonus for the party was that because the whole National News Service operation did not need to show a profit, and with much of the work done by volunteers, it cost only about $6,000 a month. Lipset reported that a privately run organization of a similar size and complexity would easily have cost $20,000 a month.[19] It was a steal.

While Lipset and Code were working their magic, Bennett took other actions to try to shape the coverage of him and his party. Bennett would later become notorious for his unwillingness or inability to hide the contempt he felt for journalists. He often insulted and bullied them and once even threatened to jail a roomful of them. John Bassett Sr. once remarked, "Mr. Bennett likes the radio better than newspapers because the radio cannot talk back."[20] Despite his obvious lack of respect for reporters, Bennett understood the power of the newspapers that employed them. It had been part of the reason he had tried to buy control of the *Calgary Herald* so many years before.

It was Bennett's appreciation of the power of the press that led him to again use his personal wealth to buy the party a foothold into the near monopoly of Liberal-friendly papers. In 1928, he signed as the guarantor of a $2,500 loan to back Port Hope, Ontario's, *Canada News*. He also arranged a list of 20,000 Conservative Party supporters to be forwarded to the newspaper's office to begin its search for subscribers. The weekly began on Dominion Day 1928 and every issue was, not surprisingly, effusive in its support of Bennett and the party and scathing in its criticism of Mackenzie King's Liberals. Unfortunately for the party and for Bennett's bank balance, the paper folded after a year.

But Bennett was not done. In order to gain traction in vote-poor Saskatchewan he directly invested $344,000 of his own money to bankroll the creation of the *Regina Daily Star*.[21] It hit newsstands in July 1928 and stood in stark contrast to the city's other blatantly pro-Liberal papers. Its readership grew quickly as the paper was distributed free of charge. Bennett was convinced that the *Regina Daily Star* played a significant role in the defeat of Saskatchewan's Liberal government in 1929.

In December 1919, Quebec City Conservative Party organizer Thomas Mahar had made a bold move and created a new weekly paper that he called *Le Journal*. By the late 1920s, it boasted a circulation of 22,000 and was an unapologetic voice for the party. It printed many flattering photographs and stories about Bennett and prominent Quebec Conservatives, and scathing stories about Mackenzie King's government. Despite growing readership, and the fact that Mahar and two friends continued to pour revenue and their own money into it, by early 1930 *Le Journal* was losing money every week. Finally, when it was clear that Bennett would not approve party funds to support the paper nor cough up his own, Mahar allowed it to flounder and fail. It was an opportunity lost.

Another unfortunate decision was made in Rainville's arranging for the party to financially support Montreal's *Le Miroir*, *Le Chameau*, and *Goglu*. The moves made sense as all three were anti-Liberal, and for a time the Conservative Party drew benefit from their editorial slants. However, it became increasingly clear that all three were fascist and racist.

Adrien Arcand published the papers. Arcand was a young, failed journalism student who had dropped out of McGill University. He admired Adolf Hitler. He believed that Quebec should adopt legislation to create a pure French-Catholic society with all non-French speaking, non-Catholics forced to leave the province. Arcand's papers reflected and spoke to the anti-Semitism that had found a home in the hearts of a disturbing number of Quebecers who looked with favour upon the supposed advantages of creating a society populated solely by those who were "pure wool."[22]

There is no evidence that Bennett knew of the racist editorial stands of the papers. There is a great deal of evidence, however, that Bennett held no racist views and that he was personally opposed to such views in B.C., Saskatchewan, and Quebec. In response to a series of anti-

Catholic articles and editorials in the *Regina Daily Star*, for instance, Bennett wrote, "Nothing could be more injurious to this country than that religious differences should become the line of division between political parties!"[23] Bennett later severed ties with Arcand. The loss of the little papers was barely felt, for the party's direct action to provide research-based content, coupled with the good press that Bennett was creating with his many tours and speeches, was influencing what Canadians were hearing about the old party and the new leader.

Directly linked to Bennett's efforts at rebuilding the party were his responsibilities in Parliament. As the leader of His Majesty's Loyal Opposition it was ostensibly Bennett's job to hold the government's feet to the fire, ensuring that all legislation passed was as good as it could be. In reality, of course, his job was to prick and prod the government's front benches, seek weaknesses in their programs, contradictions in their arguments, holes in their research, hints of scandal or wrongdoing, or anything else that could be used to embarrass the government in order to, by extension, enhance the reputation of him and his party.

As when Bennett had been posing questions to Mackenzie King's previous government, the underlying theme to his' questions as Opposition leader supported greater intervention by the federal government into the economy to improve the lives of Canadians. He asked about pensions, about unemployment insurance, about creating federally sponsored research facilities, and about greater federal support for education, farmers, and fishermen. In all that he said it was clear that his elevation to party leader had not shaken his belief in the federal government existing as a force for good. His concomitant conviction was that the good it could be doing was being squandered by a prime minister who often appeared more of a squeamish manager than an audacious leader. Despite his frustration with Mackenzie King, Bennett was consistently positive in his interactions in the House. He seldom downshifted to mere partisanship and, somewhat uncharacteristically given his nature in the past, brought a refreshing balance of wit and good cheer to debates.[24]

Bennett's first sustained attack focused on government estimates. These are the figures brought to the House to provide details regarding spending. Bennett came to the Opposition leader's role with an already firmly established reputation as a quick study, powerful speaker, and nimble debater. His relentless criticism of the estimates built upon that reputation as he drew on his business expertise to find holes and contradictions in many of the numbers and percentages. In a trend that would continue throughout his time as leader, Bennett was on his feet nearly every day and he dominated his party's portion of question period and debates. Everything seemed to be going well. Then everything changed.

THE CRASH

Stock markets are motivated by fear and greed and operate much like a teeter-totter: when one motivating factor goes up, the other goes down. Greed breeds bulls and fear breeds bears. By the middle of the 1920s, it had become evident to prudent professional investors that the drunken party of greed they had been enjoying was coming to an end. In this way, the 1920s were like the 1980s leading to the crash of 1987, or the decade preceding the 2008 crash. Former American Federal Reserve chair Alan Greenspan summarized all three eras well in explaining the 1990s as a time of irrational exuberance. Conditions and attitudes created a situation in which insatiable greed led normally intelligent and moderate investors to be seduced by easy money and skyrocketing share and asset values into believing that nearly anything was possible and that rules no longer mattered.[25] When the greed end of the teeter-totter smashes to the ground, the impact and spiralling fear reverberate for years.

As was the case in 1987 and 2008, the 1929 stock market crash was more a symptom of the economic woes than a cause. Hindsight indicates that throughout the 1920s many sectors of the economy had based their projections and investments on the idea that growth would be steady and permanent. Credit became too easy to get and corporations and individuals borrowed to buy and build and to purchase stocks on margin. All bet that loans would be paid by the profits and rising commodity and property values that for years had seemed too simple and simply certain. The overconfidence and oversupply of easy money led to overproduction. For instance, by the late 1920s the Canadian automotive industry was producing 400,000 cars a year, despite the fact that over a million were already on the road and that the most that had ever been sold in a year was 260,000.[26]

After the postwar recession had ended and before growing protectionist barriers had begun, Canadian farmers had joined in the party.

Much of Europe had been devastated by war and revolution and was slow to recover from both, creating an unprecedented need for Canadian grain and wheat. For a brief period, and it was brief indeed, farmers planted fencerow to fencerow, enjoying prices and returns that had never been as high. The old Canadian staples of iron ore, lumber, fish, and pulp and paper were all along for the ride. The railways kept building more lines to take everything to markets that could not seem to get enough of Canada's stuff. The new movies, lively jazz, and outrageous flappers in notoriously sinful Montreal, the enthusiastic flouting of prohibition laws and old-fashioned decorum, all seemed to reflect good times that, like all good parties and periods of prosperity, appeared to be asking no price and promising no end.

There had been trouble in the spring of 1929. Stock prices began to bounce wildly for reasons that few could explain. As Europe recovered and a glut of wheat flooded the world market, the price for it and other commodities had begun to drop. Manufacturers began to feel the pinch caused by tariff policies that were rendering their products more expensive in world markets. Companies responded by reducing production and laying off workers. Many also issued more and more increasingly questionable stock to raise revenue, protect profit margins, and please shareholders. It was the beginning of a circle of rational and irrational reactions that effectively wound an ever-tightening noose around the necks of businesses big and small. It couldn't last. It didn't.

Wall Street laid an egg on the twenty-ninth of October 1929. While stories of New York speculators throwing themselves from high buildings were apocryphal, the shock of the sudden evaporation of wealth was certainly real and widely felt. The crash actually occurred over three days—October 24, 28, and 29. There was a brief and exciting rally four days later but then a slow slide that lasted a full month. On the crash's first day, $4 billion in American investment vanished. Canadian markets collapsed as well. While estimates vary, it is generally agreed that by the end of 1929 Canada saw about five billion dollars simply disappear. By early the next year, the top fifty companies in the country saw their worth devalued by 50 per cent.[27]

Through the winter of 1929–30, the Canadian corporate and political elite made only minor adjustments to long-term plans, hoping to get by on hoping for the best. Many experts believed that the crash was just a temporary adjustment and that the fundamentals of the Canadian economy in general and Canadian businesses in particular were such that it had created a brief storm that would be easily weathered. The Canadian Bankers Association, for instance, published an article in its January 1930 journal arguing that the economic problems would perhaps affect the sale of luxury items but that the growing unemployment that was beginning to be seen particularly in the West was a seasonal thing that would quickly right itself. The article predicted little more than a slight and short recession.[28] That same month, Toronto's *Globe* published an op-ed piece by the highly respected Sir Edward Beatty, who, from his position as president of the Canadian Pacific Railway, wrote that the current challenges were merely a necessary economic adjustment that would prove to be short lived and result quite soon in a stronger economy benefiting all.[29]

Prime Minister Mackenzie King chose to listen to those whose economic predictions matched what he needed to be true just months before he would go to the people. That he missed the significance of the stock market crash is indicated by the fact that on the day of and following the calamity heard round the world, his diary speaks only of his trip to the West.[30] Not a mention is made of the twentieth century's most significant economic event.

Meanwhile, unemployment was growing as plant gates closed and unsold wheat rotted. All economic indicators were beginning to coalesce into a consensus of doom. Canadians were coping with the crisis largely on their own as there was no social safety net to catch those falling from prosperity to despair. There was no national unemployment insurance, or health care, no maternity leaves, or child care benefits, or welfare, and old-age pensions and relief were spotty and inadequate.

Day after day, Bennett and Woodsworth hammered the government in the House with demands for action, but Mackenzie King continue to smile and weave circuitous responses that said as little as possible. The prime minister had decided, like too many corporate and financial leaders, to do nothing while betting his bottom dollar that the sun would come out tomorrow.

1930 ELECTION

Politics is tough. Intelligently analyzing options then aligning the most persuasive alternative to a political strategy is one thing. First attaining power and then trying to remain true to one's principled analysis in the implementation of that strategy is entirely another. For instance, Stephen Harper came from the University of Calgary school of Canadian neocons that found big government and deficit spending anathema. In the late 1990s, he was president of the National Citizens Coalition, selling the idea of a balanced-budget constitutional amendment and proudly proclaiming the group's slogan: More freedom through less government. That was easy. In January 2009, Prime Minister Harper was moved by economic and political events to abandon all in which he had once believed in an effort to save his minority government and deal with the worst economic crisis since the Great Depression. His budget dramatically jacked up spending and announced an end to the era of surpluses with a planned $85 billion deficit. He and his equally doctrinaire minister of finance Jim Flaherty explained that circumstances allowed them no other option.

Like Harper, Mackenzie King was an intelligent and principled man who had taken the time to carefully develop a thoughtful political philosophy. In 1918 he had published the turgid, largely unreadable, but intellectually important *Industry and Humanity*. The book analyzed economics from the perspective of the interplay between labour and industry, and promoted social welfare legislation as making economic and moral sense. He had negotiated labour contracts, arbitrated strikes, and cleaned up after messes such as the 1907 Vancouver race riot. He understood economics at a micro and macro level and how corporate, financial, and government action and inaction affected peoples' lives.

In the 1920s and 1930s, Mackenzie King's public utterances and actions suggested a baffling inability to comprehend, or perhaps just admit, what was happening. Like Prime Minister Harper in the fall of 2008, Mackenzie King either failed to understand the enormity of the calamity that had befallen the country or was unable, for whatever reason, to be direct with Canadians about it. Author Bob Plamondon wrote, "[Harper] appeared aloof, lacking empathy, and failed to acknowledge the carnage that was taking place."[31] Similarly, in February 1930, Mackenzie King had responded to Bennett's relentless questions by telling the House that the escalating economic crisis was just ". . . a few temporary circumstances prevailing at the moment . . . in particular localities."[32]

As winter turned to spring and the economy continued to worsen,

Mackenzie King continued to ignore or trivialize all that was falling to pieces around him. As American president Herbert Hoover was doing in the White House, he seemed intent on allowing the markets to correct themselves. Like Hoover, he waited patiently for the recovery to arrive from just around the corner, but also like Hoover, he waited and waited as it stubbornly refused to show up. It appeared to more and more Canadians that the prime minister just didn't get it. One of Mackenzie King's biographers, the respected Blair Neatby, made two related points in trying to understand the prime minister's determined inability or unwillingness to act. He argued that despite Mackenzie King's education, training, and experience, he was rather orthodox and old-fashioned in his thoughts on economic matters, with ideas no more sophisticated than the average Canadian's. Further, and tied to that point, is that the only time he recognized social or political problems is when they presented themselves to him as political threats or opportunities.[33] Bruce Hutchison, an earlier biographer, considered the stubborn refusal to act or to even acknowledge a need to act and postulated, "A student of his life is inclined to conclude that the explanation was really quite simple— King's timing, for once, was just wrong."[34]

No leader could have, at that moment, addressed the calamity in its entirety, but an inability to do everything is never an excuse to do nothing. Bennett attacked Mackenzie King day after day for doing just that— nothing. The prime minister still boasted, with pre-Keynesian pride, that he was a sound keeper of the country's books, which remained in surplus despite the ever-mounting economic challenges that he still insisted would soon pass. The combination of worsening economic conditions and Mackenzie King's unwillingness to address, or even admit, their profundity, worked to Bennett's favour.

After hammering Mackenzie King in the House every week, every Friday afternoon Bennett boarded a train to spend the weekend on his never-ending tour of the country. He was indefatigable. He was relentless. He was intent on demonstrating that, unlike the prime minister, he not only understood the hardships that Canadians were facing, but also that he had solutions to the economic problems that were at the root of those hardships. Most important among those ideas was something in which Bennett had always believed and that had been included in the Conservative's Winnipeg platform—greater trade with Britain and other

Commonwealth countries through the creation of preferential tariff and trade treaties. Bennett was cleverly able to tap into the core of Canadian pride in its British heritage, which in 1930 was still palpable, while accusing Mackenzie King of wanting only to increase trade with the United States, thereby touching that hint of anti-Americanism that is always sellable.

King may have been somewhat confused about Canada's material reality but he was still a cunning politician. His February 1930 budget laid two yawning, grass-covered holes before Bennett and invited him to go for a stroll. Finance Minister Charles Dunning stood there in his new shoes and read out the government's intention to seek imperial trade preferences for Canadian manufactured goods, raw materials, and food products. Dunning then boasted that the government intended to raise tariffs on a number of goods that were currently imported from the United States in order to protect Canadian businesses and consumers.

Mackenzie King had opted to try to use the economic woes of Canadians to his narrow partisan advantage. He decided that he would use the budget not so much to deal with the crisis but to force an election. He snidely recorded in his diary: "It will be a real bombshell into the Tory camp."[35] A couple of weeks later he sat late in the evening, alone in his Laurier House study, and wrote, "We must introduce enough 'free' [products without tariffs] under Br. preference to make Tories fight us vigorously and that we surely have got [them] this time . . . What will Bennett have left to talk on when trade with Grt. Br. [is] being increased with our proposals & trade with U.S. decreased."[36]

On its face, the budget proposals indeed appeared to be the very ideas that Bennett had been proposing on his speaking tours, but he was not about to tumble into the trap. In his dynamic response to the budget, Bennett criticized the government. The proposed imperial tariff was a desperate half measure that would not work, he argued, for it was inconsistent with other existing trade policies. You must change it all, Bennett said, and not simply tinker, as the budget proposal promised to do. To undertake a program of comprehensive trade reform, he continued, a conference was needed at which Britain and the other dominions could develop a mutually beneficial and unified structure of trade preferences. Bennett tore into the Liberal proposal and thundered in the House, "The changes embodied in it are founded upon no consistent economic principle and are a crazy quilt of higher protectionism and freer trade."[37]

The prime minister listened to the budget debate and said little, allowing Dunning to respond to all questions, jabs, and insults. He slowly sensed that the post-budget jousting was doing all that he had wanted it to do. He was confident that Bennett had talked himself into a corner by arguing for tariff and trade reform but against the Liberal changes to those policies. The prime minister believed that Bennett would be unable to extricate himself from that corner and even confided to his diary that he felt sorry for the Tory leader.[38]

Meanwhile, Mackenzie King employed procedural tricks that allowed little substantive debate about unemployment. Of the worsening economic situation felt first in the prairies but spreading like a plague throughout the land, he spoke only of "seasonal slackness." When pressed by Winnipeg Labour MP Abraham Heaps to at least acknowledge that jobs were being lost throughout the country, Mackenzie King retorted, "There is no evidence in Canada today of an emergency situation."[39]

While Bennett was good at bringing the unemployment issue to the fore, James Shaver Woodsworth was masterful. J. S. Woodsworth is among the most fascinating of Canadians. He was born in Ontario but travelled west as a young Methodist minister to do social work in Winnipeg's hard and tough slums. He wrote bestselling books about the plight of Canada's forgotten working class and earned credibility when he took employment at a number of difficult jobs, including a stint as a Vancouver longshoreman that saw him lifting and throwing bundles heavier than his slim 130 pounds. His political career had begun as a leader of the ill-fated Winnipeg General Strike, then later as one of two Labour Party MPs to win office in 1921. While he would be among the guiding founders and first leader of the Cooperative Commonwealth Federation, it was as a highly respected and articulate Labour MP that he refused to allow Mackenzie King to play parliamentary rope-a-dope and say nothing about the growing problem of unemployment. In this determined effort he indirectly helped Bennett.

Standing behind his desk with the unimposing look of the preacher he had been, the slight man with the greying, thinning hair and well-clipped beard demanded that the government explore the viability of instituting a system of unemployment insurance. Mackenzie King had avoided declaring himself on the issue by pronouncing, accurately, that such an undertaking was a provincial matter. But under Woodsworth's relentless badgering he relented at least a little in saying that if the provinces initiated such a program and then asked the federal government to help coordinate it across the country, he would consider the invitation. It was a line of dominoes with each bearing the word "if." Finally, in May, with unemployment getting worse and plans for the upcoming election already in place, Mackenzie King pledged to call a conference on unemployment to help his government better understand the issue and to develop policies to address it. But the conference would not take place until after the election. And it would happen only if he won—it was yet another domino in the line.

The unrelenting pressure to do something about unemployment led to one of Mackenzie King's rare verbal blunders—a slip that may have cost him the election before the writ had even been dropped. The prime minister said,

> So far as giving money from this Federal Treasury to the provincial governments is concerned, in relation to the question of unemployment as it exists today, I might be prepared to go a certain length possibly in meeting one or two of the western provinces that have Progressive premiers at the head of their governments . . . but I would not give a single cent to any Tory Government . . .[40]

The gasps among members on both sides of the House were echoed by those from the public gallery. It is a unique moment indeed when a prime minister makes a statement of such partisan ruthlessness. In a single phrase, Mackenzie King had repainted himself as the leader of the Liberals rather than of all Canadians. Cries of shame and derisive shouts cascaded down upon him from the Opposition benches. He could have retracted or clarified, but with the hole dug he instead began pulling the dirt in upon himself. In direct response to Harry Stevens, who had yelled that the prime minister should be ashamed of himself, Mackenzie King continued and actually upped the ante:

> May I repeat what I have said. With regard to giving money out of the Federal Treasury to any Tory government in this country for these

alleged unemployment purposes, while these governments are situated as they are today with politics diametrically opposed to this government, I would not give them a five-cent piece.[41]

The prime minister's blunder piled upon a gaffe was like Christmas morning for Bennett and the Conservatives. The next week found Mackenzie King on a pre-campaign tour trying to ignore both his recent outrageous remarks and the unemployment issue itself. He quickly found that he could do neither. In Peterborough, he finally conceded that unemployment was a problem. Two days later, in Montreal, he admitted that it was a crisis. He then claimed in Halifax that, despite his "five-cent" remark, he was willing—and in fact had long been anxious— to help any province but that none had asked. His campaign then took another blow when Alberta's Conservative premier John Brownlee released documents proving that he had indeed been asking for help since February but had been unable to even arrange a meeting with the appropriate federal ministers. The jig was up. Brownlee proved that the five-cent remark was not merely a slip—it was policy.

The political bungle was perceived by many as another example of the prime minister simply ignoring reality. Even worse—and like Prime Minister Harper in December 2008—Mackenzie King had been caught sacrificing the needs of Canadians for blatant partisan advantage. With Canadians waiting for news of what Harper would do to help the spiralling economy, his government released an economic statement that included plans for scuttling pay equity for women, banning public sector strikes, and ending the manner in which political parties were funded. When Harper's cynical tactics were revealed by the shaky threat of a Liberal-NDP coalition, few Canadians seemed to want another election or Liberal leader Stéphane Dion as prime minister. It was equally clear, however, that in challenging economic times when people are worried about keeping their jobs and paying their mortgage, few are willing to excuse a prime minister more anxious to play political games than tend to the pressing affairs of state. Harper managed to dance out of the political crisis he had created for himself. Mackenzie King was not so lucky.

In the spring and early summer of 1930, the economy was continuing to spiral downward. Mackenzie King had no grand vision or even short-term plans for arresting the trend. Given the economic and political circumstances, it is difficult to imagine a worse time to have to call an election. However, Mackenzie King had decided that he needed a new mandate before the Americans raised tariffs yet again, and before the imperial conference planned for the fall. Believing victory would be his, he visited the Governor General, asked that Parliament be dissolved, and that an election be held on July 18, 1930.[42]

THE CAMPAIGN

Bennett entered the campaign expressing great confidence. All of the work he had been doing to organize the party and to raise his personal profile in the country was about to be tested. Campaigns cost money and he donated another $600,000 of his own to the cause. Beyond this substantial sum, Bennett and his new political machine had begun to prove effective as a fundraiser. His connections with the Bank of Montreal and the CPR helped to secure donations totalling $100,000. His connections with Montreal's corporate elite helped to win an additional $575,000.[43]

Mackenzie King realized that Bennett would be a formidable campaigner. All had observed his growth as party leader. Even Sir Robert Borden, certainly no fan, wrote to Beaverbrook just four weeks before the election, "During the past two years Bennett has developed fine qualities of leadership. To a very great extent he has overcome his temperamental handicap; and he has ruled with a firm hand, displaying fine courage on occasions when it was demanded."[44]

The manner in which Bennett led the 1930 campaign harked back to Macdonald and Laurier in that the leader's personality outshone the party. Liberal Conservative candidates sold themselves as "Bennett men" and party policies became "Bennett's ideas." Charles Gavan "Chubby" Power, who would rise to prominence first in Quebec and then in federal politics, observed, "There is no doubt that Bennett's high character, his great reputation, his forceful utterances and his eloquence on the hustings had more to do with the victory in 1930 than the allegiance of the electorate to the principles and policies of the Conservative party."[45]

Bennett returned to the Winnipeg Amphitheatre Rink to kick off the campaign. On June 9, he spoke to seven thousand people and even more over the radio that carried his voice through a trans-Canada hookup to five cities in Ontario, two in Quebec, and four in the Maritimes. The radio audience was estimated to have been one million.[46] The use of radio was like nothing that had ever been seen in Canadian politics. If Franklin Roosevelt is credited with showing Americans what smart political leaders could do with radio, then Bennett must be given the credit for teaching Canadians. That night he reviewed all that he had been saying in the House and on his speaking tours about the importance of national unity and prosperity as goals, and about imperial trade as a way to pursue them both. He spoke of broad visions for the future greatness of the country, noting his support for more efficiency in the railway system and for the construction of the St. Lawrence Seaway that together would take Canadian products to the world.

Remarkably, Bennett delivered over one hundred major speeches. His oratorical skills were in full force and he was something to behold. He still occasionally slid into past bad habits and appeared to become lost in the thundering cadences of his own voice. Reading his speeches today leads one to wonder if Bennett sometimes tested the attention span and political and economic knowledge of his audience. One is also left with the conviction, however, that unlike too many politicians today, he respected the people by never "dumbing down" his message. He explained rather than sold and challenged rather than pandered.

Bennett was honest; he would never be caught in a lie or a politician's hedging even when shading the truth may have been to his advantage. And he never changed his language or emphasis depending on where he was. Bennett's stump speech, for instance, that he more or less repeated at each of the stops on his first western swing, spoke proudly of his passion for Britain but also of his patriotic love for Canada. He said, "I give place to no man in my love of Empire. But there is a greater love in my life, and that is my love for Canada. Judge me by this. And those who condemn me for it, withhold your support."[47] He later said the same thing in Quebec.

To western farmers who had since the days of Laurier opposed nearly all tariffs, he bluntly stated that they might not like them but that he and his party believed they were best for the country. In words few politicians ever hear themselves say, Bennett told western audiences that they were wrong. He said, "And although I know you were wrong even then, I agree that perhaps the fault was as much ours, as yours, that we did not make ourselves better understood. . . ."[48] He then went on to explain that his support for tariff protection was based partly on his desire to protect commodity prices, especially for food and grain products.

It was on this first tour of the West that Bennett uttered a phrase that captured the nation's attention and invigorated the already animated campaign: "You have been taught to mock at tariffs and applaud Free Trade. Tell me, when did Free Trade fight for you? You say our Tariffs are only for the manufacturers. Now I'll make them fight for you as well. I'll use them to blast a way into the markets that have been closed to you."[49]

Anyone who understood tariffs, and Bennett understood them well, knew that tariffs do not blast one's way into markets, but rather are most often a blunt instrument for keeping others out of yours. The only way they might wheedle products into a market is by using tariffs not as dynamite sticks but as bargaining chips. An examination of Bennett's private and public words and the policies he had promoted throughout his public career demonstrates that he understood this fact completely. In a private letter to Winnipeg lawyer H. R. Drummond, for instance, he argued that a new regiment of tariffs and non-tariff barriers based upon a fundamental overhaul of Canada's trade policy with Britain, the United States, and the world was essential to economic renewal. Accepting the reality of growing American protectionism, he advocated imperial trade preferences as the first step in that process. But he was also realistic enough to know that absolute free trade with Britain and Commonwealth countries would be a difficult goal to make progress toward, impossible to actually obtain, and perhaps not in Canada's interest. Freer but not free trade must be the goal. He wrote, ". . . it would be quite impossible for this country to maintain its industrial life if we had complete free trade with Great Britain."[50] He was not a political schemer but a true believer.

It was over the issue of tariffs that Bennett experienced another of many periodic spats with his old friend. Beginning in early 1929, Beaverbrook had initiated a campaign that he called the Empire Crusade. It was based largely on the idea of Britain remaining as the central power in the empire and overseeing a system of free trade among it and the dominions as a bulwark against the rising power of the United States.

The idea sprang from Beaverbrook's misty-eyed notions of empire and his visceral mistrust of Americans.[51] He spent a great deal of political capital making speeches, infuriated a number of powerful enemies in promoting and opposing various leaders and candidates, and spilled a good deal of ink in papers promoting his idea. Bennett, on the other hand, had made clear many times that he was an imperialist but a Canadian first and, recognizing the evolving power relationships within the empire, supported a system not of free trade but of preferential trade and tariff agreements that would benefit all while allowing for increased trade with the United States. When asked by a reporter about Beaverbrook's Empire Crusade, Bennett was blunt. Speaking for the Conservative caucus, he said, "In our opinion Empire Free Trade is neither desirable nor possible, for it would defeat the very purpose we are striving to achieve."[52] Beaverbrook reacted by granting interviews with the *Globe and Mail* and Dafoe's *Winnipeg Free Press*. In both cases, he spoke of the value of Empire Free Trade and suggested that the views of Mackenzie King's Liberals appeared to be closest to his own and best for Canadians. For months afterwards, Beaverbrook's letters to Bennett went unanswered.

In the 1930 campaign Bennett was not advocating tariffs as protectionism, which would destroy trade. Rather, he proposed the more intelligent use of tariffs as a way to increase Canadian and international trade. This more intelligent use of tariffs had been made necessary by America's protectionist trade legislation, which had spurred countries around the world to erect their own barriers to trade. Bennett was not advocating the creation of similar Canadian barriers; he was presenting a way in which those barriers could be overcome.

The argument was complex, but the phrase resonated with Canadians. "Blasting one's way" certainly promised dramatic action. The phrase had been suggested to him by adviser Bill Herridge, about whom much more will be said later, and Bennett had decided to include it in his initial address in Winnipeg. When it received a loud and positive reaction, he repeated it at every stop. One does not throw away a good applause line.

The phrase shocked and worried a good number of people, even some of those who supported him and his idea. By July 9, there had been enough questions raised in newspapers by Liberal candidates, and even by Conservatives, that Lipset felt the need to forward a three-page letter to all Conservative candidates and senators clarifying what Bennett meant. He explained that Bennett was proposing a policy that was consistent with the Conservative platform established in Winnipeg in 1927. He further noted that the *Ottawa Citizen*, which he called Mr. Mackenzie King's organ, was playing a major role in twisting the truth about Bennett and tariffs and doing all it could to confuse matters. In an attempt to provide Conservative candidates with ammunition to use against those who would attack them on the tariff issue, Lipset argued, as Bennett had, that when Britain eventually realized that preference for Canadian grain, meat, and dairy products would be matched by preferences for their goods, a deal would be struck that would benefit the people of both countries. And this, he wrote, is blasting one's way to prosperity.[53] That the phrase garnered so much press and so much discussion meant that it was a good one: Bennett was setting the agenda and forcing Mackenzie King and the Liberals to react. And in any political campaign, when you start reacting you start losing.

Bennett's speeches always concluded with five pledges. All were economic and all regarded increasing trade for Canada as a way of addressing the country's current challenges. He ended with a rhetorical flourish worthy of a circuit-riding evangelist who never failed to bring audiences to their feet:

> A land endowed by heaven with incalculable wealth. A people free and brave and strong with the strength that comes from the mountains and the prairies, the rivers and the sea. Both untouched by age. A shrine— this Canada—which holds inviolate those laws of truth, justice and equality brought with us when we ourselves came first to this western world. The three, a trinity of power. The task of government—its great right and privilege—to support this power, to be diligent in the trust you will impose upon it, to achieve, that your labours may not be fruitless, to work, that you may know some leisure, to hold before your eyes the vision that is drawing nearer, the vision built out of a common understanding and a common purpose, with tools forged in the workshops of steadfastness and faith, the vision of the Canada soon to be.[54]

As the campaign ground on, Bennett honed his speech to state that there were really only three issues at hand. The first was the embarrassing record of Mackenzie King's government, the second was the conspicuous inadequacy of the 1930 budget, and the third was the difference between the goals of the Liberals and Conservatives for the upcoming Imperial Economic Conference, to be held in London that September.

Bennett's energy on the campaign trail was remarkable. For instance, on July 3 he was in Nova Scotia, where he celebrated his sixtieth birthday by acting as a man of far fewer years. He travelled about 250 miles and delivered three major addresses to large and enthusiastic crowds. All three meals involved meetings, questions, and remarks. To the dozens who sent cards and telegrams acknowledging his birthday he personally dictated many and hand-wrote many more notes of thanks with the assertion that he and the party were doing quite well. He observed that everywhere he travelled it looked like the Liberals were losing ground. Like many other successful people, Bennett seemed to somehow have available to him more than just twenty-four hours each day.

With the tide perceptively breaking his way, the final weeks of the campaign saw Bennett channel Shakespeare in coming not to praise the Liberal Party but to bury it. He said, "Be fair to Liberalism, and judge it not as it was, [but] by what it has become. You old time faithful Liberals, think of your warring champion of other days, and hide your eyes from the spectacle of its corpse, gibbeted by its sworn leaders. The Conservative Party, pledged to oppose it, would never have decreed for it, so horrible an end."[55] These were the wise words of a politician who was sure of his base. He was now going after the undecideds and disaffected Liberals— and winning them.

Mackenzie King had the advantage of the prime minister's office and it always helps to go to the people from that position of power. But this time it was an empty weapon. His speaking style had improved, but it was not yet what it would later become and he still stumbled and mumbled through remarks haltingly read to restless crowds. His voice was thin and reedy and in outdoor settings people beyond the first rows had trouble hearing him even when a microphone was present. In Quebec it was a problem that he spoke no French. More than that, however, was the perception among many Canadians that Mackenzie King still did not fully comprehend the hardships with which growing numbers of unemployed people and their families were suffering each day. His apparent last-minute conversion to an imperial trade scheme, his unwillingness to admit that a Depression had gripped the land, his seeming callousness regarding the unemployed, and of course, what had become known as the five-cent speech, made attacking or dismissing Mackenzie King and the Liberals just too easy.

As if all of that was not enough, shortly after the dropping of the writ, a Liberal scandal hit the papers. With Liberal party coffers empty, party bagmen had approached those in charge of Quebec's Beauharnois hydroelectric-power plant that was to be constructed on the St. Lawrence River. A deal was made involving campaign contributions, promises of government contracts, and power-rate arrangements. Mackenzie King denied that the deal making had taken place, but when more and more of the principals admitted to what had transpired, he appeared to be either lying or out of touch. Both options were lethal in the middle of a campaign.

Mackenzie King's life on the campaign trail was made even more miserable by McRae's decision to send R. J. Manion to shadow his every stop. Manion arrived at every city and town, and spoke at the same venue a day or two after the prime minister had left. Like a one-man truth squad Manion refuted every attack and slammed every idea that Mackenzie King had left behind. Manion's effectiveness was measured in the ferocity of the Liberal press's attacks upon him.

Any election involves candidates attempting to frame the question upon which the campaign should be based, and then selling a particular answer to that question. Bennett was clever in stating that the primary question of the day was how to deal with unemployment. He argued that unemployment was not really the problem itself but the symptom of a deeper problem. And that deeper problem was trade. While he sincerely believed in the efficacy of tariffs as a way to address the crisis, as the campaign began to gather support and energy he tended to oversell himself and his ideas. His promise to blast his way into markets that were obviously quite able to withstand any such attempt was not Bennett's only descent into hyperbole. On a number of platforms, he promised to eliminate unemployment or "perish in the attempt." With respect to railroads, a guaranteed applause line was "Competition Ever,

Amalgamation Never!" He campaigned under the banner "Canada First." It really did not matter what the slogan meant. It was a Rorschach statement meaning whatever the listener wanted it to mean—as empty and effective as "Just Society" or "Yes We Can." To Canadians, Bennett's vigorous, muscular slogans promised action and it was action for which many Canadians yearned.

Bennett's crowds continued to grow in size and enthusiasm. He mocked Mackenzie King's wan promise to create a committee to investigate unemployment after Canadians had voted, saying, "Mackenzie King promises you a conference, I promise you action. He promises consideration of the problem of unemployment; I promise to end unemployment. Which plan do you like best?"[56] In Vancouver he said, "So I will, when the Government is mine, continue to blast a way through all our troubles and difficulties. What else would I be there for? To cringe with others with soft words and to recoil from each rebuff? That is not Canada's way. That is not my party's way."[57]

Bennett's sister Mildred was committed to the campaign and often travelled with him. She met people at rallies and hosted political tea parties. She also visited a Toronto recording studio and made a record extolling her brother's virtues and those of the Conservative Party. She told what she believed would be endearing stories about her brother in an attempt to somewhat humanize the man whom many were coming to respect but not necessarily to know. Part of the record was also instructional. Mildred told women how to set up political tea parties and the best ways to persuade guests to vote for the local Conservative candidate. The record's effectiveness is difficult to measure, but many tea parties did indeed take place, especially in small towns across the country.

Before it was over, Bennett would travel 14,000 miles. He would often halt his car to get out and greet even small groups of people. On country roads he would stop and lean over a fence, speaking with a farmer in one of those long, slow conversations that afford rural life its grace. In Katevale, Quebec, while touring the main street on foot, he stopped at a small shop and bought them out of chocolate bars. He then continued his stroll, handing out a treat to every child he saw.

The rigours of the campaign and the enormity of the stakes, however, did not move Bennett away from those things he valued and the man that he was. One Sunday evening, for instance, found Bennett arriving at North Bay, Ontario, for an event the next day. A hundred people had gathered at the train depot to greet him. An aide entered Bennett's car and informed him that when he emerged, the people would demand a speech. For the good of the campaign, the aide continued, Bennett would need to break his rule against working on the Sabbath and oblige them. Bennett said no. He travelled but never campaigned on Sundays.

He stepped off the train to great applause and began to shake the hands of those who surged forward. Soon there were cries of "Speech!" from the crowd. At first Bennett ignored their behest, but as more and more people joined in he could no longer avoid a response. He raised his hand, the crowd quieted, and he said, "Men and women. Many years ago my mother taught me that no good would come of breaking the Sabbath. I am getting on in years now, but I have never disobeyed my mother's wish. I hope none of you will ever forget the lessons you learned at your mother's knee."[58] With that, he waved, the crowd cheered, and he was off to his hotel.

Bennett paid attention to all regions of the country but afforded special consideration to Quebec. Twice he toured through the province and was met both times with good crowds, to whom he spoke in both English and gamely read in his limited French. Quebec's farmers, its industrial workers, and its James Street business elite were slowly drawing together in an alliance of English-speaking Conservatives and French-speaking nationalists who saw a partner in Bennett.

Mackenzie King often simply had bad luck. Rain plagued his Quebec tour in June, forcing the cancellation of three outdoor rallies. A rally in the Eastern Townships was moved inside but then flopped because the rain on the building's tin roof made it impossible for his audience to hear him. A month later, July 12 to 15, Bennett was welcomed by blue skies and mild temperatures. Bennett's second Quebec swing saw him arrive in many towns at the head of a parade of sometimes a hundred cars filled with supporters who had followed him from the last town. His rallies were often attended by thousands and usually more than lived in the host towns. In St. Pierre, as just one example, the town of 12,000 saw 20,000 at the boisterous Conservative rally. At indoor gatherings, loudspeakers were always installed so those unable to get in could hear. And everywhere it could be arranged, Bennett's voice was also heard live over the radio. It was not quite Trudeaumania, but it was close.

While Bennett was the sun, and everything and everyone else involved with the Conservative campaign merely reflected his heat and light, there were many others who made essential contributions. Stevens worked industriously in British Columbia and the prairies. In Ontario and Quebec, Guthrie and Manion travelled from riding to riding supporting promising candidates, with Manion also dogging Mackenzie King. The Ottawa office continued to spread the word and Perley continued to bring in money.

The final days of the tour found a weary Bennett back in Calgary. He visited his office, dropped in on friends, and delivered two speeches. His riding was in the bag. There was nothing left to do but wait for Canadians to make their decisions.

There were no polls in 1930. Instinct and intuition were the only ways that everyone from voters, to reporters, to party leaders could predict the swaying mood of the country. Still, few were surprised with the results when the vote counting finally ended on July 19. In the 245-seat House, the Conservatives won the majority with 134, followed by the Liberals with 90, and 21 others representing Progressives, Labour, independents, and farm interests. Bennett's party won seats in every province. He could take pride in the fact that Canadians had decided to send more Conservatives to Ottawa than any time since Macdonald's last campaign. Further, in 1926, Quebec had sent only four Conservatives to Ottawa; in 1930, it would send twenty-four.

While the results appeared to be a smashing victory for the new Conservative leader, the popular vote told a somewhat more cautionary tale. Despite a gain of 43 seats, the Conservative popular support had risen only from 46.2 per cent to 49.0 per cent. And while the Liberals had lost 26 seats, their popular support had actually gone up slightly from 43.6 per cent to 43.9 per cent. With his advocacy of an activist, engaged government, Bennett had stolen votes from the parties on the fringes of the Canadian left. In 1926, 10.2 per cent of voters supported the left-leaning, smaller parties, whereas in 1930, only 7.1 per cent voted in that way. The Conservatives had won a commanding majority, and Bennett, under the arcane political system that was and is Canada's, a strong mandate to govern.

Politicians are elected by raising expectations regarding what they can accomplish; but then they must bear the momentous burden of living up to those expectations. Disappointment is almost inevitable. Bennett understood that twist and was open and honest about his thoughts and feelings, especially given the challenging times. He said in the House shortly after taking office: "Next to a battle lost, in my mind the saddest thing is a battle won. There are disappointments of hopes, there are changed conditions, there are other outlooks."[59] With the economy in worse shape at the end of the campaign than at the beginning, and all indicators continuing to head south, it might have been better for Bennett's career and reputation had he lost. In summing up Mackenzie King's response to being sent to the political woodshed, where he could sit out the worst of the Depression years, Bruce Hutchison observed that Opposition was the most comfortable residence. But Canadians had tired of Mackenzie King's immobility and been moved by Bennett's clarion call for action. If Bennett's bluster was all a bluff, they were about to call it.

PREPARING TO GOVERN

Bennett tidied up his business and legal affairs in Calgary and patiently answered hundreds of letters from across the country and around the world. With the help of Alice Millar and his staff, he responded to them all with a similar message of thanks. It is a tribute to the man that he answered a handwritten note from a Sudbury miner with the same attention and personal touch or two as from a respected captain of industry.

After a week, he made his way back to Ottawa. Mildred was again at his side and settled into her rooms next to his at the Château Laurier. Bennett's personal habits did not change. He still rose early in the morning and was at his desk by eight. He still read himself to sleep at midnight. Bennett never exercised except for the short walk from the hotel to the east block and back. He enjoyed a massage every morning to keep his muscles limber and he retained his love of chocolate creams. He seldom listened to music and never tuned in to the popular radio comedies or dramas of the day. He rarely attended plays, movies, or concerts. He read voraciously but nearly always to inform rather than entertain. He pored over political biographies and could not get enough of English statesmen—especially Disraeli. He still neither drank nor smoked. He had his hair cut once a week and he shaved with his straight razor twice a day. His handmade suits were old-fashioned tail coats and he kept a full wardrobe at his office, as he often completely changed his clothes three times a day. He was never seen, even in the most casual of circumstances, without a crisp shirt and firmly affixed tie. He never removed his jacket in his office or at meetings. It was a different time, but even then he was a different sort of man.

Bennett's first task as prime minister was to choose his cabinet. The job is never easy. Merit is only one, and sometimes a secondary, consideration when making cabinet appointments. In Bennett's day, race and gender were not on his or any other politician's radar and besides, the caucus from which he had to choose was all male and all white. However, he needed to consider regional representation and to assuage those who had supported and opposed him in the leadership race that was still for many a fresh and painful memory.

All prime ministers take cabinet construction seriously. Sir John A. was legendary for his ability to create alliances through cabinet appointments and is credited with keeping Nova Scotia in Confederation by appointing and thus silencing the dangerous and impertinent Joseph Howe. That Macdonald was fully aware of his skills in this regard was revealed when he attended a conference in the United States. In checking in to his Washington hotel, he was asked to record his occupation in the register. He wrote "cabinet maker."

In Macdonald's league was Brian Mulroney who, when he became prime minister, was in a similar situation to Bennett. For him, the most important among his leadership rivals who needed to be brought within the tent was former party leader and prime minister Joe Clark. In his memoirs, Mulroney wrote, "I was determined to work closely with the former prime minister and his key supporters to ensure that any leadership race bitterness was banished and forgotten. My overriding goal was to build a strong united government that could win elections and face challenges at home and abroad in times of crisis."[60] Even when the country turned against him and his popularity was at its nadir, Mulroney's cabinet and caucus remained steadfastly loyal.[61] Bennett knew what Macdonald and Mulroney knew.

Winnipeg's Hugh Guthrie had been the party's interim leader and

Winnipeg convention chair and he had come second in the leadership race. He deserved a prominent position and as justice minister he got one. The choice would have surprised no one: Guthrie excelled as an intelligent and skilled administrator and parliamentarian. Another leadership contender had been northern Ontario's Dr. R. J. Manion. As minister of railways and canals, he would bring to the table experience as a former government whip and service in Meighen's cabinet. Edgar Rhodes was a former Nova Scotia premier and House of Commons Speaker, so it was with an eye toward his eastern roots and political acumen that he was appointed minister of fisheries. In 1932, Rhodes would become minister of finance. Former Canadian High Commissioner to London Sir George Perley was named minister without portfolio and deputy prime minister. Perley had excelled as an organizer and fundraiser during the campaign and was also an English-speaking Quebecer whose influence in that province was significant. Also from Quebec was Charles Cahan, who became secretary of state. He brought to cabinet his strong connections with the Montreal corporate elite. That took care of the serious leadership contenders.

From the Ontario business community came former Dunlop Tire and Rubber Company president Edmond Ryckman as revenue minister. He had served with distinction in Meighen's cabinet. The talented and hard-working Robert Weir was new to Ottawa but had served in the Saskatchewan provincial cabinet and would prove a valuable asset as minister of agriculture. There were other ministers, but of lesser consequence. (For a full list of Bennett's cabinet appointments see the appendix.)

Then there was Harry Stevens. Bennett's old friend had certainly earned a place in cabinet, but he had been defeated in his Vancouver riding. Bennett nonetheless appointed him to a post that, given the promises of the campaign just ended, would be among the most important: minister of trade and commerce. He then found a safe Conservative riding, persuaded the sitting member to retire, and applauded as Stevens won the hastily called Kootenay East by-election. There was logic in taking such extraordinary measures to gather him into the cabinet. Stevens was hard-working, intelligent, extremely popular in the West, and among the best debaters in the House. His abilities were to prove quite important; other than Bennett himself, Stevens was the only member of the cabinet who could respond to the quick cut and thrust of Parliament in a way that did honour to the government. It was his ability to faithfully and dexterously represent the government that led Bennett to dispatch him to speaking engagements not only in Canada but around the world, and to trust him as he trusted no others. Bennett's use of Stevens in this way would later come back to bite him.

Bennett raised a few eyebrows when he appointed himself president of the Privy Council, minister of finance, and secretary of state for external affairs. It was not the first time that a prime minister had taken a portfolio for himself, but it was the first time that a prime minister had appointed himself to three posts. It was also the first time that a prime minister had considered himself to be the most qualified member of his caucus and thus become his own minister of finance.

Bennett's nineteen-member cabinet contained five from Quebec (although only three were French speaking), seven from Ontario, and one from each of the other seven provinces. As in all cabinets there was talent and there was deadwood.

Howard Ferguson was not a federal member of Parliament, but he deserved to be rewarded for the role he had played in bringing Bennett to power. He was appointed Canada's High Commissioner to London. The job was a plum but it unfortunately took him far from the muck of Canadian politics that he had such a flare for slogging through. Bennett would have benefited from his counsel closer to home.

Bennett could not seem to do anything for General McRae. McRae had played an essential role as an organizer at the convention, in the reorganization and modernization of the party, and finally in the campaign. But in putting such a mammoth effort into these activities he had ignored his own riding, and his constituents punished him for his oversight by handing him a defeat. McRae was offered the Senate and the High Commissioner's job in London but turned them both down. The one job he seemed to want was Canadian representative in Washington, but Bennett had already decided to give that post to Bill Herridge. Later, when Bennett made the decision first to scale down then to all but end the party's Ottawa office, McRae quit in disgust and returned to the private sector. Bennett and the Canadian people lost a skilled and dedicated public servant.

Bill Herridge would play a major role in Bennett's administration.

Bennett had met him just before the campaign through Mildred, whom Herridge was dating and would later marry. He was born in Ottawa, the son of a Methodist minister. From his father he internalized the precepts of the Social Gospel. As a young man he came to know and, although he was quite a bit younger, form a friendship with Mackenzie King, who was his family's Gatineau Hills neighbour. After having served in the First World War, he entered public life by forming the Canadian League to help returning veterans. His involvement with veterans brought him into contact with Governor General Byng, who recognized his talent and potential. Despite the difference in their ages, the two became close. It was this friendship that led to his split with Mackenzie King. Herridge believed that his neighbour had mistreated Byng, who had been an honest broker throughout the constitutional flap of 1926.

Herridge used his connections and skills to establish and build a lucrative Ottawa law practice. It was at a party that the young lawyer met Mildred Bennett. After beginning his courtship with Mildred, she recommended his services as a political advisor to her brother. Herridge became close to the Bennett inner circle and finally a role player within it. He impressed Bennett with his quick mind and political acumen. His value increased as the campaign progressed. His advice was sought on a daily basis and he was soon writing at least portions of Bennett's speeches. The ambassadorship in Washington was his reward.

Another person in need of a noteworthy position was Arthur Meighen. He was cold and cantankerous and had nearly driven the convention into the ditch on its first afternoon, but he was a former leader and prime minister. Although never close, the two were in regular contact for the first two years of Bennett's term. In February 1932, Senator and Minister of Labour Gideon Robertson became seriously ill. Bennett gave the labour file to Wesley Gordon and appointed Meighen to the Senate and to the cabinet as a minister without portfolio. Meighen immediately became the Conservative Party's Senate leader. His appointment was important, for Meighen was able to directly push and punish the three Liberal senators who had been involved in the Beauharnois scandal and thereby guard Bennett's flank, while later giving him cover for controversial legislation. Meighen's effectiveness in the Senate, and Bennett's willingness to allow him his political reins, was seen in the fact that during his term, sixteen bills that originated in the Senate's Red Chamber came to the floor of the House of Commons—more than during any other administration.

With office won, cabinet and other appointments made, personal advisers in place, and greater economic challenges arising by the day, Bennett set to work. His ability and willingness to work exceptionally hard and long was noted by even his most fervent political enemies. Mackenzie King marvelled at Bennett's work ethic and ability to accomplish a great deal in a short period of time, calling him a "driving power."[62] Years later, when Stevens had a great deal about which he could be bitter, he still conceded that Bennett was indefatigable.[63] Even as he advanced in age, the fourteen-hour workdays that were typical throughout his youth remained the norm. He employed seventeen secretaries who dealt mainly with correspondence, dictation, and other general duties. They took shifts to keep up with him. Arthur Merriam was his private secretary and Andrew MacLean was in charge of correspondence. Bennett's office was run by the loyal, efficient, and untiring Alice Millar.

Bennett continued to eschew vacations. As he had with his law practice and with all of his business interests, he linked travel with work. His cabinet and caucus colleagues often sought information from Millar regarding Bennett's travel schedule and ensured that they booked golf games or personal time for days when their boss was away. But they were often called by a prime minister who was still thinking of work no matter where he was. Manion once quipped, "R. B. holidays by getting his teeth fixed at Toronto. What a hell of a holiday."[64]

Bennett brought a fascinating and perhaps dangerous mix to the prime minister's office. Add parsimonious personal habits and the lessons of a lifetime spent creating opportunities for himself to the absence of a family or distraction of hobbies, and toss in a workaholic's obsession with issues large and small, and you had a man with little room left for others. In this we have the paradox of a man who was by nature a shy loner, driven by the lessons of his stern mother and the dictates of his strict Wesleyan faith to draw strength from his monastic lifestyle while simultaneously seeing the reaching out to improve the lot of others as a moral imperative.

In his impatient desire to do all that he could in a day, he was often guilty of intruding on ground that under other prime ministers would have, and perhaps in Bennett's case, should have been left to cabinet ministers. Ministers were often angered but then amazed when they discovered that Bennett knew their files as well or better than they did. But Bennett rankled many a colleague by making decisions that were clearly within the purview of a particular minister without even the courtesy of consulting the man.

Bennett saw the cabinet as akin to a corporate board of directors. He even referred to it as such during debates in the House. He had support for this opinion among his colleagues, many of whom had come from the world of business.[65] Manion, for instance, later referred to cabinet using a similar metaphor.[66] If Bennett saw the cabinet as a board of directors, then it followed that he saw himself as chairman of that board. He performed his role as if he were also the majority shareholder. He listened and sought opinion, but in the end, his was the only voice that really mattered.

While Bennett could perhaps be faulted for acting in an authoritarian manner in this regard, it must be acknowledged that he is not the only leader to have done so. Abraham Lincoln once famously called for a vote in his cabinet and noted that every member voted no with his the only yes vote. He solemnly looked up from the ledger on which he had recorded the lopsided tally and, according to legend, said quietly, "Well, gentlemen, the yes side has it." Bennett would have liked that. Prime Minister Jean Chrétien would have liked it too. In his first political memoir, entitled *Straight From the Heart*, Chrétien wrote of a humiliating experience that almost ended his career in 1978. He was Pierre Trudeau's finance minister, but one evening while at his cottage he listened with the same surprise as the rest of Canadians as the prime minister announced a $2 billion cut to federal expenditures. There had been no consultation. Years later, Finance Minister Paul Martin was home on his Eastern Townships farm listening to Rex Murphy's *Cross Country Checkup* on CBC radio. He was stunned to hear Murphy announce that Chrétien had fired him from cabinet.[67] Again, there had been no communication. These and other examples do not mean that Bennett's dominant style was polite or the best way to lead—but it was not unique. And it was not without cost.

The Opposition and newspapers quickly recognized the power that Bennett felt comfortable in drawing to himself and some were critical of his forming what they called a one-man government. *Maclean's* magazine, for instance, noted in 1933, "He is still the government taking upon himself the work of his Ministers or of many of them, trying to be in a dozen places and to do a dozen things at the same time."[68] A January 1931 editorial cartoon in the unapologetically Liberal *Winnipeg Free Press* by the famously anti-Bennett scribbler Arch Dale showed a cabinet room where every man at the table was Bennett, as were two assistants and even the portraits on the wall. The cartoon was reprinted in papers across the country. A joke that also became nationally known and was spun into many versions went something like this: A group of tourists was walking on Parliament Hill when they saw a lone man pass quickly by, muttering to himself. "Is that man alright?" one tourist asked. "He's fine," said the guide. "That's just Prime Minister Bennett conducting a cabinet meeting."

The accusation of running a dictatorial, one-man government would stick and be used against Bennett many times in the press, in the House, and to devastating effect in the 1935 election. While the stereotype had traction, however, like all stereotypes it was only acquainted with the truth. Bennett's cabinet ministers worked hard and were consulted frequently. Sometimes cabinet meetings lasted for hours on end and sometimes all day long as details were debated fully and by all. Deputy ministers and their staffs were worked ragged as more information was demanded and more reports ordered. Throughout his time in office the full cabinet met, on average, eighteen times per month. With respect to the Senate, Meighen later wrote, "To the credit of Mr. Bennett, I want to add that no man ever gave another freer scope than he gave me; no Prime Minister ever before committed to the Senate constructive work of such consequence or accepted from it with so good a grace a formidable catalogue of amendments to legislation initiated in the House of Commons."[69]

Nonetheless, in the House it was Bennett's voice that was heard more than any other. Due to his holding three important cabinet portfolios as well as the prime ministership, it was natural that Bennett would find himself on his feet a great deal. However, during question period and debate, Bennett quite often rose when questions could, and under most other prime ministers, would have been deferred to appropriate cabinet ministers. As the trend turned to standard operating procedure, few could help being impressed as day after day and regarding issue after issue Bennett spoke without notes about intricate details of policies and initiatives that fell within the purview of any and all departments.[70] If his domineering nature frustrated some in his caucus, it infuriated many on the opposite side of the aisle. Chubby Power, later an influential Liberal cabinet minister and senator, was both awed and appalled with Bennett and told a reporter, "In this house he often exhibits the manners of a Chicago policeman and the temperament of a Hollywood actor."[71]

Important to note—and with a nod to the point made regarding the loyalty that Mulroney maintained despite hard times—is that nearly all of Bennett's nineteen minsters remained in their original posts throughout the full five years of the administration. Most of the changes involved those necessitated by illness, such as the moves involving Ryckman and Robertson, and when Bennett himself surrendered the finance ministry to Rhodes in 1932. No one crossed the aisle. Ironically, it was only Harry Stevens, the man whom Bennett had known the longest, most intimately, and trusted the most, who would leave the cabinet under a cloud of anger.

Bennett also had to deal with his caucus. The caucus is always a tough group. It comprises ambitious and talented people who want to serve their constituents while doing right for the country but at the same time believe that they deserve a cabinet seat. Caucus meetings, consequently, are partly gladiator games in which members struggle to impress the boss as issues are debated. Prime ministers lead both the government and their party, and this dual role means that they must be constantly thinking about the long-term needs of the country and short-term political, partisan considerations. If ever one outweighs the other in the minds of caucus members, there can be hell to pay. The prime minister must persuade and cajole, slap backs and twist arms, all the while mustering the range of political skills that brought him to the apex of power in the first place. Losing the loyalty of those in the caucus room is the first step to losing it all.

A problem was that Bennett had risen to power based more upon impressing those around him with his intellect, prodigious memory, and oral abilities than through his charm. People had always come to him, not the other way around. He was an introvert forced to play a team sport—as player, coach, captain, and cheerleader. It would have been unfair to expect the man to suddenly adjust the core of what he was to become the smiling herder of caucus cats that a prime minister must be to keep members happy and unified who, by their nature, are unruly and needy. Bennett cared about pursuing goals and accomplishing tasks related to the vision he held for the country and was willing to sacrifice his time, fortune, and health in that pursuit. He had little sympathy and even less empathy for those who were not similarly passionate and driven. Those around him who needed the emotional sustenance offered by a back-slapping, head-patting boss were out of luck; Bennett simply did not have the aptitude, time, or desire.

Many prime ministers have been accused of ignoring the feelings of others while drawing too much power to themselves, including Prime Minister Stephen Harper. Among the chorus of those accusing Harper of the same tendency for which Bennett was criticized was Retired Justice John Gomery who said, "We have a government where one man seems to have an ever-increasing influence upon what government policy is going to be. If you look back historically at prime ministers in the past, I don't think they had the same hold over their party and Parliament that the present prime minister has."[72] Historian Bob Plamondon agreed, arguing that Harpers's ". . . inclinations were to motivate through intimidation, fear and raw intellectual power."[73]

While the image of Bennett as a one-man band was not completely accurate, it was based on certain truths. He held all those portfolios. He dominated caucus meetings as he dominated cabinet meetings and as he dominated the House. He may have listened carefully to cabinet and caucus colleagues but he sometimes found doing so troublesome, time consuming, and unworthy of concerted effort. Three incidents tell the tale.

First, he carefully prepared for caucus meetings, and when members were speaking he often took voluminous notes. He cared what MPS had to say as it was a valuable source of information. Once, however, it became evident that the content of caucus discussions, which are always supposed to be in camera, was making its way into the press. Bennett berated the caucus and then suspended meetings for a matter of weeks. He did not miss them. Second, a stenographer's error once led Bennett to sign a letter to a Conservative backbencher's wife in which he expressed condolences over the death of her husband. The still very much alive MP was understandably miffed that the prime minister had not even noticed him in the House or at the caucus meeting earlier that day. Third, and most significantly, francophone MPS grew increasingly unhappy with the fact that caucus meetings were held exclusively in English. Many Quebec MPS came to see this tradition, when coupled with there only being three francophone cabinet ministers (Minister of Marine Alfred Duranleau, Solicitor General Maurice Dupré, and Post Master General Arthur Sauvé), as Bennett's failing to value Quebec opinion.[74]

In treating backbenchers as there to simply vote and do the cabinet's bidding on committees, Bennett evidently saw MPS as Trudeau did, nobodies when only yards from Parliament Hill. This perception led Bennett, like Trudeau, to miss a tremendous opportunity to exploit the talent that rested in his caucus while using MPS to hear and more thoroughly understand the thoughts and fears of Canadians.

Among the enormous powers of the prime minister is that of making appointments to Canada's bureaucracy. Those appointed to high-level positions in the many departments that comprise that sprawling organization know that a change of government often means a change in employment. A prime minister, after all, is naturally inclined to want to surround himself with senior civil servants who are not only highly skilled and efficient administrators, but who also share his vision—and whose loyalty both to him and that vision can be relied upon. It was Macdonald who once turned an associate down for a post when the man promised to support him when he thought he was right. Macdonald insisted that he needed men who would support him even when he was wrong. Those elite bureaucratic positions can also offer an effective way for a prime minister, who is also the party leader, to reward service.

Bennett was no different than any other new prime minister in that a number of political and personal appointments were made. Bill Herridge's appointment to serve as Canada's ambassador to the United States was, for instance, a blatant act of nepotism. Many years later, of course, Prime Minister Chrétien determined that his nephew Raymond was the best man for that coveted ambassadorship. It should be noted that both Herridge and Chrétien served with distinction.

But Bennett was not a blind partisan, filling every position with loyal Conservatives. He was quite willing to keep meritorious senior civil servants even if they had been appointed by the previous Liberal administration. An example can be seen in Bennett's decision to keep Oscar Skelton as undersecretary of state. Knocks against Skelton included first that he was a Liberal and second that he had been appointed by Mackenzie King. Skelton was, nonetheless, a well-respected scholar and was a Queen's University politics and economics professor when in 1925 he had become the undersecretary of state for external affairs. The post rendered him second in power only to the minister and he had served with distinction. Bennett later told Lester Pearson that he had intended to replace Skelton, but that after just a few weeks he had shown himself to be exceptionally capable and indispensable to the new administration. He had overlooked those other considerations and left him at his post.[75] Skelton served admirably until his death in 1941.

Pearson had left his position as a University of Toronto history professor to accept an appointment at the tiny Ministry of External Affairs in 1927. A small, fastidious, witty, highly intelligent man, Pearson, like Bennett, impressed those with whom he worked with his attention to detail, capacity for work, and ability to analyze and synthesize complex material. His mind was such that, much later, he won President John Kennedy's confidence with his encyclopedic knowledge of arcane baseball names and statistics. Pearson's time at External Affairs was a storied one, capped with a Nobel Peace Prize for his involvement in averting a third world war over the Suez Canal in 1956.

Pearson's position at External in the 1930s led him to work closely with both Mackenzie King and Bennett. This experience, coupled with his notorious integrity, renders him a credible judge of their characters and the manner in which they handled those in the bureaucracy. Pearson found Bennett good, and Mackenzie King a difficult man with whom to work. He reported that Mackenzie King would seldom be honest with those bringing him news he did not like and left civil servants unsure of themselves, their performance, or their security. Bennett, on the other hand, Pearson came to like as a man and trust as a prime minister. In his memoirs, Pearson related the story of Bennett once calling him to his office quite upset that the young bureaucrat had been responsible for the insertion of information in the Royal Commission on Grain Futures

Report that was both inaccurate and politically embarrassing. Bennett's famous temper was momentarily on display as he berated the young man for his error. When Pearson explained the situation and suggested somewhat bravely that the prime minister was wrong, Bennett heard him out then immediately apologized. The two moved on.

Pearson was impressed by Bennett's intelligence, directness, and willingness to admit error and to beg forgiveness from a subordinate. One of the tenets of strong leadership, after all, is to deflect all praise and absorb all blame. Pearson observed, "I got to know Bennett better than I had known Mr. King. . . . He was also an easier man to get to know. He was more out-going, more straight forward. . . . His storms were rough, but they were usually of short duration and often cleared the air . . . [Bennett] was a man of wide ranging interests, confident, and catholic in his expertise."[76] The two got on famously and Bennett had Pearson along on many of his foreign trips, allowing the two to enjoy each other's company on the long voyages across the Atlantic.

Bennett had his government—and that is what he called it: not "the" government but "his" government—in place. From childhood he had dreamt of being prime minister and now the dream had come true, but in the worst economic nightmare in the country's history. It was time for the action he had promised Canadians and for which he had been preparing his entire life.

CHAPTER FIVE

BLASTING HIS WAY

1930–1935

Fidel Castro once told a joke to explain why Cuba's economy disintegrated after the 1959 revolution. He said that he had told his advisers that he needed an economist. They thought he said he needed a communist and sent him Che Guevara.[1] There was a cautionary note in Castro's quip. That is, running a complex, modern, national economy is not for amateurs. While Bennett was a skilled and successful financial entrepreneur, businessman, and lawyer, he was not an economist. He had no experience in managing anything as complex as the Canadian economy at any time, let alone in a time of crisis. But there he was, both prime minister and finance minister, looking squarely into an economic morass that was becoming worse by the week.

Among the problems Bennett faced was a lack of specificity about the challenges he faced. In the fall of 1930 there was an absence of firm empirical data. Today, any teenager with a laptop has access to more detailed current economic data about her own country and others than the 1930s' best-informed economist. Imagine a prime minister today making economic decisions without the instant digital communications that have killed time, the satellite communications and televisions that have killed distance, and the daily polling that has killed instinct. Imagine a prime minister considering options without guidance from a large bureaucracy that can base advice upon detailed, up-to-the-second statistical analysis of the Canadian economy's various sectors and of even the most minor changes in foreign markets or policy shifts by other governments. Like his contemporaries, Bennett worked with the facts he had. But the facts available were, at best, guesses.

As an illustration of the fog in which Bennett had to operate, consider that before Statistics Canada, and even before the Labour Force Survey was created in 1945, information regarding unemployment was merely an estimate arrived at by collecting numbers from a few hundred businesses across the country. The Dominion Bureau of Statistics did the best it could to extrapolate patterns in the numbers and then declared regional and national unemployment rates and other financial trends. Because the data collection process was both time consuming and difficult, all economic statistics were released only once a year, in June. The numbers were obsolete the moment they were printed. Anecdotal evidence was far more reliable than the most carefully formulated data.

But no matter what method one used to reach conclusions about the problems Canadians were enduring, the conclusions were much the same. A slowly developing and distressing story was being told from one ocean to the other. The Great Depression was cruel. And it was not fair. It hit different parts of the country, different industries, and different people to different degrees, and in different ways. Women felt it more than men and ethnic minorities more than anyone. It proved that misery does not really like company after all.

For many Canadians, the Depression years were just fine. Those who managed to keep their jobs, even if hours or pay were reduced, benefited from low and in some cases plunging prices. From 1930 to 1934 there was an aggregate drop in retail prices of an astounding 24.8 per cent.[2] But everyone was affected.

In the history of every family whose story goes back to those years, there are tales that illuminate the depression era better than books or numbers. My grandfather, for instance, was one of the lucky ones. During the 1930s he had his hours cut but kept his job as a moulder in the Dofasco steel mill in gritty east end Hamilton. He purchased a two-storey brick home in a good working-class neighbourhood for just over $4,000. He spoke fondly of my grandmother and him going to dances every Saturday night for a dime and the places being packed with men in suits and women in long dresses enjoying the latest in big band and swing tunes. He even saw Dorsey. Bread was 4 cents. A glass of beer was a nickel.

But my grandfather also told me of walking home from work along the train tracks in order to fill his lunch pail with small chunks of coal to help heat their Houghton Street home. He told of a neighbour who also managed to hold his job but saw his hours and wages significantly reduced. One winter the man's picket fence slowly disappeared as it was brought inside, a few slats at a time, to feed the stove.

And closer to home, my home at least, one summer day two women came by saying that in the early 1930s the place had been theirs. They enjoyed the tour of the old house and related the story of their dad leaving home during the Depression to ride the rails and look for work. Their mother, meanwhile, dug up the entire backyard to plant vegetables to help feed her children. In the fall, though, the family was kicked out of their rented house because their mother had sought to augment her few meagre relief dollars by selling some of the vegetables at the local market. Someone turned them in for breaking the strict municipal relief rules. They were homeless.

No, the Depression was not fair. While many places in the country were hurt, the West was ravaged. Nowhere was it worse than Saskatchewan. The proud and hard-working people of that province were hit by a perfect storm of collapsing commodity prices and natural disaster. In 1928, the province produced 321.2 million bushels of wheat for a total value of $218 million. In 1931, total production had dropped to 132.4 million bushels and only $44.4 million. In 1929, Saskatchewan farmers earned $1.60 for a bushel of wheat, but by 1932 the price had fallen to 28 cents. It cost more than that to grow the stuff.

But Mother Nature had also weighed in. By the end of 1930 fully one-third of Saskatchewan was suffering from drought, a rust infestation, and a grasshopper plague. The Biblical swarms of locusts were so massive that when in flight they would blot out the sun in a buzzing, chomping, ravenous eclipse. Entire fields representing a year's work and investment would be devoured in minutes. One farmer told of the grasshoppers eating the leather belts, hoses, and seat from his tractor and another of them eating the corn bristles from a broom, leaving only gnawed hickory behind.[3]

And the rain stopped. The fields that had for decades drawn the desperate and adventurous from around the world—allowing them to fulfill their dreams while bringing forth harvests that had both built a country and fed millions—had turned to dust. The dark, rich soil became sand and blew away. Trains sometimes needed snow-removal equipment to move through blazing July afternoons. Duststorms were such that at midday people occasionally needed to switch on their headlights to navigate. There was a story told that one could tell how bad a duststorm was by throwing a gopher into the air. If it fell immediately to the ground then the storm was not so bad, but everyone was in for a mean one if he started digging a hole up there.

The joke was cute, but not for those who watched their dreams and those of their forebears vanish in a single season. In 1928, the net cash income per Saskatchewan farm was $1,614. This was good money at a time when the average per capita income in Canada in 1929 was only $471 and 60 per cent of male urban workers earned below $1,000. But by 1933 the average net income of a Saskatchewan farm had dropped to only $66. Banks stopped the traditional cycle of advancing money to buy seed with the bridge financing paid off in the fall. Companies selling fuel for machinery or coal for home heating began demanding cash on delivery. In many Saskatchewan municipalities more than 50 per cent of taxpayers were in arrears and as a result services were cut. With savagely reduced income and no one to buy their bonds, many prairie towns teetered on the edge of bankruptcy.

An argument regarding who had it worse was not worth winning, but Saskatchewan farmers could certainly have contested Maritime fishermen. The total value of all fish sold in the three Maritime provinces in 1928 was $19.8 million. In 1933, it had dropped nearly by half to $10.2 million. Meanwhile, the average annual income for the New Brunswick farm had dropped to a mere $20. That the people of the Maritimes had started poorer than the rest of the country and so their economic slide had, on percentage terms, not been as precipitous was of little comfort.

Companies as well as individuals suffered as the wheels of economic activity ground and slowed. Canada's economy, then as now, depended upon exports, and from 1929 to 1933 export prices on almost everything fell by an average of 40 per cent. It was a dreadful spiral: as prices dropped, production slowed, causing wages to fall and spending to decline, and around and down it went. The spiral was felt by nearly all companies. Let one tell the tale. The Ford Motor Company of Canada had sales of $45.8 million in 1930 but only $17.2 million in 1932. The company's declining sales led to reduced production and layoffs. The cuts rippled through small steel, tire, glass, base metals, and other companies that supplied Ford. At the same time, the myriad of service industries that were based partly on the wants and needs of the families who had worked for all those companies suffered.

These corporate and large and small business declines and collapses effected, and were affected by, tremors in the financial sector. Banks had begun to look at loans differently. Investment houses saw company after company losing millions as stock prices collapsed and shareholders received word that they would be earning no dividends for the first time in years. The manner in which stocks, shares, and bonds could be purchased on margin was ended. The unregulated financial structure of the postwar years, which had been based on avarice and starry-eyed assumptions, began to crumble as waves of causes and effects overlapped each other and drowned, even for companies whose fundamentals were sound.

Canada's gross national product (GNP) fell from $6.1 billion in 1929 to only $3.5 billion in 1933. The country's per capita income from 1929 to 1933 fell by 48 per cent. The unemployment rate from 1927 to 1929 was a low and consistent 3 per cent, but in 1931 it hit 30 per cent. Lawyers went hungry as fewer people divorced or bought houses or started businesses. Teachers and nurses took salary cuts. Doctors saw their incomes fall and many performed services for free or followed the practices of other professionals and began bartering.

Only 1,403 athletes competed in the 1932 Los Angeles Olympics, the fewest since 1904. Only thirty-seven countries could afford to send teams, nine fewer than four years before in Amsterdam. Even professional sport was affected. National Hockey League (NHL) players accepted a salary cap and teams agreed to cut their rosters to fourteen. The league shrank as previously successful franchises such as the Ottawa Senators folded.

In the summer of 1930, no one, including Bennett, could guess at the magnitude of the economic and social devastation that had just begun and would soon leave Canada scared, scarred, and tattered. The state was failing the nation. It was up to Bennett to make it right.

BENNETT TAKES CHARGE

The prime minister's office that Bennett proudly moved into was a large, dark oak-panelled room with a deep blue carpet and a large polished oak desk. When he settled himself behind that desk it was in the chair that Sir John had used in his Kingston and Toronto law practices and then as prime minister. Arthur Meighen, a keen amateur historian, had noticed the chair being taken to a dumpster during a redecoration of offices. He had saved the oak chair with the dark blue upholstery and presented it to Borden when he became prime minister in 1911. In July 1930, an amusing flurry of letters indicated that Borden, Meighen, and George Kingston of the Worker's Compensation Board all claimed ownership of the chair, although at the time it rested in Borden's library. The only thing all could agree upon was that they wished Bennett to have it.[4] An oddity in Bennett's office was a First World War German anti-aircraft gun that had been sent to him by a supporter, along with a box of live ammunition which he kept in a desk drawer. He took great delight in regaling all who asked with details about the gun's history and capability.

As Bennett stood gazing out the bank of windows over the wide expanse of the Parliament Hill lawn below, he could, of course, not know all that was befalling the country at that time or predict all that would soon and forever alter the lives of the people he had just earned the privilege to lead. But he knew that things were bad and getting worse, and that the country deserved something beyond the false optimism of King's wait-and-hope-for-the-best policies. Rather than waiting patiently for market forces, the very forces that had played an enormous role in causing the crisis in the first place, to eventually right things, it was time to begin the "blasting."

Action began when he recalled Parliament for a special session on September 8, 1930. New MPs barely had time to set up constituency offices before heading to Ottawa and once there found little time to even locate the washrooms. Bennett set a punishing pace and demanded a furious amount of work from his staff and government departments.

Parliament began with one of the more unusual speeches from the throne in Canadian history. There was no flowery language or partisan jabs. Bennett simply had twenty lines read into the record then got to work. He began the special session with words that could have been torn from the pages of his campaign stump speech. He promised to use the power of the state to provide relief, end unemployment, and increase trade through tariff manipulation. It was the strategy that Franklin Roosevelt would employ three years later: deal first with the human tragedy through immediate relief and attempts to spur employment, and then later restructure the relationship between the government and economy so as to prevent a similar crisis in the future.

The special session saw the passage of two important initiatives: the Unemployment Relief Act that sought to create jobs by shovelling money to Canadians in what would now be called a stimulus package; and amendments to existing customs and tariff laws that promised to promote business activity by protecting Canadian companies and increasing trade. The two were important in themselves but also for what they revealed about the new direction that Bennett was taking the country.

The relief bill came first. It pledged $20 million of direct aid for Canada's unemployed. While the amount seems tiny by twenty-first-century standards, it was indeed a large sum at a time when the annual federal budget was only about $500 million. Of significance is that until that point in Canadian history, helping those hurt by economic conditions had been the role of municipal and provincial governments, charity groups, and churches. The federal government had played no significant part. This legislation represented an important step in the evolution of the collective consensus suggesting that social welfare is the responsibility of the federal government.

In the politician's "handbook" *The Prince*, Machiavelli famously observed, "There is nothing more difficult to manage, or more doubtful of success, or more dangerous to handle than to take the lead in introducing a new order of things."[5] With the relief bill, Bennett was taking that risky leap and there were indeed dangers and challenges waiting to greet him. Among them was that the federal government's constitutional power to involve itself directly in such a program was questionable. The desperate straits in which each of the nine provinces found themselves led all to put those questions aside for the moment and take the money—but that acquiescence regarding federal intrusion into areas of provincial jurisdiction would not last. A related problem was that there was no mechanism in place to disperse the money. Borden's

Union government had budgeted nearly $2 million for financial support and job creation during the postwar recession. But Borden's bill had stipulated that the funds would be attached to infrastructure projects that the municipalities and provinces would choose, manage, and help to fund. While this spending created jobs, only 20 per cent of the allocated funds were reserved for direct relief to the most needy. Provincial governments had promised to use that 20 per cent to top up their already existing relief programs, but there was no oversight process to measure whether they actually used it as Borden had intended or, in fact, if they used it at all. Bennett ordered the creation of just such an oversight mechanism as he sought to ensure that the funds got from Ottawa into the pockets of the needy.

Besides being apprehensive about the money getting to where he wanted it to go, Bennett also worried about the enormity of expenditure. He did not want other levels of government or the Canadian people to surrender their own responsibilities or self-reliance. Further, he was concerned that the large outlay of money was throwing the federal budget into deficit. Consequently, the bill was clear in stating that the program was an emergency measure that would end when the economy recovered.

An Act to Amend the Customs Act, and An Act to Amend the Customs Tariff, were the special session's second and third pieces of legislation. The acts were designed to protect Canadian jobs by protecting Canadian companies. They represented bold action in raising some 130 tariffs on nearly every domestically manufactured item. The boost in tariff levels was the largest increase since Macdonald's National Policy in 1879. The acts also addressed the practice of many countries, especially the United States, that were dealing with overproduction and employment issues by dumping products into Canada at prices far below their true value, while at the same time raising tariffs to keep Canadian products out of their markets. Bennett defended the acts as not about blind protectionism, as some critics claimed, but rather about fairness to Canadian workers in a harsh and increasingly protectionist international economic environment. He also promised that the two acts were merely first steps in a greater overhaul of Canada's tariff and trade policies that he would introduce in the next session. Bennett predicted that the acts would create at least 25,000 new jobs.[6]

Beyond their significance as economic tools of recovery and progress, the acts represented the reversal of a trend that had seen Canada moving away from the emotional and historical links to Britain and toward closer ties to the United States. After Vimy Ridge and Passchendaele, and after Borden had secured Canada's place at the League of Nations, the country was seen, and saw itself, as moving from colony to nation. The trend continued in 1922, when Canada was asked by Britain to send troops to help with the trouble with the Turks at the seaport town of Chanak; for the first time the government said no. The 1923 Halibut Treaty saw Canada ink a fishing deal with the United States without Britain as co-signer—another first.

At the 1926 Imperial Conference, all of Britain's dominions had met to discuss the future of the empire in light of the new nationalist pride that was puffing chests, especially in South Africa, the Irish Free State, and Canada. With an eye to much of the Canadian electorate that, like Bennett, wore imperial ties to Britain as a badge of honour, Prime Minister Mackenzie King worked to ensure that while Canada became more sovereign, the word "independent" was struck nevertheless from the final declaration. Instead, each of the dominions was deemed autonomous and equal in status. In what became known as the Balfour Declaration, even Britain was confirmed to be equal to all others.

As an expression of Canada's growing independence, in 1926 Mackenzie King had bolstered the Department of External Affairs. Acting as his own Secretary of State for External Affairs, he worked with the brilliant Oscar Skelton to oversee the creation of a diplomatic corps, the expansion of the Canadian High Commission Office in London, and the establishment of embassies, beginning with Paris and Washington.

Accompanying the country's slow drift from Britain was the equally slow slide toward America. A number of American branch plants had been established or expanded in the 1920s and their fingers were reaching ever deeper into the Canadian economy. In 1922, American investment in Canada surpassed British investment. By the end of the decade, 68 per cent of Canada's imports came from the United States, and Americans bought 46 per cent of Canadian exports. Further, American unions were organizing in the quickly developing Canadian manufacturing plants.

The growing influence of the United States was also felt in social spheres. American styles were pouring over the border as young Canadian women dressed like flappers and Canadian families listened to American jazz and radio plays. Canadians flocked to see American vaudeville stars. At the new movie houses they laughed at the antics of Chaplin and Keaton and commiserated with the latest hardships of compelling characters created by Toronto-born Mary Pickford, who had ironically been dubbed America's Sweetheart. American magazines flooded the Canadian market and many Canadian newspapers relied on the American foreign wire service as their eyes to the world.

The combination of these two trends—toward greater Canadian sovereignty and independence from Britain, and an unconscious surrendering to the American sphere of influence—presented significant challenges for Canada. Britain unwittingly made the shift easier by making itself increasingly difficult to deal with. In the decade following the war, the country ripped through six governments and struggled with its own foreign and economic policies.[7] Unfortunately, Canada's relations weren't any easier with its neighbours to the south. If dealing with Britain was growing tougher, substantive interaction with the United States was becoming nearly impossible.

In 1922, a protectionist and isolationist American Congress had fashioned the Fordney-McCumber Act. It raised tariffs and promoted a "Buy America" policy. America's trading partners reacted by raising tariffs on American goods. Germany and Italy, for instance, raised tariffs on American wheat so high as to effectively end its importation, while France stopped the automobile trade by raising its tariff to 100 per cent. Canada, meanwhile, raised tariffs on products affecting 30 per cent of its American trade.

The actions and reactions were punishing and self-defeating but there was more to come. In the spring of 1929, Oregon Republican congressman Willis Hawley and Utah Republican senator Reed Smoot weaved the Hawley-Smoot Tariff Act through Congress. The act, which quadrupled tariffs imposed on over 20,000 imported goods, was protectionism personified. Thirty-four countries, including Canada, had sent letters of protest to President Herbert Hoover during the debate, and each had erected even higher tariff and non-tariff barriers to block the importation of American products. On June 17, 1930, two months before Bennett became prime minister, Hoover had signed the act to show that he was doing something about the Depression. The "beggar-thy-neighbour" policies adopted by all industrialized countries in reaction to Fordney-McCumber and Hawley-Smoot saw an astonishing two-thirds reduction in world trade from 1929–1933. Canada's foreign trade, the basis of its financial prosperity, was to drop in those years by 65 per cent.

It was in this poisoned atmosphere, stuck between the closing doors of both Britain and the United States, that Bennett had campaigned for prime minister and promised to blast Canada's way into foreign markets, and then enacted the amendments to the customs and tariffs acts. On a personal level, Bennett made no secret of his love of all things British. As prime minister, he brought to the office a realistic assessment that if Canada was to fight the Depression through increasing trade, the only option was to pursue a closer trade relationship with Britain. The American actions had left few other options.

In an interview with *Maclean's* magazine in 1931, Bennett responded to those who accused him of American-style protectionism by reminding Canadians of his promise to deal with trade in order to tackle the depression. He said that if the new tariffs were ". . . giving Canadians an equality of opportunity with others who are building up their country to enable us to build up our Dominion, and to give fair competition to the worker in Canada, be it a man or woman, then it is protection that we propose."[8]

The special session ended with the bills passed easily by the large Conservative majority. While there had been perfunctory debate, few in the Opposition had done much to challenge the bills. Finally, it appeared, something was being done. In his speeches in the House and in comments later to reporters, the prime minister urged patience while the measures worked their way through the economy and slowly brought about their desired effects.

Despite the challenges and thanklessness of leadership Bennett was enjoying himself as prime minister. Stress and hard work were things that he had been used to for years and the sacrifices demanded by the job fit perfectly with his sincere belief in public service. As he noted in an

October 1931 speech, "I am not interested in politics. I am here as Prime Minister today, and I may be gone tomorrow! I don't care! Life has given me about everything a man can desire. I am sixty-one, old enough to sit back and enjoy what I have. But what I have, I owe in a considerable degree to Canada, and if I can do anything for Canada, that is what I want to do. When the Canadian people are finished with my services, I am also content."[9]

Bennett's cheerfulness was on display one sunny afternoon as he strolled along Wellington Street on his way from the Rideau Club back to his office with Herridge and two other colleagues. He was stopped by a First World War veteran named Hill, who was selling Legion raffle tickets and obviously did not recognize his prime minister. Bennett asked where Hill had served and when told asked if he had ever met General Stewart, who commanded the corps. Hill was surprised at the stranger's knowledge, and Bennett smiled upon realizing that the man had no idea who he was. When Bennett revealed his identity, Hill just laughed and said he did not believe him. Hill insisted that he had seen the prime minister's picture in the newspaper and he was certainly not him. It was then Bennett and Herridge's turn to share a laugh. Bennett reached into his pocket, purchased tickets, and then gave them back to Hill with a wish for luck on the draw. Hill's story made it to the *Ottawa Citizen* with his observation that Bennett was ". . . very nice, laughing and joking all the time."[10]

Short walks such as that remained his only form of exercise while he continued to eat like two men and work like three. Despite his vigour and the joy which he brought to his work, he admitted to more than one correspondent that there were times when he grew quite tired.[11] He was to become more tired still as he prepared for his first foreign trip as prime minister.

THE LONDON CONFERENCE

Bennett sailed for England on September 22, 1930, immediately following the end of Parliament's special session. With him were Mildred and her new husband, Bill Herridge. Minister of Justice Hugh Guthrie and minister of trade and commerce, the omnipresent Harry Stevens, were also there, along with a tiny contingent of aides and advisers including Lester Pearson. The ever-grumbling Quebec wing of the Conservative caucus grumbled some more over the fact that no one in the small group spoke French.

Bennett travelled first-class and enjoyed a large stateroom and sumptuous meals. He walked the deck each day for exercise, read, and engaged in lively discussions with those in his party and often with others he met aboard. Never really isolated, even at sea, Bennett sent and received cables dealing with government issues as well as personal and business affairs. He was in constant contact with Alice Millar who, in his absence, was afforded wide latitude in handling a good deal of his personal and business matters. She often merely reported to Bennett on actions she had taken on his behalf. The trust Bennett place in Millar seemed to have no bounds. But to him she was always Miss Millar and to her he was Mr. Bennett. There was never even the hint of a crack in their professional formality.

Britain had arranged the conference two years earlier, in 1928. It was to be part of the process of affording greater independence to its dominions through negotiating what was to become the Statute of Westminster. Despite the progress that had been made by Borden and then Mackenzie King in codifying and deepening Canada's independence, there was much left to be done. In order to end Britain's legal ability to legislate for Canada, for instance, the Colonial Laws Validity Act needed to be repealed. The act had been passed by the British Parliament in 1865 and was meant to ensure that laws passed by a colonial government were consistent with British laws, while at the same time ensuring that Parliament still had the power to legislate within its dominions. The law was clever; it allowed for self-rule while keeping the British Parliament supreme. Canadian provincial governments liked the Validity Act because it restricted the Canadian federal government's power. The premiers were unanimous, therefore, in the opinion that the Validity Act be retained. Bennett knew, of course, that it had to go if Canada was to join with the other dominions in the next step toward independence.

Bennett's willingness to ignore the desires of the provinces and to exert federal power in order to accomplish what he deemed best for the country would place him in league with other centrist prime ministers such as Macdonald and Trudeau. Macdonald's view of federal-provincial relations was seen in his locating the predominance of state power with the federal government and in his willingness to disallow provincial legislation. Further, when provincial premiers set up what was to be the country's first federal-provincial conference, Macdonald simply refused to attend. Trudeau fought the provinces throughout his tenure. He later criticized Mulroney's Meech Lake and Charlottetown Accords' constitutional amendments as reducing the power of the federal government and bolstering that of the provinces, leaving Ottawa to be nothing more than a head waiter catering to their whims. Bennett would have agreed.

The clauses and language of the Statute of Westminster were eventually hammered out, with Bennett playing an important role. His influence was unsurprising given his knowledge of constitutional law and that he was the first minister of the largest and richest dominion. When the statute was finally ratified in 1931, it granted the dominions full extraterritorial jurisdiction. No Parliament within the Commonwealth could pass legislation that would have any constitutional legality in any other dominion—including Britain.

Many analysts at the time and since have declared that the Statute of Westminster was of such significance that it would be more appropriate to celebrate 1931 as Canada's birth rather than 1867. But the statute's Section 4 still allowed for British laws to become legal in a dominion if that dominion approved. Further, upon returning to Canada, Bennett found premiers unanimous in their opposition to the Statute and the death of the Colonial Laws Validity Act. Bennett knew that he needed the support of the premiers to battle the Depression and so sought to put a favour in the bank by asking Britain for a special Canadian exemption. The British Parliament acceded and created an amendment in the Statute of Westminster allowing that nothing in the document could supersede any agreements made since 1867 between the Canadian provinces and the federal government with respect to minority rights. At little real cost Bennett had allowed constitutional progress to proceed while calming the always choppy federal-provincial waters that could have swamped that progress.

Something that would come back to haunt Bennett was that the Statute of Westminster allowed London's Judicial Committee of the Privy Council to retain its power to overrule Canada's Supreme Court. In the late 1920s, concerns had been raised by many in the Canadian legal community regarding the belief that the statute would mean nothing without a provision that rendered the Canadian Supreme Court Canada's actual court of last resort. Bennett found no support for such an idea among his dominion colleagues, however, and so the idea was not tested at the conference.

Another reason that the statute did not do all that some claimed it had done was that the power to amend the BNA Act remained with the British Parliament. Again, Bennett measured the political price that would be paid in terms of federal-provincial relations for even mentioning the issue at the conference and remained silent. Only Pierre Trudeau's audacious actions that led to the 1982 repatriation of the constitution dealt with that last vestige of colonialism.

Even given these reservations, however, Bennett's negotiating skills and political acumen moved Canada along the road toward fuller constitutional independence—but not too far and not too quickly. His accomplishment is even more impressive when one considers that, at the same time as he was negotiating delicate constitutional and imperial changes, he was also trying to get Britain and the other dominions to come to Ottawa for a conference devoted to establishing a Commonwealth trade preference arrangement.

Before recessing Parliament, Bennett had assured the House and his cabinet that he was sincere and steadfast in his belief that with the United States shutting its doors, new trade and tariff arrangements with Britain and other Commonwealth members offered the best avenue to renewed prosperity. He would, therefore, pursue them with vigour. He sincerely believed that only this form of action would protect Canadian industries from American protectionism and from the prices of American goods that were lower due to the economies of scale present in an economy ten times Canada's size. Canada had to secure markets for its commodities and manufactured goods while Canadian businesses that extracted, grew, or made them were protected from unfair international competition. The playing field needed to be levelled. It was Macdonald's idea being stirred back to life to meet new circumstances in an old way. The core of the old National Policy was being resurrected by another prime minister who was thoroughly convinced that an activist, progressive government using the full power of the state was the only vehicle through which economic prosperity could be created then protected.

Bennett's idea initially received a cool reception from conference delegates. Britain, for one, wanted something completely different. It was keen on having all of the dominions agree to another conference, but only to discuss the idea of a common defence plan. Bennett had to be quite careful to avoid being drawn into agreeing to such a conference or even to engaging in any in-depth discussion of the plan. He believed it would be bad for Canada, possibly entangling it in wars. At the same time, however, he had to promote the idea of the trade conference. The problem left him sitting taciturn through long deliberations when the notion of a common defence was being discussed. He was careful to commit to nothing.

One evening he was back at his hotel after a full day of talks about the common defence idea and grew angry when reading the minutes of the day's sessions. He found that they reported his support for the establishment of a committee to investigate the idea of imperial defence and stated that Canada wished to be a member. He dashed off a note to committee secretary Maurice Hankey, stating unequivocally that Canada would never join and that the minutes were wrong in suggesting that he had agreed upon Canada's membership. He demanded that the minutes be amended and, even more, that his and Herridge's names be stricken from the record so that it would appear that Canada was not even there.[12]

Meanwhile, Bennett and his team continued to work the backrooms to sell the notion that a pan-Commonwealth trade alliance was in everyone's interest. Herridge proved especially adept at such meetings and he impressed Bennett. Herridge met delegates in lounges, over coffee, in their rooms, and just before and after formal meetings. When comparing notes each evening, the two were pleased to see momentum gathering for Bennett's idea. The negotiations progressed sufficiently well that Bennett felt confident enough to address the plenary session. He said, "I offer to the Mother Country and to all other parts of the Empire, a preference in the Canadian market in exchange for a like preference in theirs."[13] It was a bold challenge that caught all, especially Britain, by surprise in its being offered so openly. However, before the conference ended, Bennett had secured an agreement from every dominion that they would attend an economic conference in Ottawa dealing exclusively with imperial trade. Britain was left with no option but to concede. It was agreed that Bennett would organize the conference and then chair it.

That Bennett had distinguished himself at the Imperial Conference was seen in the fact that he was the only dominion prime minister asked to address the British people on the BBC. Of course, one can never ignore the influence of Beaverbrook in setting up such an appealing opportunity for his friend. Bennett jumped at the chance.

He began the radio address with some pleasant comments about English hospitality and the accomplishments of the conference, but quickly turned to the crux of his message. He spoke of the importance of a new imperial trade arrangement that would benefit the people of Britain as well as those in her dominions. Like a patient lawyer laying his case before a suspicious jury, he began with emotion. He acknowledged those who, due to the Statute of Westminster, feared the disintegration of old imperial ties. He then argued that trade and tariff agreements would be one way among many to ensure that those ties would never be broken.

Bennett then moved to facts and spoke of the possibility of a 10 per cent tariff on all goods to all countries outside the Commonwealth, but low or no tariffs at all on goods traded within. Bennett used wheat as an example. He spoke of the importance of wheat to the Canadian economy, explaining that wheat prices and sales were plummeting due to the recovery of European crops and the dumping of massive amounts of wheat and other food products on the world market by the Soviet Union. Many Commonwealth countries, especially Australia, he said, shared the Canadian farmers' pain. A preferential Commonwealth tariff system would address the same pain felt by their brethren in lands around the world. But, he argued, Britain should never do something simply to help its Commonwealth partners without also helping itself. The preferential trade agreement would only work, and Britain should only accept it, if it was mutually beneficial. Bennett said, "But if there is an agreement, inspired by sentiment, and buttressed by definite, and lasting and mutual advantages, then it will not fail, for it will be our common wish, and for the benefit of each and all, to support and sustain it."[14]

Without polling, as would be an inevitable follow-up to such a speech today, it is impossible to gauge the reaction of his audience. However, Bennett's ideas had been bandied about at the conference, and he had more fully elucidated them with his radio address. They were well understood by members of the British public and cabinet. Cabinet secrecy being as it is, no one knows for sure what exactly was said at Westminster. But with leaks being as common over the pond as they are here, then as now, it became widely known that at least one British cabinet minister, Dominion Secretary James Henry Thomas, derided Bennett's trade ideas as humbug. Whether that characterization represented cabinet consensus is not known. Regardless, the squabbling family was coming to Ottawa and that was all that mattered.

With the Imperial Conference over and the address completed, Bennett was free to enjoy London. It was late October and the weather was grand. He did some sightseeing and enjoyed multi-course dinners with some of London's movers and shakers. He went shopping with Mildred, who helped him to choose some fine silk hosiery and a dapper new pinstriped suit. This was the second clothes-shopping expedition the two had embarked upon. On their first, they purchased a formal suit for Bennett to wear when, on October 17, he was sworn in as a member of the King's Privy Council. Mildred had been on his arm.

Mildred was also there for the launching of the *Skeena*, a destroyer built for the small Canadian navy. She was given the honour of smashing a large bottle of champagne over the hull, gleefully splashing the Thorneycroft yards. Bennett was the guest of honour at the Cutlers' Feast in Sheffield, Yorkshire, and later donned cap and gown to receive honorary doctorates from the University of Edinburgh, Queen's in Belfast, and Dublin's Trinity College. He also managed to hop the channel to be deeply moved by a visit to the Vimy battlefield and several Canadian cemeteries.

Bennett returned to Canada pleased with all that he had accomplished in London. At a federal-provincial conference that Bennett convened in April 1931, the premiers expressed disappointment in the end of the Colonial Laws Validity Act, but supported his refusing to even discuss imperial defence. A joint press release also stated that Bennett had been right in leaving issues such as the Supreme Court, repatriation, and an amending formula for another day. While all seemed pleased, no one's smile was quite as wide as that of Quebec's premier Louis-Alexandre Taschereau, who had been more vocal than the others in warning Bennett, before he had even set sail for the conference, about the importance of respecting provincial rights and responsibilities.[15] In refusing to entertain some ideas to which the premiers objected, Bennett had maintained federal-provincial peace not so much for what he did but rather for what he had decided not to do. Further, meeting with premiers before he left, and then again on his return, had paid dividends. It helped maintain, if not the peace, then at least a temporary ceasefire.

While he was away, Bennett had read reports and received briefings from staff. Upon his return he heard more dispiriting stories from caucus and Opposition members regarding the growing despair felt by more and more Canadians. His perception about just how dark the skies had become was also shaped by the thousands of Canadians who wrote directly to their prime minister explaining their lot, pleading for help, or venting their rage. The letters are fascinating. There were hundreds of them over the years but a few tell the tale of a time when ordinary Canadians saw their prime minister differently than they do today and where contact was still not just possible but seemed natural.

A woman from Rose Bay, Lunenburg, Nova Scotia, sent the prime minister four small wool mats, explaining that she was making and sending them to people in the hope that they would return $7 to help feed her family. She had confidence in Bennett, she wrote, as it had been written in a Halifax paper that he was a good man who helped ordinary people out in small ways. Bennett sent Mrs. Risser a handwritten thank-you note and $7.[16] A gentleman named W. W. Phelps from Port Hope, Ontario, wrote saying that he had terrific maple syrup. Bennett wrote back with an order for 3 gallons, which Phelps gladly sent along to Ottawa in return for Bennett's cheque for $2.[17]

These warm responses were the norm, but to some Bennett revealed his thin skin and sarcastic wit. For example, radical labour leader and communist A. E. Smith wrote to take exception to several points Bennett had made in a recent speech. Bennett replied, in part, "I am sorry you feel my address open to so severe a criticism. . . . I fear that your prejudices somewhat obscure your vision, but at any rate I appreciate you have written me, for a word of condemnation to a public man is not unusual and to receive praise from you would probably be a shock."[18]

Many other letters told of the Depression's appalling toll. From an unemployed Edmonton accountant came a plea for a job as an income tax auditor. The fraught husband and father wrote, "I have come to the end of my resources, my daughter lies dangerously ill in hospital with spinal meningitis, my wife has [had] a nervous breakdown and my little son is getting no care. I must get an appointment. My last court of appeal is to you. . . ."[19] A man had held a job with the Manitoba Telephone System since high school graduation but was suddenly let go. He wrote to his prime minister,

> . . . I have been unemployed for 26 months and am married and have three children all sick ages 4 years, 2 ½ years and 14 months. We have lost our home, furniture and all. . . . On the 20th of February the city of Winnipeg refused to give me further assistance . . . the result is that we have had many a hungry day since then and now the landlord has placed us upon the Street and that is where I am now with my family. . . . We are hungry, tired and desperate and cannot hold out any longer . . .[20]

The times were such that nearly all personal letters were hand written. Some would apologize for having letters typed, as they appeared colder and less personal. It was a time when correspondents would beg forgiveness and sign off as humble servants. And it was a time of wrenching desperation. Many who touched Bennett's heart would find a $5 bill slipped into the envelope with his response. Most letters were respectful in tone. But then there were others. A Sudbury man wrote, "Since you have been elected, work has been imposible (*sic*) to get. We have decided that in a month from this date, if thing's are the same, We'll skin you alive, the first chance we get."[21] The letter reflects the frustration felt by those who watch their dreams evaporate, their pride shrivel, and their families hurt by an enemy they cannot see. Many people reacted by seeking someone to blame. By the end of 1931 it was becoming evident that, for many, Bennett was serving as that someone. As prime minister, he was responsible for the amorphous ghosts that caused the problems plaguing them, their family, their community, and their country.

The Liberal press was only too happy to present Bennett as the focus of all anger and blame. This tendency was seen, for instance, in the *Winnipeg Free Press*, which hammered Bennett on a nearly daily basis with critical editorials and the withering wit of Arch Dale's cartoons. In September, a Dale cartoon had shown Bennett with his suitcase, indicating that he was off to London, but hopping over an enormous wall inscribed with the words "high tariff."[22] A November cartoon showed French customs officials looking with dismay as a ship's porter wheels a large barrel of blasting powder to their wicket, followed by a pompous-looking Bennett striding down the gangplank.[23]

It was not just the Liberal press that was harsh. Relations between Bennett and the entire press corps were cold at best and he sometimes said things that dropped the temperature even further. One afternoon, Bennett was sparring in the House with Mackenzie King over having been misquoted in the press. Bennett said that too often one newspaper would make an error in something he said and then other papers would reprint the error until finally what people were reading had little to do with what was originally stated. With respect to the instance to which Mackenzie King was specifically referring, Bennett said, he was pleased that the remarks were made on the radio as the reporter's interpretation of his words could be corrected by all the others who had actually heard him. He noted the example as proving the extraordinary value of radio.[24]

No member opposite, many of whom had probably been misquoted from time to time themselves, thought to take him up on his comment. However, it ignited an indignant firestorm in the press. Reporters claimed to be insulted. A number of editorials slammed what they said was his attack on the veracity of the press. Bennett received letters and telegrams asking him to retract his statement. He ignored them.

Eight months later, Bennett was having lunch in the Château Laurier with the Liberal's Senate Opposition leader after having heard Dr. Herbert Tory address a meeting of the League of Nations Society. A reporter from the *Ottawa Citizen* overheard Bennett repeating his preference for radio, saying again that newspapers often missed the main points of his speeches. The bold scribe approached the table and asked the prime minister exactly what he would write about the speech they had all just heard. Bennett smiled, snatched the young man's pencil and pad and whipped off three paragraphs that summarized what Tory had said. He then returned the items and with a laugh dared him to print exactly what he had just written. The reporter thanked the prime minister and the next day's paper had Bennett's words just as he had written them. The *Citizen* bragged about having in their temporary employ a very distinguished journalist indeed.[25]

Another bright spot in the normally dark press coverage of Bennett and his administration came when Robert Borden composed and released to the press a long letter supporting the government's fiscal and trade policies. He argued that the policies were not new, but had been Bennett's and the Conservative Party's for over twenty-five years. They were based upon a desire to build Canadian prosperity while promoting trade, and support the Empire while building Canadian independence. The letter concluded with praise for Bennett's dedication to duty and with an acknowledgement that the former prime minister had known the current holder of that office for nearly three decades and had admired him from their first meeting.[26] It was welcome praise from a still-respected figure. But it was about the only positive note being sung about Bennett as Canadians waited for the economic improvement that he had promised. Their resentment toward him grew every day that the turnaround failed to materialize.

As the snows melted and the birds returned, Bennett continued to urge Canadians to wait for the changes he had made thus far to have their desired effect. But a great number of factors had conspired to take the economy further into depression than anyone had anticipated. The prairies continued to be hardest hit. The conditions were such that the three prairie wheat pools teetered on bankruptcy. The year before, pools had guaranteed farmers one dollar a bushel, but the price had since plummeted to only 57 cents. The pools borrowed several times to make up the difference, but finally banks refused to extend more credit and provincial governments found their coffers empty. If the pools failed, the entire western wheat and grain industry would collapse. While farmers suffered, more and more workers found factory gates locked, more miners saw hours cut, and more fishermen decided their catches were not worth catching.

Parliament was called back into session in March 1931. The Throne Speech was a longer affair this time and promised more action to deal with what for the first time was admitted to be a depression. The speech promised, and then the House soon began to debate, a number of new tariff initiatives designed to battle it. The most significant raised tariffs and laws involving automobiles. Taxes were raised on large luxury cars and it was made illegal to import used cars from the United States for sale in Canada. Also of significance to mining areas of the country—

especially Cape Breton and other areas where most homes were heated and factories powered by coal—were tariffs raised significantly on imported coal, while subsidies were given to domestic producers.

The session saw Bennett struggling with an alarming fiscal crisis. The deficit for 1931–1932 would end up at $114 million, and the next year it would rise to $221 million. In 1933–1934, the last full year of Bennett's administration, it was reduced to $134 million. The numbers are laughably low to modern observers used to measuring government accounts in the billions, but they were startling at the time. Bennett worried that while stimulative, the fiscal imbalance would erode Canada's reputation abroad and ultimately slow the rate of recovery.[27] The troubling situation was rendered much more difficult as revenues continued to fall, expenditures continued to rise, and most costs remained fixed. The annual payments to war pensions, for instance, were $46 million and could not be lowered or postponed. Bennett was left with the Gordian knot conundrum of hating deficits but needing to spend.

With the 1931–32 budget, Bennett attempted to minimize the deficit through reducing expenditures by $37 million. All departments were cut. Federal government civil servants' pay was reduced by 10 per cent and the size of the bureaucracy was trimmed by eliminating all part-time jobs and vacant positions. All existing programs were examined to find inefficiencies that might lead to cost-saving changes. For instance, some direct payments to farmers such as the wheat bonus, which had never really worked as intended, were eliminated. Further, the position of comptroller of the treasury was created and afforded the power to oversee all expenditures and to report on waste.

Bennett also addressed the other side of the ledger by imposing tax increases. He raised corporate taxes rates from 8 per cent to 10 per cent. In 1932, they were raised again to 11 per cent, then in 1933 to 12.5 per cent. The sales tax that corporations paid went from 1 per cent to 4 per cent, then in 1932 to 6 per cent.

As part of his efforts to address the growing fiscal problems, Bennett had Sir George Perley, as deputy prime minister, write to the premiers announcing reductions in relief transfers. The letter explained that the improving conditions of the economy made the move advisable, but the premiers were not fooled. To the expected backlash, Bennett explained that in future budgets he might have to further reduce the amount that the federal government contributed to relief. He said that he needed to be responsible with the peoples' money and that the provinces should endeavour to do the same. The premiers saw Bennett's action for what it was: the old trick of the federal government attempting to bring its books into balance by downloading fiscal responsibilities to the provinces. Premiers would recognize the trick again in the 1990s when Finance Minister Paul Martin promised to defeat the deficit come hell or high water and forced them to deal with both.

Although the ideas of John Maynard Keynes had been growing increasingly well known and more widely accepted for years beforehand, the Cambridge-educated economist would not write his seminal book, *The General Theory of Employment, Interest and Money*, until 1936. The book changed economics with its radical new idea that at a time of economic crisis governments needed to use the fiscal tools at their disposal and ramp up spending, going into deficit if necessary, to increase demand, spur inflation, and promote business activity.[28] Bennett's policies of accepting deficit financing while promoting interventionalist economic and social policies were ahead of their time in that they reflected Keynes's ideas. But, like his contemporaries, Bennett could never completely escape his pre-Keynesian fear of temporary stimulative deficits.

While he tried to ensure that the deficit would be no higher than absolutely necessary, Bennett did take a number of initiatives that showed he was a pioneer in moving Canada into the brave new Keynesian world. For instance, he tried to stop the bleeding in the agricultural sector. First, he appointed John McFarland as general manager of the Central Selling Agency, responsible for handling all wheat pool transactions. Second, he guaranteed lenders that the federal government would underwrite all wheat pool loans. The crisis abated and the farmers got their money. But the federal government's budget, already tough to manage, was suddenly tied directly to the world price of wheat, and that price continued to fall. As it fell, borrowing became necessary to keep the whole scheme afloat. It was all a tremendous gamble. McFarland proved indispensable in managing the complexity involving domestic and foreign supply and demand. He was an intelligent and prudent administrator who had been the president of Bennett's Alberta Pacific Grain Company and a friend. Few criticized the cronyism of the appointment, though, for McFarland did a brilliant job. While prices remained low, at least there was some salvation when the constipated financial pipelines opened and wheat was planted, harvested, and sold. If only he could have made it rain.

Spring also saw Bennett overseeing a number of new initiatives designed to battle unemployment. Among them was a public works program. The idea had come from a number of meetings in which Bennett had sought advice from many quarters. Cabinet had finally agreed that with the increase in the world price of gold, the federal government could afford to increase the number of dollars in circulation without causing dangerous runaway inflation or a collapse of the dollar. Besides, it was decided that with deflation having such a negative effect on the economy, the infusion of capital would artificially create a situation in which prices could recover and potentially spur growth. Money was used to hire companies to do work on roads, bridges, buildings, docks, and more. One project, for instance, involved the building of a waist-high stone wall around the Governor General's property. Bennett's initiatives employed Keynesian tactics and programs similar to those for which Franklin Roosevelt would later earn great praise.

Bennett also amended the Unemployment Relief Act, which had been passed during the special session only months before, so that the federal government would pay half rather than a third of the cost of infrastructure programs involving the four western provinces. Another $8 million in direct relief payments was also arranged and was soon on its way to the suffering people of the West. Meanwhile, by March the price of wheat had dropped to only 39 cents a bushel. Bennett promised a 5-cent-a-bushel federal subsidy for all farmers. It was a desperate gambit meant to help a desperate people.

Bennett also acted to fulfill a campaign pledge in making changes to what had been a totally inadequate old-age pension system. Payments went slightly up and qualifications were altered so that, unlike previously, nearly everyone was eligible at age seventy. Because other provinces had not and still did not partner with the feds to support the idea, the plan involved only Ontario and the four western provinces. Months later, when one at a time provincial governments declared trouble meeting their pension obligations, Bennett arranged to increase the federal government's portion of the payments from 50 per cent to 75 per cent. He also altered the manner in which the money was transferred, getting it to them move quickly. Two years later, PEI signed on and the next year seniors in Nova Scotia welcomed cheques that offered a little more dignity to their retirement years. Too many seniors still lived with too little money, but even a small candle is welcomed to a dark room.

SAVING THE RAILWAYS

Both a symptom and a cause of the worsening economic conditions were the dire straits in which the railways found themselves. The railway has a romantic and mystical place in Canada's ethos. Macdonald claimed with some justification that without the line to the Pacific, British Columbia would not have joined Confederation and the Americans would have claimed the West. From Pierre Berton's inspirational books to Gordon Lightfoot's towering "Canadian Railroad Trilogy," the railways are a part of Canada's culture. They reflect her strength, vision, and determined effort to audaciously forge a country against overwhelming odds. Even those untouched by the railway's romantic allure cannot help but respect its presence and power. The 1896–1897 Crow's Nest Pass Agreement set rates and a formula for reviewing them that played a significant role in determining prices, products, and lifestyles for the whole country. From the late nineteenth century, railways were enormously important to anyone seeking to understand and develop the Canadian economy.

The 1920s were a time of exploding expansion for both Canadian railways. The Canadian National Railway had been owned by the government since the First World War, while the Canadian Pacific Railway was privately owned. Both were seduced by the decade's frenzied prosperity and expanded services and laid track to handle more freight and entice more passengers. Both saw revenues rise. The CNR built luxurious hotels, purchased ships, and expended borrowed capital on money-losing passenger services. The CPR followed suit with hotels such as the Château Laurier, Banff Springs, and more, while burning through even greater piles of money by extending lines and services of its own. The CPR, for instance, hosted fun but loss-leader music and folk art festivals to attract guests to its hotels. And the money kept piling up. In the heady years of the 1920s, the CNR saw, for the first and only time, two years in which it earned enough profit to pay more than just the interest on the debt it had been carrying since its inception.

Richard Bedford Bennett, in Hopewell Cape, age seven. (National Archives C-003867)

Bennett's beloved sister, Mildred. (Glenbow na-1351-5)

Upon being elected to the Alberta provincial legislature, in March 1909.
(Glenbow na-861-1)

Conservative Party representative, Calgary, 1911. (Glenbow na-3171-2)

Lord Beaverbrook and Bennett tour the Canadian barracks during an official visit to London and the battlefields of France in 1915. (National Archives PA-022714)

Bennett and Prime Minister Borden speak with a member of the Scottish Highlanders during a tour of London and the battlefields of France in 1915.

(Glenbow na-1135-60)

Entering the Conservative Party convention with Arthur Meighen, October 10, 192
(National Archives C-023539)

Prime Minister Bennett surrounded by members of the Cabinet, speaking by
telephone to Sir George Perley at the British Empire Trade Fair at Buenos Aires,
March 1931. (National Archives C-009076)

With President Roosevelt at the White House, April 1933. (National Archives C000198)

Prime Minister Bennett and long-time rival William Lyon Mackenzie King at a ceremony celebrating the centennial of the incorporation of the City of Toronto, March 6, 1934. (National Archives PA-148532)

On the campaign trail with Mildred, 1935. (National Archives C-021528)

A campaign stop at the Red Cross hospital in Calgary, Alberta, 1935.

(Glenbow NA-3087-7)

Speaking at the Calgary Highlanders' dinner, on January 3, 1939, as part of his farewell tour. (Glenbow na-2362-51)

Bennett's new home at Mickleham, Surrey, circa 1940. (Glenbow na-4507-3)

An official portrait completed on June 23, 1941, after receiving his peerage and becoming Viscount Bennett of Mickleham, Calgary, and Hopewell.

(National Archives e000756538)

But the onset of the Depression and the concomitant reduction in passengers and freight hurt both overextended companies. As happened with corporations in the late 1970s and again in the early years of the twenty-first century, the easy money and unprecedented profits had hidden the gaping cracks in poorly thought through business plans, inefficient management styles, and profligate compensation packages. Good luck had been confused with brains. Clarity began to emerge when gross revenue for the two dropped 17 per cent from 1929 to 1930.[29] Of the two the CNR was on shakier ground and forecasted a deficit of $70 million in 1932, with predicted losses in 1933 of an astronomical $1 million a week.[30] Most companies would have already been in receivership, but the banks, the Bank of Montreal in particular, continued to direct money to them through the sale of government-guaranteed bonds. The railways were too big to fail; their demise could have taken the banks and thus the entire country with them. Even so, bankruptcy was a genuine concern as share prices for both companies raced toward zero.

In the midst of the crisis, Bennett's old crony and CPR president Sir Edward Beatty accused the CNR of price-fixing and other fraudulent schemes intended to win market share. Beatty also raised a complaint that he had been voicing for years: the CNR was being kept afloat by taxpayers, and since his company paid enormous taxes it was in the crazy position of actually subsiding its own competitor. CNR president Sir Henry Thornton shrugged off the arguments and accusations while denying any wrongdoing. Public statements made it clear that he and Beatty could not agree upon what was causing the problems with their companies, let alone solutions.

Arguments swirled around the future of the railways. Bennett feared that if they were saved through amalgamation, the resulting monopoly would see rates rise as service fell. Further, if the publicly owned CNR was allowed to fail or to be absorbed by the CPR, the government would lose its influence in the most essential of Canada's essential services. In Bennett's mind it was therefore in the interest of the country to save the railways and to have them continue as two competing companies. A consensus had not formed around Bennett's ideas, but few doubted his beliefs regarding the gravity of the situation. Bennett said to a group of railway labour leaders, "No language would be too extravagant to describe the seriousness of Canada's railway problem."[31]

His years in Calgary with the CPR had rendered Bennett an expert on railways and their problems. He and Beatty had spent many quiet social evenings together, had travelled together, and had sat on the board of directors of the Bank of Montreal together. They also shared a mutual dislike of the CNR's Thornton. Thornton was a charismatic man with a dominating personality, but he was also a bad manager with extravagant tastes.

Bennett worked with Minster of Railways and Canals R.J. Manion to establish the Select Standing Committee of Railways and Shipping. Chaired by R.B. Hanson, it began its work in late 1931. But Bennett was pressured to amalgamate the two railways even before the committee reported its findings. Among those that pressed for amalgamation were the Bank of Montreal and the CPR. Bennett found himself in a sticky situation; not only was he friends with both company presidents, he also knew that he would need the same financial support that both had afforded his party in the last election in the next, in just a few years' time.

The pressure on the prime minister was enormous and was recognized by friends and foes alike. He had stated in a number of speeches in the 1930 campaign that he stood for competition ever and amalgamation never. The *Winnipeg Free Press* ran an editorial cartoon that showed Bennett standing with a paintbrush before a sign that he had just doctored to say "competition Never and amalgamation Never."[32]

The committee's hearings aired both railroads' dirty laundry with stories of wasteful spending and extravagant, outrageous upper-management salaries, especially those of the two presidents. The CNR's Sir Henry Thornton came under particular criticism, for his company also provided him with a seemingly bottomless expense account and even a free mansion in which he and his family lived. Thornton was shattered by the investigation and public questioning of his character. He burned his papers rather than submit them to the committee. After a visit from a group of Conservative MPs that he dubbed the Wrecking Brigade he tendered his resignation. Bennett was happy to see the back of him, but his departure solved nothing. Thornton died of cancer in New York City only eleven months later, penniless and broken. Bennett did not attend the funeral.

The committee tabled its final report in May 1932. Although it did not suggest amalgamation, Thornton's public humiliation and resignation led Beatty, the Bank of Montreal, and others to renew public pressure in promoting just such an option. Bennett told Manion and the rest of cabinet that he maintained his belief that the two companies should not amalgamate but that he would change his mind if there were sufficient evidence to support his doing so. And so with Manion's encouragement, Bennett created the Royal Commission to Inquire into Railways and Transportation to investigate all options. He appointed the Right Honourable Chief Justice Lyman Duff as chair.

The Duff Commission worked exceptionally quickly and reported to the House in late September 1932. It recommended the continuation of two separate companies but suggested that the two should cooperate with respect to schedules, machinery, facilities, and processes so as to reduce the operating expenses of both. It also recommended that the government oversee the transition and ensure that the savings were passed on to customers so that freight rates would drop and thus profits to farmers and manufacturers might increase. Bennett and Manion discussed then approved the recommendations, and the prime minister ordered that legislation be drafted to implement them.

While reaction to Bennett's support of the Duff Commission recommendations was generally positive, there was still some opposition. Besides those who had wanted amalgamation, there was worry from others concerned about railway company job losses. Bennett met with representatives from the Railroad Brotherhoods on January 26, 1933. They presented much the same advice as they had given to a Senate committee that had been investigating the matter the previous fall. They wanted to see the establishment of a five-person board, including representatives from labour who would oversee the changes that were coming, so as to ensure that none of them would lead to more downsizing. W. L. Best from the Brotherhood of Locomotive Firemen and R. J. Tallon of the American Federation of Labor Railways Employees Department, stressed that since 1929, 51,663 railway employees had lost their jobs and that it would be better for their membership and, in fact, the entire country, if the government increased its subsidy to the railways. When Best had made the same point during the group's Senate presentations, Arthur Meighen had responded that the government could not afford to continue to subsidize the railways at current levels, let alone increase the corporate welfare. Further, Meighen had explained, if the actions recommended by the Duff Commission were not implemented in whole or at least in large part, then there was a real possibility that one or both of the railways would go broke, resulting in far more unemployment among those whom Best represented.

Expecting to receive much the same response from Bennett, Best had brought along J. B. Ward from the Locomotive Engineers of the Canadian Pacific system and Frank McKenna, chairman of the CPR's Federated Shopmen. It was a clever ploy, but Best misunderstood Bennett. He failed to realize that if Bennett could not be pressured by his old friends who ran and financed the CPR, he would certainly not be moved by those who ran the company's unions. And he was not. Best and the others asked that Bennett consider "the human element" in the decisions he was about to make and not "further aggravate our social conditions."[33]

Bennett politely heard the delegation's complete presentation without interruption then paid them the compliment of a direct and honest response. Bennett said he agreed that the situation with the railways was threatening the stability of the entire Canadian economy. He explained that all the work being done to bolster international trade would be largely wasted without a healthy rail system to move goods across the country. He repeated Meighen's point about the consequences of losing both railways, which he stressed was a real possibility, and said that the efforts of the government were focused on saving them both. He stated, though, that in rescuing the companies, there would be adjustments that would inevitably lead to more job losses. He said, "But it will be a common sacrifice, and everyone will have to suffer."[34] Best and the others left empty-handed, but they had been heard and their points of view had been validated and respected.

Even as the railway legislation was working its way through the House, Mackenzie King and Liberal newspapers continued to insist that it was a smokescreen and that Bennett was tricking the country. The prime minister was really just a slave to the Montreal business elite, he argued, and would eventually deliver the amalgamation that they so coveted. From the beginning, Mackenzie King had also believed that Bennett's actions were motivated solely by a desire to get rid of Thornton and place Conservative people in charge of the CNR.[35]

Bennett and Manion believed Mackenzie King and the Liberals would do all they could to politicize and destroy, or at least delay, the railways legislation, and so Bennett gave it to Meighen to present through the Senate. In so doing, he robbed himself of the publicity and credit for something he had worked so hard to bring about. The legislation that passed the Senate and finally came to the House created a Joint Co-operative Committee to oversee both companies. It had representation from both and, in what must have made Best smile, a representative from labour. The committee was to see that responsible cost cutting and cooperation, especially with respect to passenger service, occurred in ways that helped the companies' bottom lines while also helping the Canadian economy as a whole. Mackenzie King by this time had spun and claimed that Bennett was trying to wreck the CNR.[36] But the Liberal caucus was split and so Mackenzie King retreated and gave only cursory opposition to the bill.

With the legislation passed and cooperative efforts beginning, Manion delivered two powerful speeches, first in Smiths Falls, Ontario, and then in Belleville, Ontario. In both he reviewed the crisis that had precipitated the Duff Commission and the government's stepping in to force the CNR and the CPR to play nice. Manion said that the option of amalgamation had never been seriously considered. He concluded, without fear of contradiction, that the Canadian economy was on firmer ground due to actions that had saved the railways and kept the Canadian National in public hands.

Later, 1938's Transport Act strengthened what Bennett had begun by rendering more of the Duff Commission's recommendations law and amending some key regulations. Among the changes that Bennett's legislation had introduced, but the Transport Act more firmly enforced, was the necessity for railways to negotiate freight rates so that all of one particular customer's goods could travel on one line, thus reducing shipping costs. The legislation and regulations were important steps taken down the path toward economic stability and prosperity that Bennett had forged.

THE OTTAWA CONFERENCE

While balancing the various challenges that competed for his attention, Bennett prepared for the Ottawa Imperial Conference. Originally intended for 1931, it was finally scheduled to take place from July 21 to August 20, 1932. Its goal was to help each of the Commonwealth's dominions to address their ravaged economies through reducing or eliminating trade barriers between members while raising them against the rest of the world. The notion of increasing trade with Britain and the Commonwealth through preferential tariff arrangements was something that Mackenzie King had been planning well before the 1930 election. On April 5, 1930, he had pondered the imminent election and confided to his diary that ". . . the Imperial Conference will lie ahead as something which [the] liberal Gov't that favours free trade within Br. Empire & less with the U.S. I believe we can sweep the country with it."[37] While there is no evidence that he and Bennett discussed inter-Commonwealth trade, it was clear that both agreed on its necessity.

Bennett had sold the idea of the conference to his Commonwealth colleagues on his belief that with the United States having led the trend toward cutting international trade, the dominions had no choice but to turn to each other. It was to be an imperial circling of the wagons based not upon misty-eyed nostalgia but rather a clear understanding of the shifting tides of power that were buffeting all players on the world stage—including Canada. A Canadian nationalist, Bennett believed that he could react to American isolationism while exploiting the fact that Britain's glory days were behind it and that Canada's were yet to come. Indicating the degree to which he understood the shifting Canadian-British paradigm, he said:

> The day of the centralized Empire is passed. We no longer live in a political Empire. I found people looking forward to the Conference in the belief that we will lay at Ottawa the foundation of a new economic empire in which Canada is destined to play a part of ever-increasing importance.[38]

Bennett's proposed trade arrangement was a confluence of his faith in the power of tariffs to bring about economic benefits, his imperialist belief that the familial ties between Canada and the old Empire could be developed into a profitable synergy, and his nationalist fear of the growing power of the United States. The three were linked by his Tory inclination that the government must act to intervene vigorously in the economy.

Bennett had been expressing these nuanced and overlapping ideas for years. For instance, near the end of 1910, he had written a long letter to Aitken, stating: "In Canada the situation is really acute. We have gone on and made commercial treaties with the nations of the world and are now thinking of reciprocity with the United States. That means political union in 25 years because the West must be the dominating partner in the life of this dominion within that time unless we can maintain close commercial union between the East and West as confederation fails."[39] Bennett went on to express his yearning for a day when young men, supposedly such as he, would be able to take the reins of power and create what he called an "Imperial Federation." Such an organization, he argued, could bring benefits to Canada while standing against the ever-present pressures of American domination or even annexation.

Before he left Canada to live and work in Britain, Beaverbrook had expressed similar ideas. In fact, he publicly admitted that his foray into the newspaper business was made primarily to promote the notion of an imperial free-trade arrangement.[40] With his Empire Crusade, he had insisted to any and all who would listen, and old and trusted friend Bennett listened a great deal, that the scheme would render the newly created Commonwealth self-sufficient in terms of raw materials, finance, markets, and perhaps most importantly, food.

Beaverbrook burned through political capital in his relentless promotion of his rather simplistic scheme of imperial free trade. He and Bennett's friendship slid into one of its periodic schisms when Bennett insisted that his complex preferential trade and tariff idea was more attainable and beneficial. During the 1930 campaign, a bitter Beaverbrook initiated *Globe and Mail* and *Winnipeg Free Press* interviews and expressed support for Mackenzie King. Bennett visited Beaverbrook in November 1930 after the Imperial Conference. They agreed to disagree.

Upon his return to Canada, Bennett had held a press conference and without prompting told reporters about Beaverbrook's Empire Crusade. He explained it in some detail, noting that it was something he and his old friend had discussed for years, but that he could still not support it as the way to increase Canadian trade. Canada, he said, needed both the Commonwealth and the United States as trading partners.[41] It would be a delicate balance.

Bennett's thoughts on that balance were seen years before in his enthusiastic opposition to Laurier's 1911 Reciprocity Treaty that promised free trade with the United States and had been his first chance to sing on the national stage of his rejection of the pull of continentalism in favour of greater Canadian nationalism as expressed through stronger imperial ties. It was a song that he would pull from his repertoire often in the 1920s. For instance, in 1928, he had said in an exchange in the House with Mackenzie King, "I am for the British Empire next to Canada, the only difference being that some gentlemen are for the United States before Canada. I am for the British Empire after Canada."[42]

In January 1932, Britain's chancellor of the exchequer Neville Chamberlain, acting as the equivalent to Canada's minister of finance, and reflecting Britain's growing protectionism tendencies, had brought forward a revenue tariff bill which imposed a 10 per cent duty on nearly all products imported into Britain. The bill made exceptions only for wheat, meat, and some other commodities. Bennett was upset by the bill, seeing that it so obviously contradicted his views on and hopes for enhanced imperial trade while it would also hurt Canadian producers and exporters. He wrote to Chamberlain expressing his displeasure. Bennett was pleased to receive a quick response stating that the bill would not come into effect until after July's Ottawa Conference, which would afford him a chance to amend or even kill it. Chamberlain explained to his prime minister and cabinet that only Bennett's letter and logic had resulted in the delaying of the imposition of the tariff.[43]

On February 3, 1932, accepting cabinet's contention that he was stretched too thin, Bennett had appointed Edgar Rhodes to succeed him as finance minister. Rhodes was given the job of helping to prepare for the Ottawa Conference. He appointed respected Queen's University professor William Clifford Clark to assist in the effort. They worked with Stevens to organize staff to research and write preparatory reports and briefing books.

Among the more distressing documents that emerged from the process was a report regarding American branch plants in Canada. It was written by bureaucrats at the Dominion Bureau of Statistics. It noted that the first branch plants had appeared in 1860 and that by 1922 there were 259. The late 1920s had seen an explosion of new branch plants. The report outlined the magnitude of the economic issue with a list of 964 manufacturing companies that in early 1932 were located and operating in Canada but with head offices and majority shareholders in America. A report to the American Congress had indicated that at the end of 1929, American investment in branch plants in Canada totalled US$540.6 million.

The Canadian report concluded that the two main reasons for the establishment of branch plants were to augment profits through jumping Canadian tariffs by having goods manufactured in Canada, and to use Canadian plants to export products to Britain.[44] The report raised questions as to what exactly constituted a Canadian product. Bennett also read that in 1930, American investment in Canadian manufacturing represented 17.74 per cent of the country's total industrial investment and that branch plants employed 114,505 Canadians. That number meant that 24.3 per cent of all wages earned in the Canadian manufacturing sector was earned in American branch plants.[45] This point raised questions about Canada's economic sovereignty. The statistical analysis laid bare the limited manoeuvring room that Bennett really had in advancing Canadian trade. In many ways the report can be seen as the dawning of the intricacy of economic globalization forcing its way into public policy decision making.

Despite the hard work done by diligent men, some delegates were critical of the fact that while international conference agendas are usually agreed upon up to six months in advance, the Ottawa agenda was not wired until July 7. Many delegates had already left for Ottawa when summaries were cabled to them.

Finally, after a few hectic days of switching some lodgings and dealing with minutiae, the delegates assembled in the House of Commons and the gavel's bang announced the conference was to begin. In London, Bennett had accepted the invitation to act as chair. He had also decided to lead the Canadian delegation. This dual role put him in the difficult position of having to mediate discussions and allow all opinions and delegations to be heard while also speaking for Canada. It was a balance that he did not always handle well. The brusque manner that had allowed him to succeed so spectacularly in both the worlds of business and politics was neither effectual nor well received in the tactful and sensitive milieu of international diplomacy.

As the conference moved slowly through its long agenda at plenary and breakout sessions, Bennett appeared to be everywhere and doing everything. Behind the scenes, though, he was delegating intelligently. When a British delegation complained about negotiations led by Commissioner of Taxation R.W. Breadner, Bennett had him replaced by Hector McKinnon and then was pleased to see him work out a schedule of reduced tariff rates with his British counterpart. Minister of Trade and Commerce Harry Stevens had been given authority to oversee all trade negotiations. His staff worked late into, and sometimes through, nights in hammering out agreements where possible and summarizing disagreements where they were not. They reported to him early each morning and he, in turn, briefed Bennett.[46] In most cases, Bennett accepted what had been agreed to by Stevens and his staff. There were incidents, however, where Bennett rejected or amended draft agreements. For instance, Stevens brought him a deal involving British and Canadian steel and iron that Bennett thought gave too much while offering Canada too little. He rewrote parts of the agreement and insisted on a tariff on British boilerplates. The changed deal upset the British and irked Stevens and his staff. In the end, however, when the deal was signed according to Bennett's new draft, it brought considerable benefit to an important Canadian industry.[47]

While the international press was present and working hard to bring news to their respective countries, the Canadian press found itself stymied by a prime minister who believed it in the country's best interest to keep silent until the conference's final communiqué. This decision frustrated Manion, who had been put in charge of managing the conference's press relations. Manion delegated press briefings to Pearson. Quickly discovering that he was unable to extract any information from Bennett, the ever-resourceful civil servant turned to Malcolm Macdonald, a friend and his counterpart in the British delegation. At the conclusion of every session, Pearson spoke to Macdonald and then to the Canadian press.[48] The trick allowed Pearson to give them only what they could have discovered through diligent inquiry but at least be seen to be giving them something.

While Bennett's voice was the only Canadian one that mattered, and thus the Canadian delegation was a picture of disciplined unity, the British delegation was a feuding dysfunctional family. Both Prime Minister Stanley Baldwin and Dominion Secretary J.H. Thomas opposed imperial free trade in principle and Bennett's preferential tariff ideas. But it was clear that the most powerful voice of the contingent was Chancellor of the Exchequer Neville Chamberlain, who was supported by British Board of Trade president Walter Runciman. Bennett was pleased by Chamberlain's evident clout. In the reticent but crafty politician he had a fellow traveller who shared his views on the importance of pan-imperial trade preferences.

The matter of tariffs on meat and other food products was one of many important issues that split the British delegation. Baldwin worried about losing the support of his cabinet and caucus in London if taxes imposed on non-Commonwealth food resulted in higher domestic prices. He worried too that every rural riding would be lost in the upcoming election if food from the dominions were allowed in without tariffs, thereby affecting British food production profitability. Chamberlain later wrote that the conference's turning point was August 15, when the Australians joined the British splinter group and refused to deal on tariffs regarding foreign meat.[49] While product after product was agreed upon, food was always the point of departure at the end of every day and it was always the British that seemed to block genuine progress.

The conference ended with many bilateral agreements in hand but without the overall trade arrangement that Bennett had envisioned. Still, many were pleased with what was accomplished. At the conclusion of the conference, Bennett received a number of congratulatory letters from friends and political allies, as well as Canadian farm and business leaders. Warmly worded telegrams also arrived from the British and Australian delegations congratulating Bennett on his leadership throughout the difficult negotiations. He answered them all by making the same point in slightly altered phrasing: "It is my earnest hope that we have laid the foundation for greater Empire trade and that in the future we may see economic as well as sentimental ties binding the different parts of the Empire closer together."[50]

Canadian newspapers experienced a rare moment of consensus as they found themselves in agreement regarding both the conference's success and Bennett's leadership throughout. Typical of the editorial comments from papers was one found in the *St. Thomas Times-Journal* which began, "Except for super-partisans who hate to admit that a political opponent ever does any good, the people of Canada must, metaphorically speaking, take their hats off to Rt. Hon. R. B. Bennett, Prime Minister of Canada. . . . Canadians should be proud of him. He has earned an imperishable place in the role of a builder of Canada and a builder of Empire."[51] *The Globe*'s managing editor Harry Anderson was effusive in his praise, noting in a private letter to the prime minister, "First let me send, very heartily, a handshake of congratulations on the achievement of the conference. Surely a sound and lasting foundation has been laid for great progress and development in Empire trade."[52]

But all was not wine and roses, for a great deal of frustration furrowed the brows of participants as they boarded ships for home. Perhaps most importantly, Baldwin was angry at how things had worked out and returned to London believing that his party would blame him for not making more progress on trade. But his heart had not been in the negotiations from the outset. Upon arriving in Ottawa he had met with Mackenzie King and told him that he had hoped that simply raising tariffs in England would result in lower tariffs generally.[53] He also predicted, correctly as it turned out, that his inability to see his way through the mire of conflicting interests in order to create a trade plan that would at least begin to address the issue of preferential imperial trade would lead to his downfall as party leader. In a vain attempt to save his political skin, Baldwin began a campaign to blame Bennett for his own failures in Ottawa. Baldwin's manoeuvre was stymied, however, by his reputation for having only a casual regard for the truth.[54] If indeed the conference frustrated expectations, there was blame enough to go around. Chamberlain later admitted to not understanding many of the financial issues under discussion, while the entire British delegation was so muddled and divided that Bennett needed to help and direct them from behind the scenes.[55]

Baldwin told British reporters that Bennett entered the room each day with a new brainwave that had little to do with what had been previously agreed upon and, in fact, led to agreements ending in shreds with no progress made. Chamberlain, it must be added, also blamed Bennett for the failure to make more progress. He found Bennett smug and irritable. Chamberlain wrote, "Most of our difficulties centred round the personality of Bennett. Full of high Imperial sentiments, he has done little to put them into practice. Instead of guiding the conference in his capacity as Chairman, he has acted merely as the leader of the Canadian delegation. In that capacity he strained our patience to the limit."[56] It should be noted that Chamberlain and Baldwin had similarly negative things to say about Australian prime minister Stanley Bruce who, like Bennett, worked tenaciously to bring benefit to his country.[57]

Canadian historians who have examined the Ottawa Conference have formed a consensus that seems to support Chamberlain's critical statement and Baldwin's condemnation of the event as a failure.[58] Indeed, Bennett had organized the conference to create a system of preferential tariffs within a united Commonwealth and to bring economic recovery to Canada; neither happened. However, a fair analysis must concede that at least partly as a result of the bilateral agreements that were made at the Ottawa Conference, and Bennett's obsession with increasing trade, Canada's trade with Britain and other conference participants substantially increased in the period following the gavel's final fall.[59] Exports to Britain in the two years after the conference rose from 28 per cent to 38 per cent, and to all other Commonwealth countries from 36 per cent to 48 per cent of all exported goods.[60] Other statistics told a similar story. From April to October 1931 aggregate imports totalled $64 million; by April to October 1934 imports from Commonwealth countries had risen to $68.1 million. From April to October 1931 aggregate exports to them were $105.3 million and from April to October 1934 they were $166.2 million.[61] Even where unreliable statistics fail to inform, there remains a consensus that the conference spurred business and boosted employment through creating a renewed confidence among many business leaders that at last and at least something was being done to get Canada out of the economic mud in which it had been stuck for too long.[62]

CONTINUING TO BLAST HIS WAY

At the Ottawa Conference Bennett had managed to create a climate where progress on trade and tariff policy had been made without surrendering the protection needed for Canadian manufacturers and wheat producers.[63] Further, the agreements signed and personal relationships forged at the conference also allowed for subsequent small, behind-the-scenes trade activities. For instance, Stevens discovered that while dried fruit from Australia was just as good and just as cheap as the same products from California, the Americans were much better at packaging their produce. Stevens made contact with his Australian counterparts whom he had met in Ottawa. The packaging issues were quickly addressed, and soon Canadians were enjoying dried fruit from down under.[64]

Stevens performed brilliantly before, during, and after the conference in pursuing trade opportunities such as these. That did not mean that he and Bennett did not clash from time to time. Months after the Ottawa Conference, for example, Bennett called Stevens to his office one day to report that he had been told that Canada's trade commissioner in New Zealand had been acting in ways that were hurting the Canadian steel industry and that he should be fired. Stevens heard the prime minister out and then left to initiate an investigation. He discovered that the commissioner had, in fact, acted quite appropriately but in so doing had upset a couple of prominent Canadian steel men. When Stevens returned to tell Bennett of the situation, the prime minister exploded, saying, "Mr. Stevens, I am the Prime Minister of Canada, and as the Prime Minister I instruct you to dispose of the services of this man Cole in New Zealand."[65]

Stevens wrote a letter to Cole that dismissed him, but stated clearly that in his opinion it was without cause. He apologized for simply following the orders of the prime minister, who did not fully understand the situation. He put Cole's copy in a file and sent another copy of the absolutely inappropriate letter to Bennett, stating that he was awaiting Bennett's final decision. The letter led to another meeting, which allowed Stevens to again explain the pertinent details. Bennett heard him out then changed his mind. Cole served out his term. The incident demonstrated Bennett's temper but also the degree to which he would listen and act upon advice from trusted colleagues and, as always, his willingness to take stands contrary to those demanded by big business.

Despite their occasional personal troubles, Bennett and Stevens continued to be an effective team in seeking new markets for Canadian goods. Stevens sent a number of messages through appropriate channels indicating his eagerness to deal in matters of trade with any country willing to negotiate a mutually advantageous arrangement. These entreaties led to trade deals being signed in late 1932 with Germany and France and later with Poland and Austria. Bennett sent emissaries to Latin America and soon thereafter inked trade deals with Bolivia,

Guatemala, Panama, Costa Rica, and Haiti. At the same time, more deals were made with Commonwealth partners Hong Kong, South Africa, Ireland, and India.

Given the meetings, speeches, travel, and conferences, the reports, debates, and arguments, and all the good press and bad, one is left to conclude that there was little Bennett had left undone in his efforts to increase trade. But while noteworthy progress had been made, it was not enough. Britain's removing itself from the gold standard—something that will be addressed later—had destabilized global currency markets and negatively affected the previously widely accepted efficacy of tariffs. Commodity prices continued to plummet. And the only clouds over the prairies held not rain but grasshoppers. All of Bennett's best efforts simply could not stabilize global prices or currency rates, or invent customers, or conjure rain.

By early 1933 it had become evident that the higher tariffs and trade deals were helping the manufacturing and mining sectors, which were located mostly in central Canada. Regardless of the positive effects of Bennett's actions, however, Ontario's average per capita income had fallen 44 per cent. That precipitous drop was painful, to be sure, but when compared with other regions where the tariff policies had more limited effects, incomes had fallen even more. Recall that Saskatchewan's had dropped by 72 per cent and Alberta's by 61 per cent.[66]

Farmers needed more help. In an effort to provide it, Bennett used the contacts he had made at previous international conferences to push for another. In August 1933, he chaired the World Wheat Conference. Delegations from wheat-producing countries hoped to do something about the collapse of world prices. Canada, the United States, Argentina, and Australia had agreed in advance that they would attempt to raise prices by reducing production. It was an old trick that relied on the older truth of supply and demand. At the World Monetary and Economic Conference held in London just the month before, Bennett had signed a deal with Australia, Peru, Mexico, China, India, Spain, and the United States to keep 35 million ounces of silver from the world market for four years. Bennett had ordered the federal government to begin purchasing Canada's silver to meet its silver quota. Based on the silver precedent, participants agreed to another quota system that would reduce worldwide wheat production by 15 per cent. Bennett agreed to cap the amount of wheat Canada would place on the world market at 200 million bushels a year.

There was great consternation from many quarters within Canada when the conference's communiqué was announced, much of it from Bennett's own cabinet. There was an even greater uproar when Bennett explained that an emergency wheat control board would be created to oversee the limits to production and to enforce the 200-million-bushel cap. The most vocal criticism came from Charles Cahan. Once again he spoke from the perspective of a believer in laissez-faire economics who saw the agreement and the new government agency as anathema.[67]

Bennett listened to critics, but his belief in the necessity of the government to intervene in the market in order to combat the Depression, and in this case to try to raise the price of wheat, was not changed. He acted to blunt the ideologically based criticism. Before leaving for the conference, he had taken a politically intelligent step and fully briefed western premiers. He had their support in hand before making his proposals in London. The premiers helped sell the idea of manipulating production to farmers; consequently, Bennett had the only constituency that really mattered on his side.

In a sad irony, there was another reason that the criticism ebbed. Even before the regulations needed to be fully enforced, the combination of drought, grasshoppers, and rust had taken more than enough farmland out of production to ensure that the cap wasn't exceeded. Meanwhile, many farmers had already done as Cahan and the free market advocates had argued would happen if government stayed out of the way. They had seen the price of wheat continuing to drop and switched to more profitable crops or left farming altogether. In the end, then, the wheat conference agreement was not painful for Canadian farmers. But neither did it bounce the price.

Just before Christmas 1933, Bennett wrote a long letter to each Conservative member of Parliament and senator and dozens of party officials. All said much the same thing. He began by thanking each recipient for his or her service to the country and party and acknowledged how difficult the year had been for all. He then noted the hurricane of criticism that had been endured for the previous three years by all members of the government and the Conservative Party. He wrote of hopeful economic indicators suggesting that there were signs of recovery ahead and that they needed to remain united. He wrote, "If our Party will act as a unit, forget differences and consolidate our efforts, bearing in mind that Conservative principles will endure as long as there is a world, and that loyal and devoted souls will always stand at the crossroads to ensure that our future is protected by the experience of the past, I am confident we will eventually succeed."[68]

It was reassurance from a boss and a pep talk from a coach. Bennett received a number of thank-you letters in return, all expressing gratitude for his message of hope and encouragement. It was evident that support for Bennett and his government was slipping among Canadians, but caucus support was holding. This support held despite the fact that there had been a sex scandal brewing.

During the July-August 1932 Ottawa Conference a rumour had circulated. Mrs. Hazel Beatrice Colville of Montreal had told friends that she and Bennett were soon to be married. She was preparing her trousseau. The forty-three-year-old Colville was the daughter of Sir Albert Kemp, who had served with Bennett in Borden's cabinet. She was attractive, intelligent, wealthy, and well connected. Mackenzie King discussed the rumour with Baldwin and others with the added speculation that following the wedding Bennett would resign as prime minister and move to England.[69] The rumours turned to scandal when it was discovered that Mrs. Colville was Roman Catholic, had been twice divorced, and was known for her many romances. Bennett said nothing to the press, which, unlike today, respected his privacy.

Bennett and Colville had, in fact, begun a romantic relationship five months before. On the day the Ottawa Conference ended, she and Bennett met for a week's holiday at her elegantly refurbished eighteenth-century seigneurial house at Mascouche, Quebec. He spent much of his summer there. They continued to see each other when they could and a number of tender letters were exchanged. An obviously smitten Bennett wrote, for example, "I miss you beyond all words & I am lonesome beyond cure without your presence."[70]

Rumours of the affair were fascinating to many Canadians who had grown used to the fact that both the prime minister and opposition leader were bachelors. There were many jokes about it, including in the

House. One afternoon there was a long and somewhat tedious debate led by a Conservative member who was upset about the apparent habit among some Doukhobor women of sometimes appearing naked on their isolated farms during torridly hot summer days. The member sought to draw Mackenzie King into the debate and asked what he would do if he were at his home enjoying a pleasant afternoon when he suddenly spied a number of naked Doukhobor women dancing on his lawn. Mackenzie King replied quickly, and to roars of laughter from both sides of the aisle, that he would send immediately for the leader of the government.[71]

In the spring of 1934, Colville ended the affair. Bennett wanted her to give up cigarettes, drink, and Montreal's nightlife and she refused. The relationship demonstrated that Bennett was indeed capable and desirous of love but, alas, it was not to be. Shortly after the breakup, in August and September 1934, Bennett sailed for England. He combined political and business meetings with a much-needed time out. As usual, his leisure activities involved shopping in London with his sister Mildred and time in conversation about books, politics, and business with Beaverbrook.

Upon his return in early October 1934, Bennett was moved to comment in a speech that his travels had convinced him that while troubles and challenges remained, Canada had been faring better than almost every other country in the world. He credited the trade deals inked at and flowing from the Ottawa Conference as the primary factors in that success; they protected the country from ruthless competition and provided preferred markets for commodities. He noted, "The fact that Canadians avoided panic and kept their heads throughout the darkest days stands as a lasting memorial to Canadian character and sanity."[72]

He was encouraged by the fact that since the end of 1932, unlike during the final years of Mackenzie King's administration and the first two years of his, Canada was again in a positive balance of trade—selling more than it was buying. Bennett took pride in the new Commonwealth trade agreements, which helped with the turnaround. While overall economic recovery was frustratingly uneven and slow, trade numbers continued to improve. He had noted in a Toronto speech in April 1934 that imports and exports had gone up $132 million over the previous year and that 60 per cent of that trade had been within the Commonwealth. Exports of commodities from food products to minerals to newsprint were all up, some substantially. He summarized the statistical analysis on exports as astonishing.[73] Similarly, Bennett expressed tremendous satisfaction with the additional agreements that his government had forged with other Commonwealth countries, singling out the substantially increased trade with South Africa and New Zealand.[74] The progress was steady but unemployment and related hardships still plagued far too many Canadians. More needed to be done.

THE UNITED STATES

In the 1970s, Prime Minister Trudeau initiated actions that sought to promote what he called a "third way." While acknowledging the importance of economic interaction with the United States, he sought to increase trade with the rest of the world so as to render the country less dependent upon, using his metaphor, the twitches and grunts of the elephant with which Canada was sharing a bed. Prime Minister Chrétien did the same thing with the many Team Canada trade missions that he led in the 1990s. Bennett understood the same thing that Trudeau and Chrétien did: while it is good for Canada to diversify its trade by increasing the number of partners, the essential trade relationship with the United States can never be forgotten.

Bennett had gone as far as he could in promoting and advancing Commonwealth and other international trade. While the numbers indicated success, and the manufacturing sector began to feel the warmth of recovery, a larger strategy to find markets for Canadian goods had to be developed. That new strategy had to ignore the protectionist walls that presidents Harding and Hoover had been erecting and directly engage the United States.

The year 1932 had witnessed transformative change in the United States. The November elections represented a repudiation of Hoover and the Republican Party's handling of the economy. Democrats won a commanding congressional majority, taking 100 seats in the House of Representatives and 12 in the Senate. The Democrats held the largest majority in the Senate since 1869 and in the House since before the civil war. Fifty-year-old former New York governor and former assistant secretary to the navy Franklin D. Roosevelt crushed Hoover to become the country's thirty-second president. FDR won the largest portion of Electoral College votes in more than one hundred years and the highest percentage of the popular vote ever. Roosevelt's sunny optimism, sparkling charisma, and promise to deliver a New Deal to Americans had inspired hope and optimism. Many Americans were convinced that with FDR in the White House, things would improve.

Like Bennett only three years before, Roosevelt came to office in the depths of an economic and moral collapse. He promised an activist administration that would seek innovative solutions to simultaneously help people while saving capitalism from itself. FDR's core political beliefs were consistent with Bennett's own ideas. The Canadian prime minister also shared the new president's tireless energy and willingness, if not eagerness, to explore new options in the face of new problems. Franklin Roosevelt was America's R. B. Bennett.

Roosevelt had campaigned on the promise to end the restrictive trade practices of the past, but regardless of the winds of optimism sweeping northward, Bennett continued to approach America quite warily. His misgivings were based not only upon the ties to Britain and the Commonwealth that were such an important part of Canada's political culture as well as his personal beliefs and political imperatives, but also on a distrust of America's power that he shared with many Canadians. In a speech delivered in October 1934, for example, he argued that the United States had taken it upon itself to establish a continental defence in which it protected itself by also protecting Canada from air and sea threats. He admitted that the American policy had benefits for Canadian security but asked how long Canada could accept that protection and still control not only its own defence and foreign policies but also its natural resources. Pondering the future of Canadian sovereignty, he wondered, "If the resources of this country of which we boast so proudly are to be ours to hand to those who come after us, it is time we begin to direct our thinking to the factors that are involved in their defence and security."[75]

Despite these qualms, Bennett was realist enough to know that, regardless of all he had been doing with the imperial trade initiatives and in the face of the tit-for-tat tariff war that Smoot-Hawley had exacerbated, trade with Canada's neighbour was an essential part of reinventing prosperity.[76] Like FDR, who in his presidential campaign had expressed his support for trying anything, Bennett was willing to try everything.

Complicating attempts of all national leaders to address international trade issues, however, was the quickly developing corporate globalization that was rendering it increasingly difficult to determine the nationality of particular companies and thus how trade between countries could be influenced. For instance, Ontario's Electro Metallurgical Company of Canada made graphite electrodes used by steel and chemical companies in electric furnaces. They were manufactured in Welland, Ontario, and sold in Canadian dollars through an agent called the Canadian National Carbon Company. In 1930, sales to the UK totalled a quarter of a million dollars. However, the British Customs office undertook an investigation and found that both the Electro Metallurgical Company of Canada and the Canadian National Carbon Company were wholly owned subsidiaries of the American Union Carbide and Carbon Company. As such, neither was deemed Canadian and so the products they were manufacturing and selling fell outside the parameters of the imperial trade regulations. The company would be forced to lose British contracts or pay about $60,000 in duties each year. With those contracts lost, Canadians jobs would be lost. The company's vice-president wrote to Bennett, beseeching him to intercede on the company's behalf by reducing empire content rules on products manufactured by companies not owned wholly within the empire.[77] Bennett acted on the company's behalf with letters to the British government. But the larger points are as clear today as then—the Canadian and American economies were inexorably linked, and while the United States needed Canada, Canada needed the United States more.

In those days, the new president took office not in January but in March. In February 1933, Bennett announced to the House of Commons that with a new president apparently willing to turn away from the protectionist trade policies that had been erected in the 1920s and willing to at least explore new opportunities, the Canadian government was initiating negotiations with the United States to see if mutually beneficial trade agreements could be signed. He sent Canada's ambassador to the United States, Bill Herridge, to meet with president-elect Roosevelt. The ostensible purpose of the long-scheduled meeting was to discuss the St. Lawrence Seaway Treaty, but Herridge was instructed to also raise the possibility of new trade deals with the vibrant American leader. Herridge was pleased to report that FDR believed that new trade arrangements deserved attention.

After a number of discussions with American and Canadian officials about the possibility of increased Canadian-American trade, Bennett travelled to Washington to meet Roosevelt. He was there with a number of other heads of state for what was called the Washington Conversations: preparatory meetings for the upcoming World Monetary and Economic Conference to be held that summer in London. Bennett and Roosevelt met in the White House on April 27, 1933. Unlike after his meeting with Hoover in January 1931, Bennett encouraged the taking of a photograph. Roosevelt and Bennett were quite different in temperament but they got along well, as the president's natural ebullience was joined by the grace and charm that Bennett could muster when necessary. Although the relationship was not nearly as warm as the one FDR would later establish with Mackenzie King, the two concluded business efficiently and agreed that increased trade was in both their best interests. A joint communiqué announced, "We have agreed to begin a search for means to increase the exchange of commodities between our two countries."[78]

The American press afforded coverage of the meetings with Roosevelt. Typical was a front-page story in the *Evening Independent* which spoke of the two leaders seeking ways to attain reciprocal reductions in tariffs under the headline "Tariff Truce Discussed to Bring World Action to Restore Prosperity."[79] Bennett accepted an invitation to address Americans over the CBS radio network and in his speech he heaped effusive praise on the new president and spoke of the mutual advantages of greater trade and lower tariffs between the two countries.

Bennett then ordered Herridge to initiate low-level trade discussions with congressmen and the members of the executive branch. The two exchanged a number of letters discussing and debating the various meetings and tactics to be used. Despite his meeting with the president and his reaching out to American business and political leaders, Bennett remained hesitant to forge new trade ties with the Americans too quickly. At one point, Herridge responded to Bennett's urging him to go slow with a letter that betrayed impatience with his brother-in-law: "We cannot afford to wait. For economic nationalism in Canada is just another name for economic ruin."[80]

In June 1934, Roosevelt signed the Reciprocal Trade Agreements Act. He had been pushing congressional leaders for the bill for months, and throughout that time Herridge had been telling them of Bennett's support. The act allowed the United States to offer any trading partner a mutual 50 per cent reduction in tariffs on agreed-upon goods. Bennett gave Herridge the responsibility to approach State Department officials to test whether a mutually beneficial bilateral trade agreement could be reached on a number of products that would benefit Canadian producers. For months Herridge tried to negotiate in good faith, but he was perturbed by American officials who were inexplicably unwilling to deal.

On November 14, after months of getting nowhere, Bennett took the rare move of going over the heads of the lower-level negotiators and wrote directly to Secretary of State Cordell Hull. The letter, no doubt composed with the advice of, or perhaps even written by, Herridge detailed every sticking point that had been raised over the months of unproductive talks. Bennett explained that the Ottawa Conference had erected no barriers to Canadian-American trade and that Canada had never defaulted on loans held by American banks. The letter ended adroitly with the acknowledgement of the purpose of the Reciprocal Trade Agreement Act and the Senate's Trades Agreement Committee, which, not coincidentally, was scheduled to begin talks on bilateral trade with Canada the very week that Bennett's letter arrived.[81] The letter was received and politely acknowledged. It led to more negotiations, but again nothing substantive was obtained. Bennett and Herridge nonetheless maintained their pressure and back-channel meetings.

Bennett had decided that progress on increasing trade with the United States had its best chance of being realized through closed-door negotiations away from the spotlight of public scrutiny. Lester Pearson, who had gained a great deal of experience in dealing with the Americans throughout the late 1920s and 1930s, agreed with Bennett's decision in this regard. He later wrote, "Contrary to the popular belief that secret negotiations were evil and dangerous, especially for the weaker party, my own experience has been that Canada, in settling her differences and resolving her problems with the United States, usually did better through quiet, rather than through headline diplomacy. Indeed, the latter is not diplomacy at all, but international public relations."[82] Bennett's decision to keep the details of the talks quiet was perhaps best for the country, but it eliminated the possibility of using them to demonstrate to Canadians that he was doing all that could be done to increase trade.

For two years the talks dragged on and on, bringing forth few substantive matters of agreement. Those months saw only slow and uneven economic recovery in Canada and a drastic reduction in Bennett's popularity. Increasing numbers were blaming him personally for the slow recovery and some even for the onset of the Depression in the first place. In December 1934, Bennett delivered speeches that foreshadowed a new bluntness—a tone that he would use to explain changes he believed necessary to spur a speedier recovery and build a more secure future. And in January 1935, he famously delivered five radio addresses that outlined his ideas. The press dubbed his program Bennett's New Deal. In the parliamentary session that immediately followed, Bennett oversaw the introduction of a number of bills designed to put those ideas into practice, as discussed in detail in chapter 8.

While moving his legislative agenda through Parliament, Bennett decided that he had finally had enough of the glacial pace of the American trade talks. He needed to do something bold to get things moving. With an election on the way, perhaps in a matter of months, and with his popularity continuing to plummet, reminding Canadians that he was still attempting to increase trade with the United States was not a bad political move.

On February 16, 1935, he delivered a speech before the Canadian Society of New York City in which he explained his belief that greater trade and commerce between Canada and the United States would benefit both countries. He began by praising President Roosevelt and Congress for the actions being taken to combat the Depression. He stated that both in the US and Canada, emergency measures were adopted first and reform legislation was enacted later so as to avoid ever again experiencing the worst that the Depression had served up. He reminded his audience that in the first eleven months of 1934, American trade with Canada was greater than with any other country. He argued that he had always believed in the positive use of protective tariffs but that the tariffs between Canada and the US were currently too high. He argued that American tariff changes of the 1920s had not helped international trade or American workers. Bennett noted that when Congress passed the Reciprocal Trade Agreements Act of 1934, however, it had handed the president great latitude to deal with those tariffs and to negotiate new trade agreements, such as the one that he was proposing. He then stated that both countries would benefit from greater bilateral trade and investment, and so trade barriers needed to be addressed and tariffs needed to be lowered on wood, fish, wheat, and a host of other products. He dangled the hopefully tempting idea that Canadian natural resources were such that their wealth could not even be accurately measured and would be of great benefit to America.[83] The speech led to more low-level trade talks but still no breakthrough.

In an interesting turn of events, Harvard University's Professor William Elliot unofficially visited Ottawa four months later and met with Mackenzie King. The State Department representative told the Liberal leader that his government was preparing to sign a treaty that would eliminate a host of tariffs in a unilateral action that would bring great benefit to the economies of both countries. Roosevelt had wanted Mackenzie King to know that the trade talks were going well and that he believed a deal would be signed before the upcoming Canadian election. He wanted the Liberals to prepare for the news to avoid being embarrassed by it. Mackenzie King asked Elliot to have the president wait until after the election to sign a trade deal to keep from helping Bennett. Elliot promised to do what he could but told him that it was believed that the Liberals would win the election with or without the trade agreement. Confirming that part of the reason for the American foot dragging in the trade negotiations was their anger at Bennett's imperial preference ideas, Elliot told Mackenzie King that if the Liberals represented Canada at the next Imperial Conference, and did as the Americans wished, Canada could expect even more reductions in tariffs.[84] This was not the last time that a Democratic president worked to help a Liberal leader. Kennedy did what he could to help Pearson and Clinton's speech criticizing separatism helped Chrétien. It was proof that behind FDR's charm and smile was a tough political operator who played politics as a contact sport. Unfortunately for Bennett, the Elliot visit proved that the game was on. The Democrat would not support the Conservative.

Unaware of the Mackenzie King–Elliot meeting, Bennett continued to encourage the talks with the same determination that the American negotiators used to stall them. Herridge became exasperated with the petty details that some of the talks were reduced to deliberating upon while avoiding main issues. In one report to Bennett, for instance, he complained about Americans wanting to talk about tariff reductions on items such as blueberries and cream while refusing to discuss fish or lumber. In another he wrote, "The impression was derived that the United States officials did not appreciate the sweeping character of their requests in relation to the limited number of valuable concessions offered to Canada."[85]

Bennett again tried to move things along by submitting a list of products that Herridge could take to the table that he believed would help both countries.[86] Herridge brought the list forward but nothing came of it. Bennett submitted a new list. It too went nowhere. Finally, on October 8 the American trade negotiators suspended talks until after the Canadian election.

In November 1935, just days after assuming office, Prime Minister Mackenzie King signed a comprehensive trade agreement with the United States. It gave Canada "most favoured nation" status and it dramatically lowered tariffs on over a thousand products, most importantly wood, fish, and wheat. The agreement was good for Canada. It was good for the United States. It was essentially the deal that Bennett and Herridge had been proposing for nearly two years.

Mackenzie King spoke proudly of a new day for Canada. It was a new day made brighter by more advantageous tariff and trade policies, numerous bilateral trade agreements, more direct trade with Britain and the United States, and four years in a row of rising exports and increasingly positive trade balances. As Canadians enjoyed the sunshine of those actions, Bennett watched from the opposition bench shadows.

CHAPTER SIX

CREATING CANADIAN ICONS

1931–1935

IN A DEMOCRACY such as Canada's, voters choose their political leaders according to a number of factors. Among them is the belief that a particular candidate will be able to handle with calm, reason, and resolve whatever challenges the Fates may devise. Voters sometimes think they are choosing a leader but end up with a manager. Good managers are those whose experience, values, and character are such that when difficult decisions arise, they are able to intelligently pick the best option given the facts known at the time. Good leaders are those who are able not only to do that, but more. They are also able to shape events and bring to fruition novel ideas and, in so doing, steer that which they lead in a new direction and thereby bring benefit to all. Good managers choose well between options while inspired leaders create new options from which to choose. Important leaders do more than play the rules of the game well—they change the game. R. B. Bennett was such a leader.

While working throughout his tenure as prime minister to provide relief to suffering Canadians and increase international trade to spur an economic recovery, Bennett was also creating three institutions that have become icons in Canada's statehood. In so doing, he changed the way Canadians relate to each other and the manner in which the Canadian state does business. In one way or another, and to different degrees and in different ways, each of the three brings benefit to the Canadian nation and state to this day.

Bennett helped to protect and promote Canadian culture and social uniqueness through his creation of what became the Canadian

Broadcasting Corporation (CBC). He moved Canada toward becoming a global trading power while helping virtually every sector of the economy through advancing the construction of the St. Lawrence Seaway. Bennett also created the Bank of Canada, which modernized the Canadian economy by providing an instrument through which monetary policy would be more professionally and centrally managed, with the inevitable boom-bust capitalist cycles rendered less extreme and destructive.

In all three cases, Bennett found many important and powerful people and groups advising or even threatening him to slow down or to do nothing at all. Those on the political right in his cabinet and caucus did all they could to stop him from putting his Tory principles so blatantly into practice. Those on the left, meanwhile, were frustrated by his unwillingness to do more or do it more quickly. In each case it would have been easier and more popular to do nothing. But effective leaders do not shrink from challenges or wilt in the face of criticism.

CANADIAN RADIO BROADCASTING CORPORATION

By the mid-1920s, commercial radio was thriving in Europe and the United States. Like early television and later the Internet, radio was not just a technological marvel and source of entertainment but also a new and exciting conduit through which those within a country gathered news and opinion and so engaged in a grand civic conversation. At its best, radio was a means through which citizenship could be enhanced. Beginning in Scandinavia, then catching on in western European countries and finally Britain, these notions regarding the importance of radio as a public good led to the regulation of stations and networks and various models of state financing and ownership. In the United States all stations remained in private hands, but the government conceded the civic value of radio and so the public was granted the ownership of the airwaves that they enjoy to this day.

Despite these actions taken by other governments, by the early 1920s radio in Canada was in terrible condition. As is the case with too many issues, Canada was a victim of its geography, for it had too much; money, because it had too little; and, at a critical moment, weak leadership that trembled in the face of those twin challenges. Radio signals were strong near the few small transmitters that dotted the largest cities, but grew weaker as one travelled farther from urban centres. Radio transmissions were absent in rural communities and merely a dream on isolated farms.

All of these facts were not enough to move Prime Minister Mackenzie King. But in 1928 he surrendered to pressure from the Catholic Church, which had been upset by radio broadcasts promoting the ideas of the Jehovah's Witnesses and criticizing the Catholic faith, and by J. S. Woodsworth, who was critical of the government's reacting to the spat by revoking the offenders' radio licences. The prime minister established the Royal Commission on Radio Broadcasting chaired by former Imperial Bank of Commerce President John Aird. Also on the commission were electrical engineer and educator Augustin Frigon and Charles Bowman, editor of the *Ottawa Citizen*. The commission's mandate was to offer advice on how Canada could catch up to the industrialized world while also investigating the viability of a state-owned radio broadcasting network. After a great deal of work and through studying what was being done in other countries, the Aird Report on Radio Broadcasting recommended that the government finance the creation of seven publicly owned stations not to replace, or even to offer competition to, but to augment the sixty-two commercial stations that existed at the time. To allow this to happen, it suggested that the government finance the creation of more wavelengths since at the time there were only forty-two in Canada. This meant that only forty-two stations could be on the air at any one moment. Such an investment would, the commission argued, boost the paltry 27,500 watts of total transmission power that existed in the country.

There was objection to the Aird Report. It came mostly from wealthy individuals who owned radio stations and who saw a public system as unfair competition. Opposition was also heard from those who saw publicly owned anything as smacking of socialism or even communism. There was no groundswell of support to counteract the loud voices of opposition. Mackenzie King decided to do with the report as is done with many: he put it on a shelf to gather dust.

In his response to Mackenzie King's February 1930 Speech from the Throne, opposition leader Bennett noted that in the previous session of Parliament the government had instituted several commissions and yet none of their findings or recommendations had found their way into the new agenda. Bennett made specific reference to the Aird Commission

Report. He said he had read it, supported its recommendations, and was saddened that the prime minister had decided to ignore it. In so doing, Bennett labelled himself a friend of public radio.[1]

Shortly after moving into the prime minister's office, Bennett asked Alfred Duranleau, his minister of marine and fisheries—under whose jurisdiction radio in Canada rested at the time, since it was so new and no one really knew where else to put it—to investigate the state of radio in the country. Duranleau and Bennett spoke several times about the issue and shared reports and letters. One such report was from eight commercial radio operators and manufacturers. It stated that there were 185,000 Canadian radio sets sold in Canada, but that 118,000 of them had been made in the United States. The report asked for the tariff to be raised on imported American radios to build the incipient Canadian industry.[2] The tariff recommendation aside, the report demonstrated the growing popularity of radio in Canada.

What the report did not mention, but that anyone listening to his or her newly purchased and probably American-made radio soon discovered, was that the majority of the voices emanating from the box had American accents. The Columbia Broadcasting System (CBS) and the National Broadcasting Corporation (NBC) were already being investigated by the United States Congress for their monopolization of the airwaves. Although American senators did not much care what signals were spilling over the northern border, Bennett's mailbag was filled with letters from many Canadian listeners who seemed to care a great deal about two large and growing American corporations adding to the infiltration of Canada by American culture and commerce. And the trend that was disturbing so many people was not about to stop. In fact, in November 1929, NBC had inaugurated a service operating out of CKGW in Toronto. All of its programming was American. So successful was the station that only three months later, NBC was in negotiation with Quebec's Marconi Radio Company to create another American station to broadcast 100 per cent American content at CFCF in Montreal.

In December 1930, the two-year-old National Council of the Canadian Radio League (CRL) had begun to make itself heard. It was a large group, with representation from every province and nearly every sector of society. It comprised a loosely tied amalgam of representatives from many groups, including the Royal Society of Canada, the Trades and Labour Congress, the Canadian Legion, and the Imperial Order Daughters of the Empire. On its board was president of the Canadian Bar Association and eventual prime minister Louis St. Laurent; W. M. Birks, who had turned his jewellery store into a successful national chain; First World War hero General Sir Arthur Currie, who was at that time the principal of McGill University; Cairine Wilson, president of the National Council of Women; and a rich cross-section of others representing Canada's elite, including senators, captains of industry and finance, labour leaders, and university presidents.

The CRL let it be known to Bennett, and anyone else who would listen, for that matter, that it supported the recommendation of the Aird Commission and wanted the creation of public radio. It argued, as the Aird Commission had, that private radio should continue to exist in Canada for it served a valuable purpose. But because private radio exists to earn a profit it cannot provide the educational and public service programming that is needed to tie together a country as vast as Canada. Nor, it argued, could private broadcasters be expected to lose money by extending their signals into remote areas. These services addressed the public good and thus should be undertaken by the government on the public's behalf.

In January 1931, Bennett received a copy of the RCA News. It spoke of the tremendous growth and popularity of radio in the United States. Of special interest to Bennett, given the important role that radio had played in his election just months before, was that President Hoover had used radio twenty-seven times to speak directly to Americans. Further, the report stated, 193 government officials had similarly taken their messages to the people.[3] It was another voice supporting the idea that radio could be a bulwark of democracy and an invaluable educational tool.

With the CRL making noise and Bennett privately, and occasionally publicly, stating his support, opposition to the idea of public radio began to again coalesce. As radio would do when TV appeared, and as TV would do when the Internet surfaced, newspaper owners saw new communications technology as a threat to their bottom lines. After the publication of the Aird Report, they had been among those who had petitioned Mackenzie King, demanding that he ignore the recommendations. Around Christmas of 1930, they began to organize again, this time to fight not just public radio but radio itself. A group of powerful editors told all other Canadian editors that they should refuse to print the names of or accept advertising from firms that also used radio advertising. They believed that every dime of advertising spending going to radio was being taken from them.[4] Choking the revenue stream would kill the usurper that was competing for ad dollars and the public's attention.

No sooner had the newspaper owners begun to fall together, however, than they fell apart. Like the precious few progressive thinkers of any transitional time, enough of them began to see that they could make more money cooperating with radio than fighting it. Some even began to seek opportunities to invest in new stations. The conglomerates that today own the companies that produce and then distribute product did not invent the notion that if you can't beat them, buy them.

With the newspaper opposition to radio and public radio fraying, others took the lead and organized letter-writing campaigns. Some argued from an ideological point of view, imploring Bennett to keep the hands of the state away from the radio industry. Others said that all of the government's attention and money should be directed toward economic matters related to ending the Depression. As MPs saw more and more negative letters arriving, many began to speak against public radio in weekly caucus meetings. In January 1931, William Tummon, Conservative MP from Hastings South, Ontario, told Bennett that he had received four hundred letters from constituents, all stating their opposition to public radio.[5] A Belleville MP claimed to have received nearly a hundred such letters.[6] Letters from business people from coast to coast poured in with nearly all opposed to the idea.

In March, Canadian private radio broadcasters weighed in with a nineteen-page pamphlet entitled *Radio Broadcasting Under Private Ownership*. It outlined the benefits that private ownership had brought to Canada. It then presented an argument against the recommendations of the Aird Commission. The arguments were persuasively stated, although they all distorted what the commission report had actually said. The arguments can be understood simply by knowing that they were peppered with words and phrases such as "monopoly," "censorship," "lack of choice," "increased licence fees," and "discrimination." The pamphlet went on to use similar sophistry to attack the recommendations of the CRL. The final page listed forty-seven companies that had expressed support for private radio. Among them were Imperial Tobacco, Simpson's, Lowney, Neilson, Quaker Oats, Pepsodent, Silverwoods Dairy, Dominion Stores, Massey Harris, Shirriff's, Fuller Brush, and Supertest Petroleum. And, the list concluded ominously, many others.[7]

With the economic collapse robbing the government of revenue, a host of complex issues demanding Bennett's time, and in the face of such organized and potent opposition, it would have been understandable if Bennett had taken Mackenzie King's lead and let the matter drop. But he did not. He made it clear to those around him that he wanted the matter of public radio pursued. He was supported in this goal by Rod K. Finlayson, the Winnipeg lawyer who sat on the executive committee of the CRL. Bennett had met Finlayson during the 1930 campaign and had been impressed with his intelligence and wit. Shortly after the election Bennett sought Finlayson's advice on several matters and each time had been rewarded with pithy, articulate replies. He was to become one of Bennett's most trusted advisers.

Bill Herridge was another supporter of public radio. On April 14, 1931, after a long courtship, Herridge had married Bennett's beloved sister Mildred. The wedding was a major social event with many of the country's political and business elite in attendance at the grand reception at the Château Laurier. Bennett beamed as he stood at the hotel's door and watched his sister acknowledge the crowd of Ottawa citizens that had gathered on Wellington Street to wish her well. The festivities were splendid but the honeymoon brief. Bennett took but a few hours off to attend the ceremony and part of the evening's reception but then was back upstairs to pore over his briefing books. Herridge and Mildred were soon on an official trip to England with Bennett, then off to their new home in Washington.

While in London with Bennett, Herridge had been cabled by the CRL's Graham Spry. Spry was aware of Bennett's desire to use Britain to stand against American influence in trade. He sought to use that inclination to encourage Bennett to see radio as a way to protect Canada against being swamped by American culture. Herridge spoke to Bennett about the issue. Bennett cabled Spry, telling him that he wanted him to investigate the notion of public radio further and that there would no more commercial radio licences granted at least until he had returned to Canada.[8] Bennett's next cable was to Duranleau, with the instruction to issue no more licences.[9]

Just as the move toward public radio was beginning to proceed, however, it was stopped. It was temporarily frozen by a court case brought against the federal government by the government of Quebec. Quebec insisted that the granting of radio licences was a provincial jurisdiction. If Quebec was right, then public radio was doomed. Bennett, however, insisted that under Section 91, Subsection 29, of the BNA Act, radio fell under federal jurisdiction. The scrap was on and the case quickly found its way across Parliament Hill to the Supreme Court— housed at that time in a dilapidated, leaky old building that would be demolished just as the court itself was growing to become more relevant. Bennett ordered a vigorous defence. Government lawyers were helped by the CRL, which paid the expenses of Brooke Claxton, who presented a compelling case in support of the federal government's argument. He made two main points. First, he noted that the Constitution's residual power clause granted responsibilities that were not specifically allotted to either level of government to the feds. This clause, he argued, gave the federal government the power to regulate radio. Second, and an even more persuasive argument, was that in 1927, Canada and seventy-eight other countries had signed the International Radio Telegraph Convention. The legality of that treaty, along with the fact that only the federal government had the constitutional power to enter into treaties, meant that the regulation of radio was within the federal government's power. The Supreme Court agreed.

Quebec was not satisfied, however, and began an appeal process that saw the case land with the Judicial Committee of the Privy Council's office in London, with its power to overrule decisions of the Canadian Supreme Court. Meanwhile, the Americans had been watching the Canadian situation. In January 1932, the American Senate passed a resolution stating that the secretary of state should immediately undertake negotiations with governments of other North American countries with regard to allowing more American radio owners and advertisers into their markets. The senators were coveting Canadian air and American corporations were about to pounce, just as Bennett's hands were tied by another interminable federal-provincial squabble.

A month later, however, the Privy Council denied Quebec's appeal.

The decision handed Bennett the constitutional power to act. Less than a week after the ruling he stood in the House to announce the formation of a special parliamentary committee to undertake a study of not only commercial radio in Canada but also of the idea of a publicly funded radio network. He appointed noted friend of public radio Raymond Morand to be its chair. He and the other seven commissioners were drawn from business, radio, and public life, and were both Conservatives and Liberals. They set to work quickly and travelled the country hearing testimony.

Bennett's active pursuit of the public radio option, and his appointment of Morand, who had openly expressed his support for the idea, made Bennett's beliefs in the matter of public ownership clear. His conviction that the government should play a role in protecting and promoting Canada's social and cultural uniqueness had already been seen in the actions he had taken to protect Canada's infant magazine industry. In July 1931, Bennett had sought to stop the influx of American magazines into the Canadian market by proposing drastically increased duties on them. He assured Canadians that scholarly journals and those addressing themselves to religious matters and economic concerns would be exempt. He explained to the House that he was seeking to inspire Canadians to look within Canada for cultural and intellectual stimulation.[10] In February 1932, in announcing the Morand Committee, he made the same argument with respect to public radio, telling the House, "The enormous benefits of an adequate scheme of radio broadcasting controlled and operated by Canadians is abundantly plain. Properly employed, the radio can be made a most effective instrument in nation building, with an education value difficult to estimate."[11]

Knowing it had an ally in Bennett, the CRL ensured that the Morand Committee heard from witness after witness who urged the creation of a public radio network. While the committee work was being done, Bennett and Spry spoke on the phone about both the committee and about what was being done across the country to stir up interest in the public radio scheme. Spry assured Bennett that he was gathering people of influence to endorse the idea. Among those who spoke in favour of public radio, for instance, were former prime ministers Borden and Meighen. Meighen had long been a strong proponent of public radio. Meighen spoke to Bennett about the manner in which American and

Australian radio, both of which were totally in private hands, were not serving the best needs of the people and not allowing radio to meet its potential.[12] In so doing, he emboldened Bennett to be brave in the face of so much opposition.

Some of that opposition came from the many members of Bennett's caucus who were cool to the idea of public radio. Some were outright hostile. Many continued to bring the subject up in caucus meetings and others wrote letters to the prime minister expressing their opposition. From Quebec he heard that the idea was no good because the province would be swamped with English programming, and from the West he heard that it was no good because taxpayers would be forced to finance French programming. From some he heard the legitimate ideological opposition to government intervention into what had been a private realm of enterprise, and from others the excuse that the creation of public radio should be delayed until the Depression ended. Bennett listened to all, but his reactions in caucus and replies to the letters indicated that while he understood the points raised he did not agree with them.

As the Morand Committee ended its hearings and began work on its final report, opposition to public radio reached a fever pitch. Bennett was approached by a number of business people who either saw public radio as placing the government on a slippery slope toward a socialist ownership of industry or as a danger to their profit margins or both. Edward Beatty tried to dissuade Bennett from his support. He argued that a national radio network was a good idea but that private enterprise could build a better network faster and more efficiently than government ever could. Bennett received a number of letters from other friends and business associates that also warned him away from public radio. Many of the correspondents had contributed handsomely to the Conservative Party. R. W. Ashcroft from the Canadian Association of Broadcasters even promised that if Bennett killed the idea, he would enjoy an hour of free nationally broadcast radio time to deliver his New Year's message to Canadians.[13]

The Morand Committee's report was received by Bennett in late April and tabled in the House on May 9, 1932. It began by reviewing its mandate and the points made in the public and written submissions. It then recommended that the government create a radio broadcasting commission that would, through three independent commissioners, regulate all broadcasting in Canada. The commission should, it said, allow private broadcasters to continue to operate, but it should have the power to grant and cancel licences, create and purchase programming, build and operate stations, and regulate everything that went on the air including programs and advertising. Further, it recommended a national network of stations operating with optimum power. The stations should exist for educational purposes, for legitimate experimental work, and for broadcasting programs of community interest. The stations, the report said, should operate with the money made available through transmission and licence fees. In other words, they should be commercial free.[14]

Bennett acted quickly to put the commission's recommendations into law. In the debate over the bill that he had ordered to be written, Bennett foreshadowed the intention and achievement of the Canadian Radio and Television Commission. He spoke of the importance of public radio as a means to protect Canada from undue American influence while simultaneously bolstering Canadian national unity and pride through the promotion of Canadian arts and artists. Canadian artists, he argued, enable Canadians to speak with one another and of each other. Canadians needed Canadian stories told, especially given the neighbourhood. Culture is the glue of any civil society. Bennett said,

> Without such control, radio broadcasting can never become the great agency for the communication of matters of national concern and for the diffusion of national thought and ideals, and without such control it can never be the agency by which national consciousness may be fostered and sustained and national unity still further strengthened.[15]

Bennett also made an argument that would later be appropriated to justify the creation of VIA Rail and Air Canada. He said,

> Private ownership must necessarily discriminate between densely and sparsely populated areas. This is not a correctable fault in private ownership; it is an inescapable and inherent demerit of that system. It does not seem right that in Canada the towns should be preferred to the countryside or the prosperous communities to those less fortunate.[16]

The bill passed the House with only one member casting a dissenting vote. It received royal assent and became law on May 26, 1932. The Canadian Radio Broadcasting Corporation (CRBC) that would grow into the CBC was born. Bennett then moved to expedite appointments to the CRBC's commission and the drawing up of the procedures that would specify the manner in which it would pursue its broad and ambitious mandate. When the members of the commission were appointed, it quickly began planning for the establishment of 5,000-watt stations in Montreal, Toronto, Winnipeg, and Red Deer. It planned for another thirty-two stations operating with 500 watts or greater. It also recommended, and the government accepted, something that no one had before discussed: that the annual tax of one dollar that had for years been levied on each radio owner be abolished. Bennett agreed and the hated tax was gone.

The CRBC soon found itself bogged down in a morass of difficulties. Most importantly, there were technical troubles with the creation of the network, with decisions regarding programming, with the percentage of French versus English programming, and with funding. In March 1933, an act to amend the Canadian Radio Broadcasting Act was introduced. The act afforded the CRBC more independence from Parliament and greater power to spend the profits it was already making. It also gave CRBC commissioners the equivalent rank of a deputy minister. It allowed the CRBC to go outside the existing civil service to hire the experts it needed. The bill's purpose, Bennett explained, was to allow the CRBC the power and flexibility it needed to pursue its goal of promoting excellence in Canadian radio for the benefit of Canadians.

Bennett was pleased with the work the CRBC was doing but, as was typical for him, he wanted more and he wanted it faster. To see what could be done, he turned to a man who would play a significant but shadowy role in Canadian history—Gladstone Murray. Born in British Columbia, Murray was a graduate of McGill University who had earned a Rhodes Scholarship to study at Oxford. He came to Bennett's attention as a journalist writing for Beaverbrook's *Daily Express*. Beaverbrook supported his career and Murray joined what became the state-owned British Broadcasting Corporation (BBC). He was quickly promoted to the point where, when Bennett called upon him, he was the BBC's manager of political relations.

Bennett asked Murray for his opinion on the CRBC and in June 1933 Murray responded with a well-researched report. He assured Bennett that the CRBC's problems were all fixable. He said that a clearer mandate, more secure funding, and time were the antidotes. His report concluded, "In the development of public service broadcasting on a co-operative constructive basis, with management on efficient business lines and State control remote yet secure, Canada will be in a position to add immeasurably to the amenities of civilization and also to produce a decisive new instrument of national unity and stability."[17]

Bennett was quick to make Murray's report public as it supported both the fledgling CRBC and his ideas regarding public radio that had led to its conception and establishment in the first place. He also saw to it that some of the report's recommendations were implemented with more amendments to the CRBC's operating mandate. Funding, however, remained a significant challenge. The scant resources available to the government in the midst of the Depression were an insurmountable hurdle.

The funding problems that faced the CRBC offer an interesting insight into the behind-the-scenes operations of the Bennett cabinet. On two occasions, cabinet took actions against the CRBC when Bennett was not present. In June 1933, when Bennett was in London, cabinet cut its funding through an order-in-council. When Bennett returned he rescinded the order and funding was restored. In May 1935, when Bennett was ill and convalescing, cabinet violated the law by approving radio licences and American programming on newly created stations. Ministers loyal to Bennett informed him of cabinet's action and Bennett again came to the CRBC's defence and reversed the decision. Despite these acts of insubordination, no one was fired.

More attacks against the CRBC, many well earned and others driven by blind ideological opposition, were launched throughout the remainder of Bennett's time in office. Despite the misgivings about public radio and the exceptional difficulties the CRBC experienced in making the vision a reality, Bennett never lost faith in the vision itself. He was proud of his work in establishing the national broadcasting network and demonstrated that fact by taking time to appear whenever he could at the inauguration of new stations. On Saturday, December 1, 1934, for instance, the prime minister travelled to Winnipeg and spoke at the opening of

CKY. It boasted a 15,000 watt transmitter, making it greater than any other operating in the country at the time. Bennett praised the daring initiative because it was pursuing a goal he had when he established the radio commission two years before: to bring radio to all Canadians but especially to those in rural areas. He saw such a service, he said that day, as playing an important role in strengthening Canada's social fabric.[18]

In 1935, Mackenzie King could very well have killed the CRBC. Instead, he moved to re-form and improve it. It became the Canadian Broadcasting Corporation (CBC) with a more precise mandate regarding news and public education, more secure funding, and a more masterful manager in Gladstone Murray.

ST. LAWRENCE SEAWAY

The St. Lawrence River was the first trans-Canada highway. After providing a trade and transportation route for Native nations for thousands of years, it took the first European adventurers into the interior for gold and souls. Those of the economic determinist school of Canadian historical scholarship have based careers upon the argument that through the quest for furs, the mighty waterways and especially the St. Lawrence played a more significant role in the creation of Canada than political decisions made in Paris, London, or later, Ottawa. Renowned historian Harold Innis, who was the father of what became known as the Laurentian thesis, wrote in 1930, "The present Dominion emerged not in spite of geography but because of it."[19] Canada was, according to the title and thesis of Donald Creighton's seminal book, the "empire of the St. Lawrence." And yet, as important as the river had always been, by the 1920s the St. Lawrence was still largely unchanged. While there were power plants and canals, docking facilities and bridges, much of the river remained an untamed torrent singing with the crash of mighty rapids. It was romantic alright, but mostly unnavigable. Many saw the potential in a great St. Lawrence project, but many more thought it unimaginable.

When finally completed in 1959, the St. Lawrence Seaway took its place among the world's great technological, economic, and political achievements. It allowed mammoth ships to take cargo to nearly the centre of the country: a distance equal to that of the transatlantic voyage itself. The seaway's construction took five years, 22,000 workers, and

$470 million, with cooperation from the governments of Canada, America, Ontario, Quebec, and New York. Soon, about 40 per cent of American and about 67 per cent of all Canadian export goods travelled through the seaway to the world. Manufactured goods from Ontario factories, iron ore and other such products from the north, and grain, wheat, and corn from the prairies all made their way through the seaway. Meanwhile, electrical power made possible by the construction lit homes and factories.

The vision for the creation of a seaway along the St. Lawrence can be traced to Dollier de Casson, who in 1680 brought his talents and money to an attempt to build a canal around the Lachine Rapids. The realization that Canadian-American cooperation would be needed to realize the vision was seen in the 1892 attempt by Minnesota congressman John Lind to initiate an investigation into a joint project to create a water route from the Great Lakes to the mouth of the St. Lawrence. In 1921, an International Joint Commission recommended to both governments that a cooperative effort should be undertaken to construct dams, canals, and power plants along the river. In Canada, it was argued that the seaway would create direct benefit for Quebec City and Montreal, as they would become important international ports. It was suggested that Ontario would benefit from the additional power capacity while its manufactured goods, as well as products from the West, could make their way through the province to the wider world.

Like most things Canadian, however, even when the benefits are clear, the old squabbles about federal-provincial jurisdiction had to first be endured. Questions about which level of government owned the water, or the riverbed, or the river's banks, and which level should pay for the construction and later own the seaway's many facets, or be responsible for the maintenance and repair of all that would be built, all needed to be agreed upon. Further, if power was to be generated, who would own the plants and the power? If the power was sold, what would be the price and who would profit?

These questions and more landed on Prime Minister Mackenzie King's desk in early 1923. It is clear from the actions he took and confidences he shared that he weighed the economic potential against the political challenges and decided to shelve the International Joint Commission Report and do nothing. Mackenzie King confided to his

diary, "I believe the project will come about someday but is full of uncertainties begetting its technical aspects—power—water canal etc. &
possibilities of international friction in joint ownership of anything so
vast."[20]

Quebec's Liberal premier Taschereau and Ontario Conservative
premier Ferguson disagreed about nearly everything, but with respect
to the possibility of moving forward with the seaway they found themselves in anomalous harmony. Together they pressured Mackenzie King
to at least discuss the concept. The prime minister stalled all that he
could and then came upon a terrific delaying tactic. In April 1928, he
asked the Supreme Court to settle the federal-provincial jurisdiction
question. The court was vague and suggested that a political decision
needed to be made because a constitutional one was not viable.

Unable to delay discussions any longer, Mackenzie King finally
agreed to meet with two provincial delegations in January 1930. It was
clear from the beginning of the meeting, however, that his intention
remained to stop the seaway. In addition to his earlier fears, he had
somehow persuaded himself that because the project would necessitate
negotiations with Washington and New York State, it would result in a
surrender of Canadian sovereignty that could ultimately lead toward
American annexation.[21]

Mackenzie King attempted to derail the meeting by digging out a
two-year-old letter from Ferguson in which the premier had urged the
building of a power plant on the St. Lawrence to provide electricity for
Ontario at a cost favouring his province. Power generation was of particular importance to Ferguson as Ontario desperately needed electricity for its manufacturing plants in the rapidly growing region hugging
Lake Ontario's western shore from Toronto to Niagara Falls, known as
the Golden Horseshoe. Meanwhile, Quebec had just witnessed the creation of the Beauharnois power plant, which was privately owned and
generating more power than it needed. The Quebec government stood
to make a tidy profit if demand could continue to outpace supply.
Keeping Ontario from erecting a plant on the St. Lawrence was essential
to this scenario.

Mackenzie King had shown the letter to his Quebec lieutenant
Ernest Lapointe and Finance Minister Charles Dunning, who were understandably upset that Ferguson had been speaking with him about a

partnership without involving Quebec in the discussion. Their anger meant the plan was perfect. Mackenzie King was happy to have found this way to, as he put it, "corner" Ferguson, anger Taschereau, and scuttle both the meeting and progress on the seaway.[22] The meeting blundered on but soon fell apart in recrimination and bad feelings.

It was eventually agreed that the premiers would repair to their capitals and compose letters to him outlining what they thought the three had agreed upon. The two wrote that Mackenzie King had agreed that the provinces owned and enjoyed full proprietary rights on the river's beds, banks, and waters and that the federal government would bear the lion's share of the costs. Mackenzie King responded that nothing of the sort had been agreed to and so progress that had appeared to be afoot was halted.

Meanwhile, Quebec's Beauharnois power plant was the subject of intense scrutiny in the House of Commons. Alberta MLA Robert Gardiner had noted that in 1927 the federal and Quebec governments had approved the project and the use of 40,000 cubic feet per second of river water with the estimate of it basing its operations on $1.2 million in capital assets. By early 1930, Gardiner alleged, the company had $30 million in capital assets. He wondered if money was being illegally pocketed or if secret deals had been made and demanded an inquiry into the dealings of the man at the centre of the deals: R. O. Sweeney. The Mackenzie King government swayed and dodged and an inquiry was avoided.

After the 1930 election, Gardiner brought the issue to the House again, but this time Prime Minister Bennett agreed to an investigation. Bennett was interested in getting to the bottom of what appeared to be a shady scheme. Bennett had known Sweeney for some time and, in fact, Sweeney had approached him with a ridiculously low offer to purchase his interest in the E. B. Eddy Company. The two men intensely disliked each other.

The inquiry reported in July 1931 that deputy minister of public works Harold Bonner handled the details of the federal grant of water rights to the Beauharnois Power Corporation while he was also serving as the corporation's general manager. Further, it was found that the grant had enabled investors to turn a quick $2.1 million profit on their initial outlay while they also arranged to control a majority of the stock worth an additional $17 million. Beyond that, the corporation had funnelled about $650,000, through two Liberal senators, to the Liberal Party for use in the 1930 campaign while also picking up the tab for Prime Minister Mackenzie King's stay at a swanky Bermuda hotel. Upon hearing that his hotel receipt was about to be made public, Mackenzie King had rushed to Bennett's office and asked that the evidence be suppressed to protect the dignity of the Prime Minister's Office[23] Bennett agreed, but the damning receipt was nonetheless public within days. To Mackenzie King's excuse that he did not know who had paid for his vacation, Bennett reminded all that the person who receives criminally obtained benefit is usually the criminal.[24]

At this point, Bennett probably would have been excused had he let the seaway project disappear into the vortex of the Liberal and corporate scandal, spinning with the seemingly endless federal-provincial snits and constitutional spats. After all, he faced the same political, technical, and jurisdictional challenges that had turned Mackenzie King's feet to stone. Everything suggested that he should have just let the seaway dream fade away.

But by the time he became prime minister, Bennett had been showing an interest in the project for over a year. In January 1929, the still relatively new Conservative opposition leader had read two reports contained within the *McGill University News*. The first detailed the technical challenges inherent in building the seaway and the second attempted to make sense of the political labyrinth through which anyone wishing to realize or at least advance the project would need to pass. It was clear from the reports that the political challenges outweighed the technical. To understand similar challenges, Bennett asked his staff to provide him with information regarding the manner in which the French had failed and the Americans had succeeded in building the Panama Canal.

Throughout the 1930 campaign, Bennett had argued that the seaway would be good for Ontario in providing power, good for Quebec in creating jobs and bolstering communities touched by the development, good for the West in reducing the costs of shipping goods, and good for the country as a whole. Within a stump speech that was repeated throughout the country, he had spoken of the St. Lawrence River and asked why a proper canal and seaway to the world's markets had not already been built. Anticipating opposition, he'd stated that it could and should be built with no threat to Canadian sovereignty. He argued that the only reason it had not been built was that the Liberal government did not choose to build it, and that it had refused only because Mackenzie King was not sufficiently daring. He challenged his listeners to share his intrepid vision, saying,

> See this great water route as the carrier of half the world's trade. See the factories that grow up on its banks, their wheels spun by the harnessed stream. See the people come to man them: The purchasers of your products. See the growth of the cities lying within its basin: They, your assured market in all the years to come. I once called the St. Lawrence basin the Ruhr to be of Canada. I should more properly have termed it, the Ruhr of North America.[25]

Bennett slammed Prime Minister Mackenzie King for his refusal to believe that it is government's job to make such investments and undertake such projects. He criticized him for having stated that the seaway system was not needed because there was not sufficient trade. Bennett argued that the seaway would increase trade and thus the traffic would meet the capacity. If they built it, the ships would come. He showed political courage in making these points not only in Ontario and Quebec, where the benefits were obvious and direct, but everywhere.

Bennett received a good deal of mail from those who had been confused and infuriated by Mackenzie King's inability or unwillingness to move the seaway project forward. O. E. Fleming, for instance, president of the Canadian Deep Waterways and Power Association, was one of many who had publicly expressed frustration with Mackenzie King for doing so little since the publication of the International Joint Commission Report eight years before. He wrote to Bennett noting that Mackenzie King had not even mentioned the St. Lawrence project in his 1930 Throne Speech. After all the work that had been done, Fleming wrote, that obviously intentional oversight had led him to give up on the man.[26]

In expressing interest in the project, Bennett also aroused the critics to whom Mackenzie King had listened. Many slammed the seaway project as having benefits that could not be balanced against the enormous costs of despoiling a beautiful river, destroying valuable farmland, flooding people's homes, and spending outrageous amounts of public money. They were valid arguments. Others said that its construction was technically impossible. Much of the opposition to the seaway was based upon suspicion about the United States. Some saw a seaway agreement, no matter how it was structured, as surrendering sovereignty to the Americans. Still others believed, perhaps accurately, that the United States was interested in the project only to secure more electrical power for itself. Americans were talking about improved navigation only to placate Canadians; the real objective was to have Canada pony up some of the cash that would allow New York State to meet its growing power needs. No one, after all, had ever accused New York's governor, the brash and charismatic Franklin D. Roosevelt, of being dumb.

Bennett understood the political, economic, and technological challenges but was intimidated by none of them. He had become certain that the benefits would outweigh the costs and the technical issues could be resolved. The only point he conceded was that he could not understand the American attitude toward the project. He was sincerely baffled by the Americans' reluctance to share his vision, to be bold, to rebel against timidity by putting shovels in the ground and getting on with it.[27] And in Canada, like Mackenzie King, he knew the costs and risks associated with entering the gauntlet through which he would have to pass to move the project forward. But unlike Mackenzie King, he summoned the political courage to do so.

The first action on the seaway file that Bennett took as prime minister was to ignore those who pressured his government to stop or slow the construction of southwestern Ontario's Welland Canal. The Welland Canal is a technological marvel. It was dug in 1829 and allowed an end to the portage around Niagara Falls. From its inception, it was seen as the initial step in a dream that would be realized with the completion of locks that would tame the St. Lawrence and provide a highway of fresh then salt water to Europe and the world. In 1841, the colonial government of Upper Canada had seen the value in the people owning and controlling such a vital resource and had purchased all of the canal's private stock. More canals were built with another stage begun in 1913, stopped during the First World War, but then started again in 1919.

When he took office, Bennett found that the expansion of the canal was years behind schedule and vastly over budget. He ordered Manion, his minister of railways and canals, to put pressure on those who were involved with the project to complete it on time, according to a new set of deadlines, and to better control costs.

With Manion taking a direct interest, the canal expansion was finished in 1931, at a cost of $130 million. Bennett delayed its grand opening to coincide with the 1932 Ottawa Imperial Trade Conference. Specially outfitted trains were arranged to take dignitaries to the event. Governor General Lord Bessborough was the host and in attendance were the leaders of all attending nations. Bennett made a fine and inspiring speech, as did Britain's Stanley Baldwin, and both speeches were transmitted over the radio. All applauded as the 540-foot-long *Lemoyne*, carrying 540,000 bushels of Manitoba grain, passed through the canal on its way to Toronto. It was an inspiring moment that Bennett had set up to promote the St. Lawrence Seaway.

Shortly after the conference concluded, Bennett initiated contact with American president Hoover. During his 1928 presidential campaign, Hoover had spoken of the advantages of building an internal trade route from, as he mapped it, Duluth, Minnesota, to the Atlantic. Bennett was impressed with Hoover and for good reason; he brought to the presidency a wealth of experience. A blacksmith's son, Hoover had been born to limited means in a small Iowa town, but his intelligence and drive saw him graduate with an engineering degree from Stanford. He was working as a mining engineer in China when in June 1900 the Boxer Rebellion led to violence, and with his wife Lou's support he personally intervened to save hundreds of children's lives. He later led efforts to bring more than 120,000 Americans home from Europe at the outset of the First World War. After the war, he led the American Food Administration that brought much-needed food to starving millions in Europe and civil war–ravaged Russia. Europeans dubbed them Hoover rations and called Hoover a hero. He later served as commerce secretary under presidents Harding and Coolidge.

Despite Hoover's intellect, personal and political courage, and political and philanthropic accomplishments, he suffered from an image problem. He lacked charisma and personal charm. Like many self-made men, he had little patience for those he deemed lazy or foolish. These qualities, coupled with his inability to end the Depression while appearing to have little empathy for those suffering its consequences, led to his unpopularity with the majority of Americans. Like Bennett, his negative public persona would taint his term in office and trivialize all that he had done in his life.

The two leaders met in Washington in January 1931. They discussed a number of issues before Bennett raised the seaway question. Hoover had been well briefed and so was quick to propose that the two immediately establish another joint commission to negotiate a treaty that might move the project ahead. This was exactly what Bennett had told advisers that he wanted, but upon seeing that the president wanted it too, the skilful prime minister weaved about and said that a number of irritants needed to be addressed before such a commission could be contemplated. But Bennett had learned what he needed to know: the American president shared his eagerness to make progress on the seaway.

Present at Bennett's meeting with Hoover and essential in all his dealings with the Americans was Bill Herridge. He had quickly become well connected and well liked in Washington's inner circles. Herridge had presented his credentials as Canada's ambassador to the United States to President Hoover. He had arrived with instructions that among his priorities was to take whatever action he deemed prudent to advance the St. Lawrence Seaway negotiations. Like Bennett, Herridge had long been a supporter of the seaway. Even before his appointment to Washington, he had devoted many hours to reading about the project. He had invited General Andrew McNaughton, who was an engineer and acknowledged expert on the seaway, to spend a number of weekends at his cottage. The two had delved into the many technical aspects of the undertaking.

Herridge and Bennett had also devoted a good deal of time to discussing the technical and political obstacles. In one of those discussions, Bennett acceded to Herridge's request that he be given the authority to carry out negotiations alone, without the involvement of the External Affairs Department, and even without commissioners.[28] Bennett trusted him and saw value in his working alone.

It was thus with the *gravitas* of his office, the faith and direction of his prime minister, the personality of a charming and skilled negotiator, and an expert's knowledge of the political and technical challenges before him, that Herridge began his work. He knew that President Hoover remained keen on advancing the project. His meetings in Ottawa with

American ambassador Hanford MacNider had told him that. He had also met with Secretary of State Henry Stimson, who had been told by Hoover to expedite the talks and arrive at an agreement as quickly as possible. Herridge reported back to Bennett that the negotiations were going well and the two discussed some of the intricacies of what lay ahead.

As with the American trade talks, Bennett was careful to keep the negotiations' details secret, but he did let Canadians know that he was proceeding with the seaway initiative. In answer to a question in the House about the Welland Canal, he spoke about the importance of the canal's reconstruction so that it could carry ocean-bound ships. He then broadened his response beyond what the questioner had asked in bringing up the fact that a similar deepening of the Hudson River was being undertaken as well. He used the two projects to explain how both the Canadian and American governments were demonstrating a belief in canal projects as a way of stimulating short- and long-term economic activity. When the Opposition spoke against such work as foolhardy in a time of limited resources, Bennett thundered back, "Did it ever occur to honourable members that there are occasions in the lives of nations as of individuals when decisions have to be made or the opportunity is gone forever."[29] Meanwhile, Bennett asked General McNaughton to devote more time to working in consultation with Herridge on a draft treaty. By the end of June, Bennett had signed off on the McNaughton-Herridge draft.

After a series of preliminary discussions in July 1931, a secret lunch meeting took place involving Herridge and Americans Ambassador Hanford, Secretary of State Stimson, and Assistant Secretary of State Rogers. The men had developed a trusting and collegial relationship, all had done their homework, and all enjoyed the support of their prime minister and president. An agreement was quickly reached. Herridge was proud to report to Bennett that the rough outline of the agreement mirrored much of the Canadian draft proposal.[30]

The lunch agreement stated that the project would proceed, technical matters would be worked out later, and the estimated $800-million cost would be shared equally between the two countries. The agreement was quite specific and involved building a 27-foot deep channel from Lake Superior to the St. Lawrence. Dams, canals, locks, and electricity-generating power plants would be shared by both countries. It was believed that everything could be completed in eight years. While construction was proceeding, private companies would refit the ships that had previously traversed only the lakes to allow for sea travel. Port facilities along the route would be improved to accommodate them. Hoover quickly signed off on the agreement, as did Bennett.

Meanwhile, anticipating the agreement, Bennett and Manion had begun talks with Ontario's new premier, Conservative George Henry, who had taken office in December 1930. Henry had quickly moved toward agreements with Bennett regarding the amount the province would pay to build the seaway balanced with the amount it would earn through the electrical power that would be derived from it.

Only after the agreement with Ontario was made did Bennett bring Quebec premier Louis-Alexandre Taschereau to the table. Taschereau had been Quebec's premier since 1920 and had been intricately involved in all power projects and other capital improvements along the St. Lawrence. He was understandably angry about not only the fact that deals had been made with Ontario and the United States without Quebec's involvement, but also about the details of those deals. In a harshly worded letter to the prime minister, Taschereau made it clear that he believed Quebec had been betrayed. Bennett was calm in his reply and patiently responded to each of the premier's complaints. He concluded that Quebec would benefit from the seaway more than the federal government or any other province or state.[31] The condescending tone was that of a teacher to a petulant child. Bennett's letter must have worked, though, for Taschereau made no public criticism of the deal or of Bennett. On the contrary, he pledged to abide by the agreements that the prime minister had forged.

Bennett had done something remarkable, something that Mackenzie King had refused to even try. He had managed to carry out a three-way negotiation with three tough bargainers. He'd settled matters in a way that would bring great economic benefit to the country when it needed it most, while also enriching Canada's economy for decades to come. The deal promised benefits to both countries—but it was not to be.

News of the clandestine Washington lunch that had led to the secret Canadian-American deal was leaked to Governor Roosevelt. Like his Quebec counterpart, FDR was incensed that a deal had been reached without his involvement. Roosevelt had taken office somewhat cautious about the seaway. His cousin and former New York governor Theodore

Roosevelt had warned as far back as 1914 about water-power barons who would promote the enterprise to line their own pockets while bringing little benefit to the people of the state. Further, FDR had seen his predecessor, Governor Alfred E. Smith, expend an enormous amount of political capital in vainly trying to bring about progress on the project.

But FDR had sufficiently overcome his fears to at least establish a commission to study the project. In April 1931, he went further and had enacted the New York Power Authority Act, which supported the construction of power plants on the St. Lawrence to bring abundant and cheap electricity to the farms, homes, and factories of his state. Without disclosing his negotiations with Bennett, Hoover had politely but firmly told Roosevelt that a larger seaway plan would be in accord with the New York legislation and would bring the benefits to New Yorkers that FDR had hoped. But before Roosevelt had time to react, first the *Baltimore Sun* and then other American and Canadian newspapers reported the secret Canadian-American deal. Roosevelt was forced to speak against it as it entailed his state surrendering riparian rights and paying a higher percentage of the costs than his New York Power Authority Act had envisioned.

Bennett and Hoover chose to proceed through the political hurricane that their agreement had unleashed in Quebec and New York and on July 18, 1932, the St. Lawrence Deep Waterway Treaty was signed. Many newspapers on both sides of the border dubbed it the Hoover-Bennett Treaty. Canadian reaction was generally positive. Even Mackenzie King confided in his diary that Bennett had worked out a very good deal for Canada.[32]

Bennett was confident that his majority in the House would see the treaty pass through Parliament with a minimum of fuss. However, the American Constitution states that two-thirds of the Senate must ratify all treaties. When finally presented to the Senate on December 6, 1932, the Hoover-Bennett Treaty ran into three problems. First, Hoover had lost the election the month before and so was a lame duck with little power to persuade legislators as they awaited the inauguration of the next president in March. Second, President-elect Roosevelt was still cool to the idea of the seaway construction and too distracted by the demands of transition to give the treaty the support it needed, even if he had been so inclined.

Finally, the treaty became entangled in a web of intersecting regional interests. The most vocal opposition came from Mississippi Valley states, whose senators worried about the competition from New York and saw the project as one more way that the rich and powerful North was seeking to squelch the economic potential of the South, which had never fully recovered from the civil war and Reconstruction. Meanwhile, powerful railway lobbyists buttonholed senators, arguing that their businesses would be irreparably harmed and thousands of jobs would be lost by the seaway's construction.

Herridge did what he could to lobby senators, becoming a regular visitor to the halls of the grand old Capitol. Idaho's Senator William Borah chaired the powerful subcommittee of the Senate Foreign Relations Committee that was considering the treaty. Borah began as a staunch opponent and so it took a good deal of time to even come up for debate. But Borah eventually became convinced that there was merit in the project, changed his mind, and persuaded his committee to pass it. The treaty finally went to the full Senate in January 1934.

President Roosevelt had become a supporter, since as president he was considering not just what was best for the state of New York but for the country as a whole. Through the prism of his New Deal make-work projects he also saw the seaway as another public work that could create infrastructure jobs. On January 10 he signed a long letter to the Senate majority leader, requesting the ratification of what Borah's subcommittee had renamed the St. Lawrence Seaway Treaty. FDR noted that Bennett had approved construction of the Beauharnois power plant and argued that Canada was already proceeding with the project and would be enjoying its benefits while the American government was missing an opportunity to help its own people. He carefully detailed the economic benefits that would accrue to all regions of his country and pleaded with senators, as he had with Borah, to look beyond regional interests and adopt a broader view. He wrote, "On the affirmative side, I subscribe to the definite belief that the completion of the seaway will greatly serve the economic and transportation needs of a vast area of the United States and should, therefore, be considered solely from the national point of view."[33]

The treaty came to the Senate floor for a vote on March 12, 1934. The sectional interests remained, however, and the voices of corporate lobbyists were heard. The treaty was defeated by a vote of 46 to 42. It had won the majority but not the constitutionally demanding two-thirds. Herridge reported to Bennett that the lobbyists and special interests had been too powerful to overcome. He wrote,

> The Treaty's fate was determined by the combined pressure brought to bear by the railway companies, port authorities, and power interests in the States along the Atlantic seaboard . . . the Treaty was beaten mainly through the activities of the transportation and power interests, successfully operating to establish an appearance of a sectional cleavage of interest.[34]

President Roosevelt would later attempt to initiate construction of the seaway as necessary for the war effort. He tried to move its funding through Congress as a defence measure in an attempt to negate the need for the two-thirds vote, as it would no longer be a treaty. But even this tactic gained little traction and he abandoned the effort rather than be linked to a failure.

With the seaway killed by the American Senate, Quebec and Ontario lost their incentive to cooperate. Premier Taschereau stated that he was opposed to any further talk of seaway construction. In Ontario, newly elected premier Mitchell Hepburn stated that the province was rescinding its cost allocation agreement with the federal government.

With no support from the United States and none from Quebec and Ontario, ideas regarding the building of the St. Lawrence Seaway were put on the shelf. Power projects such as the Beauharnois generating station, the dredging of American ports and canals, and other minor improvements to the waterway proceeded. But a generation would pass before others finally caught up with Bennett's prophetic vision.

Bennett's not having turned a silver shovel's worth of Quebec soil to mark the beginning of the seaway's construction can be seen as failure only if one considers a single monarch butterfly a failure for not completing the entire trip to Mexico. Bennett moved the journey along. When meaningful negotiations resumed after the Second World War, Canadians and Americans began where Bennett had left off. The final bilateral agreement that Prime Minister Louis St. Laurent and President Dwight Eisenhower oversaw was based directly on the Hoover-Bennett Treaty.

BANK OF CANADA

The colonies that would become Canada abandoned pounds and pence for dollars and cents in 1858. At Confederation in 1867, like nearly every other country, Canada was tied to the gold standard. That international gentleman's agreement meant legitimacy for the Canadian currency in world markets based on the understanding that 25 per cent of the country's paper money could be issued up to $50 million, and then for each dollar printed after that a dollar in gold had to be purchased and physically stored. This practice meant that the paper money was actually worth something and varied in value only with the price of gold, which fluctuated very little. Whenever the world's major economies suffered from rising inflation, there was talk of raising the fifty-million limit, or raising the 25 per cent, or even abandoning the gold standard altogether, but little changed.

Canadian chartered banks also wielded enormous influence. They set interest rates, and they worked with their counterparts abroad to influence foreign exchange rates. Further, along with the government, the chartered banks printed and issued money. As late as 1920, of the total $298.3 million in circulation, the banks had issued $132.4 million and the government $165.9 million.[35] The banks decided on their own how many notes to put into circulation according to what they deemed best for both the economy and their bottom lines. Canadians paid for goods and services not only with Canadian money but also with Bank of Montreal or Bank of Commerce notes. The federal government's role was simply to ensure that only reputable firms became banks and that each had capital in hand equal to the amount of money they printed. The system was fine as long as banks and the government all maintained their gold reserves. The system held through mild domestic fluctuations and even major international crises, mostly stemming from financial problems in the United States in the 1890s and again in 1907.

Britain had had a privately owned central bank, called the Bank of England, since stealing the idea from the Dutch in 1694. The American central bank, called the Federal Reserve, was established in 1913 and based upon Alexander Hamilton's eighteenth-century National Bank of the United States.

Following the creation of the American central bank, Robert

Borden's government pondered the viability of such an institution for Canada. York South MP William Maclean did some research and submitted it to caucus, but the idea went nowhere. A new Finance Act was passed that provided greater legislative direction for Canada's banks, but Borden had decided that a central bank was unnecessary. As a result, Canada's chartered banks continued to wield enormous power over the country's economy.

The world's financial system was irrevocably knocked off kilter by the First World War. In July 1914, even before the war began, the British government ended the convertibility of its Bank of England currency to gold in order to help pay for the war everyone knew was coming. All governments were forced to react. In Canada, the Borden government did the same thing while also loosening the regulations regarding the amount of currency chartered banks could circulate. The actions caused inflation. This was exactly the point, for it rendered the enormous war expenses easier for governments to handle.

With the war's conclusion all industrialized countries were dealing with inflation, debt, and the uncertainty of a post–gold standard world. In 1922, a conference was held in Genoa. Participants, including Canada, discussed the many intersecting issues facing them, and among the solutions put forth regarding the financial instability was the establishment of central banks. Prime Minister Mackenzie King's representative had supported the idea in Italy but then nothing was done.

There was a perfect opportunity to address the issue. The Bank Act, which needed to be amended if a Canadian central bank was to be created, had to be renewed every ten years and it was up again in 1923. But Mackenzie King watched the fastball coming down the middle and let it sail by. He allowed the act to be renewed with nary a mention of a central bank.

The worldwide depression that began in late 1929 refocused attention on international financial practices, while every government sought to address its own economic challenges. By the time Bennett took office in July 1930, Canada was in the throes of an economic collapse and with the country's financial system a contributing factor.

As international trade slowed and commodity prices dropped, companies began laying off workers and people bought fewer goods and services. Saving rates went up as even folks with money worried about the future and slowed spending. Sound companies delayed investments. At the same time, personal, business, and corporate loans that had been granted with the least security began to go bad. Banks did as they always do in such situations and called in the loans they could, foreclosed on those in arrears, and stopped lending to all but those with the most solid of credentials. They also stopped lending to each other. To get a loan you had to prove you did not need one, and even then your chances were not good. Canadians who could still afford a house, car, or farm found it difficult to secure affordable loans to make those big-ticket purchases. Even companies with good books and capacity were often unable to borrow for expansion.

Illustrative of the banks' situation was that of the Royal Bank, the country's largest. The loans on its books went from $640.5 million in fiscal 1929 to $384.6 million in fiscal 1933.[36] The numbers are small by today's standards but they represented a 40 per cent drop in outstanding loans. When added to similar drops in the other banks, this figure goes a long way toward explaining the financial squeeze that was put on the Canadian economy. The money had dried up. The swirling multiplier effects of decreased consumer spending and decreasing industrial capacity spun the economy further down and faster. Canadians could take some small pride in the fact that while approximately four thousand American banks declared bankruptcy throughout the Depression, and many took their depositors' money with them, not a single Canadian bank closed its doors. But the price paid to keep those doors open was steep: the banks helped to move the country from recession to depression.

In the financial crisis that began in 2008, most governments moved swiftly to bail out failing banks and corporations while tossing stimulus money out the door in an attempt to get businesses to invest and people to spend. Interest rates were dropped to the point where they approached zero, creating nearly free money. It was a concerted effort to get cash flowing again. These actions were based on the lessons of the 1930s. Bennett, however, had no lessons on which to draw. Still, what he needed to do was clear. He needed to get more money into the economy to create inflation. It wasn't that the country was insolvent or the currency was not sound. Bennett needed commodity and other prices to rise so that they would be profitable to produce again. The rise in prices would loosen the banks' restriction on credit, which would in turn work as a financial laxative and get everything moving again.

Bennett considered allowing the fiduciary issue of banknotes—permitting more money to be created beyond that which could be backed by the gold held by banks or the government. But he rejected the idea, believing that it would not address the issue of unemployment. Further, he worried that the action would devalue Canada's currency on world markets, which could in turn lead to increased costs on current debt and trouble selling bonds to raise additional revenue in the future. Mackenzie King agreed and the action was not taken.[37]

Bennett's decision to hold the line on the creation of money was based on his commitment to the orthodox notions of the gold standard. But his fealty was shaken by actions taken in Britain. Britain had ended the gold standard in the First World War, but re-established it in 1925. In September 1931, Prime Minister and First Lord of the Treasury Ramsay MacDonald announced that Britain was abandoning the gold standard again and would allow its currency to float on the world market. He believed that the action would increase the value of the pound and stabilize domestic prices. Other countries, including the United States, which owned much of the world's gold, quickly followed the British lead. The decision caused all currencies to fluctuate wildly. With Canada's economy tied so closely to Britain and the United States, the manner in which the Canadian dollar was valued was of paramount importance and so Bennett was left with few options. He made the decision to allow the Canadian dollar to float independently of gold as well. It moved from close to par with the American dollar to settling two weeks later at about 90 cents. The change was of immediate benefit to Canadian manufacturers for their goods, and through the rippling multiplier effect the many people and companies involved in their construction became cheaper to American customers and therefore, despite the high tarriffs, their order sheets began to fill. While this consequence was welcome, the end of the gold standard meant that Canadian financial policies and practices, which were on shaky ground before, grew even more uncertain, harder to predict, and impossible to control.

The overlapping issues would be tricky even today, with all the economic levers that could be pulled and with all national governments playing according to at least similar fundamental rules. But for Bennett, and other national leaders at the time, it was a whole new ball game. Old rules no longer seemed to apply and new ones were yet to be written. The abandonment of the gold standard, coupled with ongoing international and domestic financial instability throughout the winter of 1931–32, led Bennett to explore the option of a Canadian central bank.

Today it is difficult to ponder the economy without the Bank of Canada. While the government is in charge of fiscal policy, through which it influences the economy by manipulating taxing and spending, the Bank of Canada exerts its influence through controlling monetary policy. Broadly put, monetary policy involves managing the number of dollars in the economy by manipulating the ease with which credit is available. It performs that trick through raising or lowering the interest rate that it demands from the chartered banks that borrow money from its coffers and thereby influences the rates that banks charge their customers. Through these actions, the bank tries to control inflation and keep the economy stable. It influences the value of the dollar and renders international business transactions predictable and reliable. It also controls the look and production of money. The bank operates independently from Parliament so that it is free from the temptation of politicians who might wish to manoeuvre monetary policy for short-term political gain. Former American Federal Reserve chair Alan Greenspan has quipped that a central bank's job is to see when the party is slowing down and take in a spiked punch bowl and, conversely, when the party looks like it may get out of hand, to go back in and remove it.[38] Teetotalling Bennett needed to offer spiked punch to Canadian bankers.

Bennett was unable to concoct the brew, however, because at that time the Canadian government controlled only fiscal and trade policies. He needed the power to control monetary policy. Bennett's business and legal background, coupled with his experience on the board of the Royal Bank, allowed him to understand well how banks worked. He personally knew many of those who ran them. In the early spring of 1932 Bennett wrote to several of his friends and contacts in the banking industry about the notion of a central bank. Among the responses he received was a well-researched and thoughtful essay from Randolph Nobel. Nobel was the Royal Bank's long-serving and well-respected assistant general manager. His March 1932 letter suggested that the government needed to take actions that would allow it to win control of monetary policy and then to use that power to increase the money supply, thereby easing the credit crunch that had helped to cause the Depression and was playing a role in impeding recovery. Nobel also suggested that with control of the money supply, the government could reduce the value of the Canadian dollar, which would make Canadian exports cheaper on the world market and thereby increase their quantity. Unemployment would then fall. All of this, Nobel concluded, could only be done through the establishment of a central bank.[39]

Bennett demanded more information and sought more experts with whom he could speak. One such expert was Clifford Clark, a Queen's University economics professor. He had impressed Bennett with a paper that he had written in advance of the Ottawa Conference in which he advocated ideas quite similar to Nobel's. In October, Bennett appointed Clark as his deputy minister of finance. Bennett then asked a number of university economics professors and civil servants in the Finance Department to comment on the papers by Nobel and Clark. He was pleased when there was near unanimity in support of the proposals. American president Harry Truman once joked that he yearned for a one-armed economist, for every time an economic adviser would say something was so, he would immediately add, "But on the other hand. . . ." By the fall of 1932, it appeared that Bennett had assembled a dream team of one-armed economists unanimous in their support for the creation of a central bank.

As word inevitably spread that Bennett was entertaining the notion of a central bank, there arose the equally inevitable negative reaction. Several provincial and many municipal governments entered the debate in ways that caused confusion. A number of cities, for instance, wondered if they might be able to issue their own scrip. In his replies to questions and suggestions, Bennett was always polite but not above occasionally stating bluntly that the writer was dead wrong with respect to facts, premises, or assumptions. While many provincial premiers sought to understand, Quebec's Taschereau applied his typical ready, fire, aim approach. In a *Montreal Gazette* article, he argued that a national bank would destroy Canada by giving too much power to the federal government.[40] While Taschereau was expressing the old question of balancing federal and provincial powers from Quebec's unique viewpoint, opposition to the idea of a central bank began to coalesce around the ideological argument that government should leave banking in private hands and to the dictates of the free market.

Bennett consulted broadly, meeting with many people and most often with Clifford Clark and Finance Minister Edgar Rhodes, who had taken over the ministry from Bennett nine months before. Finally, in November 1932, Bennett decided to attempt moral suasion spiced with a little bribery. He informed every chartered bank that, with the authority of the Finance Act, he was going to have them borrow $5 million from the government, which they could then lend to their customers. It was a measured attempt to increase the money supply, spur some inflation, end the financial constipation, and get some dollars flowing through the economy again.

The action did little of consequence. The Canadian dollar fell briefly to 80 cents against the American greenback, which promised some relief for exports, especially warming Ontario's manufacturing sector, but the decline was temporary. The action failed largely because every bank reacted the same way and kept their interest rates and loan policies the same. They all took the new money and spun it back to pay down their own existing loans. The unsuccessful attempt at prodding the banks so as to influence monetary policy demonstrated that Nobel, Clark, and all of the others were right. A modern, complex, industrial, and predominately urban economy needs a central bank. And to get out of the Depression Canada needed one right away.

While Canadian banks were refusing to play a positive role in addressing Canada's monetary crisis, in June 1933 Bennett and representatives of sixty-five other countries met in London's Geological Building at the World Monetary and Economic Conference. Its goal was primarily to determine a strategy to end the damaging fluctuations in currency rates. Many of the participants, including Bennett, had met President Roosevelt at the White House in April and found a gathering consensus around the pursuit of that goal.

However, while the delegates gathered in England, FDR boarded a 45-foot schooner called the *Amberjack II* and with a small crew dead-reckoned his way 400 miles up the eastern seaboard to his cottage at Campobello, New Brunswick. While enjoying his holiday, he had been receiving cables from London that he did not like. He called the ever-present reporters to his side and told them that he believed it best for the

American economy that the United States dollar not be pegged to gold or any other standard. It should continue to float against world currencies. He chatted amiably through his smile and asked that the conversation be off the record, but Roosevelt knew exactly what he was doing.[41] The announcement reflected Roosevelt's belief that a side agreement being hammered together between France and Britain to temporarily return to the gold standard would hurt American efforts to bring inflation to the American economy and, more fundamentally, that monetary policy should be the purview of central banks and not governments.[42]

The next day, on July 1, 1933, the bombshell of an announcement was the *New York Times*'s headline. Roosevelt's musings all but ended the World Monetary and Economic Conference since without the cooperation of the United States, any attempt to gain monetary control of the world's currencies was futile.

FDR's policy statement and the conference's failure meant that there would be no international cooperation to return to the predictability of world currency rates that the gold standard had afforded and some new regime might allow. The United States would not be the world's banker. Every country was on its own. Bennett's call for a Canadian central bank became more urgent than ever.

In July 1933, with the conference limping on, Bennett had Finance Minister Rhodes announce the establishment of a Royal Commission on Banking and Currency to investigate the advisability of creating a Canadian central bank. Bennett chose Lord MacMillan from the British House of Lords, who had chaired a similar commission in Britain, to be its chair. Other hand-picked members included banker Beaudry Leman from Quebec, Ontario's Sir Thomas White, who had served as Borden's finance minister, and Britain's Sir Charles Addis, who had been a director of the Bank of England. Rounding out the commission was Alberta premier John Brownlee representing the West and farmers.

MacMillan took his commission on the road and heard deputations in thirteen cities. Like all royal commissioners, the men heard reasoned arguments, screeching protests, and clunky metaphors, in both verbal and written forms. Although there were many negative opinions expressed, the commissioners had a relatively easy time of it, for the depth of the Depression had created a mood that allowed nearly any fresh idea to be welcomed as a possible remedy to the hard times.

It was also clear that the commission allowed Canadians a venue to express anger at the banks that many, especially those who had been thrown out of homes or off farms, had come to hate. This deep-seated enmity had led many Canadians to join Americans in celebrating the adventures of Bonnie and Clyde and Pretty Boy Floyd, who had become Depression-era folk heroes by robbing banks and, while their sacks were being filled, taking the time to burn mortgage and loan records. Most of these Robin Hood tales are more legend than fact, but when confronting an enemy as faceless as the Depression and as powerful as banks, legends are sometimes more necessary than facts. A story circulated that a banker got a young farmer's daughter in trouble but then offered to marry the girl. The farmer said no; he would rather have the shame of a bastard child in his family than a banker.

Despite his experience with banks and bankers, Bennett made it clear to all that in this apparent war between the banks and the people, he sided with the people. Bennett was inundated with letters from small-business people and farmers asking him to personally intercede on their behalf to force banks to extend or make loans. Bennett always replied politely and almost always in the negative, as nearly every request was beyond his legal purview, but there were many occasions when the cases were such that he had his staff investigate and then take appropriate action. Sometimes the cases in which Bennett took personal action concerned large companies and large sums, but often they involved individuals being treated by local bank branches in ways that irked Bennett's sense of fair play.

One example illustrates the point. In July 1935, Gravelbourg, Saskatchewan, wheat farmer Howard Irvine needed $50 in bridge financing for three months to cover the premium on his crop insurance. Despite the fact that Mr. Irvine was not in arrears with any other loans, his Bank of Toronto branch in Bateman followed instructions from its head office and said no. It had been told to end all loans for such purposes. To the Saskatchewan MP who brought the Irvine case to his attention, Bennett wrote that it was ". . . a striking instance of the lack of understanding on the part of some of our banks."[43] Mr. H. Howard, the general manager of the Bank of Toronto head office, then received a stern letter from the prime minister asking for an explanation and stating bluntly that he regarded the bank's decision in the Irvine case and the overall policy that led to it as wrong. Bennett then not so subtly reminded Howard that there was a growing movement throughout the land, begun by the CCF but finding traction among left-leaning Liberals and Conservatives as well, to nationalize all banking operations. He wrote, ". . . that your bank refused to loan him [Irvine] money for this purpose has caused great antagonism to banks and strengthens the forces which are endeavouring to nationalize our financial institutions."[44] There was a vapid response to Bennett's letter from Howard's assistant manager followed by the prime minister snapping back, "Unfortunately, expressions of good-will if accompanied by a refusal to advance $50.00 to a farmer who feels he is in need of it, are not calculated to satisfy the farmers that the good intentions are very real."[45] The farmer eventually got his fifty dollars.

While being publicly demonized throughout the country, the Canadian Bankers Association kept its head high and was the only professional organization that stood with the chartered banks in opposition to the idea of a central bank. It explained directly to Bennett, and through depositions to the MacMillan Commission, that it and the banks were naturally upset about what they predicted would be a loss of their wealth and power. Bennett had stated, for instance, that if a central bank was created then all of the gold held in all of the chartered banks would be physically transferred to the central bank. Plus, they would no longer be able to, quite literally, print money.

But more than looking after the interests of the banks, the Canadian Bankers Association expressed fear that a central bank would hurt Canada. It claimed that the chartered banks had served Canada well for years and should not be punished. They had, for instance, kept unprofitable branches open in small towns and rural districts. If the central bank were established and bank profits suffered, they threatened, those branches would need to be closed. It also raised fears that a syndicate of some sort would get control of the bank. The Bankers Association argued that the government should await economic stabilization before making such a move. Particularly, the re-establishment of the gold standard should be promoted then given time to take effect. Further, it expressed worries about fluctuating exchange rates. It argued that with so many European countries in such dire economic straits, an inexperienced central bank would be easily overwhelmed with a run on the currency and be unable to deal with the crisis.[46]

Bennett had predicted the opposition presented by the banks and its association and knew that he needed to summon the political courage to persevere in the face of it. In a May 1934 private letter to bank presidents and the chair of the Canadian Bankers Association he had written, "You must realize that the reason we have had no central bank in Canada is because the chartered banks were powerful enough to prevent it, and they are accepting it now under protest."[47] Bennett's letter could not have been clearer in going on to suggest that they were on the wrong side of history and that they should, in effect if not in fact, shut up and get out of the way.

Despite the organized objections raised by the banks, and some that saw any government intervention in the economy as anathema, the MacMillan Commission seemed to be hearing what Bennett needed it to hear. But he realized that he would also need bipartisan political support in the House to get it done. It was essential if he was to keep the confidence of Canadians and the domestic and international markets. Accordingly, Bennett kept Mackenzie King and J.S. Woodsworth apprised of the commission's work and of his leaning toward the necessity of creating a central bank. He encouraged both opposition leaders to meet with Lord MacMillan, and at least two such meetings took place.

Cooperative Commonwealth Federation leader Woodsworth was already on board. The CCF's founding document, the Regina Manifesto, had outlined a socialist agenda for Canada including an unequivocal pledge to eradicate capitalism. It also stated a desire to socialize banking and to create a central bank.[48] While Woodsworth mattered due to his presence and stature in the House as a widely respected party leader, Mackenzie King's opinion was even more important. In two meetings with the opposition leader, MacMillan sold the notion of a strong central bank operating outside the Finance Department as a means to afford long-term financial stability. Mackenzie King was persuaded.[49] Bennett's politically adroit decision to include the two was successful, for when the time came, Mackenzie King worked to bring his caucus around to supporting the notion of a central bank.

Bennett meanwhile continued to read scathing editorials in papers and vicious letters that attacked him for doing nothing to help Canadians. He ignored the criticism, secure in the realization that the uninformed needed to stay that way just a while longer. Finally, on November 20,

1933, Bennett spoke on the radio and made it clear that he supported the establishment of a central bank and that, in fact, the bill to create the bank was already being drafted. The address caused a flutter among the chartered banks that again claimed that their views had not been adequately heard or understood. The bankers demanded that they have an opportunity to scrutinize the bill before first reading. Bennett was cool in response, basically telling them to calm down.[50]

Bennett did all he could that winter to persuade Canadians that the notion of a central bank was a good one. By April 1934, he was still working hard. He spoke in South Oxford, Ontario, for instance, and presented the idea of a central bank to those about to vote in the federal by-election. He touted the bank as necessary for Canada to promote and maintain sound economic fundamentals and to conduct its own exchange transactions. He promised that it would more responsibly and humanely regulate credit and interest rates. As a result of its power and actions, he told his audience, the bank would do much to avoid a repetition of the financial disaster that had so recently gripped the country. He then wrapped the bank in the flag, stating: "I look upon a central bank as a great forward step taken by this country, which is an essential condition of its taking its place amongst the great countries of the world."[51]

The MacMillan Commission Report was finally released later that spring and, to the surprise of no one, recommended the establishment of a Canadian central bank. The only dissension came from Commissioner White, who argued that while a central bank was needed, a period of such economic adversity and uncertainty was not the time for such a dramatic reform. He also argued that Canada should ignore the moves of Britain, the United States, and others, and look for stability in its monetary affairs through a return to the gold standard. The only other commissioner to show any support for Sir Thomas White's view was Beaudry Leman. And his only concern was that a central bank might not be constitutional.

Both the report and the positive reaction to it from one coast to the other gave Bennett the support he needed. In the summer of 1934, a Bill to Incorporate the Bank of Canada was introduced into the House. Bennett was clever. He had Finance Minister and Senator Edgar Rhodes introduce the bill in the Senate and then ask only that the Senate and

House support the establishment of a central bank in principle. Bennett promised to bring forward and offer for debate further details after they had been hashed out by the committee on banking and commerce. The parliamentary tactic ensured that critics of the bill, such as the Canadian Bankers Association, had a less conspicuous target at which to shoot and so their objections would have less resonance. The bill received Royal Assent on July 3, 1934.

A comparison of the report and the final act shows that Bennett decided not to take all of the commission's suggestions but rather to begin slowly. All the powers that the commission recommended, or that the bank would later be afforded, were not in the bill. In making this decision, Bennett may have expected to be criticized by the commissioners but, in fact, he received congratulations from Commissioner Leman, who wrote,

> I am afraid that, after a few years' experience, it may be found necessary to broaden the statutory powers of the Central Bank. On the other hand, it may have been an act of wisdom to shackle and fetter the new species introduced in the Canadian fauna, in order that no one be scared. As it becomes evident that the animal is tame, it will no doubt be found desirable to loosen and even remove some of the chains.[52]

The act stated that the Bank of Canada would regulate internal credit and foreign exchange, use monetary instruments to stabilize levels of production, trade, employment, and prices, and provide expert advice to the government. It would operate as a public trust working for the benefit of the country and would be divorced from those interested only in profit or political gain. As Bennett said in the House in June, "We confidently believe that freed from political control and with the merit determined by the experience of those who are engaged to manage the bank, it will discharge the obligations from which it was created and thereby bring improved conditions to the Canadian people."[53]

The act also stated that the bank would be privately owned, with shareholders limited in the amount they could own and by their citizenship. Five million in shares would be offered to Canadians for $50 each, with one person allowed to own only one share. Critics said the ownership scheme was wrong, for it would lead to shareholders demanding monetary policies based on the profit that would accrue to the Bank of Canada rather than what was best for the country. Bennett countered that private ownership was needed to keep it beyond the influence of politicians who might find ways to bend the law and regulations that were there to keep it at arm's-length reach from political interference. He knew well that the manipulation of interest rates for political purposes had been for decades quite common in Canada. He received many letters, even after the Bank of Canada was in operation, suggesting that he should raise or lower the interest rate for sometimes the most sinister of reasons and sometimes for the most flippant. Consider, for instance, the manager of Halifax's Elmwood Hotel, who urged Bennett to raise interest rates to 7 per cent because it would ". . . win quite a few votes for you especially from the Ladies who expressed themselves very strongly upon getting such a small return on their savings."[54] An independent, privately owned Bank of Canada, Bennett reasoned, would never cave to pressure from Canada's powerful political or corporate elite.

The bank was widely supported across the country and by all parties in the House. But the idea of private ownership was not popular. Both Woodsworth and Mackenzie King attacked it as unnecessary. Some critics noted that the issuing of shares was cynical, as not many Canadians had $50 in disposable income with which to purchase a share.

Bennett was unmoved by the arguments. Due to his large majority in the House, the bill passed with the provision for private ownership intact. The day the shares were made available they were snapped up. The bank was soon fully subscribed. Bennett was then able to use the private ownership of the bank to quiet those who wanted him to directly influence it in one way or another. He replied that he was not a shareholder in the bank and therefore had no vote.

The act stated that the bank would be operated by a governor, who would have similar powers to those of a general manager at a chartered bank. The governor would be assisted by the deputy and assistant deputy governors and answerable to a nine-member board of directors. In September 1934, Bennett appointed thirty-seven-year-old Royal Bank general manager Graham Towers to be the Bank of Canada's first governor. Once in office, the talented and charming Towers wrote to Bennett recommending J. A. C. Osborne, at that point the secretary of the Bank of England, as his deputy. Bennett concurred and Osborne got the job.

A board of directors then needed to be chosen. The act stipulated that three directors should have experience in and represent industry, production, and commerce, with the remaining three from other endeavours. Bennett believed that the selection of directors should be based upon merit rather than allowing the political considerations of language, ethnicity, region, or religion to be considered. He received visitors to his office and letters by the score from those suggesting themselves, family members, or cronies for a directorship position. Many had qualifications that were weak and sometimes laughable. Many who opposed the creation of the bank swung quickly and attempted to become a director to exert influence from within. The Canadian Chamber of Commerce, for example, had instructed those within its network of local chambers to write letters and appear at MacMillan Commission meetings to stop the creation of the bank. But in December it spun and drew up a slate of candidates which it presented to Bennett with the insistence that it be installed as the bank's directors. The chamber did not help its case by including among its slate R. A. Wright of Drinkwater, Saskatchewan. He had earlier enraged farmers by fighting against the establishment of the wheat pool while repeatedly attacking Bennett's Marketing Act. Both actions had even caused the Liberals in his riding to condemn him as he unsuccessfully sought the Liberal nomination. The chamber's slate was ignored.

Many others misread the selection as an election and so initiated full-fledged campaigns with flyers and even advertisements in newspapers. The most enthusiastic in this regard was General Motors senior executive Lorne Ardiel, who set up supporters from coast to coast then oversaw the publication of a campaign-like booklet that reviewed his life and bragged of his qualifications. It included excerpts from speeches in which Ardiel had spoken of the important role of central banks in stabilizing national economies. Another aggressive candidate was Ottawa's Archibald Kains, a retired banker, who also published a pamphlet explaining why he was eminently qualified. He had it distributed to each of the bank's shareholders and of course he, like Ardiel and others, ensured that the campaign bumph was mailed to the prime minister's office.

A board of directors for the Bank of Canada was finally selected but there was still work to be done before the bank became operational. A number of statutes needed to be done away with or radically altered, such as the Dominion Notes Act and the Finance Act. Regulations and standard practices and procedures needed to be changed. The old chartered bank money needed to be taken out of circulation and new banknotes had to be designed, printed, and distributed. Bennett personally oversaw all that was done. Despite the complexity and the enormity of the undertaking, it was completed over the course of just a few months. Canadians watched as Bank of Montreal three-dollar bills made their way to museums where they rest now beside the old Bank of Canada ones and twos.

In one of his five radio addresses to the Canadian people in January 1935, Bennett explained his creation of the Bank of Canada as a necessary and important step in the long-term restructuring of capitalism in Canada that would bring more stability to the economy. He called the bank,

> . . . a powerful instrument of social justice: because it will be the means of insuring a greater measure of equity in the dealings of class with class; because it will aid in correcting the disabilities in the old system; because it will be an independent source of advice and assistance in all matters relating to finance; because it begins a new chapter in the history of Canada's financial life.[55]

The new chapter began when the Bank of Canada commenced its work on March 11, 1935. But that did not mean that the chartered banks stopped fighting it. The next and final battle was fought over the transfer of gold. According to the statute creating the Bank of Canada, all chartered banks were to transfer their gold holdings to the bank and receive payment at fair market value. If the Bank of Canada later decided to sell any of the gold then it would reap and keep the profits. The process seemed simple enough.

In early March the physical transfer of gold to the new central bank began. The Bank of Montreal led the way, transferring $13 million of gold coin and bullion from its main branches in Montreal, Toronto, Ottawa, Winnipeg, and Vancouver. In writing to inform Governor Towers and Finance Minister Rhodes of the transfer, Bank of Montreal president C. B. Gordon concluded, "The said transfer is made in conformity with and pursuant to the said Section but is so made under protest inasmuch as we have been advised that said Statute is *ultra vires* of the Parliament of Canada in so far as it requires transfer of said gold to you on the terms therein stated."[56]

The legal claim was based not only on the Bank of Montreal's belief that it and the other chartered banks deserved more money for its gold, but also upon an opinion rendered the previous December by the bank's solicitor. The opinion was predicated on the notion that no law had ever existed stating that the banks had a legal obligation to hold gold in reserve. They had done it only to maintain strong reserves. Consequently, the argument followed, it was beyond the power of the government to, in effect, confiscate the banks' gold.[57]

The Dominion Bank added nuance to the fight when the letter announcing its gold transfer stated the expectation to receive any profits that the Bank of Canada made on any future sale of any of "its" gold.[58] For good measure, the Dominion Bank's letter also noted that the transfer of gold was *ultra vires*. One at a time, each of the banks submitted their letters and each claimed aggrieved status. Each cited in various ways that they should not be forced to relinquish their gold as sections 28 to 30 of the Bank of Canada Act were illegal and, further, that any profit on the sale of "their" gold was theirs.

The legal and constitutional matters had been argued months before and Bennett had considered them settled. Rhodes had his officials review the legalities of the act and it was determined again that the banks' arguments were specious. They were basing their argument about future profits on their claim that all of the gold they owned was held against liabilities outside of Canada, which was absurd. But that being said, there was power in their argument regarding the need to negotiate the amount of compensation for gold that had been held against domestic liabilities. The Conservative caucus began to lose its nerve. James Herbert Stitt, MP for Selkirk, for instance, questioned Bennett suggesting that the banks be allowed to keep the gold. Bennett replied in caucus for all to hear, "Jimmie Stitt, you quit worrying. We are going to get that gold and it is just about time for us to find out whether the banks or this government is running this country."[59]

Unfortunately, progress was delayed due to Bennett's suffering a heart attack in March 1935 and enduring a period of convalescence throughout the spring. When he returned to work in June, he saw that both the public, through the Bank of Canada, and the shareholders of the chartered banks were dealt with in a fair manner in accordance with both the law and sound accounting practices. He took a personal hand in renegotiating the chartered banks' compensation for the gold. Finally, after years of bickering and harsh words, the matter was concluded and everyone set to making the new system work.

Of all those involved with the banking industry, however, only the Canadian Bank of Commerce's Samuel Logan wrote to Bennett to acknowledge the prime minister's latest efforts at fairness for all. After acknowledging payment of $3.6 million in compensation for the bank's gold transfer, Logan wrote, "I feel that you took a great personal interest in this and I fully appreciate everything that was done."[60] A tired-sounding but palpably grateful Bennett responded that throughout his five years as prime minister, Logan's letter was the only one he had ever received from a chartered bank expressing appreciation for anything that he had done.[61]

Prime Minister Mackenzie King had supported the bank but never agreed that it should be owned by Canadians. Once in office, he had the Bank of Canada Act amended and the government purchased every share. The government became the bank's sole owner. He did not, however, alter its independence from Parliament or anything else of significance. He did not seek to reduce its powers to control Canada's monetary policy and through that power to exert a stabilizing and positive influence on the economy and financial system. He knew, as did every prime minister who succeeded him, that Bennett had created an indispensable Canadian institution—an icon.

In his 1993 *The Bank of Canada: Origins and Early History*, bank researcher George Watts stated without fear of contradiction, "The founding of the Bank of Canada in 1934 appears to have been largely due to the initiative of one person—Prime Minister Bennett."[62] In his creation of the Bank of Canada, Bennett demonstrated his conviction that monetary policy was a cause of—and would be part of the solution to— the Depression's ravages. In this way, he presaged the arguments of monetarists such as Milton Friedman. Years later, the esteemed University of Chicago economist wrote that problems with the money supply were among the chief causes of the Depression and that dealing with monetary issues faster and better could have shortened the length and limited the depth of the crisis.[63]

As with the CBC and the St. Lawrence Seaway, in creating the Bank of Canada, Bennett had not simply chosen among expedient options, he had created new ones—he had changed the game. In standing against naysayers and powerful big-business interests, even those to whom he owed political debts, Bennett had proven himself not just a competent manager but a bold and effective transitional leader.

CHAPTER SEVEN

STRENGTH TO STUBBORNNESS:
ON TO OTTAWA TREK AND HARRY STEVENS
1934–1935

A N EFFECTIVE LEADER must be strong. He can demonstrate strength through a determined adherence to core principles even when the siren song of expediency offers the fleeting popularity of an easy battle easily won. He must allow for tactical flexibility and remain confident when others lose faith in his principles, goals, strategies, tactics, or even him. The effective leader must also recognize when his strength crosses the ever-shifting, invisible line and becomes stubbornness. Stubbornness suggests not a dedicated allegiance to the principled attainment of a goal but rather a surrendering to ego, leading to a refusal to entertain new facts, contrary opinions, or novel options. It reveals itself in a willingness to intimidate and micromanage. The stubborn leader sees the victory of another as his own defeat, for he sees power not as a means to an end but rather as a finite resource to be gathered and ruthlessly guarded behind the fortress of a smile.

Two issues with which Bennett had to deal in the last two years of his administration offer insight as to whether Bennett can be deemed a strong or a stubborn leader. They also allow a deeper understanding with respect to the degree to which Bennett's Tory principles informed all that he did throughout his political career. The first was a protest movement that began in April 1935. The year before, Bennett had created camps in remote areas to house and provide work for employed, single young men. While thousands had taken up the offer of the relief camps, many became unhappy. The protest began in British Columbia as a request for improved camp conditions, but it soon grew to include demands for more direct government action to help the unemployed everywhere. By June, hundreds of protesters were on trains heading toward Ottawa to take their concerns to Parliament Hill. The second issue began with Bennett's old friend Harry Stevens, who in his capacity as minister of trade and commerce brought to the country's attention what he considered the misused clout of large retailers. His actions led to an inquiry, then a Royal Commission, and finally to misunderstandings and unfortunate clashes that resulted in his resignation and an irreparable split in Conservative ranks.

UNREST AND REACTION

The Vancouver Strike, the On to Ottawa Trek, and the deadly Regina Riot that ended it all began four years earlier with Bennett's attempts to address problems related to unemployment. By the late spring of 1931, a number of factors were coming together in ways that made many parts of Canada resemble a tinderbox yearning for a spark. Things got worse when the number of unemployed Canadians reached disastrous new heights. In 1933, the official national figure reached 30 per cent, but that was merely a guess. In many regions and in some sectors it was higher. And the numbers are just numbers—cold and remorseless. It was the people behind the numbers who mattered. Each individual mattered, each one was hurting, and each one had a family who shared that pain.

Thousands of men roamed the country in a dangerous and desperate search for work. They slept on benches. They ate from garbage cans or in soup kitchens. There were many complaints about the soup kitchen food, the conditions, and servers who were either too gruff or ladled their soup along with evangelical appeals to find Jesus. Many municipalities were finding it increasingly difficult to finance relief payments when the numbers demanding and deserving relief kept going up as precipitously as their tax rolls kept tumbling down. They could hardly help their own residents, let alone the growing number of job-searching transients. Municipalities screamed to their provincial capitals for help; the provincial governments, in turn, demanded assistance from Ottawa. But all levels of government were experiencing the same fiscal problems.

Added to the economic hardships were intersecting social strains that were tearing at the fabric of civil society. Marriages were breaking up. Many that should have were dissolving into violence and acrimony. Parents were unable to feed and clothe their children. Many grown and married children who wanted to be on their own could not afford it and ended up staying with parents long after they should have moved out. Crime, alcoholism, and violence were on the rise.

Unemployed men rode from city to city on top or beneath freight trains, looking for work. Riding the rails was illegal and dangerous. Around every city and town of any size grew makeshift camps where homeless men stayed for a day or two, searching for work. The jungles, or Bennett boroughs, as these camps were often called, were hellish places of petty crime, violence, and vice. On occasions too numerous to count, the local police, RCMP, or sometimes even bands of vigilantes smashed through the jungles rousting the men and destroying their shacks. The goal was simply to keep them moving. But more came on the next day's train.

In a detailed letter to Bennett in June 1931, Minister of Labour Gideon Robertson spoke of the conditions he found in British Columbia and Alberta. The tale he told was horrific. He spoke of unrest among approximately four thousand unemployed people when the Edmonton and Calgary city councils cut off all forms of relief. The army needed to be called out to prevent violence. The problems among the unemployed were being stirred to a fever pitch, he argued, because communist agitators were exploiting desperate men locked in seemingly hopeless situations.

Robertson suggested enforcing the ban on free train travel that was part of both railways' regulations. Further, he said, the federal government should do something to provide employment for the growing number of young, single men. He advocated the establishment of work camps. Continuing, Robertson suggested to Bennett that municipal and the two provincial government leaders with whom he had consulted would support a program of deporting "aliens" who were unemployed but had lived in Canada for only two or three years.[1]

In the fall of 1931, Bennett asked R.J. Manion, minister of railways and canals, to look into the issue of men riding the rails. Manion went beyond that narrow mandate and consulted with social workers and with his friend General Andrew McNaughton about the problems caused by the presence in Canadian cities of so many unemployed, transient young

men and the suffering they were subjected to. McNaughton is a fascinating Canadian. He was a brave leader in the First World War and an
able and important general in the Second, but he was more than that. He
was a slight man with piercing brown eyes that appeared to be serious and frowning even when in the best of moods. He graduated from
McGill with degrees in science and engineering and was later inducted
into the Canadian Science and Engineering Hall of Fame for having invented the cathode ray, which led to the discovery of radar. In the early
1930s he became involved with civil aviation and represented Canada at
a number of international conferences dealing with aviation, engineering, and military matters. He was earning respect for his work on the
St. Lawrence Seaway project. Now Manion needed him to help out in
another way.

Like Robertson, Manion was appalled not only that there were so
many single, unemployed people, but also that they seemed to be losing
hope in their country and in themselves. He feared that there would be
more unrest if something was not done with and for them. Every revolution in history has at its root angry and inconsolable young men with
time on their hands and nothing left to lose. McNaughton knew that
and shared Manion's fear. He also recognized a perfect confluence of
needs: Canada needed stability while also needing airstrips to create a
national system of civil aviation, while mayors needed unemployed
young men out of their cities, and those young men needed housing
and work. Consequently, he agreed with Robertson's idea that work
camps could hire and house young men, and thereby give them the morale boost they needed. They would do work that would benefit the
country, and, by removing them from the cities, the possibility of their
causing trouble would decrease. Along with respected Alberta social
worker Charlotte Whitton, Manion and McNaughton made presentations to Bennett, who asked a number of probing questions of each and
then approved the idea.

An order-in-council was passed on October 8, 1932, and the planning for the camps began in earnest. The Department of Labour would
be responsible for them, but the Department of National Defence (DND)
would build and run them. This arrangement was seen as the cheapest
and most efficient way to proceed because the military had experience
with prisoner-of-war camps and could easily adapt their plans and

procedures to the new enterprise. It was decided that 237 camps would be built, beginning in British Columbia and Alberta. They would be constructed far from cities and towns. They would be deep in the woods that were to be cleared as part of the work projects for the men. Cabinet approved $668,000 for camp construction costs.

It was agreed that camp rules would be strict. To be admitted to a relief camp one needed to be single, over eighteen years of age, male, living outside the family home, and healthy. Although the term was not defined, a young man could not be a "political agitator." Transportation was provided to the camps at no charge. Upon entry, young men were given clothing, soap and towels, a bed, three meals a day, and the use of showers and toilet facilities—again all without charge. For all of this the men were expected to work forty-four hours a week at whatever job was assigned. They would be given 20 cents a day for spending money and 1.3 cents a day for cigarettes. The money was not meant to be and was never called wages. Their work was unpaid. Free courses for all men who wanted them were set up through Frontier College. It was made clear that the men would not be allowed to form camp committees and that any complaints had to be brought on an individual basis to the foreman. Further, a man could leave the camp at any time, but once gone he could not return. The rules were explained to all who entered the camps and then conspicuously posted.

Men began arriving at the first ninety-eight camps in British Columbia's interior in the late fall of 1932. They were put to work clearing trees, building roads, and constructing airstrips. The camps were originally set up to accommodate two thousand men. They were so quickly and overwhelmingly subscribed that within two years more camps had been built and over eleven thousand young men were living in and working around them. By the time they were closed by the Mackenzie King government in 1936, 170,248 unemployed young men had spent time in the camps.[2]

Bennett had a difficult time discerning whether the camps were successfully meeting their goals because every letter and report he received seemed to contradict the last. Some detailed rampant corruption. McNaughton and Manion acknowledged problems and addressed them by transferring some men, banishing others, and tightening procedures. By June 1934, McNaughton was able to report that the camps were doing what they had been set up to do. He wrote that they were financially feasible. More importantly, he stated they had played a significant role in saving many Canadian cities from social unrest that would have necessitated a military presence to maintain or restore order.[3]

Meanwhile, however, complaints continued. A Liberal member from Winnipeg, for instance, spoke in the House of deplorable conditions at the Riding Mountain, Manitoba, camp. Bennett listened to a sorry tale of the camp's housing consisting of a dimly lit, windowless, tarpaper structure that was 79 feet long and 24 feet wide. It held stoves in its narrow centre aisle which separated rows of straw-filled, rough-hewn bunk beds. Eighty-eight men stayed in the smoky, smelly, and dirty structure. The conditions were such, it was argued, that even those running the place worried about the long-term emotional scars that the men would suffer.

But those condemning camp conditions were matched by those who claimed that the conditions were really not that bad. Undisputed friend of the working class and the unemployed J. S. Woodsworth spoke many times about the camps, but his greatest complaint was that they were run by the DND. He worried that the military, used to dealing with soldiers or prisoners, was exerting too much control over the lives of the men. With respect to living conditions, though, he stated in March 1934, "I can quite understand that life in these camps may be superior to that in every cheap lodging and around the soup kitchens that have been established in our cities . . ."[4] Bennett investigated every complaint but, as Woodsworth's thoughts showed, the reality of the camps became increasingly difficult to ascertain.

An issue that needed to be addressed was that, in British Columbia, there were really two camp systems. Although all were built by the DND, some were administered by the provincial government under the direction of R. G. Fordham. While rules and conditions were similar, it became generally accepted that the Fordham camps were superior in terms of the quality of food and accommodations and the general treatment of relief workers. As unions and the Communist Party cleverly infiltrated the camps and began to secretly organize workers, they exploited the differences and demanded changes in the DND-run camps. The problems led to the B.C. government removing itself from the administration of some camps and a levelling of all to DND standards. Understandably, many union leaders and communist organizers used what had become slight temporary differences between the camps to stir unrest.[5]

By the beginning of 1933, some camps had already seen wildcat strikes. Building on these strikes, many organizers and workers ignored the restriction on camp committees and the Relief Camp Worker's Union (RCWU) was born. By July 1933, it had representation in every British Columbia and Alberta camp and even in some in Saskatchewan and Ontario.

Often the RCWU organized written lists of complaints that were submitted to administrators and many times those complaints were addressed. Sometimes there were wildcat strikes over minor issues and these too often led to minor changes. In September 1933, for instance, a number of strikes over the tobacco ration led to a DND decision that tobacco would be provided free of charge to all relief camp workers. Another example of the government's flexibility when pushed came in March 1934 when a number of strikes led to a complaint making its way to the prime minister's office. Bennett was advised by B.C. premier Duff Pattullo that many relief camp workers who had been thrown out due to their involvement with strikes or violence had actually been goaded into misbehaviour by outside communist agitators and so should be allowed back in if they applied and went through a review process. Bennett accepted the advice. Many found life back on the street worse than camp life had been after all, and so were allowed to return.[6]

Meanwhile, the mercurial Liberal premier Pattullo continued to hound Bennett with complaints about the number of unemployed men on the streets of his cities. He wondered if the federal government could not simply round up these men and force them into camps. When more premiers and mayors wrote with similar complaints and suggestions, Manion asked McNaughton to investigate the idea of imprisoning unemployed single men. McNaughton began drawing up plans for the creation of camps of detention. By mid-1934, plans had proceeded to the point that McNaughton had scouted out locations, such as Kingston's Fort Henry. Manion's staff had composed an order-in-council for cabinet's consideration. But when Bennett heard of the plans he found the idea abhorrent and shut it all down before it began.

But unrest in the camps continued. With the growth of RCWU came a corresponding increase in the number and intensity of camp disturbances. Camp administrators reminded relief workers that if they were unhappy with the rules, or food, or 20-cent-a-day allowance, or anything else about the camp, for that matter, they were free to leave. The option was somewhat disingenuous, as many municipalities had ended all support of transient unemployed and the RCMP and many local police departments had begun to strictly enforce trespass laws in the cities, towns, and on railways. The result was that many young, unemployed transient men found relief camps to be de facto compulsory.[7]

Bennett demanded more reports on the camps. He continued to defend them and the policy that had brought them about. On April 12, 1934, for example, Bennett spoke in South Oxford, Ontario, supporting the Conservative candidate in a by-election. He acknowledged the hard times that all people of Canada had been experiencing and noted that, while the worst seemed to be past, a great deal of work still needed to be done. He acknowledged also that the government had made some mistakes but on the whole was proving itself more successful in dealing with the global crisis than most other national governments. He pointed to several areas of particular pride; one of them was the relief camps.

The prime minister told those assembled that the camps were a part of the government's overall emergency relief effort. He said they were meant to help single men by preserving their dignity and morale while keeping them healthy and active, and retaining their suitability for employment. He boasted that he had just received a report noting that about fifty thousand men had moved through the camps since they had been opened and that that number alone proved their value.[8]

By the end of 1934, despite Bennett's efforts to clearly explain their purposes and benefits, the relief camp program had become almost as widely unpopular as the prime minister who had created them. Recently elected Liberal premiers continued to make partisan hay by criticizing the Bennett government for the conditions and optics of the camps. Adding to the negative cacophony were those of the increasingly popular political left, represented by the CCF, the unions, and the communists. One of the most frequently heard complaints was about the provision of 20 cents a day for expenses. Many argued that it was insultingly low pay and that regular hourly wages should be instituted. Bennett spoke in the House and wrote a number of letters explaining over and over again that the 20-cent stipend was not and had never been intended to be pay. The camps, he patiently explained again, had been set up to provide housing, clothing, food, and work for unemployed and transient young men. Bennett even found himself having to defend the camps to his own backbenchers, who in the growing gale of criticism seemed unable to admit to a basic grasp of the camp's intentions. Responding to sharp questions from Ira Cotnam, the Conservative member from Ontario's Renfrew North, for instance, Bennett wrote, "No one suggests that the amount paid is for wages. It is merely a little pocket money for those who are on relief, and we receive letters daily from men who are not able to obtain work who speak in the warmest terms of what is being done for them."[9] Despite his clarity and best efforts, Bennett was losing control of the narrative.

Meanwhile, the RCWU's power continued to broaden and deepen. Part of the reason was the involvement of Arthur "Slim" Evans. A wiry little man with a sharp tongue and acidic wit, Evans had been born in Toronto but grew up in the American and Canadian West. In 1912, when only twenty-four years old, he had served time in a Kansas prison for the role he played in organizing an International Workers of the World free speech protest. He was behind bars again in Drumheller, Alberta, for leading a violent strike for the One Big Union movement. In 1933, Evans was incarcerated yet again for embezzling union funds in Penticton. Upon leaving jail he was hired by the Communist Party of Canada to organize the National Unemployed Workers Association. Through that work he became involved with the camps and a bane to the prime minister.

On December 7, 1934, Evans and some others organized a five-hundred-person protest rally outside Victoria's picturesque legislative buildings. They brought demands and a 30,665-signature petition to Premier Pattullo. Later that day, Evans met alone with DND officials and repeated his demands. Days later there were more protests, some involving the occupation of DND offices in Nanaimo, Vancouver, and Victoria. Evans insisted that men hated the camps. His main demands were that the 20-cent stipend be replaced with work for wages and that the hundreds of men who had been forced from the camps—he called them blacklisted—be allowed to return. It is not clear if Evans understood the irony in his requests. Bennett ignored them.

The unrest that was moving out of British Columbia's camps and into the cities led to more letters pouring into the prime minister's office. Over the Christmas break, Pattullo made a number of contradictory requests. In one letter, the premier asked that the camps be ended. In another, he asked for concessions to improve conditions. In yet another, he asked that all unemployed single men be rounded up and imprisoned. Bennett wrote back saying that he appreciated Pattullo's thoughts and ideas but that the current policies regarding the camps were sound and would continue.

Bennett's firm stand appeared to be effective. By January 3, 1935, nearly all relief workers who had left the camps had returned and been allowed to resume their work. Many, after all, had just gone home for Christmas. The only exception was about a hundred workers whom administrators had deemed dangerous agitators. They were not allowed re-entry, despite their expressed desire to return. For a couple of months, peace graced the camps and a great deal of valuable infrastructure work was accomplished.

But those organizing the men continued to work diligently. On March 15, Evans and delegates from camps in B.C. and Alberta assembled for a conference in Kamloops. They drew up a long list of demands including, most importantly, better camp conditions and work for wages. Others, meanwhile, continued to organize in the camps and persuaded more workers to support joint action. Organizers worked in cities and towns attempting to shape public opinion. Some newspaper editors began to publicize the RCWU complaints while some found themselves threatened if they did not. The newspaper in Princeton, B.C., for instance, published an editorial critical of the RCWU, but after being visited by a number of union "representatives" printed a retraction the next day.[10] Businesses found themselves similarly intimidated. Even a Princeton brothel became involved. When one of the men enjoying himself upstairs was found to be a cook in a relief camp that did not support the RCWU, a union leader had the madam throw him out.[11]

In June 1935, Bennett reported to the House that since the camps' inception 12,601 men had been asked to leave for inciting disturbances. More than that number had replaced them and were doing valuable work. Bennett defended the camps, arguing that inspectors had visited and reported that conditions were good. Where problems were found they were fixed. He praised the camps as tending for single, homeless, unemployed young men in a humane and caring way and said that social workers from other countries had seen the camps and expressed their "warm approval."[12]

The camps were neither as bad as some reports claimed nor as good as Bennett insisted. Conditions were shabby enough and at enough of them, however, that the camps became useful for those wishing to use them as examples of the hardships that depression-strapped Canadians were facing. Their very existence allowed them to be exploited as examples of the failure of democratic capitalism and thus to promote particular political and ideological agendas. The problem for Bennett was to decide whether the complaints that he read about camp conditions were reasonable requests for reasonable actions or the propaganda of agitators. A third option was whether the reports from those responsible for the camps were accurate or the spin of those trying to protect their jobs and reputations. In this highly charged atmosphere, Bennett erred on the side of seeing foreign-born rabble-rousers and communists behind many of the complaints and demands for change. As he wrote to Manitoba's Liberal premier Jimmy Gardiner, "The government's goal is to maintain the fabric of society and the institutions of our country against the illegal threats and demands of the Communists and their associates."[13]

This orientation should have surprised no one. Bennett had little sympathy for anyone who disobeyed the law, no matter what circumstance led to their decision to do so—including workers striking for what they believed to be right. This belief ran on a parallel track with his conviction that those who immigrated to Canada owed their adopted land the respect that is shown through obeying its laws. Those immigrants who fail to demonstrate respect in that fashion, he reasoned, should reconsider their decision and return to their home. He even reserved the right, legally his, to deport immigrants who had not yet completed the naturalization process but were found guilty of crimes either at home or in Canada. He had made his beliefs in such matters plain four years before. In his response to a question about the growing influence of communists in organized labour, Bennett had told the House in February 1931,

If the government is given reason to believe that there is a settled purpose
in the minds of a considerable number of people—not large, numerically,
but scattered over the various parts of Canada—to take action against the
maintenance of law and order . . . then we will take such action . . . and
free this country from those who have proven themselves unworthy of
our Canadian citizenship.[14]

To afford the government the power to deal with what he saw as
troublemakers, Bennett applied Section 98 of the Criminal Code. The
section had been created by order-in-council after the tragedy of the
1919 Winnipeg General Strike. It was enacted in legislation by Mackenzie
King in 1927. Intent upon maintaining law and order while ridding
Canada of revolutionaries, Section 98 rendered it illegal to hold meetings or publish material that promoted force or violence as a vehicle for
political protest or change. A linked amendment to the Immigration
Act allowed for the deportation of those deemed unworthy of citizenship due to their actions or perceived danger, including violating the
provisions of Section 98. That Bennett supported the spirit of these
amendments was seen in his including a section in the 1931 Relief Bill
that allowed the federal or any provincial government to take whatever
action was deemed necessary to preserve order. Bennett had defended
the Relief Bill provision by standing in the House with a copy of the 1914
War Measures Act in his hand and exclaiming, "This is a land of freedom where men may think as they will and say what they will, as long
as they do not attack the foundations upon which our civilization has
been built."[15]

Section 98 had been controversial from the start. Critics claimed
that it smacked of authoritarianism as it allowed the government to
punish anyone for even thinking in a way the government did not like.
In November 1932, a reporter asked Bennett about Section 98 and his
response was not only printed the next day but read by Woodsworth
into the public record. A "sound bite" that would haunt the prime minister was thus created. Bennett said, "We know that throughout Canada
this propaganda is being put forward by organizations from foreign
lands that seek to destroy our institutions and we ask every man and
woman to put the iron heel of ruthlessness against a thing of that kind."[16]
Those who hated Section 98 and the power it gave the government—

and hated Bennett for expressing his willingness to use that power—had a new nickname for the prime minister: Iron Heel Bennett.

The propaganda and threat to which Bennett was referring was communism. When Bennett took office in 1930, only seventeen years had passed since Vladimir Lenin had led the Bolshevik Revolution. Only sixteen had passed since Borden had sent 6,000 Canadian soldiers to Russia to support the anti-Bolshevik forces in the civil war that lasted years and killed thousands. Only nine years had passed since the Canadian Communist Party had been created. Like all other communist parties around the world, the Canadian party at that time was a child of the Soviet Comintern and took direction and funds from Moscow. In 1928, Josef Stalin publicly and proudly had the Comintern direct all communist parties to work to become the sole voice of the working classes of all capitalist countries by moving into labour unions and destroying the socialist parties that were competing for the hearts and minds of workers.[17]

By 1929, the Communist Party of Canada had infiltrated labour cells in factories across the country. Its *Canadian Tribune* regularly advocated support for Stalin and the Soviet Union, and urged workers to reject the gradualism of labour and socialist parties while moving quickly to overthrow the democratic-capitalist system. By 1931, it had become a powerful force among many intellectuals and many working-class people, especially in urban centres such as Winnipeg, Montreal, Toronto, Hamilton, Thunder Bay, and Windsor. It claimed in 1933 to have played a role in 75 per cent of Canadian strikes.[18]

In August 1931, Bennett used Section 98 to have Communist Party leaders Tim Buck, Sam Carr, and six others arrested for unlawful association and seditious conspiracy. It was as blatant a demonstration as one could imagine both of Bennett's conviction that communism was a dangerous force in the country and his determination to do something about it. For others, regardless of its legality, it was a bald demonstration of Iron Heel Bennett's ruthless use of undemocratic power. All those arrested were convicted and spent two and a half years in Kingston's maximum-security prison—they became known throughout Canada as the Kingston Eight.

Within weeks of his imprisonment shots were fired into Buck's cell, narrowly missing him. Rumours spread among communist sympathizers that Bennett had ordered him assassinated. With his arrest and narrow escape Buck was becoming an unlikely folk hero.

In response to Buck's arrest, an organization was established calling itself the Canadian Labour Defence League. It comprised a disparate group of men and women all concerned with addressing the needs of the working class and having the imprisoned men released. The league was a front organization for the Communist Party of Canada.[19] In November 1933, a delegation travelled to Ottawa and secured a meeting with the prime minister. It began politely enough, led by the Reverend A. E. Smith, a well-known communist and former minister from Saskatchewan. But it quickly degenerated as Smith and others berated and insulted the prime minister, and Bennett lost his temper. Bennett was forced to call an abrupt end to the meeting and have the delegation forcibly removed.

A play called *Eight Men Speak*, about Buck's arrest and the attempt on his life, was performed at the Standard Theatre in Toronto just a couple of days later. The local police shut it down after one performance, stating that it was distasteful. Police in Winnipeg threatened to revoke the licence of a production company that announced it would stage the play. Meanwhile, Smith had been making speeches in which he spoke of the need to replace the government and accusing Bennett of having ordered Buck's murder. He was arrested and charged with sedition under Section 98. Canada was gathering political prisoners.

The fiasco of Smith's meeting with Bennett, the cancelling of the play, and Smith's arrest led to another influx of letters to the prime minister. Many were from the same unions and organizations as before and focused upon Buck and the Kingston Eight and demanded their release. Most simply completed and mailed in a preprinted form adding only the name of their organization or local, the names of the signing officers, and the date.

Smith was acquitted. His trial had provided him with a pulpit from which to speak of communist goals and to rail against Bennett. While much that he said was dismissed by mainstream media, there were some who saw merit in his criticism of the government. The *Toronto Herald*, for instance, published an editorial stating that it disagreed with everything Smith stood for. It continued,

But we are glad the jury squelched the proposal to send him to jail for venturing to air his opinions. If we are going to send every man to the pen who holds views contrary to our own or who ventures to severely criticize the government in power, we will have to build bigger and better jails to hold them all.[20]

An unpopular prime minister's ham-fisted attempts to protect the country from communism were rendering him even more unpopular. Among Bennett's literally hundreds of Christmas greetings that year was a small card boasting an illustration of a young boy in a cap holding a hammer and sickle. The card stated, "Revolutionary Greetings from B.C. Canada 1933–4—For a New Year of Decisive Struggles Against Capitalism." Inside was a quote from Tim Buck which said in part, "The future holds only fear for dying capitalism and its henchmen, for before them stands their doom, the inevitable world victory of the workers against the capitalist system of anarchy, poverty and war."[21] In January 1935, with Bennett focused primarily on his New Deal radio addresses and attendant legislation, another 186 resolutions and letters arrived. They were almost all worded exactly the same: the eight imprisoned communists were either war or political prisoners, and must be released.

The next weeks brought yet another effort whereby a number of unions and locals again used exactly the same form to put forth resolutions demanding that Section 98 be torn up and that all persons still held in custody under the section be immediately released. It was easy to see that much of the effort was organized by the Communist Party simply to have Tim Buck and other communists released from prison. No doubt many of the correspondents were sincere in their belief that Section 98 violated Canadian values. It was difficult, however, to divide those whose protests were sincere from those seeking merely to exploit the situation to promote an ideological point of view. A letter in a category of its own stated, "If you refuse to release all the political prisoners within one week's time, YOU SHALL SURELY DIE." It was signed "Jesus Christ." Unfortunately neither the envelope nor letter contained a return address.[22]

Upon Buck's release in November 1934 he was welcomed as a martyr to the communist cause. To mark the occasion, a rally was organized. Seventeen thousand people packed Maple Leaf Gardens and eight thousand more had to be turned away at the door. Buck mesmerized the audience with a blistering attack on Bennett and the forces of the bourgeoisie that he was said to represent. Seated on the stage during the address was Liberal Ontario premier Mitchell Hepburn.

The Communist Party grew more powerful—and infiltrated more unions—with the positive publicity Buck had earned and the hard work he and others had done. Their message resonated with many workers suffering the hardships of the Depression. By 1935, twenty-five communist candidates had won municipal and school board elections. Blairmount, Alberta, elected an entire slate of communists to fill its council and its first bylaw was to rename its main street Tim Buck Boulevard. The party infiltrated so many of Ontario's CCF riding associations that in 1936 Woodsworth dissolved the Ontario CCF. In recognizing the Communist Party's goals and growing power, Bennett was clearly not using a bogey to frighten but acknowledging a social force with which to be reckoned.

Growing alongside the power of the Communist Party was a trend toward violent strikes. While throughout his public and private careers Bennett had fought for the rights of those without economic clout or political power, he had little use for those unions, whether communist dominated or not, that used the threat of strikes to bring about improvements in the working lives of their members. From time to time Bennett would meet protesters, labour leaders, or others who were advocating what he considered radical ideas. He once met in a large room with a clear view to the front of the Parliament Buildings. Bennett set it up so that the delegation with whom he was meeting would be intimidated by the naked display of state power; in sightlines past him and out the windows, he arranged to have an RCMP paddy wagon and several mounted and armed officers standing at attention and staring back through the window.

During his tenure as prime minister, Bennett needed to deal with a number of strikes, many of which turned violent. With each unfortunate instance his disdain for violence and especially for the efforts of outsiders grew. A coal miners' strike in Estevan, Saskatchewan, was particularly ugly. In September 1931, he received a number of reports about the growing unrest. He read that the leaders of the coal miners' strike were not local men but members of the Communist Party, many of whom were from out of town and some from out of province. One such leader was James Sloan, who made impassioned speeches in which he encouraged men to stop at nothing to get what they wanted. Sloan and others planned a parade through town, but the municipal council saw trouble coming and voted against allowing a permit. Sloan ignored the council's wishes and led the parade anyway. Many strikers said later that they would not have marched had they known that what they were doing was illegal. But march they did and when they were a block from the town hall the chief of police ordered them to stop and disperse. Soon voices were raised, then fists, then the local police and RCMP billy clubs. Bricks and bottles flew at the police as they sought to arrest the more belligerent of what had become a mob. The police were slowly backed against the steps of the town hall. Only then did they form a line and fire shots over the heads of those attacking them. When men continued to rush the police line, bullets were fired into them, with the order to aim low. Three striking miners were killed and several suffered leg wounds.

The Estevan riot initiated a spate of fifty-three resolutions, letters, and telegrams to the prime minister. One of particular note came from the National Unemployed Workers Association in Victoria. It called what happened at Estevan "bloody murder" and "a slaughter." Its resolution stated in part, "This meeting recognises in this outrage the commencement of Bennett's Blank Check Reign of Terror, by which he hopes to force the Canadian workers to accept without protest the capitalist attack upon the standard of living of the Canadian worker. . . . The end of capitalism has been hastened; the hysterical and murderous bourgeoisie cannot long hope to maintain their rule by perpetrating atrocities of this nature. LONG LIVE THE REVOLUTIONARY WORKERS OF CANADA."[23]

Another strike that informed Bennett's attitudes involved miners in Corbin, British Columbia. They went on strike on January 20, 1934, demanding safer working conditions and improved pay. The strike went on and on and on. A year later, in January 1935, Bennett received a report stating that, according to the Workers Protective Association, the RCMP had viciously attacked workers who had been staging a peaceful and legal action. The police had first closed the highway so that no assistance or medical attention could reach the workers. Bennett received a number of resolutions that used harsh language condemning him and the RCMP. One from the Workers Protective Association of Princeton said, "This brutal attack upon working people signifies there is no limit to the extent your Department will go in its mad attempts to subjugate the toiling people to poverty and want."[24] Bennett's reaction to the Workers Protective Association could probably have been predicted, but it can also be guessed that he would have been moved by the Women's Auxiliary of Calgary writing him the very next day expressing, albeit in more polite language, a similar opinion of the police and his government's actions.[25] Others wrote to Bennett calling the actions atrocities while still others used the words "terror" and "fascist" to describe the government and police. In all, 790 resolutions from various groups and individuals found their way to Parliament Hill. Not a single one supported the police or the government.

There was yet another violent clash between police and strikers that November. In Innisfail, Alberta, farmers went on strike demanding decent grading for their wheat and grain. The RCMP took strike leader George Palmer into custody, beat him, tarred and feathered him, and left him in a field. Farmers and others concerned with what had happened met in public halls the next day in twenty-two Alberta communities. In Calgary, a thousand people assembled to speak against the actions of the police. Each meeting sent a resolution to Bennett demanding action to rectify the problem and to condemn the RCMP.[26] Bennett responded perfunctorily to each piece of correspondence, revealing sympathy for pain suffered and regret for damage incurred. Unions and the RCMP both appeared to be losing control of themselves. The phrase "police riot" was entering the popular lexicon.

There were many other large, long, and bitter strikes involving, for instance, the Toronto Garment Workers, the Halifax Sewer Workers, and, in one that was sure to affect Bennett, the International Paper Union at the E. B. Eddy Company. His reaction reflected his thoughts on strikes and strikers. Eddy workers threatened to strike in early August 1935 if wage demands were not met. As a director and major shareholder in the company, Bennett wrote to company president Victor Drury suggesting that if a strike were forced upon the company, the public would rally behind management. He suggested that Drury tell a priest in Hull that he planned to shut the plant and reopen it with other workers. Drury was to let the priest attempt to get the men to call off the strike and, if he failed, to carry out the bluff.[27] The strike did not materialize.

VANCOUVER STRIKE

It was with his clearly formed and publicly articulated opinion of strikes and outside agitators, his suspicions about unions, his belief in the obligation of the state to protect law and order, and his conviction that the Canadian Communist Party represented a legitimate danger to the country all clearly established in his mind, that Bennett learned that the Vancouver strikers were receiving support from the Communist Party of Canada. Just days after they were released from prison, in November 1934, communist leaders Tim Buck and Sam Carr had travelled to Vancouver where they met with strike leaders. Four months later, Buck and Carr returned to the city, where they expressed their fulsome support for the strike in addresses before a mass meeting.

In April and May 1935, work in all B.C. relief camps slowed or stopped as nearly all of the men left. While some went back home, between one and three thousand did as the union had asked them to do and assembled in Vancouver. The union set up barracks at four downtown halls. Evans was in charge of arranging food and shelter as well as the political organization for the assemblage. He met with municipal and provincial political leaders as well as newspaper editors to urge support for the men.

Evans and other leaders demanded that the city pay relief to all the workers, but Vancouver's mayor cried poor and refused. To raise money to feed the men, Evans organized a tag day where workers stood on street corners collecting donations and pinning a small piece of paper on donors' lapels. In a single day, workers gathered an amazing $4,000.

In New Westminster, city council banned tag days, but Evans planned one anyway. The police chief tried to stop it by having a number of organizers arrested. Evans sent a hundred workers to storm the police precinct where their comrades had been jailed. The chief broke down and released them all. The tag day occurred. New Westminster was a moral victory for the strikers, but also it was seen by many as a turning point: with Wild West tactics, the strikers had, for the first time, broken the law. Meanwhile, pamphlets and posters were printed and distributed throughout Vancouver and the surrounding area trumpeting the strikers' demands and gloating over their facing down the enemies of the working man.

By the middle of April 1935 there were approximately 1,500 strikers in Vancouver. Evans and the others organized rallies in public parks at which many clergy, municipal, and provincial leaders, as well as CCF and communist representatives, pledged their support to cheering throngs. Often there were spontaneous parades down streets or even through stores, as strikers chanted "End to Slave Camps" and "Work for Wages."

Nearly every day the men would set out from what they called their divisional headquarters and parade around the city's downtown core. Stores hired guards to stand at their thresholds to keep the marchers out. On April 26, a large group passing the Seymour Street entrance of the two-storey Hudson's Bay Company store noticed that it was unguarded. So they swept in. Accounts from marchers, police, and shoppers as to what happened next differ, but the facts are that speeches were made, displays were ransacked, police and marchers clashed, shoppers had to scurry for safety, and arrests were made. Later, Mayor Gerry McGeer stood at the First World War memorial in Victory Square and, quite literally, read the riot act: disperse or face arrest. The strikers withdrew.

The next day, however, strikers were back with a renewed demand that city council grant them relief payments. To again press their case, to both Bennett and the city, they organized three simultaneous marches, which split the police. The tactic enabled them to take over the City of Vancouver Museum at Main and Hastings. As five hundred men occupied the building, strike leaders negotiated with McGeer, who finally relented and promised three days of food rations if the men would leave the museum undamaged.

The violations of the law, the marching, disruptions to businesses, and finally the disturbance at the Hudson's Bay store and the occupation of the museum had robbed the strikers of a great deal of their public sympathy and support. And yet May 1, the day of labour's traditional recognition of working peoples' struggles and contributions, saw a huge demonstration of support. High school students and city workers were among those who joined a large parade down Burrard Street and cheered at a boisterous rally at the Malkin Bowl. The May Day parade showed that the public's attitudes toward the strikers were waxing and waning. Battles were being won, but as overall goals remained unmet the war was being lost.

At that moment Bennett was dealing with a number of other matters, including moving his New Deal legislation through Parliament and trying to push the Americans to increase trade. He also needed to decide upon a date for a federal election, which, despite the low and still-tumbling popularity of both himself and his government, the constitution demanded he soon call. And he was still recovering from a heart attack that he suffered in March that had all but removed him from the day-to-day operations of his government during April and May and left him constantly tired.

Despite the distractions and from his sick-bed, Bennett focused upon a number of letters he and his cabinet had received from Vancouver's mayor and B.C.'s premier. All begged for federal help. But Bennett had already decided that the best course of action would be to do nothing. For one thing, he had deemed that the responsibility for maintaining order rested with the city and the province. It was made clear to Premier Pattullo that if he believed he could no longer handle the situation, he would need to transfer all power to do so to the federal government. Bennett would then be able to take action in a constitutionally sound manner.[28]

On May 20, Bennett made his thoughts on the tense situation clear in a cable to Mayor McGeer, who had been sending him a number of alarming and sometimes threatening letters and telegrams. Bennett wrote that any man who wished to accept the conditions of the camps could do so, while any man who found the conditions unacceptable was free to leave. If they decided to leave, he explained, then their welfare became the responsibility of the province and city in which they resided.[29] McGeer may have been correct in his response that Bennett was failing to grasp the seriousness of the situation in Vancouver. The mayor tried again to urge the prime minister to understand that communists and outside agitators had stirred the situation to the point where he feared riots and widespread violence. Only through increased funding that no city and no province could handle without federal assistance could such terrible ends be avoided. He concluded with an ominous thought: "If you persist in attitude laid down in your telegram trouble is inevitable and responsibility must rest on you."[30] Bennett was not moved.

Slim Evans and Richard Bennett, two intelligent and determined men, had reached an impasse. With neither willing to compromise, only one could win. Evans moved first. He recognized that the strike was fall-ing apart. Between three to four hundred strikers had left, fed up with bad food, crowded quarters, and a lack of progress. Many headed for home while others returned to their camps. To stem the tide, a meeting was held in Hamilton Hall on May 30 in which he delivered a speech meant to rouse his followers; they must become more militant, he ar-gued, or admit defeat.[31] A vote was called and 70 per cent raised their hands in favour of continuing the strike. From the floor came a sugges-tion that they leave Vancouver, put all of the men on trains, and move the protest directly to Bennett in Ottawa. The idea was quickly adopted and plans began to be made. The On to Ottawa Trek was born.

THE TREK

The strikers left the city in three groups on the third and fourth of June. Many were demoralized upon their arrival at Kamloops when they dis-covered that nothing was prepared nor did anyone really seem to want them. As a camp was hastily established at a municipal park, many talked of abandoning the struggle, but Evans spoke persuasively about commitment and so not a single man left. During the afternoon many trekkers spread out and spoke to various people and groups about what they were up to, and that evening a rally was held at the park. The meet-ing won them support, food, tobacco, and even donations to cover fu-ture expenses. A number of young men joined the trek when it left the next morning. Kamloops taught the leaders a lesson. From that point on, advance men were sent ahead of the trekkers to incite the locals and inform the police.

The most talented advance man was a young Saskatchewan native named Matt Shaw. He was as determined as any of the strike leaders, but the secret of his success was his beguiling charm. For instance, in April, with the strike just under way, Shaw had arranged to corner Governor General Lord Bessborough on a Vancouver train platform. For ten min-utes Shaw impressed upon His Majesty's representative all of the prob-lems and demands of the relief camp strikers. The two warmly shook hands at the end of the conversation with each wishing the other good luck. Shaw's advance work, and his personality that made it possible, was indispensable.

Due mostly to Shaw's efforts, two days later the strikers were welcomed in Golden, B.C., with an enormous feast. Abundant pots of hot coffee and other drinks awaited. Hanging between two trees and suspended over a large fire was a bathtub filled with gurgling beef stew. They were similarly welcomed in Medicine Hat, where, like at every other stop, they were carefully watched by police but cheered by crowds offering food, clothing, and support.

In Calgary, they were bivouacked at the Exhibition Grounds, but the meals that Shaw had arranged failed to materialize. This led to trouble, ending with trekkers taking control of a provincial relief office and holding employees hostage until the city agreed to provide food and food coupons. Threats such as this became standard procedure. Shaw had developed a blackmailing technique that was proving quite effective. He would arrive at a city a couple of days in advance of the main party, meet with the mayor, and demand money and food coupons for each of his men. If granted, he promised they would stop but leave on the same train. If refused, he threatened to camp in the city, run tag days, and do whatever else was needed in order to secure food and other needs.[32]

There were a number of RCMP spies within the ranks of the trekkers who informed the prime minister that the trekkers' operation was gaining strength as it moved. It was drawing support from the people of each city and town passed through, and additional numbers from relief camps and unemployed young men. Plans were being made for even more supporters who would be joining them in Winnipeg and Toronto before the final push to Ottawa.[33]

The trek had begun to stir the public's imagination across the land. Bennett was asked about it nearly every day in the House, but he stuck to his argument: he regretted that so many young men were falling under the spell of communists. He called those on the trains trespassers and noted that several communist societies, operating under various names, had been demanding to negotiate with him but that he had refused each offer.[34]

In the first week of June 1935, the full cabinet discussed the situation at length and a consensus was reached: the trek was communist inspired and led, it was wreaking havoc in every city it descended upon, and it should not be allowed to continue. The decision was made to end it. The best place to stop the trek, it was decided, was in Regina. The location made sense because Regina was the western headquarters of the RCMP, meaning that communications would be easier and reinforcements readily available. Letters were written informing the RCMP in Regina, the city's mayor Cornelius Rink, and Saskatchewan's Liberal premier Jimmy Gardiner. Gardiner expressed rage over Bennett's decision that the trek would be stopped in his capital city. He wrote to Bennett pleading with him to allow the trekkers to move through his province.[35] Bennett offered him no choice.

The plan was not secret. The next day, Minister of Justice and Attorney General Guthrie rose in the House and announced to the country that the trekkers were under the direction of communist elements, were trespassing on the trains, were attempting to disturb the peace, order, and good government of the country, and were breaking several laws including Section 443 of the Railway Act. Therefore, he explained, the RCMP had been asked to stop them in Regina. They would be told to stop violating the law and to return to their homes or relief camps.[36]

The announcement shocked many people. There was concern about Bennett having decided to stop the trek and about Regina as the site of the showdown because of the RCMP's poor reputation in the city and province. In 1928, the Saskatchewan government had been forced by financial considerations to eliminate its provincial police and had asked the RCMP to take over policing duties. Three years later, the RCMP found itself embroiled in controversy when its officers used lethal force, killing three striking miners in Estevan. In 1933, a relief camp that had been set up in Saskatoon's Exhibition Grounds was raided by the RCMP and in the riot that erupted several unemployed men were injured. A number of police officers were also hurt and one died from his wounds. Regardless of who was to blame for the confrontations and violence, by 1935 few in Saskatchewan or Regina harboured much love for the Mounties.

Meanwhile, the trekkers moved closer and closer. Their numbers continued to grow. On June 12, they were in Moose Jaw, where townspeople organized a parade and offered tents that had been set up on the sports field. And on they came. On June 14, they arrived in Regina.

Their welcome was like in most other towns. Clapping and cheering crowds met them at the station and more people lined the streets of a makeshift parade. Tents and food had been prepared at the Exhibition Grounds. It looked like it would be another triumphant stop on a long journey of increasingly exuberant success. The trekkers arrived 2,500 strong, and were soon joined by five hundred more strikers from the Dundurn Camp. The city afforded them relief, so that more food was made available. At a mass meeting, local communist, CCF, and union leaders spoke in support of their actions. Crowds cheered the trekkers the next day as they paraded downtown. Meanwhile, the RCMP finalized their plans and prepared their men.

It was high noon. One can almost hear the Ry Cooder music swelling with Bennett and Evans standing on a dusty main street in some spaghetti-western movie. But then, at the last minute, there was a reprieve. Bennett sent Minister of Railways and Canals R.J. Manion and Minister of Agriculture Robert Weir to speak with trek leaders. Manion was chosen due to the trekkers using the railways, and Bennett sent Weir because he was a Saskatchewan MP, well respected by westerners not only for his military service (he had served with distinction and was wounded at Passchendaele) but also because of his support for farmers and the West.

Manion and Weir met with a delegation for two hours on the evening of June 17. Manion sent a telegram to Bennett that evening reporting that the trek leaders had six demands. They wanted work that paid at least 50 cents an hour with union rates for skilled labour and specified daily, weekly, and monthly hours. They demanded that the compensation act cover all relief camp work and that first aid be available at all camps. They wanted worker committees formed in each camp and all camps to be removed from the purview of the Department of National Defence. They wanted a program of national unemployment insurance. Finally, they demanded that all relief camp workers be guaranteed the right to vote. They also wanted to speak directly with the prime minister.

Manion indicated to Bennett that the people of Regina appeared to be largely with the trekkers and that, in dealing with the situation, Gardiner's government was ineffectual. He suggested that a cooling-off period might allow a peaceful resolution of the affair. Bennett approved the paying of first-class fares for the delegation to travel to Ottawa to meet with him and the cabinet. Meanwhile, trekkers who wished to stay in Regina would be fed at the federal government's expense and those who chose to return to their homes or camps would be offered free train fares to do so. Several cables were exchanged between Ottawa and

Regina until late in the evening Manion sent a final message noting with some surprise that the trekkers' delegation had agreed to all of the conditions and would be coming to Ottawa.[37]

On June 22, eleven men walked into the dark-panelled cabinet room to meet with the prime minister and eleven members of his cabinet. The cabinet sat on one side of a large table with Bennett in the middle. Directly across from Bennett was Evans with his men and one woman— Margaret Richmond—on either side of him. If either man were intimidated by the other he did not show it. One of the more extraordinary meetings involving a Canadian prime minister was about to commence.

It all began politely enough. Bennett allowed Evans to speak at great length. His demands were listed, explained, and defended. Manion corrected a couple of points. Then Bennett weighed in. He asked the age and birthplace of each delegate, noting that only Evans was Canadian. He then suggested that each of their demands had either already been met or that they were based on a misunderstanding of the purpose of the relief camps. He accused the trek leaders of being irresponsible citizens in violating laws and in stirring others to do the same. James "Red" Walsh, leader of the Relief Camp Workers Union, snapped that he and the other leaders had done "their damnedest" to avoid breaking the law but that the government's refusal to negotiate had led them to take the actions they had. If anyone was hurt, he said, it would be the government's fault.

Bennett sounded very much the lawyer in replying that Walsh had just provided all the proof that was needed to establish that he, Evans, and the others had been prepared from the beginning to engage in illegal activities. Bennett then recalled that Evans had been sent to prison for embezzling funds from the union he had once led. Evans lost his temper and snarled,

> You are a liar. I was arrested for fraudulently converting those funds to feed the starving, instead of sending them to the agents at Indianapolis, and I again say you are a liar if you say I embezzled, and I will have the pleasure of telling the workers throughout Canada I was forced to tell the premier of Canada he was a liar. Don't think you can pull off anything like that. You are not intimidating me a damned bit.[38]

It was an astounding outburst that proved the meeting was going nowhere. But in losing his temper, Evans had ceded victory to Bennett who carried on with the logical presentation of his case. He noted that Evans had been arrested a second time under Section 98 of the Criminal Code for leading miners in an illegal strike. Trek marshal and Scottish-born Jack Cosgrove began protesting Bennett's concern over the fact that the delegates were foreign-born, or that Evans had a criminal record. That the trek was led by hotheaded, foreign-born outsiders, like so many of the other strikes with which the government had been dealing over the years, was exactly what Bennett was trying to establish for his colleagues. Except for Manion, who said little, cabinet members sat as silently as a jury, listening to the prime minister drawing damning testimony from the increasingly agitated witnesses before him. Cosgrove jumped to his feet and twice Bennett asked him to sit down. Again, a loss of temper, as always, led to a surrendering of the point at hand.

Bennett returned to his argument that in demanding work for wages the men were misinterpreting the purpose of the relief camps. He admitted that some abuses had crept into some camps and that they had been addressed, but he argued that the camps' main function—providing housing, food, and useful activities for single young men—was being accomplished. With that established he said, "You cannot go and take the government by the throat and demand that anything that pleases your sweet desire will be done."[39]

He then went point by point through the rest of the six demands, explaining how they were either unreasonable, beyond the scope of the federal government, or had already been addressed through legislated programs. For instance, he outlined the various programs the government had initiated to provide work for wages for unemployed Canadians. He spoke of public works programs that had been made available and stated that relief camp workers could leave at any time to take those jobs. With respect to camp committees, he said that any man in any camp was free to bring grievances to those running the camp, but that the committees the trekkers demanded would not be allowed, for they would only serve as vehicles through which propaganda that would encourage unlawful strikes and agitation could be dissembled. And regarding the demand that workers be given the right to vote, Bennett pointed out that any relief camp worker who met the regulations of the Franchise Act already had the right to vote. By the end, each and every demand of the trekkers had been carefully and fully addressed. Bennett concluded with a warning. He said, "That is all that can be said. I want to warn you once more, if you persist in violating the laws of Canada you must accept full responsibility for your conduct." Evans simply said, "And you also."[40]

Bennett understood the threat in Evans's words. The prime minister responded,

> In order that there be no misunderstanding you might make known to all those who are with you whether at Regina or elsewhere that they will be able to go back to their camps, and that as work develops on highways or on any public undertaking, to the extent to which the opportunity may offer, they will have the opportunity to work, but a continuance of illegal trespassing upon the property of the railways involving the interruption of mails, the loss of life, and injury to property will not be tolerated. Good day gentlemen.[41]

Evans then spoke more to his own people than to Bennett. He said that in raising the "red bogey" the prime minister had the "red horrors." He said, "Our responsibility is we must take this back to the workers and see that the hunger programme of Bennett is stopped."[42] And with that they left. Good to his word, Bennett allowed them to return to Regina. The trekkers and the RCMP both prepared for the confrontation they knew would come.

Bennett rose in the House on June 24 and explained the cabinet's meeting with representatives from what he called "the so-called marchers." He began by telling the House that seven of the eight were foreign-born and that the leader had a long criminal record. He explained how their demands had either already been met or could not be met by his or any other government. He expressed sympathy for the many young men who were being exploited by men such as Evans, who sought only to further their own "sinister purposes." Bennett again defended the temporary relief camps and said that while earlier problems had existed they had been fixed and that the camps had for some time been fulfilling the purposes for which they had been created. He explained that the government had offered the creation of a temporary camp to take care of those now assembled in Regina so that they would have work, food, and accommodation while arrangements were made for them to return home or to a relief camp of their choosing. Bennett concluded with the thought that had informed all of his decisions in the matter. He said,

> ... the government is fully seized of the seriousness of the situation and believes as firmly as it is possible to believe that the present movement of these marchers upon Ottawa in defiance of the law is in reality an organized effort on the part of the various communist organizations throughout Canada to effect the overthrow of constituted authority in defiance of the laws of the land. The government is determined to maintain law and order by all the means within its power and calls upon all law abiding citizens to assist to that end.[43]

In case anyone still failed to understand, Bennett repeated that the RCMP had been ordered to stop the trek. It would also assist the railways to ensure that no one illegally used the rails again.

THE RIOT

The first of July was Dominion Day. Evans and many of the same people who had been with him in Ottawa spent the afternoon meeting with Saskatchewan's premier. Gardiner was still enraged with Bennett's decision to stop the trek in Regina but shared his desire to end the standoff without violence, so he offered support for any who wished to leave or move to the temporary camp then being set up. He offered no false hope regarding the trekkers' cause.

At eight o'clock that night, about five hundred trekkers and supporters from the city met in Regina's Market Square. As Evans was addressing the crowd, three unmarked vans took up positions at the square's perimeters. At the sound of a whistle the van doors flung open and RCMP officers wielding bats poured out. They charged the crowd and soon it was an orgy of screams and blood and bone-cracking blows. With the square quickly cleared, the trekkers tried to reassemble and reorganize on the adjoining streets, but mounted police who had been held in reserve moved in. As what had become a roiling, brawling riot spilled into the neighbouring streets, a number of storefronts were smashed and cars overturned. Makeshift barricades were thrown up and rocks rained down on the police as they charged. Soon the trekkers and others caught up in the melee were throwing not only rocks but bottles, pieces of metal, and anything else they could lay their hands on. A brigade was quickly assembled and some men gathered projectiles and brought them to the men at the barricades who immediately launched them at the police and their horses. There was tear gas. There were gunshots.

As the sun rose on Regina the next day, its glow revealed a horrible sight. The streets resembled a battlefield of smashed windows, over-turned cars, the ruins of barricades, bits of tattered clothing, and, in places, the dark stains of spilled blood. More than a hundred people were in jail, including Evans, Shaw, and other leaders who were appre-hended just minutes after it all began. Thirty were in hospital. Constable Charles Millar had been hit over the head with some sort of club and killed.

When the trekkers roused themselves at the Exhibition Grounds site they saw that Mounties armed with Vickers machine guns sur-rounded them. Gardiner met with Evans, released on bail, and other trek leaders. Final plans were made to evacuate the men as quickly as possible according to the deal worked out with Bennett and Manion two weeks before. Within three days the Exhibition Grounds was empty and the men were on trains moving east and west. On a train heading back to Vancouver, an effigy of Bennett was constructed and hung outside the window. It flapped in the wind with a sign around its neck declaring that it was indeed Bennett who would rot in hell.

The day after the Regina Riot saw, not surprisingly, both Mackenzie King and Woodsworth on their feet in the House decrying all that the government had done to cause the tragedy. Bennett rose in the govern-ment's defence and reiterated many of the same points that had been made before the riot occurred. He conveniently ignored the fact that the RCMP had started the melee and said that the violence was unfortunate but that it justified his government's conviction that those who called themselves marchers were willing to use any means to bring about their foul ends. Further, the trek leaders were too powerful in swaying other-wise right-minded Canadians to employ methods far beyond what they would otherwise see as proper. He again outlined the purpose of the camps and noted that conditions were the same as at a well-run lumber camp, except even better, for education through Frontier College was encouraged and arranged. Bennett made the point that those in the relief camps had been working well until outside communist agitators entered and began organizing them based upon trumped-up charges of mistreatment. He said that by the time the strikers reached Saskatchewan it was no longer a strike or protest or sporadic uprising but "a revolutionary movement." Also, he went on, the railway companies had asked the government for help. The three trains that left Vancouver to begin the trek had no effect on the proper operation of the railways and the delivery of mail, but by the time the trekkers were in Saskatchewan the railways and mail delivery were being seriously hampered. This disruption broke federal laws. Bennett compared himself to American president Grover Cleveland, who in 1894 had stepped in to end the Pullman Strike when it had similarly led to tampering with railways and the mail in Illinois. As in the United States, he concluded, illegal acts demanded action no matter who was doing them or the motive behind them. In such cases, the police and government had no option but to act.[44]

The story ends with one set of facts and the reports of two commissions. With respect to the facts, Bennett had been advised by Manion, Premier Pattullo, and several RCMP reports that the leaders of the Vancouver Strike and the Ottawa Trek were communists. They were. Arthur "Slim" Evans had been associated with the Communist Party of Canada before the strike and trek and would maintain his ties afterwards. A year after Regina, he was hired by the Communist Party to raise money and recruits for the Mackenzie Papineau Battalion, which was being organized to fight on the side of the communists against the fascists in the Spanish Civil War. Evans undertook a gruelling schedule of one-night stands, speaking in fifty-three British Columbia communities. Four others who were members of the delegation that met Bennett—Red Walsh, Peter Neilson, Paddy O'Neill, and Tony Martin—were also party members and involved in stirring interest in the war and support for the communists. All four volunteered and fought in Spain. O'Neill and Neilson were killed.

Mackenzie King agreed with Bennett that the strike and trek had been led by communists. Upon hearing of the Regina Riot, he had sat with trusted colleague Ernest Lapointe and determined that they had to be very careful in criticizing Bennett's handling of the entire affair. They did not want to be seen as supporting the trekkers too vehemently lest they be branded as supporting communism. They elected to let Woodsworth lead the debate in the Commons.[45]

The truth was revealed in the commissions. The Royal Commission on Relief Camps, British Columbia, was chaired by the Honourable William A. Macdonald. It had been created by the British Columbia government to investigate relief camp conditions and it had submitted its findings just as the strike was beginning. The commission's report criticized Bennett's policy of having camp work done for free and providing only spending money. It stated that those leaving the camps had to do so with very little or no money in their pockets, which made life back in cities quite difficult and the men easy to exploit.[46] Ironically, however, given the fact that the state of the camps was the ostensible cause of the Vancouver Strike and all that followed, the report found that, beyond some easily rectified problems, camp conditions were fine. It found that the rules were clear and generally followed and that a great deal of valuable work was being done. The commission also concluded that accusations and complaints such as mail tampering, restricting the movement of workers in and out of camps, denying workers the right to vote, and poor or inadequate food, were unfounded. It had concluded that the camps were doing exactly as they had been designed to do and doing it quite well.[47]

A second commission, the Regina Riot Inquiry Commission, was established by the Saskatchewan government. In November 1935, after the federal election that would return him to the opposition side of the House, Bennett travelled to Regina and, following a series of meetings, felt compelled to telegram Justice Minister Lapointe. He reported that the commission had been taken over by communists and communist sympathizers and that the federal government had reversed an earlier commitment and appointed counsels for the RCMP who both were well-known Liberals. Lapointe laconically responded that the Saskatchewan government had appointed the commission and so the Mackenzie King government could do nothing about it.[48] Bennett was not reassured and maintained his belief that the commission was little more than a partisan hatchet job.

Despite Bennett's concerns, the commission's final report exonerated him. It stated that he and his government had acted responsibly, legally, and constitutionally throughout the incidents related to the Vancouver Strike, On to Ottawa Trek, and the Regina Riot. The RCMP, however, was skewered for actions that it took to initiate the riot. Evans, who testified at the hearings, was criticized for saying things that could not have been true, such as claiming to have witnessed the killing of the constable when at the time he was nowhere near the area in which it happened. Evans also testified that, despite all that he had said during the strike and trek, that camp conditions were not really a problem.[49] He who had accused Bennett of being a liar had admitted to lying to incite his followers and had been caught lying again, but this time under oath.

Bennett had made it clear before, and stuck to his conviction later, that he believed it was his duty to do all that he could to protect society from violence and disorder. In carrying out that duty he had ordered the trek stopped, but he did not plan or direct the actions that the police took. He had been appalled by the violence but that had not dissuaded him from his belief that the government was right to act to protect society when that society is under threat. Only four days after the riot, he had written a letter to a Belleville reporter named W. Wilbur. In it, he used an argument and language similar to that which Pierre Trudeau employed to explain his use of the War Measures Act in October 1970. On the steps of the Parliament Building's Centre Block, Trudeau told a reporter, ". . . it is more important to keep law and order in the society than to be worried about weak-kneed people who don't like the looks of an army. . . . I think that society must take every means at its disposal to defend itself. . . ."[50] Bennett was rather less strident but made the same point when he wrote, "It is not the intention of this Government to allow such demonstrations as will interfere with the maintenance of law and order throughout the country."[51]

Bennett had been right about the strike and trek being led by communists and outside agitators who often used trumped-up charges regarding camp conditions to incite the men. And two commissions had found that he had done nothing improper in his handling of it all. Nonetheless, Bennett was hurt by the affair.

The perception that had been planted years before—and was based upon Bennett's own well-known attitude toward strikes and his use of Section 98—was that "Iron Heel" Bennett had little concern for the working man. Many saw his involvement in the strike, trek, and riot as support for an opinion of Bennett that they had already come to believe. The media didn't help. The week after the Regina Riot, for example, the *Winnipeg Free Press*'s Arch Dale editorial cartoon showed Bennett picking out new clothes by looking at storefront manikin models of Hitler, Mussolini, and Stalin. The display was named the "Dictatorship Outfitting Company."[52]

Others interpreted Bennett's actions and attitudes as motivated merely by political expediency, given that there was a federal election in the offing. Consider the editorial in the *Regina Daily Star* published ten days after the riot:

> In my judgement that riot and its accompanying disturbance was deliberately planned and purposely brought about in order to provide a dying Government with a Red bogey. Mr. Bennett's is not the first tottering Government which has instigated a war in order to win an election. . . . Blood has flowed in the streets of Regina in order that the Conservative press may declare that "our national life is at stake" and that Mr. Bennett is the "saviour of the nation."[53]

With polling not yet available, it is difficult to ascertain the degree to which Canadians at the time supported or opposed Bennett's handling of the strike, trek, and riot. But Liberal papers and his political opponents were quick and ruthless in using it as ammunition against him in the election that followed only months later, with the blood on Regina's streets still fresh in the nation's collective memory.

HARRY STEVENS

On July 2, 1935, the day after the Regina Riot, the House debated the violence and the events leading to it at great length. In the evening session Harry Stevens delivered a long speech and supported much that Bennett had done in his creation of the camps. He explained that he had visited several of them and found conditions good and the men generally happy in their work. But over the course of the previous months much had changed in the Bennett-Stevens relationship. Stevens had gone from trusted colleague and cabinet minister to the prime minister's bitter personal enemy and rogue Conservative MP, banished from both the cabinet and the caucus. Those changes coloured the rest of his assessment of Bennett's handling of the strike and trek. Stevens said that the prime minister had overestimated the ability of communist leaders to brainwash young unemployed men. He argued that most of those striking in Vancouver and then riding the trains to Ottawa were intelligent young men who were not misled, misguided, or deceived. Stevens continued, swooping in for the kill, that Bennett's suggesting that the trekkers were little more than communist dupes and then ordering the RCMP to stop them in Regina probably persuaded more young Canadians to become communists. Stevens said, "I say that as a creator of communism the Prime Minister takes the cake. I think he has done more to create communists in Canada than any other ten men, and that would include Evans, Buck and Collins or whoever they are."[54]

These were harsh words indeed. The very public way in which the Bennett-Stevens relationship had soured was another reason for the prime minister's troubles in the 1935 election. It is also another intriguing case study in considering Bennett as a leader and a man.

His name was Henry Herbert Stevens, although he was often referred to as H. H. by colleagues and as Harry by friends. He was a rather slight, fit, balding man, with deep-set dark eyes and thin lips that often curled into a slight smile that could both disarm and dismay. Stevens was born in England in 1887, but when he was a child his family emigrated to settle in Peterborough, Ontario. He enjoyed Sunday services at a downtown Methodist church presided over by Reverend Edwin Pearson, whose son Lester was also part of the congregation. When Stevens was only seven, the family moved to Vancouver. Stevens was never wealthy but he made a good living in the real estate and insurance business. He began his political career as a Vancouver alderman and, like Bennett, was first elected to the House of Commons in 1911. The two rookie MPs became close. For a time they roomed together, had offices adjacent to one another, and were deskmates in the House. Stevens served as Meighen's minister of trade. He and Bennett did important committee work together and in 1927 Stevens assisted Bennett in his quest for the party leadership. In 1930, Bennett worked hard to find his old friend a seat and placed him in his cabinet as minister of trade and commerce.

Bennett's troubles with Stevens began innocently enough. In September 1933, Stevens was driven from Toronto to a conference in Couchiching by Jim Walsh, the outspoken general manager of the influential Canadian Manufacturers Association. While en route Walsh regaled Stevens with stories of how small businesses were being hurt by big retailers that were able to buy in bulk and thereby sell products at retail prices that were less than what small independents had to pay for them wholesale. Stevens later learned that Montreal and Toronto sweatshops were flooding the market with clothing that also undercut small retailers, rendering their ability to stay in business tenuous at best.

Stevens took the issue to the prime minister and suggested that perhaps the government should do something about the pricing practices that he deemed to be unfair. Bennett was hesitant to act, noting that the big retailers were doing nothing illegal. Besides, regulating hours, pay, and work conditions for all workers, including those in sweatshops, was the responsibility of the provinces. Stevens left the meeting with the knowledge that Bennett wanted nothing to be done. For weeks after the meeting, however, he received numerous entreaties from various quarters providing more examples of inhumane sweatshops and predatory pricing practices. Stevens did as he had been told to do—nothing—but he continued to gather facts.

Bennett had been scheduled to speak at the National Shoe Retailers' Association annual meeting in Toronto on January 15, 1934. As he was home in Calgary after spending Christmas with his sisters in Vancouver and had decided to remain there to tend to personal business, he contacted Stevens and asked him to speak in his place.

Stevens stood behind the podium, surveyed the crowd, and unleashed a maelstrom that would change Canadian history. He laid out, in excruciating detail, all of the facts about unfair retail pricing that he had been collecting. He explained how it affected the garment and dry-goods trades but extended also into goods associated with the production of grain and livestock. Although he did not specifically name any particular business or business person as perpetrators, he stated emphatically that the large department stores were the worst offenders. Perhaps things would have been different had he stopped there—and his planned remarks indeed ended at that point. But maybe it was the adrenaline within him or the receptive audience before him that tempted him to go on. He pledged that the government would soon undertake a full-scale investigation of unfair pricing and production practices and that changes would be made to rectify the wrongdoing.

Stevens must have been pleased with the response to his speech from his audience that night, from the press the next day, and from politicians and business leaders across the country. As disparate a group as the premier of Ontario, Vancouver's city council, and business groups such as the Calgary Merchants Association and the Toronto Retail Meat Dealers Association wrote to applaud the Stevens reform pledge. His office was inundated with appreciative mail from workers who told tales of toiling long hours producing goods for the big retailers and being paid pennies only to find the goods they made priced outrageously high in catalogues and stores. Small-business owners wrote of being unable to compete when their wholesale prices were higher than the retail prices at the big stores.[55] The situation was the same as the one that small independent retailers today face when a competing big-box store comes to town.

Bennett did not share the enthusiasm of his minister's new fans. Days after having delivered the incendiary speech, Stevens was called to the prime minister's office and greeted with an explosion of fearsome temper. Bennett was understandably upset that his minister had simply contrived government policy on the fly without consultation with the caucus, cabinet, and most importantly, his boss. Bennett did not fire him but asked rhetorically, "I suppose you know what happens when a Minister of the Crown makes an announcement of policy without the consent of his fellow Ministers?"[56] Stevens declared that he understood and left the room.

The next day Bennett received Stevens's letter of resignation. It was certainly not contrite. Stevens wrote, ". . . I fear that you have allowed certain problems of a more or less international or general character to so obsess your mind and your attention that it has made it impossible for you to appreciate some of these pressing Canadian problems which, while difficult of solution, are quite within the power of parliament."[57]

Bennett was presented with a complex problem. The issues Stevens was raising were worthy of concern and Bennett had agreed that the mess needed attention. But he was worried that Stevens was being used by powerful interests, such as the Canadian Manufacturers' Association, the Canadian Chamber of Commerce, and others, that were perhaps acting on selfish motives. For this very reason, Meighen and others advised him to be wary of believing the charges that Stevens had made in his January speech.[58] Further, he worried about handling the situation in light of the false but unshakable stereotype that had dogged his political career and was affecting his unpopularity as prime minister: that he cared disproportionably for the interests of big business. In a letter to Ontario's minister of mines, Charles McCrea, he noted his support for Stevens's bringing the issue to national attention, but observed, "I am hopeful that . . . we may be able to take some action that will be helpful to the country generally and disabuse the minds of the people that we are thinking only of the large interests . . ."[59]

Rather than accepting Stevens's resignation, Bennett sought ways to retain his loyalty, serve the government, and address the issue at hand. Bennett spoke with Manion, who then met with Stevens, bringing with him the prime minister's apologies for any slight or misunderstanding. Further, Manion was instructed to tell Stevens that Bennett had considered the price spread issue that had sparked his resignation in the first place and believed that it deserved government attention. Manion said that Bennett believed that a royal commission, as Stevens had demanded, was not the best way to focus that attention but proposed instead the creation of a select committee of the House with Stevens as its chair. Stevens was happy with the idea, but, showing either enviable brass or blind arrogance, demanded that he should write the committee's terms of reference. Manion returned to Bennett's office with the news. The prime minister agreed.

The Stevens Price Spreads Committee began its work on February 16, 1934, and sat for fifty-three days of testimony. It quickly became evident that the big retailers, Eaton's and Simpson's in particular, would be in for a rough ride. Sad tales of women and children slaving in their kitchens for pennies while the clothing they made sold for high prices at stores in which they could not afford to shop touched the hearts of Canadians. The large retailers were savaged for using loss leaders, that is, offering a few well-placed or advertised items priced to sell at a loss to attract customers in the hope they would make additional purchases. In the wording of their questions to those brought before the committee Stevens and his colleagues did not attempt to mask their biases.

Small-business people were treated with dignity and deference while big retailers were afforded little respect and their answers subjected to sarcastic rebukes. It was populism gone wild and as the press reported it across the country, Stevens became the little guy's hero.

While all of this should have been positive news for Bennett, the committee placed him in a difficult position for he was stuck in the middle of a suddenly split caucus. Those with a leaning toward the left wing of the party applauded the committee as the most populist and popular action the government had taken to date. The committee demonstrated the government's support for Canadians who were trying to make ends meet but were being hammered by big business. For some, especially during economic hard times, it is nice to see the well off receiving a public rebuke. And for Conservative MPs, it was refreshing to finally be getting good press and receiving supportive mail.

Others in the caucus, however, complained that Stevens was out of control. In particular, Secretary of State Charles Cahan, Deputy Prime Minister Sir George Perley, and Minister of Finance Edgar Rhodes, each of whom had close ties to corporate Canada, beseeched Bennett to rein in their maverick colleague. They saw Stevens as a demagogue representing an ideological bent with which they fervently disagreed. Most vehement among them was Cahan, who saw the Depression not as the collapse of the capitalist system but as a necessary and inevitable correction. He never swayed from his belief in the value of self-reliance, hard work and in laissez-fair capitalism as the best way to protect the opportunity for all to make the most of themselves. The role of the federal government was to butt out and let the markets handle temporary turbulent situations—this included the use of labour and pricing.[60]

Bennett found himself between the extremes of his party, and shaken by the fervour that Stevens was arousing with his populist appeal to the disenfranchised. As much as he had dedicated such a substantial amount of his talents and energy during his public career toward helping the working and middle class, Bennett was suspicious of those who sought to stir class strife. He had written in 1930, "The first step towards dictatorship was a prejudicial appeal to the little man."[61]

Meanwhile, Stevens had established the terms of reference for his committee with such latitude that it was able to move far beyond the garment and retail industries. As it did so, it became clear that more time would be needed to hear all of the evidence that was deemed necessary to make a full report. Because a parliamentary rule dictated that a select committee could not continue after a recess of Parliament, Stevens asked that the committee be converted to a royal commission. There was a long cabinet discussion regarding the request. It was decided that the committee's work had received such positive press that to shut it down would be perceived as the government's trying to stop further investigation. On July 7, 1934, Stevens's committee became the Price Spreads and Mass Buying Commission that he had wanted at the outset. Bennett had sided with the populists.

An explosion came on the second of August. The *Winnipeg Free Press* and the *Toronto Star* published accounts of a tempestuous speech Stevens had made the previous June in which he had personally lambasted Sir Joseph Flavelle. Flavelle had been born to a humble and troubled family in Peterborough, but by age forty-five was a millionaire. He was president of the Hudson's Bay Company, chairman of the Canadian Bank of Commerce, and founder and president of the National Trust Company. An active citizen, he was also chair of the Toronto General Hospital's board of trustees and was on the board of the University of Toronto. Further, he had served during the war as the chair of the Imperial Munitions Board. Stevens knew all that and also knew that Flavelle was a generous contributor to and influential voice in the Conservative Party. He nonetheless attacked Flavelle for his controlling interest in the Robert Simpson Company—Simpson's. With partners Harris Fudger and Alfred Ames, Flavelle had purchased Simpson's in 1897 and turned it into a tremendously successful business. Stevens attacked Flavelle personally and accused Simpson's of supporting price-fixing and unfair, unhealthy labour practices. The comments violated the law regarding parliamentary committees and royal commissions, as members are bound to keep their minds open and mouths shut until all evidence is heard. Even then they must first state their opinions with a written report that is properly tabled before Parliament.

Bennett was outraged that Stevens had made the inflammatory remarks and that he had sabotaged his own commission. But his anger grew as he realized that Stevens had not simply been overheard whispering to a colleague but had, in fact, expressed his ill-conceived thoughts in carefully prepared remarks which he then worked to publicize. The scandal began as a speech delivered to sixty-five Conservative caucus members known as the Study Club. A member of the Hansard staff had copied the speech in shorthand and later shown it to Stevens who made edits to the copy. Brigadier General Stewart, MP for Lethbridge, Alberta, was chair of the Study Group and he made copies for each member, taking care to mark each as confidential. But it did not stop there. Several members asked Stevens for more copies. Stevens then asked the Bureau of Statistics to make three thousand copies and personally paid for the printing. However, he made no request regarding confidentiality. Consequently, the bureau manager followed standard operating procedure and sent twelve copies to Stevens's office and copies to all those on the usual mailing list, which included all MPs, senators, party supporters, and all of Canada's newspaper editors.

Among those who eventually received a copy of the pamphlet and immediately contacted Bennett to express righteous indignation was Sir Joseph Flavelle. He was furious that a minister of the Crown had publicly accused him and his company of immoral and perhaps criminal behaviour. Flavelle demanded that Bennett do something about the loose cannon firing wildly from the Conservative decks. Bennett lamely suggested that he sue the newspapers for slander and promised nothing.

But the second Bennett hung up the phone he called Stevens. He curtly expressed his displeasure at both the speech and its distribution. Stevens relented only slightly by claiming somewhat weakly that he had never intended for it to be issued as it was. Bennett extracted a promise from Stevens that no more copies would be made or mailed.

That Bennett clearly understood the depth of the trouble in which Stevens had placed the government was expressed in a letter he wrote to Senator James Haig, in which he complained, "The difficulty is that the statements in the document are incorrect, and when they are corrected it places the Minister in a very difficult position and the Government in a worse one . . . there is never any difficulty in facing facts, but it is perfectly clear that if we seek justice we must do justice. . . ."[62]

Bennett was left with the same situation he had found himself in with Stevens's resignation letter. If he fired his minister he would be accused by the Liberals and the Liberal press of getting rid of a man who was fighting for the little guy against the powers of corporate Canada. On the other hand, if he allowed Stevens to carry on he would be excusing his minister's flagrant disregard for fairness and balance as well as parliamentary rules. Further, a number of people, such as Flavelle, would be incensed by the fact that Bennett was standing by a man who had brought such damage to themselves and their companies.

The timing was such that the situation did not need to be immediately addressed. Since it was summer, Parliament was not in session and so the Opposition did not have question period available to them to focus their attacks and the attention of the country. Further, Bennett was scheduled to sail to Europe to attend a meeting of the League of Nations in The Hague. Today, with the media ravenously devouring public people in its frantic need to feed the monster of the twenty-four-hour news cycle, the Stevens scandal would play out much differently. But before Watergate changed the rules, cable changed the needs, and technology changed the means, Bennett had the luxury of literally sailing away from the problem. It did not follow him. But it waited.

The first cabinet meeting upon his return was a stormy one. At the October 25, 1934, meeting, Bennett expressed regret that the Stevens speech had been made, that it had been copied and distributed, and further that the speech had contained what had subsequently been proven to be errors of fact in the sections defamatory to Simpson's and Flavelle. Bennett demanded that Stevens's first action at the resumption of the commission hearing must be an apology for what he had done and a statement correcting the factual errors. Stevens looked slowly around the silent room and saw not a single cabinet colleague ready to support him. He reacted with a slow boil and asked for a day to consider whether he would be prepared to do as asked. Saying no to a prime minister is an option of which few ministers ever avail themselves.

Over his coffee the next morning Stevens found, on the front page of his *Ottawa Citizen*, an accurate and detailed account of everything that had been said at the cabinet table the day before. Bennett's demand of an apology and correction was there for the country to see. Stevens assumed that Cahan had been the leaker, but the guilty party was never definitively ascertained. Who had broken cabinet solidarity did not really matter; the damage had been done.

That afternoon saw Bennett glaring at his cabinet ministers while Stevens's chair sat conspicuously empty. Bennett held in his hand yet another letter of resignation from Stevens. The letter announced his desire to relinquish his cabinet post and chairmanship of the Price Spreads Commission. This time Bennett granted his old friend's wish. Bennett then took the time to read aloud a long letter that he had composed to Stevens that morning. It outlined all of the mistakes Stevens had made from the day the price spreads issue was first raised at the Couchiching speech, to the present. Ministers sat in stony silence while the prime minister read the lengthy letter. They offered no comment when he finished.

Bennett had his letter delivered to Stevens, who then composed one of his own. Again showing his unwillingness to adhere to normal political practices, Stevens released his letter to the media. Stevens denied that he had resigned, insisting that he had been fired. Bennett would not be called a liar, so he released both the resignation letter and his response. He laid the entire blame for the scandal on Stevens, accusing him of ignoring the principles of British justice and fair play and of knowingly publishing inaccuracies and refusing to correct them.[63] Stevens replied with yet another letter that defended his actions while portraying himself as the champion of the working man standing against faceless corporate power. To be sure that he would hurt the man who had hurt him, Stevens also released his letter to the press.

All of Canada saw the depths to which the two former colleagues had fallen. Bennett's government, already much maligned, seemed to be falling apart. Meanwhile, Bennett demonstrated that while Stevens had acted inappropriately and had earned his punishment, the government still recognized the importance of the work that the now-disgraced minister had begun. He appointed William Kennedy, a Winnipeg MP, to assume the chairmanship of the Royal Commission. In November, New Brunswick's Richard Hanson was appointed the new minister of trade and commerce.

While the appointments meant the important work of the ministry and commission would proceed, the political storm surrounding Stevens, including whether he should remain a member of the Conservative caucus, continued to swirl. He had become a dangerous distraction. While he blamed Cahan for causing his departure, he pulled few punches whenever asked about Bennett. He told one reporter who encouraged a resolution of the spat, "Ye shall not hitch an ox and an ass together."[64] There was too much important work to do and Bennett and the party were already unpopular enough without the Stevens scandal suggesting to Canadians that, besides apparently being unable to solve the riddle of the Depression, the prime minister could no longer even control his own cabinet and caucus. And yet the two stared eyeball to eyeball and nothing was done to resolve it.

The impasse continued through the winter of 1934. The government's popularity continued to slide while Stevens was hailed by many in the press and even many Conservative Party stalwarts as a man of the people. Bennett delivered his New Deal radio speeches in January 1935 and promised, among other things, to shape policy and legislation on the findings of the Price Spreads Commission that, he reminded Canadians, he had initiated and seen to its conclusion. But in the shadow of an impending election, Bennett's popularity continued to decline as Stevens's rose. Bennett was told that reconciliation was essential for the legislative and electoral success of his government.[65] But he still refused to budge.

Finally, Manion, Minister of Immigration and Colonization Wesley Gordon, and Postmaster General Arthur Sauvé grew frustrated with the poisonous situation and took matters into their own hands. They approached Vancouver MP Leon Ladner, who besides sharing Stevens's hometown was well known as a conciliatory man, to speak with both Bennett and Stevens. He was to see if a rapprochement could be arranged for the good of the government and party.

Ladner met first with the prime minister and after some small talk mentioned that he had heard that Stevens's daughter Sylvia was terminally ill with colitis. Bennett exploded with rage and pounded his large desk at the mere uttering of Stevens's name. He did not even mention poor Sylvia. Ladner sat patiently waiting for the storm of anger to pass then bravely suggested that party whip Tom Simpson needed the prime minister's instructions as to whether Stevens should be invited to the caucus meeting that was scheduled to convene in three days. Ladner argued that the party would benefit from Stevens being invited, for if he chose not to attend, at least the prime minister would look magnanimous. Bennett's first reaction was renewed anger. He said that Stevens had caused him irreparable harm.[66] But then he stood and for several moments stared silently out the large window overlooking the Parliament Hill lawns. One can only imagine his wrestling with the personal and political considerations that tore him from one option to the other.

Finally he turned and in a quiet voice said that Stevens should be both invited and welcomed.

Ladner immediately made his way to Stevens's office. Stevens was in an ugly mood, which did not improve when Ladner asked if he was planning on attending the caucus meeting. Stevens huffed that he had not been invited. Ladner then made his exact argument in reverse. He said that Bennett had invited him and that the former minister would appear fair and generous if he were to accept. Stevens played hard to get and insisted that he had not been formally invited. It was a petulant standoff.

Three days later there was palpable tension in the caucus room as members shared the normal chats before the prime minister entered and business began. There were audible sighs of relief when Stevens entered and took a seat inconspicuously in the corner. Minutes later, Bennett strode past the reporters who had gathered outside the caucus room door. He swept into the room and took his seat at the front, arranged his files before him, and called for the first order of business. As the meeting began and the first issue was being addressed, Stevens suddenly rose and, without a word, left the room. With the slamming of the door, the Conservative Party was torn asunder.

Stevens later explained to Ladner that when Bennett ignored him, he waited fifteen minutes before deciding that he could no longer endure the humiliation. Bennett later said that he had entered the room and not seen Stevens and, concerned with the issues of the day, merely started the meeting as usual. He swore that the first time he saw Stevens was when he rose and left. If he had seen him earlier, he said, he would have approached him and shaken his hand. Ladner later wrote, "Perhaps it was the Whip, who had sent out the invitation to Stevens and should have taken great care to be present, or have someone present to make sure that each of these able and distinguished leaders in the Conservative Party knew that the other was present in caucus, and that the party's future might depend upon a hand-shake and a smile."[67]

Perhaps Stevens should have holstered his petulance. Maybe Bennett should have tried harder and recognized the importance of stroking the man's ego for the good of the party. But it was too late. Regrets and would-have-beens mattered little as the next day's headlines screamed that the Conservative Party was broken. It would take a generation to mend.

With all hopes for reconciliation dashed, Stevens repaired to Vancouver to, for all intents and purposes, sulk. In the spring he was told by caucus chair John McNickle that he could do a great service to the party, to the leader, to himself, and to the country, if he would return to caucus. More than that, McNickle reported that seventy-two MPs had signed a letter stating that they would support him in the next leadership race. On at least three other occasions Stevens was approached by Rhodes, Gordon, and Manion, who assured him that Bennett's days were just about over and that he would have their support in replacing the old man. Meanwhile, an underground movement began with Stevens's tacit approval. Small-business people in ridings across Canada organized a whisper campaign and people were urged to write to their Conservative MPs urging support for Stevens as Bennett's successor.[68]

At the same time, Stevens was entertaining offers to leave the party. A group of businessmen including Garment Manufacturers president Warren Cook and Montreal printer Thomas Lisson met Stevens in Ottawa and tried to convince him to lead a new party. Stevens was flattered. He was even more tempted when other business leaders approached him, including the CPR's Sir Edward Beatty and multi-millionaire financier and Conservative stalwart Sir Henry Holt. Beatty and Holt put $3 million on the table for Stevens to betray the Conservatives and start his own party. Stevens again demurred.

Much of the move toward Stevens was inspired not only by disappointment in Bennett's performance as leader and prime minister, but also by the rumours that had been circulating about Bennett's wishing to retire. Unusually for Ottawa, this time popular rumours were actually true. In May 1935, emerging from his period of convalescence following his heart attack, Bennett had, in fact, decided to retire from public life. He had worked too hard for too long and his health had suffered. He was tired. Upon his return from King George's Silver Jubilee celebrations he had approached both Edgar Rhodes and Arthur Meighen about succeeding him. Both had said no. Rhodes had already decided to leave politics himself, partly due to his grief over the recent death of his wife. Meighen was happy in the Senate and had no desire to return to the leadership of a divided party in the midst of Canada's worst economic calamity. Bennett knew that if he left he would be opening the door for Stevens to succeed him and he was having trouble stomaching that eventuality.

On June 19, 1935, surrounded by talk of replacing him, Bennett was moving important legislation through the House and directing Herridge's trade negotiations with the Americans. Meanwhile, the On to Ottawa strikers waited in Regina as Slim Evans and his colleagues were about to arrive in Ottawa. Stevens chose that day to publicly confront Bennett. Stevens had risen to slam legislation that he claimed paled next to the promises that the prime minister had made in a series of radio addresses the previous January. Bennett rose and in a voice and with a passion that reminded some of the days when he was called "Bonfire" Bennett he tore into his old friend. He accused Stevens of being irresponsible in demanding legislation for which there was no widespread support and which would clearly be deemed unconstitutional. Bennett accused him of being a demagogue and promising Canadians things he knew he could not deliver. He questioned Stevens's plans, his work, his principles, and his character. He said, "If the people of the country have been led into the belief that this parliament can pass any kind of legislation it likes regardless of the constitution then the age of lawlessness is upon us."[69]

When Bennett took his seat it was to a standing ovation from every member of the government benches. The Opposition sat stunned. There have been few times in Canadian history when a leader, let alone a prime minister, levelled such a long, articulate, and devastating attack on a member of his own party—and this one a former friend and colleague.

That night, buoyed by the positive reception for his declaration of war on not only Stevens but upon any who were contemplating joining the maverick, Bennett attended a party caucus dinner. In his speech following dessert, he noted the rumours of the political backstabbing regarding Stevens possibly replacing him or forming his own party, and he dismissed them. He claimed that his experience had taught him that it was unwise to believe rumours. He then made it clear that the fight with Stevens had ended his contemplation of retirement. The prime minister assured all that he had completely recovered his health and that he was looking forward to leading the party to victory in the next election. When reporters later asked about his future, Bennett angrily snapped, "I'll die in the harness rather than quit now."[70]

So Stevens and Bennett were as two bulls in the barnyard: too obstinate, too brave, or perhaps too proud or dumb to forgive or make up. There is a great deal that Bennett could have and should have done differently, but he was handling himself much as several of his fellow leaders would in similar situations. In June 2002, for example, Prime Minister Jean Chrétien was contemplating retirement after a long and storied political career that included two majority governments, but he faced a recalcitrant finance minister whose poorly hidden leadership ambitions were splitting the Liberal caucus. The challenges to his leadership, especially from Paul Martin, but also from others who were testing the waters at the time, stirred his fighting spirit. He decided to fight another day. In his memoirs, Chrétien wrote, ". . . I was damned if I was going to let myself be shoved out the door by a gang of thugs. By trying to force me to go, they aroused my competitive instinct, ignited my anger, and inadvertently gave me the blessing I needed from Aline [his wife] to fight a third term."[71] He remained leader and won a third straight majority.

Perhaps in these matters Bennett was even more like another millionaire bachelor who came to the prime minister's office with a reputation for intelligence leaning toward arrogance. Pierre Trudeau was similar to Bennett in many ways: he was a shy, introspective man in a profession that demanded personal interactions that he could pull off but that often appeared forced and unnatural. They were both introverts in an extrovert's game. In the fall of 1975, Finance Minister John Turner was upset that Trudeau was affording him and his agenda inadequate support and decided to leave cabinet. One is tempted to picture Trudeau's explanation of what followed as Bennett speaking of Stevens. Trudeau might have been able to talk Turner into staying, but he allowed the resignation to stand. In his *Memoirs* Trudeau observed,

> You can tell me I handled it badly, tell me I should have got down on my knees and begged him to stay. But that's not the way I saw politics, then or now. Politics is a difficult game and you have to have your heart in it. And if his heart wasn't in it for one reason or another . . . or because I was his leader, then perhaps it was right that he leave politics. Another type of leader might have handled it differently, but I have always believed that if an adult has thought carefully about his future, then he knows what is best for himself.[72]

Perhaps so late in his term and with the core issue such a blatant breach of protocol, Bennett was simply unable to summon the fortitude necessary to address the emotional needs of colleagues in order to maintain support and loyalty. But this instance cannot be used to make the point that this was a consistent weakness. There is a good deal of evidence suggesting that Bennett understood well the importance of dealing with his MPS in a gentle and supportive manner in ways that would have done the master, Sir John A., quite proud. Consider one of many examples. Following a young MP's maiden speech, Bennett penned a note stating, "I am so sorry that I did not see you before you left. I wanted to talk to you about the speech which you made the other evening when I was out of the House. It was a most moving appeal and expressed the ardent convictions of a youthful idealist, with a power rarely equalled."[73] Bennett then went on to comment on each of the young man's salient points. This note was not written by a man unaware of the importance of such communications or incapable of involving himself in the art of supportive, empathetic leadership.

The Stevens debacle hurt Bennett in several ways, one of which was that it allowed the perception to develop that the prime minister had been upset not with his wayward minister but with the work and thrust of the Price Spreads Commission. The accusation was made that he was cutting his old colleague loose because Stevens was flying too close to the sun, which housed many of Bennett's high-powered corporate friends. Somehow lost in the rancour and unfortunate messiness of the situation was that, as Bennett often reminded people, it had been he who had authorized the investigations in the first place. Further, as early as the 1930 Imperial Conference, it had been Bennett who brought sweatshop labour and slavelike wages forward as both moral and economic issues. They needed to be addressed, he had argued, not only because it was right, but also in order to level the playing field between countries that were to be involved in fair and freer trade.

The Price Spreads Commission's final report was left for staff to complete. As secretary to the commission, Lester Pearson had worked diligently in organizing research material for the commissioners and in later synthesizing all the written and oral submissions into manageable and comprehensive formats. He also took the lead in compiling and writing much of the final report.

The Royal Commission Report laid out in excruciating detail the degree to which Canadian economic power had become concentrated in just a few hands. Political economist Wallace Clement would later dub those who held such concentrated wealth and power Canada's "corporate elite," whose remarkable clout was enhanced, protected, disguised, and exerted through a web of interrelated corporate directorships.[74] The Price Spreads Commission confirmed that those exerting linked and massive power did so in ways that led to unfair competition, pricing, wages, and working conditions. In so doing, the report served as an important analysis of and warning about the evolution of the modern Canadian economy in particular and society as a whole.

When the Price Spreads Commission's final report was presented, Bennett was pleased with the work that had been done and the recommendations that had been made. He forwarded it to the Justice Department with the instruction that it was to draft legislation to implement every one of the report's recommendations that were deemed constitutional. As a result, a number of bills were drafted that would be brought to the House the next spring. Many of those bills would form the core of what became known as Bennett's New Deal. Perhaps the most important among them was the 1935 Companies Act that addressed unfair pricing practices, working conditions, holiday time, and minimum wages.

The legislation being created demonstrated once more Bennett's belief that the ideas Stevens had first presented as worthy of discussion in his January 1933 speech were indeed important. The two were in fundamental agreement in terms of not only policy but also with respect to the Tory principles upon which the ideas and legislation rested. Rather than politics, it was pride and ego that fuelled their split. It became personal and it became nasty. When Stevens's daughter died in December 1934, Bennett neither attended the funeral nor sent a card.

Both shared a responsibility for splitting the Conservative Party when in mere months it would be going to the people to seek a renewed mandate. Both men were strong. Both men were stubborn. At least one of them should have been stronger.

CHAPTER EIGHT

A NEW DEAL AND A NEW GOVERNMENT

1934–1935

O
N THE SECOND OF JANUARY 1935, approximately 800,000 Canadians had finished their dinner, hustled their kids off to bed, and settled down with their radios. It had been widely advertised that the prime minister had something to say. Newspaper and radio reports and Conservative Party mailings and phone calls had ensured that people knew this would be the first of five important speeches, all well worth hearing. At nine o'clock an announcer introduced the prime minister. Bennett's voice was familiar. While to many his message was welcome, to some it was jarring. To others it was blasphemy. Taken together, the five speeches announced what came to be called Bennett's New Deal.

Much was made of what Mackenzie King dubbed Bennett's "deathbed conversion" to the political left, and of the urgent, populist tone, and of the speeches' radical content. The speeches were certainly at odds with the image of Bennett that, after nearly five years in office, had become cemented in the public's mind. Was Bennett not, after all, the millionaire bachelor and staunch defender of capitalism and big-business interests? Was he not the conservative who believed that government should do little while waiting for the market to correct itself? Was he not "Iron Heel" Bennett with no conscience, concern, or understanding of working peoples' problems? If so, then who could believe the man suddenly pretending to be Franklin Roosevelt?

Yet there he was, boldly announcing that capitalism was broken, that corporate Canada had let the country down, and that radical reform was needed to put things right. To those who had accepted the stereo-type Bennett appeared to have torn off the ideological clothes of a conservative, sped past the wardrobe offered by liberalism, and dressed himself as a democratic socialist. Perhaps it was all just a cynical political prank. Maybe he meant not a word and was only doing whatever he could to redeem himself, after years of failure, in a daring and reckless attempt to retain power.

However, the accusations of political gamesmanship made by opponents and commentators then and many historians later were dead wrong. All that Bennett said in his radio addresses was consistent with the Tory principles he had espoused throughout his political career. The five speeches were a conversation, not a conversion. They expressed determination, not desperation. And they encouraged purpose, not panic.

Bill Herridge is, and was at the time, credited with persuading Bennett to make the radio addresses. Herridge had been in Washington from the last days of the Hoover administration and saw first-hand the new vitality that gripped the city when Roosevelt arrived. As seen in 1960–61 with John F. Kennedy, and again in 2008–09 with Barack Obama, the months between FDR's election and inauguration were electrified with the sincere belief that things were about to change for the better. Seldom does such emotionally charged positive anticipation survive the arrival of the event, but in FDR's case his administrations' energy and daring exceeded expectations. From Roosevelt on, all American presidents, and to a lesser degree Canadian prime ministers, are measured by what they accomplish in their first hundred days.

FDR had suggested in his March 1933 inaugural address that an activist government was essential to address the country's economic ills. Roosevelt's first hundred days brought a bank holiday followed by the Emergency Bank Act that restored America's faith in their banks and financial system. It brought the end of Prohibition and the start of relief for those hardest hit by the Depression. From March to June 1933, thirteen substantive pieces of legislation were passed and their implementation began to be felt. The regenerative, restorative, optimistic feeling came from the new belief that simply by taking action things were going to get better. Perhaps the new president had been right in suggesting that fear was indeed the only thing Americans had to fear.

Herridge had become friends with many of those close to FDR. In his chats around dinner tables, and even more informal settings, he came to recognize that Roosevelt and his people were far more similar to Bennett than Hoover and his crowd had been. He explained to Secretary of State Dean Acheson, Vice President Henry Wallace, and others that while Bennett led a party called Conservative, his administration believed in a robust, activist government and his reaction to the Depression had been like FDR's in first providing immediate relief then long-term structural change. He was proud that Bennett was as courageous as Roosevelt in his willingness to try just about anything, to risk alienating his party, and to be called a traitor by those who believed he was in office to speak only to and for their interests.

But Herridge's many conversations and keen political sense led him to a conclusion. Because he was so well attuned to feelings in both capitals, he knew that Roosevelt was reaching people less on an intellectual and more on an emotional level. Due to the trust and respect upon which their relationship had come to be based, Herridge felt confident in sharing this observation with the prime minister. In April 1934, he wrote to Bennett: "The spirit of the New Deal is what has really mattered . . . the hope and promise of a new heaven and a new earth remain . . . the Canadian people must be persuaded that they also have a New Deal, and that that New Deal will do everything for them *in fact* which the New Deal here has done *in fancy*." [italics his][1]

Herridge went on to argue that for a Canadian New Deal to work, the Canadian people must believe in their hearts that Bennett was the one who could lead them from what he called "the wilderness of the depression." He recommended that Bennett need not lay out the specifics of a program but rather just sell the idea of a viable and vigorous package of reforms. He wrote, "The leader could promise all things—a new system, regulation, control, and so forth—and ask for a mandate to bring them about. But under no circumstances say how you propose to achieve the new order of society, don't be specific or definite. Stick to generalities."[2]

Herridge's numerous and often long-winded letters to Bennett suggested how and why to sell the ideas to Canadians while making it clear that the product to be sold was consistent with Bennett's long-held beliefs about government's role in the economy. In laying out his case for the Conservative Party to remain on the ideological left of the political spectrum, Herridge was preaching to the converted; he was making a point that Bennett had been making throughout his public career. Channelling the ideas of John Maynard Keynes, Herridge wrote, "I do believe that the days of *laissez-faire* are over. I do believe that the capitalist or profit system can never work again as it once worked. I believe that government is in business to stay."[3]

Bennett was initially cool to the idea of wrapping all the new legislative ideas that he was contemplating into a single bundle. While he respected Roosevelt's political skills, he believed that his New Deal was a hodgepodge of half-formed ideas. He told trusted personal aid Rod Finlayson that the American New Deal was the work of "fanatics and crackpots."[4] However, Bennett was also aware that his government was, despite all that it had done and was doing, still being blamed for doing too little to combat the Depression. He knew too that his leadership was being quietly challenged by caucus members, and that Stevens was publicly undermining him, the party, and the government. These considerations led Bennett to allow Herridge's notions of a Canadian New Deal more consideration than might otherwise have been the case.

Both Finlayson and Herridge continued to pressure Bennett to accept the necessity of a new strategy to regain the political initiative. Only through the success of such an effort, they told him, could he possibly continue to make the substantive changes to Canada's political economy that he envisioned as essential to building a secure prosperity. Bennett finally agreed. He asked Finlayson and Herridge to draft speeches that would put the strategy into motion. The principles and policies were to be those on which he had based his entire career, but they would be repackaged in a more saleable way.

The speeches were written over a matter of months. Herridge and Finlayson began in the summer of 1934. At a long weekend retreat at the Herridge family cottage on the shores of the picturesque Harrington Lake, the two consulted a host of books and Bennett's old speeches and engaged in spirited debates and discussions that ranged well into the night. By the time the outlines of the speeches were ready, Herridge had to be back to Washington, so it fell to Finlayson to carry on with their preparation.

That the work was being done became widely known in the government's inner circles and many weighed in on the arguments. All opinions were considered. For weeks, every lunchtime in the Château Laurier's cafeteria became the site of a makeshift, ad hoc study group whose members constantly changed but whose topic of discussion remained the same: the speeches and what should be in them. Finlayson kept Bennett apprised of the debates and progress and took his input back to the fluid group.

Meanwhile, Bennett was continuing to do as he had done for years. He not only pursued aggressive legislative reform in the House, but also used speaking engagements as opportunities to tout reform as essential to ending the Depression and the need to permanently restructure the economy to avoid another. In a speech to the Rensselaer Polytechnic Institute in New York State, for instance, Bennett spoke of reforms that would have made Keynes proud. He also undertook a short tour in which, without saying so, he previewed much of what he would soon be telling all Canadians. He was received well in Halifax, Montreal, Brockville, Toronto, and back in Ottawa.

In October 1934, Bennett brought nuance to the ideas he had been expressing for years before. He spoke of the need to save capitalism from two enemies. One was the socialists who sought to increase the power of government in order to destroy it. He said that socialism was dangerous, for the will of the state was encouraged to supersede the desires of individuals. The other enemy was the corporate elite who sought to negate the power of government in order to preserve their own, but then manipulated the levers of government when such manoeuvring was to their advantage. He saw this concentrated and intelligent corporate power as more dangerous than socialism. He warned of ". . . the Empire of finance outside the realm of Government which threatens to make individuals mere cogs in a machine."[5]

Herridge also played a role in preparing Canadians for the speeches that he and Bennett knew, and in fact hoped, would be somewhat startling. In December, he addressed the Canadian Club in Ottawa and laid out the skeleton of what Bennett and he had decided would be five separate radio speeches. In his audience were reporters, cabinet members, and MPs, but also Mackenzie King, Supreme Court Chief Justice Lyman Duff, Borden, Quebec premier Taschereau, and Bennett himself. Using the rhetorical style and flourish of his preacher father, Herridge enthusiastically presented the reform package. Presaging the words and evangelical tone that he and others were writing for Bennett, he assessed capitalism's ability to meet the current crisis. He said,

If we looked more to spiritual leadership and less to capitalist leadership; if we made business less our religion and religion more our business; if we proclaimed by deeds the eternal truths of the Christian faith, we might find that this system did not work so badly after all . . . the form is unimportant so long as it responds to the one true test of its effectiveness: the greatest good of the people as a whole.[6]

Bennett's speeches and Herridge's Canadian Club remarks were all widely reported upon. Even the *New York Times* picked up the story with a December 23 article entitled "Cry for New Deal Rising in Canada." Canadian newspapers noted the decidedly reformist and, some said, radical nature of much of what the prime minister and his closest adviser were saying. If anyone failed to predict what was coming, they were not really listening.

The five half-hour radio broadcasts were entitled *The Premier Speaks to the People.* Bennett spoke from CRCO in Ottawa and was linked to thirty-eight stations across the country on the CRBC radio network that his administration had created—an interesting fact that is overlooked by those claiming that the speeches were a sudden shift to the left. Approximately 800,000 heard the first speech, with each subsequent speech earning a greater audience. The five broadcasts cost $11,000 and Bennett paid the bill out of his own pocket.

The addresses aired on the second, fourth, seventh, ninth and eleventh of January. They were carefully structured as one long narrative. Bennett began by stating the problem in broad and explosive terms. The old system was discredited and gone, he argued, and radical changes were needed to create a new system in its place. He explained actions his government had already taken, based upon that premise and goal, and then moved on to outline an extension of his reform program intended to focus on Canada's short- and long-term economic difficulties. He preempted criticism of the actions that he was proposing by criticizing the Opposition for having nothing better to offer. The final broadcast ended with Bennett issuing a challenge to his own party, Canadian citizens, and business, farm, and labour leaders to support his ideas.

To understand Bennett's message and Canadians' reaction to it, one must consider his actual words at some length. In the first broadcast, which set the stage for all that would follow, Bennett said,

The time has come when I must speak to you with the utmost frankness about our national affairs for your understanding of them is essential to your welfare. . . . In the last five years, great changes have taken place in the world. The old order is gone. It will not return. We are living amidst conditions which are new and strange to us. Your prosperity demands corrections in the old system, so that, in these new conditions that old system may adequately serve you. The right time to bring about these changes has come. Further progress without them is improbable.[7]

Bennett went on to say that the purpose of the speeches was to fully explain the program of reform that he believed was needed to address Canada's many problems. He wanted Canadians to have plenty of time to consider it before they voted in the next election. He was then blunt in outlining the philosophical underpinning of the reforms. He suggested that the Canadian people, through their government, could act or continue to be acted upon. While avoiding ideological labels, he argued that only an adoption and adaptation of the Tory principles in which he had always believed, would bring about long-term prosperity in a fair and just society. While not mentioning his name, he laid out a case that supported Keynesian interventionalism. His government had always been about this kind of change and now more change was needed. All that was new was the incendiary language, passion, and urgency. He said,

And in my mind reform means government intervention. It means government control and regulation. It means the end of laissez faire. Reform heralds certain recovery. There can be no permanent recovery without reform. Reform or no reform! I raise that issue squarely. I nail the flag of progress to the masthead. I summon the power of the State to its support. . . . And when the system is reformed and in full operation again, there will be work for all. We can then do away with relief measures. We can then put behind us the dangers of the dole. . . . If we cannot abolish the dole, we should abolish the system.[8]

Bennett's words and message were remarkable. No Canadian prime minister, before or since, has been so bold in stating, in such nuanced detail, his assessment of current problems or proposed solutions. The complexity in what he said paid Canadians the compliment of assuming that they had the attention span to listen and the intelligence to understand. No prime minister, before or since, has through his passionate espousal of his beliefs appeared so naked before the Canadian people and so willingly placed his reputation and political future squarely in their hands.

There was an overwhelming reaction to the first speech. Bennett received dozens of congratulatory letters and telegrams. Many came from businesses big and small. Many noted agreement with his aims and ideas and several stated that Bennett had taken an important step toward re-election. Some, such as the one from Stephen Leacock, were from opponents or critics who until that point had found precious little good to say about Bennett or his government. Leacock is better known today as a humorist, but he was also the founding head of McGill's Department of Political Economy. To Leacock, Bennett replied that he had received many letters and telegrams but included a more personal note. He wrote, ". . . I write you very frankly that I appreciate none of them more than your own kind message of good-will. I realize that my declaration involves me in much hard work and that I am no longer young. Nevertheless, I propose to go forward with my proposals to the fullest extent of my ability."[9]

Bennett also received a good amount of mail condemning all that he had said. The most commonly expressed criticism was that he was moving toward the CCF in proposing socialist solutions to the country's ills. President Obama weathered similar attacks as some called his proposals for increased government intervention socialism. Prime Minister Trudeau was accused of the same thing with his attempts to use government's power to combat the economic challenges of the 1970s. At the time of Bennett's speeches, FDR was fending off the same accusations for the same reasons. Many of Bennett's correspondents in 1935 could have been writing to Roosevelt in 1934 or Trudeau in 1975 or Obama in 2009 in expressing their fear that while regulation was a part of the capitalist system, he was actually advocating a move toward dictatorial government regimentation. One correspondent called Bennett's ideas "decapitalisation." The *Montreal Gazette*, for instance, opined in its editorial that Canada was not prepared ". . . to fly the flag of Socialism, side by side with the historic banner under which Conservatism heretofore has always made it's appeal to sober-minded Canadians."[10]

Bennett answered each letter in much the same way. He explained that his actions were far from the goals of socialists or communists in that he wished to save and strengthen the very capitalist system that they sought to destroy.[11] To many other correspondents he attempted to encourage historical and international perspective. He stated that even if the government were to carry out all of the social reforms that he mentioned in the speech, and more that would be explained in subsequent speeches, Canada would still be far behind Britain with respect to its social policies.[12] Bennett drew attention to Britain's Widows', Orphans', and Old Age Contributory Pensions Act of 1925 and the Royal Commission on Unemployment. The latter led to the passage of the Unemployment Act of 1934, which had moved the country toward a national unemployment insurance program.

While thousands of Canadians heard the first speech, the leader of the Opposition did not. Mackenzie King was home at Laurier House that night but decided not to tune in. He had spent part of the afternoon reading a staff report on the speech based on an advance copy that Bennett had provided opposition party leaders. The speech inspired a rant in his diary. He wrote, "In its egotism it is nauseating. . . . if the country stands for this kind of bombast, I feel like dropping out of its public life—but I have no doubt as to the reception it will get."[13] That night Mackenzie King dreamt of "politics and interference" and in the morning he read a book which referred to a Bible passage about being wary of doctrine. This led him to pick up a pen and write down his thoughts on the value of laissez-faire economics.[14]

But Mackenzie King's political instincts were keen. He recognized that Bennett was doing again what he had been doing since becoming his party's leader: establishing the Conservatives securely to the left of the Liberals. Mackenzie King's reaction indicated his understanding that in the coming election he would be going to the people supporting right-wing laissez-faire attitudes and policies while Bennett would be attacking him from the left. It would be 1930 all over again.

The second speech was delivered a week later. Even more Canadians tuned in as the first speech had become the talk of the nation. Folks heard their prime minister speak passionately of the abomination of child labour, inhuman conditions in sweatshops, the hardships of long workdays and -weeks, and the vast difference in income between producers and workers. Something had to be and would be done, he promised, to fight these scourges of Canada's modern capitalist society.

These were hardly new issues. In fact, it was Macdonald's Liberal-Conservative government that had first presented legislation to address them. The issues had been the subject of debate in Britain for some time as well, and parties of all stripes had sought to take them in hand. Similarly, Theodore Roosevelt had supported the Progressive reform movement in enacting legislation to deal with the issues at the turn of the century. Later, his cousin Franklin had dealt with them through much of his New Deal legislation, programs, and agencies. From its inception in Calgary in 1932, and throughout the fiery rhetoric of its Regina Manifesto, Canada's CCF had made it clear that these issues were at the core of its mission. Bennett referred a number of times to the Price Spreads Commission's work of the previous year, that had brought the issues again to the fore. The social policy ideas that Bennett was proposing were clearly less radical than humane.

The second speech also spoke of the ravaging social and personal effects of unemployment that stole bread from supper tables while robbing people of their dignity and pride. Bennett quickly reviewed all that his government had done to help those who, through no fault of their own, had lost their jobs. He spoke of some of the actions taken to try to create employment. But, he said, unemployment remained a problem and the government needed to do more to end it and to help those victimized by it. He stated that a national systematic program of unemployment insurance had to be created. He warned that the program would not reward laziness but rather offer a bridge to those who wanted to work but temporarily had no work to do. He said, ". . . no man must be left to the uncertainties of private charity or to the humiliation of government gratuity. . . . As a member of our economic society, he should have security, provided always that he is willing to work. . . . This security will be provided by means of unemployment insurance. For this reason, I believe in unemployment insurance, not as a means of bolstering up a faulty system, but as an element in establishing a sound modern one. . . ."[15] He went on to link the same moral and economic logic to his government's Old Age Pensions Act. Then, long before Tommy Douglas took power in Saskatchewan and three decades before Prime Minister Pearson would introduce Medicare, he said, "Likewise, health insurance and accident and sickness insurance must be developed in the same way."[16]

The third speech focused on fairness. He spoke of the necessity of fairness in the farm credit system and returned to the work done by the Price Spreads Commission. He argued that better systems for economic statistical analysis were needed and proposed the establishment of the Economic Council of Canada to oversee them. He then went on to explain and defend the Marketing Act and the Natural Products Marketing Act as needed to promote economic activity while encouraging fairness in that activity.

In an attempt to cut off critics who might argue that he was acting too quickly or too late, he explained that it would have been folly to contemplate such reform measures while the country was suffering through the worst of the Depression. There was a need for immediate relief and the restoration of a measure of stability before restructuring. He then said, "I say that, as a matter of fact, there is no haste at all, either in thought or action. There is urgency, but that is another matter. This is the right time for reform."[17]

The fourth speech dealt with finance. Bennett outlined all that he had done in creating the Bank of Canada and called it ". . . an instrument of social justice."[18] He explained that with his Dominion Companies Act, corporations that sought investments from Canadians needed to provide full and transparent financial information to ensure that informed investment decisions could be made. He said tricky accounting processes designed to deceive and hide toxic debt and manipulate stock prices had to stop. He anticipated the quarters from which criticism would come, revealing his understanding that the greatest opponents of change are always those with the most to lose. In words that resonate with anyone who watched in silent rage the white-collar perp walks of the crooked and greedy in the 1980s and then felt the bile rise again in 2008 when millionaire automobile CEOs arrived in private jets to sit before American senators to beg taxpayers to subsidize their arrogance and spectacular ineptitude, Bennett said,

> Selfish men, and this country is not without them,—men whose mounting bank rolls loom larger than your happiness, corporations without souls and without virtue—these, fearful that this Government

might impinge on what they have grown to regard as their immemorial right of exploitation, will whisper against us. They will call us radicals. They will say that this is the first step on the road to socialism. We fear them not.[19]

The fifth and final speech was political and philosophical. Bennett pre-empted the partisan attack that was to come and, in fact, had already begun. He painted himself as the leader of action and the Liberals as apologists for inertia, big business, and a failed system. Bennett could not have been blunter:

> If you are satisfied with conditions as they are, support Liberalism. If you want no changes in the capitalist system, declare yourself for that party. If you are against reform, back Liberalism with all your might. For Liberalism, as you see, has no intention of interfering with big business. For Liberalism stands for *laissez faire* and the unrestricted operation of the profit system and the complete freedom of capitalism to do as it thinks right or to do as it thinks wrong. So, if you believe in a Party of inaction; if you desire a Party which supports reaction; back Liberalism. . . . For my Party . . . stands for the freedom of the individual and private initiative and sound business, but it stands with equal certainty for permanent and better relationships between the people and those instruments of commerce and finance which are set up to serve them. It stands not for traditions which are outworn or practices which belong to another age or for economic faiths which, if pursued now, mean economic hardships. My party stands simply for the greatest good for the greatest number of people. And it shapes and will continue to shape its policy of reform to make that sure.[20]

While the speeches were heard by Canadians from coast to coast, and each sparked front-page coverage and editorial commentary, Bennett had already planned to ensure that all could read and carefully ponder his words. All five speeches were printed in book form. The book's foreword was written by Stephen Leacock. Echoing what he had written to Bennett after the first speech, Leacock stated that Bennett's speeches had ". . . quickened the spirit of the country to a new life and a renewed energy."[21] He went on to praise Bennett, saying that all Canadians had been doing their bit in the struggle against the Depression but that, ". . . none of us [has] shown better heart in this struggle than the members of the government of Canada, and above all, the Prime Minister . . . by widening the channels of Empire trade he has sought to alleviate the ill fortune it was not yet possible to remove. Through all of this time Mr. Bennett has never uttered a word that was not full of hope and ultimate confidence in the future."[22]

There was a fascinating reaction to Bennett's speeches. A great deal of it was positive. Many letters of congratulation poured in from Conservatives. Among those Bennett received was one from an ambitious Saskatchewan lawyer named John Diefenbaker who reported that the speeches were enthusiastically received throughout his province.[23]

Not surprisingly, since much of what Bennett had said was consistent with his beliefs and those that formed the core of the recommendations of his Price Spreads Commission, Harry Stevens also expressed support. He told the *Globe* that he welcomed the prime minister's words. The speeches made it clear, Stevens said, that Bennett understood the problems facing Canada.[24]

Much of the press reaction, however, was negative. Most that were critical had been surprised by the program's ideas, but even more by Bennett's blunt assessment of the capitalist system. For instance, Wilfrid Heighington wrote in *Saturday Night*, "The great asset of the Conservative Party . . . has been that of reliability. The moment that the Rt. Hon. Mr. Bennett took the microphone for those all-shattering speeches in January 1935 . . . that priceless attribute disappeared in a veritable cloud of confusion, doubt, and despair. The staunchest of party workers was blanched, the normally Conservative voter was dismayed, and the great body of silent and unbiased electors wagged their heads."[25] That assessment seemed to sum up the media consensus.

A number of newspapers were critical of the speeches in a way that helped to create an impression of Bennett that was far removed from the facts. It was erroneously argued that the left-wing ideological thrust of the speeches represented a mad swing away from all that Bennett had ever advocated in a desperate attempt to position himself for the upcoming election. Their interpretation echoed Mackenzie King's contention in the House on January 21 that the "death-bed conversion" was simply a pre-election ploy.[26] The *Winnipeg Free Press* claimed that

Bennett had "suddenly" discovered that the capitalist system had flaws and asked, "... how does it happen that Mr. Bennett finds out this interesting fact on the eve of a general election?"[27] The *Montreal Gazette*, which normally supported the Conservative Party but was also the voice of the St. James Street corporate elite, wondered the same thing. Its January 30 editorial stated, "If there exists a confusion of thought throughout Canada as to what all this is about, and what it actually portends, the origin of that confusion is to be found in the programme which Mr. Bennett has been discussing, if it can be called a programme."[28] *Saturday Night* magazine stated more bluntly that "Consistency, it has been stated, is the bugbear of little minds, and no one can accuse Mr. Bennett of consistency. His mind is not made that way. His thoughts are continually active and in politics, continually erratic."[29]

It is understandable why partisan enemies would want to characterize the speeches as representing a dramatic shift in Bennett's beliefs and policies. In politics, after all, the accusation of changing one's mind on an issue, of flip-flopping, is often fatal. Pierre Trudeau learned that lesson when he campaigned against wage and price controls in 1974 only to implement them when in office. The "flip-flop" was used as a powerful weapon against him in the next election and was one of the factors that resulted in his losing in 1979. Few survive as Brian Mulroney did when he railed against free trade with the United States before later becoming its champion. The fact—and it is a fact—that the New Deal radio addresses represented ideas that were consistent not only with what Bennett had been saying since entering public life before the First World War and the bills that he had brought to the House since becoming prime minister in 1930, was simply ignored by his critics.

Perhaps the negative reaction had less to do with the bogus charge that Bennett was somehow veering madly off a course on which he had been set for decades, and more to do with people being scared by the notion of a Canadian New Deal. It was a poker metaphor. It promised a new start, a do-over. The metaphor was Roosevelt's, of course, and its promise of new opportunity coupled with the frantic activity of his government's first hundred days was embraced by most Americans. In Canada, however, perhaps the metaphor was frightening because it did not soothe but challenge; it did not promise but demand. Perhaps, too, it rankled because it was American and so was automatically suspect.

Further, because the label was FDR's, it suggested that Bennett's ideas must be stolen as well as foreign. It is important to note, however, that not a single time in any of the speeches leading up to the radio addresses, nor in any of the five, did Bennett call his ideas or policies a New Deal—not once. The phrase "Bennett's New Deal" was the invention of the media and his political opponents.

Of more immediate importance for Bennett than the reactions of newspapers and partisan critics were those of his cabinet and caucus colleagues. And in managing that reaction, Bennett erred. He had consulted neither caucus nor cabinet before the first speech and he did not meet with them until the fifth had been broadcast. Some, nonetheless, supported all that Bennett had said. Manion was most important and positive among Bennett's supporters. Many cabinet members were incensed by what Bennett had said but all were by the fact that he had not brought them into his confidence so they could properly react to questions. Bennett tried to joke his way through the first caucus meeting following the speeches. As he entered the room he hung his arm over Sir George Perley's shoulder and called him comrade. Few laughed.

The most vocal cabinet critic was, not surprisingly, that old free marketer Charles Cahan. Cahan told all who would listen that Bennett's proposed legislation would ruin the party's chances in Quebec; it was so close to socialism that the Catholic Church would be forced to stand against it. The Church had already demonstrated its willingness to involve itself in Canadian politics. On the pope's directive it had organized pulpits throughout the country to demand that no one consider voting for the CCF. It was stated in churches on Sunday mornings that one could not simultaneously be a good Catholic and a good socialist.[30] Cahan threatened to resign over the speeches although he later reconsidered and stayed on.

Cahan's reaction could have been predicted. Most of the corporate and business community to which he gave voice in cabinet agreed with his dismay at the prime minister's attack on laissez-faire capitalism. But there were many others in the Canadian business community who saw merit in Bennett's appraisal and approach. Despite what the speeches said about capitalism and, by extension, their role in it, many business people wrote to indicate their support for what he had said and how directly he had said it.[31]

WORKING THE PLAN

With the speeches delivered, Bennett set out on the next phase of the plan that he, Bill Herridge, and Rod Finlayson had discussed for nearly a year and signed off on the previous November. According to the plan, the radio addresses would be followed by the reconvening of Parliament and a Throne Speech. The Throne Speech would echo the reformist tone and rhetoric of the radio addresses. Bennett would cast himself in the role of reformer. He would leave Mackenzie King to play the part of defender of laissez-faire inaction and corporate interests which the Price Spreads Commission had so effectively savaged and Bennett's speeches had promised to put right. Bennett would then call an election for April and cruise to victory on the great ship of reform.[32] It was a worthy plan, but the mighty ship quickly smashed against some hefty rocks.

The first rock was hit as Bennett sat for a number of meetings with Finlayson and Herridge. He became increasingly upset with his brother-in-law, Bill Herridge, whose growing arrogance was becoming grating even for those who had for years known and liked him. At one point the three were working on a speech and Bennett was demanding wholesale changes to the draft. A frustrated Herridge hissed that Bennett should leave the speech to him and Finlayson, for without them Bennett could never write a good speech on his own. Bennett snapped. His temper darkened the room. Herridge was subjected to a long and explosive tirade and told to leave the office. He never came back.

From Washington, where Herridge continued his work in the Canadian embassy, Herridge wrote a number of increasingly pitiful letters. First he offered advice and pretended the split had not happened. Then he asked forgiveness. Bennett did not answer a single one. In Bennett's rigidly compartmentalized mind, Herridge had simply ceased to exist. Bennett and Mildred had seen less and less of each other since her marriage and move to the United States, and the tiff with Herridge made things worse. In the last years of his life Bennett acquired a yappy little dog that followed him everywhere. He named the dog Bill.

Herridge's departure robbed Bennett of his most skilled speech writer and, along with Finlayson, a clever, nimble, and able political adviser. Herridge understood the hurly-burly of Parliament and the difference between goals, strategies, and tactics. To lose such an important adviser with a politically hazardous session of Parliament and election both on the horizon was an injury from which Bennett would not recover. Most tragic was that the injury was self-inflicted; his temper had caused the rift and his pride maintained it.

The rock was hit but the ship moved on. The sixth and final session of Parliament convened on January 17, 1935. The Speech from the Throne used less provocative language than Bennett's five radio addresses, but the points raised were the same. The Governor General's monotone listed six programs that the speeches had introduced, including legislation to bring about unemployment insurance, minimum wages, old-age pensions, workplace reform, and changes to regulate companies and to help farmers sell their products. In the Throne Speech debate, Bennett responded to opposition members who called the ideas radical. He reminded them of the seriousness of the economic and political challenges that Canada still faced and of the need for the government to take full responsibility for addressing them. He rhetorically asked if opposition members really believed that when Canadians were facing hardships on so many fronts, the government should do nothing. The strategy seemed to be working out perfectly; but the second rock loomed.

For Bennett's plan to work as envisioned, Mackenzie King needed to play his part. He needed to take the Throne Speech's bait, vote against it, and allow Bennett to call an election. But Mackenzie King was too adroit for that. He and his caucus made critical comments but refused to vote against the government. Unable to engineer the pulling down of his own government to fit the timetable he preferred, Bennett was left with no option but to move to implement the policy statements that he had presented to the Canadian people. Mackenzie King was rather proud of himself for seeing through Bennett's trick and in his diary wrote, "I thought the thing to do would be to call the bluff on the address . . . not let Bennett get away with promises this time—demand performance, & at once."[33]

NEW DEAL LEGISLATION

With the House still unexpectedly in session, Bennett was forced to present a budget and bills to put meat on the skeleton he had presented to Canadians, but that he had hoped to first troop around the country in a campaign. Some bills were ready because they had been worked on in the months before the January speeches, but others were rushed to the House. Like under-rehearsed plays, some of the legislation suffered from the speed at which it was brought to the stage.

The first bill of significance sought to create a system of unemployment insurance. The idea was not new and so none should have been surprised. In fact, Bennett had ordered Finlayson and Deputy Finance Minister Clifford Clark to develop an unemployment insurance plan shortly after he took office. He had brought the notion to the January 1931 federal-provincial conference, but premiers could not agree among themselves, let alone with Bennett, as to how it should be financed. Three months later Bennett had stated in the House that establishing a national system whereby employers and employees contributed to an unemployment insurance fund remained a goal of his government. In the fall of 1934, Bennett again set Finance Department officials to work on drafting a scheme along the lines that he had been discussing for years. They had the outline of the bill ready before Christmas and it was presented to the House in late January 1935.

The Employment and Social Insurance Act proposed a system whereby employers, employees, and the federal government would contribute to a fund that would enable the federal government to support those who were forced from their jobs due to the economic circumstances of their employers. The act was a statement as clear as the July prairie sun that the government should care for and about the welfare of the governed. There were strict rules and restrictions regarding eligibility, but the legislation was a bold step forward and much as unions and others who supported such legislation had been advocating for some time.

In Bennett's speech presenting the bill, he reminded the House of the economic and social costs of unemployment and stated his belief that the government owed it to the people of Canada to assist those who were suffering through no fault of their own. He noted that in bringing forward a scheme of compulsory unemployment insurance, Canada was following the lead of many countries that had already instituted similar legislation, including Austria, Bulgaria, Germany, Great Britain, Northern Ireland, the Irish Free State, Italy, Poland, Australia, and Switzerland. Many of those unemployment insurance systems, he explained, had been put in place even before the Depression. He went into great detail explaining the manner in which the British government came to the decision to implement a similar policy and how it worked.[34] He sold the legislation as good economic policy while also morally correct in a compassionate, democratic society.

The unemployment insurance bill reflected Bennett's final step away from the federal government providing direct relief to Canadians. In one of Bennett's first acts as prime minister, he had allocated $20 million for direct relief and the 1931–32 budget had set aside another $50 million. He had said at the time that the program was temporary and the funds would end when the economy recovered. The relief programs were problematic from the start since the money was inadequate to meet the need and because of the financial and administrative strain they placed on provincial governments. Further, the enormous price tag was helping to push an already high deficit even higher. The unemployment insurance scheme would relieve the pressure on the provinces, and with 80 per cent of the costs coming from premiums, reduce the burden on the federal budget.

Bennett had planned his presentation so as to leave no obvious targets at which the Liberals could aim an attack. But Mackenzie King did not need targets in order to triangulate fire. In a demonstration of his absolute mastery of the House, he had already asked two innocuous-sounding questions that revealed the manner in which he would criticize the unemployment insurance bill and, in a broader way, focus his attack on Bennett in the next election. First, in the debate following the Throne Speech, he wondered how secure services for the people would be if the foundations of Canada's democratic government were being shaken by the manner in which the reform messages had been brought forward. The question made it apparent that Mackenzie King would attack Bennett for having brought the New Deal ideas to Canadians directly through the radio addresses rather than through Parliament. Bennett's attempt to be honest and direct with Canadians through the radio speeches would be used as trumped-up evidence of his disdain for democracy and Parliament in his continuing to run a one-man, dictatorial government.

Mackenzie King's second question came during the debate on the unemployment insurance bill. It began when former justice minister and attorney general Ernest Lapointe asked if Bennett had taken the plan to the provinces. Bennett replied that he had discussed it with them at the federal-provincial conference the previous year but that jurisdictional problems had arisen and so it had gone no further.[35] If Lapointe was the left jab then Mackenzie King was the right cross. He asked if Bennett had submitted this proposal or any others that the Throne Speech had mentioned to the Supreme Court to test whether they were within the constitutional purview of the federal government.[36] Bennett replied that he had not and did not plan on doing so, for he was confident that the legislation was within what he called the "competence" of the federal government.

Bennett instantly recognized the trap. He explained at some length that he'd based his constitutional opinion on three facts. First, the federal government had signed the Treaty of Versailles in June 1919, and one of its provisions, Article 23, stated that governments must do what they can to assist labour and fight unemployment. Second, and tied to that signing, was that Section 132 of the BNA Act assigned the federal government the responsibility of seeing that treaty obligations were fulfilled. Third, Bennett noted that in a recent challenge to radio and aviation legislation, Britain's Judicial Committee of the Privy Council had ruled that the residual clause of the BNA Act should be broadly interpreted in terms of federal power and that this precedent afforded judicial support to all of his social legislation.[37] In other words, the legislation was well researched and indeed within the constitutional purview of the federal government.

Bennett's response was masterful but wasted. The exchange revealed to those paying attention that Mackenzie King's second campaign strategy would be to argue that the New Deal legislation was unconstitutional. The impending campaign would be 1926 all over again, with the constitution playing a major role. As a bonus, Mackenzie King would be able to use Bennett's apparent disregard for the constitution as yet another example of his dictatorial rule. Throughout the rest of the parliamentary session, Mackenzie King kept hammering the same two points, linking them with Bennett's leadership style, and biding his time.

Days later, after having brought forward the Employment and Social Insurance Act, Bennett rose to introduce its companion piece, the Minimum Wages Act. The act was relatively modest in scope but nonetheless offered to set wages for a number of trades. It passed through the House with a minimum of debate.

With the first two bills working their way through the parliamentary process, Bennett dealt with a number of big and small decisions that are part of executive power, prepared the next bills in his legislative agenda, and set out to continue to sell his ideas to Canadians. He established a gruelling schedule where he would rise early to deal with correspondence and meetings all morning, appear for important debates and question period until the late afternoon, and meet with cabinet and staff to direct the preparation of the next pieces of legislation. On Friday afternoons he would catch a train to deliver an out-of-town speech or two, then immediately return to do it all again the next week. Late into each evening in his hotel suite or on the train he dealt with telegrams, letters, briefings, and phone calls. It was a punishing pace.

In January, he spoke three times in Montreal: on the fifteenth to the Young Conservatives Club, on the twenty-third to the board of trade, and then to the Canadian Construction Association on the twenty-sixth. He spoke to the Toronto Board of Trade on the twenty-ninth. On February 16, he spoke to New York City's Canadian Society and then in Kingston, Ontario, on the nineteenth. He travelled to Toronto on the twenty-third, where he was scheduled to address the Young Conservatives Club, but that afternoon he fell ill and had to cancel. He spent that day, night, and next morning in the hotel. He was attended by a doctor and advised to rest. The next morning he returned to Ottawa.

Back at the Château Laurier, the prime minister skipped his morning massage, left correspondence unanswered, and missed his morning appointments. He was examined by his doctor that afternoon. Bennett was diagnosed with an acute respiratory infection and sent to bed. The illness was disturbing personally but disastrous politically. At the very moment that he most needed to be speaking with Canadians, he was silenced. For the remainder of February and the first week of March he took crucial calls and dealt with urgent correspondence, but for all intents and purposes he vanished.

Bennett's absence left cabinet members scrambling. They were in the midst of writing the budget and preparing and shepherding through the House the most ambitious package of reform legislation that Parliament had ever seen and they were suddenly without their leader. Not only that, but Bennett had delegated little in terms of crafting the various pieces of legislation or in planning for their passage. Acting

Prime Minister Sir George Perley took a number of actions that kept the cabinet and caucus together but it was well known that he did not support many of the New Deal initiatives or the political philosophy at their core. Further, he was getting old and his effectiveness as a leader in the House was waning. Manion was among many who believed that Perley was letting Bennett down by not being more vigorous in his promotion of the New Deal legislation.[38] Perley's ineffectiveness resulted in Rod Finlayson stepping to the fore. He coached the cabinet and later individual ministers as to the best way forward.[39]

Under such trying circumstances, the cabinet did an admirable job. Finance Minister Rhodes worked furiously with Finlayson and his staff to create a budget. The final wording was completed just the evening before it was presented in the House. The budget contained more promises than substantive change, but it did as Bennett had pledged and raised taxes on the richest Canadians by hiking corporate taxes by one percent and imposing new surtaxes on investment incomes of over $5,000. It reflected Bennett's belief that a period of economic crisis is not a time to worry about balancing the government's books in that it allowed another deficit. The deficit was projected to be the highest in the Bennett years: $17 million.

The cabinet then worked to bring forward the reform bills that Bennett had only sketched out in principle. The Prairie Farm Rehabilitation Act promised to create an advisory board that would investigate then recommend ways to help farmers whose land had been devastated by the drought. Another relief bill added more funding to the program created in 1934. The Relief and Public Works Construction Act offered funding to more federal, provincial, and municipal infrastructure projects. In deference to the deficit, and because Bennett was not able to personally push for more, the amount offered was only $30 million. Finally, the Economic Council of Canada was established. It would conduct research and provide advice to the prime minister and cabinet regarding economic and social changes affecting Canadians.

The budget and each piece of legislation was met by insipid responses and general support from the Liberals. They were disciplined in following their leader's orders to do nothing disruptive in the House while preparing to fight in the election.[40] Bennett, meanwhile, was forced to merely listen to reports from Finlayson, guess at opposition strategy, and send instructions back to colleagues. Things were bad but they were about to get worse.

On the morning of March 7, 1935, Prime Minister Bennett suffered a heart attack. For years he had been overworked, overstressed, overtired, and overweight. All of this, when coupled with his lack of exercise and terrible diet, meant that his abstinence from drinking and smoking were good but not enough. He had for some time been a heart attack waiting to happen. His last complete physical examination had been in Calgary by Dr. R. S. Stevenson in August 1934. The electrocardiogram had indicated that Bennett had an irregular heart rhythm with a particular problem in the left ventricle, or in medical terms, "auricular fibrillation, left ventricular preponderance."[41] The doctor had, for some reason, prescribed no medicine nor recommended any change in lifestyle. It is unlikely that Bennett would have listened anyway. Now, however, his doctors ordered complete bedrest.

Bennett had been out of the public eye, but at least directing things from behind the scenes, since the twenty-third of February. But with the heart attack he was totally out of the picture for another three weeks. Finlayson and the cabinet were left completely on their own. By mid-March, Bennett was again dealing with some matters of state from his suite, but to the public he was still the invisible man. As he slowly recovered, he was able to do more work but he tired easily. He was capable of no public appearances. He could not appear in the House.

The government continued to manage the nation's affairs. On March 14, only one week after his heart attack, another of Bennett's reform bills, the Weekly Day of Rest Act, was introduced. It stated that workers were owed one day off a week and that day should normally be Sunday. It set fines for companies that violated the act by forcing employees to work seven days a week. Bennett was kept up to date with daily briefings, and made suggestions throughout the act's drafting and introduction, but said nothing to the press. The act passed with little debate.

On April 16, Bennett invited a group of reporters whom he had grown to trust a little more than others to his suite and undertook a press conference. It had been nearly two months since he had spoken to a reporter or since he had been seen or heard from by Canadians. In the short chat, he expressed full support for all the government had been doing in the House, but he said little of consequence. The purpose was simply to demonstrate to the Canadian people, and perhaps to those in his party, that while he was a little thinner, a little paler, and that his eyes showed strain, he had recovered and was still the leader.

Beginning that afternoon, people were introduced to a different, less guarded Bennett. Perhaps it was that he had just stared death in the face. Perhaps he was feeling the reflective calm that moving through one's sixty-sixth year allows. Or perhaps he was predicting that his days as prime minister were over. There is no evidence as to his sharing his thoughts on the cause of his change in demeanour, but the change was nonetheless evident. He was less combative and more relaxed. He pondered questions more thoughtfully and spoke with less urgency. Even political foes noticed a change. Bruce Hutchison, for instance, who was by no means a fan, wrote an editorial in the *Calgary Herald* in which he observed, "The fire is still there, but it is no longer a consuming flame, which often burned friend and enemy alike and all but consumed Mr. Bennett himself."[42]

Two days later, Bennett left for New York on his way to King George v's silver jubilee in London. While leaving Canada at such a critical juncture was risky, he had never made a secret of his love of the monarchy and of all things British. Plus, protocol demanded the presence of the prime minister of the Commonwealth's largest dominion and not a surrogate. And, the trip offered more time to regain his strength.

Bennett enjoyed the trip immensely. One of his proudest moments came on a gloriously sunny spring morning when he rode through the streets of London with Prime Minister Hertzog of South Africa in the long royal procession's second car, just behind the king himself. The celebrations included a service at St. Paul's Cathedral in which Bennett was seated in a place of honour near the front. It also included a weekend at Windsor Castle with the Archbishop of Canterbury and the royal family. He spent time alone with the king. One can only imagine the thoughts of the boy from Hopewell Cape as he laid himself down to sleep in the Edward III Tower. In a letter of thanks to the king that he wrote from his London hotel before departing for home, one can sense his being nearly overwhelmed by all he had experienced. He wrote,

Perhaps you would permit me to add that I valued very highly the
opportunity so freely given to discuss with my Sovereign matters of
concern. I state the simple truth when I write that I came away from the
Castle with an even deeper feeling of affection and devotion for my King
and Queen, and I shall continue to aspire more earnestly to serve the
Crown to the best of my ability, sustained by the conviction that my
Royal Master expects His servants to do the best within them.[43]

Mildred was with him in London as was Alice Millar and a small
group of staff that again included Pearson. Bennett stole some time for
sightseeing and shopping with Mildred. He also spent time with
Beaverbrook, who arranged for his friend to see his personal physician.

Bennett found the days travelling over the Atlantic and back aboard
the French liner *Paris* to be especially pleasant. While dealing with work
in the mornings and evenings, he whiled away afternoons speaking with
other passengers and with staff about things other than the challenges of
governing. It was while aboard the *Paris* that Bennett worked on yet another expression of the Canadian tie to Britain. Before the trip, he had
decided to reinstate the practice of submitting names to the Crown for
the bestowal of Royal Honours as a way to recognize achievement.
Bennett had asked his cabinet to submit suggestions for those who should
be honoured first. In quiet moments in his cabin he pared it down to a
final list. He then invited a rather seasick Pearson to look over his decisions. The nauseous young man was surprised to find his name among
the nominees. Despite his illness, Pearson remained sufficiently shrewd
to notice that his boss, Oscar Skelton, was not on the list, so he asked that
his own name be removed. Those who finally received Royal Honours
included Frederick Banting (scientist), Ernest Macmillan (musician),
Arthur Beauchesne (House of Commons clerk), Lyman Duff (chief justice of the Supreme Court), Charles Saunders (scientist who invented a
new hybrid wheat, allowing the West to boom), and Charlotte Whitton
(Alberta social worker and later long-time Ottawa mayor).

The trip back offered Pearson another surprise when a pleasant
afternoon was spent on deck with a French gentleman who engaged
the prime minister in a long and rather detailed discussion about
wine. Despite the fact that Bennett had always eschewed any type of
liquor, including wine, he was a polymath who impressed all with his

meticulous knowledge of the fine liquid in which he himself had never indulged.[44] But soon, probably sooner than all would have liked, it was back to Canada and the political firestorm that waited.

Bennett's illness, then the heart attack, and then the silver jubilee, had effectively removed him from the public eye from late February until late May. Without Bennett travelling the country and selling his program, the political high ground had been abandoned to the Liberals. The *Canadian Annual Review* noted: "That had given his opponents ample time to undermine his social reform platform. Just so, in 1911, had Sir Wilfrid Laurier lost the Reciprocity Election by attending King George's Coronation, thus giving the Conservatives six months in which to fight the trade compacts with Washington."[45]

When he returned first from his sickbed and then from London, he was feeling tired and lethargic. He was honest with reporters about his health. In a May press conference in Ottawa he confided to reporters, "I saw two specialists in London and they reported that my heart was organically sound. It was, however, a tired heart. Just what it will be capable of accomplishing remains to be seen."[46] Two weeks later, Bennett was even more direct in a letter to old friend Howard Ferguson in which he admitted, "I really should not be at work. . . . I doubt very much whether I will be able to go on. If I get half a chance to rest for six months, I will be all right, but as there is an election before that time, it looks to me as though I might have to retire. I will know definitely before prorogation."[47]

On May 20, there was thunderous applause from both sides of the House when the prime minister took his seat. Parliament had been recessed for nearly five weeks. With Bennett back at work and directing cabinet, another flurry of reform legislation found its way to the House.

On May 23, Guthrie introduced the Criminal Code Amendment Act. Based upon recommendations from the Price Spreads Commission, it stated that companies could not engage in false advertising, or set salaries lower than the legislated minimum wage, or set the prices of their products such that they were designed only to harm or eliminate competition. Penalties were high. The predatory pricing provision, for instance, promised fines of up to $5,000 and a month's jail time.

Two weeks later, Bennett rose to introduce legislation to create the

Canadian Wheat Board. The act augmented the Wheat Board Act passed the year before, but this time proposed that the government take control of all grain elevators to further control the purchase and distribution and, consequently, the price of prairie wheat and grain. It established headquarters in Winnipeg. The board would determine how much of each product should be grown or extracted while establishing standards for quality. The act promised greater government power in the economy with the proviso that it could move to handle more products, such as barley, oats, and rye, if deemed advantageous to producers and consumers. Bennett argued that the act was really just creating in name what had been operating for over two years under the brilliant leadership of John McFarland.

The Liberals stood against the wheat board with the same argument they had used against the Criminal Code Amendment Act: the government was becoming too powerful and inserting itself too radically into the marketplace. That insertion, however, was exactly the point. The very next day, before Mackenzie King had time to organize the debate, Minister of Trade and Commerce Richard Hanson moved second reading on the Dominion Trade and Industry Commission Act. Taking its inspiration from the Price Spreads Commission, the act afforded more power to the Tariff Board and to the National Research Council. Further, it stated that the Industry Commission would have the power to investigate businesses that were suspected of engaging in unfair practices. It also detailed a Canada standard for goods that companies marketed, thereby establishing the now well-known CSA-approved label for Canadian products. Again, the Liberals were aghast at the government promising to intervene so actively in the marketplace.

Only ten days later, Agriculture Minister Robert Weir introduced the Farmer's Creditors Arrangement Act. It amended the act passed the previous year so as to help farmers gain the credit they so desperately needed. It gave them more flexibility in negotiating how loans could be repaid and a greater likelihood of securing loans in the first place.

A week later, the furious pace continued with the introduction of Natural Products Marketing Act amendments. Intended to address low and still fluctuating commodity prices, the act expanded similar 1934 legislation by affording the government the power to assist not only farmers but also the forest industry through regulations that allowed the selling of products at more stable and predictable prices. It also brought the pulp and paper industry under the protection of the regulations.

The Dominion Housing Act offered federal money to help banks and prospective first-time homeowners arrange mortgages. The act came from a committee that Bennett had established the year before. It promised $10 million for a program that loaned money at a low 3 per cent interest to builders of a new home if they were able to raise at least 20 per cent of the cost on their own. It was meant to help people to purchase a new home while stimulating job growth in the construction trades. The program was eventually directly responsible for the construction of 5,000 homes and countless jobs for Canadians.

Finally, Bennett introduced the Companies Act Amendment. It was based upon the belief that among the reasons for the Depression had been the tricks played by banks and corporate boards involving accounting practices, stock-price manipulation, and corporate governance. The act provided more transparency for investors by forcing companies to be forthright in reporting shifts from common to preferred shares, and changes in ownership and board membership. It provided that company directors had to emerge from the shadows and that an annual and audited financial statement had to be presented to shareholders with a copy sent to the secretary of state.

Only five months had passed since Bennett's final radio address. Bennett had fallen ill, suffered a heart attack, and gone to England. Despite all of that, he had overseen the delivery of a Throne Speech and the creation and passage of a budget, juggled the challenges presented by Stevens and the growing relief camp, strike, and trek troubles, directed trade negotiations with the United States, and managed the presentation of fourteen significant pieces of legislation. It was a remarkable achievement.

As the late-spring sun began to warm the land and urge Canadians to shake off memories of yet another cold winter, would it all matter? The Canadian people were about to decide if they wished to change or repeat the decision they had made five years before in choosing Bennett to lead them from the cold chill of the Depression.

PREPARING FOR THE 1935 ELECTION

Every prime minister does his or her best according to their wit, wisdom, and character. Similarly, each worries, when election time nears, as to whether those efforts were good enough to earn the trust of Canadians one more time. Bennett knew that times had been tough, and he was open with many about the degree to which he took responsibility for errors that had been made. To a supporter in Winnipeg, for instance, he had written with pride and humility, "I have given my best to the country during the last five years, and I believe there is written a record of which no one need be ashamed, although it is quite probable that we have made mistakes as all poor human creatures must."[48] It was now up to the voters.

Bennett began the campaign with troubles that no incumbent needed. Important among them was dissension within Conservative ranks. The Stevens affair was the most damaging, but there was trouble with others too. During a warm June afternoon House debate regarding unemployment among veterans, for instance, things were slogging along when R.J. Manion rose and questioned the veracity of a report that had been tabled by Mr. Justice Hyndman. There is nothing wrong with such a question, but it is usual practice to raise such things in caucus or, in this case, in cabinet where the report had already been discussed. When Manion had taken his seat, Bennett leaned over Guthrie, glared at Manion and whispered, but in a voice heard by all, that such remarks by a member of his own government had no place in the House. Manion snapped back that he would express his opinion whenever and wherever he pleased and that if Bennett wanted his resignation, he could have it right then and there. Bennett, of course, should have ended the exchange, but his blood was up. He retorted that if Manion wanted to resign immediately he would accept it. The men slumped back into their chairs like scowling red-faced brothers in a back-seat spat, with Guthrie as the poor sib between to keep them apart.

The confrontation was all over the next day's papers.[49] The sparks amounted to nothing, but they had been sufficiently bright to cast light on a government under extreme stress, a splintering cabinet, a proud minister willing to take unfounded criticism from no one, and a prime minister who despite his age and position still occasionally let his temper get the best of him. The public fight with Manion, the public criticism against the January speeches from Cahan, and the longer, more significant split with Stevens all revealed that the support Bennett had once enjoyed from his colleagues had been shattered.

On July 5, 1935, Parliament was adjourned. Two days later, Stevens announced the formation of a new political party with himself as its leader. The Reconstruction Party was born. On August 15, Bennett visited Governor General Bessborough and an election was set for October 14.

Bennett had hoped to allow himself time to rest and plan, and for the country to enjoy what was left of the summer. But headlines through the spring and summer of 1935 screamed of discontent. May was the Vancouver Relief Workers Strike, June the On to Ottawa Trek, and July the Regina Riot. If that was not enough, unemployment was still high and optimism was still low. It is hard to imagine a tougher set of circumstances for an incumbent facing the electorate.

But there was even more. When Bennett looked to the party organization that would enable him to take his case to the Canadian people, he found it a shambles. The organization that had been so brilliantly put together using Bennett's money and McRae's talents had been taken apart shortly after the 1930 election. All provincial offices had been closed. Most riding associations across the country had stopped meeting. Lists of electors, supporters, and contributors had been allowed to go stale and in many cases were lost. The *Canadian*, which had been so effective in the 1930 campaign as a means of presenting the Conservative Party view, had printed just one issue after the election and had been allowed to fold. The National News Service, which was so powerful a tool, had been shut down to save money. If that was not sufficiently ill advised, Bennett had also ordered the plates to be broken up so that they would not fall into the wrong hands. The party's headquarters in Ottawa had closed. The men who had made it and the entire 1930 campaign work—Redmond Code, Robert Lipset, General McRae—had left for the law, the press, and the Senate, respectively.

Good people departing due to an inability to retain even part-time employment with the party was seen everywhere, and everywhere it hurt. A party works on people and structure and in the early 1930s both had been allowed to fall away. The structure could perhaps have been rebuilt, but once the experienced people were gone, it was difficult to have them surrender the often much better paying positions they had found to return to a party that had proven itself to be nothing but a part-time and disloyal employer.

The organization had died not due to neglect or incompetence but because Bennett had ordered its death. He had decided to dedicate none of his time to party matters as he focused on the affairs of the state. On January 6, 1931, just three months after winning office, Bennett had written a long and blunt letter to the party chief and chief whip in which he explained decisions he had made regarding the party's central organization. He noted that the only money supporting the organization was coming from his own pocket and that he was ending his personal sponsorship. He offered one month's expenses to effectively shut the operation down. He further argued that the work of spreading news regarding party policies and government actions could be more effectively and cheaply done through local riding associations.[50]

Shutting down the central organization did not stop the requests for funds. Bennett continued to receive letters and guests in his office asking that he personally finance their political careers. Bennett responded to all stating that as of June 1930 he had contributed half a million dollars to the Conservative Party and that no one should expect him to spend more. To prospective Toronto Conservative candidate T. A. McAuley, for example, Bennett explained, "I have spent more money now, I think, than any other man in the Party and I feel certain my Toronto friends will realize my position."[51]

Bennett had been urged to keep an eye on party affairs. He had been told of the need to keep the offices open, the *Canadian* in production, the riding associations vibrant, and the voting and donor lists current.[52] But the letters urging such action stopped when it became clear that Bennett's mind had been made up. The organization that had played such an enormous role in making him prime minister was gone. In the summer of 1935, with a new election dawning, he realized the mistake he had made. He later wrote, "I gave too much time to the problems of government and too little to the interests of my Party."[53]

This is not to say that absolutely nothing had been done about party organization for five years, for indeed there had been some sound and fury. In the fall of 1934, Bennett had asked cabinet ministers Stevens,

Manion, and Gordon to establish a committee to plan for the next election. But the committee came to nothing as the three bickered about budget and authority. Gordon quit. Bennett received a series of recommendations from Stevens and Manion, but there is no indication that he did anything with them.

In December 1934, Toronto backbencher Earl Lawson had written to Bennett expressing frustration with the sorry state of the party and offering to become its national organizer. Bennett quickly accepted and the appointment was made. Lawson began in January 1935 by setting up an office in Ottawa and assembling a two-person staff. He hired friend and reporter Fred Edwards as the director of publicity and charged him with the responsibility of reinventing the machine that had proven so effective in 1930. Edwards did what he could, but with old files and little money he was stymied from the start. He managed to produce three new issues of the *Canadian* and to send copies of Bennett's New Deal speeches to friendly individuals and groups across the country. The efforts were laudable and better than nothing, but they were ad hoc at best.

More could have been accomplished and in a timelier manner, but there was simply not the money to do so. Lawson had not appointed a fundraiser. Then, as now, money was the grease that allowed a political party's wheels to turn, and the Conservative party had little. Bennett's generous donations had been good for the party but had created long-term problems by alleviating the necessity to develop other sustainable sources of revenue. In the late spring of 1935, Lawson and his tiny staff struggled to develop a fundraising plan, but it was far too late in the game for any strategy, no matter how well inspired or intelligently implemented, to gather the necessary funds.

In August, with the writ dropped, the paper-and-paste organization that Lawson had put together nearly fell apart. He could hardly be blamed. He needed to return to his Toronto riding to fight for his political life and so was seldom in the office or in day-to-day control. He had appointed the talented Lou Golden as party general secretary, and he had instantly become the de facto national party organizer. Late in the summer, however, Golden fell ill with a potentially fatal bone disease and had to leave his post. Lawson scrambled and, just eight weeks before voting day, young Richard Bell was appointed to take over. Bell worked long hours and quickly won Bennett's respect as he arranged the leader's tour, oversaw all party communications, attempted to strengthen the ties to and between what had been moribund provincial offices, and saw to the last-minute approval of candidates.

By late September, working with what Golden had begun, Bell assembled a reliable mailing list of 400,000 names. A quarter of those were in Quebec. Mailings went out, reporters' questions were answered, and an enormous amount of work was done by the tiny but dedicated staff. But communications between hastily appointed provincial directors and the central office suffered during the transition to Bell and never really recovered. Chaos and frustration were heightened as Bennett and Finlayson often ignored Bell's central office and spoke directly to candidates and provincial directors. Calls to provincial offices and to the national office were often directed elsewhere. Many trivial and some important questions went unanswered. And everyone asked for more money. All were told that there simply was no more.

Bennett had for years rejected many ideas presented to him regarding fundraising. Important among them, for what it says about his integrity as a man and a leader, was the age-old and commonly practised trick of awarding government contracts to those who made contributions to the party. The practice encourages regular and generous contributions from those companies and others wishing to latch on to the patronage teat. But Bennett rejected the whole sordid idea. Shortly after becoming prime minister, for instance, he had been told of a series of contracts to be awarded in Montreal that had the potential to bring significant funds to party hampers.[54] Bennett turned the opportunity down. He opened those and all other contracts to a fair and transparent tendering process. Bennett paid a steep price for his integrity.

The Conservative Party's growing problems were seen in the by-elections it had been losing. The party had held its own in the first two by-elections when it lost Three Rivers–St. Maurice but won in Hamilton-East. In 1932, it broke even again, winning in Alberta's Athabasca and in New Brunswick's Royal, but losing contests in Montreal-Maisonneuve and Ontario's South Huron. But the next year saw the beginning of the swing against Bennett and the Conservatives. There were three by-elections and the party lost them all: in Saskatchewan's Mackenzie, New Brunswick's Restigouche-Madawaska, and Quebec's Yamaska. In 1934 and early 1935, there were six more federal by-elections; the Conservative Party candidates lost all except the one in Toronto East.

Meanwhile, Conservative governments had been voted out of office in Ontario, Saskatchewan, and New Brunswick. The party had only managed to hold on to Prince Edward Island. But in 1935, that government fell too, with not a single Conservative earning a seat.

Even when money, organization, and support were gathered and focused on a particular project, it did not seem to matter. In Ontario's South Huron, after all, five cabinet ministers, including the nationally popular Stevens and Manion, had stumped enthusiastically for the local Conservative candidate. Volunteers were plentiful and some of the budget was left in the bank on Election Day—but it was to no avail. The Conservative candidate was trounced. By the late spring and early summer of 1935, four ridings were without representation in Ottawa. Bennett let them sit empty rather than risk more defeats.

In the spring of 1935, when everyone including Bennett knew full well of the challenges the election would hold, a fascinating idea surfaced. In early March, Bennett heard rumblings about the creation of a coalition government, much like the one that Borden had formed to fight the First World War. Toronto Conservative MP Frederick Morrow explained to the prime minister that Liberal stalwart Ernest Lapointe had approached him with the notion that the Liberals and Conservatives should form a national party to combat the Depression. He reported that a number of Liberal MPs were ready to endorse the idea. An unsubstantiated rumour even circulated that if Mackenzie King decided not to involve himself then he could either continue as Liberal leader or room would be made for him as president of McGill University. Morrow was quick to point out, however, that Lapointe could not really be trusted. He had had shady dealings in the past and was in desperate need of money and so would do just about anything to secure a Senate appointment or jump at any other opportunity that would afford him a steady and reasonable income.[55] Bennett did nothing to encourage the idea, not surprisingly since he had opposed the first unity government so vehemently. The notion went nowhere.

In the end, it was apparent that if Bennett were to win re-election he would need to do it with his record and himself as the only assets on which he could rely. As had been the case throughout most of his po-

litical career, he prepared to face the people with little organization, few
allies, little money beyond his own, and the odds against him.

THE CAMPAIGN

The Liberals began the campaign by laying a fourteen-point platform
before the Canadian people. It was intriguing, for many of the points
were from Bennett's January speeches and the legislation he had subsequently brought to the House. They were simply reworked and made
more palatable by divorcing them from their urgent rhetoric. The
Liberals promised, for instance, to bring forward a plan for unemployment insurance and public works programs. There was a promise to
eliminate unfair trade practices and price-fixing and to extend trade
with Britain through a preferential tariff. The Canadian National Railway
would be kept separate from the CPR, maintained as a publicly owned
railway, and run with greater efficiency. There was even a promise to
"create" a central bank. Some of the platform was a veiled attack based
on false stereotypes regarding Bennett and his leadership style, such as
the promise to end "autocratic powers" and to restore the power of
Parliament. Finally, there was a pledge to repeal Section 98 of the
Criminal Code. Overall, it was an anemic effort; what was not vague
was stolen, and what remained was either misleading or qualified by the
phrase "as opportunity offers."[56]

A Liberal campaign poster that was also used as a newspaper ad
stated that people should vote Liberal for five reasons. Like much of the
platform, each played on the negative perception of Bennett's reputation that the Opposition and critical newspapers had been helping to
construct over the previous five years. One said, "You do not want a
one-man government." Another said, "You do not want the 'iron heel' of
ruthlessness in Canada."[57]

The Liberals were not alone in inflammatory rhetoric on their campaign posters. A Conservative poster that found its way to the telephone
poles of the West exclaimed in an odd use of bold print and capital letters, "Vote for Mr. Bennett in the next election—Save Canada from
Annexation and Absolute Destruction—The opposition Leader, Mr. M.
King Must be kept out at all costs—All Loyal citizens should uphold Mr.
Bennett which means good leadership, law and order, and a prosperous
country. The Ottawa Conference was the Greatest Achievement in

Canadian History."[58] The gloves had definitely hit the ice.

The sixty-one-year old Mackenzie King entered the campaign well rested and, after months of careful dieting he had lost 40 pounds and was more fit and energetic than he had been in some time. With the baby fat gone from his face and the frenetic, high-pitched voice from his speeches, Mackenzie King appeared to be a new and improved candidate, certainly different from the man Canadians had voted from office five years before. He presented himself as a calm, reliable presence and leader of a strong Liberal team. He repeated in many speeches, "What this country needs is not the fist of the pugilist but the hand of the physician."[59]

The campaign began in earnest after Labour Day with a series of four radio speeches that Bennett delivered from Toronto. They were unlike the January speeches in tone and quite specific in laying out plans for his next administration. Among the policies he promised to pursue if re-elected was more trade with the United States but higher tariffs to other countries outside the Commonwealth, lower interest rates, easier loans for homeowners, job creation, and the establishment of a mandatory retirement age of sixty. He also promised improved public radio and the creation of a more efficient civil service. He pledged to deal firmly with communists and others who threatened peace, order, and the country's continued economic recovery.

The opening speech made clear that, if re-elected, Bennett intended to continue to lead from the left of the political spectrum. For instance, he promised to create a commission to look into transportation issues including, most importantly, the railways. He said that if the commission recommended amalgamation or nationalization, he would seriously consider the options but that he would take the ideas to Canadians before proceeding, as they were CN shareholders. Also, he promised that the newly created Economic Council of Canada would investigate the future of energy needs with a specific look at the creation of pipelines. The council would be charged with determining ways that energy needs could be met and make a recommendation to Parliament that would allow the country to ". . . avoid the present competition, the present unprofitable production, the present prices, by devising a scheme of coordination and elimination of duplication."[60]

Not flinching from attacking his opponents while defending his record, he said, "The Conservative Party stands upon the bedrock of performance; the opposition parties upon the changing sands of political expediency."[61] He then hinted at the array of new political parties that were presenting themselves as political options for Canadians. He sarcastically noted, "Political arguments of the day include the case for capitalism, reformed capitalism, Socialism, Communism, and some rare economic creations for which, perhaps, we cannot find a name."[62]

Bennett also responded to Mackenzie King's accusations of his having run a one-man government: "When he talks in this way, who is he trying to frighten? You? Me? Himself? I really don't know whom. It is too absurd. It is not even a good joke."[63] He went on to say that there would never be a dictator in Canada as long as Canadians were Canadians and concluded, "So do not let us be childish and talk about things that have no substance, when we all know that there are things of grave importance which should engage our every waking hour."[64]

Bennett tried to address the schism created by the Stevens affair. He said that Stevens had fought throughout his entire political life for Conservative policies and expressed regret that he had left the party. He then noted that the Reconstruction Party's objectives were the same as those of the Conservative Party, but that Stevens was advocating untested and impracticable means to pursue them while at the same time trying to initiate a class war. Bennett argued, "National objectives cannot be obtained by arousing class prejudices and by repudiation and destruction."[65]

He ended with a list of what he believed to be the most noteworthy accomplishments of his administration: the establishment of the Bank of Canada, the Natural Products Marketing Act, farm loans, the Farmer's Creditors Arrangement Act, unemployment insurance, minimum wages, the eight-hour day, a day of rest, the Economic Council of Canada, the Dominion Housing Act, the Board of Commerce and Industry, amendments to the Companies Act and the Criminal Code, protections for investors, the abolition of unfair labour and pricing practices, and the creation of the Canadian Wheat Board and the CRBC.[66]

None of this was new and all was consistent with the ideological view that Bennett had held throughout his political career and stated most bluntly with the January speeches. But it was a lot to swallow. He had hit every opponent and anticipated every possible attack. Rather than simplifying his platform into just a few priorities, he had laid out a large and complex set of ideas. Although it was in harmony with his past work, it nonetheless had the appearance of yet another new program—the third in nine months. Further, in outlining so many priorities it appeared that he had none in particular.

On September 19, a cheering crowd of between five and six thousand people met Bennett's train as it pulled into the Calgary station at 11:30 a.m., forty-five minutes late. A loud ovation rose from the crowd when he appeared, raised his hat, and beamed a large smile. Police formed a cordon around him as he moved slowly through the crowd shaking hands and greeting many people by name. The Native Son's Band played the national anthem and "For He's a Jolly Good Fellow" as he arrived at the Palliser Hotel where hundreds more had gathered to welcome him. After briefly freshening up, he gulped a quick snack then addressed seven hundred people at a formal luncheon hosted by the Canadian Club. He spoke for an hour and used much of the speech to warn of the dangers that the world presented for Canada. He spoke of the dictators of Europe. He warned of the peril that communism posed for the world. He used this warning to segue into a point he had raised in his campaign's opening address. He stated that Russian leaders had recently boasted that 90 per cent of the strikes that had occurred recently in Canada had been organized by communists. He made specific reference to the On to Ottawa Trek, stating that it had been part of a communist plan to overthrow Canada's constitution, institutions, and traditions. He went on to argue that the problems faced by Canada were different from those at Confederation and so constitutional amendments were needed to afford the federal government the power to address those problems.[67]

On his second day in the city he presented a number of scholarships to deserving secondary school students. At 3:00 p.m. one thousand loyal Conservatives packed the Elks Hall for the perfunctory nomination meeting. Mayor Andrew Davidson was there and among those who spoke were the Conservative candidates for Calgary East, Bow River, and Medicine Hat. Bennett surprised no one when he won the nomination for Calgary West by acclamation. He then delivered yet another one-hour speech.

With victory in his home riding in the bag, he embarked on a tour of the country that would have staggered a younger and healthier man. He showed courage by beginning in Regina. He was pleased with and proud of his reception. He also visited Vancouver, Victoria, and Winnipeg. He then headed back east where he was applauded for speeches in Quebec City and Montreal, much of which he delivered by reading well-practised French. In all he made forty major addresses and visited every province.

Bennett's rallies were well attended and for the most part the audiences were enthusiastic and well behaved. His speeches were written primarily by Finlayson. Bennett had even acceded to Finlayson's repeated requests and allowed Bill Herridge to help with the drafts. Bennett himself often significantly reworked them before they were delivered. At every stop he proudly outlined his record of achievement. He noted that since 1930, exports were up and unemployment was down. He explained how the Bank of Canada and the regulations that had been imposed on banks, the stock market, and corporations had greatly reduced the chances of Canada ever seeing another prolonged depression. He listed the many pieces of legislation that had forced businesses to improve wages and working conditions, and policies that had provided jobs and relief to desperate Canadians. He took credit for the Price Spreads Commission and told how much of his recent legislation was based on its recommendations. He bragged about public radio and how Canadians were being brought together to celebrate their culture rather than being swamped by programs from over the border.

Mackenzie King, meanwhile, stuck diligently to his game plan. The Liberal campaign slogan was a simple alliteration: King or Chaos. At every campaign stop he urged audiences to remember the hard times of the Depression and to tag Bennett as having been unable to alleviate them. He attacked what he called Bennett's "dictatorial style." He promised to do away with what he said was Bennett's excessive use of orders-in-council, that he claimed had usurped the power of the House. He spoke of getting rid of the Criminal Code's Section 98, which, he argued, had the potential to steal the rights of all citizens. He asked Canadians to affix all blame for all problems on the doorstep of his opponent. A favourite line, and similar to one used by presidential candidate Ronald Reagan forty-five years later, was, "You have now had five years of the Bennett government. I wonder if any of you are as well off now as when it started?"[68]

Mackenzie King offered ideological mush. He spoke of freer trade but not free trade. He promised a balanced budget but no significant tax increases or spending cuts to achieve it. He pledged several programs that had, in fact, already been put in place, and even the creation of a central bank. He knew that the promises were less important than in 1930 because Canadians were already in the mood to toss Bennett out of office. From the outset he planned to use this perception to his advantage by focusing on avoiding gaffes and letting Bennett lose. He had told his caucus in June, "The main thing from now on is to realize that the people vote against, rather than for something and to keep their mind focussed on Bennett and his mismanagement of things."[69] In that way he was like Jean Chrétien running against the despised Conservatives in 1993 or Pierre Trudeau running against the hapless Joe Clark in 1980. As he slid beneath his coat in the back seat of a car that was about to whisk him away, Trudeau had joked that he was the shadow.

The other parties spoke mostly to their limited constituencies, and they all struggled with small staffs and very little money. Led by the universally respected J. S. Woodsworth, the CCF took its 1932 Regina Manifesto to the hustings and promised to eradicate capitalism through the nationalization of businesses such as banks and insurance companies, and to end the contradictions of a government that it said was claiming to want to help people with relief but then attacked them with the RCMP and legislation such as Section 98. The Social Credit Party earned its reputation as the "funny money party" by pledging to mail a $25 cheque to every Canadian every month. They could not really explain where they would get the money and how the scheme would not devalue the currency, but those details did not seem to matter. Ex-radio preacher and Social Credit leader "Bible Bill" Aberhart had ridden his populist message to the premiership of Alberta and so was removed from the campaign, but he leant his persuasive voice to radio addresses that were especially attractive to a good number of Depression-scarred westerners. The Social Credit Party would govern Alberta until 1971. Stevens's Reconstruction Party played the populist card by attacking big business and promising a program based to a large degree on the findings of the Price Spreads Commission. It nominated candidates in ridings across the country but few were well qualified. Many were strangers even in their hometowns. A host of small labour parties and the communists also fielded candidates.

The CCF, Social Credit, and Reconstruction parties had some appeal across the country, and pockets of substantial support among socialist intellectuals, working-class Canadians, and alienated western farmers. All were similar in that they offered programs to the left of the political spectrum. With Bennett's personal convictions, the 1927 Winnipeg convention, the record of his administration, and most blatantly with his words and legislation of 1935, Bennett had also situated the Conservative Party on the crowded ideological left. All Canadians who saw value in such a political point of view, and the programs that view inspired, had a host of electoral choices. Meanwhile, Mackenzie King had for years been inching the Liberals to the centre-right. The 1935 election, therefore, saw the Liberals alone in drawing support from the right and centre, with the Conservatives scrambling for votes on the splintered left. This fact made the wisdom of Mackenzie King's shadow campaign seem wiser still.

Most campaigns see cabinet ministers and provincial premiers travelling to ridings deemed important because a belief develops that they can be won or that a particular candidate deserves support. Such trips help the local candidate, bring prestige to the minister and premier, and take pressure off the leader who, after all, cannot be everywhere at once. No such relief came in 1935. Despite requests and later pleas from Finlayson, and sometimes from Bennett himself, ministers stuck to their own ridings. They declared that they could not afford a day away if they hoped to hold their hotly contested seats. Further, cabinet ministers Rhodes, Macdonald, Sauvé, Duranleau, Guthrie, and Matthews had decided not to seek re-election. They had gone back to private life or to patronage appointments and all sat out the campaign. The recently appointed ministers who had replaced them had no national profiles and so would be no help; besides, like the others in the caucus, they had their own seats to worry about. Bennett even asked Meighen to help, but the former prime minister claimed that as a senator he should not be involved in the partisan race. Bennett was on his own.

The necessity of his appearing alone at campaign events played into Mackenzie King's portrayal of the prime minister running a one-man government. Mackenzie King, on the other hand, promised a strong Liberal team. To hammer the point home he ensured that he was surrounded by prominent Liberals at every campaign stop. At a large rally at Toronto's Maple Leaf Gardens, for example, he was introduced via a radio hookup by eight Liberal premiers. He spoke of the Liberal team taking on the one-man government of the autocratic R. B. Bennett.

The one-man-show notion had dogged Bennett from the beginning of his administration, and Mackenzie King had presaged in a series of 1934 speeches that he would try to exploit it for electoral advantage. At a time when the world was trembling with the realization that Hitler, Mussolini, and Stalin were imposing ruthless totalitarian dictatorships upon their peoples and threatening the world with violence and death, Mackenzie King's decision to link Bennett to the word "dictator" was cynical indeed. But in April, Mackenzie King had spoken in Toronto and said, "We have in Canada to make our choice; we must decide whether we want a dictatorship or whether we want to carry on the old system of Parliamentary representation."[70] The next day he went further still in his outrageous claims, saying that Bennett's policies were geared to getting rid of Parliament altogether and that he was even attempting to craft a bill that would do away with the need for elections.[71] Months later he was still at it. The *Ottawa Citizen* ran portions of Mackenzie King's September 17 speech in which he said, "The great struggle today is between democracy and dictatorship. . . . During these past four years in Canada the free institution of parliament has gradually been subjected to a change which permitted many of the abuses rampant in dictatorship."[72] More such messages were repeated throughout the 1935 campaign.

An unfortunate decision by Fred Edwards back in the messy and scrambling national party headquarters in Ottawa, meanwhile, had handed Mackenzie King a gift to help with his message. The August issue of the revived *Canadian* had contained a cartoon by A. Racey that showed Bennett wearing rain gear and a smug grin, alone on a ship, hands firmly on the wheel, with a hurricane-like storm raging behind him. The caption read, "Stand By Canada." The same cartoon, with variations on the caption, became a party ad in newspapers and magazines, the cover of candidate speaker's notes, and a feature of campaign literature. Unfortunately, there was no one on the ship but Bennett. It was clear inside and outside the party that the election was to be based on Bennett as leader. Mackenzie King's message of a one-man government was thus afforded resonance.

Meanwhile, the radio was used in the 1935 campaign as it had never been used before. Every party leader delivered nationally aired half-hour speeches. Edwards went further and had a six-part radio drama carefully and cleverly scripted and then performed by professional ac-tors. They portrayed small-town folks who had previously voted Liberal but with the help of a "Mr. Sage" were switching to Bennett and the Conservatives. The radio plays were as clever as they were cruel. They were ostensibly non-partisan, quite articulate, and used value-laden language and issues of the heart to attack Mackenzie King while linking support for Bennett with intelligence, confidence, loyalty, and patriot-ism. The first two plays aired in September in vote-rich Ontario and Quebec. Their terrific popularity led to the last four being nationally broadcast. A short excerpt from one of the plays is indicative of them all. At one point Sage told his friend Bill that he had been staying with his brother-in-law in Quebec and had heard of Liberal tactics during the war. He explained, "Mr. King's henchmen used to call up the farmers and their wives in the early hours of the morning and tell them their sons would be conscripted for war if they voted against King." Sage then went on to show disgust over the Beauharnois scandal. "Yes, Bill—over $700,000—and that's from the man who wants to be Prime Minister of Canada. Can you beat it?"[73]

Never during any of the broadcasts was it mentioned that the plays were produced by and for the Conservative Party. Mackenzie King's anger with the Mr. Sage dramas led him to redraw the mandate of the CRBC and turn it into the CBC in 1936. One of the new rules banned political dramatizations but allowed time for free political broadcasts for all par-ties with the proviso that the party affiliation be clearly stated at the end of each segment.[74]

But while radio was important it was also expensive and neither the Liberals nor the Conservatives had the money that they had employed in 1930. As the campaigns progressed, however, both parties managed to raise not the funds they would have liked but at least the funds they needed.[75] While Bennett spent some of his own money in the campaign, he did not lay out anywhere near what he had five years previously. Of the dollars he did take from his own pocket most went to his own riding and to the ridings of other Alberta candidates.[76]

That there was money available, however, did not mean that the Con-servative Party efficiently used it.[77] Provincial directors still complained about bad communications and a lack of funds. In the latter stages of the campaign some Conservative radio spots were cancelled, some ads pulled, and two mailings stopped due to a lack of money.

In the campaign's last two weeks, with running for office and running the government competing for Bennett's focus, world events intruded. Throughout his term, Bennett had acted as his own external affairs minister and essentially left most day-to-day operations to the very capable O. D. Skelton and his small but able staff. This arrangement was a reasonable reflection of the fact that Canada's foreign service was tiny and its foreign policy still largely determined by Britain. Even this degree of independent Canadian action on the world stage was more than many of Bennett's cabinet colleagues wanted when in 1930 they had pressured him to do away with the External Affairs department altogether. Bennett had insisted that it remain and had prevailed.[78]

The first major international crisis with which Bennett had to deal was Japan's 1931 invasion of Manchuria. The blatant expression of Japan's desire to create a Pacific empire represented the real first shots of the Second World War. If one abandons a Eurocentric view of that epic struggle, then it was already eight years old by the time Hitler's blitzkrieg swept into Poland. Japan's attack on China led directly to Pearl Harbour, the fall of Hong Kong, and eventually to the horrors of Hiroshima and Nagasaki. Japan's initial aggressiveness posed a problem for the League of Nations, for both it and China were members and there was a reluctance to antagonize either. There was subtle pressure exerted by member states in a futile effort to have Japan withdraw, but it was ignored.

At that point, a consensus began to develop for imposing economic sanctions on Japan. Skelton supported sanctions but Bennett had said no. He wanted Britain to take the lead and have Canada follow. In December 1931, Secretary of State Cahan spoke at the League on behalf of Canada and echoed the empty words of the British and all other delegations in saying that Japan had no desire to permanently occupy Manchuria and that the League's interfering would only complicate matters and possibly prolong Japan's presence there. The League dithered. Weak sanctions were eventually imposed but to no effect. Japan moved on Manchuria and later the world slept as Nanking was raped.

Bennett's second major international crisis came in early October 1935, just days before the Canadian election. The League of Nations, and through it Canada, was again asked to stand up to aggression. Benito Mussolini, a barrel-chested former teacher and newspaperman, had swaggered his way to power in Rome in 1922. It was he who had established fascism as an ideology based on fear and constant warfare against seen and unseen foreign and domestic enemies. He had even given it its name. Mussolini's foreign adventures were partly an attempt to regain the glory of ancient Rome with the establishment of a new Italian empire, and partly an expression of his elephantine ego. Italy invaded Ethiopia, then called Abyssinia. Ragtag Ethiopians, armed with nothing but spears, antiquated rifles, and a faith in their emperor, the charismatic Haile Selassie, charged 400,000 Italian infantry, supported by modern tanks and aircraft. Their bold attempts at defence were as brave as they were foolhardy. They didn't have a chance. Mussolini had gambled that the League of Nations, and through it the world community, would talk but do nothing. He was right.

Howard Ferguson, Canada's head of the High Commission in London, and Dr. W. A. Riddell, Canada's representative at the League, both cabled Ottawa asking for direction. The League was contemplating sanctions against Italy that would have ended their supply of oil and thus the war. They needed to know how Canada was to vote. Mackenzie King expressed a lack of trust in Canada's representatives at the League and said they should agree to nothing until parliament could decide. Bennett agreed and so instructed Skelton, who notified Ferguson and Riddell. The problem was that the prime minister and cabinet were engaged in the election campaign and Parliament had been dissolved.

Riddell quite accurately predicted that Hungary and Austria would probably abstain but that all others would support the imposition of sanctions. Riddell also predicted that Canada would be asked to sit on a committee to investigate and advise the League on questions related to sanctions. Skelton summarized Riddell's report in a cable to Bennett and advised that Canada should not support sanctions or become a member of the committee. Bennett initially disagreed, believing the timid response to Japanese aggression in 1931 had been wrong, and that the world needed to finally and firmly stand up to a bully. But he relented, and accepted Skelton's advice. With the election less than a week away, Bennett ordered Riddell to essentially stall for time until a new Canadian parliament had been sworn in. Canada should serve on the committee if asked but not actively seek membership. Then, whether on the committee or not, Riddell was to simply refuse to vote, or abstain, or do anything else he could to avoid establishing a Canadian position regarding sanctions.[79]

Canada was indeed offered membership on one of two committees and Riddell, frustrated by Bennett's refusal to support the sanctions he believed necessary, somewhat disingenuously reported that there was no longer an option but to become a member of the sanctions committee. The committee moved quickly to explore the possibility of imposing oil sanctions on Italy and lifting the arms embargo that had been imposed on Ethiopia. Again Riddell cabled Ottawa, and in a somewhat more insistent tone asked for direction. He was again told to stall.

The day before Canadians were to go to the polls Bennett changed his mind. He ordered that Riddell be cabled in Geneva and that when the issue came to a vote, Canada should support sanctions.[80] It was the lawyer as much as the diplomat in Bennett who had finally reasoned that Canada had signed the covenant that had created the League of Nations in the first place and that since Italy, another signatory, was clearly in violation of that covenant, it was incumbent upon Canada to take a role in punishing Italy.

The next day, Bennett's Conservatives were defeated. Ferguson resigned and Riddell was told that there would be no further instructions coming from Ottawa. The government's defeat put Riddell in an impossible position. He was feeling enormous pressure at Geneva and had to do something. He operated according to his last instructions, which had been to support sanctions. Riddell decided, quite on his own, to propose to the committee that the League's cutting off Italy's oil would be the most effective economic punishment. The idea was adopted and dubbed the "Canadian proposal."

Upon taking office, Mackenzie King had the option of maintaining support for the League and the Canadian proposal that Bennett had encouraged and Riddell had created. But he looked at the Catholic-based support that Italy enjoyed in Quebec and the divided public opinion in the rest of the country and decided that politics mattered more than principle. With political advice from Quebec's respected Ernest Lapointe, and with a somewhat one-sided memo from Skelton, the prime minister announced a change in Canada's policy. He publicly and internationally embarrassed Riddell and Canada by stating that Canada's spokesperson had acted without instruction and so Canada was rescinding its support for sanctions.[81] The decision was another small nail in the League of Nations' coffin.

Months later, Mackenzie King went to Geneva and in a speech at the League of Nations stated that it was Canada's belief that the organization should only ever seek to mediate world problems and should never take actions that punished members. Mackenzie King's words, along with the League's feckless response to Mussolini, demonstrated that the League was doomed. The noble idea at its core would rise again in San Francisco with the birth of the United Nations. It was an idea that Bennett tried—too late and with too little, but at least finally— to support.

But this was in the future. Even while consulting with Finlayson, Skelton, and Riddell, and deciding Canadian policy regarding Italy and the League, Bennett had maintained a punishing pace on the hustings. At the campaign's end, a tired Bennett offered a nonetheless typically roaring speech at a large and well-attended rally at Toronto's Maple Leaf Gardens. His last speech of the campaign took place in Belleville. With that the work was over. There was nothing left to do but board the train for Ottawa to rest and await the verdict.

ELECTION DAY

Election Day dawned with good weather almost everywhere. Seventy-five per cent of eligible voters found their way to the polls. Bennett listened to the radio in his East Block office. There were no reporters. There were no cameras. He was accompanied only by Mildred, whose husband the diplomat diplomatically stayed in Washington. The results arrived one time zone at a time. They were dispiriting. Before Manitoba results were announced, and with British Columbians still voting, the verdict was unequivocal. Bennett's Liberal-Conservatives had been demolished and Mackenzie King's Liberals would win a majority.

Bennett kept track of the results at his desk and noted that twelve of eighteen Conservative cabinet ministers had lost their seats. He was pleased to notch his own riding in the win column but chagrined that Stevens had won his seat as well. The only positive in that victory, for Bennett, was that Stevens was the only successful Reconstruction Party candidate.

When all the counting was done, the magnitude of Bennett's loss began to sink in. Mackenzie King's Liberals had won 173 seats, which was up from 90 in 1930, while Bennett's Conservatives had their count shrink from 134 to only 39. Most of the party's support came from British Columbia, southern Ontario, and the English-speaking parts of Montreal. The party had won only one seat in New Brunswick, Saskatchewan, and Manitoba, and Bennett's in Alberta. The party was skunked in PEI and Nova Scotia. The weakness in support among francophones that had been felt throughout Bennett's administration was reflected in his party's not winning a single contest in a predominantly French-speaking riding. The party lost popular support in both urban and rural ridings. By any measure, it was the worst defeat in the party's history. It would not be outdone until Kim Campbell led the party to only two seats in 1993.

1935 Election—Seat Results

Liberal	173
Liberal Conservative	39
Social Credit	17
CCF	7
Independent Liberal	5
Liberal Progressive	2
Reconstruction	1
Independent Conservative	1

The seat numbers were one thing, but, as is often the case, the popular vote told a different story. The Conservative Party's popular vote had crashed from 49 per cent in 1930 to 29.8 per cent. However, the Liberals' popular vote in 1930 had been 43.9 per cent and in 1935 the party captured only 44.4 per cent. These figures make it clear that while voters did indeed abandon Bennett, they had not moved to Mackenzie King. A full 25.8 per cent of the Canadian electorate had placed their X beside a candidate from one of the small protest parties—more than in 1930. The CCF had captured 8.9 per cent of the popular vote, quite impressive when one considers that it was but two years old. The other parties were in the single digits. In total, 56 per cent of Canadians had voted for the Conservatives or another party of the left. The ideas did not lose— Bennett's Conservatives did.

But seats dictate power in Ottawa, and Mackenzie King had won a majority. He was anything but magnanimous in victory and, in fact, continued to sell his campaign theme with overblown hyperbole. He called the election a "victory for democracy" and "an end to one-man government, mistaken policies and autocratic leadership . . . it proclaims the end of the superman idea."[82] It was junk, of course, but it didn't matter. The only thing worse than a sore loser is a sore winner.

Bennett had worked exceptionally hard throughout the campaign. At each event he spoke powerfully and well. He met hecklers everywhere he went but he swatted them like flies, drawing applause for his quick wit and good humour. The positive fighting spirit that Bennett brought to the campaign and maintained even in the face of such monstrous adversity was noted by all.

But while he kept his spirits high and campaigned magnificently, he had seen the writing on the wall. The anti-Conservative and anti-Bennett feelings in the country were palpable. He felt them, but had trouble understanding them. Late in the campaign, Bennett had found himself back home in Calgary and took time to enjoy a leisurely dinner at the Palliser Hotel. He bumped into an old friend named Frank Holloway who naturally asked how the campaign was going. Bennett looked down and in a nearly inaudible voice had whispered, "I wouldn't say this to anyone, Frank, but I think we've lost. And one man has crucified the party: Stevens."[83] In case one might conclude that it was the dark opinion of a man understandably tired and commenting from the depths of the exhausting rigours of the gruelling campaign, one is left to consider a letter Bennett wrote a full year later, after having had time to rest and reflect. He wrote of Stevens, "Perhaps one might be able to use the words of Balfour regarding Peel: 'He committed the unforgivable sin; he broke up his party.'"[84]

Bennett was not alone in that assessment. Howard Ferguson wrote to Beaverbrook that he too blamed Stevens for the loss. He estimated that Stevens and his Reconstruction candidates stole between 75 to 100 seats.[85]

A careful analysis, however, supports neither Ferguson nor Bennett. In offering Canadians his Reconstruction Party candidates, Stevens no doubt siphoned votes that might well have gone to the Conservatives. However, even if every single Reconstruction vote is added to the Conservative total, the two add up to less than the number won by the Liberals. Of course in the "first past the post" Canadian electoral system it is the individual riding numbers that count. The numbers indicate that in twenty-five Ontario ridings, seven in Quebec, five in Nova Scotia, three in New Brunswick, three more in B.C., and one in Saskatchewan, a combined Conservative and Reconstruction vote would have defeated Liberal candidates. These ridings would have added another 48 seats to the Conservative total, bringing it to 88, which is significant. But if the 48 is added to the Conservatives and subtracted from the Liberals, the Liberals would still have won 123 seats. If everything else had remained equal, the Liberals would still have formed the government. Bennett still would have lost.

Perhaps a better assessment of Stevens's effect on Bennett and the Conservatives' defeat would be in terms of factors that cannot be empirically measured. One can consider the effects of the split in the Conservative Party in terms of people's perception of the party as a unified organization existing to give voice to their needs and concerns. If the party could not run itself, some must have asked, how can we trust it to run the country? Further, one must take into account the number of grassroots volunteers and contributions of money and goodwill that were drawn from the party by the Bennett-Stevens rift. And given the state of the Conservative Party organization, this siphoning was something that was ill afforded.

Bennett was not blind to these numbers and ideas. Neither was he so bitter as to refuse to see nuance. He was, in fact, willing to shoulder some of the responsibility for the loss. As he confided to former Conservative MP Brigadier-General A. E. Ross three years after the election, "I am not unaware of my own limitations. I have made many mistakes, but I served this country as disinterestedly as any man who ever occupied public office, and I never expected more than loyalty from those with whom I was associated. That I did not receive it may perhaps be a criticism of myself."[86]

The Ross letter reveals that beyond the myriad problems he faced when entering the campaign, and even when factoring Stevens into the mix, there was another electoral factor—Bennett himself. Every Canadian knew the "Iron Heel" he had shown the On to Ottawa trekkers and knew of those he had imprisoned and deported with Section 98. All knew the cartoon image of Bennett as the voice of big business despite all that belied it. Mackenzie King had kept the canard of the one-man government alive. And perhaps most damning of all, Canadians knew what Bennett buggies were, and Bennett blankets, and Bennett coffee, and more, and more. After sweeping into power with promises to "end unemployment or perish" and to "blast" his way into world markets and thus back to prosperity, the five years in which he had been prime minister were harder than anyone could ever remember. Statistics showed that by the fall of 1935 things were getting better, but like all recoveries the process was long and slow with many areas of the country yet to feel its warm rays. Employment is a lagging indicator in any economic recovery and where jobs remain absent, a respect for political leaders is seldom present. In hard times, the leader is always blamed; and Bennett was. Perhaps it was not even Bennett's Conservatives that had lost. Perhaps it was just Bennett himself, who in a similarly unfair Mulroney-like fashion had come to personify all that Canadians found wrong with the government, politics, and the country in general.

Bennett understood his role in the defeat. In a reflective letter he wrote to G. H. Clarke, a Queen's University professor, only a month after the election, he explained people voting against him as the only way that they had available to express their anger at the general conditions of the day. He was willing, he suggested, to be the country's punching bag, and proud that he had not taken the coward's way out and left the leadership before the election.[87]

But even after time granted him the gift of distance and reflection and with his willingness to at least shoulder a portion of the blame for his party's defeat, Bennett retained a belief that Stevens was the villain of the piece. He went to his grave convinced that, had members of the party stood up to Stevens, the party would have been in much better shape going into the 1935 election and quite possibly would have won. He insisted to many that he saw Stevens's actions, as not a betrayal of him personally but of the party itself. The election was lost because the party was wrecked by Stevens's actions, and that destruction was the fault not only of him but also of those party members who encouraged or at least allowed him to undertake his devastating moves.[88]

A fascinating "what if" in Canadian history is to ponder whether the Conservatives would have fared better had Bennett resigned in 1934. Stevens no doubt would have ascended to the leadership, the party split would not have happened and so all that the Reconstruction experiment took from the Conservatives would have remained in that camp. With Stevens as the leader, however, the party would have no doubt moved even further from the Tory left to the populist left and perhaps caused a split with Cahan and those on the right wing of the party. The election would have seen the same crowded field on the ideological left, with Mackenzie King still allowed that open right lane to victory. If Stevens had started to organize the party in late 1934 it is by no means certain that he would have had enough time. Further, and perhaps most importantly, even with Bennett gone the Conservatives might still have borne the brunt of the blame for the five worst years of the long depression. Or, perhaps Stevens would have united the Canadian left—as Peter MacKay and Stephen Harper later united the right—and under his fresh leadership kept votes from shifting to the small parties that shared so many of his party's ideas. Perhaps.

But all of this speculation is moot. Not only did Bennett not resign, he was proud of the fact that he had remained at the helm. Shortly after the election he wrote to Robert Borden, "I will be responsible for the disaster that has overtaken our Party. I went down with the ship and did not seek to evade punishment."[89]

And punished he was. Richard Bedford Bennett had dreamt his whole life of being the prime minister, and the Canadian people, in their ultimate wisdom, had taken that dream from him. Bennett was sixty-five years old. What was a man who had reached retirement age and accomplished every dream he had ever dreamt to do next?

CHAPTER NINE

THE FINAL YEARS

1935–1947

D IFFERENT PEOPLE REACT differently to defeat. But the grief of rejection often reveals personality and character as much or perhaps even more than the joy of victory. Trudeau pitted his strength against nature on a long canoe trip, and returned tanned, relaxed, and bearded. Macdonald binged and was not seen for weeks. If anyone had expected Bennett to shamefully skulk away after his October defeat they would have been disappointed. He was saddened but not immobilized. He still had work to do and so he got to it.

Bennett dictated letters to all victorious and defeated candidates and to those who had helped in the campaign. He wrote personal notes to many others. He returned to Calgary where he tended to business matters. Bennett's mother would have been proud to hear him say to a number of those who inquired that he was carrying on in public life due to "a sense of duty."[1] Without missing a step, Bennett was charging into the next phase of his life and career with the same verve, focus, and determined effort that he had brought to all others.

Bennett returned to Ottawa for the opening of Parliament on October 23, 1935, just nine days after the election. He demonstrated that he had learned an important lesson in defeat when he ordered that the national party office remain open. Jane Denison was appointed national director. With no staff and an annual budget of only $4,000, she worked exceptionally hard. She kept the party lists up to date, improved communications with provincial offices, which also stayed operational, and oversaw a number of mailings to party faithfuls and newspapers.

Denison also produced new issues of the *Canadian*.

More could have been done at the national level but Bennett argued that the party should strive to organize itself from the grassroots up. Work should begin, he said, at the constituency level, helped by provincial offices. Only when they became strong should substantive money and effort be devoted to the national office. He reasoned that with a majority government in Ottawa there would be no federal election for at least four years, where there would be an election in nearly every province in the next three.[2]

While the plan had merit it would have been bolstered had Bennett supported it by travelling the country to help with the implementation. But he did not. Fundraisers could have been organized. They were not. Morale-boosting rallies for volunteers, possible donors, and potential candidates could have been staged. They were not, either. Bennett received a number of letters from provincial party leaders and rank-and-file members that bemoaned the sorry state of the party in their part of the country. But he stayed in Ottawa. While pouring himself into his responsibilities and appearing to colleagues and the public as still burning with the old passion and drive, he confided to friends that he was tired. Perhaps the man who had worked for so long and so hard, suffered a heart attack just months before, and still shouldered the responsibilities of various businesses and the leadership of the official opposition deserved a break.

While in Ottawa, he remained seated on his wallet. He made it clear that he would no longer be funding party operations from his personal fortune. This decision created problems as the party had ended the 1935 campaign $170,000 in debt. Bennett encouraged Denison and provincial directors to undertake fundraising initiatives that would be essential for the party's future. But, as in the past, he refused to personally participate. He was adamant that he would never take part in the fundraising dinners that had become a new and lucrative practice for the Liberals.[3]

While leaving responsibility for the day-to-day party organization and operation to others, Bennett took a sincere personal interest in his post as leader of His Majesty's Loyal Opposition. He explained his dedicated work as the most important person on the opposition benches in a letter, in which he wrote, "Democracy is only possible if in Parliament there is an opposition with some knowledge of public questions, and even though small in numbers, with courage to criticise measures that may be submitted."[4]

The Conservative caucus that he led was drastically different from the one he had known as prime minister. First, of course, was that there were only thirty-nine members. Second, nearly all of his former cabinet colleagues—who had taken much of the workload and upon whom he could depend for sage advice—were gone. Those remaining arrived fatigued, while warhorses such as Perley and Cahan were over seventy and showing their age. The caucus was predominantly young men who were keen but inexperienced. Although of dubious health and no longer a young man, Bennett remained the hardest working and most able of the bunch. His energy and dominance over the caucus was evident; he was in the House every day and on his feet for every issue. He spoke far more than any of his younger colleagues. Hansard shows extended passages of his extemporaneous remarks posing questions, raising points, and presenting arguments. Together they demonstrate that his passion and wordsmith skills were as fervent and impressive as at any time in his career.

His domination of the small caucus and his towering presence in the House disturbed some Conservative MPs and revived the accusation of one-man rule. Bennett received a good deal of advice regarding the need to delegate. A letter from Conservative MP Wilfrid Heighington related well the point made by many. Heighington wrote,

> . . . whether you like it or not, you must appreciate the fact that there is need for consultation with those in the lesser ranks of the party's activities who perhaps could not only assist you in the performance of your duties but help you guide the party to a prosperous future. . . . I am steadfastly behind you and the Conservative party. I only write to ask you please to consult those who share with you the future of the party and to clear yourself of the charge, which I feel is all too justly made, that you are conducting the destinies of the party on your own, disregarding those who have nothing but personal goodwill towards you and who share all your hopes and expectations for the ultimate triumph of our party.[5]

The response to Heighington's rather courteous and constructive criticism betrays much about both Bennett's thin skin and his still-broad network of reliable political informants. He replied that he indeed consulted broadly, since responses to all bills were considered in caucus and all members encouraged to state their views. Further, he argued, he also sought the views of friends of the party outside caucus. He then must have stung Heighington by noting that he was unable, as opposition leader, to play any role in helping him to obtain the appointment that he had heard the MP had been recently seeking. Having wounded his correspondent by impugning his motives, Bennett then swooped in for the kill. The charge that he ran the party without consultation, he wrote, was groundless and the spreading of such rumours circulated only by those with sinister purposes.[6]

Bennett continued to rise in the House nearly every day. He showed sincere consternation for Liberal attempts to unfairly blame his administration for problems that Mackenzie King was facing, for taking credit for legislation created by his government, and, most often the case, for offering a bill that contradicted something that his government had done. In many cases he seemed to be defending old ideas due to a sense of pride rather than a careful reading of the political landscape or with an eye to increasing the political popularity of his party. For instance, he even stood to attack Mackenzie King's rescinding the widely despised Section 98 of the Criminal Code and to decry the closing of the hugely unpopular relief camps. Simply remaining quiet while Mackenzie King made the changes would have been the politically wise thing to do. But he spoke up—over and over again. As noted by Bennett biographer Peter Waite, "Bennett scorned hypocrisy. He had the dangerous habit of saying what he really thought. What drove Bennett was his own mind, not what others thought."[7]

BENNETT'S LONG SHADOW

Within two weeks of coming to office, on November 4, 1935, Prime Minister Mackenzie King referred all of Bennett's New Deal legislation from the previous parliamentary session to the Supreme Court. The court's decision would colour Bennett's legacy.

In bringing the reformist legislation to the House that spring, Bennett had reasoned that because, collectively, the acts were based on a broad interpretation of the federal government's constitutional power, they would likely be challenged. His Minimum Wages Act, Employment and Social Insurance Act, Natural Products Marketing Act, and Hours of Work Act all contained provisions and promised regulations that moved into provincial areas of jurisdiction. He had already seen many of Roosevelt's New Deal programs crash against the wall of the U.S. Supreme Court and get torn asunder due to the federal government overstepping its constitutional bounds. Bennett, of course, was a skilled lawyer and had argued cases before the Supreme Court and the Judicial Committee of the Privy Council; he was confident that a broad interpretation would break his way. He had said when introducing the legislation that the federal government's right to act was based upon its constitutional obligation to provide peace, order, and good government, and upon its international treaty obligations to protect the rights of labour.[8]

The Canadian Supreme Court, however, disagreed. It found much of the New Deal legislation *ultra vires* due primarily to the federal government infringing on provincial property and civil rights as listed in the British North America Act's Section 92. Bennett followed the case quite closely. Every day, Finlayson provided detailed accounts of the intricacies of the arguments being made. He noted especially the persuasiveness of Ontario chief justice Newton Rowell and respected Quebec constitutional lawyer Louis St. Laurent, both Liberal and both destined to play large roles in the country's future, who were arguing the federal government's case. Bennett predicted that all the legislation would stand. Both he and Finlayson were surprised when the Supreme Court ruled against the government.[9]

Mackenzie King could have let the case die, but he recognized that the issues at stake were actually of greater importance than the legislation itself and so he took the next step and referred it all to the Judicial Committee of the Privy Council. On January 28, 1937, the council supported the Supreme Court by deeming nearly all of the New Deal legislation *ultra vires*. It argued that since the Depression was not a national emergency, the federal government had no right to use its treaty-making powers or the peace, order, and good government clause as justification for so broadly interpreting its powers under Section 91. The Farmer's Creditors Arrangement Act was the only law left untouched. The Privy Council's decision reversed the trend toward centralizing political power in Canada that it had established with the radio and aviation cases and upon which Bennett had relied.

The decision angered Bennett. He believed that it flew in the face of precedent, and altered the court's views on the relationship between the federal government and the provinces. He said that the decision further emasculated the federal government by destroying its jurisdiction with respect to treaties in a way that embarrassed the country and weakened future governments.[10]

Bennett was not overreacting. The decisions of the Canadian Supreme Court and the Privy Council were indeed momentous. Two freight trains, each representing a different vision of the country, had for years been charging toward each other. The judicial review of Bennett's New Deal package of legislation invited a collision of those trains, and the crash would change Canada.

The first of those trains contained arguments regarding Canada's ability to decide legal and constitutional matters for itself. The Canadian Supreme Court had been established in 1877, but in the 1930s its decisions could still be appealed to London's Judicial Committee of the Privy Council. Criticism of the Privy Council's power had been growing in Canada for some time and had reached a fever pitch in the 1920s. Manitoba's Justice A. C. Galt was among those in the Canadian legal community who argued that the reason for the institution's waning respect was in its having overturned twenty Canadian Supreme Court decisions from 1911 to 1921.[11] The issue could be seen as concomitant with the country's burgeoning national pride. The events of the 1930s had turned the developing consensus into a critical mass of scholars, lawyers, and others in civil society insisting that the national government simply had to have the constitutional power it needed to respond to a national crisis in a nationally unified way.

The Privy Council's overturning so much of Bennett's legislation rallied those who argued that the council had overstepped its bounds again. Many said that it had been too narrow and formalistic in its interpretation and—not for the first time, but more fervently than ever—should be done away with once and for all. In a radio address that saw excerpts published in mainstream newspapers across the country, University of Manitoba president Sidney Smith captured the mood of the legal community, and of a growing number of Canadians, when he said,

It does appear that we cannot expect from the Privy Council an interpretation of the constitution that will enable the Dominion to take over some of the social services and the regulations of industrial activities which the provincial legislatures, with insufficient revenue, are unable to undertake [due to its] narrow legalism.[12]

Smith's words, and similar arguments that were being made across the land, vindicated Bennett's broad and centralist interpretation of the constitution and the legislative package upon which it had been based. A group of influential lawyers and university professors calling themselves the Canadian Legal Realist Movement was formed in 1937. It dedicated itself to ending the Privy Council's power in Canada. More articles were written in scholarly journals and the mainstream press, and many letters arrived on the desks of parliamentarians arguing that with the quashing of Bennett's New Deal legislation, the Privy Council had proven once and for all that it did not understand the unique needs of Canadians.

Despite his feelings for Britain and his belief in the importance of the emotional ties that Canada had to its mother country, Bennett agreed with the chorus of those demanding an end to the Privy Council's power. In a 1938 letter to Regina's F. W. Turnbull, he wrote that the Privy Council's jurisdiction over Canadian legal decisions must end. Bennett observed, "Of course, to permit a body of men in England to make a constitution for us is absurd."[13]

But the Privy Council's power to overturn decisions of the Canadian Supreme Court would not end quickly. It was not until 1949 that the Canadian Supreme Court became Canada's court of last resort and the country stepped one more rung up the ladder toward constitutional maturity. Bennett's New Deal legislation had played a role in advancing the debate that led to that important step.

The second freight train that was smoking its way forward carried questions regarding a fundamental vision of Canada as a nation-state. Macdonald and the others ensconced in Charlottetown and Quebec City had based their work on the conservative philosophies of Edmund Burke and their observations of the Americans, who were at that moment ripping themselves apart in a civil war fought essentially over the issue of states' rights. These influences led Macdonald and the Canadian

founders to locate predominant state power with the federal government. Macdonald included an introductory statement in the BNA Act's
Section 91 list of federal powers. It stated that Parliament would be
responsible for the "Peace, Order and Good Government of Canada, in
relation to all Matters not coming within the classes of the Subject of
this Act assigned exclusively to the Legislature of the Provinces."[14] The
phrase was meant to say that the federal government would assume
responsibility for any area of jurisdiction that might arise later. The specific powers listed in Sections 91 and 92 were simply illustrative of the
types of areas that the two levels of government could tend to in carrying out their responsibilities.

However, beginning shortly after Confederation, in decision after
decision, the Privy Council had sided with whatever province brought
questions to its bench. In case after case, it separated the phrase from
the list of powers that followed and decided that the items in the list
could not be superseded by it.[15] By the late 1920s, the teeter-totter of
power had shifted so that the clout of the federal government had declined precipitously as that of the provinces had risen.

Macdonald would have wept. Bennett got mad. He believed that for
the country to operate efficiently and the government effectively, especially in a time of crisis, the federal government needed all the power
that Macdonald had intended for it. Bennett worried that so much power had devolved to the provinces that the federal government had been
emasculated and left unable to deal with the economic crisis at hand.
The twin arguments that he had laid out in January 1935 were his rallying call to that interpretation. Bennett realized that while the provinces
had constitutional authority for a number of social responsibilities—
such as education, social assistance, and labour—their financial powers
to raise money did not match those responsibilities. The Depression had
shone a light on the disparity between the provinces' social responsibilities, as allowed by the British court's narrow constitutional decisions,
and their financial capacity, as dictated by economic reality. The many
programs that Bennett had instituted, such as direct emergency relief,
had been his reaction to that disparity. In 1930, only British Columbia
and Prince Edward Island collected taxes on corporations, but by the
Depression's end all nine did. Some introduced income taxes and others
gasoline taxes, but all those efforts and more had proven inadequate.

The federal government, in the meantime, was able to raise significant revenue through corporate taxes, income taxes, excise taxes, and its sales tax, which went from 1 to 8 per cent. It also had a greater capacity to take on debt and run deficits to meet temporary challenges and then, through various programs, ship that money right back to the provinces.

Bennett wrote to the editor of *Maclean's* in December 1935, stating that he wished he could have been better at explaining the constitutional and fiscal problems that the country faced and the solutions that he had been offering. He described the problems Canada would face if it did not soon rectify the issue of the constitutional separation of federal and provincial powers in a responsible fashion. In a statement that could have been written by prime ministers from Trudeau to the current occupant of the Sussex Drive mansion, Bennett warned, ". . . unless firm action is taken in the way of bringing home to the Provincial Governments a sense of their own responsibility, we will have Federal financial obligation with local authorities expending the money, without regard to how it may be obtained."[16]

The Privy Council's overturning of the New Deal legislation said that Macdonald and Bennett were wrong. The centralist view was wrong. Its decision was welcomed by those adhering to the compact thesis. It postulated a system of devolved power and held that the provinces must constantly be wary of any federal intrusion into their jurisdictions. Those advocating that point of view see Canada as a treaty or compact between provinces. Prime Minister Joe Clark supported this view when he called Canada "a community of communities." Every provincial premier from René Lévesque to Ralph Klein who has railed against federal power sees the country this way. In 2001, before becoming prime minister, Stephen Harper had shown himself to be a supporter of this school when he signed a letter supporting the building of a "fire-wall" around his home province of Alberta. Pierre Trudeau, on the other hand, channelled Sir John and Bennett when he warned that the federal government's role in such a country would be that of playing head waiter to the provinces. He fought for the centralist vision while in office, and then afterwards with his carefully reasoned and influential opposition to the compact thesis that lay at the heart of Prime Minister Mulroney's Meech Lake Accords and Charlottetown Amendments.

The two trains met. By the late 1930s, a growing number of influential

Canadians had become tired of the provinces jealously guarding constitutional responsibilities while being unable to meet them. And they were quite sick of the empire striking back. In August 1937, with the full support of opposition leader Bennett, Prime Minister Mackenzie King created the Royal Commission on Dominion-Provincial Relations. It was first chaired by Ontario chief justice Newton Rowell, and when he resigned due to illness, by constitutional law professor Joseph Sirois—it became commonly known as the Rowell-Sirois Commission. Its mandate was to examine political decisions made during the Depression and the constitutional arguments rendered regarding Bennett's New Deal legislation. It would determine if the distribution of powers as constituted enabled the federal system to fulfill its obligations to Canadians while promoting national unity. For three years the commissioners travelled widely and consulted broadly.

The Rowell-Sirois Report was a stunning repudiation of the compact thesis and afforded nearly unqualified support for the centralist view that Bennett had espoused throughout his career and that informed his New Deal legislation. The report stated that for Canada to create a modern society in a responsible way, it must adopt a more centralist constitutional approach to power sharing. The federal government simply had to have the jurisdictional powers needed to enact the social and economic policies and programs that a modern society demanded and Canadians deserved. As Bennett had said in word and deed, constitutional powers must be shifted, or at least more broadly interpreted, so that a match could be forged between social responsibilities and fiscal capacity. The wide disparity in the wealth of provinces, the report argued, meant that the power to raise revenue and thereby meet those responsibilities must rest with the federal government. In other words, the report suggested that in terms of what Bennett had been trying to do with his economic and social policies based on his centralist vision of the country, he had been right.

One of the recommendations made by the Rowell-Sirois Report was that the federal government be afforded the responsibility for providing relief to the unemployed. In 1940, Mackenzie King acted on the recommendation. A constitutional amendment was made, and a federally operated unemployment insurance program was instituted. It was based entirely on the program that Bennett had created.

In January 1941, Mackenzie King convened a federal-provincial conference to discuss the report more fully. As one might have expected, provincial premiers were loath to surrender any power. The commissioners may have smiled when the richest provinces declared themselves most vehemently opposed to even discussing constitutional changes such as the report suggested, but the poorest—Saskatchewan, PEI, and Manitoba—were quite willing to have the federal government assume more fiscal powers and to be the recipients of more financial aid. Most were frustrated by the conference, although there was progress on unemployment insurance. It took the Second World War, and the need for the federal government to take the power needed to respond to that new crisis, to change minds. Slowly, the report's recommendations were adopted and the centralist view of Canada that Bennett had espoused came to form the collective consensus nearly everywhere for two generations.

As the struggle toward the adoption of an altered vision of Canada was moving apace, Bennett's wise and visionary leadership should have become apparent. The two trains became one with the federal government its engineer. Canada moved forward with an enhanced ability to decide its own constitutional progress and with greater federal power to meet the burgeoning needs of an increasingly urban, complex, and vibrant country. Esteemed historian Frank Underhill later reflected on the consensus among those analyzing Bennett's New Deal, and the crucial role it played in this transformation, and noted, "It inspired all subsequent social legislation."[17]

RESIGNATION

In the spring of 1937, London was the place to be. On the evening of May 11, thousands of enthusiastic monarchists spent the night in Trafalgar Square so that they would not miss a thing. The occasion was the coronation of King George VI. The event was rather unexpected, as King Edward VIII had taken the throne after the death of his father just the previous December. But he had announced his abdication in a dramatic radio address, explaining that he could not carry out his responsibilities as sovereign without the woman he loved. For the king to marry a divorced woman, and an American at that, was simply unimaginable. He and Mrs. Wallis Simpson left to live a life of quiet contemplation and Bennett left to attend the lavish ceremony.

Accompanied as always by Mildred, Bennett found respite on the ship. He was merely one among a large contingent of Canadians, and Prime Minister Mackenzie King naturally drew more attention. But there was a new king and a blushing young Queen Elizabeth to be celebrated in royal and spectacular fashion at Westminster Abbey. Again Bennett and Mildred enjoyed the theatre and the magnificent shopping that London had to offer. He also travelled to Germany to consult a world-famous heart specialist. After a thorough examination, the doctor told him that he was fine but that he should contemplate a quieter life, away from the stresses of political leadership. Bennett enjoyed a taste of that life with another extended stay at Beaverbrook's estate. It was then off on an invigorating world tour of a number of Commonwealth countries, including Australia, New Zealand, and South Africa. Bennett later spoke of being most impressed with New Zealand and of being proud to see loyalty to the Commonwealth everywhere. South Africa, however, disturbed him. He warned of the dangers of racism and said that his experience there reminded him of the virtues of diversity.[18]

With Bennett absent from the country, the knives came out. There was great speculation about his political future and much of it was fuelled by Conservative senator John Haig who, without Bennett's knowledge, had spoken in Winnipeg about the Conservative leader's intention to soon step down. He had not a clue what he was talking about. The speech nonetheless set backrooms and the chattering class chattering.

Bennett had not made a decision about his political future, but news of Haig's speech, which reached him in England, persuaded him to ruminate on the issue. He added fuel to the fire of speculation by making broad hints to a number of British correspondents about his belief that a younger man should perhaps take up the leadership of the party. Another point made casually to a number of correspondents, including to such important party supporters as the president of the Crown Life Insurance Company, was that he had grown physically and emotionally tired of public life. He wrote, "At my age I have no ambition to be Prime Minster again and I have a clear appreciation of the thanklessness of the task in which I was for so long engaged."[19]

As news that he was considering resigning swept back across the

Atlantic to Canadian newspapers, Bennett felt great pressure from individuals, business people, and even unions, complimenting him on his service to his country and encouraging him to stay. He responded to each politely. A short sentence in one letter seemed to sum up all of the well-conceived and carefully expressed reasons for his impending decision. To a correspondent in Bolton, Ontario, Bennett admitted, "I am tired."[20]

But he was rejuvenated by his holiday and by so many friends and supporters encouraging him to remain at his post. Shortly after his return he told all who asked that he'd made the decision to remain as party leader. He explained that he did so because he wished to put aside health concerns and did not want to be seen as a quitter or coward. He summoned the courage and energy, or perhaps the tenacious stubbornness, to continue. He claimed to many that he took no feeling of satisfaction from remaining as Conservative leader but rather believed it to be his duty.[21]

So it was back to work. For seven months Bennett assiduously dedicated himself to his duties. However, just as his heart was physically weak it was perhaps metaphorically weakened as well. He occasionally appeared distracted. He still spoke often in the House but sometimes without the old passion that had been so consistent for so long. As a hard winter dragged on, with an election looming closer, and with more medical tests having been done, Bennett made another decision. While his heart was adequate to meet the demands of an opposition leader, he decided that it was not sufficiently strong to sustain him on the campaign trail—and that trail was coming, sooner or later.

In early February 1938, Bennett assembled the caucus. In a closed-door meeting he formally announced that he was resigning, effective immediately. The stunned silence in the room was quickly replaced by enthusiastic pleas that he stay on. The meeting continued until finally, late in the afternoon, Bennett relented and agreed to remain, but only with the promise from those assembled that a convention would be held to replace him a quickly as was practical.[22]

Whatever happens in caucus is supposed to stay in caucus, but then as now it is a leaky vessel. The next day, newspapers reported again that he was leaving. Bennett spoke to no journalists but answered a great number of letters with a similar message. He told all who pleaded with him to reconsider that his decision this time was final due to his weakening heart.

To many correspondents he confessed a struggle in his mind between trepidation regarding his mortality and his devotion to duty. To one supporter he revealed himself more than was common. He wrote,

> I am sure you realize how reluctantly I am retiring from active participation in public life. I believe I could truthfully say that I would not be concerned about dying in harness but I do not like to contemplate the possibility of being an invalid or, what may be worse, find myself at a critical point in a general election unable to discharge the duties of my position, which would undoubtedly affect the fortunes of my Party.[23]

Meanwhile, Bennett saw to party and succession matters. All seemed to agree that the party was in better shape than it had been in between the last two elections, but also that there was a great deal of work left to be done. The first order of business was to hold another national convention to stir grassroots interest, grab headlines, and determine a platform. As Bennett had not formally announced his decision to leave, there were no overt plans made regarding a leadership contest. A date was picked that would allow time to prepare. Planning was based largely on the structures and processes established prior to the hugely successful event in Winnipeg eleven years before. As in 1927, General McRae oversaw the whole affair and, as before, his preparations were flawless.

In March 1938, 150 delegates made up of Liberal Conservative MPS, senators, and senior party people from every province assembled in Ottawa to plan the party's second national convention. Committees were established to examine the major challenges facing the party. It was decided that a national organization needed to be permanent and that a national council had to be established to coordinate the central and provincial offices. It was also decided that more publicity and regular communications with party members was needed. The Policy and Convention Committee suggested that a convention involving people from the grassroots of the party should be convened in order to hash out new party policies on a number of issues. All agreed, as most had in 1927, that women needed to play a much greater role in the proceedings. The committee also brought forward a suggestion that, due to the plethora of parties on the scene, including three with the word "Liberal" in their name, that the party change from the Liberal-Conservative to the National Conservative Party.

As planning proceeded smoothly, Bennett remained in the background. When most of the big decisions were made, he deemed it time to formally announce that he planned to resign as party leader. As with the caucus, there were many who urged him to reconsider. But this time, and with these people, there were fewer doing so. Their urgings seemed more polite than sincere. It was a fascinating moment. If a rousing cheer, a resolution, or even a series of positive statements had been made, it is possible that Bennett might have again changed his mind. But this time, with not just the MPs but the party faithful hearing of his wish to resign, the room remained largely silent. And that silence said more than words ever could. Bennett was done.[24] He issued a press release that repeated what he had told the delegates: that he was resigning due to doctor's orders following a diagnosis of a weakness in his heart.

Just as the final decision had been made, a tragedy struck. Mildred died. She had taken ill weeks before and had been whisked to a hospital in New York City where she was treated for breast cancer. Bennett had travelled south to visit her and stayed for several days. She appeared to be recovering from what doctors described as respiratory troubles acquired during her recovery. All were assured that she would soon be discharged.

While in New York, Bennett had met with Bill Herridge. Herridge had sent numerous letters to Finlayson and some directly to Bennett during the 1935 campaign. Bennett had acknowledged the soundness of his advice by often following it, but he had never written back. While they dealt together with Mildred, the two former close friends and colleagues were civil but did not speak of politics. Bennett left New York with the assurance from Mildred's doctors that she was improving.

He was back in Ottawa for only a few days when the telephone rang. It was Herridge. Bennett wept openly when informed of his sister's death. She was only 49. He sat alone in a darkened room and read aloud the entire Book of Ruth. According to friends, his mourning never ended, for in losing Mildred he lost more than a sister. He lost his closest friend and confidante. It is easy to trace his reduced interest in Canadian public affairs to the moment of Mildred's death. For days he was not seen outside his Château Laurier suites. For the first time in his life, work went undone. Letters of condolence flooded his office but most were answered by Alice Millar. For a long while he was inconsolable.

CONVENTION

On a hot fourth of July morning, co-chair John MacNicol banged the gavel to commence the proceedings of the second Liberal-Conservative Party national convention. The 1,597 delegates comprised riding representatives, MPS, senators, MLAS, and a number of ex-officio members of the party that included many former politicians. Every riding association had played a part in preparing for the convention. Letters were written, meetings held, and finally, pre-conference committees arranged to establish five standing committees to lead the convention. Publicity, resolutions, organization, nominations, and credential committees began their work.

Scarred by the Bennett-Stevens-Cahan ideological split that had caused such damage to the party in the lead-up to the 1935 election, the Resolutions Committee cautiously worked its way through the ideas presented to it by riding associations and individuals. It was careful to ensure that policies were clearly in the middle of the political spectrum. They were quite tepidly worded to avoid specifics. When the platform was finally ready, it was clear to all that the committee had been successful in ensuring that the party's right, left, and centre would find nothing too objectionable. Of course, something that is designed not to offend is also certain not to excite. The platform was bland enough to do neither. Bennett signed off on it all after making only minor amendments.

Even after such careful preparation, some parts of the platform found trouble when they reached the floor. The most serious issue went to the core of a problem that Bennett had been unable to address: the French-English cleavage. It presented itself at unlikely moments, such as the platform debate regarding support for British Commonwealth flyers to be trained in Canada. Bennett had spoken in support of the initiative in the House. Meighen stood at the convention and announced his support for the plan, couching it as necessary to demonstrate that Canada was still loyal to Britain. The Quebec delegation, however, was outraged that the party would so blatantly ignore its province's desire to play no role whatsoever in any joint British-Canadian defence scheme just as it appeared that the world was stepping toward another European war. At that point, after all, Hitler had already taken the Rhineland and Austria. Of lesser importance, it seemed at the time, was that Japan had taken Manchuria. With thoughts of war in the air, a compromise that pleased no one and said little was finally adopted. It pledged only that Canada would remain loyal to the Crown and that the defence of Canada could be best protected in consultation with all members of the Commonwealth. There was applause from the floor when the resolution passed, but the Quebec delegation remained seated and silent.

Bennett's farewell speech was short and vague. He reviewed his major accomplishments and restated his love for and faith in the country. He thanked supporters and all Canadians for the honour of having served. The speech demonstrated his realization that the convention was about the future, and that he was already of the past and needed to sweep the spotlight from himself. He was not, as had been the case in 1927, destructive like Meighen, but neither was he instructive like Borden. The understated remarks were barely like Bennett.

The speech inadvertently revealed that despite all of his adroit work in the province, Bennett still did not completely understand Quebec. He said, "My friends from Quebec you and I are British subjects together, not English or French, but British subjects, and in that proud name I ask you to join with other British subjects not only in Canada but in every part of this great world, to ensure the prosperity of Canada and the safety of the Commonwealth."[25] Bennett had chosen to utter those words in English. Once again the Quebec delegates sat as those around them stood and applauded. In saying what he did, Bennett acknowledged the French-English cleavage but also that he was unable to comprehend the ethnic nationalism that was pumping the heart of a tiny but growing number of Québécois. Bennett was neither the first nor last Conservative leader to boldly proclaim a fundamental misunderstanding of this vital Canadian issue. Consider Diefenbaker writing in his memoirs in 1976, the year that Quebecers put René Lévesque into the premier's chair, ". . . not one syllable, not one word, not one line in any speech I ever delivered conveyed any other idea than that I was for 'one Canada, one nation.' I have never uttered a disparaging word about French Canada either indirectly or at all."[26] He just had. And like Bennett he didn't even know it.

Five men stepped forward to replace Bennett. Denton Massey was first elected as a member of Parliament in 1935, but he brought with him years of public service in Toronto, and as a son of the family that had co-founded the Massey-Harris Company, he was heir to a fortune along with powerful, corporate connections. Earl Lawson had come to Ottawa in 1928. He was best known and respected for the yeoman's work he had done in party organization. Joseph Harris was another Toronto MP. He had earned the respect of many through his adept chairing of the politically explosive Commons Committee on Railways, Canals, and Telegraph Lines. Murdoch MacPherson was a Regina lawyer and had been an MLA and Saskatchewan's Attorney General. MacPherson was an appealing choice as a talented westerner who had been born in Cape Breton, but he had lost his seat in the 1934 provincial election and had recently suffered a bout of poor health. Best known and qualified of the bunch was Dr. Robert J. Manion. Manion had lost his seat in the last election, but his travels to nearly every riding in the land, his work in three cabinets, his raw intelligence, and his eighteen years in Parliament convinced most delegates that he was the man to beat.

Other names that rose and fell included Stevens, Meighen, and Bennett himself. Among those who came to believe that Bennett actually wanted the job and could succeed himself was the influential J. W. Dafoe. He had heard the rumours that Howard Ferguson and Bill Herridge were active both before and during the convention in trying to garner support to draft Bennett. In the weeks leading up to the convention, Bennett had, in fact, received numerous letters encouraging him to remain as leader, but he had answered each one with a polite thank-you and assurance that his decision was final. But his Wednesday-evening farewell speech, even though subpar according to his standards, had persuaded a good many delegates that he was still the best man for the job. Word began to circulate that if all the other candidates would withdraw from the race, Bennett would accept a draft and remain. The conversations about Bennett became feverish.

Only an hour before first-ballot voting was scheduled to begin there was still no word on whether Bennett's name would be among the candidates. Meighen was called to Bennett's room and was shocked to hear Bennett say that he might consider a run to succeed himself. Meighen counselled against it. He told Bennett that Manion had support from every region's delegates. He reported that the Quebec delegates had all donned bilingual Manion buttons and would vote as a block. Bennett heard him out then said that he had no intention of allowing his name to stand. Meighen left with Bennett's assurance and let the word filter through the hall.[27] The race was wide open. Whether Bennett had seriously considered placing his name in nomination or was playing some political game will never be known; he tipped his hand to no one either publicly or privately.

As the slate of candidates delivered their speeches, a number of minds were changed. Murdoch MacPherson had arrived with no organization whatsoever. He had even pondered withdrawing his name from contention. But his speech was the best of the evening. Beyond the passion of his delivery, MacPherson was the only candidate to adopt Bennett's entire Red Tory program as his own. Manion's speech was competent but less inspiring. His policy promises nonetheless showed that, like Bennett, he was a reformer on the party's left. His speech offered more vague platitudes than specifics, which, to be fair, reflected the party's new platform. But it was no way to win a nomination.

Bennett had a decision to make. Many delegates were waiting to see which candidate he supported in order to determine their own votes. Manion had spoken to Bennett and asked directly for his endorsement but Bennett had demurred. After MacPherson's speech, Bennett's mind was made up. He then discovered that Meighen had also decided to back Saskatchewan's native son. Bennett told a couple of supporters and within minutes his intentions had swept through the hall.

The first ballot saw Manion win 726 votes to MacPherson's second-place 475, with the rest far behind. On the second ballot, both men drew support from the two remaining Toronto candidates, but more went to Manion. He won on the second ballot with 830 to MacPherson's 648. Bennett had backed the wrong horse.

MacPherson later solicited Bennett's opinion regarding what he should do to advance his career now that he had missed his opportunity to lead the party. The former leader's advice was interesting for what it said about Bennett himself. He told MacPherson that perhaps losing the race was a gift, for it would be better at that stage in his life if he concentrated on his law practice, built up some wealth, and then later re-entered politics. Bennett contended that it was impossible to keep a practice going in the West when seconded to Ottawa as an MP. A career as an indigent politician, which he himself would have been had he not built assets and wealth before entering the federal arena, was not something that he wished upon anyone, especially his young friend.[28]

The newly named National Conservative Party had a new leader. Manion said everything one would expect him to have said in accepting the convention's decision, but all could sense that there was trouble ahead. Two former prime ministers, including the departing leader, had spoken and voted against him. Like Meighen, Manion was a dignified, intelligent, and honest man, but could not inspire passion. Like Bennett, he was a principled, thoughtful, and articulate spokesman for the reformist wing of the party, but could not build unity. He was the best of the lot, but doomed for a short and troubled tenure. All good soldiers do not make good generals.

Mackenzie King was polite with Manion and did something that he had never done with Bennett. He invited him to lunch at Kingsmere, the prime minister's private estate just north of Ottawa in the picturesque Gatineau Hills, where he communed with nature and concentrated on the leisurely creation of a fake ruins assembled from bits of rock gathered from famous sites around the world. The gracious prime minister recommended that Manion restrict the number of people he saw each day and work to preserve his strength, for the job he had just taken on was physically and emotionally taxing. It was a friendly start, but in due course Mackenzie King would act to destroy him.

As Bennett was no longer the leader of the Conservative Party, a number of offers came his way. Among the more substantial suggestions with which he wrestled were appointments to the Senate or Supreme Court, or the presidency of a university. He had once yearned for a Senate appointment and toyed with the idea of a place on the Court, but he turned down all entreaties to even consider the moves. While the academic offers were no doubt legitimate, those discussing the appointments to the bench or Senate were probably dreaming; it was quite unlikely that Mackenzie King would have made either.

THE LONG GOODBYE

With a new Conservative Party leader in place and Bennett nearing the end of his long political career, it fell to the press, party, and Canadian people to consider their thoughts on the man. People seldom get to hear their eulogies, but a politician often does—and with those leaving from beneath a dark cloud of unpopularity it is always interesting to see whether the feelings engendered by the public man remain as his public life ends.

Bennett had never been on good terms with the press and always believed that he was unjustly treated. He thought that nearly all newspapers and periodicals printed inaccuracies and were unfair in their assessment not just of him but of most politicians. He held *Maclean's* as the most unfair with respect to his administration.[29] Bennett wistfully, or perhaps hopefully, later wrote to one correspondent, "I do not suppose, in the whole history of Canadian political life, any man has been attacked as I was during the five years I held office . . . many who were not too kindly disposed in days gone by are now realizing that, after all, I had no selfish purposes to serve and desired only to do my best for the country in which I was born and in which I have lived all these years."[30]

No longer being at the helm of the party, however, allowed Bennett to relax somewhat with the press. He accepted a number of requests for interviews, some of which were quite wide ranging. In each, the interviewer left impressed with Bennett's verbal ability and mental acuity. His powerful personality overwhelmed the uninitiated. For instance, Bruce Hutchison explained one conversation as beginning with Bennett's speaking about Canadian politics and linking Canada's economic future to trade, which itself depended upon developing global links in an increasingly interdependent world. He pressed his point by speaking of the situation in South Africa, then moved on to minute details of a British military campaign, and then to a history of the Boers. He drew a connection to the importance of trade with China, which led to his speaking in precise detail about the history of the Ming dynasty and its contributions to art and pottery, then to Alexander the Great, then to ancient Rome, and finally to summing up with quotes from Theodore Roosevelt and a review of the Monroe Doctrine. Hutchison wrote that it was as if Bennett's mind raced faster, recognized more complexity, and illustrated points with more historical connections than any listener could follow. Hutchison concluded his piece with a point that must have pleased Bennett. He wrote, "Mr. Bennett should write a book. . . . Then, perhaps, history would understand him, for his public record will not reveal him. . . . The interesting, the unique thing, is not what Bennett has done or not done, but Bennett himself. We may look on greater men, but not on his like again."[31]

Laudatory letters poured into his office. Bennett answered each with sincere gratitude and humility. Esteemed University of Toronto economist Harold Innis, for instance, was one of many academics who took time to send his thoughts to Bennett. Innis wrote,

> Your leadership of the party especially during the years when you were Prime Minister was marked by a distinction which has not been surpassed. . . . No one has ever been asked to carry the burdens of unprecedented depression such as you assumed and no one could have shouldered them with such ability. I am confident that we all look to those years as landmarks in Canadian history because of your energy and direction.[32]

Even though many articles and letters were written as if he were already gone, Bennett was, in fact, still quite active. He remained the member of Parliament for Calgary West and while speaking less, his voice still often filled the chamber. One of his more memorable remarks came when Mackenzie King rose to answer questions regarding the leak from a Vancouver paper regarding Britain's request to establish pilot training sites in Canada. The prime minister was opposed to the idea, believing that it would draw Canada more deeply into the war that everyone knew was on the horizon. He stirred Bennett's wrath when he argued that the sites would negatively impact Canada's sovereignty.

Bennett caught the eye of the Speaker and rose to his feet. He stated that Canada had a responsibility to Britain and, in fact, to the world, to do all that it could to help in the preparation for the conflict. He thundered in his conclusion,

> If it was the last word I ever uttered in this House, or with the last breath in my body, I would say that no Canadian is worthy of his great heritage and his great traditions and his magnificent hopes for the future who would deny to the old partner who established us the right in this country to create those centres, which she may not have at home, to preserve her life and the life of every man who enjoys freedom and liberty under the governing aegis of that flag.[33]

Mackenzie King immediately relented and there on the floor of the House, without consulting anyone, he changed his government's policy and announced that Commonwealth pilot training sites would indeed be established in Canada.[34] The sudden policy shift showed Mackenzie King acting like—dare it be ventured—a one-man government. The clash was not the first time that Bennett demonstrated a better instinct for the threats to world peace than the new prime minister. After attending King George VI's coronation and the Imperial Conference in 1937, Mackenzie King had travelled to Germany and met with Hitler, who had been Germany's chancellor for four years. While Hitler's opinion of the prime minister was not recorded, Mackenzie King famously observed that the Nazi leader was ". . . a simple sort of peasant, not very intelligent, and no serious danger to anyone."[35]

Bennett, on the other hand, had demonstrated a prescient understanding of the dangers that the world faced from the madmen of Europe. In 1935, four years before Britain declared war on Hitler—a war that saw more civilian deaths than military—Prime Minister Bennett attended a conference in New York City. It dealt with the storm that all intelligent and alert people saw gathering in Europe. Bennett warned those assembled of the dangers he saw in Hitler, Stalin, and Mussolini, and equated fascism and totalitarian communism for the savagery at their core. He predicted a new and horrible war and even outlined the nature of the conflict to come. His words have even more profundity now as images of Dachau, the Blitz, Hamburg, Dresden, Hiroshima, and Nagasaki come to mind. He said,

> Many millions of men and women within the sound of my voice, of every race and clime, have come to appreciate that their lives are the pawns with which the game is played. These millions should know that another great war will be a conflict not primarily between armies or between navies, not between craft fleets. It will be a conflict of peoples against peoples in which the scientific skill and perfected mechanism of each country is organized to destroy, maim or cripple the entire population of the other.[36]

His New York speech was not the only time Bennett spoke of the dangers of scientific progress being used for terrible ends. On June 16,

1934, he had travelled to the United States to make a similar point in an address to the Rensselaer Polytechnic Institute's graduating class of engineers. He urged people of science to turn their talents and energies to goals benefiting mankind. He asked the young graduates to ponder whether, as scientists, they believed that science and technology had outpaced the social order. He issued a challenge to the young engineers:

> And so I make a bold suggestion to you as men of science, trained in the application of its principles, that you should play your part in the restoration of the equilibrium of human forces by the application of a scientific attitude to problems of human behaviour which may seem to be outside your direct sphere . . . [for] of what avail to be able to count the stars, if man starves in the midst of plenty; if he must languish in idleness when so much remains to be done; if he must fight when he knows now that war means destruction and desolation alike to victor and vanquished.[37]

He had seen it coming. The year 1938 brought frightening military action from Germany, Italy, and Japan, appeasement from some, and war preparations from others. Meanwhile, Bennett felt frustrated that he had much to say in a world going mad but that he had lost the pulpit from which to say it. As opposition leader his efficacy was minimal and as an opposition member of Parliament it was even less.

Shortly after the Conservative Party convention had ended, Bennett had travelled to England. After toying with the idea for decades, he had made the decision to retire there. He had briefly considered California, and more seriously thought about South Africa or Australia, but decided on England due to his love of all things English, because Beaverbrook was there, and because England was at the centre of world activities.[38]

Another consideration was that with his service in Canada over, perhaps in England he could still contribute. Bennett made this point in a December 1938 article. A reporter was preparing a piece on Bennett and sent him a proof for approval. A first draft contained a sentence regarding his decision to leave Canada that read: "A great Canadian . . . is leaving it, not because he loves Canada less, but because England has for him a greater appeal." Bennett changed little in the article but he took pen in hand and edited that sentence to read instead: "He is leaving it because he believes that his activities of the past mitigate against his usefulness as a private citizen."[39]

Bennett spent late August to early November 1938 meeting with old friends and acquaintances in London and searching for a home. Beaverbrook played host at his palatial Surrey estate. After seeing many ostentatious country homes, Bennett settled on the one that Beaverbrook had suggested at the outset. It was right next door. Juniper Hill was a tired but still magnificent old house surrounded by 100 acres and containing outbuildings, gardens, a large pond, and three cottages. The house boasted four reception rooms, nineteen bedrooms, a formal library, and a winter garden room. The estate was 20 miles south of London, halfway up a large hill, and offered a commanding view of the Mickleham valley.

That Bennett was ready to retire and happy to be soon back with his old childhood friend was seen in a letter he wrote to Beaverbrook from the ship heading back to Canada in November. He admitted,

> It pleases me beyond words to think that in my old age I am a neighbour in a strange land of the great man whom I used to know as a mere lad—of promise, I then thought—in the Old Manse at Newcastle and who amid all the changing scenes of life has never ceased to remember the old days and his ever grateful friend. [He signed the warm letter "Dick."][40]

Bennett arranged for £40,000 of improvements to be made to the house and grounds including the installation of an elevator and a theatre projection room. A grand gazebo was constructed in a newly created garden that boasted an array of flowers, shrubs, and banana trees. Beaverbrook hired architect Robert Atkinson to oversee the work. The house represented an enormous change for Bennett. It would be the first house in which he had lived since his family home in New Brunswick. After all, for decades he had called hotels home in both Calgary and Ottawa. His suite of rooms at Calgary's Palliser and Ottawa's Château Laurier were spacious enough but they were nonetheless at hotels that took care of his laundry, meals, and more. Even though Juniper Hill would come with a staff, the change in Bennett's lifestyle and routine would be momentous.

When word reached Canada that Bennett had purchased Juniper Hill and that the rumours that he would be leaving the country were indeed true, he was swamped with speaking invitations. Upon his return, he and Alice Millar carefully sorted through them all and accepted many in what became a coast-to-coast tour; a victory lap of kind words and good wishes. Bennett was quite aware that it was his promise to retire from both public life and the country that was at the root of the warm responses he was receiving from old friends and foes alike, even from many reporters who had never had a good word to say about him. He later wrote, "I am quite certain that the politicians opposed to me would not have taken part in these gatherings had they not assumed that I was permanently taking up my residence in England."[41]

The January 1939 farewell tour was spectacular for the size and conviviality of the crowds that met him at every stop. Among the many cities he visited, none was more special than Calgary. A large crowd of six hundred well-wishers met his train at the station on a cold January afternoon. That evening he attended a dinner at the Palliser Hotel hosted by the Kiwanis Club. In his remarks, he slightly altered the story he had been telling for months and claimed that he was leaving politics not so much because of his health, or what he called a bothersome heart, but rather that he wanted to retire, for he believed it unfair to remain with Manion as leader. He would not do as Diefenbaker did after losing the leadership in 1967, for instance, and remain in the House undermining the new leader's authority. He was also leaving Canada, he said, because he did not think it fair as a former prime minister to be involved in Canadian businesses or even in his Calgary law practice. To use his name and the prestige of the office would be undignified and sully that office.

Another reception was held at the Calgary armouries. There, he praised the city and its growth, noting that it was known and admired even in England. He concluded by advising his audience to avoid drink and to work hard but to never measure success simply by the money and things that one managed to accumulate. He said, "I feel that if your whole aim in life is material ends, you have lost out in life."[42]

He accepted gifts and emotionally charged applause at events in Edmonton, Lethbridge, and more. At the Vancouver Hotel's Crystal Ballroom, 1,250 people purchased tickets to pay tribute to the former prime minister. As the orchestra played "God Save the King," members of the city and provincial elite stood on chairs to get a better view and applauded fulsomely as Bennett entered the room. Many people jammed themselves onto the balcony to watch and many others were turned away at the doors from what was the largest reception ever held in the city.

He was soon back in Calgary for one last dinner and one final speech. Again at the Palliser Hotel, Bennett chose sacrifice as his topic. He explained that the road to salvation for Canada was not simply better trade policies or other legislation that might address the issues of the day, but rather a long-term dedication by all Canadians to making their country better. Beyond this, he said, "I believe in democracy, but, to be successful it must be efficient, and this can only come through a willingness of individuals to make sacrifices for freedom. This is my last word to you."[43]

Finally it was time to leave the city that had been his home for decades. A large crowd gathered at the station and Bennett slowly made his way through it to the train. A woman yelled out, "You'll be back, R.B." and a number of people cheered. But Bennett shook his head. With darkness falling, and a chilling wind rising, Bennett responded, "I don't know about that. I can't say whether I'll ever be back, but I expect not."[44] He shook hands with a good number of folks and paused for chats with members of the Palliser Hotel staff that had come to see him off. As he finally reached the platform of the rear car and stood looking out at the crowd, wearing a thick overcoat and gloves but bare-headed, a band struck up "Auld Lang Syne." As the song concluded and the applause ended, Bennett said, "I'm sorry my own active days are over. I would like to make some contribution. When I think I may not come this way again, the thought fills me with great sorrow. For your confidence and good will I thank you. Farewell, and if forever, still forever fare thee well."[45] As the train huffed and began to pull away, the crowd cheered and the band struck up another tune. The old man waved as tears streamed down his cheeks.

There were more events and more speeches. One of the more memorable took place on January 16 at Toronto's Royal York Hotel, when the Conservative Party elite gathered to pay tribute. The dinner was as ostentatious as the surroundings. The speeches, including Bennett's, revealed little of consequence. An exception was that of Arthur Meighen. Meighen was the keynote speaker and he began by praising Bennett and arguing that he had done a wonderful job as prime minister. He noted that no man could have done more to govern the country through the economic crisis that he had inherited. He praised Bennett for his fealty to the truth and for always concerning himself more with the interests of the country than the pursuit of popularity. He said that to win a victory at the polls at the expense of what is best for the people is not victory at all. Meighen then coldly appraised Bennett and his New Deal with an observation that was perhaps accurate but certainly rapier sharp. He said,

> There are many excellent citizens who have still something of a horror of what is called the New Deal programme of 1935. I am a long way from being a visionary radical, but I know something about that legislation, and make the statement that in all its important features it was sound and timely. Our guest will not be offended when I say that what a lot of people have still in their minds like a nightmare is not the legislation, which was enlightened, but the speeches, which frightened.[46]

Beyond bland thank-you notes, there is no evidence indicating Bennett's reaction to the event or to Meighen's assessment. Perhaps his silence speaks all the volumes we need.

In his final appearance in the House, charitable words were spoken on both sides of the aisle. Bennett thanked all, but even in his gratitude betrayed some of the bitterness that had come to inhabit his soul. To a carefully worded farewell from Mackenzie King, he responded, "I shall never forget your kindness at times or your cruelty at others. . . ."[47]

Bennett must have been moved by the deluge of congratulatory letters that came his way. One that was noteworthy arrived from the Veterans' Association of the RCMP. It thanked him for the resolute support he had afforded the force and for significantly improving benefits and retirement compensation for officers. The letter said in part, "During your many years of public life, particularly in Western Canada, you have always been a powerful and sympathetic friend of the Royal Canadian Mounted Police and its predecessors the Royal North West Mounted Police and the North West Mounted Police. We, the Veterans' Association, however, are mainly desirous of recording our gratitude and recognition of what you were able to do for the ex-members of that Force."[48]

Considering his relationship with the press, Bennett must have been either pleased or amused when several newspaper editors wrote convivial letters and printed equally laudatory editorials. Many said much as the *Halifax Herald*, whose editor wrote, "What you were able to do for this country, and certainly for the Maritime Provinces, during your leadership, was great and unforgettable . . . you will be followed overseas, not only by the sincere good wishes, but by the affection of armies of friends and admirers. . . ."[49]

Mackenzie King was happy to see Bennett go. King accepted an invitation to a Rideau Club tribute luncheon for Bennett only with the proviso that he not be asked to speak. In his diary he wrote, "I confess that the H. of C. Parliament proceedings and public life itself seem entirely different today with Bennett out of the way. It was as though the house had been freed from something loathsome."[50] Perhaps his pleasure at seeing Bennett gone was partly due to the personal enmity between the two, but also due to Bennett's effectiveness in the House. Mackenzie King admitted as much in another diary entry in which he observed, "I felt a power and freedom in speaking today that I have not had, at any time, in Parliament. Part of it was having Bennett out of the House of Commons . . ."[51]

There were more luncheons and dinners, including large affairs in Montreal, Quebec City, Fredericton, and St. John. Bennett finally found himself in Halifax with a first-class ticket for the ship that would take him from the land of his birth. Halifax's January 30 luncheon was co-hosted by the Canadian Club and Dalhousie University in the luxury liner *Monclare*'s main dining room. Bennett's speech was somewhat shorter than usual. He made the same point he had been making in many of his recent addresses in noting the importance of Canadian unity. As he had throughout his career and certainly most explicitly with his New Deal legislation, he advocated a strong federal government and an end to provincial parochialism as the means to attain that unity. He said, "Unity is essential and unity means one sovereignty and one Dominion of Canada. It does not mean nine sovereignties. . . . I invite you to a wider patriotism than that of a mere provincial life . . . if we are to endure as a people we must fill our minds with a sense of unity and with a sense of compromise and see [that] narrow provincial boundaries do not divide us."[52] He concluded, "I still have the hope of my youth. I still have faith that the genius of our people is equal to the task."[53] With those words his voice cracked. His eyes welled up. He retook his seat to thunderous applause.

While in Halifax he penned a letter to his riding association and one to Manion. He resigned his Calgary West seat. Then it was time. He waved to the crowd assembled at the Halifax pier and made his way up the gangplank. He walked alone. As he did, he felt a shower of confetti and so turned to wave an acknowledgement. He was then bombarded with even more of the messy stuff as well as a host of ribbons and streamers. He smiled when it became apparent that he was caught up in a wedding party that happened to be boarding the ship at the same time. When the guests had recognized the distinguished gentleman in their midst they had unleashed their ammunition upon him. With one final wave to the crowd he disappeared from the deck. And he was gone.

ENGLAND

Bennett moved into one of his Juniper Hill estate's cottages and with the same focus and drive that he had brought to bear on all other aspects of his life, oversaw even the tiniest details of the ongoing renovations in his new grand house. He would not move into his still-unfinished and largely unfurnished home until the first of October. To the surprise of others, and perhaps himself most of all, he developed a love of and talent for gardening. He tended to flowers a little, but with the help of his gardener became quite expert in the cultivation of vegetables. He spent many hours poring over gardening books and seed catalogues, and he bored dinner guests with tales of his asparagus or beets or whatever else happened to be ripe for their enjoyment.

Also for the first time in his life, Bennett acquired dogs. He purchased two Scotties and named them Peggy and Pat. It is interesting that his old rival Mackenzie King also named all of his dogs Pat. After Pat and Peggy both met untimely deaths, Bennett purchased another dog, this time a small cur that he named Bill. For years, Bill and Bennett were inseparable and wandered Juniper Hill's grounds together as close companions.

Bennett also purchased four Highland cows. He knew little about their care but often visited and spoke with them as they grew fatter from the rich grasses of his meadows. When he was informed that the time had come to have them slaughtered he first agreed but then demurred.

He could not let it happen and so they lived long and supposedly happy lives.

He came to enjoy shopping. To that point he had always just accompanied his sister Mildred or Alice Millar, enjoying the afternoons and exercise while they made all the decisions. But this was new. He had never valued material possessions, but in addition to his continuing to seek out books he became an enthusiastic collector of art. He was always careful to spot a bargain. His library shelves soon groaned with political biographies and he often made gifts of books that he had particularly enjoyed. His art collection was never valuable, and consisted mostly of pastoral scenes, but he hung new finds with great relish.

Bennett personally sought out and purchased many of Juniper Hill's furnishings. The story of one particular shopping trip is worth retelling for what it reveals of the man. One afternoon, he purchased fourteen antique chairs from a dealer in Kent. Bennett expressed disappointment that the complete set of eighteen was not available and the dealer was quick to suggest a local artisan who crafted reproductions. Bennett was pleased and ordered four. Little did the dealer know, however, that Bennett sought out the artisan and visited his shop where it quickly became obvious that all fourteen supposed antiques were, in fact, reproductions. The flummoxed dealer flatly denied the charge whereupon Bennett filed a statement of claim. The dealer made numerous offers to buy back the fourteen chairs but Bennett demanded justice in an admission of guilt. Finally, the dealer admitted his deceit. With that, Bennett dictated a letter to that effect which was filed with the court. He then demanded not a penny in compensation: he kept the chairs, and he paid his bill in full. He had wanted only what was honest and right to be done. There is no record of another merchant attempting a similar swindle with the well-dressed Canadian.

Miss Alice Millar remained in Bennett's employ and in Ottawa. She continued to handle his still-voluminous correspondence. His long relationship with Millar was a fascinating one. She became his personal secretary shortly after he won the party leadership in 1927. Bennett trusted her implicitly, and business and political friends and foes often wrote directly to her in order to gain the attention of her boss. Bennett relied on her for discretion, of course, but also on her ability to prioritize and forward information to him in letters that were pithy in their summaries of complex issues. Bennett entrusted her with personal business matters and regularly had Millar receive dividend and other payments, deposit them in his name, and pay bills for him of sometimes substantial sums. He often had her speak and negotiate with business associates on his behalf.

Bennett had an insatiable appetite for Millar's well of juicy political gossip that never seemed to run dry. She often spiced her otherwise tedious political or business letters with news about who was not speaking with whom. Moreover, Bennett admired her political acumen. Among the numerous letters she sent over the pond were many assessing current political events and personalities based not upon newspaper accounts or political wags but upon the often more reliable thoughts expressed by taxi drivers and servants. Bennett took all such news quite seriously.[54] Millar was Bennett's political inside trader.

So well known and influential did Millar become that in May 1939, with Bennett already in England, complaints were made. It was reported in several newspapers that Millar had improperly conducted Bennett's private business from her personal suite in the Château Laurier at the same time as she had also been conducting his political business. This situation was, according to the *Ottawa Citizen*, a small thing but represented an abuse of parliamentary privilege nonetheless. Bennett wrote to Millar essentially telling her not to worry about it and suggesting that she do as she had always done and ignore requests for interviews.[55] The non-scandal blew over.

The considerable number of cables and letters between them after Bennett moved to England, and the detail in their content, indicate the degree of trust that he had in her and the power that that trust enabled her to wield. It also indicates how much he needed her. After a number of requests, and with the harshness of the silly and insensitive scandal in her mind, Millar agreed to move to England.

In June 1939, Bennett ordered the renovation of the largest of Juniper Hill's three cottages. Noting Millar's worries about the notoriously dubious English heating systems, he arranged for fifty-six radiators to be installed. With everything set, she packed her belongings and took the *Empress of Britain* over the Atlantic. Staying with Bennett at his temporary quarters until her cottage was fully renovated and redeco-. rated, she oversaw the building of an addition, the laying of carpets in the hallways, and the creation of a small library. Millar adjusted well to life on the English estate; she planted a garden and even raised a few chickens. She also took up where she'd left off and acted as Bennett's buffer from the world.

In June 1947, Bennett paid for Millar to take a long cruise. It was her first exotic holiday. She penned many rambling hand-written notes back to Juniper Hill describing her exploits, unique meals, and more. It is interesting that only in these notes was there an ever-so-slight melting of the professional tone that was typical of all their correspondence. Millar even ended a note, "I do hope you are well and being made comfortable and happy. My regards to your visitors and staff and animals and to you. Affectionate respects and regards."[56] She then signed the note "Alice Elizabeth Millar—spinster still _____." Throughout their years together she always referred to him as Mr. Bennett and he always addressed her as Miss Millar. They did not see each other socially. Like him, she never married.

In his preparations for his move to England, Bennett had divested himself of his companies, directorships, and law firm. The E. B. Eddy Company was unique in its complexity, however, and so he remained a major investor and company director. From Juniper Hill he maintained regular contact with the company president, Montreal's Victor Drury.

At that time, E. B. Eddy was vibrant and growing. It boasted liquid assets of $3.2 million and debts of only $94,000.[57] But Bennett was not happy with how the company was being managed or with the manner in which Drury's succession was being planned. Eddy's complex corporate structure was such that the Gatineau Power Company owned 49.7 per cent of the company. In December 1938, Bennett wrote to Gatineau Power's president Gordon Gale and asked him to take over the presidency of Eddy after Drury's impending retirement. It should have been easy. However, there were hard feelings between Gale and Drury. Other board members became involved and picked sides. Finally, Sid Kidd, Eddy's senior manager, had to write to ask Bennett to step in and fix the succession mess. Bennett wrote to Gale, and apologized for whatever part he had played in causing the problems. He suggested that he himself could become president so that Drury would resign without protest, thereby allowing Gale to become president in a year's time. The bluff did not work and the tensions continued. At the May 1939 board of directors meeting, it was decided that Drury would remain president, and Gale vice-president. Bennett was unpleased but from so far away there was little he could do.

The next month, Bennett confided to Alice Millar that his reading of all the company documents indicated that there was still something fundamentally wrong with the management of the Eddy company.[58] By October, his displeasure was such that he elected to sell 4,900 of his common shares and in mid-November, he sold his 15,000 preferred shares for £24 per share. He cleared C$1,785,000. His remaining shares allowed him to continue as a director and, while he allowed Gale to vote as his proxy, he still closely monitored company activities.[59] The massive liquidization of his investments was not only profitable but afforded him one more step away from entanglements with Canada.

With business concerns becoming more simplified, and his estate nearing completion, Bennett could finally concentrate more on what he would like to do than what he had to do. From the moment he had announced his intention to move to England he had been the recipient of a great number of fascinating offers, including running for office, joining the board of several companies, and investing in various ventures. He turned down nearly all with polite notes, but in late June he began to accept a few that he had filed away. He, for instance, regularly read Bible lessons at Mickleham's nearby church. He accepted an appointment as the county of Surrey justice of the peace and on a regular basis took his place on the bench, hearing a range of cases. Bennett was even offered a safe Tory seat in London's Marylebone district that would have assured him a place in the House of Commons. But he declined, explaining that his days of running for office were over.

PUBLIC MAN AGAIN

On the first day of September 1939, England declared war on Nazi Germany. Ten days later, Canada did the same. The Pacific theatre had already been ablaze since Japan invaded Manchuria in 1931. Soon, the whole world was at war. It was a conflagration borne of the failure of politics, a surrender to fear, and the triumph of evil. It was what Bennett had been warning about for some time and it was already taking the tragic course that he had foreseen. Even before the formal declaration of war, Bennett's quiet repose had been disrupted numerous times by squadrons of planes skimming the treetops overhead. No one knew if those planes might soon be German, but many discussed the possibility. The war made the decision as to what Bennett would do with his time and talents. He had to help.

He let his willingness to pitch in be known to Beaverbrook. While serving in several capacities with the Chamberlain administration, when Winston Churchill became prime minister in March 1940, Beaverbrook found himself in the cabinet. He was minister for aircraft production for a year, then minister of supply, for a few months minister of war production, until a cabinet shuffle in December 1942 saw him reassigned as Britain's envoy to Washington.

With Beaverbrook touting his talents, Bennett was appointed chair of the London Advisory Committee of the Canadian Red Cross. He led an investigation into the advisability of employing skilled but interned enemy aliens. He represented the British government on the board of a munitions manufacturer. He also travelled back to Canada to embark on a cross-country speaking tour, encouraging all Canadians to support the war effort and young men to enlist.

Back in England, he became Beaverbrook's assistant at the Ministry of Aircraft Production. Some of Bennett's contributions in this capacity involved acting as a member of a number of boards of directors, doing the same sort of work for the public that he had done to generate personal profit back in Canada. The British Manufacturing and Research Company (MARC), for instance, had been created in 1938 to build 20 mm guns and ammunition. Two factories were built and the first guns were produced by January 1939. Bennett administered the construction of two more factories. While production was going well, Bennett noted problems in efficiency levels. In July 1940, the company was shaken up. Bennett was appointed to the board of directors. In this capacity, he led the reorganization of MARC to streamline the purchasing and shipping of raw materials, the manufacturing process, the treatment of workers, and the shipment of product. Production went up, profits went up, and the workers received medical and health benefits.

Bennett's work often involved his being swamped with the excruciating sorts of details that he had always delegated to others. For example, he was charged with managing the enlargement of the Radlett Aerodrome. He found himself working to hire tradesmen in the midst of a labour shortage. He secured contracts for all of the raw materials that were needed to build bases for planes, for the construction of factories to manufacture the planes, and then for the material needed to build the planes themselves. Bennett became the point man in sourcing wood, magnesium, aluminum, steel, and everything else that was needed for the wide-ranging operation. These negotiations would have been complicated in peacetime: they were especially tricky with Nazi planes and submarines destroying trade routes, and with Britain's traditional suppliers of many important materials falling into enemy hands. Refined cryolite, needed for the production of aluminum, for instance, had come from Denmark. When it fell to the Nazi army, Bennett needed to find a new and reliable source and that search led him to negotiations with the Aluminum Company of Canada (ALCAN).

The ALCAN deal was the first of many contracts that Bennett sent Canada's way. Some Canadian companies, however, seemed naively to believe that they were in for special treatment because they were dealing with the former Canadian prime minister. They were all quickly disabused of that assumption. Bennett managed to secure large contracts for spruce, for instance, from Vancouver's Sitka Spruce Lumber Company. Charles Labrie, the purchasing agent who acted to set up the deal, made it clear that, while he was happy for the contract, he was miffed that Bennett had driven such a hard bargain in securing the lowest possible price for his British project.[60]

Bennett was also called upon to oversee the investigation of a tragedy. On August 9, 1940, an aircraft manufacturing factory was under construction when thirty-nine trusses fell into the 600-foot-long structure and it all collapsed. Six men were killed and another twenty injured. The architect and consulting engineer were both on the site the next day arguing over whether one of them, both of them, or the wind was to blame. A three-person committee of inquiry was established and Bennett was appointed its chair. Over a matter of weeks a series of witnesses was called and while all three commissioners played a role, Bennett led the questioning. He meticulously edited all the commission's documents, effectively writing its final report. The commission finally found the accident to be just that: tragic, but no one's fault.[61]

Despite being pulled in so many directions, Bennett made a habit of touring factories not just to inspect but also to boost morale. He often arranged in advance to have workers gathered and would then address them in his old barnstorming manner. His point was always the same: that everyone from the soldier on the front line, to the pilot patrolling London's skies, to the factory worker toiling at a machine, was working for the same end. They were all saving civilization by destroying Hitler. His oratorical skills were as undimmed as his memory, allowing him to speak without notes and with great effect. He drew on his knowledge of British, European, and military history to stir patriotic pride in his audience's hearts and pry guilty donations from their wallets. At one luncheon alone, Bennett's remarks were credited with persuading patrons to write cheques to the Manchester Aircraft Fund that totalled £65,000.[62]

Newspapers spoke highly of his visits and inspirational speeches. The *Stratford Express*, for instance, reported on Bennett's visit to the Thames Refinery in Silvertown and observed, "There is nothing halfhearted about Mr. R. B. Bennett, Canada's ex-Premier . . . he expressed in no mincing way what the British Empire must do to save itself and civilization generally from destruction by the evil thing threatening them . . . the already enthusiastic personnel were keyed to a further (sic) pitch by his straight talk of what must be done to the enemy."[63]

On the few days that he was home, Bennett dealt with details regarding the never-ending house renovations and enjoyed time in his gardens. He dealt with correspondence each morning. As the war and his involvement escalated, the number of letters rose and their handling took up a greater portion of each day. Alice Millar organized it all the night before and then every morning Bennett either read his letters or had her read them aloud. As he had done since his Calgary days, he dictated replies to most and hand wrote responses to some.

Letters from old political friends and foes were among those filling his mailbag. Senator Arthur Meighen was a constant correspondent who despaired at Mackenzie King's handling of the country and the war. Bennett was polite with all and afforded each the respect of prompt and thoughtful replies. It was only occasionally that he allowed his old, dangerous sarcasm to surface. For instance, Bennett said in a number of replies to Meighen that keeping up with correspondence was not only a problem for him but that the content of the senator's letters was perhaps testing national security. To Meighen's complaining of the hardships of wartime, he tried to encourage some perspective by closing an April 1941 letter with the thought "I will try and write you a long letter just as soon as I can get to it. Of course you realise as fully as anyone that none of us know whether or not we will be here to-morrow, for the bombs of the Hun fall in almost every county of the Kingdom and no house, 'in town or country', is secure from possible destruction."[64] The volume and content of letters that continued to arrive at Juniper Hill suggest that neither Meighen nor Bennett's many other Canadian correspondents seemed to get the hint.

An old friend who could not have possibly missed what was certainly more than a subtle insinuation—and one that also revealed the bitterness still crowding the corners of his mind—was Charlotte Whitton. She opened her mail one day to find this sharp rebuke in response to a letter she had written, asking if Bennett might ever consider returning to Canada:

> Don't you think I was given a furlough by the Canadian people in 1935? They rejected me and all my plans and ideas and hopes. Haven't I the right to accept the views of doctors? . . . as for wanting me back that is sheer nonsense, Charlotte, and you must know it. They gave me a great 'send off' for many reasons. Some for real regard; some glad to be rid of me. But it just became a bit of mob manifestation; Hosanna in the highest and 'Crucify Him Crucify Him' a week later.[65]

Bennett did not know, and there is no evidence to suggest he ever found out, that in February 1941 he was the subject of a fascinating discussion in Ottawa. Canadian Pacific Railway president Sir Edward Beatty visited Mackenzie King in the prime minister's office. He suggested that in order for Canada to fight the war with a united government, a wartime cabinet should be assembled containing the best people possible, regardless of party. He suggested that Bennett be appointed finance minister, not only because he was eminently qualified, but also to allow Mackenzie King to demonstrate to the Canadian people just how serious he was about the initiative. The prime minister decided to hear him out and promised to consider the matter, but as Beatty pressed he became impatient. Finally, King cut Sir Edward off and stated flatly that he would never do such a thing. And even if he did, he would never invite Bennett to join his government. Within an hour of arriving, he said, Bennett would be trying to take over everything and run it himself. Beatty left disappointed.[66]

LORD BENNETT

Mackenzie King was not, however, through with Bennett. Never one to shrink from exploiting a relationship, Lord Beaverbrook approached colleague and personal friend Prime Minister Winston Churchill. He asked that Churchill grant Bennett a peerage and appoint him to the House of Lords. Beaverbrook spoke of Bennett's service as Canada's prime minister, his generous donations to worthy causes and institutions throughout his life, the wealth and jobs he had created, and of course his stellar work in the British war effort. Churchill agreed but, respecting process, he wired the Canadian prime minister for his blessing. The disdain with which Mackenzie King still held Bennett bubbled to the surface. To the privacy of his diary he scoffed Bennett's even wanting such an honour. He wrote, "It reveals the ambition of the man's life; his own glorification and his readiness to use his country to that end, even to the extent of leaving it completely at a time of its greatest need. I shall be amazed if, among the thinking people of Canada it does not create a revulsion of feeling toward Bennett. . . ."[67]

The practice of honouring Canadians with peerages was stopped in 1919. It is why Borden is the last Canadian prime minister called "Sir." Bennett brought the tradition back in 1934, but with his election the next year, Mackenzie King reverted to the old policy. Churchill, however, was a difficult man to turn down, so Mackenzie King eventually made an exception to his own rule and supported Bennett's elevation to the House of Lords.[68]

On June 23, 1941, draped in sartorial splendour, Richard Bedford Bennett became Viscount Bennett of Mickleham, Calgary, and Hopewell. He was nervous. According to tradition, he needed to be formally introduced to his fellow lords by two viscounts and he had chosen Lord Hailsham, a former lord chancellor, and fellow Canadian Lord Greenwood. When his name was announced, he nodded graciously, acknowledging the warm applause from his peers in the ornate red chamber.

The honour was one that he had long coveted. In fact, at the conclusion of the 1932 Ottawa conference, British delegate James Thomas had told Bennett that upon his return to England, the king would be sure to ask if there was anything Bennett wanted in recognition for his service as Canada's prime minister and for his efforts at the conference. Bennett had replied that upon his retirement he would like to live in England and to be awarded a peerage.[69] And now it was his—another dream had come true.

Bennett attended sessions as often as most and enjoyed his time there. His maiden speech was not well received; it was deemed too long and thought to employ too familiar a tone. But he learned quickly and was soon a well-respected member of the upper chamber.

Of the many speeches that he delivered in the House of Lords, a February 1942 address is of particular interest, for it makes clear the beliefs that lay at the heart of the policies he had supported throughout his public life. He spoke of the importance of maintaining imperial ties and of the absolute necessity of the increased role of the state. He acknowledged that all members of the Commonwealth had grown and prospered under what he called "methods of laissez faire," but after the Depression, and with the challenges of a whole world at war, those methods needed to be put to one side. He said, "It seems to me obvious that in the world of the future the organised community and state, or groups of states, must displace, whether in peace or in war, the unorganised, just as machine production has displaced hand production."[70] He went on to say that he was not advocating socialism but merely organized government action and policies which would protect freedom and thus allow free men to work for their own benefit and the benefit of a free society.

Bennett returned to this theme to support Sir William Beveridge's report regarding the viability of wide-ranging social welfare legislation. It had been tabled in the House of Commons and received support from the government, but was being scathingly attacked by Conservative newspapers and politicians. Bennett rose to add his voice to the chorus of those supporting the principles at the report's heart. He was careful to say that the war must be won first. With victory, he said, will come the challenge of rebuilding and debt. But with these obviously substantial obstacles overcome, the principles of the Beveridge Report should be pursued through the creation of bold new social programs. He then outlined legislation that he had brought forward in Canada as proof of, and a model for, how a mature and modern state took responsibility for the well-being of its people.[71] The Beveridge Report went on to become the basis of the British social welfare state.

Bennett also spoke a number of times of the need to create a civil air transportation system after the war. In February 1943, he drew on his experience with the Canadian railway system and what he had learned working with Britain's Aircraft Ministry to thoroughly examine the challenges and opportunities. He argued that while there was agreement that an air transportation system should be established, serious discussions should immediately take place regarding whether there should be public or private ownership, and many companies or a monopoly. He said government should play a significant role regarding regulation and subsidization. In raising these and other issues in such a frank and thoughtful manner, he earned attention and positive press in Britain as well as in Canada and the United States, which at the time were wrestling with similar challenges.

The British Overseas Airways Corporation (BOAC) had been in existence for several years, having grown from a 1939 act of parliament that created the company to operate all overseas air service. After Bennett's House of Lords speeches on the future of civil air travel, he was invited to address leading members of the British air industry. He did so in April 1943. He so impressed those assembled that days later he was invited to assume the chairmanship of the corporation.[72] Bennett turned the offer down, citing his many wartime commitments.

His interest in the matter remained, however, and he continued to raise the issue of civil air transportation in the House of Lords and to be involved in a number of meetings with political and business leaders discussing and planning for the future of the industry. He was part of the group that established the British Joint Air Transport Committee. It was this committee that determined the future of civil aviation in Great Britain.

REMAINING TIES TO CANADA

Bennett's correspondence always included letters from Canadians as well as the Canadian schools and organizations to which he remained tied. Despite his dedication to his adopted country, his homeland was never far from his mind. He had company. In early 1942, with Hitler's war in its third year but fortress Europe still impregnable there were approximately 190,000 Canadian military personnel stationed in Britain. Bennett seldom turned down an invitation to speak with Canadians stationed in and around London. On one occasion he addressed a dinner celebrating the New Brunswick Regiment at a large London pub. He told the young soldiers how proud he was of their devotion to duty and how happy he was that they would soon be going home. Enthusiastic applause punctuated his words throughout his address. As he was wrapping up, he shouted over the din what he thought was a rhetorical question. He asked if there was anything else he could do for them. With testosterone-dripping soldierly camaraderie the young men bellowed in unison, "More beer!" Bennett laughed heartily and, despite his personal aversion to suds, gestured to the waiters and yelled, "More beer!"

Bennett's remaining business interests also kept him linked to Canada. But they would soon end. By the winter of 1942, Bennett had grown frustrated by decisions being made at the Eddy company and with his inability to influence those decisions from so far away. In 1943, he sold his remaining Eddy shares to Willard Weston. Part of the deal placed Bennett on the Weston company board of directors, a post he retained for only a year. With that resignation, while some investments remained, his business dealings with Canada joined his political connections in that they were completely severed.

Those broken ties did not mean that Canada and Canadians were divorced from his mind, or, perhaps more accurately, from his heart. He was an exceedingly generous man who had made charitable giving a part of his life even before he had earned his wealth. His well-deserved reputation for selfless philanthropy resulted in his constantly being asked to support one cause or another, be it a symphony orchestra or a little girl in need of an operation. He once told a Calgary audience that he received letters every day asking for money. On a typical week he was asked for $10,000.

He obviously had to be selective about his giving. He was a softie when it came to churches, schools, libraries, and deserving groups from small towns. As before and during his time as prime minister he was also quite often moved by personal appeals from individuals. He answered each request politely and sometimes with a cheque. To those who received nothing he offered his support but begged to be forgiven with an understanding that the number of requests that found their way to his desk each week was simply overwhelming.[73]

Bennett valued education and supported it with his money. At one point during the Depression, he was helping eighteen young men to complete their university education, some with the payment of their full tuition. Several did not even know their benefactor by name. Others were the children of friends such as Colonel D.G.L. Cunningham, whose son was studying at the Royal Military College. Bennett's generosity grew even greater after his move to England. When in Calgary he had started a scholarship grant to deserving secondary school students and he increased the value of those grants in 1940. Every June he provided cash grants to deserving students from each of Calgary's secondary schools and in 1942 he endowed $15,000 to support the Viscount Bennett Scholarship for a deserving Calgary student who would be attending the University of Alberta. He and Beaverbrook also endowed a number of scholarships supporting worthy students in England.

Bennett supported Canadian universities through numerous and substantial donations, with special attention to Dalhousie in Nova Scotia and Mount Allison in New Brunswick. His greatest concern was for Dalhousie. In 1920, he had joined its board of governors. He was a member of the library committee that established a new library, and he made a munificent donation to allow the purchase of more books than had been planned. He followed this with annual donations to the library for yet more books.

Believing that young women deserved support in order to fulfill their educational aspirations, Bennett also involved himself in the planning and financing of the Shirreff Residence for Women at Dalhousie University. He was on the fundraising committees that saw the erection of a fine new residence for the university president.

Typical of the manner in which Bennett arranged the donations was that in April 1943 Alice Millar and his brother Ronald arrived unannounced at the office of Dalhousie president Stanley with a cheque for $725,000 and with a promise of more to come. Bennett believed that while buildings and facilities were important, a university's strength was in its faculty, so he asked that the money be used to create an endowment to pay the salaries of four new professors. He asked for a Dean Weldon chair of law, a Harry Shirreff professorship in science, a Mrs. E. B. Eddy professorship of medicine, and a Viscount Bennett professorship in law. Millar was clear on Bennett's insistence that there be no publicity as to who had donated the funds. Stanley respected Bennett's wishes to the point that he did not even tell his board chair.

In 1944, Bennett donated another £230,000 to Dalhousie and Mount Allison with no strings attached. Mount Allison's board elected to use its share to endow a chair of history and five scholarships that were named after Bennett's mother and each of his siblings. Dalhousie's gift was the larger of the two. The board used the money to bolster their endowment for the library and the women's residence and to create new endowments for chairs of epidemiology, law, and chemistry.

Bennett's donations often took the form of bank loan guarantees to those trying to scratch out a start in business. He also made material gifts, such as the purchase of a stained-glass window for his sister Evelyn's Vancouver church with a plaque in her honour. He donated funds to allow the restoration of the church that he and his family had attended back in Hopewell Cape. From the day he had become prime minister, Alice Millar was responsible for seeing to it that any child born in Canada and christened with the name Richard Bedford received an inscribed Birks silver mug. He also gave generous annual gifts to the Canadian Council on Child Welfare, the Protestant Infants' Home and Hospital, the Ottawa Welfare Bureau, and, although he never attended a performance, the Ottawa Symphony Orchestra. The Calgary Stampede was also the recipient of his generosity, and every year the event's Best All-Around Cowboy won the R. B. Bennett Trophy.

THE END

Bennett continued to fulfill his duties in the House of Lords and his responsibilities to the war effort, but he was beginning to feel his age. The winter of 1942–43 was long and difficult. Hitler learned the same lesson as Napoleon when Russia's bitter cold and endless snow again became its saviour. While not as harsh in England, the winter at Juniper Hill never seemed to end and Bennett's health suffered.

When buds finally found the trees, Bennett was a different man. He was seventy-three years old. Letters were frequently left unanswered and, while never missing an appointment, he often failed to take the initiative in meetings or ask probing questions. He turned down more speaking engagements than he accepted. He began to enjoy longer trips to London where he would visit doctors and spend afternoons attending theatre performances. He walked alone down London's streets and sometimes saw two plays a day.

Back at Juniper Hill, on March 15, Bennett called Alice Millar to his study. He dictated a long memorandum explaining that he wanted all his remaining stocks, bonds, and shares to be sold and, except for his home, all assets of any kind to be liquidated. He then outlined more donations and gifts that he would like made in his name. He instructed her that there must be no publicity regarding any of the gifts. He wanted no newspaper coverage or brass plaques. The list was extensive.

More money was given to schools, including $5,000 to the University of New Brunswick, $5,000 to the New Brunswick Normal School, and $100,000 to the University of Alberta for scholarships for students living near the university. A gift of $200,000 was awarded to Mount Allison University for the establishment of what became the Bennett-Stiles Chair. Dalhousie University received another $25,000. In gifts to his old profession, Bennett donated a hundred shares of Royal Bank stock to the Law Society of Alberta, and a hundred shares of both Royal Bank and Bank of Commerce stock to the Canadian Bar Association. He gave $5,000 to the Law Society of Upper Canada and another $5,000 to the Law Society of New Brunswick for prizes for young lawyers. In nods to towns in which he had lived, he sent $17,500 to the Hopewell Cape Church and Library, paid the mortgage of Calgary's Central United Church, his old place of worship, and $50,000 to the city's Protestant asylum. He also gave money to individuals including friends, business associates, his brother, and each of his fifteen godchildren.

Signing the cheques may have warmed his heart but it could not strengthen it. Bennett's health continued to deteriorate and in early 1944 he was diagnosed with diabetes. He came to know the stresses of monitoring his diet with fastidious care and the pains associated with that dreadful disease. But as he continued with his many responsibilities, few knew of the physical strains he was facing with such quiet courage.

In May 1944, while in London to attend a war conference with Churchill and other Commonwealth leaders, Mackenzie King met Bennett at a luncheon at Guildhall. They had not seen each other in years. The prime minister spotted Bennett across the room. When they finally met, all they could muster was a wan handshake as they each asked, "How are you?" Neither answered. Neither smiled. Neither said another word. The prime minister wondered if Bennett had even recognized him. He noted that Bennett had aged dramatically and had what he called a "cut to pieces appearance."[74] The two men would not see each other again. It is easy to believe that Mackenzie King did not regret that fact, for even as late as New Year's Eve in 1942 he had been reflecting in his diary over the good blessings the previous years had bestowed upon him and on the short list was that Bennett was safely out of the country.[75]

Later that spring, Bennett welcomed his brother Ronald's two sons to Juniper Hill. He was happy and proud that they'd followed their father's lead and enlisted in the Canadian army. He was later shaken when told that both nephews were killed in the fighting at Normandy on the Caen-Falaise Road. The deaths made a sad man even sadder.

At the war's conclusion many of his responsibilities were wrapped up and he was awarded the gift, or perhaps curse, of leisure. While still taking his responsibilities in the House of Lords quite seriously, Bennett allowed himself to slow down. More invitations were declined than accepted. After spending the Christmas of 1946 at home, he moved to a hotel in Sidmouth, Devon, where he could be closer to a doctor. But his health did not improve. In March, he returned home and the domestic staff noted a loss of weight and vitality.

Bennett continued to rise early and dress the part of the country gentleman. Millar continued to arrive each morning and together they waded through his still-considerable correspondence. He enjoyed most afternoons in his garden both directing the gardener and from time to time getting his own hands dirty. His aging old dog Bill remained a faithful companion.

He continued to receive many invitations to speak and to write but he accepted fewer and fewer. His enduring interest in the future of the

Commonwealth inspired him to pen an article for the *Imperial Review* that was published May 1947. In it, Bennett expressed many of the principles and ideas that had guided his political career. He also related his abiding faith in the ability of well-meaning people to sit and make valuable decisions and again proposed a conference as a way to address international challenges. In the last article that he would write, Bennett argued,

> It is quite clear that it is impossible to maintain the partnership relation unless the policy is one supported by all the nations of the Commonwealth. It is obvious to every citizen that we cannot have a partnership with the other nations of the Commonwealth and promote and support separate policies. There must be united action for a common purpose. . . . In these critical days, is it not the duty of the senior partner to call an Imperial conference for the purpose of dealing with the difficult and complex problems connected with the maintenance of the British Commonwealth of Nations?[76]

Bennett rallied himself to attend certain functions, such as the City of London lunch for Princess Elizabeth on June 11, 1947. It was there that he spoke briefly with the future queen, who presented Bennett with the City of London's Medal of Freedom for his work during the war. He remained in London for the week following the ceremony and again passed solitary afternoons seeing plays and movies. Six days later he attended one of his last speaking engagements. Ironically for a non-drinker, but appropriately for a Canadian who had once done quite well through investments in the Calgary Brewing and Malting Company, the meeting was the annual dinner of the Institute of Brewing.

Two weeks later he appeared as lead counsel before Westminster's Judicial Committee of the Privy Council, representing the Canadian Bankers Association. He looked tired, pale, and a little weak, but nonetheless presented a spirited case arguing the constitutionality of the Alberta Bill of Rights Act, which had been passed by the Social Credit government. Upon the case's conclusion, and while awaiting the final decision, E. J. Chambers, with whom he shared the case, was so confident of their efforts that he suggested a celebration. Bennett said no; he was feeling quite tired. He begged off and made his way home to Juniper Hill.

The next day Beaverbrook paid him a visit, but again Bennett said he was fatigued. Beaverbrook cut his stay short and promised to return the next day to look in on his friend. That evening Bennett took a slow walk through his garden accompanied only by the ever-faithful Bill. He then repaired to his favourite room in the grand house—the library. He sat in silence with an unopened book on his lap and gazed out a window at the darkness, or perhaps his reflection. At ten-thirty, as usual, he made his way to the elevator that took him to his room. He slowly undressed and as he climbed into his large bed, Bill, as was his custom, curled up at the end. His long-serving butler, Mr. Epps, wished him good night and saw him turn to his Bible as he did each night.

Epps found Bennett the next morning in his bathtub, with the water running over the sides. He had a peaceful look on his face indicating that he had died without pain or trauma. Dr. Thomas Cotton later confirmed that the cause of death was auricular fibrillation. His heart had simply stopped beating. It was June 26, 1947. The next week he would have turned seventy-seven.

On June 30, Bennett was laid to rest in the local churchyard down the hill at Mickleham. There was a short and private funeral. The next week a grand memorial service was held at Westminster Abbey. The king and queen were there joined by dignitaries from Britain's political and business elite, a number of distinguished Canadians, and representatives from a number of the world's governments. Mackenzie King, conspicuously, stayed home. The next week another memorial service was held at Lincoln's Inn Chapel, specifically for members of the British law society.

A good number of pleasant things were said about the man, as is only right under such circumstances. Canadian newspapers eulogized him with kindness. But perhaps Bennett himself had written the most honest epitaph of all nearly thirty years before. In a letter to Prime Minister Borden, written in 1918 when he thought his public life was over, Bennett had observed,

> I have corrupted no man. By no man was I corrupted. I have expressed
> my opinions on public questions with some degree of candour. . . . I am
> fully conscious of my own limitations. I have not the disposition that

enables me to readily compromise my opinions or accommodate my views to mere expediency. I might almost say with the first Lord Westbury 'From my youth up I have truckled to no man and I have been independent to a fault.' Measured by the standards of the hour my public life has been a failure. Yet I am comforted by the thought that one of the greatest thinkers has pointed out that one of the real perils of Democracy is the readiness with which men sacrifice principles for place and power. Nor have I forgotten the value that so great a philosopher and statesman as Lord Morley attaches to fidelity to conviction. . . . I can say with a clear conscience that I have at no time sought honours: But I have desired useful and honourable service. I can challenge the criticism alike of friend and foe as to the disinterested character of my efforts to serve my day and generation to the best of my ability. At the end of long years of struggle I am discredited. My experience is wasted.[77]

At his death, and after all taxes and expenses were paid, his estate's net value was pegged at $1.2 million. In the couple of years prior, he had given more than that away. The bulk of his estate was divided between his sister's two sons, who were his only living relatives. He also provided for the Royal Empire Society, the Royal Society for the Encouragement of Arts, the New Brunswick Museum, his favourite charities and schools, and members of his staff.

Upon Bennett's death, nearly every letter of condolence streaming in from around the globe was addressed to Miss Millar. She received and replied to all of the kind notes, many of which mentioned her personal grief and sorrow after such a long and dedicated service. She continued to arrive at work each morning to tie up Bennett's business affairs, as many with legal and financial concerns forwarded their letters not to lawyers handling the estate but to her. Millar then began to gather and organize his papers so that the future might not forget the man to whom she had dedicated so much and expressed so little.

The papers offer a glimpse of the man but as through darkened glass. He personally burned those that could have been most revealing. So we are left with the political and ideological values that had remained so consistent throughout his life expansively and publicly expressed, but his deepest personal beliefs, as always, well hidden. The secrets are gone. He took his private thoughts with him to the grave, which itself reflects the life he led. The stone sarcophagus marking the spot stands before a humble church, proud but apart from the people and country he served. It stands unvisited. It stands alone.

APPENDIX

THE CABINET OF PRIME MINISTER
RICHARD BEDFORD BENNETT

AUGUST 7, 1930, TO OCTOBER 23, 1935

PRIME MINISTER

Rt. Hon. Richard Bedford Bennett

MINISTER OF AGRICULTURE

Hon. Robert Weir August 8, 1930 – October 23, 1935

SECRETARY OF STATE FOR EXTERNAL AFFAIRS

Rt. Hon. Richard Bedford Bennett August 7, 1930 – October 23, 1935

MINISTER OF FINANCE AND RECEIVER GENERAL

Rt. Hon. Richard Bedford Bennett August 7, 1930 – February 2, 1932

Hon. Edgar Nelson Rhodes Senator February 3, 1932 – October 23, 1935

MINISTER OF FISHERIES

Hon. Edgar Nelson Rhodes August 7, 1930 – February 2, 1932

Hon. Alfred Duranleau Acting Minister February 3, 1932 – November 16, 1934

Hon. Grote Stirling Acting Minister November 17, 1934 – August 13, 1935

Hon. William Gordon Ernst August 14, 1935 – October 23, 1935 ˙

MINISTER OF IMMIGRATION AND COLONIZATION

Hon. Wesley Ashton Gordon August 7, 1930 – February 2, 1932

Hon. Wesley Ashton Gordon Acting Minister February 3, 1932 – October 23, 1935

SUPERINTENDENT-GENERAL OF INDIAN AFFAIRS

Hon. Thomas Gerow Murphy August 7, 1930 – October 23, 1935

MINISTER OF THE INTERIOR

Hon. Thomas Gerow Murphy August 7, 1930 – October 23, 1935

MINISTER OF JUSTICE AND ATTORNEY GENERAL

Hon. Hugh Guthrie August 7, 1930 – August 11, 1935
Vacant August 12, 1935 – August 13, 1935
Hon. George Reginald Geary August 14, 1935 – October 23, 1935

MINISTER OF LABOUR

Hon. Gideon Decker Robertson Senator August 7, 1930 – February 2 1932
Hon. Wesley Ashton Gordon February 3, 1932 – October 23, 1935

MINISTER OF MARINE

Hon. Alfred Duranleau August 7, 1930 – July 19, 1935
Vacant July 20, 1935 – August 29, 1935
Hon. Lucien Henri Gendron August 30, 1935 – October 23, 1935

MINISTER OF MINES

Hon. Wesley Ashton Gordon August 7, 1930 – October 23, 1935

MINISTER WITHOUT PORTFOLIO

Hon. John Alexander Macdonald Senator August 7, 1930 – August 13, 1935
Rt. Hon. Sir George Halsey Perley August 7, 1930 – October 23, 1935
Rt. Hon. Arthur Meighen Senator February 3, 1932 – October 23, 1935
Hon. Onésime Gagnon August 30, 1935 – October 23, 1935
Hon. William Earl Rowe August 30, 1935 – October 23, 1935

MINISTER OF NATIONAL DEFENCE

Hon. Donald Matheson Sutherland August 7, 1930 – November 16, 1934
Hon. Grote Stirling November 17, 1934 – October 23, 1935

MINISTER OF NATIONAL REVENUE

Hon. Edmond Baird Ryckman August 7, 1930 – December 1, 1933
Vacant December 2, 1933 – December 5, 1933
Hon. Robert Charles Matthews December 6, 1933 – August 13, 1935
Hon. James Earl Lawson August 14, 1935 – October 23, 1935

MINISTER OF PENSIONS AND NATIONAL HEALTH

Hon. Murray MacLaren August 7, 1930 – November 16, 1934
Hon. Donald Matheson Sutherland November 17, 1934 – October 23, 1935

POSTMASTER GENERAL

Hon. Arthur Sauvé August 7, 1930 – August 13, 1935
Vacant August 14, 1935 – August 15, 1935
Hon. Samuel Gobeil August 16, 1935 – October 23, 1935

PRESIDENT OF THE PRIVY COUNCIL

Rt. Hon. Richard Bedford Bennett August 7, 1930 – October 23, 1935

MINISTER OF PUBLIC WORKS

Hon. Hugh Alexander Stewart August 7, 1930 – October 23, 1935

MINISTER OF RAILWAYS AND CANALS

Hon. Robert James Manion August 7, 1930 – October 23, 1935

SECRETARY OF STATE OF CANADA

Hon. Charles Hazlitt Cahan August 7, 1930 – October 23, 1935

SOLICITOR GENERAL OF CANADA

Hon. Maurice Dupré August 7, 1930 – October 23, 1935

MINISTER OF TRADE AND COMMERCE

Hon. Henry Herbert Stevens August 7, 1930 – October 26, 1934
Vacant October 27, 1934 – November 16, 1934
Hon. Richard Burpee Hanson November 17, 1934 – October 23, 1935.

http://www.pco-bcp.gc.ca/mgm/dtail.asp?lang=eng&mstyid=15&mbtpid=1#FTNote4 November 16, 2009.

NOTES

PROLOGUE

1. R. J. Manion. *Life is an Adventure*. Toronto: The Ryerson Press, 1936. 289.
2. Address of R. B. Bennett, cited in *The Family of Nations*. New York: Carnegie Endowment for International Peace, Division of Intercourse and Education, 1935. 12. *Bennett Papers*. NAC. Reel 1400.
3. Bruce Hutchison. *Mr. Prime Minister, 1867–1964*. Toronto: Longmans, 1964. 240.
4. Bennett speech to convention accepting nomination. Minutes of the Winnipeg Convention, October 11, 1927. 198–199. *Bennett Papers*. NAC. Reel 909.
5. Robert Borden. *Letters to Limbo*. Toronto: Macmillan Press, 1971. 258.
6. P. B. Waite. *The Loner: Three Sketches in the Personal Life and Ideas of R. B. Bennett, 1870–1947*. Toronto: University of Toronto Press, 1992. 104.
7. Blair Neatby. *The Politics of Chaos: Canada in the Thirties*. Toronto: Macmillan, 1972.
8. Michael Bliss. *Right Honourable Men: The Descent of Canadian Politics from Macdonald to Chrétien*. Toronto: HarperCollins, 2004. 108.
9. Ibid. 110, 113.
10. Gordon Donaldson. *The Prime Ministers of Canada*. Toronto: Doubleday. 1994. 132.
11. James Struthers. "Canadian Unemployment Policy in the 1930s," in *Readings in Canadian History: Volume Two*. R. Douglas Francis and Donald B. Smith, eds. Toronto: Nelson, 2002. 334.
12. Bennett, Jaenen, and Skeoch Brune. *Canada: A North American Nation*. Toronto: McGraw Hill Ryerson, 1987. 558.
13. Jim Christopher. *The North Americans*. Toronto: Oxford University Press, 1988. 439.
14. Thomas Walkom. "Stephen Harper, meet R. B. Bennett." *Toronto Star*. October 18, 2008.

CHAPTER ONE:
THE EARLY YEARS, 1870–1910

1. P. B. Waite. "Bennett, Richard Bedford." *Dictionary of Canadian Biography Online*. (John English, General Editor.) Toronto: University of Toronto, 2000.
2. James Gray. *R. B. Bennett: the Calgary Years*. Toronto: University of Toronto Press, 1991. 8.
3. It should be noted that Sir John A. Macdonald had formed and named the Liberal-Conservative Party. To a modern ear it sounds like something of an oxymoron. From its inception, most people called it the Tory or Conservative Party. For the sake of simplicity, this book will employ the common vernacular and refer to it as the Conservative Party.
4. Interview with Mrs. Robinson. *Bennett Papers*. NAC. Reel 443.

5. Beaverbrook, Lord. *Friends: Sixty Years of Intimate Personal Relations with Richard Bedford Bennett*. London: Heinemann, 1959. 9.

6. Watkins, *R. B. Bennett, A Biography*, 27.

7. Beaverbrook, *Friends*, 9.

8. Bob Plamondon. *Blue Thunder: The Truth About Conservatives From Macdonald to Harper*. Toronto: Key Porter Books, 2009, 149.

9. Waite, "Bennett, Richard Bedford."

10. Beaverbrook, *Friends*, 25.

11. Ibid., 6.

12. Ibid., 13.

13. Watkins, *R. B. Bennett, A Biography*, 31.

14. Ibid.

15. Ibid., 32.

16. Gray, *R. B. Bennett: the Calgary Years*, 31.

17. *Calgary Herald*. January 12, 1939. *Bennett Papers*. NAC. Reel 3144.

18. Beaverbrook, *Friends*, 5.

19. Andrew MacLean. *R. B. Bennett: Prime Minister of Canada*, Toronto: Excelsior Publishing Company Limited, 1935. 76.

20. MacLean, *R. B. Bennett: Prime Minister of Canada*, 36.

21. Gordon, *R. B. Bennett, M.L.A., 1897–1905*, 8.

22. *Calgary Herald*. April 6, 1899. Cited in Gray. *R. B. Bennett: the Calgary Years*, 52.

23. *Regina Leader*. April 6, 1899. Cited in Gordon. *R. B. Bennett, M.L.A.*, 26.

24. *Calgary Herald*. April 7, 1899. Cited in Gordon. *R. B. Bennett, M.L.A.*, 26.

25. Gray, *R. B. Bennett: the Calgary Years*, 53.

26. *Calgary Herald*. July 7, 1902. *Bennett Papers*. NAC. Reel 545.

27. Robert Borden. *Robert Laird Borden: His Memoirs*. Toronto: Macmillan Company of Canada Ltd., 1938. 9.

28. Bennett to Ives. February 11, 1903. *Bennett Papers*. NAC. Reel 3141.

29. Bennett to Maclean. March 2, 1903. *Bennett Papers*. NAC. Reel 3141.

30. Bennett to Macdonnell. March 10, 1903. *Bennett Papers*. NAC. Reel 3141.

31. Borden. *Robert Laird Borden*, 90.

32. Bennett to Sanford Evans. May 1, 1903. *Bennett Papers*. NAC. Reel 3141.

33. Bennett to Borden. May 4 and June 22, 1903. *Bennett Papers*. NAC. Reel 3141.

34. Bennett to McCarthy. February 24, 1905. *Bennett Papers*. NAC. Reel 3141.

35. Bennett to Borden. August 27, 1904. *Bennett Papers*. NAC. Reel 3141.

36. Bennett to Roblin. October 7, 1905. *Bennett Papers*. NAC. Reel 3141.

37. Bennett to Borden. November 15, 1905. *Bennett Papers*. NAC. Reel 3141.

38. Bruce Hutchison. *Mr. Prime Minister, 1867–1964*. Toronto: Longmans, 1964. 245.

39. Bennett to Bohmer. June 5, 1903. *Bennett Papers*. NAC. Reel 3141.

40. Bennett to Rev. W. E. Dunham. June 22, 1903. *Bennett Papers*. NAC. Reel 3141.

41. Bennett to Rev. Thomas Powell. December 18, 1903. *Bennett Papers*. NAC. Reel 3141.

42. Beaverbrook, *Friends*, 24.

43. Watkins. *R. B. Bennett*, 78.

44. A.J.P. Taylor. *Beaverbrook*. London: Hamish Hamilton, 1972. 36.

45. David Adams Richards. *Lord Beaverbrook*. Toronto: Penguin Books, 2008. 88.

46. Richards, *Lord Beaverbrook*, 27.

47. Ibid., 77.

48. Ibid., 78.

49. Ibid., 46.

50. Ibid., 65.

51. *Edmonton Journal*. March 3, 1910. Cited in Gray. *R. B. Bennett: The Calgary Years*, 102.

52. Quoted in Watkins, *R. B. Bennett*, 65.

53. Watkins, *R. B. Bennett, A Biography*, 71.

54. Gray, *R. B. Bennett: The Calgary Years*, 115.

55. Joseph Schull. *Laurier: The First Canadian*. Toronto: Macmillan of Canada, 1965. 530.

56. Ibid.

57. Beaverbrook, *Friends*, 23.

58. Ibid., 24.

59. Bennett to Aitken. November 13, 1910. Quoted in Beaverbrook, *Friends*, 30–31

60. Aitken to Bennett. February 16, 1911. *Bennett Papers*, NAC. Reel 3142.

61. *Eye Opener*. August 12, 1911. *Bennett Papers*. NAC. Reel 3141.

CHAPTER TWO:
PUBLIC FIGURE, PRIVATE MAN, 1911–1925

1. Bennett to Aiken. November 18, 1911. Bennett Papers. NAC. Reel 3142.

2. Hansard. Ottawa: Debates in the House of Commons. November 20, 1911.

3. Ibid.

4. Ibid.

5. Beaverbrook, *Friends*. 33.

6. Hansard, June 2, 1913.

7. Ibid.

8. Roger Graham. *Arthur Meighen: A Biography. Volume I*. Toronto: Clarke Irwin, 1960. 80.

9. Ibid., 97.

10. Hansard, May 15, 1914.

11. Ibid.

12. Ibid.

13. Ibid.

14. Ibid.

15. Mackenzie King diary. May 14, 1914. (http://king.collectionscanada.ca/EN/PageView.asp)

16. Hansard, February 16, 1914.

17. Hansard, February 11, 1914.

18. Beaverbrook, *Friends*, 35.

19. Tim Cook. *Shock Troops: Canadians Fighting the Great War, 1917-1918. Volume Two*. Toronto: Penguin Books, 2008. 3-4.

20. Waite, "Bennett, Richard Bedford."

21. Richard Gwyn. *The Northern Magus: Pierre Trudeau and Canadians*. Markham: Paper Jacks. 1981. 30.

22. Bennett to Aitken. June 8, 1917. *Beaverbrook Papers*. NAC. Reel 1759.

23. Gray, *R. B. Bennett: the Calgary Years*, 96.

24. *Bennett Papers*. NAC. Reel 1273.

25. Borden, *Robert Laird Borden*, 611.

26. Robert Craig Brown. *Robert Laird Borden: A Biography, Volume 1, 1854 -1914*. Toronto: Macmillan of Canada, 1975. 62.

27. *Bennett Papers*. NAC. MG 26 K Vol. 1.

28. Ibid.

29. Borden, *Robert Laird Borden*, 627.

30. Ibid., 697–98.

31. Ibid., 713.

32. Bennett to Borden. April 17, 1918. *Bennett Papers*. NAC. Reel 3174.

33. Beaverbrook, *Friends*, 38–39.

34. Ibid. 39.

35. Bennett to Borden. April 17, 1918. *Bennett Papers*. NAC. Reel 3174.

36. Graham, *Arthur Meighen, Volume I*. 80.

37. Borden to Bennett. January 1, 1917. *Bennett Papers*. NAC. Reel 3174.

38. Beaverbrook, *Friends*, 38.

39. Bennett to Borden. April 17, 1918. *Bennett Papers*. NAC. Reel 3174.

40. Ibid.

41. Ibid.

42. Beaverbrook, *Friends*, 40.

43. Waite, "Bennett, Richard Bedford."

44. Mackenzie King diary. August 28, 1907. (http://king.collectionscanada.ca./EN/PageView.asp)

45. Mackenzie King diary. July 8, 1920. (http://king.collectionscanada.ca./EN/PageView.asp)

46. Bennett to Meighen. May 23, 1921. *Meighen Papers*. NAC. Reel 3220.

47. Beaverbrook, *Friends*, 43.

48. Bennett to Aitken. March 13, 1922. *Bennett Papers*. NAC. Reel 3174.

49. *Halifax Morning Chronicle*. October 10, 1921. Cited in R. MacGregor Dawson, *William Lyon Mackenzie King: A Political Biography 1874–1923*. Toronto: University of Toronto Press, 1958. 351.

50. Beaverbrook, *Friends*, 43.

51. Ibid.

52. www.albertasource.ca/lawcases/civil/bennettlougheed/bennettlougheed.htm June 22, 2007.

53. Ibid.

54. Ibid.

55. Watkins, *R. B. Bennett*, 102.

56. Meighen to Bennett. June 8, 1925. *Meighen Papers*. NAC. Reel 3463.

57. Bennett to Meighen. June 10, 1925. *Meighen Papers*. NAC. Reel 3463.

CHAPTER THREE:
ON TO LEADERSHIP, 1925–1927

1. Bennett to Alexander. December 23, 1922. *Bennett Papers*. NAC. Reel 3174.

2. For a discussion of this tendency see J. Brodie and J. Jenson, "Piercing the Smokescreen: Brokerage Parties and Class Politics," Alain-G. Gagnon and A. Brian Tanguay, eds. *Canadian Parties in Transition: Discourse, Organization and Representation*. Scarborough: Nelson, 1989. 24–44.

3. http://pm.gc.ca/eng/media.asp?id=2333, November 22, 2008.

4. Watkins, *R. B. Bennett*, 78.

5. Hansard, February 15, 1926.

6. Ibid., March 11, 1926.

7. Hansard, March 26, 1926.

8. Ibid.

9. *Montreal Evening Standard*. October 7, 1926. *Bennett Papers*. NAC. Reel 3174.

10. Graham, *Arthur Meighen: A Biography*, 432.

11. Gray, *R. B. Bennett: the Calgary Years*, 264.

12. Ibid., 261.

13. Watkins, *R. B. Bennett*, 124.

14. Bruce Hutchison. *The Incredible Canadian: A Candid Portrait of Mackenzie King: His Works, His Times, and His Nation*. Toronto: Longmans, Green, 1953. 116–17.

15. Hansard, February 18, 1927.

16. Borden's remarks. Minutes of the Winnipeg Convention. October 10, 1927. 23. *Bennett Papers*. NAC. Reel 909.

17. Ibid., 26.

18. Graham, *Arthur Meighen*, 498.

19. *Stevens Papers*. NAC. Vol. 162 A.

20. Bennett to Aitken. November 10, 1927. Cited in Lord Beaverbrook. *Friends*, 49.

21. *Stevens Papers*. NAC. Vol. 162 A.

22. Tilley remarks. Minutes of the Winnipeg Convention. October 11, 1927. 192. *Bennett Papers*. NAC. Reel 909.

23. Bennett speech. Minutes of the Winnipeg Convention. October 11, 1927. 197. *Bennett Papers*. NAC. Reel 909.

24. John R. MacNicol. *The National Liberal-Conservative Convention*. Toronto: Southam, 1930. 55.

25. Bennett speech. Minutes of the Winnipeg Convention, October 11, 1927. 267. *Bennett Papers*. NAC. Reel 909.

26. Ibid.

27. Ibid.

28. Beaverbrook, *Friends*, 49.

29. *Globe*. October 12, 1927. *Bennett Papers*. NAC. Reel 909.

30. *Saturday Night*. October 22, 1927. *Bennett Papers*. NAC. Reel 909.

31. Cited in Watkins, 126.

32. Leo Zakuta. *A Protest Movement Becalmed: A Study of Change in the* CCF. Toronto: University of Toronto Press, 1964. 237.

33. See Janine Brodie and Jan Jenson, "Piercing the Smokescreen: Brokerage Parties and Class Politics," in *Canadian Parties in Transition: Discourse, Organization and Representation*, Alain-G. Gagnon and A. Brian Tanguay, eds. Scarborough: Nelson, 1989. 24–44.

34. Conrad Winn and John McMenemy. *Political Parties in Canada*. Toronto: McGraw Hill Ryerson, 1976. 2.

35. See J. L. Granatstein, *The Politics of Survival: The Conservative Party of Canada, 1939–1945*. Toronto: University of Toronto Press, 1967, and John English, *The Decline of Politics: the Conservatives and the Party System. 1901–1920*, Toronto: University of Toronto Press, 1993.

36. See Gad Horowitz, *Canadian Labour in Politics*. Toronto: University of Toronto Press, 1968. Chapter 1.

37. R. B. Bennett. *Canadian Problems as Seen by Twenty Outstanding Canadian Men*. Toronto: Oxford University Press, 1933. 30.

38. Larry Glassford. *Reaction and Reform: The Politics of the Conservative Party Under R. B. Bennett 1927–1938*. Toronto: University of Toronto Press, 1992. 25.

39. Ibid.

40. Minutes of the Winnipeg Convention. October 9, 1927. 131. *Bennett Papers*. NAC. Reel 909.

41. See John Boyko, *Last Steps to Freedom: The Evolution of Canadian Racism*. Winnipeg: Gordon Shillingford, 1998. Chapter 2.

42. Minutes of the Winnipeg Convention. 142. *Bennett Papers*. NAC. Reel 909.

43. Borden's speech. Winnipeg Conservative Convention Minutes. October 10, 1927. 23. *Bennett Papers*. NAC. Reel 909.

44. *Ottawa Journal*. January 25, 1928. *Bennett Papers*. NAC. Reel 909.

CHAPTER FOUR:
OPPOSITION TO PRIME MINISTER, 1927–1930

1.   Belanger to Bennett. October 15, 1927. *Bennett Papers*. NAC. Reel 921.

2.   Bennett to Willis. April 10, 1928. *Bennett Papers*. NAC. Reel 18.

3.   McRae to Bennett. December 20, 1929. *Bennett Papers*. NAC. Reel 18.

4.   Guthrie speech to Conservative Business Men's Club. January 6, 1927. *Bennett Papers*. NAC. Reel 18.

5.   Cahan to Beaubien. December 7, 1926. *Bennett Papers*, NAC. Reel 18.

6.   Bennett to Dion. May 28, 1927. *Bennett Papers*. NAC. Reel 242.

7.   Bennett to Favreau. February 4, 1928. *Bennett Papers*. NAC. Reel 18.

8.   Bennett to Blondin. June 16, 1928. *Bennett Papers*, NAC. Reel 18.

9.   Hogarth to Bennett. April 7, 1930. *Bennett Papers*. NAC. Reel 3176.

10. Bennett to Tolmie. August 29, 1929. *Bennett Papers*. NAC. Reel 16.

11. Ibid.

12. McRae to Bennett. February 12, 1930. *Bennett Papers*. NAC. Reel 242.

13. McRae to Ryckman. May 30, 1930. *Bennett Papers*. NAC. Reel 242.

14. Ibid.

15. Election in Sight. *Bennett Papers*. NAC. Reel 242.

16. Lavine, Allan. *Scrum Wars: The Prime Ministers and the Media.* Toronto: Dundurn Press, 1996. 158.

17. Ibid., 159.

18. Waite, "Bennett, Richard Bedford."

19. Report from the director of publicity of the Conservative Federal Headquarters—Organization: The Press, 1930. *Bennett Papers*. NAC. Reel 18.

20. Ibid., 151.

21. *Bennett Papers*. NAC. Reel 11607.

22. See John Boyko, *Last Steps to Freedom: The Evolution of Canadian Racism.* Winnipeg: Gordon Shillingford Publishing. 1998. Chapter 3.

23. Bennett to MacMillan. May 14, 1928. *Bennett Papers*. NAC. Reel 14.

24. Waite, "Bennett, Richard Bedford."

25. Alan Greenspan. *The Age of Turbulence: Adventures in a New World.* New York: Penguin, 2007. 466.

26. L M. Grayson, and Michael Bliss. *The Wretched of Canada: Letters to R. B. Bennett, 1930–1935.* Toronto: University of Toronto Press, 1971. vii.

27. www.canadianeconomy.gc.ca July 14, 2008.

28. "Must Recession Follow." *Journal of Canadian Bankers Association* 37. (January 1930): 125–26. Cited in Horn, *The Dirty Thirties*, 32–33.

29. Edward Beatty, "Transportation Earnings Must Suffer Temporarily But Extensions Continue." *Toronto Globe.* January 3, 1930. Cited in Horn, *The Dirty Thirties*, 34–36.

30. Mackenzie King diary. October 29–31, 1929. (http//king.collectionscanada.ca/EN/PageView.asp)

31. Plamondon. *Blue Thunder*, 461.

32. Hansard, February 24, 1930.

33. Blair Neatby. *William Lyon Mackenzie King, 1924-1932: The Lonely Heights.* Toronto: University of Toronto Press, 1963. 310-11.

34. Hutchison. *Incredible Canadian*, 161.

35. Mackenzie King diary. March 29, 1930. (http://king.collectionscanada.ca/EN/PageView.asp)

36. Ibid., April 5, 1930. (http://king.collectionscanada.ca/EN/PageView.asp)

37. Hansard, April 6, 1930.

38. Mackenzie King diary. April 6, 1930. (http://king.collectionscanada.ca/EN/PageView.asp)

39. Hansard, April 3, 1930.

40. Hansard, May 6, 1930.

41. Ibid.

42. Neatby, *The Lonely Heights*, 327.

43. McRae to Ryckman. May 30, 1930. *Bennett Papers*. NAC. Reel 242.

44. Borden to Beaverbrook. July 2, 1930. Cited in Beaverbrook, *Friends*, 56.

45. Norman Ward (ed). *A Party Politician: The Memoirs of Chubby Power*. Toronto: Macmillan, 1966. 265.

46. Waite, "Bennett, Richard Bedford."

47. Bennett stump speech (untitled and undated). 8. *Bennett Papers*. NAC. Reel 946.

48. Ibid., 11.

49. Ibid., 15.

50. Bennett to Drummond (undated). *Bennett Papers*. NAC. Reel 946.

51. Taylor, *Beaverbrook*, 59.

52. Ibid., 295.

53. Lipset to candidates and senators. July 9, 1930. *Bennett Papers*. NAC. Reel 921.

54. Bennett stump speech (untitled and undated). 22–23. *Bennett Papers*. NAC. Reel 946.

55. Ibid.

56. Blair Neatby. *The Politics of Chaos: Canada in the Thirties*. Toronto: Macmillan, 1972. 55.

57. Watkins, *R. B. Bennett*, 134.

58. MacLean, *R. B. Bennett*, 108.

59. Hansard, September 9, 1930.

60. Brian Mulroney. *Memoirs 1939-1993*. Toronto: McClelland & Stewart, 2007. 317.

61. Plamondon, *Blue Thunder*, 349.

62. Mackenzie King diary. June 16, 1933. (http://king.collectionscanada.ca/EN/PageView.asp)

63. *Stevens Papers*. Vol. 163. 1955 interview.

64. *Manion Papers*. Vol. 105. Diaries, 1914–1942. July 1, 1932.

65. Hansard, July 29, 1931.

66. R. J. Manion. *Life is an Adventure*. Toronto: Ryerson Press, 1936. 308.

67. Martin, Paul. *Hell or High Water: My Life In and Out of Politics*. Toronto: McClelland & Stewart, 2008. 236.

68. "Backstage at Ottawa." *Maclean's* 45. April 15, 1933. Cited in Glassford. *Reaction and Reform*, 100.

69. Roger Graham. *Arthur Meighen: No Surrender. Volume III*. Toronto: Clarke Irwin, 1965. 25.

70. Gratton O'Leary. "Conservatism's New Prophet," *Maclean's* XL, November 15, 1927. 46.

71. Cited in Glassford, *Reaction and Reform*, 109.

72. *Toronto Star*. May 14, 2008.

73. Plamondon, *Blue Thunder*, 349.

74. Barrette to Bennett. May 19, 1931. *Bennett Papers*. NAC. Reel 1115.

75. Pearson, Lester. *Mike: The Memoires of the Rt. Hon. Lester B. Pearson, Vol I*. Toronto, University of Toronto Press, 1972. 71–72.

76. Ibid. 73,

CHAPTER FIVE:
BLASTING HIS WAY, 1930–1935

1. Fidel Castro. *My Life*. New York: Allen Lane, 2007. 248.

2. All the statistics in this analysis are from the Rowell-Sirois Report, the Price Spreads Commission Report, Statistics Canada website www.statcan.ca, and James Gray, *Men Against the Desert*. Saskatoon: Modern Press, 1967.

3. Barry Broadfoot. *Ten Lost Years: Memories of Canadians Who Survived the Depression*. Don Mills: Paper Jacks, 1973. 40.

4. Kingston to Bennett. July 31, 1930. *Bennett Papers.* NAC. Reel 3143.

5. Niccolò Machiavelli. *The Prince, and Other Writings.* New York: Barnes and Noble, 2004. 25.

6. Hansard, September 12, 1930.

7. Gregory A. Johnson, and David A. Lenarcic, "The Decade of Transition: The North Atlantic Triangle During the 1920s," in *The North Atlantic Triangle in a Changing World: Anglo-American-Canadian Relations, 1902–1956,* McKercher and Aronsen (eds). Toronto: University of Toronto Press, 1996. 83.

8. *Maclean's.* August 1, 1931. *Bennett Papers.* NAC. Reel 3153.

9. MacLean, *R. B. Bennett,* 86.

10. *Ottawa Citizen.* September 10, 1931. *Bennett Papers.* NAC. Reel 3153.

11. Bennett to Borden. October 7, 1931, *Bennett Papers.* NAC. Reel 3174.

12. Watkins, *R. B. Bennett,* 149.

13. Waite, "Bennett, Richard Bedford."

14. Broadcast message. October 1930. *Bennett Papers.* NAC. Reel 1401.

15. Cahan to Gauthier. April 9, 1931. *Bennett Papers.* NAC. Reel 1341.

16. Risser to Bennett. March 11, 1930. *Bennett Papers.* NAC. Reel 3143.

17. Phelps to Bennett. March 17, 1930. *Bennett Papers.* NAC. Reel 3143.

18. Bennett to A. E. Smith. June 11, 1931. *Bennett Papers.* NAC. Reel 3143.

19. Johnston to Bennett. June 10, 1931. *Bennett Papers.* NAC. Reel 1323.

20. Bronson to Bennett. June 21, 1931. *Bennett Papers.* NAC. Reel 1320.

21. McWilliams to Bennett. June 21, 1931. *Bennett Papers.* NAC. Reel 1320.

22. Arch Dale. *Five Years of R. B. Bennett.* Winnipeg: Winnipeg Free Press, 1935. 3.

23. Ibid., 5.

24. Hansard, January 30, 1931.

25. *Ottawa Citizen.* May 14, 1931. *Bennett Papers.* NAC. Reel 3153.

26. *Bennett Papers.* NAC. Reel 3174.

27. Glassford, *Reaction and Reform,* 118.

28. Michael Bordo, Angela Redish, and Ronald Shearer. *Canada's Monetary System in Historical Perspective: Two Faces of the Exchange Rate Regime.* Vancouver: University of Vancouver Press, 1999. 2.

29. *Press Clippings Scrapbook* 81. *Manion Papers.* NAC. Vol. 96.

30. http://socserv.mcmaster.ca/maclabour/article.php?id=550

31. Ibid.

32. Dale, *Five Years of R. B. Bennett,* 21.

33. http://socserv.mcmaster.ca/maclabour/article.php?id=550

34. Ibid.

35. Mackenzie King diary. September 22, 1932. (http://king.collectionscanada.ca/EN/PageView.asp)

36. Mackenzie King diary. March 14, 1933. (http://king.collectionscanada.ca/EN/PageView.asp)

37. Mackenzie King diary. April, 5, 1930. (http://king.collectionscanada.ca/EN/PageView.asp)

38. Watkins, *R. B. Bennett,* 149.

39. Bennett to Aitken. November 13, 1910. *Beaverbrook Papers.* NAC. Reel 1759.

40. Beaverbrook, *Friends,* 29.

41. Bennett press conference. December 1930. *Bennett Papers.* NAC. Reel 1040.

42. Ibid., 54.

43. Sir Grahame Keith Fieling. *The Life of Neville Chamberlain.* London: MacMillan, 1946. 205.

44. American Branch Factories in Canada 5. *Bennett Papers.* NAC. Reel 1172.

45. Ibid., 19.

46. *Stevens Papers.* 1955 interview. NAC. Vol. 167.

47. Ibid.

48. Pearson, *Mike*, 74.

49. Fieling. *The Life of Neville Chamberlain*, 179.

50. Bennett to Price. August 24, 1932, *Bennett Papers*. NAC. Reel 3173.

51. *St. Thomas Times-Journal* editorial. August 24, 1932, *Bennett Papers*. NAC. Reel 3173.

52. Anderson to Bennett. August 23, 1932, *Bennett Papers*. NAC. Reel 3173.

53. Mackenzie King diary. July 19, 1932. (http://king.collectionscanada.ca/EN/PageView.asp)

54. Fieling. *The Life of Neville Chamberlain*, 181.

55. Ian Drummond. *Imperial Economic Policy, 1917-1939: Studies in Expansion and Protection*. Toronto: University of Toronto Press, 1974. 30-31.

56. Beaverbrook, *Friends*, 76.

57. Drummond, *Imperial Economic Policy*, 234.

58. See as examples Michael Bliss, *Right Honourable Men*. Toronto: Doubleday Collins, 1994. 114, and J. L. Granatstein, and Norman Hillmer. *Prime Ministers: Ranking Canada's Leaders*. Toronto: HarperCollins, 1999. 109.

59. Drummond, *Imperial Economic Policy*, 286.

60. Harold Innis. *The Fur Trade in Canada: An Introduction to Canadian Economic History*. Toronto: University of Toronto Press, 1930. 445.

61. Trade and Commerce Report. December 1934. 24. *Bennett Papers*. NAC. Reel 1401.

62. Drummond, *Imperial Economic Policy*, 287.

63. William L. Marr and Donald G. Paterson. *Canada: An Economic History*. Toronto: Macmillan, 1980. 388.

64. *Stevens Papers*. Tenth interview. NAC. Reel 1195.

65. Ibid.

66. Report of the Royal Commission on Dominion-Provincial Relations, Book 1, *Canada: 1867–1939*. Ottawa: King's Printer, 1940. 144.

67. *Bennett Papers*. NAC. Reel 1401.

68. Bennett to J. C. Moore. December 27, 1933. *Bennett Papers*. NAC. 1401.

69. Mackenzie King diary. August 26, 1932. (http://king.collectionscanada.ca/EN/PageView.asp)

70. Bennett to Colville. May 21, 1932. *Bennett Papers*. NAC. Reel 1401.

71. Manion. *Life is an Adventure*, 213.

72. Bennett speech. October 9, 1934. 1. *Bennett Papers*. NAC. Reel 1401.

73. Bennett speech to Toronto St. George's Society. April 13, 1934. 1–3. *Bennett Papers*. NAC. Reel 1401.

74. Ibid.

75. Bennett speech. October 14, 1934. 10–11. *Bennett Papers*. NAC. Reel 1401.

76. Drummond, *Imperial Economic Policy*, 234.

77. King to Bennett. August 13, 1934. *Bennett Papers*. NAC. Reel 3143.

78. Cited in Glassford, *Reaction and Reform*, 117.

79. *Evening Independent*. St. Petersburg, Florida, April 27, 1932. *Bennett Papers*. NAC. Reel 3143.

80. Herridge to Bennett. April 7, 1934. *Bennett Papers*. NAC. Reel 1025.

81. Bennett to Hull. November 14, 1933. *Bennett Papers*. NAC. Reel 1025.

82. Pearson, *Mike*, 68–69.

83. Bennett speech to Canadian Society of New York. February 16, 1935. *Bennett Papers*. NAC. Reel 1400.

84. Mackenzie King diary. June 4, 1935. (http://king.collectionscanada.ca/EN/PageView.asp)

85. Herridge to Bennett (undated). *Bennett Papers*. NAC. Reel 1024.

86s. Bennett to Herridge (undated). *Bennett Papers*. NAC. Reel 1024.

CHAPTER SIX:
CREATING CANADIAN ICONS, 1931–1935

1. Hansard, February 24, 1930.

2. Memorandum Concerning the Canadian Radio Industry. December 17, 1930. *Bennett Papers*. NAC. Reel 1289.

3. Montgomery Wright, "Radio Becomes a Primary Link Between Government and the People." RCA *News*. New York: Corporation of America, 1931. 1. *Bennett Papers*. NAC. Reel 1289.

4. Robertson to Bennett. January 7, 1931. *Bennett Papers*. NAC. Reel 1289.

5. Tummon to Bennett. January 17, 1931. *Bennett Papers*. NAC. Reel 1289.

6. Weese to Bennett. January 17, 1931. *Bennett Papers*. NAC. Reel 1289.

7. Ewart Greig (ed.). *Radio Broadcasting Under Private Ownership*. Toronto: Canadian Association of Broadcasters, 1931. *Bennett Papers*. NAC. Reel 1289.

8. Bennett to Spry. February 11, 1931. *Bennett Papers*. NAC. Reel 1289.

9. Bennett to Duranleau. February 11, 1931. *Bennett Papers*. NAC. Reel 1289.

10. Hansard, July 7, 1931.

11. Hansard, February 14, 1932.

12. Meighen to Bennett. August 5, 1935. *Bennett Papers*. NAC. Reel 350.

13. Ashcroft to Bennett. December 21, 1931. *Bennett Papers* NAC. Reel 1289.

14. Second and Final Report of the Parliamentary Committee on Radio Broadcasting. *Bennett Papers*. NAC. Reel 1289.

15. Hansard, May 9, 1932.

16. Ibid.

17. National Radio in Canada, Report from Gladstone Murray. June 3, 1933. 7. *Bennett Papers*. NAC. Reel 1293.

18. Bennett speech. December 1, 1934. *Bennett Papers*. NAC. Reel 1293.

19. Innis, *The Fur Trade*, 262.

20. Mackenzie King diary. January 23, 1923. (http://king.collectionscanada.ca/EN/PageView.asp)

21. Mackenzie King diary. January 23, 1930. (http://king.collectionscanada.ca/EN/PageView.asp)

22. Ibid.

23. Mackenzie King diary. April 18, 1930.

24. Hansard. Ottawa: House of Commons Debates. July 30, 1931.

25. Bennett stump speech (untitled and undated). 6. *Bennett Papers*. NAC. Reel 946.

26. Fleming to Bennett. January 20, 1928. *Bennett Papers*, NAC. Reel 946.

27. Bennett to Logan. April 20, 1928. *Bennett Papers*. NAC. Reel 946.

28. Herridge to Bennett. April 8, 1931. *Bennett Papers*. NAC. Reel 1467.

29. Hansard, May 12, 1932.

30. Herridge to Bennett. July 8, 1931. *Bennett Papers*. NAC. Reel 1467.

31. Bennett to Taschereau. July 11, 1932. *Bennett Papers*. NAC. 1467.

32. Mackenzie King diary. July 16, 1932. (http://king.collectionscanada.ca/EN/PageView.asp)

33. John T. Wooley and Gerhard Peters, *The American Presidency Project* (online). Santa Barbara: University of California, 1999.

34. Herridge to Bennett. March 17, 1934. *Bennett Papers*. NAC. Reel 1023.

35. Bennett speech to the annual meeting of the Board of Trade of the city of Toronto. January 23, 1933. 8. *Bennett Papers*. NAC. Reel 1400.

36. Duncan McDowall. *Quick to the Frontier: Canada's Royal Bank*. Toronto: McClelland & Stewart, 1993. 245.

37. Michael Bordo et al., *Canada's Monetary System*, 21.

38. Greenspan, *The Age of Turbulence*, 111.

39. Nobel to Bennett. March 17, 1932. *Bennett Papers*. NAC. Reel 1104.

40. *Montreal Gazette*. October 31, 1932. *Bennett Papers*. NAC. Reel 962.

41. Jean Edwards Smith. *FDR*. New York: Random House, 2008. 340.

42. Charles Poor Kindleberger. *The World In Depression 1929–1939*. Berkeley: University of California Press, 1986. 216.

43. Bennett to Turnbull. August 2, 1935. *Bennett Papers*. NAC. Reel 962.

44. Bennett to Howard. August 2, 1935. *Bennett Papers*. NAC. Reel 962.

45. Bennett to Marsh. August 6, 1935. *Bennett Papers*. NAC. Reel 962.

46. White to Bennett. November 3, 1935. *Bennett Papers*. NAC. Reel 962.

47. Bennett to W. M. Smith and Southam. May 9, 1934. *Bennett Papers*, NAC. Reel 1040.

48. *Regina Manifesto*. The First CCF National Convention: July 19–23, 1933. Regina, Saskatchewan. 3. http://www.saskndp.com/assets/File/history/manifest.pdf

49. Mackenzie King diary. September 27, 1933. (http://king.collectionscanada.ca/EN/PageView.asp)

50. Bennett to Logan. November 23, 1933. *Bennett Papers*. NAC. Reel 962.

51. Bennett speech at South Oxford. April 12, 1934. 3. *Bennett Papers*. NAC. Reel 1401.

52. Leman to Bennett. June 7, 1934. *Bennett Papers*. NAC. Reel 963.

53. Hansard, June 27, 1934.

54. Meagher to Bennett. June 28, 1935. *Bennett Papers*. NAC. Reel 962.

55. The Premier Speaks to the People. The Fourth Address. January 9, 1935. Cited in *The Bennett New Deal: Fraud or Portent?*, J. R. H. Wilbur (ed.). Toronto: Copp Clark, 1968. 88.

56. Gordon to Rhodes. March 11, 1935. *Bennett Papers*. NAC. Reel 963.

57. Gordon to Towers. March 8, 1935. *Bennett Papers*. NAC. Reel 963.

58. Dawson to Rhodes. March 11, 1935. *Bennett Papers*. NAC. Reel 963.

59. Waite, "Bennett, Richard Bedford."

60. Logan to Bennett. July 10, 1935. *Bennett Papers*. NAC. Reel 963.

61. Bennett to Logan. July 15, 1935. *Bennett Papers*. NAC. Reel 963.

62. George Watts. *The Bank of Canada: Origins and Early History*. Ottawa: Carleton University Press, 1993. 8.

63. Charles Calomiris, "Financial Factors in the Great Depression." *Journal of Economic Perspectives* 17:2 (Spring 1993): 62.

CHAPTER SEVEN: STRENGTH TO STUBBORNNESS: ON TO OTTAWA TREK AND HARRY STEVENS, 1934–1935

1. Robertson to Bennett. June 19, 1931. *Bennett Papers*. NAC. Reel 1433.

2. Liversedge, *On To Ottawa Trek*, viii.

3. McNaughton to Finlayson. June 22, 1934. *Bennett Papers*. NAC. Reel 1457.

4. Hansard, March 15, 1934.

5. Bill Waiser. *All Hell Can't Stop Us: The On-to-Ottawa Trek and Regina Riot*. Toronto: Fitzhenry & Whiteside Limited, 2003. 36.

6. Bennett to Pattullo. March 2, 1934. *Bennett Papers*. NAC. Reel 395.

7. Lorne Brown. *When Freedom Was Lost: The Unemployed, the Agitator and the State*. Montreal: Black Rose Books, 1987. 50.

8. Bennett speech at South Oxford. April 12, 1934. 2–3. *Bennett Papers*. NAC. Reel 1401.

9. Bennett to Cotnam. May 14, 1934. *Bennett Papers*. NAC. Reel 1497.

10. Liversedge, *On To Ottawa Trek*, 56.

11. Ibid., 57.

12. Hansard, June 24, 1935.

13. Bennett to Gardiner. June 27, 1935. *Bennett Papers*. NAC. Reel 1090.

14. Ibid., February 1, 1931.

15. Hansard. Ottawa: House of Commons Debates. July 29, 1931.

16. Ibid., November 11, 1932.

17. Norman Penner. *Canadian Communism: The Stalin Years*. Toronto: Methuen, 1988. 188–89.

18. Ivan Avakumovic. *Socialism in Canada. A Study of the CCF-NDP in Federal and Provincial Politics*. Toronto: McClelland & Stewart, 1978. 286.

19. John Manley, "'Audacity, audacity, still more audacity': Tim Buck, the Party, and the People, 1932–1939," *Labour/Le Travail* 49. (Spring 2002). 11.

20. Cited in Morris Wolf. *Tim Buck Too. Canadian Forum*. December 1991.

21. Christmas card from Angus Murray to Bennett. *Bennett Papers*. NAC. Reel 991.

22. Christ to Bennett. Undated. *Bennett Papers*. NAC. Reel 991.

23. Resolution of the National Unemployed Workers Association. October 4, 1935. *Bennett Papers*. NAC. Reel 1090.

24. Protest Resolution from the Workers Protective Association of Princeton B.C. to Bennett. April 19, 1935. *Bennett Papers*, NAC. Reel 1090.

25. Anderson to Bennett. April 20, 1935 *Bennett Papers*. NAC. Reel 1090.

26. Resolution from E. E. Van Horne to Bennett. November 17, 1934. *Bennett Papers*. NAC. Reel 1090.

27. Bennett to Drury. August 21, 1935. *Bennett Papers*. NAC. Reel 1090.

28. Perley to Pattullo. March 26, 1935. *Bennett Papers*. NAC. Reel 1497.

29. Bennett to McGeer. May 20, 1935. *Bennett Papers*. NAC. Reel 1497.

30. McGeer to Bennett. May 21, 1935. *Bennett Papers*. NAC. Reel 1497.

31. Ronald Liversedge. *Recollections of the On To Ottawa Trek*. Toronto: McClelland & Stewart, 1973. 83.

32. Mackenzie to Gordon. June 11, 1935. *Bennett Papers*. NAC. Reel 1090.

33. Commanding General Military District 13 to Adjutant General in Ottawa. June 9, 1935. *Bennett Papers*. NAC. Reel 1090.

34. Hansard, June 7, 1935.

35. Gardiner to Bennett. June 12, 1935. *Bennett Papers*. NAC. Reel 1090.

36. Hansard, June 13, 1935.

37. Manion to Bennett. June 17, 1935. *Bennett Papers*. NAC. Reel 1090.

38. Report of the Regina Riot Inquiry Commission, Vol II. Ottawa: King's Printer, 1935. *Bennett Papers*. NAC. Reel 1497.

39. Ibid.

40. Ibid.

41. Ibid.

42. Ibid.

43. Hansard, June 24, 1935.

44. Hansard, July 2, 1935.

45. Mackenzie King diary. July 1, 1935. (http://king.collectionscanada.ca/EN/PageView.asp)

46. Macdonald Commission Report. 11. May 23, 1935. *Bennett Papers*. NAC. Reel 1497.

47. Ibid. 16.

48. Ernest Lapointe to Bennett. November 22, 1935. *Bennett Papers*. NAC. Reel 1497.

49. *Proceedings of the Regina Riot Vol. VIII*. Ottawa: King's Printer, 1935. *Bennett Papers*. NAC. Reel 1497.

50. George Radwanski, *Trudeau*. Toronto: MacMillan, 1978. 326.

51. Watkins. *R. B. Bennett*, 226.

52. Arch Dale. *Five Years of R. B. Bennett*, Winnipeg: Winnipeg Free Press, 1935. 73.

53. *Regina Daily Star*. July 10, 1935. *Bennett Papers*. NAC. Reel 1497.

54. Hansard, July 2, 1935.

55.   *Stevens Papers.* NAC. Vol. 58.

56.   Bennett to Stevens. October 26, 1934. *Bennett Papers.* NAC. Vol 101.

57.   Watkins, *R. B. Bennett*, 201.

58.   Ibid. 202.

59.   Ibid. 202–3.

60.   Hansard, January 21 1935.

61.   R. B. Bennett et. al. *Canadian Problems as Seen By Twenty Outstanding Men of Canada.* Toronto: Oxford Univ. Press, 1933. 11–31.

62.   Bennett to Haig. August 13, 1934. *Bennett Papers.* NAC. Reel 100.

63.   Bennett to Stevens. October 26, 1934. *Bennett Papers.* NAC. Reel 1097.

64.   Glassford. *Reaction and Reform*, 380.

65.   Ibid.

66.   Watkins, *R. B. Bennett*, 213.

67.   Ibid.

68.   Cook to Stevens. March 15, 1935. *Stevens Papers.* NAC. Vol. 125.

69.   Hansard, June 19, 1935.

70.   Watkins, *R. B. Bennett*, 224.

71.   Jean Chrétien. *My Years as Prime Minister.* Toronto: Knopf, 2007. 259.

72.   Pierre Trudeau. *Memoirs.* Toronto: McClelland & Stewart, 1993. 194.

73.   Andrew MacLean. *R. B. Bennett.* Toronto: Excelsior, 1935. 109.

74.   Wallace Clement. *The Canadian Corporate Elite.* Toronto: McClelland & Stewart, 1975. Intro.

CHAPTER EIGHT:
A NEW DEAL AND A NEW GOVERNMENT, 1934–1935

1.   Herridge to Bennett. April 12, 1934. *Bennett Papers.* NAC. Reel 1025.

2.   Ibid.

3.   Herridge to Bennett. July 18, 1934. Bennett Papers. NAC. Reel 1025.

4.   Bennett to Finlayson. May 2, 1934. Bennett Papers. NAC. Reel 1025.

5.   Bennett speech. October 14, 1934. *Bennett Papers.* NAC. 1401.

6.   Cited in John R. Wilbur. *H. H. Stevens, 1878–1973.* Toronto: University of Toronto Press, 1977. 149.

7.   *The Premier Speaks to the People.* The First Address. January 2, 1935. Cited in J. R. H. Wilbur (ed.), *The Bennett New Deal: Fraud or Portent?* Toronto: Copp Clark, 1968. 80.

8.   Ibid. 81.

9.   Bennett to Leacock. January 6, 1935. *Bennett Papers.* NAC. Reel 1401.

10.   *Montreal Gazette.* January 4, 1935.

11.   Bennett to Huestis. January 4, 1935. *Bennett Papers.* NAC. Reel 1401.

12.   Bennett to B. B. Graham. January 8, 1935. *Bennett Papers.* NAC. Reel 1401.

13.   Mackenzie King diary. January 2, 1935. (http://king.collectionscanada.ca/EN/PageView.asp)

14.   Ibid. January 3, 1935.

15.   Ibid. The Second Address. January 4, 1935. Cited in J. R. H. Wilbur. 84.

16.   Ibid.

17.   *The Premier Speaks to the People.* The Third Address. January 7, 1935. Cited in J. R. H. Wilbur. (ed.). 86–87.

18.   Ibid. The Fourth Address. January 11, 1935. Cited in J. R. H. Wilbur. 88.

19.   Ibid., 89.

20.   *The Premier Speaks to the People.* The Fifth Address. January 11, 1935. cited in J. R. H. Wilbur (ed.). 90.

21.   Ibid. *Bennett Papers* 2. NAC. Reel 1402.

22. Ibid.

23. Denis Smith. *Rogue Tory*. Toronto: Macfarlane, Walter and Ross, 1995. 79.

24. John R. Wilbur. *H. H. Stevens, 1878–1973*. Toronto: University of Toronto Press, 1977. 151.

25. Ernest Watkins. *R. B. Bennett: A Biography*. Toronto: Kingswood House, 1963. 220.

26. Hansard. January 21, 1935.

27. *Winnipeg Free Press*. January 30, 1935. Cited in J. R. H. Wilbur. 102.

28. *Montréal Gazette*. January 30, 1935. Cited in J. R. H. Wilbur. 104.

29. Donald W. Buchan. *Saturday Night*. January 12, 1935. Cited in J. R. H. Wilbur. 105.

30. Seymour Lipset. *Agrarian Socialism*. Berkeley: University of California Press, 1950. 138.

31. Ballantyne to Bennett. January 8, 1935. *Bennett Papers*. NAC. Reel 1402.

32. Herridge to Bennett. January 18, 1934. *Bennett Papers*. NAC. Reel 1995.

33. Mackenzie King diary. January 15, 1935. (http://king.collectionscanada.ca/EN/PageView.asp)

34. Hansard. January 29, 1935.

35. Ibid.

36. Ibid.

37. Ibid.

38. R. J. Manion to James Manion. March 22, 1935. *Manion Papers*. Vol. 18.

39. Finlayson to Perley. March 22, 1935. *Bennett Papers*. NAC. Reel 1096.

40. Mackenzie King diary. January 30, 1935. (http://king.collectionscanada.ca/EN/PageView.asp)

41. Watkins. *R.B. Bennett, A Biography*, 221.

42. Hutchison. *Calgary Herald*. September 19, 1935. *Bennett Papers*. NAC. Reel 3144.

43. Ibid. 137.

44. Pearson. *Mike*. 73.

45. Watkins. *R.B. Bennett, A Biography*, 222.

46. Ibid., 223.

47. Ibid.

48. Bennett to Richmond. July 16, 1935. *Bennett Papers*. NAC. Reel 1041.

49. Manion to Price. June 6, 1935. *Manion Papers*. NAC. Vol. 98.

50. Bennett to party chief and chief whip. January 6, 1931. *Bennett Papers*. NAC. Reel 3177.

51. Bennett to McAuley. June 7, 1930. March 11, 1930. *Bennett Papers*. NAC. Reel 3143.

52. Code to Bennett. August 23, 1930. *Bennett Papers*. NAC. Reel 1113.

53. Bennett to Reid. August 23, 1938. *Bennett Papers*. NAC. Reel 1478.

54. Pitfield to Bennett. October 9, 1930. *Bennett Papers*. NAC. Reel 3177.

55. Morrow to Bennett. March 1, 1935. *Bennett Papers*. NAC. Reel 3143.

56. Hutchison, *Incredible Canadian*, 193.

57. *Bennett Papers*. NAC. Reel 1401.

58. Liberal-Conservative campaign poster—1935. *Bennett Papers*. NAC. Reel 3144.

59. Hutchison, *Incredible Canadian*, 198.

60. *Calgary Herald*. September 16, 1935. *Bennett Papers*. NAC. Reel 3144.

61. Ibid.

62. Ibid.

63. *Calgary Herald*, September 16, 1935. *Bennett Papers*. NAC. Reel 3144.

64. Ibid.

65. Ibid.

66. Ibid.

67. *Calgary Herald*. September 20, 1935. *Bennett Papers*. NAC. Reel 3144.

68. Cited in Glassford, *Reaction and Reform*, 181.

69. Mackenzie King diary. June 16, 1935. (http://king.collectionscanada.ca/EN/PageView.asp)

70. *Toronto Globe*. April 11, 1934. *Bennett Papers*. NAC. Reel 3175.

71. *Border Cities Star*. April 12, 1934. *Bennett Papers*. NAC. Reel 3175.

72. *Ottawa Citizen*. September 18, 1934. *Bennett Papers*. NAC. Reel 3175.

73. Cited in Sandy Stewart. *From Coast to Coast: A Personal History of Radio in Canada*. Toronto: CBC Enterprises, 1985. 26.

74. Ibid.

75. Price to Bennett. October 15, 1935. *Bennett Papers*. NAC. Reel 3173.

76. Memo to Miss Millar. Undated. *Bennett Papers*. NAC. Reel 416.

77. K. Z. Paltiel. *Political Party Financing in Canada*. Toronto: McClelland & Stewart, 1970. 30.

78. Waite, "Bennett, Richard Bedford."

79. Bennett to Skelton. October 14, 1935. *Bennett Papers*. NAC. Reel 1402.

80. Bennett to Skelton. October 20, 1935. *Bennett Papers*. NAC. Reel 1402.

81. Hansard. February 11, 1936.

82. Bruce Hutchison. *Incredible C anadian: A Candid Portrait of Mackenzie King: His Works, His Times, and His Nation*. Toronto: Longmans, Green and Company, 1953. 200.

83. Watkins, *R. B. Bennett*, 227.

84. Ibid., 228.

85. Glassford, *Reaction and Reform*, 199.

86. Bennett to Ross. April 1, 1938. *Bennett Papers*. NAC. Reel 1401.

87. Bennett to Clarke. November 12, 1935. *Bennett Papers*. NAC. Reel 1401.

88. Bennett to McLure. May 7, 1938. *Bennett Papers*. NAC. Reel 3143.

89. Bennett to Borden. October 31, 1935. *Bennett Papers*. NAC. Reel 3174.

CHAPTER NINE:
THE FINAL YEARS, 1935–1947

1.   Bennett to Challies. June 13, 1936. *Bennett Papers*. NAC. Reel 145.

2.   Ibid.

3.   Lawson to Bennett. December 23, 1937. *Bennett Papers*. NAC. Reel 416.

4.   Bennett to Irish. September 27, 1937. *Bennett Papers*. NAC. Reel 416.

5.   Heighington to Bennett. February 24, 1938. *Bennett Papers*. NAC. Reel 3143.

6.   Bennett to Heighington. April 4, 1938. *Bennett Papers*. NAC. Reel 3143.

7.   Waite, "Bennett, Richard Bedford."

8.   Hansard, January 29, 1935.

9.   Finlayson to Bennett. January 25, 1936. *Bennett Papers*. NAC. Reel 3144.

10. Bennett to Robinson. February 13, 1937. *Bennett Papers*. NAC. Reel 1498.

11. *McGill Law Review*, 47:566.

12. Ibid., 47:571.

13. Watkins, *R. B. Bennett*, 217.

14. Canada Act, Section 91 (http://www.gov.ns.ca/legislative.legc/canada82.htm)

15. See Bora Laskin. "Peace, Order and Good Government Re-Examined," in *The Courts and the Canadian Constitution*. Toronto: McClelland & Stewart, 1964. 66–104.

16. Bennett to Moore. December 17, 1935. *Bennett Papers*. NAC. Reel 3177.

17. Frank Underhill. *In Search of Canadian Liberalism*. Toronto: Toronto University Press, 1960. 126. See also Eric Adams. "Canada's Newer Constitutional Law and the Idea of Constitutional Rights," in *McGill Law Journal* 51. 2006.

18. *Calgary Herald*. April 16, 1937. *Bennett Papers*. NAC. Reel 3144.

19. Bennett to Ross. March 29, 1937. *Bennett Papers*. NAC. Reel 3182.

20. Bennett to McCort. April 26, 1937. *Bennett Papers.* NAC. Reel 3182.

21. Bennett to Davies. August 12, 1937. *Bennett Papers.* NAC. Reel 3182.

22. Bennett to Streight. February 8, 1938. *Bennett Papers.* NAC. Reel 1477.

23. Bennett to Keyes. March 12, 1938. *Bennett Papers.* NAC. Reel 3182.

24. M. Gratton O'Leary. "Who Will Succeed Bennett?" *Maclean's.* May 1, 1938. 10.

25. Convention proceedings 154. *Bennett Papers,* NAC. Reel 1401.

26. John Diefenbaker. *One Canada: Memoirs of the Right Honourable John G. Diefenbaker, Years of Achievement 1956-1962.* Scarborough: Signet Books, 1976. 23.

27. Meighen to Bennett. July 12, 1938. *Bennett Papers.* NAC. Reel 1496.

28. Bennett to MacPherson. August 29, 1938. *Bennett Papers.* NAC. Reel 3143.

29. Bennett to Turner. March 9, 1936. *Bennett Papers.* NAC. Reel 3144.

30. Bennett to Cox. March 9, 1935. *Bennett Papers.* NAC. Reel 3144.

31. Bruce Hutchison. *Calgary Herald,* September 19, 1935. *Bennett Papers.* NAC. Reel 3144.

32. Innis to Bennett. April 16, 1938. Reel 3145.

33. Hansard, July 1, 1938.

34. Blair Neatby. *William Lyon Mackenzie King, 1932-1939: The Prism of Unity.* Toronto: University of Toronto Press, 1976. 282.

35. Hutchison, *Incredible Canadian,* 226.

36. Bennett speech. Cited in *The Family of Nations.* New York: Carnegie Endowment for International Peace Division of Intercourse and Education, 1935. 13. *Bennett Papers.* NAC. Reel 1400.

37. Bennett speech at Rensselaer Polytechnic Institute. June 16, 1934. *Bennett Papers.* NAC. Reel. 1401.

38. Watkins, *R. B. Bennett,* 236.

39. Ibid., 231.

40. Beaverbrook, *Friends,* 89–90.

41. Watkins, *R. B. Bennett,* 237.

42. *Calgary Herald.* January 12, 1939. Bennett Papers. NAC. Reel 3144.

43. Ibid.

44. Ibid.

45. *Calgary Herald.* January 14, 1939. Bennett Papers. NAC. Reel 3144.

46. Meighen speech at Bennett dinner. Toronto, January 16 1939. *Bennett Papers.* NAC. Reel 3176.

47. Hansard, Januar y 16, 1935.

48. Nash to Bennett. January 9, 1939. *Bennett Papers.* NAC. Reel 3153.

49. Dennie to Bennett. November 25, 1938. *Bennett Papers.* NAC. Reel 3153.

50. Mackenzie King diary. January 12, 1939 (http://king.collectionscanada.ca/EN/PageView.asp)

51. Mackenzie King diary. January 16, 1939 (http://king.collectionscanada.ca/EN/PageView.asp)

52. *Halifax Herald.* January 31, 1939. *Bennett Papers.* NAC. Reel 3144.

53. Ibid.

54. Millar to Bennett. March 17, 1939. *Bennett Papers.* NAC. Reel 3153.

55. Bennett to Millar. May 18, 1939. *Bennett Papers.* NAC. Reel 3153.

56. Millar to Bennett. June 19, 1947 *Bennett Papers.* NAC. Reel 3153.

57. *Bennett Papers.* NAC. Reel 3162.

58. Bennett to Millar. June 12, 1939. *Bennett Papers.* NAC. Reel 3153.

59. *Bennett Papers.* NAC. Reel 3163.

60. Labrie to Bennett. October 25, 1940. *Bennett Papers.* NAC. Reel 1498.

61. *Bennett Papers.* NAC. Reel 1498.

62. Hill to Beaverbrook. March 6, 1941, *Bennett Papers.* NAC. Reel 3174.

63. *Stratford Express.* August 2, 1940. *Bennett Papers.* NAC. Reel 1498.

64. Bennett to Meighen. April 9, 1941, *Bennett Papers*. NAC. Reel 3176.

65. Cited in Glassford, *Reaction and Reform*, 244.

66. Mackenzie King diary. February 19, 20, 1941. (http://king.collectionscanada.ca/EN/PageView.asp)

67. Mackenzie King diary. April 22, 1941. (http://king.collectionscanada.ca/EN/PageView.asp)

68. This practice would come to light again in 2001 when later, disgraced and jailed media mogul Conrad Black worked to finagle himself a peerage, but Prime Minister Chrétien refused to allow him to accept it as it violated the law and practice as Mackenzie King had re-established it. Black opted to surrender his Canadian citizenship to become Lord Black of Crossharbour.

69. Beaverbrook, *Friends*, 92.

70. Bennett speech to the House of Lords. February 16, 1942. *Bennett Papers*. NAC. Reel 3173.

71. Bennett speech to the House of Lords. March 1, 1942. *Bennett Papers*. NAC. Reel 1498.

72. Farey-Jones to Bennett. April 16, 1943. *Bennett Papers*. NAC. Reel 1498.

73. Bennett to Atkinson. May 28, 1930. *Bennett Papers*. NAC. Reel 3143.

74. Mackenzie King diary. May 10, 1944. (http://king.collectionscanada.ca/EN/PageView.asp)

75. Mackenzie King diary. December 31, 1942. (http://king.collectionscanada.ca/EN/PageView.asp)

76. Watkins, *R. B. Bennett*, 254.

77. Bennett to Borden. April 17, 1918, *Bennett Papers*. NAC. Reel 3174.

BIBLIOGRAPHY

ARCHIVAL SOURCES

National Archives of Canada (NAC)

Richard Bedford Bennett Papers
Lord Beaverbrook Papers
Arthur Meighen Papers
Dr. R. J. Manion Papers
Diaries of William Lyon Mackenzie King (online)
Hansard: Debates in the House of Commons

NEWSPAPERS AND PERIODICALS

Calgary Herald
Eye Opener
Globe and Mail
Maclean's magazine
Ottawa Citizen
Ottawa Journal
Saturday Night
Toronto Star
Vancouver Sun

SECONDARY SOURCES

Adams, Eric M. "Canada's Newer Constitutional Law and the Idea of Constitutional Rights." *McGill Law Journal* 51. 2006.

Avakumovic, Ivan. *Socialism in Canada. A Study of the CCF-NDP in Federal and Provincial Politics.* Toronto: McClelland & Stewart, 1978.

Beaverbrook, Lord. *Friends: Sixty Years of Intimate Personal Relations with Richard Bedford Bennett.* London: Heinemann, 1959.

Bennett, R. B. et. al. *Canadian Problems as Seen by Twenty Outstanding Canadian Men.* Toronto: Oxford University Press, 1933.

Bliss, Michael. *Right Honourable Men: The Descent of Canadian Politics from Macdonald to Chrétien.* Toronto: HarperCollins Ltd., 2004.

———. "Privatizing the Mind—The Sundering of Canadian History, the Sundering of Canada," *Journal of Canadian Studies* 26:4. (Winter 1991–92).

Borden, Robert. *Robert Laird Borden: His Memoirs*. Toronto: Macmillan Company of Canada Ltd., 1938.

———. *Letters to Limbo*. Toronto: Macmillan Press, 1971.

Bordo, Michael, Angela Redish, and Ronald Shearer. *Canada's Monetary System in Historical Perspective: Two Faces of the Exchange Rate Regime*. Vancouver: University of Vancouver Press, 1999.

Bothwell, Robert and Hillmer, Norman (ed.). *The In-Between Time: Canadian External Policy in the 1930s*. Toronto: Copp Clark Publishing, 1975.

Bowering, George. *Egotists and Autocrats: The Prime Ministers of Canada*. Toronto: Viking Press, 1999.

Boyko, John. *Last Steps to Freedom: The Evolution of Canadian Racism*. Winnipeg: Gordon Shillingford Publishing, 1998.

———. *Into the Hurricane: Attacking Socialism and the CCF*. Winnipeg: J. Gordon Shillingford Publishing, 2006.

Brebner, J. *Canada: A Modern History*. Ann Arbor: University of Michigan Press, 1960.

Broadfoot, Barry. *Ten Lost Years: Memories of Canadians Who Survived the Depression*. Don Mills: Paper Jacks Ltd., 1973.

Brodie, J., and J. Jenson. "Piercing the Smokescreen: Brokerage Parties and Class Politics," in *Canadian Parties in Transition: Discourse, Organization and Representation*, Alain G. Gagnon and A. Brian Tanguay, eds. Scarborough, ON: Nelson Canada, 1989. 24–44.

Brown, Lorne. *When Freedom Was Lost: The Unemployed, the Agitator and the State*. Montreal: Black Rose Books, 1987.

Brown, Robert Craig. *Robert Laird Borden: A Biography, Volume I, 1854-1914*. Toronto: Macmillan of Canada, 1975.

———. *Robert Laird Borden: A Biography, Volume II, 1914-1937*. Toronto: Macmillan of Canada, 1980.

Calomiris, Charles. "Financial Factors in the Great Depression." *Journal of Economic Perspectives* 17, no. 2, (Spring 1993): 62.

Castro, Fidel. *My Life*. New York: Allen Lane, 2007.

Careless, J. M. S. *Canada: A Story of Challenge*, rev. ed. Toronto: Macmillan Press, 1970.

Clement, Wallace. *The Canadian Corporate Elite: An Analysis of Economic Power*. Toronto: McClelland & Stewart, 1975.

Chrétien, Jean. *Straight From the Heart*. Toronto: Seal Books, 1986.

———. *My Years as Prime Minister*. Toronto: Alfred Knopf Canada, 2007.

Cook, Tim. *Shock Troops: Canadians Fighting the Great War 1917-1918. Volume Two*. Toronto: Penguin Books, 2008.

Creighton, Donald. *John A. Macdonald: The Old Chieftain*. Toronto: Macmillan of Canada, 1955.

Dale, Arch. *Five Years of R. B. Bennett*. Winnipeg: Winnipeg Free Press, 1935.

Dawson, R. MacGregor. *William Lyon MacKenzie King: A Political Biography*. Toronto: University of Toronto Press, 1958.

Diefenbaker, John. *Memoirs of the Right Honourable John G. Diefenbaker: The Crusading Years 1895–1956*. Toronto: Signet Books. 1975.

———. *One Canada: Memoirs of the Right Honourable John G. Diefenbaker, Years of Achievement 1956–1962*. Toronto: Signet Books, 1976.

Donaldson, Gordon. *The Prime Ministers of Canada*. Toronto: Doubleday Press, 1994.

Drummond, Ian. *Imperial Economic Policy, 1917-1939: Studies in Expansion and Protection*. Toronto: University of Toronto Press, 1974.

Duffy, John. *Fights of our Lives: Elections, Leadership, and the Making of Canada*. Toronto: HarperCollins Publishers Limited, 2002.

English, John. *Arthur Meighen*. Don Mills: Fitzhenry and Whiteside, 1977.

———. *The Decline of Politics: the Conservatives and the Party System, 1901–1920*. Toronto, University of Toronto Press, 1993.

Feiling, Keith Grahame, Sir. *The Life of Neville Chamberlain*. London: MacMillan and Co. Ltd. 1946.

Foster, Donald, and Colin Read. "The Politics of Opportunism: The New Deal Broadcasts." *Canadian Historical Review* 60, no. 3. 1979.

Glassford, Larry. *Reaction and Reform: The Politics of the Conservative Party Under R. B. Bennett 1927–1938.* Toronto: University of Toronto Press, 1992.

Gordon, Stanley. *R. B. Bennett, M.L.A., 1897–1905: The Years of Apprenticeship.* Calgary: University of Calgary, 1975.

Graham, Roger. *Arthur Meighen: A Biography.* Toronto: Clarke, Irwin & Company Ltd., 1960.

———. *Arthur Meighen: The Door of Opportunity, Volume 2.* Toronto: Clarke Irwin and Company, 1963.

———. *Arthur Meighen: No Surrender, Volume 3.* Toronto: Clarke Irwin and Company, 1965.

Granatstein, J. L. *The Politics of Survival: The Conservative Party of Canada, 1939–1945.* Toronto, University of Toronto Press, 1967.

Granatstein, J. L., and Norman Hillmer. *Prime Ministers: Ranking Canada's Leaders.* Toronto: HarperCollins, 1999.

Gray, James H. *Men Against the Desert.* Saskatoon: The Modern Press, 1967.

———. *The Winter Years: The Depression on the Prairies.* Toronto: University of Toronto Press, 1967.

———. *R. B. Bennett: the Calgary Years.* Toronto: University of Toronto Press, 1991.

Grayson, L. M., and Bliss, M., eds. *The Wretched of Canada.* Toronto: University of Toronto Press, 1971.

Greenspan, Alan. *The Age of Turbulence: Adventures in a New World.* New York: Penguin Books, 2007.

Guillet, Edwin C. *You'll Never Die John A!.* Toronto: Macmillan of Canada, 1967.

Gwyn, Richard. *The Northern Magus: Pierre Trudeau and Canadians.* Markham: Paper Jacks Ltd. 1981.

Hoar, Victor. *The On To Ottawa Trek.* Toronto: Copp Clark Publishing Company, 1970.

Horn, Michael. *The Dirty Thirties: Canadians in the Great Depression.* Toronto: Copp Clark Publishing Company, 1972.

Horowitz, Gad. *Canadian Labour in Politics.* Toronto: University of Toronto Press, 1968.

Hutchison, Bruce. *Incredible Canadian: A Candid Portrait of Mackenzie King: His Works, His Times, and His Nation.* Toronto: Longmans, Green and Company, 1953.

———. *Mr. Prime Minister, 1867–1964.* Toronto: Longmans Canada Limited, 1964.

Innis Harold. *The Fur Trade in Canada: An Introduction to Canadian Economic History.* Toronto: University of Toronto Press, 1930.

Johnson, Gregory A., and David A. Lenarcic. "The Decade of Transition: The North Atlantic Triangle During the 1920s," in *The North Atlantic Triangle in a Changing World: Anglo-American-Canadian Relations, 1902–1956.* McKercher, Brian James Cooper, and Lawrence Aronsen, eds. Toronto: University of Toronto Press, 1996.

Kealey, Linda et al. "Teaching Canadian History in the 1990s: Whose 'National' History are We Lamenting?" *Journal of Canadian Studies* 27, no. 2, (Summer 1992): 129–31.

Kindleberger, Charles Poor. *The World In Depression 1929–1939.* Berkeley: University of California Press, 1986.

Laskin, Bora. "Peace, Order and Good Government Re-Examined," in *The Courts and the Canadian Constitution.* Toronto: McClelland & Stewart, 1964.

Levine, Allan. *Scrum Wars: The Prime Ministers and the Media.* Toronto: Dundurn Press, 1996.

Lipset, Seymour. *Agrarian Socialism: The Cooperative Commonwealth Federation in Saskatchewan—A Study in Political Sociology.* Berkeley: University of California Press, 1950.

Liversedge, Ronald. *Recollections of the On To Ottawa Trek.* Toronto: McClelland & Stewart, 1973.

Machiavelli, Niccolò. *The Prince, and Other Writings.* New York: Barnes and Nobel Publishing, 2004.

MacLean, Andrew. *R. B. Bennett.* Toronto: Excelsior Publishing, 1935.

MacNicol, John R. *The National Liberal-Conservative Convention.* Toronto: Southam, 1930.

Manion, R. J. *Life is an Adventure.* Toronto: The Ryerson Press, 1936.

Manley, John. "'Audacity, audacity, still more audacity': Tim Buck, the Party, and the People, 1932–1939," *Labour/Le Travail* 49 (Spring 2002) 9–411.

Marr, William L., and Donald G. Paterson. *Canada: An Economic History.* Toronto: Macmillan, 1980.

Martin, Lawrence. *Iron Man: The Defiant Reign of Jean Chrétien.* Toronto: Viking Canada, 2003.

Martin, Paul. *Hell or High Water: My Life In and Out of Politics.* Toronto: McClelland & Stewart, 2008.

McDowall, Duncan. *Quick to the Frontier: Canada's Royal Bank.* Toronto: McClelland & Stewart, 1993.

Morton, W. L. *The Kingdom of Canada, A General History from Earliest Times.* Toronto: McClelland & Stewart, 1963.

Mulroney, Brian. *Memoirs 1939-1993.* Toronto: McClelland & Stewart, 2007.

Neatby, H. Blair. *The Politics of Chaos: Canada in the Thirties.* Toronto: Macmillan, 1972.

———. *William Lyon Mackenzie King: 1924-1932, The Lonely Heights.* Toronto: University of Toronto Press, 1963.

———. *William Lyon Mackenzie King: 1932-1939, The Prism of Unity.* Toronto: University of Toronto Press, 1976.

O'Leary, Gratton, ed., *Unrevised and Unrepented: Debating Speeches and Others by the Right Honourable Arthur Meighen.* Toronto: Clarke, Irwin & Company, Ltd., 1949.

———. *Recollections of People, Press, and Politics.* Toronto: McClelland and Stewart. 1977.

Paltiel, K. Z. *Political Party Financing in Canada.* Toronto: McClelland & Stewart, 1970.

Pearson, Lester. *Mike: The Memoirs of the Rt. Hon. Lester B. Pearson, Vol. 1.* Toronto: University of Toronto Press, 1972.

Penner, Norman. *Canadian Communism: The Stalin Years.* Toronto: Methuen, 1988.

Plamondon, Bob. *Blue Thunder, The Truth About Conservatives from Macdonald to Harper.* Toronto: Key Porter Books, 2009.

Prang, Margaret. "The Origins of Public Broadcasting in Canada." *Canadian Historical Review* 46, no. 1. 1965.

Radwanski, George. *Trudeau.* Toronto: MacMillan Company of Canada, 1978.

Richards, David Adams. *Lord Beaverbrook.* Toronto: Penguin Canada, 2008.

Safarian, A. E. *The Canadian Economy During the Great Depression.* Ottawa: Carleton University Press, 1970.

Schull, Joseph. *Laurier: The First Canadian.* Toronto: MacMillan Company of Canada, 1965.

Skelton, Oscar Douglas. *The Life and Letters of Sir Wilfrid Laurier.* Toronto: Oxford University Press, 1921.

Smith, Dennis. *Rogue Tory: The Life and Legend of John G. Diefenbaker.* Toronto: Macfarlane, Walter and Ross, 1995.

Smith, Jean Edwards. *FDR.* New York: Random House, 2008.

Singer, Barnett. *The Great Depression.* Don Mills: Collier MacMillan, 1974.

Stewart, Sandy. *From Coast to Coast: A Personal History of Radio in Canada.* Toronto: CBC Enterprises, 1985.

Struthers, James. "Canadian Unemployment Policy in the 1930s," in *Readings in Canadian History: Volume Two.* R. Douglas Francis and Donald B. Smith, eds. Toronto: Nelson, 2002.

Taylor, A. J. P. *Beaverbrook.* London: Hamish Hamilton, 1972.

Thompson, John Herd, and Allen Seager. *Canada 1922-1939: Decades of Discord.* Toronto: McClelland & Stewart, 1985.

Trudeau, Pierre. *Memoirs.* Toronto: McClelland & Stewart, 1993.

Underhill, Frank. *In Search of Canadian Liberalism.* Toronto: University of Toronto Press, 1960.

Waiser, W. A. *Saskatchewan: A New History.* Calgary: Fifth House, 2005.

———. *All Hell Can't Stop Us: The On To Ottawa Trek and Regina Riot.* Calgary: Fifth House, 2003.

Waite, P. B. *The Loner: Three Sketches of the Personal Life and Ideas of R. B. Bennett, 1870–1947.* Toronto: University of Toronto Press, 1992.

Ward, Norman, ed. *A Party Politician: The Memoirs of Chubby Power.* Toronto: Macmillan, 1966.

Watkins, Ernest. *R. B. Bennett: A Biography.* Toronto: Kingswood House, 1963.

Waite, P. B. "Bennett, Richard Bedford." *Dictionary of Canadian Bibliography On-Line.* Toronto: University of Toronto, 2000. John English (General Editor). http://www.biographi.ca/009004-119.01e.php?BioId=42132. January 21, 2009.

Watts, George. *The Bank of Canada: Origins and Early History.* Ottawa: Carleton University Press, 1993.

Wier, Austin. *The Struggle for National Broadcasting in Canada.* Toronto: McClelland & Stewart, 1965.

Wilbur, John R. H. *The Bennett New Deal: Fraud or Portent?* Toronto: Copp Clark, 1968.

———. *The Bennett Administration 1930–1935.* Ottawa: Canadian Historical Association, 1969.

———. *H. H. Stevens, 1878–1973.* Toronto: University of Toronto Press, 1977.

———. "R.B. Bennett as a Reformer." *Canadian Historical Association: Historical Papers,* 1969. 103-111.

Winn, Conrad, and John McMenemy. *Political Parties in Canada.* Toronto: McGraw Hill Ryerson, 1976.

Wolf, Morris. "*Tim Buck Too.*" *Canadian Forum.* December 1991.

Zakuta, Leo. *A Protest Movement Becalmed: A Study of Change in the CCF.* Toronto: University of Toronto Press, 1964.

INDEX

9|23